MW01069870

# THE CANONICAL PATH OF OPUS DEI

---

*The History and Defense of a Charism*

A. de Fuenmayor • V. Gómez-Iglesias • J. L. Illanes

# THE
# CANONICAL
# PATH
# OF
# OPUS DEI

*The History and Defense of a Charism*

Translated by William H. Stetson

**Scepter Publishers**
Princeton, New Jersey

**Midwest Theological Forum**
Chicago

Published in the United States of America by

SCEPTER PUBLISHERS, INC.
20 Nassau St.
Princeton, NJ 08542

and

MIDWEST THEOLOGICAL FORUM
1410 W. Lexington St.
Chicago, IL 60607

First American Edition: 1994

Printed in the United States of America

ISBN 0-933932-70-7

# INTRODUCTION

On March 19, 1983, the process of erecting Opus Dei as a personal prelature reached its end. In a solemn liturgical ceremony in the Roman basilica of St. Eugene, the papal nuncio in Italy presented to Opus Dei's prelate, Monsignor Alvaro del Portillo, the Apostolic Constitution *Ut sit*, of John Paul II, by which the Prelature of the Holy Cross and Opus Dei was established. This culminated not only a legal process begun in 1979 when the Roman Pontiff was asked to transform Opus Dei into a personal prelature, but also a much longer history. Its juridical journey began the day Opus Dei came into being on October 2, 1928. On that day in Madrid a young priest, Josemaría Escrivá de Balaguer *saw*, with unforgettable clarity and light, what God wanted him to do. He was to spread the call to holiness and apostolate in the world among people of all races and social conditions teaching them to use their work and all other circumstances of daily life in the pursuit of this goal.

"I continued to work with souls," Msgr. Escrivá would recall many years later, evoking the time following that October 2nd. "Thus little by little from the firm rock of the mandate from God— I could not doubt nor have I ever doubted—there flowed like a spring, the customs, the different manifestations of the Work's good spirit, its characteristic practices of piety, the way for each to be apostolic in the world, with one's peers."

"Thus the first ones who gathered at my side acquired the interior life proper to consistent Christians.... They struggled to be virtuous, faithful to the Church's teachings, carrying out their work in an effective professional manner, a source of holiness in apostolic work, especially with their colleagues, in the middle of the street."[1]

A pastoral phenomenon of sanctity and apostolate in the world began to take shape. From the first moment Opus Dei enjoyed the good will and blessing of the Bishop of Madrid in whose diocese Msgr. Escrivá lived at that time and where he began to lay the foundations of Opus Dei. As it developed and spread, however, it needed broader approvals.

Thus began a process whose stages were: the diocesan approval as a pious union in 1941; the diocesan erection of the Priestly

---

[1] *Letter*, Dec. 29, 1947/Feb. 14, 1966, no. 22

Society of the Holy Cross as a society of common life without vows in 1943, after obtaining a *nihil obstat* of the Holy See; its approval as a secular institute of pontifical right in 1947 and 1950; the petition for a change of canonical form presented first in 1962 and repeated in 1979. The definitive step was the official presentation of the Apostolic Constitution *Ut Sit* to Msgr. del Portillo on March 19, 1983.

The process was not only long, but also complex, even "complicated," as the Founder of the Work once said.[2] Each approval was for a specifically different juridical form. A cursory glance could overlook the foundation underlying these changes, seeing them as whims or mere historical accidents. The fact is, however, that reasons for the steps not only existed but made them necessary. "Our *iter iuridicum* (canonical itinerary)," Msgr. Escrivá commented, "may seem tortuous to human eyes. But with time it will be seen to have been successive advances when viewed from God's perspective.... Thanks to ordinary divine providence, little by little a path is made that eventually leads to a definitive one: one that will preserve the spirit and re-enforce apostolic efficacy."[3]

Later, when the legal process was nearing the end, he added, "What we earnestly desire is only this: to harmonize the charism— the specific vocation we have received from God—with the legal norm. We seek an adequate legal framework that we can rightly use with internal and external firmness before God, the Church, and our fellow men."[4]

A profound unity underlies this long process. We could call it fidelity to the foundational charism, to the light received from God in 1928. It was a quest for a legal configuration suited to this charism. The configuration did not exist and that was the problem. Therefore, time had to pass and developments had to take place in the Church in order to open up new canonical possibilities.

From the perspective of those who view events with hindsight the underlying unity appears as the effort to be faithful to the original inspiration or light, which unfolds its full potential little by little. For the founder the experience and realization of this unity implied all of this and much more: to let oneself be filled with the gift, to incarnate it in one's own life, to transmit it to others, and to defend it in the face of all possible and real misunderstandings. It also meant doing this without closing in on oneself but rather

---

[2] *Letter*, Dec. 8, 1949, no. 12

[3] *Letter*, Dec. 29, 1947/Feb. 14, 1966, no. 163

[4] *Letter*, May 25, 1962, no. 77

opening oneself up to the whole Church, letting oneself be judged by her. Only in the Church is there a guarantee of truth; only in and through the Church can every particular Christian mission achieve its objective. Such over the centuries has been the lot of those to whom has fallen the *onus et honor*: the burden and honor, the suffering and joy, of contributing to a deeper understanding and rejuvenation of Christian living. So it will remain in the future. Such was the lot of Msgr. Escrivá. He saw himself called not to travel well-trodden paths but to forge ahead and mark out new ones.

In the final analysis the question is none other than the relation between charism and institution, more precisely, the relation between the spirit animating an activity and the institution meant to serve and spread this spirit. From that interaction arises a pastoral phenomenon with its social relevance that finally calls for ecclesiastical regulation and a legal-canonical framework. Needless to say, our objective is not the theoretical study of this important ecclesiological question. Rather we will study a particular reality: the history of the legal steps of Opus Dei. Whenever necessary, however, we will make wider reflections. The method we follow is primarily historico-legal but sometimes we will go beyond the law. We will deal then with sources: the legal texts (regulations, constitutions, statutes...) and other documents that present the spiritual phenomenon reflected and reinforced by the legal texts. Any attempt to study the legal evolution of a spiritual and apostolic institution requires such an approach. This method is even more necessary when the institution, as in Opus Dei's case, introduces important new considerations. There simply was no adequate canonical category, and therefore it had to be carved out. The legal steps arose from the inspirational principle, which transcended the legal phase especially in the first stages. What Msgr. Escrivá "saw" forms the background for any analysis and understanding.

In the first part of the book we seek to sketch the basic outline of Opus Dei's pastoral projection as set forth in the earliest texts. As far as possible the historian tries to capture the original foundational charism as it begins to take root and blossom. Only that inspiration explains subsequent events and serves as a touchstone for any legal steps.

In the second part we examine the early legal approvals at the diocesan level. While these steps were provisional and in many aspects inadequate, they reflect in an important way, especially the first one in 1941, the efforts of Opus Dei's founder to embody in legal formulas the spirit and apostolic practice he had been living. We consider and describe how the founder undertook this process of approval. Let us bear in mind that Msgr. Escrivá was not only a holy priest and a deep spiritual author but also no less an excellent jurist. We examine therefore the tension between charism and law, given the non-existence of appropriate channels for Opus Dei.

The third part is dedicated to papal approvals. They represent a decisive milestone and in some respects a bending of form. With the approvals that came in 1947 and 1950 Opus Dei achieved full papal recognition of its spirit and apostolate, plus an interdiocesan and international legal personality. This aided its expansion, both geographic and social; by the end of the '50s it was universal not only *de iure* but also *de facto*. (From the start Msgr. Escrivá saw Opus Dei charged with promoting among men and women of all countries and social classes, the call to holiness and apostolate in their occupations and particular states in life.) These approvals allowed the pastoral phenomenon to develop in a way that made possible the subsequent canonical steps.

The formula according to which these papal approvals were granted, that of a secular institute, was less inadequate than preceding ones, but it did not fully conform to the reality of Opus Dei. Thus further steps would be required to reach a definitive status. Opus Dei could take these steps in the '60s both with the authority attendant upon its broad extension and within the movement for renewal of ecclesial life and canon law generated by the Second Vatican Council.

The fourth and last part of this study deals with the consequences of that stage. We analyze some of the fundamental characteristics of the status Opus Dei received as a personal prelature inserted in the pastoral and hierarchical structure of the Church: a structure made up of priests and lay people for promoting Christian life in the world by personally striving to sanctify the ordinary circumstances of each one, man or woman.

Although the specific object of our work is to study the legal steps taken by Opus Dei until it achieved its definitive canonical configuration, we will also refer to its spirit and the development of its apostolate and therefore to its history in general. Without this background, its legal path—or that of any other spiritual and apostolic institution—would not be fully understandable. We will point to larger matters only to the extent that they shed light on the juridical questions that more directly occupy us.

With respect to the sources or documents used, we have to mention first of all the regulations, constitutions and statutes that correspond to the different approvals received by Opus Dei beginning in 1941 until 1982-1983. In addition we will use many reports, opinions, letters, etc., written by those who intervened in the diverse stages. Among these sources a principal place is held by those texts of the Founder of Opus Dei himself, which can be grouped in three categories:

a) Intimate notes from the early years and other writings or letters of a personal character from that time or later found in the general archives of the prelature.[5]     b) *Letters* and *Instructions* meant to help form members of Opus Dei since the beginning. We will quote them with the word *Letter* or *Instruction* followed by the date and the number of the paragraph or paragraphs cited.[6]

c) Books and writings that have been published. *Spiritual Considerations* (mimeographed 1932; first printed Cuenca 1934); *The Way* (Valencia 1939); *Conversations with Msgr. Escrivá de Balaguer* (Madrid 1968); *Christ is Passing By*, Homilies (Madrid 1973); *Friends of God* (Madrid 1977); *Furrow* (Madrid 1986); *The Forge* (Madrid 1987); etc. We will cite them in the usual way by page or paragraph number. Other texts, books or studies on Opus Dei or on the founder's life, theological and juridical studies of related questions, etc., will be quoted according to usual practice.

Besides, to complement the study there is an appendix of documents: a series of texts from the various stages of the legal evolution. Faced with numerous documents, we have made a careful selection. The 73 documents form a representative selection from the different historical moments and of the process as a whole. The appended texts are given in the original language. Throughout the book, however, they have been translated whenever this would facilitate their reading.

Since in this study canonical and theological questions are interwoven, both research and writing was done by a team. The frequent exchange of ideas and the common examination of texts

---

[5] These archives contain not only the writings of Msgr. Escrivá de Balaguer but many other texts and documents to which we will also refer in our study. The archives are divided into several sections of which we are interested above all in two:

- the founder's historical registry, which contains writings and documents having reference to his life and activities, the testimony of people who knew him, etc.; these citations will bear the initials RHF, followed by the number of the document;

- the juridical section consists of documents referring to the legal process; it will be cited using the initials AGP, Sezione Giuridica, followed by the number of the document.

[6] The *Instructions* offer experiences and practical details referring to particular aspects of the formative and apostolic work, together with underlying criteria. The *Letters* have a more expository tone and deal ordinarily with aspects of spirit which Msgr. Escrivá glosses and comments on with the authority proper to a founder; in other cases they relate to points of Opus Dei's history on which he thought it important to leave a factual record or to record how he reacted to those facts. As Msgr. Escrivá said in one of the *Letters*: "They are not a treatise but a family conversation to give you God's light and...to share some details of our internal history" (*Letter* Dec. 29, 1947/Feb. 14, 1966, no. 13); their familiar tone does not stop them from offering many historical details and above all a mind and criteria that endow them with particular hermeneutic value. In fact we will often quote from them.

makes ours a work of collaboration for which the authors jointly take responsibility.  The work has been wide-ranging, and we have tried to proceed with historical rigor.  Nonetheless the depth of the topic and the closeness of some of the events admit of further investigation and reflection as with any research project.  Future studies may provide new data, prompt the analysis of new questions or emphasize complementary facets.  The underlying principle, however, does not leave any room in our judgment for doubt.

The authors of this work to a greater or lesser degree personally knew Msgr. Escrivá de Balaguer.  We thus perceived the dispositions of his soul, his profound faith, and his total dedication to the Christian and priestly mission to which he saw himself called since October 2, 1928.  Our research has but confirmed this judgment; the sources document the dedication with which he always strove to carry out the foundational charism entrusted to him.  At the outset we wish to declare our profound admiration and veneration for this outstanding figure.  We also want to manifest our filial affection for Opus Dei's present prelate, Bishop Alvaro del Portillo, who directly collaborated with the founder for so many years.  To him fell the task of faithfully consummating the canonical path whose history we have tried to trace.

Rome, October 2, 1988

# CONTENTS

## PART TWO

## DIOCESAN APPROVALS

### CHAPTER III

### THE 1941 APPROVAL

### CHAPTER IV

### THE DIOCESAN ERECTION OF 1943

## PART THREE

## PONTIFICAL APPROVALS (1947 AND 1950)

### CHAPTER V

### OPUS DEI AS A SECULAR INSTITUTE

## CHAPTER VI

### PREPARATIONS FOR
### A NEW PONTIFICAL APPROVAL

## CHAPTER VII

### THE PONTIFICAL APPROVAL OF 1950

## PART IV

## TOWARDS A DEFINITIVE LEGAL SOLUTION

### CHAPTER VIII

### IN SEARCH OF NEW WAYS

## CHAPTER IX

### THE SPECIAL GENERAL CONGRESS

## CHAPTER X

### OPUS DEI, A PERSONAL PRELATURE

Part One

THE BEGINNING

# Chapter I

## WITH THE STRENGTH OF
## THE FOUNDATIONAL CHARISM

1. The foundation of Opus Dei
2. With the certainty of faith
3. Vistas of holiness and apostolate
4. Opus Dei's organization
5. Essential characteristics of Opus Dei

# Chapter I

## WITH THE STRENGTH OF
## THE FOUNDATIONAL CHARISM

### 1. The foundation of Opus Dei

The winter of 1917-1918 witnessed a lasting change in life for Josemaría Escrivá de Balaguer. He was around 16 years old, a young man in the last years of high school. He was a cheerful boy with a good Catholic upbringing from his family and teachers; a normal, somewhat pious boy without any special religious interests. One wintry day he saw footprints left by a discalced Carmelite in newly fallen snow in the city of Logroño where he lived at that time. This event unleashed an interior awakening.[1] God was getting into his life and asking from him a deeper faith, and even more, a radical availability to carry out whatever God might show him. These were the first "inklings" of divine Love as he would say.

He began to intensify his life of prayer and piety and soon decided to become a priest, thinking this the best way to prepare himself for whatever God wanted. A succession of supernatural gifts intensified his conviction that God wanted something of him. Clearly what, however, had to wait till October 2, 1928. On that

---

[1] To situate properly the theological-legal questions that make up our study, it will be necessary to make reference on occasions to the environment or historical circumstances of the life of Msgr. Escrivá. For further information on the events referred to in the text or subsequent ones, several biographical works on the founder of Opus Dei can be consulted. Salvador Bernal, *Mons. Escrivá de Balaguer, Apuntes sobre la vida del Fundador del Opus Dei*, Madrid 1976 (English translation *Profiles of Msgr. Escrivá de Balaguer*, New York 1977); F. Gondrand, *Au pas de Dieu. Mons. Escrivá de Balaguer fondateur de l'Opus Dei*, Paris 1982 (English translation *At God's Pace*, New York 1989); A. Vázquez de Prada, *El Fundador del Opus Dei*, Madrid 1983; P. Berglar, *Opus Dei. Leben un Werk des Grunders Josemaría Escrivá*, Salzburg 1983; A. Sastre, *Tiempo de Caminar. Semblanza de Monseñor Josemaría Escrivá de Balaguer*, Madrid 1989; D. Helming, *Footprints in the Snow*, New York 1986; H. de Azevedo, *Uma luz no mundo. Apontamentos sobre a vida de monsenhor Escrivá de Balaguer*, Lisboa 1988.

fateful day he received a light that became the central event of his
life. Earlier events—his childhood, youthful inklings, seminary training, ordination and pastoral work, studies of civil law, and his
transfer to Madrid[2] all fell into place as preparations for that signal
event in 1928. The clarity of vision that overtook him on that occasion was *the* principle and motive that governed all of his subsequent actions.

What happened on October 2, 1928? No dated account from
that day exists, but there are several later statements by the founder.
The earliest writing comes three years after the event, a handwritten note: *"Three years ago today* (I received the illumination *about the
whole Work*, while I read those papers. Moved by this I knelt down.
I was alone in my room between conferences and I gave thanks to
the Lord and I remember with emotion the ringing of the bells of
the parish of Our Lady of the Angels), while at the convent of the
Vincentian Fathers, I tried to arrange into some sort of pattern the
loose notes I had been taking up until that time; from that moment
on the mangey donkey *became aware of* the burden, beautiful and yet
weighty, that the Lord in his inexplicable goodness had placed upon
his shoulders. This day the Lord founded his Work. From that time
on I began to deal spiritually with young lay people, whether stu-

---

[2] Without entering into details (these can be seen in the works cited in the previous
note), Josemaría Escrivá de Balaguer was born in Barbastro, Spain, on January 9, 1902;
he studied in Logroño and Saragossa; he was ordained a priest in 1925, incardinated in
the archdiocese of Saragossa. Several years before his ordination, with the permission
of his archbishop, he began to study civil law in the state university of that city and
obtained the licentiate in 1927. In that same year he asked for permission to move to
Madrid to study for a doctorate in law, then only obtainable in the capital. In Madrid
he combined his work of research with grueling pastoral activity. This work and his
dedication to the task of founding Opus Dei prolonged his stay in Madrid, obtaining
in 1929, 1930, and 1931 the necessary permissions from the archbishop of Saragossa
and the bishop of Madrid. The latter was granted for a period of five years. In 1934 he
was named rector of the Foundation of Santa Isabel, an institution in Madrid dating
from the 16th century. This appointment was renewed in 1942 within the process of
review and renewal of appointments following the conclusion of the civil war in 1939.
The Foundation of Santa Isabel had been part of the Palatine jurisdiction, which on
April 1, 1933, under the republic had been assumed as part of the diocese of Madrid.
The complex political situation in Spain during the years of the republic made it advisable that the canonical confirmation of the appointment as rector of Santa Isabel be in
the beginning only verbal, because of which Fr. Josemaría continued incardinated in
the archdiocese of Saragossa. His pastoral work, however, was dependent upon the
bishop of Madrid. On February 11, 1942, canonical appointment was conferred and he
thus became incardinated in the diocese of Madrid, where he continued to live until he
moved to Rome. The documents referring to these events are to be found in the archives of the diocesan curias of Saragossa and Madrid and of the Patrimonio Nacional.
Some historical data on the Palatine Jurisdiction can be found in M.V. Quero, "Capilla
Real," in *Diccionario de Historia Eclesiástica de España*, Vol. 1, Madrid 1972, pp. 338-339.

dents or not. I formed groups, I prayed and got others to pray. And to suffer . . ."[3]

"Illumination," "light," "realize," "see": these are expressions the Servant of God[4] always used to evoke what happened on that decisive day. God thrust himself once again in his life, but this time not with hints and inklings but with an overpowering and definitive light. From that time on he knew what God wanted of him, what the task was to which he should dedicate his whole life.

Don Josemaría discovered first of all an apostolic dimension: that of Christians spread throughout the world dedicated to the most diverse tasks and occupations. Sometimes they are conscious of their faith and consistent with its demands; at other times they are forgetful of the life conferred upon them in baptism, allowing, at least in practice, a gap to develop between their faith and their daily life woven of desires and secular interests. At the same time he discovered a call, a mission: God wanted him to invest all his energies into promoting an institution—a "Work," to use the term he used from the beginning—whose aim is to spread among all Christians living in the world a profound awareness of the God-given call inherent in their baptism. This work was to be identical to the pastoral phenomenon it promotes. It was to be a work made up of ordinary Christians who discover the meaning of the Christian vocation and commit themselves to communicate this discovery to others. Thus they spread in the world a conscious awareness that faith can and ought to enliven all facets of human existence: work,

---

[3] Two points will help to understand better some of the phrases from the text: a) On October 2, 1928 Fr. Escrivá was taking part in a retreat for the clergy of Madrid in the convent of the Vincentian Fathers in that city; b) he often used at that time the phrase "mangey donkey" in his prayer and intimate writings to refer to himself, expressing thereby humility, his unworthiness for the divine mission received, yet his desires and resolutions of fidelity.

From 1917 or 1918 Opus Dei's founder began to make entries in notebooks of his interior experiences, ideas that arose in his prayer, etc. The first of these notebooks is no longer preserved; beginning with the second, started in March 1930, these *intimate notes* are kept in the general archives of Opus Dei. To make their use easier numbers have been assigned to the different paragraphs. Thus the note of 1931 just quoted is found in paragraph no. 306.

For a general orientation, cf. J. L. Illanes, *Dos de Octubre de 1928: alcance y siqnificado de una fecha*, in Various authors, *Mons. Josemaría Escrivá de Balaguer y el Opus Dei*, Pamplona 1985, pp. 65ff.

[4] Ugo Cardinal Poletti, papal vicar for the diocese of Rome, inaugurated the cause of beatification and canonization of the Servant of God Josemaría Escrivá de Balaguer by decree of February 19, 1981. It can be seen in the *Rivista diocesana di Roma*, 22 (1981):372-377. Its first phase was solemnly closed in Rome on November 8, 1986.

(*Translator's note*. On May 17, 1992, His Holiness John Paul II solemnly proclaimed Josemaría Escrivá de Balaguer *Blessed*.)

family, social life, research and culture, civic life, professional relations, etc. The light received by Fr. Escrivá on October 2, 1928, was
clearly an illumination of a foundational nature, a charism that
made him a founder. From that moment he knew he was called to
promote an institution, a work. This work would not consist in an
organization with certain limited objectives, but an undertaking
that would arise from a deepened understanding of the universal
call to holiness contained in the gospel. It would give rise to a
wideranging pastoral phenomenon, an apostolic enterprise. All of
this is contained in the foundational charism of Opus Dei whose
nucleus we seek to understand.

However, the powerful grace which Fr. Escrivá received on October 2nd was not limited to the above-mentioned elements. It
extended to other aspects to which we must now make reference.
We hope to present a relatively complete though summary description of the founder's mind during the first years. Let us proceed
historically.[5]

## 2. With the certainty of faith

A fact that stands out clearly in the life of Josemaría Escrivá is
the certainty and conviction with which, relying upon God, he acted
from the very beginning. He passed through very difficult situations; he experienced on occasions tiredness, interior dryness, and
even sorrow and bitterness. Yet the firm certainty of God's will
shown to him on October 2, 1928, never faltered. Contemplating
the vast panorama of people of every race and nation making present
in all the world's environments and occupations Christ's light, warmth,
and truth was second nature to his mind and heart, encouraging
and moving him to action. He would think, write, say, and even
sing: *Regnare Christum volumus*: we want Christ to reign, we want his
grace and love to bear fruit in history. Also, *Omnes cum Petro ad
Iesum per Mariam*, All with Peter to Jesus through Mary: may all be
united to Peter, living for and off a united Church; enlivened by a
tender devotion to the blessed Virgin Mary, may they draw closer
to Christ. May all identify themselves with Him until they know
and feel themselves to be beloved children of our Father God and
therefore brothers of one another, servants of each other, striving
ceaselessly to be sowers of peace, joy, and fraternity.

These ideals filled his soul, especially at the hour of prayer.
More than once in his notes and other personal writings he inter-
rupts the thread of his thoughts to interject *Regnare Christum volumus*
or *Omnes cum Petro ad Iesum per Mariam*. He then continues without

---

[5] For this we rely on the *Intimate notes* described in footnote no. 3 of this chapter,
supplemented at times with other early texts or writings of the founder from later
years that evoke his first steps.

further interruption. This profound interior fire, feeling himself committed—even more, fused with God's will as revealed to him that October day—soon found expression in deeds.

The above text where he says he began to deal spiritually with young people is no rhetorical statement. This reality is echoed in the written testimonies of many of those young people themselves or of other people who knew him at that time.

At the beginning he aimed his apostolate at men: he thought the God-given mission referred only to men. A new light given him on February 14, 1930, made him understand that was not the case. He should also extend to women the spiritual message and calling that define and give substance to the Work of God. On the other hand that first light had shown him not only lay people, single or married in Opus Dei, but priests as well, since the mutual cooperation of priests and lay people is essential to the fullness of the Christian apostolate. In fact, among the first to join the Work at the start were not only a few lay men and women but also a priest: Fr. Norberto Rodríguez, whom he had met in connection with various pastoral assignments.

Every new venture ordinarily exacts effort and determination to overcome difficulties. Opus Dei was no exception. The young priest Josemaría Escrivá reached many people with his ministry. As soon as there were signs of their being able to understand, he shared with many of them the apostolic panorama opened in his soul on October 2nd. Some of them followed him. Others did not heed him. Still others heard him but either did not understand or, after giving signs of having understood, did not persevere, choosing to follow other paths. "Souls slipped through my fingers like eels," he would comment many years later.[6] Moreover he experienced long stretches of spiritual aridity, seasoned now and then by moments of great joy and new illuminations from God. Among these one merits special note because it directly corroborates the nucleus of the foundational charism of Opus Dei. It took place on August 7, 1931, while he was celebrating the sacrifice of the Mass. Shortly after the event he wrote: "August 7, 1931: Today this diocese celebrates the feast of the Transfiguration of our Lord Jesus Christ.[7] As I prayed for my intentions in Holy Mass fixed on the interior changes the Lord has wrought in me during these years of my residence in Madrid. . . . And all this in spite of me: without my

---

[6] With regard to these events, as well as to the suffering and interior maturing which the foundational process worked in Josemaría Escrivá, we refer readers once again to the works mentioned in the first note of this chapter.

[7] The reference is to the diocese of Madrid-Alcalá, where August 6 is celebrated as the feast of SS. Justin and Pastor, patrons of the diocese. For this reason the feast of the Transfiguration is transferred to the 7th.

cooperation, I can say. I believe I renewed the resolution of pledg-
ing my whole life to the fulfillment of God's will: the Work of God.
(A resolution I now renew with all my soul.) The moment of consecration arrived: when I raised the sacred Host, without losing
due recollection, without distractions (I had just made mentally an
offering to the Merciful Love), there came to my mind with extraordinary force and clarity that passage of Scripture: *Et si exaltatus
fuero a terra, omnia traham ad meipsum* (Jn 12:32). Ordinarily when
faced with supernatural things I am afraid. Then there also came to
me the *Ne timeas*: Fear not, it is I. And I understood that men and
women of God will place the cross with Christ's teachings on the
summit of all human activities . . . and I saw the triumphant Lord
drawing all things to himself."

"Bereft of virtue and knowledge (humility is truth . . . without
posturing), I wanted to write books of fire that would race through
the world like a living flame enkindling light and warmth in men,
turning poor hearts into glowing embers to be offered to Jesus Christ
as rubies for his royal crown."[8]

The passion and enthusiasm of this passage betray Fr. Escrivá's
profound convictions. They likewise manifest the foundation, the
root of this conviction: a faith spurred by God-given lights and
inspirations and nourished by prayer until they bring about a certainty that nothing nor anyone can shake.[9]

Another series of events barely a month later completes and
develops the founder's interior world. It left deeply engraved in
his soul what became one of the more salient characteristics of his
spirit: God is our father. "I was considering," he writes on September 22, 1931, "God's kindnesses towards me, and full of interior joy
I would have cried out in the street, so that the whole world might
know of my filial gratitude: Father, Father! And if not shouting at
least under my breath I walked about calling upon him in that way
(Father!), certain that I was pleasing him."[10] A few days later on
October 17, this sentiment became even keener and sparked a pe-

---

[8] *Intimate notes*, nos. 217-218. This event and the text of St. John to which it refers have
been recalled by Msgr. Josemaría Escrivá many times; see for example *The Way*, no.
301; *Christ Is Passing By*, nos. 105, 156 & 183; *Friends of God*, no. 58; *The Forge*, no. 685.

(*Translator's note*. Cf. also, P. Rodríguez, "*Omnia traham ad meipsum*. El sentido de Juan
12:32 en la experiencia espiritual de Mons. Escrivá de Balaguer", in *Romana* 13 (1991):331-
352.)

[9] As the adverb "ordinarily", used in this text of 1931 gives witness, Msgr. Josemaría
Escrivá experienced many times in this decisive foundational period the supernatural
action of divine grace. His reaction was always the same as mentioned in this text: an
initial sensation of confusion and fear, soon overcome by the certainty that the one
who was making himself present to him was God himself who is Father and before
whom one ought not therefore to react with fear, but with love and trust.

[10] *Intimate notes*, no. 296.

riod of prayer where suffering, dryness, and living faith were rolled into one: "I wanted to pray after Mass in the quietness of my church, but I wasn't able to do so. In Atocha I bought a newspaper (ABC) and took the trolley. Hours later I still have not read more than one paragraph of the newspaper. Prayer surged up in me with copious and ardent affections. I continued this way in the trolley car until I reached home."[11]

Often he recalled the profound experiences of that autumn of 1931. It was a tense period in the political, social and religious life of Spain, where the future appeared uncertain. Besides, Fr. Josemaría was encountering troubles and misunderstandings. This background of suffering and hardship did not separate him from God; rather it led him to surrender himself even more, to identify himself completely with God's will. In this framework arose the prayer to which the previous text referred. "When the Lord gave me those blows around 1931," he later commented, "I did not understand. And suddenly in the midst of that great bitterness the words: *You are my son* (Ps 2:7), You are Christ. And I only knew how to say: *Abba Pater! Abba. Pater! Abba! Abba! Abba!* Now I see it with new light, as a new discovery, just as with the passage of time one sees the Lord's hand, the Wisdom of the all-powerful.

"You have made me understand, Lord, that to have the cross is to find happiness and joy. And the reason—I see it more clearly now than ever—is this: to have the cross is to identify oneself with Christ, to be Christ, and for this reason to be God's child."[12]

First in the trolley car, then walking through the streets, and finally in the quiet of his home, the consciousness of being God's son filled him completely. He could not read the newspaper or do anything; he could only address himself to God calling him Father. And as he walked homeward with people all around, the words "Abba, Pater, Father" come to his lips and almost break forth out loud. "They must have thought I was crazy," he later commented. Indeed an awareness of divine sonship took deep root in his soul. The founder was to draw the lesson that such paternity is the bedrock for the spirit of sanctification and apostolate amidst the world, that he saw himself called to spread.

Awareness of divine sonship sums up Msgr. Escrivá's personal life and teaching. It was the reason and stimulus for simple and confident prayer: to deal trustingly with God who is completely a Father, a Father who loves us "more than all the mothers of the

---

[11] *Ibid.*, no. 334. The church to which the text refers is that of Santa Isabel, in which he then carried out his priestly work close to Atocha Circle in Madrid. His residence at that time was located in Viriato Street, about 45 minutes from Atocha.

[12] RHF, 20787, p. 15.

world can love their children."[13]  This perspective also sheds new
light on human realities-- the normal tasks and occupations of men
and women—seeing God's goodness reflected therein.  "Divine filiation," he said in a homily in 1952 which reflects well-seasoned
ideas, "is a joyful truth, a consoling mystery.  Divine filiation fills
all our spiritual life because it teaches us to deal with God as a
Father, to know him and to love him; it fills our interior struggle
with hope and gives us the confident simplicity of small children.
Even more: precisely because we are children of God, this reality
leads us to contemplate with love and admiration all the things that
have come forth from the hands of God the Father and Creator.
And in this way we are contemplatives in the middle of the world,
loving the world."[14]  To know oneself to be a child of God is to know
that one has not been cast into the world by accident nor condemned to futility.  Rather we are called to life by love and are
therefore invited to put love into each and every circumstance of
life, no matter how humdrum or ordinary.  This God who is a
Father sees only the love that motivates our deeds.

### 3. Vistas of holiness and apostolate

Continuing to pursue the fundamental points of the spirit and
message of Opus Dei's founder we should underline another characteristic feature of his spiritual life: a highly vivid hope born of his
firm and deep faith.

"Dream and you will fall short," the founder often said to his
followers.  A man who believes cannot be cowed; he is magnani-
mous, enthusiastic for great enterprises.  Even more, he lets his
imagination feed on supernatural realities; he dreams about the
marvelous things God has promised. What he imagines, his dreams,
might not dovetail with the outcomes God brings about, but the
apostle will never be disillusioned. We can never outdo God's generosity, not even in our imagination.  God is always greater, generosity itself. Our dreams always fall short; grace always exceeds our
wishes; our prayer always ends in thanksgiving.  Msgr. Escrivá's
call to dream simply reflected his personal experience, what he
always lived, especially during the early stages of the development
of the Work.  There were difficulties, and even periods of great
interior dryness.  His eagerness to infect others with the ideal God
had revealed entailed not only dogged efforts but, more than once,
failure.  The apostle reached many, but the group that gathered
around him in a unity of ideals and toils was quite small.  Nevertheless, even when Fr. Josemaría found himself almost completely

---

[13] *The Way*, no. 267 (*Spiritual Considerations*, 1932 edition, no. 31).

[14] *Christ Is Passing By*, no. 65.

alone, a young priest not yet 30 years old, without material means, in the middle of a serious political and cultural crisis, he let his founder's imagination soar to contemplate the fruits that would come with the passage of time. The seed sown on earth by God on October 2, 1928, would take root and grow into a tree luxuriant and laden with fruit.

When Fr. Josemaría witnessed misunderstandings, even hatred of the Church—not infrequent at that time—he would cry out: "Lord, your Work!" If God's Work were already developed, so many souls would have become familiar with God, and things would have turned out differently. News in the paper, a comment in a conversation, a casual encounter with a friend, so many things of this sort led him to imagine how much good would come upon the earth if God's children with personal responsibility reflected their Father in all their doings and settings. Imagine such Christians in the press and other media, in great international corporations no less than in barber shops or on farms. . . . That is but a sample of the professions mentioned in his early notes. His heart would pound, his soul would marvel at the transforming power of grace, helping him to discover in his prayer: "It's enough to make one go crazy." A bit later he jotted down: "God's goodness does not fit in my head."[15]

Endowed also with a talent for governance and organization, Fr. Escrivá would easily move from grand outlines to small details. In these first years with nothing to show, he would describe panoramas that were impressive for their realism. Don Laureano Castán, later to become Bishop of Sigüenza, ran into Fr. Escrivá in the summers between 1929 and 1932. He recalls: "I remember one conversation when he spoke to me of the foundation God wanted which he called the Work of God. Although he was working to make it a reality, he spoke of it as though it already existed: aided by God's grace, he saw the Work clearly projected into the future. . . . I can find no other reason for perseverance in praying daily for Opus Dei," continues Bishop Castán, "than Msgr. Escrivá's overwhelming faith and the holiness that was obviously at work within him."[16]

The founder's gigantic hope not only bears witness to the lights received on October 2, 1928, but also points to the way Opus Dei works as a pastoral phenomenon. In essence this is how Fr. Escrivá proceeded: He would transmit his faith, opening up vistas of apostolate to those at his side—perspectives of a world enlivened by Christ's spirit. He would then invite them to commit themselves to this needed work and in the process discover what it really means to be

---

[15] *Intimate notes*, nos. 44 & 66. (The first text dates from June 1930; the second from the same month or the beginning of July.)

[16] L. Castán Lacoma, "Msgr. Escrivá de Balaguer, un hombre de fe" in *La Provincia*, Las Palmas de Gran Canaria, Oct. 1, 1978.

a Christian. They were needed to put Christianity into practice whatever and wherever one is, that is, as ordinary men and women engaged in the vast array of tasks that build up human society. It was in this context that he would refer to the Work as the instrument to spread this spirit, along with the possibility of binding oneself to this apostolic enterprise.

A man who dealt with the founder in 1929 and 1930 writes: "The Father [the term used by those who took part in his priestly work] spoke of *being* the Work of God, of *doing* the Work of God, rather than belonging to the Work."[17]  Msgr. Escrivá recalled in 1967: "The Work went ahead with the desire for holiness (one of the signs of a divine call) and with an eagerness to outdo oneself. . . . I didn't speak of the Work at first to those at my side: I set them to work for God, and that was it. It's what the Lord did with the apostles. If you open the gospel, you will see that at first Jesus did not speak to them of what he was going to do. He called them, they followed him, and they often conversed alone with him; on other occasions he spoke to smaller or larger groups. . . . That's how I behaved with the first ones. I said to them: Come with me . . . and some of them do not know for certain when it was that they asked to be admitted [to the Work]."[18]

Perhaps no document better reflects this reality than Msgr. Escrivá's best-known book, *The Way* (and its predecessor *Spiritual Considerations*).[19]  The author later explained the book's plan: "I tried to prepare a long inclined plane that souls would ascend little by little until they could understand the divine call of being contemplative souls in the middle of the street."[20]  These words express perfectly the interior pace of *Spiritual Considerations* and *The Way*. They begin by placing before the reader his own responsibility for giving meaning to his own life. "Don't let your life be sterile. Be useful. Blaze a trail." So begins *The Way*. Then it goes on to speak of character, self dominion, strength, toil, and excellence. Little by little it presents a panorama of prayer, Christian integrity, loving God, apostolic commitment, divine filiation, dedication, perseverance. All this is formulated in such a way as to spur the person to

---

[17] José Romeo Rivera (RHF, T-3809).

[18] RHF, 20171, p. 1368.

[19] The first version of *Spiritual Considerations* dates from December 1932, even though it incorporates many texts from 1929 and 1930. The 1932 edition—reproduced on mimeograph with a total of 246 points—was revised in 1934 giving rise to a first printing with the same title. It was later enlarged and transformed into *The Way*, which appeared in 1939. Although the number of points for meditation grew and some changed their place in the reworkings of 1934 and 1938-1939, the underlying characteristics and the general sequence of ideas remained the same throughout.

[20] *Letter*, December 29, 1947/February 14, 1966, no. 92

live this spirit where it finds him or her, where ordinary Christians should continue to live: in their workplace, their home, their ordinary social environment.

Opus Dei was born and developed as a pastoral phenomenon of Christian life amidst the ordinary circumstances of secular affairs, aimed only at promoting this reality. The institution exists to awaken those immersed in secular occupations to the grandeur and demands of the Christian vocation. This is the essential fact we must keep in mind, since it governs all of Opus Dei's history and its canonical path, which are the immediate object of our study. Even though this nucleus is essential—and precisely because it is essential—it does not express all the features that configure Opus Dei as a concrete institution. It contains its reason for being, its purpose and its fundamental nature, but that is not enough. It must be ordered and organized to carry out its spiritual-apostolic mission. Let's go again to texts and historical facts to complete the description of Opus Dei in its first stage.

## 4. Opus Dei's organization

How was Opus Dei configured? What characteristics did it have at the start? Literally, if not sociologically, the answer is very simple. First of all there was the founder. Recalling the early years, Msgr. Escrivá said all he had was his "26 years of age, the grace of God and a sense of humor." We would add, as well, an open and outgoing personality, an ability to communicate, priestly zeal, dedication often to the point of exhaustion, a deep interior life and habitual presence of God.

Secondly, there was a small group of followers. There were some seven or eight diocesan priests acquainted with the Work and on whose cooperation Fr. Josemaría counted to a greater or lesser degree. In at least one case the relationship was very brief: Fr. Jose María Somoano died a holy death in 1932. With others it lasted for years. Very quickly, however, Fr. Escrivá reached the conviction that some lay men who formed part of the Work must be ordained. Only thus would there be priests formed according to his spirit who could contribute effectively to the work.

Then, third, were a few men who belonged to the Work. Of those who had joined Opus Dei by the end of 1932 only one, Isidoro Zorzano, will be present in the later stages; another, Luis Gordon, died in November of that year; the remainder did not persevere. In 1933 the scene began to change. Several more young men joined the Work and their vocation took root and grew firm. By the middle of 1936 the founder could count on 10 or 12 men dedicated to the Work they had come to know and love.

Fourth were a few women, the first of whom joined the Work in 1932. Since Fr. Escrivá was still a young man, he thought it better to entrust the training of women members to one of the older priests who helped him. This may have been one of the reasons why he would later realize that these first women had not assimilated Opus Dei's specific spirit. In 1939 he advised them to follow other paths, while he began again the women's branch, almost from scratch. Only Dolores Fisac remained. She had come to know Opus Dei in 1937 and had not had contact with the other women.

This description could be broadened, even quantitatively, if all the persons reached in those years by Fr. Josemaría's priestly and apostolic work were included. There were hundreds of people of the most diverse backgrounds who felt the founder's spiritual influence. Yet in 1936 the nucleus of Opus Dei consisted only of the founder and a handful of young men who gave hopes of perseverance and thus of future development.

What structure or features did Opus Dei have at that time that defined it as an institution? God's Work was passing through a "period of gestation," in the founder's words. The seed had been planted in 1928 and confirmed on successive occasions, but the complete organism was still forming.

In speaking to those whom he drew towards the Work, Fr. Josemaría did not present them with something already accomplished, but with a panorama, the goals, a path, a call from God. By corresponding to this call they would have to mark out the path with their own steps. "The reality of God's will was very clear," he commented. "It was necessary, therefore, to do what the Lord enjoined. Afterwards would come the theory and the laws, born of lived experience. Thus I did not tell the first ones *what they were coming to* institutionally. Otherwise I would have had to begin with a little rule book. Not at all! The regulations came afterwards."[21]

What follows from all this? How much indetermination existed in Opus Dei in the thirties? Clearly the young priest was conscious of the provisional—more precisely, the approximate or tentative—nature of many of his reflections on how Opus Dei was to be organized. Ideas and facts would have to be evaluated and sifted. He remarks on this in his intimate notes. There such phrases appear as "Life itself in time will show us the rule"; "perhaps what has been said will have to be reformed or corrected"; "we will hold to what practice teaches us"; "God will show us"; "the Lord will inspire the solution, when he wants." In those notes we find more developed statements as well. One from March 1930 reads: "All the notes on these scraps of paper are but the seed. They bear as much resemblance to the completed being, perhaps, as an egg does to the strutting chicken that has hatched from its shell."[22]

---

[21] *Letter*, December 29, 1947/February 14, 1966, no. 23.

[22] *Intimate notes*, no. 14.

But let us ask further, what is it that changes, and how can we evaluate those changes? Another text also from July 1930, slightly later than the one just quoted, points to an answer. It contains an interpretative key that illustrates the context of Fr. Escrivá's thinking in those years. It should enlighten us on the distinction between what in his eyes still remained to be determined and therefore required his reflection and study and what, on the other hand, was established, God-defined reality. After setting forth some possible apostolic activities he writes: "This is not—how well I realize it—something definitive, an illumination, but only a sliver of light."[23] We see clearly formulated the distinction between "illuminations," the insights God grants which constitute therefore landmarks or definitive points of reference and the "slivers of light," the aspects, details, particulars that meditation, study, or experience helped him discern and even sketch out. These secondary features were undoubtedly necessary, channeling activity in certain directions, as they do, but they did not in themselves possess the self-evidence or evident truth. Rather, they were at the service of the original divine light to which they had to be compared and to which they must be accommodated.

It was no little balancing act that the founder faced. On the one hand he had to be absolutely faithful to everything related to the charism received. Who was he to obey God's will less than exactly? He must not vary anything, not in the slightest. Yet he also had to be open to new data and adapt things to changeable historical situations which was a challenge to his founder's prudence that could only be met with unconditional allegiance to essentials. Such was Fr. Escrivá's case, especially at the outset.

Opus Dei's structure was not yet fleshed out in all its details. Its organization was still developing. Nevertheless the Work was not a shapeless reality, a vague and undefined movement towards an ideal, powerful perhaps but lacking still even a minimum of structural support. Rather, it was an institution endowed at the start with very definite contours. The lights received on October 2, 1928, February 14, 1930, and August 7, 1931, and on similar occasions, determined not only the spiritual features, but also its institutional qualities. These had to be embodied in life and completed, undoubtedly, in one aspect or another, but above all with fidelity to essentials. The Work must be made wholly consistent.[24]

---

[23] *Ibid.*, no. 44.

[24] That Fr. Escrivá tenaciously clung to the foundational charism both in its overall outline and essential, specific traits is seen in an *Instruction* he wrote in 1934. At that time Spain was going through social changes and political upheavals that directly threatened religion. In response there sprang up all kinds of Catholic movements and groups and likewise calls for these to coalesce in a united front. In that context the

## 5. Essential characteristics of Opus Dei

What are the characteristics that define the Work as the founder saw it? Or at least what are its fundamental traits? We will now attempt to identify them, but not without a preliminary caution. What follows is not a synthesis or panoramic vision of Opus Dei's spirit, nor is it a sketch of the ecclesiological, theological, and existential implications that derive from its rich spiritual message. Rather we seek the attributes that make up the institutional features of Opus Dei. We thus turn to the first writings of the founder for the Work's basic nature and structure. Here begins the canonical development we want to examine and evaluate.

Even at the risk of repetition, the first characteristic must refer to sanctifying the world, establishing Christ's kingdom, impregnating all activities and temporal realities with the spirit of the Gospel. How? As a result of all kinds of men and women committing themselves to be authentic Christians. From the perspective of Opus Dei's founding, this desideratum is the end it aspires to. Better yet, that redemptive presence is the expected fruit. Such a program of peace and unity, to be completed only in the heavenly kingdom, can be advanced in some way in each historical moment by virtue of grace. This panoramic mission calls for a positive attitude to life and the world, a determined effort to reflect even now by means of faith and charity the fullness of love God has manifested in Jesus Christ.

The first essential trait immediately leads to the second: the re-evaluation of one's work or occupation, the task each person carries out in the world. Through work man takes his place in the world and contributes to its development. It is with and through his work that the ordinary Christian can bring Jesus Christ to the world. By work, Josemaría Escrivá understood not only one's job, but also the sum total of duties and commitments that make up

---

founder felt urged to emphasize to his followers the seriousness and permanence of their God-given mission. Neither he nor they could consent to diluting the Work or harnessing it to solve problems of a particular place or time.

"In talking with you," he writes, "I have often pointed out that the enterprise we are called to accomplish is no human undertaking but rather a great *supernatural enterprise*. From the very start it came endowed with the qualities that justify its being called, literally and without boasting, the *Work of God*." He goes on to say that three proposals had reached him for the Work to merge with one or another of these transitory organizations. His reaction was very precise: "There was room for only one answer. In the apostolic terrain we will always be united. At least on our part there will never be friction for we come only to carry out Christ's apostolate—not ours.

"But union as they propose — or, better said, confusion — cannot be, for we are not engaged in something human. *Our enterprise is divine.* Consequently it is forbidden for us to compromise, mutilate or change anything related to the spirit and organization of the Work of God." *Instruction*, March 19, 1934, nos. 1, 19-20.

daily life. But he always attributed a primordial importance to work in the strict sense, considering it an essential and necessary element by which man is bound to the world. Many consequences derive from this principle. Let's point out two substantive and parallel ones that deeply configure Opus Dei: first is the requirement that all of its members work, that is, engage in some occupation or professional task;[25] second is its openness to all kinds of people of any social class or condition who carry out a task or office in the middle of the world.[26] The third element is a vocational sense: the reality of a divine call inviting a person to live the Christian faith in its radical fullness and eliciting a thorough and decisive commitment. The founder never spoke of Opus Dei as an association whose purpose or scope was limited or restricted and to which one commits only a part of his life. Rather he spoke of it as a spiritual and apostolic work whose realization requires the entirety of a person, for such is the will of God. Without a doubt this is one of the reasons, and not the least important, why he called the institution he promoted the Work of God. In this way he underlined unambiguously its charismatic and divine origin. In 1934 he wrote, "Do not forget, my children, that we are not souls who have joined other souls to do a good thing. This is a lot but still little. We are apostles *carrying out an imperative mandate of Jesus Christ.*"[27] Opus Dei thus does not arise from the initiatives of a priest filled with spiritual longings; rather in its founder's eye it is the fruit of God's intervening in history. He is not calling people to take part in a well-meaning apostolic project with more or

---

[25] The activity and circumstances of the members of Opus Dei can be quite diverse: celibacy or marriage, manual or intellectual work, work in the fields of business, the arts, or sports, to mention only a few of the different possibilities. But in the life of no member of Opus Dei can there be missing the element of work. "To anyone who rejects honest human work—important or humble—saying that it cannot sanctify or be sanctified, you can tell him with a clear conscience that God has not called him to his Work." (*Letter*, January 9, 1932, no. 3). The same criteria appear several times in his intimate notes: "Man was born to work *ut operaretur*: in the Work all will work," he writes on March 19, 1933 (*Intimate Notes* no. 955). A few months later, on January 20, 1934 (*Ibid.*, no. 1119), he reiterates this norm in a more juridical tone. Years later he will use practically the same words in the statutes written in seeking the first canonical approval of Opus Dei, which, as we shall see, took place in 1941.

[26] This reality is present in an explicit way in the oldest writings of the founder. He does so by referring to various occupations quite different from one another but also with explicit declarations. Thus, for example, in early June 1930 he declares decisively that Opus Dei will never be "an association of one particular or several particular professions," because "there is room for all professions." A few days later, referring to the occupations the women who come to Opus Dei can carry out, he enumerates various—some manual, others intellectual—and concludes, "any honest work done for God." About the same time but speaking of men, he expresses himself in similar terms: "every kind of professional work, with naturalness: the ordinary thing, sanctified" (*Intimate Notes*, nos. 38, 43-44).

[27] *Instruction*, March 19, 1934, no. 27.

less intensity, as circumstances permit. Rather he calls each to make oneself fully available to God, who calls each one by his own name. Incorporation to Opus Dei presupposes knowing that one is the object of a divine vocation or call. To this God-given invitation one should respond with an unconditional dedication. From that moment one should pledge all one's might to imitate and follow Jesus Christ. And for Opus Dei members—let us not forget it—this intimacy and partnership takes place in daily work, amid the common conditions and circumstances of life in the world.

A fourth facet linked to the previous ones is a deep and definite call to personal holiness, because vocation is a summons to participate in God's intimate life, to live off Him and for Him. In June 1930 Fr. Escrivá succinctly enumerates the essential notes: "Plain Christians. Dough in fermentation. What is ordinary is ours, with naturalness. The means: professional work. Everyone saints!"[28] It is not a question of carrying out a human enterprise, but of collaborating in the divine adventure of redemption, thus above all else they strive to identify themselves with Jesus Christ. In him and through the Holy Spirit, they unite themselves with God the Father. This means holiness, prayer, interior life, faith, love shown in deeds. Thus Opus Dei comes across as a pastoral phenomenon of a full Christian life in all its aspects, ratified in the circumstances and environments common to the human condition.

A fifth essential trait is the apostolic projection. Knowing oneself called by God is, always and necessarily, to know one is sent to mankind to show them the love of which one has been the object. The discovery that God calls one to love him in and through the gamut of daily occupations leads to the desire to deal with God in every moment. But not only that, it also entails making one's ordinary life redemptive, helping others in the same setting to savor God's special love; "May your behavior and your conversation be such that everyone who sees or hears you can say: this man reads the life of Jesus Christ"; "Among those around you, apostolic soul, you are the stone fallen into the lake. With your word and example produce a first ripple . . . and it will produce another . . . and then another, and another . . . each time wider."[29] Modest behavior and conversation, example and word weave a Christian way of acting without anything strange or ostentatious. On the contrary, infusing daily events with a Christian view of life awakens the depth and richness of the faith. There thus necessarily arises the ordinary Christian's apostolic drive, what the founder of Opus Dei calls "apostolate of friendship and trust." One of the last points in *The Way* reads: "Those words whispered at the proper time into the ear

---

[28] *Intimate Notes*, no. 35.

[29] *The Way*, nos. 2 & 83 (*Spiritual Considerations*, 1932, nos. 2 & 11).

of your wavering friend; that helpful conversation you managed to start at the right moment; the ready advice that improves his studies; and the discrete indiscretion by which you opened for him unsuspected horizons for his zeal—all that is the 'apostolate of friendship.'"[30]

All the above aspects converge in a sixth characteristic: unity of life. In the founder's texts that have reached us, this expression first appears in a note dated February 6, 1931.[31] He may have used it earlier; now in any case he employs it more and more, conscious that it summarizes his spiritual message. Unity of life does not have for him a merely generic meaning, arranging one's actions and attitudes around a central point. Certainly it does mean this process of arranging things as well as the resulting spiritual unity, but it also always connotes for Fr. Escrivá the lay and secular condition of those of whom it is predicated. Thus fully understood, the expression denotes the whole spiritual program of the Work. Unity of life according to the spirit of Opus Dei means being called by God to see the world as part of His plan. Thus the world plays a part in the spiritual life of ordinary Christians, fusing thereby its theological and apostolic dimensions. "In Opus Dei unity of life is necessary to the children God has called to his Work. This unity of life has two interwoven facets: an interior, which makes us contemplatives; and an apostolic, through our professional work, which is visible and external."[32]

Still more graphically in the *Instruction* of March 1934 there appears a brief paragraph towards the end of the document outlining the "ideals" that configure Opus Dei: "To unite work with ascetical struggle and contemplation could seem impossible, but it is necessary if the world is to be reconciled with God. This daily toil is to be converted into a means of personal sanctification and apostolate. Is not this a noble and grand ideal for which it is worth giving up one's life?"[33]

A seventh characteristic going beyond the spirit outlines a pastoral need. Opus Dei is for both men and women. This calls for an internal structure with two branches. In 1928 the founder, as men-

---

[30] *The Way*, no. 973; other graphic descriptions from a later date can be found in *Christ is Passing By*, nos. 148-149, and *Friends of God*, nos. 264-265.

[31] *Intimate notes*, no. 155.

(*Translator's note.* The Decree on the Heroicity of his virtues proclaims: "The Servant of God was a pioneer of the *intrinsic unity of Christian life*." Cfr. Congregation for the Causes of the Saints, *Decree. Cause of Canonization of the Servant of God, Josemaría Escrivá*, April 9, 1990.)

[32] *Letter*, January 9, 1932, no. 14.

[33] *Instruction*, March 19, 1934, no. 33.

tioned earlier, thought his work was limited to men. On February 14, 1930, however, God showed him that the light received a year and a half earlier was to be shared also with women. He also saw that their respective apostolic endeavors should be autonomous, though united in spirit, foundational charism and, later, institutional structure. To express this reality of unity and distinction, the early writings (1930-31) speak of "two Works"; then more frequently, "two branches" or "two sections." This latter terminology ultimately prevailed.*

An eighth characteristic, also substantially affecting Opus Dei's structure, is that both celibate and married persons belong to the Work. To assure apostolic continuity, there needed to be men and women committed to living celibacy and who are thus more available for being entrusted with functions of direction and formation. Fr. Josemaría sometimes referred to this reality by distinguishing between the "general staff" and the "troops."[34] Like every metaphor, this too must be seen in context. With it he seeks to express a distinction of functions, while participating in the same apostolic enterprise. Both celibate and married members are alike called to sanctify their life's work in the habitual circumstances of daily life.[35]

A ninth essential characteristic is the close cooperation of priests and lay people. The Work is an institution promoting sanctity and apostolate among ordinary lay people, the majority of whose members are lay people with many different occupations. Fr. Escrivá saw the priest's mission in exclusively spiritual terms. They are not to direct the secular activities of the other members of the Work, but, by means of their priestly ministry, to foster the members' interior life, their Christian sense of existence and their apostolic zeal. In a text from 1931 the founder writes: "The priests will be solely *spiritual directors of souls*, and that is no small thing." These priests, he continues, will play a very important role in the Work. But this is true only in so far as they truly serve the others and as true shepherds sacrifice themselves for the spiritual sake of those entrusted to their care. They are to dedicate time to the others,

---

* *(Translator's note.* English-speakers, however, have preferred two "branches".)

[34] *Intimate notes,* no. 339 (dated October 20, 1931).

[35] We will deal more fully with this idea of unity of vocation. With respect to the expression "troops" see the commentary of Msgr. Escrivá himself in *Conversations with Msgr. Escrivá de Balaguer,* nos. 45 & 92. From it we extract a paragraph: "In an army—and this is all the comparison was meant to express—the soldiers are as necessary as the general staff and can be more heroic and merit more glory. In a word, there is a variety of tasks and all are necessary and worthy. What is really important is that each person should follow his own vocation. For each individual, the most perfect thing is, always and only, to do God's will."

forming them one by one, conscious of the divine efficacy of "this hidden apostolate."[36] From this comes the motto he set for them at the beginning: "To hide and disappear."[37] This mission of service is to be more than full time; they renounce any ambition or applause. Their only aim is to foster the Christian life of the lay men and women who seek their pastoral help.

In tenth place we point to the founder's recognition of the impact that seed ideas, underlying convictions, have on men and nations. From this arose the esteem Fr. Josemaría showed for the intellectual professions, conscious of their social impact.[38] More broadly, he prized integral formation, the development of the whole person. In this way human personality is rooted in the deepest layers of human existence and identified with the fundamental options and other decisions of the will. At the same time it implies and presupposes the free cultivation of the intellect. Chapters of *The Way* and *Spiritual Considerations* on "Study" and "Formation" are illustrative. There we find an ideal wherein spiritual life, theological knowledge, adequate grounding in the subjects called for by one's profession or occupation, and cultural enrichment are integrated harmoniously in each Christian. Thus each strives to bring about a personal synthesis that makes of him a "discerning soul" capable of acting as a Christian in any circumstance. And this is the goal for persons of every social condition and occupation.[39] From this perspective forming its members is seen to be the role that summarizes everything the Work does. Opus Dei, the founder repeated, exists only to educate and form its members and all those who avail themselves of this formation. Thus strengthened, each person can act with a Christian sense in professional and social life. This institutional preoccupation is summarized in an expression Fr.

---

[36] *Intimate notes*, no. 158.

[37] *Ibid.*, no. 96 from October 25, 1930.

[38] A priest who knew Fr. Escrivá in the late 1920s remembers a commentary that summarizes this esteem, expressed in a somewhat poetic manner. One day Josemaría asked him: "Have you seen the snowy peaks of the great mountains? They are the great ideas and the great intellects. They seem distant, remote, but from this snow comes the water that makes the valleys fertile." (Account of Fidel Gómez Colomo, in RHF, T-1364).

[39] See *The Way*, nos. 332-386. The expression "discerning soul" is found in the brief prologue included in *The Way* (expanding the one that had appeared in *Spiritual Considerations*). It summarizes the purpose of the book; the phrase where this expression appears at the end of the prologue reads: "I will only stir your memory, so that some thought will arise and strike you; and so you will better your life and set out along ways of prayer and of love and in the end you will be a more worthy soul."

* *(Translator's note.* There is a problem in this translation, because "alma de criterio" is better translated by "discerning soul." Cf . *The Forge*, nos. 450 & 840.)

Escrivá used in January 1932 and to which we will return: "We are
and we will always be a great catechesis."[40]

A new characteristic, the eleventh, completes the preceding one:
members remain free in all professional, social, and political matters. The affirmation of this freedom is present from the beginning.
Early in 1931, for example, Fr. Escrivá sketches in his *Intimate Notes*
different apostolic activities; to this enumeration he adds, "a Catholic
political party, no: differences of opinion."[41] Early in 1932 he writes:
"We are citizens the same as others: the same duties, the same
rights.—The political freedom of the members. For this reason, in
human things, a variety of opinions."[42] Following up on the first of
these texts the founder clearly indicates the only thing uniting Opus
Dei members among themselves and, consequently, their wide margin
of freedom and diversity: "unity only in the common denominator." He uses a metaphor to which we will return. What specifically
is that common denominator? The faith of the Church, the spirit of
the Work and apostolic drive. On top of these rests a most varied
numerator composed of personal traits and the choices each has
freely embraced.[43]

As the twelfth characteristic let us cite Opus Dei's universal or
international nature. The institution comes not for a specific country but rather for the whole world: its subsequent expansion is not
then a mere fact but rather an intrinsic requirement of its original

---

[40] *Intimate notes*, no. 548. As a corollary of this teaching he insisted from the very start
that "the Work does not act; it is its members who do," underlining that Opus Dei has
as its purpose not the fostering of enterprises or particular works, but principally the
spiritual and apostolic development of its members. Afterwards they, conscious of
the demands of their Christian life and with personal freedom and responsibility,
dedicate themselves to become holy and apostolic, according to their personal status
in the ordinary circumstances of life. Nevertheless this does not stand in the way of
Opus Dei's taking care of some apostolic works. These undertakings are not a specific
end of the Work, but only a means to serve the ultimate objective: the full maturity of
Christians.

[41] *Intimate notes*, no. 206.

[42] *Ibid.*, no. 158 . In the *Letter* dated January 1932, he further explains this point: "The
Work does not have a political program: this is not its purpose. Our sole goal is spiritual and apostolic, and has a divine stamp, love for freedom"; "act freely because this
is proper to our distinctive divine call to sanctify ourselves by working in ordinary
tasks according to the dictates of one's own conscience"; "the bond that unites us is
exclusively spiritual" (*Letter*, January 9, 1932, nos. 42-44).

[43] He comments on this metaphor in another text of December 1931: "I would dare to
make a diagram of the members of Opus Dei as God wants them: I would write down
a series of fractions with the same denominator (unity of formation which makes them
identify themselves with Jesus Christ) and very different numerators (autonomy), corresponding to the different circumstances of character and temperament and even to
the different paths along which Jesus Christ will lead their souls." (*Intimate notes*, no.
511).

spirit. We document this with a single text from the already quoted *Instruction* of 1934: "*We are not an organization arisen out of the circumstances of the moment. . . .* Nor have we come to fill a need of a particular country or particular time, because Jesus Christ wants his Work from the very first moment Catholic, with a universal heart."[44]

In the founder's mind the universality of Opus Dei implies a centralized and interdiocesan organization. There we have its last distinctive feature. In his *Intimate notes* he points to this character. Thus, for example, referring to the one leading it, he writes that he will need the cooperation of "a certain number of members . . . with him or spread throughout the world to help him govern the Work."[45] In these personal notes he says Opus Dei cannot have a legal status only at the diocesan level, "because of the very universal character of the Work of God."[46] And already in 1931 he foresaw that the headquarters would end up in Rome, the center of the Catholic world.[47]

The preceding characteristics do not exhaust everything that could be said of Opus Dei's spirit and activity, as we pointed out earlier. It is equally obvious that the commentary on the features could be much more extensive. Such exhaustiveness would be fitting if our objective were to set forth and study Opus Dei's spirituality or its apostolates. Since our purpose is merely to follow Opus Dei's canonical progression, the description given seems sufficient. Now let us move on to consider some of the basic ideas which we have to understand in order to grasp more exactly the pastoral phenomenon that is Opus Dei. For this we turn once again to its first years. Such an attempt will shed light too on the vicissitudes of Opus Dei's subsequent canonical evolution.

---

[44] *Instruction*, March 19, 1934, nos. 14-15.

[45] *Intimate notes*, no. 153 (February 2, 1931).

[46] *Ibid.*, no. 157.

[47] *Ibid.*, no. 220 (August 10, 1931) and no. 422 (November 29, 1931).

# Chapter II

## *A DISTINCTIVE PASTORAL AND APOSTOLIC PHENOMENON*

1. Christian faith and secular realities
2. Personal responsibility, freedom and secularity
3. Universal call to holiness
4. The Christian vocation in the world: its requirements

   a) Divine vocation and human vocation

   b) Christian value of earthly realities
5. In search of new terminological and conceptual formulas

# 6. The problem of Opus Dei's canonical configuration

# Chapter II

## A DISTINCTIVE PASTORAL
## AND APOSTOLIC PHENOMENON

### 1. Christian faith and secular realities

The object of this chapter is to highlight certain underlying characteristics of Opus Dei. Although they have already been mentioned we will now look at them in greater depth, to underline the central nucleus which illuminates the whole and makes it an articulated unity.

To analyze the legal steps taken by Opus Dei, we must have a profound grasp of the foundational charism; only from that point of view can the complete process be evaluated. We must also consider the ecclesial and theological environment that reigned when Opus Dei was born, since these circumstances influenced its varied legal stages.

One must not forget the tendency earlier in this century to identify, at least in practice, the vocation to full Christian life with the religious state or with priesthood. Moreover, from the Enlightenment onward, Europe passed through a succession of confrontations between Church and State. The spread of secularizing and laicist attitudes occasioned the birth of many movements, groups, and associations intended to foster, in one way or another, the presence and action of Christians in civic life. Surrounded by this climate, Josemaría Escrivá needed great firmness to define and defend Opus Dei's distinctive nature and specific features.

There was an abundance of Catholic groups and associations at that time. Simplifying matters, we can group these new movements in two fundamental types: on the one hand, groups for social and civic action; and on the other, educational or charitable associations. These latter were born in or around the French Revolution or in later religious persecutions with the hope that their members—lay people in some instances, religious without habits in others—would take charge of the educational and charitable works that traditional religious orders and congregations had been forced to abandon.  Some even sought to maintain Christian influence in institutions, while keeping their own condition hidden.[1]

Opus Dei's founder referred to this myriad of institutes to underline the Work's distinctiveness.  In the *Instruction* of March 19, 1934, he writes: "In stormy times many organizations and institutions arise that tend to dedicate themselves to different works of zeal, which the religious orders and congregations have had to give up in the face of persecution.  Naturally Spain now is not an exception, nor was it in the revolutionary period of the last century.  We see various and indeed many groups of men and women of good will determined to give battle to Christ's enemies with a supernatural outlook."[2]  Having thus described the panorama and after pointing out that some of these organizations can appear "externally" (this qualifier is important) similar to the Work, he gave a clear criterion to those who at the time formed part of Opus Dei: Do not concern yourself with these institutions whose future development will be what God wants.  Focus on fidelity to your own vocation where God awaits you and fidelity to what the Lord wants to foster through the Work; "let them follow their paths and let us follow ours."[3]

These words reflect neither a desire to single himself out nor a wait-and-see attitude intent on discovering what might be more prudent or fitting in a particular moment.  Rather they echo a profound conviction of the uniqueness of Opus Dei as a pastoral phenomenon.  It presupposes a doctrinal and theological foundation quite different from that of these other institutions, arising then as in other times with greater or lesser chances of survival.  Let us now examine what makes Opus Dei a distinctive entity.

What happened on October 2, 1928?  On that day Blessed Josemaría saw displayed before his eyes a vast apostolic panorama which he was being called to promote.  A multitude of men—and after 1930, also of women—were to work in many different environments thereby

---

[1] Many studies have been made on specific initiatives or movements; for an overview of the general context in which they were born, we mention a few works where further data and bibliographical references can be obtained: H. Jedin (ed.), *Handbuch der Kirchengeschichte*, t. VI, Freiburg i. B. 1973; R. Aubert (ed.), *Nouvelle histoire de l'Eglise*, t. V, Paris 1972; G. Redondo, *La Iglesia en el mundo contemporaneo*, Pamplona 1979; Various authors, *La spiritualità cristiana nell'età contemporanea*, Vol. VI, Roma 1985; Various authors, *Spiritualità e azione del laicato cattolico italiano*, Padova 1969; G. Penco, *Storia della Chiesa in Italia*, Vol. II, Milan 1978; A. Dansette, *Histoire religieuse de la França contemporaine*, Paris 1965.

[2] *Instruction*, March 19, 1934, no. 8.

[3] *Ibid.*, nos. 9-13.

helping to invigorate them with the grace and truth of Christ. To describe this reality, an apostolic and pastoral phenomenon and its eventual fruits, Fr. Josemaría fixed on a metaphor: an intravenous injection. As the liquid injected into the body regenerates it from within, so also do Christians who live up to their faith. They are an "intravenous injection in the circulatory system of society." From within the structures of society they transmit the strength of the Gospel, Christ's light and love enlightening minds, healing hearts, overflowing in goodness, unity, fraternity, progress.[4]

Fr. Escrivá's apostolic perspective always bespoke spreading Christ's message in society, establishing a harmony between Christian faith and social life and, consequently, harvesting justice, peace, and love as the fruits of acting as a Christian. Explaining this panorama, the founder often pointed to the specifics of the historical-cultural matrix where the Work was born and, above all, to the rupture between faith and life, between Christianity and earthly realities. In a 1961 *Letter* he commented: "The Lord has wanted to raise up his Work at a time when in most countries elites and entire populations seemed to be fleeing from the Source of all grace; when even in long-standing Christian countries people were using the sacraments less frequently; when whole sectors of the lay world seemed to be asleep, as though their operative faith had disappeared."[5]

He had expressed similar ideas in an entry in his *Intimate Notes* between April and June 1930: We must struggle "against laicism with an apparent laicism; against indifferentism, with an apparent indifferentism." A year later, in July 1931, he echoes the idea with somewhat different words: "a healthy lay outlook, a healthy anticlericalism."[6] Both phrases indicate not only the evil or crisis to be overcome, but also the way to overcome it. What is needed is not merely a reaction against the spiritual crisis and anti-Christian attitudes, but a deepening of one's understanding and living of Christianity. Since such a conversion would be deep and authentic, it could grasp and assimilate the positive elements contained in modernity. He later advocated neither laicism nor clericalism but a lay mentality; not secularization or sacralization but secularity. To the clerically-minded, such an attitude towards the world may seem secularized. In reality, however, it is an authentically Christian way of life, consistent with a belief in God the Creator towards whom all creation ought to be oriented. Earthly realities are not to

---

[4] This metaphor appears already in 1930 texts: *Intimate notes*, no. 14.

[5] *Letter*, January 25, 1961, no. 13.

[6] *Intimate notes*, nos. 32 & 206.

be instrumentalized or merely exploited, but the God-given nature of each must be respected.[7]

The solution to the contemporary crisis of culture calls for awakening men and women living in the world and dedicated to secular activities to the grandeur of their Christian vocation. Remaining where one is, being as it were one more among one's peers, a Christian with his full-fledged faith, ought to give new life to human realities, from within, without any religious ostentation or clericalism of any kind. From the first, Fr. Escrivá distinctly saw that the Work he was to found would contribute to this great apostolic objective. This is borne out by many of his writings. Among others the 1934 *Instruction* paints the critical panorama of Europe in the 1930's as the background against which the birth of Opus Dei must be evaluated: "Out of this worldwide cataclysm, comparable only to that wrought by Luther, God has wanted to bring forth the Work he inspired some years ago."[8]

Such quotations could be multiplied, because these sentiments were deeply rooted in Fr. Josemaría's soul. But it would be more helpful perhaps to make more precise the scope and meaning of the statements we have already quoted.

a) First, references to cultural events of the time for Opus Dei's founder, both then and later, served to underscore the urgent need for apostolic action, whether of the Church in general or of the Work. Opus Dei, however, was not conceived in response to this or that threat. The foundation is rooted only in what happened on October 2, 1928. It does not stem from his personal reflections on particular events, nor from social or cultural trends nor from temporal problems of any kind, but from a divine light that transcends history. In the 1934 *Instruction* he insists: "*The Work of God has not been thought up by a man* to solve the sad situation of the Church in Spain since 1931."

"Many years ago the Lord inspired it in an inept and deaf instrument, who saw it for the first time on October 2, 1928, the feast of the Holy Guardian Angels."[9]

b) Second, while the promise of peace and social progress resulting from spreading the Gospel played a role, even an important one, in Fr. Escrivá's preaching and life, neither his priestly activity nor the efforts of Opus Dei can be construed as a mere means to

---

[7] For a theological-canonical reflection on the lay vocation, see: A. del Portillo, *Faithful and Laity in the Church*, Dublin 1972 (2nd ed. 1981); P. Lombardia, *Escritos de Derecho Canónico*, Vol. II, Pamplona 1973; J. Herranz, G. Lo Castro and others, *Chi sono i laici. Una teologia della secolarità*, Milan 1987; Various authors, *La mision de los laicos en la Iglesia y en el mundo*, Pamplona 1987.

[8] *Instruction*, March 19, 1934, no. 41.

[9] *Ibid.*, March 19, 1934, nos. 6-7.

improve and transform society. In the founder's eyes the Christian
betterment of society is not an end, but rather a fruit. An effect may
be foreseen and even hoped for, but that does not mean that it is
sought directly. It may be a by-product of what is directly sought
and desired. Such is the meaning of a well-known point in *The Way*:
"A secret. —An open secret: these world crises are crises of saints.
God wants a handful of men of his very own in every human activity. And then *pax Christi in regno Christi*, the peace of Christ in the
kingdom of Christ."[10]

The mission entrusted to Fr. Josemaría Escrivá on October 2,
1928, was to promote among persons of all social conditions and
occupations, a profound conversion of soul which would lead them
to orient their whole life towards God. This conversion and consciousness seriously leads one to turn faith into life. Such a project
cannot help but affect the world and history, even profoundly. This
attitude underlined, confirmed and expanded earlier illuminations
especially the "If I am lifted above the earth . . ." heard on August
7, 1931, to which, moreover, the point in *The Way* alludes. But what
constitutes the direct object of the founder's pastoral action, thereby
endowing Opus Dei with its own features as he always saw them?
Ever faithful to the foundational charism, what Fr. Escrivá felt himself called to spread is found at the deepest level: each person
identifying himself with God's will, even more with God himself.

Beneath this scheme lies a keen perception of the theological
dimension of Christian existence. And it calls for a profound unity
between task and vocation, between action and intimacy with God,
between apostolate and holiness. The ultimate source of this sought-
for perfection, its inspirational nucleus, is found, as we have already said, in the illuminations granted Fr. Escrivá in 1928 and in
the following years. But there were even antecedents to these. In
fact, his spiritual restlessness began—let us not forget—during the
winter of 1917-1918. Then began a long process of acquiring maturity in his interior life.[11] From then on Josemaría Escrivá knew that
God wanted something of him. But he is not even given a glimpse
of the divine plan. This uncertainty, his theological studies and
subsequent priestly ordination, the experience of sorrow and troubles,
his early pastoral work—all these created in his soul an unconditional availability to God's will and a keen consciousness of the
worth of prayer, sacrifice and spiritual childhood.

All of this was taken up and given new impetus with the charism
received in October 2, 1928 and subsequent events. "God got into

---

[10] *The Way*, no. 301

[11] With regard to this point, as in general with respect to other details of the historical
environment, we refer to the biographical studies cited in note no. 1 of Chapter 1.

my life," he commented many times. For him history is not a succession of meaningless, heterogeneous events; rather it is the unfolding
of the Trinity's loving design. God comes out to meet humanity and
to share our human life as He did in Bethlehem, Nazareth and Cal-
vary. Again today he makes himself present when he wants and as
he wants. God is the supreme protagonist of history, not man. But
God counts on us: he awakens us to his plans and invites us to
become his collaborators. Man's attitude should be that of availability, gratitude, awe, attentively listening to what God says, actively
surrendering to what God wants. What ultimately drives history is
not human determination and effort, but divine providence, which
gives meaning to everything. Our role is to open ourselves to God's
will and to trust in his grace. From this fundamental truth derives
a hierarchy of means which Fr. Escrivá formulated in one of the
apothegms for which he had a special gift: "First, prayer; then, atone-
ment; in the third place—very much 'in the third place'—action."[12]

In promoting the Work, Blessed Josemaría practiced what he
preached. He not only set to work, but at the same time exacted of
himself much prayer and sacrifice. He likewise turned to many
others seeking their prayers. His priestly work reached many sick
people whom he habitually asked to offer their sufferings for the
development of the mission God had entrusted to him. "Opus Dei
was born," he always said, "among the poor and the sick of the
hospitals of Madrid."[13]

At the same time he thought that this foundation of personal
prayer, sacrifice, and dedication ought to animate the Work of God
throughout its history. To ensure this, for a time he proposed that
there should be "houses of prayer," as a source of strength for Opus
Dei members working in many different professional fields; they
would pray in a special way for apostolic progress. There should
also be clinics and hospitals ("houses of expiation") where patients
would receive medical attention, but where they would also discover the Christian meaning of suffering, uniting themselves spiritually to a whole gamut of apostolic endeavors and strengthening
the Work with their prayer and abandonment.[14]

Nevertheless it was not long before the founder realized that
the union of these three dimensions must be still more fundamental, such that it takes place in the life of each person. In July 1930
he wrote that action, prayer, and expiation must be genuine in each

---

[12] *The Way*, no. 82; this point is also found in the 1932 *Spiritual Considerations* where it
is no. 48.

[13] Cf. S. Bernal, *op.cit.* (Chapter 1, note 1), pp. 168 ff.; A. Vazquez de Prada, *op.cit.*
(Chapter 1, note 1), pp. 121 ff.

[14] *Intimate notes*, no. 16 (March 13, 1930).

and every one of Opus Dei's members. "Without *prayer*, without continual presence of God; without *expiation*, sought in the small setbacks of daily life; without all of this, there is not, nor can there ever be, true personal apostolic *action*."[15]

This evolution of ideas occurred all in the space of a few months. Such was the ferment of the founder's interior life during the first years. It also evidences that, no matter what the point of departure, he always returns to the same principle: the call to a living, personal encounter with Jesus Christ.[16] Dreaming of great fruits and broadening horizons for his lay followers, Fr. Josemaría's preaching always led to a full commitment to God, to self-surrender, in a word, to holiness.

His aspiration was that all Christians—whatever their condition, situation, or occupation—should see themselves called by God, urged to live the message, demands, and promises of the Gospel in their entirety. They were to do so without leaving the world—humanity's normal condition of life. In the middle of the world, by personally, intimately identifying themselves with God, Christ is brought into the world, enlivening it with his grace. Another clear example of rooting oneself in God is the text of June 1930 from which we have already quoted in part. It is very rich: "Ordinary Christians. Dough in fermentation. Our way is ordinary things lived with naturalness. The means: professional work. Let all become holy! Silent abandonment."[17]

This call to holiness should never be seen as something self-centered, leading to isolation from one's fellows. Holiness does not lie there, nor was it ever so understood by the founder. Vocation is an invitation to correspond to God, who loves the world to the extreme of giving up his Son, made man, to redeem mankind. We cannot hope to love God without imitating the generosity and abandonment of Jesus Christ. An ordinary Christian should seek to live

---

[15] *Ibid.*, no. 74. In a letter dated November 23, 1930, addressed to Isidoro Zorzano, an engineer and member of Opus Dei, he wrote: "If we are going to be what the Lord and we want, our life must be rooted before all else in *prayer* and in *expiation* (sacrifice). Prayer: never leave out meditation when you get up in the morning, I repeat; and offer as expiation all the annoyances and sacrifices of the day" (RHF, EF-301123-1). In another letter of September 3, 1931, also to Isidoro Zorzano, he returns to the same topic: "What is our present work? Each one of us must be a foundation stone. We must acquire spiritual strength by being put to the test to see if we can bear the enormous weight of the Work of God. Pray. Make expiation. I seem heavy-handed. But all of the 'science' is there" (RHF, EF-310903-1).

[16] On November 14, 1931, the founder wrote: "The Work of God is going to make men of God, men of interior life, men of prayer and sacrifice. The apostolate of the members will be an overflow of their life 'within:' they will give from their superabundance: they will never be a mere facade: they will always have less facade than dwelling place—the phrase is not very apt" (*Intimate notes*, no. 391).

[17] *Ibid.*, no. 35.

amidst secular structures in such a way as to impart a Christian dimension to human activity, thus working to restore all things in Christ.

This transformation follows only from a radical, permanent conversion. The founder of Opus Dei sought only to inflame hearts with love for Jesus Christ, to transmit to others the excitement born of discovering this infinite greatness of God's love revealed in Jesus Christ. From October 2, 1928, Fr. Escrivá knew he had been called in a special way to transmit this message to people living in the world, dedicated to secular tasks and occupations. They are called to discover in all their depth the riches of the Gospel and to see God's gift incarnated in their lives. Only thus can they plumb the depths of the ultimate meaning of the apparent minutiae of each day, turning them into encounters with God and sharing with others the love that comes from God.

Blessed Josemaría did not launch a social-action movement nor did he merely seek to recall the laity to their apostolic and social responsibilities, topped off by an invitation to have interior life as the basis for apostolate. Fr. Escrivá's was a vocational phenomenon. Through his priestly work he urged each person to reach into the depths of his soul where he finds himself face to face with God. There he hears himself called by God, invited to identify his life with Christ's. There he also sees coming together the call to intimacy with God, the God-entrusted task or mission, and the world where this task is to unfold.

Opus Dei's founder summons everyone—and Opus Dei keeps doing the same—to a full Christian life in the world that can't help but produce fruits of social transformation, of the establishment of justice, fraternity, and peace. Faith and love should overflow into deeds; grace can and ought to produce fruits of redemption now and at every moment. Yet a fully Christian life transcends these consequences since it reaches beyond time and history. It's results are secondary and gratuitous in relation to the paramount goal: radical identification with Jesus Christ, full surrender to God.

## 2. Personal responsibility, freedom and secularity

The theological and spiritual perspectives just seen place before us the pastoral phenomenon of Opus Dei. Therein we have the criteria for judging and evaluating adequately the Work's subsequent legal development and for grasping what distinguishes Opus Dei from both social movements and latter-day religious orders and other institutions considered alike. We will deal with this last question at length because, for reasons soon to be seen, the contrast will help us to understand the legal evolution of Opus Dei. Before we do, however, let us expand upon some traits of Opus Dei's apostolic action and its internal structure.

When on October 2, 1928, the young priest Josemaría Escrivá realized that he was to dedicate himself with all his strength to promoting a pastoral phenomenon of the pursuit of holiness and the carrying out of apostolate in the middle of the world, he saw at once the project's magnitude, indeed its complexity. The goal, the objective was clearly defined, but how was it to be achieved? How should the Work be organized? Some points were patent: the central role of professional work; the presence of lay men and priests; some laymen would be celibate, others married. That there were to be two branches (one for men and another for women) was made clear in a subsequent illumination. But while these elements might constitute a skeletal structure, they left much room for the details necessary for action.

As already pointed out, the founder did not proceed *a priori*, that is, he did not stop first to draw up a set of regulations. Rather he launched into apostolic work. He sought people who could understand him and to whom he opened horizons of holiness and apostolate in the world, leading them up "an inclined plane." Meanwhile he also *dreamed*, setting his imagination free to catch glimpses of what might be the future extension of the apostolate. He reflected on solutions to eventual problems; he weighed challenges and possibilities, always measuring his thoughts against the light he received on October 2, 1928 and subsequent occasions. Always he left the door open to what later experience—guided by the foundational charism—might deem opportune or appropriate.

These reflections ranged over everything relating to the organization of apostolic work: to the ways and means to foster vocations to follow Jesus Christ in the middle of the world, to awakening souls to the universal call to holiness, to assuring perseverance. Thus the mind of Fr. Josemaría went towards practices of piety, moments of prayer without which one cannot live an authentic Christian life. He asked himself if one or another form of piety were suitable to those called by God to sanctify themselves precisely in the world, occupied besides by many duties and activities. At other times his attention would focus on the world of work: all honest human occupations are doubtless open to holiness; this he saw clearly. But is it enough to lay down this fundamental principle or is something else needed?

A text from the middle of June 1930 reflects this state of mind. To further the Work it seems necessary, he writes, "to spell out well in what kinds of activities its members are going to be occupied." But immediately he adds something more, as though correcting in part what he had just written, yet returning, to affirm it again: "I understand the fervor, the zeal for God's glory, like a cyclone leading us to want to be, by Him and for Him, everywhere. These are the works of men; rather I have said it badly: it is the Work of God carried out by small men; therefore it is necessary to determine clearly the fields of action."[18]

In fact in following months he sometimes enumerates some apostolic possibilities, but he completes the list with phrases of a generic character: "any honest work done for God," "every line of work," "every kind of human activity . . ." Sometimes he points to the kinds of work each of the members can carry out in his ordinary setting. Elsewhere he refers to activities some members may promote among themselves or with other persons. He even details the characteristics these clearly apostolic but secular activities ought to possess.

The panorama he sketches is sometimes a bit complex, especially at the beginning. By 1932-33 the diagram has become more simplified as the result of greater experience. The number and solidity of early vocations to the Work had begun to grow, allowing Fr. Escrivá to reach more specific conclusions. The result is a simple scheme: Opus Dei as an institution will be concerned only with the spiritual formation of its members, but without excluding the possibility, and even appropriateness, of apostolic enterprises which serve as a support for the whole apostolate.

What we have written thus far in this chapter underscores the foundation of this blueprint and its consistency with the other elements that make up Opus Dei. Such a spiritual infrastructure would be meaningless in an organization with socio-cultural aims. Identification with Christ would be even more out of place were its objectives political. These spiritual ways and means are clearly consistent with, and even required by, an entity whose purpose is to foster a personal encounter with God in the midst of the world, in all sectors of society, in a vast array of efforts. They are consistent also with an enterprise that urges following and imitating Jesus Christ, docility to the Holy Spirit, a life of faith, authentic Christian witness.

In this as in other areas Blessed Josemaría grew both in the depth of his understanding and in the refinement of his preaching, moving towards greater and greater precision of expression. For example, we read in his personal notes for October 20, 1931: "The work of God will be a marvelously disciplined army."[19] This phrase could be misunderstood if it is separated from more specific statements. In July 1931 he states emphatically that Opus Dei will never be a "Catholic party"; and that among its members there can be and is "a diversity of opinions."[20] Thus a little more than a year later

---

[18] *Intimate notes*, no. 42.

[19] *Ibid.*, no. 339.

[20] Cf. text quoted in notes 41-43 of Chapter 1.

(March 1933) he writes in terms apparently contradictory to what he had said in October 1931: "Our organization is an organized disorganization."[21]

In 1933 as in 1931, the founder had the same thing in mind: a multitude of Christians in all walks of life, differing in character, temperament and opinions, but united in a common faith, in love for the Church, in fidelity to truth, in apostolic zeal. Only in apostolic ambition do they form a disciplined army committed to bringing to the world above and beyond all political and social differences—better yet, through those differences—Jesus Christ's light and strength. This teaching continues to develop in breadth and depth, especially in later writings where he spells out the relations between Christian freedom and history.[22]

Let us focus on a related topic about which much has been written and most often out of focus. It concerns the understanding of a main feature of Opus Dei: the reserve or discretion of its members. What we find in Opus Dei's founder is a welcome effort at consistency between the Christian faith and vocation that can be summarized in two words: humility on the one hand and naturalness or secularity on the other.

Fr. Josemaría's life and action were deeply rooted in the truth that God is the principal actor in both history and his own life: "It is for me to hide and disappear, so that only Jesus shine."[23] He always tried to live this norm and to inculcate it in others. Consequently those around him should not only count on God, but also exclude any vain desire for attention or self-aggrandizement. Let them be realists: attributing any merit and goodness to God: *Deo*

---

[21] *Intimate notes*, no. 956. The expression "organized disorganization," was interchangeable with "unorganized organization." An ample commentary can be found in *Conversations*, nos. 19, 35 & 53.

[22] See among others, *Conversations, Christ is Passing By* and *Friends of God*; see also his brief but substantial article entitled "Las riquezas de la fe" in the newspaper *ABC* (Madrid, October 2, 1969). See also D. Le Tourneau, *What is Opus Dei*, Dublin 1987; J. Herranz "Libertad y responsabilidad," in Various authors, *Cristianos corrientes. Textos sobre el Opus Dei*, Madrid 1970, pp. 70-90; C. Fabro, "El primado existencial de la libertad," in Various authors, *Mons. Josemaría Escrivá de Balaguer y el Opus Dei, op.cit.* (Chapter 1, note 3), pp. 341-356.

[23] From the start the founder, convinced he was merely an instrument in God's hands, would repeat this phrase, applied in a very particular way to himself. On April 26, 1934, he wrote to Don Francisco Morán, Vicar General of the diocese of Madrid-Alcalá, informing him about his priestly work and the imminent publication of *Spiritual Considerations*: "The clear will of God for me is that 'I should hide myself and disappear'" (RHF, EF-340426-1). And so he conducted himself to the end. On January 28, 1975, he wrote to all the members of the Work on the occasion of the 50th anniversary of his priestly ordination (March 28): "I don't want you to prepare any solemn celebration because I want to spend that jubilee in accordance with the norm that has always guided my conduct: to hide myself and disappear; this is my way, may Jesus Christ alone shine" (RHF, EF-750128-2).

*omnis gloria!* Let all the glory be for God. This is one of his earliest and most frequent phrases.[24]

Naturalness or secularity is characteristic of Opus Dei members, because they are ordinary Christians, one more among their peers, without distinctive garb, insignias, or special ways of acting. Their decision to live the faith with all of its consequences does not give rise to exterior manifestations which would be wholly inappropriate to their secular condition. Yet at the same time they avoid any hint of mystery or secrecy,[25] bearing witness to Christ with deeds, as we read in *The Way*: "'And in a pagan or in a worldly atmosphere, when my life clashes with its surroundings, won't my naturalness seem artificial?' you ask me. And I reply: Undoubtedly your life will clash with theirs; and that constrast—because you're confirming your faith with works—is exactly the naturalness I ask of you."[26]

This theological principle had special nuances during the early years. Prudence was advisable as the Work took its first steps, but also because of rampant antireligious sentiments of the time. At no time, however, was naturalness, discretion or reserve—call it what you will—in the founder's eyes a tactic, nor, still less, a strategy of concealment to facilitate apostolic plans or to mask political or temporal ambitions totally excluded by Opus Dei's sole apostolic purpose. The Work limits itself to spiritual and apostolic formation, while defending the complete political-cultural freedom of all its members.

In the final analysis different perspectives always lead to the same principle: the vision of Opus Dei as an institution aimed at fostering a radically Christian way of life among men and women, lay people of all different social levels, each in his or her own occupation according to personal circumstances, options, and tasks.

Let us turn to another of the questions related to this nucleus: what is implied and presupposed in a call to a fully Christian life

---

[24] We find it already in March 1930, one of the oldest of his personal notes that we retain: *Intimate notes*, no. 8; it appears afterwards more than one hundred times. He also used it in *The Way*, nos. 780 & 784, points already present in *Consideraciones espirituales* of 1932, where it is found in nos. 195 & 198. See also *Furrow*, no. 647; and *The Forge*, nos. 611, 639, & 1051.

[25] He repeated this on many occasions. Here are two texts taken from letters, the first dated 1930; the second 1932. "What the Lord asks of us is naturalness: if we are ordinary Christians, souls dedicated to God in the middle of the world—in the world and of the world, but without being worldly—we cannot act in any other way; to do things which in others would be strange would also be strange in us." (*Letter*, March 24, 1930, no. 8) "You would work with naturalness, without show, without trying to call attention to yourselves." (*Letter*, January 9, 1932, no. 64) We note that—as we will see later on—the words "without mystery or secrecy" are an expression Opus Dei's founder often used to rule out attitudes contrary to his spirit.

[26] *The Way*, no. 380.

amidst the world. There we find the fundamental theological problem that Fr. Escrivá had to confront in order to carry out the mission called for by the foundational charism and to obtain a suitable canonical formulation.

## 3. Universal call to holiness

The founder tells of a conversation he had with the then Vicar General of the diocese of Madrid, Don Francisco Morán, in the mid-30s. Fr. Morán had a great regard for the Work and its founder, and this mutual trust moved him to call one day on Fr. Josemaría to make known to him a criticism of which he was the object: *"They have come to me to accuse you of trying to introduce a new state [in life]."* "I explained to him," Msgr. Escrivá writes, "that just the opposite was the case: I want people to sanctify themselves as *ordinary faithful*, each one in his or her own state, each fulfilling his duties, in the exercise of his occupation and in the place he or she occupies in the world."[27]

This reply went to the heart of the problem. It answered the question and took cognizance of the lack of understanding implied in the accusation. This answer, moreover, resolved a problem while raising an even greater one. Opus Dei's founder did not in any way seek to bring about a reform in the religious state, adding a new figure to already existing orders and congregations. But that did not mean that his undertaking did not give rise to questions of some breadth. Rather, his work moved in a different direction, not that of the so-called state of perfection nor the creation of new forms or states of life. His message was all about the sanctification of Christians in the modes and states of life proper to ordinary life.

Even a summary knowledge of the history of Christian spirituality and apostolate suffices to know that the implementation of such a plan could not help but have a strong impact in the ecclesiastical, theological and canonical environment of the first third of this century. Certainly in the treatises and writings of this time no text is found that formally excludes someone living in the world from reaching the heights of the Christian life. On the contrary, one can point to authors and writings that expressly affirm this possibility.[28] Nevertheless, it is undeniable that people tended to think that holiness in the world was something exceptional. In more

---

[27] *Letter*, December 29, 1947/February 14, 1966, no. 7.

[28] It could not be otherwise, after St. Francis de Sales and St. Alphonse Maria di Liguori, among others. Still it must be recognized that the works of these and other saints, even though very important in the pastoral sphere, did not bring about a true theological clarification with respect to the topic we are examining. On this point see J. L. Illanes, *Mundo y santidad*, Madrid 1984, pp. 65ff, with the bibliography mentioned there.

general terms besides, the radical discipleship of Jesus Christ required, in itself, separation from or renunciation of secular occupations and the adoption of a state or condition of life distinct from that
common to all mankind.  As expected, this perspective gave rise to
obvious and inevitable pastoral consequences.  In preaching to ordinary faithful, for example, the emphasis was placed on moral and
pietistic aspects of the faith without unfolding all of the theological
richness of the Christian vocation.

In some of his letters Fr. Escrivá offers recollections of the spiritual climate that reigned when Opus Dei was taking its first steps.
In the 1947 *Letter* already quoted he writes, "In spite of the religious
environment of the Catholic foundation of my country, people were
still fairly far from God.  Nobody was taking care of them.  Women
ordinarily had a certain piety—or rather "pietism"—in most cases
without very much doctrinal foundation.  Men were embarrassed
to be pious.  People breathed the air of the Enlightenment and the
sad violence of the 19th century continued."[29]  In another *Letter* he
says, "Vast sectors of the laity seemed to be asleep, as though their
operative faith had disappeared."[30]  It would not be difficult to
quote studies and eye-witness reports that confirm this description
and even accentuate its negative aspects.  Nevertheless, it is not
historical processes or environmental circumstances that are under
consideration here, but rather doctrinal questions.  Even though the
general conditions already mentioned could seem to hinder vocations to the Work, it was not circumstances but rather theoretical
frameworks reflected therein that particularly influenced the events
and difficulties of the canonical path of Opus Dei.

To proclaim not only the possibility of radical Christianity amidst
the world and thus the reality of a universal call to holiness, but
also to make explicit some of the most important consequences of
this affirmation required the modification of accepted ideas and a
well established mentality.  "I began to work," the founder recalled
on October 2, 1962, "and it was not easy.  Souls escaped from me as
eels in the water.  Besides there was a most ferocious misunderstanding, because what today is ordinary teaching in the whole
world was not so then. . . .  A whole new system of thought had to
be created: theological, ascetical and legal.  Before me was a centuries long gap.  There was nothing to begin with.  To human eyes the
Work was pure madness.  That's why some said I was crazy and
others, that I was a heretic and so many similar things."[31]

---

[29] *Letter*, December 29, 1947/February 14, 1966, no. 28.

[30] *Letter*, January 25, 1961, no. 13.

[31] RHF, 20160, p. 987.

His preaching had to overcome theological and canonical mind-sets that for centuries had identified, or nearly so, the call to holiness with the vocation to the priesthood or the religious state. His whole activity presupposed and bore witness to a lively conviction that radical Christianity or full dedication should be equated neither with the priestly vocation nor religious spirituality insofar as the latter implied a greater or lesser separation from the world. He saw the call to a radical discipleship of Jesus Christ extended to every Christian and therefore capable of being embodied in secular and lay forms. Fr. Josemaría dedicated time, energy and intellectual effort to spreading this doctrine. Yet he always demonstrated not only a deep consciousness of the value and dignity of the priestly state, but also a profound appreciation for the religious state, whose importance for the Church he both recognized and taught. At the same time he clearly invited men and women to seek sanctity and apostolate right where they were.[32] With his writings and the whole of his priestly activity he contributed powerfully to opening a way in the Church for the clear proclamation of the universal call to holiness, anticipating the solemn declarations of the Second Vatican Council, to which we will later refer.

For now let us put aside historical developments and focus on the 1930's. Analyzing his texts from this period, we notice that to support the call to holiness in the world, the founder used affirmations situated on three different levels, even though they are interconnected.

1. First he taught in a direct, clear, determined way—with the forcefulness of one with a divine mission—that people in the midst of the world can and ought to aspire to holiness where they are, in and through the varied realities in which they are immersed. "Everyone is called to be a saint!" he exclaimed in a text of June 1930.[33] Still other texts affirm: "In the world, in ordinary work, in the duties proper to one's state, and there and through all of this, saints!" he writes in February 1931.[34] In June 1932 he writes: "We are interested in all souls. . . . For this we must desire to serve everyone out of love for God . . . to bring all to holiness: *estote perfecti!* (to all), to fill the world with peace and joy."[35] These are short texts to which can be

---

[32] Later we will have the opportunity to refer to other texts; let us quote here a point from *The Way* that reflects the theological, pastoral environment to which we have just alluded: "You have the obligation to sanctify yourself. Yes, even you! Who thinks this is the exclusive concern of priests and religious? To everyone, without exception, our Lord said: 'Be perfect, as my heavenly Father is perfect'" (*The Way*, no. 291).

[33] *Intimate notes*, no. 35. Cf. notes 28 of Chapter 1 and 17 of this chapter.

[34] *Ibid.*, no. 154.

[35] *Ibid.*, no. 158. The *estote perfecti* refers to the words spoken by Jesus Christ at the end of the sermon on the mount: *estote ergo vos perfecti, sicut et Pater vester coelestis perfectus est* (Mt 5:48).

joined fuller explanations such as that from the *Letter* dated March
24, 1930: "We have come to say, with the humility of one who knows
that he is a sinner and a very little thing—*homo peccator sum* (Lk 5:8)
we say with Peter—but with the faith of one who lets himself be led
by the hand of God, that sanctity is not for a privileged few: that the
Lord calls everyone, that from all he awaits love: from everyone,
wherever they are; from everyone whatever their state in life, their
profession or their occupation. Because this ordinary daily life without outward show can be the means of sanctity."[36]

Ordinarily his affirmations in this regard are not part of a reasoned discourse, but by way of assertions founded on the authority
conferred on him by the charism. However, with the passage of
time, there are theological reflections, more and more developed, to
some of which we will refer. For the moment we end with the
declaration made in 1967 to an American journalist that synthesizes
this section: "Since the foundation of the Work in 1928, my teaching
has been that sanctity is not reserved for a privileged few. All the
ways of the earth, every state in life, every profession, every honest
task can be divine."[37]

2. Second, he affirms and reiterates—also with the authority
derived from the foundational charism—that Opus Dei members
are not religious nor can they be in any way assimilated to the
religious, since they are ordinary lay faithful or secular priests according to each case. Parallel with what we said in no. 1, this is one
of his most constant affirmations over the years. Often it is formulated in very brief terms, without further commentary. At other
times he descends to particulars that reveal very well his concern to
avoid anything that could lead even remotely to obscuring the difference between one charism and the other.[38] Still elsewhere, particularly in periods after the 1930s, when events made it necessary,
his thought is expressed in more developed explanations. Thus the
central concept is interpreted or reaffirmed from different perspectives, as for example in a *Letter* from the late 1940s: "From the first
moment of the foundation of Opus Dei, my daughters and sons,
from October 2, 1928, I have always seen the Work as an institution
whose members would *never* be religious nor would they live in a

---

[36] *Letter*, March 24, 1930, no. 2.

[37] *Conversations*, no. 26.

[38] Such is the case of a text written towards the end of March 1930, or a few days later,
in which Blessed Josemaría makes some reflections about the statutes or regulations of
the Work which in time will have to be written: "It will be made clear that religious
men or women cannot be members . . . but in all the regulations the profound respect
of which Catholic religious are worthy will be made clear." (*Intimate notes*, no. 30) This
spirit and even the language will be found in many other texts.

way *similar* to the religious, nor could they be in any way *considered alike* to or considered the *equivalent* of religious."[39]

The scope of this affirmation comes into focus if we bear in mind that just because the religious charism differs from that of Opus Dei does not in any way give rise to a lesser demand in following Jesus Christ. The opposite is true. It is to proclaim that every Christian, also the one in the world, can and ought to follow Jesus Christ with a radical fullness. In a *Letter* of 1930 from which we have already quoted, he writes: "Our life is simple, ordinary, but if you live it in conformity with the demands of our spirit, it will be at the same time heroic. Sanctity is never something mediocre; the Lord has not called us to follow him along a path that is easier or less heroic. He has called us so that we may remind everyone, in any state or condition in life, in the midst of the noble toils of this earth, that they can be saints, that sanctity is something attainable. At the same time we must proclaim that the goal is very high: *Be perfect as your heavenly Father is perfect* (Mt 5:48). Our life is the heroism of persevering in the ordinary things of every day."[40]

3. Third—and in this way he closes the circle—he points out that Opus Dei is rooted in the Gospel, where the universal call to holiness is found, and there lies the justification for affirming the invitation to an explicit following of Christ in secular settings and occupations. All these occupations are to be given new life, and engaged in with a profound consciousness of mission, and endowed in this way from within with all due Christian meaning. It is in this line that we must place the answer of Blessed Josemaría to don Francisco Morán, according to which Opus Dei has not come to promote a new state of perfection or a modification of the religious state, but to achieve something quite different: the pursuit of a full Christian life, each one in his own state. This is reflected in an oft-repeated phrase of the founder: "The divine paths of the earth have been opened"; the divine paths of the earth are not only human, but also divine, opportunities to encounter Jesus Christ, to be united with him, in order from then on to continue traveling along with him the very same path, but with new depth and perspectives in the service of the divine plan to restore all things in Christ.

From another perspective there come together other texts, in which the founder points out that Opus Dei is not a stage in the process by which the religious are becoming more involved in the world. Rather the Work is rooted in a completely different process: that of awakening the laity and the secular clergy to the wider

---

[39] *Letter*, December 29, 1947/February 14, 1966, no. 84.

[40] *Letter*, March 24, 1930, no. 19.

dimensions of their vocation.[41]   Another phrase he often repeated
points in the same direction.  He presents the spirit of the Work and
Opus Dei itself as a reality "as old as the Gospel, and like the Gospel
new."[42]  This is also borne out by his frequent references to the first
Christians as the example or paradigm of life according to the spirit
of Opus Dei: "Just as observant religious are eager to know how the
first of their order or congregation lived, so as to have their model to
follow, so you too—Christian laymen—should seek to know and
imitate the lives of those disciples of Jesus who knew Peter and Paul
and John, and all but witnessed the death and resurrection of the
Master."[43]  It is among the first Christians, those men and women
who heard the apostolic preaching and lived their faith immersed in
the great Greco-Roman civilization to which they gave new life with
Christ's light and love, that ordinary Christians of today can and
ought to find their inspiration and stimulus.[44]

   The threefold affirmation  we have just analyzed, with its variety of tones, forcefulness of enunciation and frequency of use, bears
witness to the importance which the founder attributed to theses
ideas as the clear expression of something basic and decisive. He
wants to highlight the distinctiveness of Opus Dei and the implications of the message that it presupposes as well as the apostolate it
was destined to spread.

## 4. The Christian vocation in the world: its requirements

   The oft repeated affirmation of the universal call to holiness is
presented by the founder of Opus Dei as the expression of the charism

---

[41] Some similar texts are to be found in J.L. Illanes, *La santificación del trabajo*, Madrid
1980, pp. 63-64.

[42] The earliest text in which we find this expression is from January 1932: *Intimate notes*,
no. 551.

[43] *The Way*, no. 925. This point appears already in *Spiritual Considerations*, in the 1934
edition, but not in the mimeographed text of 1932, even though in his personal notes
there is a reference to the first Christians from that year (the earliest one concretely is
from October 1932: *Intimate notes*, no. 854). As a small detail in the terminology we
point out that in the earliest texts he speaks of "primitive Christians", afterwards he
prefers the expression "first Christians."

[44] As is well known the reference to the first Christian generations has been common
throughout history. Founders or reformers of religious orders and congregations have
done this. The characteristic thing for Msgr. Escrivá is not then the simple fact of this
reference, but the meaning and scope he attributes to it. Msgr. Escrivá has in mind
always the vision of the first Christians as ordinary men and women who lived in the
world in the circumstances proper to ordinary life, the life which they shared with the
other citizens of the Empire, their fellow men and women.  Other quotes and a more
extensive commentary on the importance of this reference to the first Christians in the
preaching of the Founder of Opus Dei can be found in R. Gómez Pérez, *La fe y los días*,
Madrid 1973.

or the divine gift he had received, and not as the conclusion drawn from a process of intellectual reflection. Nevertheless, it is rich in theological implications and calls for a deeper investigation of the central aspects of this Christian truth. Fr. Josemaría himself explicitly formulated some of these implications, since, as he turned constantly throughout his life to that initial light, each time he went deeper, perceiving new shades, lights and consequences. This is all the more true as events forced him to underline the uniqueness of the Work and its differences with respect to other pastoral phenomena. This is not the moment to explain extensively the whole spirit of Opus Dei, nor is it the time to interpret the contribution that it has made to the development of theology. It is appropriate, nevertheless, to point out some details that may help to highlight its originality. We will focus our attention on two points: the connection between human vocation and divine vocation, and the Christian value of earthly realities.

a) *Divine vocation and human vocation*

The whole of Christian life is based on the new birth received with baptism. Christian life is not merely the unfolding of the human person, but the development of divine life communicated by Christ. Because baptism is a new birth, a new being re-created in Christ, it affects not only some facets of life, but the whole of life, in every moment and every aspect. The newness implicit in Christian life in some cases—that of a religious vocation—may call for a separation from or a break with the normal circumstances of human life, or in other cases—that of the priesthood—dedication to ministerial tasks. Ordinarily, however, in the great majority of Christians, the novelty gives rise to a new Christian spirit in daily events, thus incorporated and integrated into Christian life.

Msgr. Escrivá saw this reality with a special depth and expressed it in many different ways. For example, let us quote from a homily for the feast of St. Joseph in 1963, where he reflects extensively on the saint's simple ordinary life and extends it to every Christian: "You, who celebrate with me today this feast of St. Joseph, are men who work in different human professions; you have your own homes, you are from so many different countries and have different languages. You have been educated in lecture halls or in factories and offices. You have worked in your profession for years, established professional and personal friendships with your colleagues, helped to solve the problems of your companies and your communities. Well then, I remind you once again that all this is not foreign to God's plan. Your human vocation is a part—and an important part—of your divine vocation."

Earlier he said: "Christian faith and calling affect our whole existence, not just a part of it. Our relations with God necessarily demand giving ourselves, giving ourselves completely. The man of faith sees life in all its dimensions from a new perspective: that which is given us by God."[45]

The light of faith, when it illuminates our whole life, leads to the discovery of its most profound dimension: its radical reference to God; and it makes known to us that the ultimate horizon of human tasks and activities is nothing other than the divine plan of salvation: even more, God himself. From this there springs up immediately for an ordinary Christian one conclusion: to be a Christian is itself a vocation. The call is not juxtaposed to daily life, but rather, inserting itself into and intermingled with daily life, it should shape it and endow it with supernatural plenitude and fullness of meaning. To walk with God and towards God, to identify oneself with Christ, does not imply in any way to separate oneself from common, ordinary life, but rather to live it with a God-centered orientation. In summary, as we have just pointed out and as Fr. Josemaría used to say in a phrase that synthesizes his thought, "the human vocation is a part, and an important part, of the divine vocation."[46]

Human tasks and situations are not a foreign environment for a God-centered life to take place. Rather they are the means and path, better still, they are the raw material that a God-centered life must take up and incorporate into its own proper dynamic.[47] The Christian life of the ordinary man or woman, whom God wants to live in the world, completely dedicated to secular occupations, presents itself as a life that has its source and foundation in grace. Secular tasks and occupations are its axis or hinge.[48] Whence the pledge implied by such a life can be summed up in one phrase: to sanctify daily life. Blessed Josemaría frequently said, in accord with the importance he gave to work, "to sanctify work, to sanctify oneself in work and to sanctify others through work."[49]

---

[45] *Christ is Passing By*, no. 46.

[46] "I have told you a thousand times," he wrote in 1948, "that the *human vocation* is a part, and an important part of our *divine vocation*, because our life can be summed up by saying that we have to sanctify our work, sanctify ourselves in our work, and sanctify with our work" (*Letter*, October 15, 1948, no. 6). See also, among other texts, *Christ is Passing By*, no. 46; *Friends of God*, no. 60.

[47] Cf. *Christ is Passing By*, no. 4; *Conversations*, no. 60.

[48] Cf. *Friends of God*, no. 62.

[49] In 1940 he wrote: "Once again I tell you, my children, the Lord has called us so that, remaining each one of us in our own proper state in life and in the exercise of our own profession or work, we sanctify ourselves in our work, we sanctify our work, and we sanctify others with our work. This is how this human work which we do can more than reasonably be considered *opus Dei, operatio Dei*, work of God" (*Letter*, March 11, 1940, no. 13). See also, *Conversations*, no. 55. Other parallel texts in addition to the one quoted in note 46 of this chapter are found in *Letter*, May 6, 1945, no. 16; *Letter*, December 24, 1951, no. 79; *Letter*, June 31, 1954, no. 18; *Letter*, January 25, 1961, no. 10; *Con-*

b) *Christian value of earthly realities*

The ideas contained in the statements made above imply and presuppose a keen consciousness of the unity of creation, insofar as it is governed by a divine plan directing all things back to God. In other words, creation and redemption are intimately united. Fr. Escrivá himself expressed this in clear and explicit ways. In a homily delivered in 1967 he said: "We must love the world and work and all human things. For the world is good. Adam's sin destroyed the divine balance of creation; but God the Father sent his only Son to re-establish peace, so that we, his children by adoption, might free creation from disorder and reconcile all things to God."[50]

He reiterated this deep theological thought more extensively in another homily three years later: "Christ Our Lord still wants to save men and the whole of creation—this world of ours which is good, for so it came from God's hands. It was Adam's offense, the sin of human pride, that broke the divine harmony of creation. But God the Father in the fullness of time, sent his only-begotten Son to take flesh in Mary ever Virgin, through the Holy Spirit, and re-establish peace. In this way, by redeeming man from sin 'we receive adoption as sons.' (Gal 4:5) We become capable of sharing in the intimacy of God. In this way the new man, the new branch of the children of God (Rom 6:4-5) is established to free the whole universe from disorder, restoring all things in Christ (cf. Eph 1:9-10) as they have been reconciled with God (cf. Col 1:20)."[51]

The texts and reflections just set forth do not constitute—we have already pointed it out—an exposition of the spirit of Opus Dei. Such an exposition, even an approximate one, would require our dealing with many other aspects: the sense of divine filiation, the union between theological and human virtues, the value of little things, contemplative life in the middle of the world, eucharistic piety and Marian devotion, and so forth.[52] With respect to the two questions we mentioned, we have tried to limit ourselves to sketching them out without an extensive interpretation.

---

*versations*, no. 70; *Christ is Passing By*, no. 46; *Friends of God*, no. 9. With respect to the teaching of Msgr. Escrivá on work one could also see, among other studies, J.L. Illanes, *La santificación del trabajo*, op.cit. (note 41 of this chapter), and P. Rodríguez, *Vocación, trabajo, contemplación*, Pamplona 1986.

[50] *Christ is Passing By*, no. 112.

[51] *Ibid.*, no. 183; see also *Conversations*, no. 70.

[52] To know the spirit of Opus Dei, the best source is of course the writings of its founder. Among the different studies, in addition to those already mentioned, one could also consult the various collaborations included in the collective volume, *Msgr. Josemaría Escrivá de Balaguer y el Opus Dei*, op.cit. (chapter 1, note 3), and in the brief synthesis written by D. Le Tourneau, in *What is Opus Dei*, op.cit. (note 22 of this chapter) pp. 27ff, with the bibliography quoted there.

The reader will have noticed that we have followed a systematic method rather than an historical one, as we had been doing up until now. We were trying—and with this we answer two observations which we have just made—to show or at least point out the theological depth of a charism. It was better to limit ourselves to a few essential points, those sufficient to catch a glimpse of the wide perspective (even though they do not exhaust it), and also to base ourselves on texts where Opus Dei's founder shows what his message implies and presupposes. In any case, and leaving aside methodological considerations, we must spend some time on these theological perspectives considered in themselves. Thus we will be able to grasp better the profound dimensions of Opus Dei's spirit and to understand consequently its distinctiveness with respect to other ecclesial realities, and therefore the determination necessary for its pastoral spreading and its later canonical configuration.

## 5. In search of new terminological and conceptual formulas

To pick up again the historical thread, during the 1930s statements about the call to holiness and apostolate *in sæculo* did not receive a spontaneous welcome in the ecclesiological-cultural environment. Moreover, the conceptual elements and the vocabulary were inadequate to express this call in an easy way. The dominant theology tended to consider secular occupations an obstacle to living a full Christian life and therefore every affirmation of secularity was thought to be a mitigation of full Christianity. It interpreted every call to holiness as an invitation to the priesthood or to separate oneself from the world in one of the forms of the religious state.

To assert the distinctiveness of Opus Dei in general terms does not exhaust the task to which the founder was called. Rather it constitutes a point of departure. In a wide range of fields—stretching from the need to find particular means of ascetical formation and specifics of apostolic action, to the determination of specific characteristics of living the virtues—Fr. Josemaría was faced with a relatively blank slate. He was led to reflect on and analyze the depths of the common Christian inheritance. Only thus would he be able to sketch out the specific lay and secular modes of achieving sanctity in the middle of the world, doing without the characteristics proper to other spiritualities.

The texts document that the founder was aware of this problem. From the very beginning he realized the strong semantic baggage deriving from the spirituality of the religious life in the form of many consecrated terms of Christian asceticism. He had to seek new terms or to broaden the meaning of older ones, to make them applicable with a fullness of meaning to this new lay and secular experience.[53] As is easily understood, the task was not always simple. The effort at conceptional and terminological renewal required not only a keenness of intellect but also the passage of time. It was not possible to give life suddenly to new modes of expression either sociologically or psychologically. Otherwise there would be a lack of communication; besides new concepts and words can arise often in confrontation with those that preceded them and frequently by means of guesswork and approximations.

We cannot be surprised, therefore, that to express the full dedication presupposed by a call to the Work, Fr. Escrivá had recourse on occasions to terms derived from the religious spirituality dominant until that time in the whole terrain of spiritual theology. Yet he always tried to refine the terms he was forced to use because there were no others. Thus, for example, in a text of 1930, he describes the members of the Work as "true *religious in re*?"[54] He uses these words just as we have transcribed them, underlined and followed by question marks. Thus he indicates very clearly—apart from the text itself, of course—the inadequacy of the expression used solely to explain the fullness of dedication. But he also suggests that it is used with a theological and spiritual background different from that of the religious. Something similar happens on other occasions when he speaks about evangelical counsels, whether in general or mentioning the classic trilogy of poverty, chastity and obedience, or analogous concepts. The context always refers to a secular and lay experience, one that is not monastic or religious. Thus he underlines that the sanctity to which Opus Dei calls them is not a mediocre or discount sanctity, but rather a full and radical sanctity. It is not less than that to which the religious state is aimed, even though carried out in another context and with other characteristics. While he unfurls a vast historical panorama where the desire of a radical discipleship of Jesus Christ is equally present, he affirms at the same time the difference between various paths or spiritualities.[55] Without the comparisons and vocabulary it was

---

[53] A single text from March 1930 will bear out what we have said: "I wanted to find a Spanish word, different from 'vocation,' which would embrace a similar meaning"; immediately after this he suggests such a word using question marks: "call" (*Intimate notes*, no. 13). This in fact was the word that he used as the title of one of the chapters of *Consideraciones espirituales* and *Camino*. With the passage of time and having separated the word "vocation" from an exclusive reference to the clerical or religious state, he had no objections to using it, even frequently, endowing it with the breadth of meaning found in the New Testament.

[54] *Intimate notes*, no. 14.

[55] This is the case of some paragraphs, with an historical-poetic style, of the *Instruction* of 1934, in which the reference to the charismatic origin of different forms of the religious state serves as the background for the assertion of a different reality, that too of charismatic origin, but different from the previous ones: the pursuit of sanctity in

nearly impossible for him to describe the dedication of the members of Opus Dei.

In the same context of conceptual clarification obtained by considerable effort, we find a question we should examine slowly, because of its particular relationship to the canonical development. We refer to the configuration given to the vocational commitment or the decision of full dedication which Opus Dei presupposes and to the bond consequently established between the members and the Work itself.

What were the surroundings? What resources did spiritual theology and canon law make available to him? In the years 1928 and following, the notion of vocational commitment was intimately bound up with the notion of the religious state or the priestly state. Ordinary Christians were the object of ordinary pastoral care. And if they could become members of different institutions, it was always a question of institutions with specific goals requiring only a partial or limited pledge. They could, without doubt, reach the peak of sanctity and many of them aspired to be saints. Yet in truth this desire was more a spontaneous aspiration than a reflective choice. The idea of a universal call to holiness and consequently that of a full vocational commitment to sanctity and apostolate in ordinary life were completely foreign to the mentality of the time. The founder could not find any point of reference allowing him to give legal form to a reality such as that implied in Opus Dei. Nowhere to be heard was a call to follow Jesus Christ fully and radically in and

---

one's own state in life. He points out first—with the metaphor that has already been commented upon—that the ordinary Christian must be "an intravenous injection in the circulatory system of society" bringing the light of Jesus Christ to the world, and, he continues: "Jesus always made his followers adapt themselves to the times: among the first Christian religious the retreat to the desert or to the monastery was a universal phenomenon.

"Francis makes universal the type of the runabout friar, going forward along the road to preach Christ. With his sons Dominic lights up the universities of Europe. Later the Theatines, the Barnabites, the Jesuits, and the Somachi—without choir and with the cassock of the secular clergy—work for souls with new forms of apostolate.

"Now, by means of a divine and universal impulse also, there is arising a militia, old as the Gospel and like the Gospel new, which has soldiers without any exterior habit, who sometimes will be monks and sometimes wandering friars who walk along all the paths of this life. Men and women who, in their own state and profession whether intellectual or manual, will be sometimes wise men and women, and always learned, well prepared; and with knowledge, with professional work and with their example of a Christian life well lived they will carry out a most fervent apology of the faith" (Instruction, March 19, 1934, nos. 42-45).

It is obvious that the expressions "monks" and "wandering friars"—the same as the reference to "soldiers"—has a metaphorical value to express the fullness of Christian life in reference, as the text itself adds, to "men and women—in their own proper state and profession."

through secular occupations, showing in word and deed from within the world itself that all men and women of every condition, work or occupation are called to union with God. Hitherto there simply had been no reality that was both vocational, of full dedication, and secular in character. What was he to do?

With regard to the basic question Fr. Escrivá did not have the slightest doubt or cavil. From the first he offered the ideal of a full dedication, calling for a commitment of the whole person and leading to a stable bond with Opus Dei. With respect to the expression or formalization of this reality, however, things were not so simple. One point, a negative one, was clear: anything implying assimilation to the religious state was to be avoided. But with regard to the positive expression many questions remained. Was it possible for there to be dedication and commitment without expressing this decision in a formal and explicit act? It was doubtless possible to act in this way, at least for a time, but not as a solution over a long period of time. Would it be possible to have recourse to vows or promises, not of a public character like those of the religious, but perhaps private? This was certainly possible. In fact it was relatively common then for lay people to make private vows on many different matters, even of obedience to one's own spiritual director. This possibility, however, was not satisfactory since the context implied was not fitting to secularity. If all of the preceding steps were excluded, then where could he turn?

At this juncture the founder decided to continue working without attempting to anticipate any more formal structure. He opened Christian horizons to the people that he dealt with and led them as it were up an inclined plane. When appropriate, he pointed to a decision of dedication. The commitment undertaken was clear in the consciousness of those who corresponded. Such a solution was viable, but as we have already indicated only in a provisional sort of way. With the passage of time and the increase of activity the need to achieve a more structured setup became more and more obvious. Around 1934, the matter became more urgent. Some of those who had responded to the call were disturbed by various priests and other people who claimed their decision was totally worthless.

In March of that year he consulted this problem with, among other priests, Norberto Rodríguez, one of the priests helping him, and with Valentín Sánchez Ruiz, S. J., his confessor, seeking a theological opinion or advice. "All were in agreement with the need to unite ourselves with a spiritual bond, which for the moment would be constituted by private vows made for one year," Fr. Escrivá recorded in his personal notes of these conversations.[56]

---

[56] *Intimate notes*, no. 1150.

He did not like the solution, but in the end he gave in. He felt almost forced to it "out of a psychological motive" (an expression used many years later) to help those coming to Opus Dei to be clearly conscious of the commitment they were making.[57] Nevertheless, he did this with one condition: these vows were to be private—"extremely private" he writes on one occasion—reserved to the conscience of the person, without their being received in any way by Opus Dei as such, which ignores or disregards them. On the other hand the bond between members and the Work is to be wrought by a simple act wherein the decision to dedicate one's life to holiness and apostolate according to the spirit of Opus Dei is manifested, "without vows or promises of any kind."[58]

Such was the criterion he adhered to and defended, not without difficulty, throughout the canonical vicissitudes of Opus Dei. As the passage of time made it more and more necessary, he emphasized in his preaching that this situation did not please him: "The Work is not interested in vows, but rather in virtues," he would repeat. On the far horizon still lay the definitive solution: the disappearance of all kinds of vows and the formulation of the relation of Opus Dei with its members by means of a bond of a contractual nature. We will develop this at the proper time.

## 6. The problem of Opus Dei's canonical configuration

We set for ourselves two objectives in this first part: to describe the fundamental elements of the foundational charism of Opus Dei, and to point out the problems that would affect its subsequent legal evolution. There remains only one question: the problem of the applicable juridical form under which to seek the approval of Opus Dei.

Canonical legislation and practice in the 1930s and following years did not recognize any juridical figure suitable to the charism proper to Opus Dei. It would have to accommodate an institution universal in scope, with a unified and inter-diocesan organizational structure, composed of secular priests and laity—men and women, celibate and married—who, in answer to a definite vocation, commit themselves, in a stable way, to live a full Christian life in the world, in their work and other circumstances proper to secular and lay life, and who, through these circumstances spread among their peers a universal call to faith, to Christian perfection and apostolate. Clearly the juridical forms proper to religious orders and congregations or to societies in some way equivalent to them whose members live a complete dedication but in a theological context of pub-

---

[57] Cf. *Letter*, December 29, 1947/February 14, 1966, no. 180.

[58] *Intimate notes*, no. 1225 (February 19, 1935).

lic consecration and, to one degree or other, of separation from the world and its activities were not suitable. Similarly inappropriate was the form of associations of the faithful of a local character and with specific and narrowly determined purposes, since these implied a partial and limited dedication.

Thus Fr. Josemaría was confronted in those years with juridical problems analogous to those of an ascetical or theological nature, as we pointed out earlier. In some ways the canonical problem was more serious, or at least more immediate. As a social phenomenon—or a pastoral one, in the case of Christian life—acquires a certain breadth of development, the need to endow it with a structure in conformity with law becomes a need that no longer can be postponed. Moreover its solution transcends intellectual and scientific reflection, since it affects the canonical system and therefore authority itself. Thus the founder was confronted with the need to fight for nothing less than a reform of canonical legislation, an objective always arduous and in any case requiring time. In the meantime intermediate solutions had to be adopted.

Because history does not stand still, apostolic needs made it necessary to endow Opus Dei with some juridical garb, even before seeking reform of the legislation. Archbishop Vincenzo Fagiolo in an article that speaks precisely of the relationship between charism and law in the history of Opus Dei has grasped the situation and the effect that it had on the founder: "Divine providence had wanted that the young Josemaría Escrivá study canon and civil law. As founder, apart from the immediate problem of seeking vocations, he was presented with another, less urgent, yet one that also had to be resolved: how to fit what God had made him see into the juridical-ecclesiastical framework? How to manage that laity and priests, men and women, celibate and married, belong to Opus Dei and constitute a single pastoral unity—organic and indivisible—not only of spirituality, formation and aims, but also of government?" There was no adequate solution and it was necessary to wait. Meanwhile, Archbishop Fagiolo wrote, "Opus Dei needed a provisional statute that would allow it to live and develop in the Church and that would not stifle or deform the message God had entrusted to the founder. To combine this double requirement was not always easy, and in this challenge Msgr. Escrivá showed the measure of his high quality as a jurist, as a holy priest and as an adept of government."[59]

Later we will see how this "high quality as a jurist" is manifested. Let us now say solely that the juridical problem was not in fact separable from the theological questions touched on earlier.

---

[59] Arch. V. Fagiolo, "Carisma e diritto nella fondazione del Opus Dei", in *L'Osservatore Romano*, June 23, 1985, p. 5.

One could only think of bringing forth the adequate canonical solution to what Opus Dei represented and represents after clearly and unequivocally laying the foundation for the universal call to holiness and the participation of every Christian in the mission of the Church. The possibility of a pastoral phenomenon fostering holiness and apostolate in the world first had to be fully recognized. Law usually follows life. The canonical legislation in effect in the 1930s reflected in fact the life of the Church for decades and centuries before. Likewise it will be the progress of life and especially the effect of the Second Vatican Council that will lead to the introduction into the canonical system of new forms that will allow Opus Dei to receive a legal configuration fully in accord with its foundational charism and with its historical projection as a pastoral phenomenon.

Part Two

DIOCESAN APPROVALS

# Chapter III

## THE 1941 APPROVAL

# Chapter III

## THE 1941 APPROVAL

### 1. Verbal diocesan approval

1933 represents a relatively important milestone in the initial stages of Opus Dei. New vocations had come to the Work, and Fr. Josemaría saw that it was feasible to take a step he had long dreamt about: to begin a secular activity with apostolic potential.

Near the end of his life, on March 19, 1975, the founder recalled the early years. To carry out what God had asked of him, he sought "strength in the poorest corners of Madrid . . . in the hospitals and, as you cannot call houses those hovels where they were, wherever the sick could be found. Meanwhile I worked and formed the first ones I had around me. Many professions and occupations were represented: university students, workers, small businessmen, artists. . . ."[1]

His words show clearly that Fr. Escrivá always sought to ground his apostolate in prayer and sacrifice. No less impressive is the breadth with which early on he conceived Opus Dei. These facets are evinced not only by his recollections but also by those who knew and dealt with him at that time.

In the mid '30s he prayerfully sifted his first experiences and apostolate. Little by little he concluded it would be better to concentrate for the time being on university students.[2] This move would not restrict the Work's universal scope as seen on October 2, 1928, but rather would expedite it. The idea was to challenge them with

---

[1] Various authors, *Mons. Josemaría Escrivá de Balaguer y el Opus Dei*, op.cit. (chap. 1, note 3) pp. 24-25.

[2] Fr. Escrivá used indiscriminately—during those years and later—the words "university students" and "intellectuals." He understood them in a broad way: not limited to a cultural elite, but comprising all those walks of life that presuppose a university degree.

the call to holiness in the world, even to the point of committed celibacy. Thus for its base Opus Dei would be able to count on a nucleus of members who were free to spread the Work to many others. These, in turn, could be celibate or married and from all social conditions and occupations.[3]

With this in mind Fr. Escrivá set up a small academy which he named DYA (Derecho y Arquitectura: law and architecture). For the founder the acronym also was an act of faith: God and Daring (Dios y Audacia). Trusting in God and daring to fulfill His will was a motif in Fr. Escrivá's preaching.[4] The Academy "DYA" opened its doors in December 1933. The move proved to be a good one, for the apostolic work flourished. Soon Fr. Josemaría saw the merit of expanding the academy and adding a student residence. This new center was launched in October 1934. The following March he sought permission from the bishop of Madrid to set up an oratory (chapel) in the residence.[5] The request was promptly granted and on the last day of the month he celebrated Holy Mass and reserved the blessed sacrament for the first time in the tabernacle in a Center of the Work. The founder was overjoyed: now he had the guarantee that Opus Dei would take shape more and more.

From the start Fr. Escrivá counted on the verbal approval of the bishop of Madrid, the Most Rev. Leopoldo Eijo y Garay.[6] He regularly kept the bishop informed through the Vicar General of the diocese, Fr. Francisco Morán, with whom he communicated frequently. Despite this benevolence and support, Fr. Josemaría took no step to obtain any written approval. He thought that at this stage verbal approval was enough.[7] To seek anything more might be

---

[3] This commitment to celibacy does not in any way imply separation from the world nor is its motive to be sought therein. Rather, it implies the discovery of the Christian value of secular activities and the consciousness of being called to sanctify oneself in and through these activities. Celibacy arises from within this lay, secular vocation to make oneself more available for tasks of formation and direction of the Work. Other reflections on a theology of the laity can be found in J. L. Gutiérrez, "El laico y el celibato apostólico," in *Ius Canonicum*, 26 (1986):209-240.

[4] See the bibliography in note 1, chap. I.

[5] This request can be found in the Appendix, document no. 1. The first reply to this request was given verbally and then on April 10, 1935, in writing (cf. Appendix, document no. 2). On July 10, 1936, permission was asked to transfer the oratory to the new domicile of the academy-residence (cf. Appendix, document no. 3).

[6] Born in Vigo (Spain) on April 11, 1878, consecrated bishop in 1914, he took possession of the diocese of Madrid-Alcalá in 1923. In 1946 he received the personal title of Patriarch of the West Indies. He died in Vigo on August 31, 1963.

[7] "Since his work did not go beyond the limits of the apostolic activity of any ordinary priest, it was enough during that foundational stage to be able to count on the approval and blessing of his bishop, at that time Most Rev. Leopoldo Eijo y Garay, Bishop of Madrid-Alcalá, which he had from the very beginning." Thus Cardinal Bueno Monreal,

precipitous and even counterproductive. Some thoughts that he jotted down in May 1934 sum up his attitude: "What would one say of a pregnant woman who wanted to register her unborn child at city hall or in the parish? What would you say if she wanted to sign the child up as a college student? Madam, they would say, wait. Let the child be born, let him grow and develop. . . . Well, in the womb of the Catholic Church there is an unborn child, with life and activities of its own, like a child in its mother's womb. . . . Be calm; the time will come to register the child, to seek the suitable approvals. Meanwhile I will always give an account to Church authorities of all our external activities—as I have done until now—without rushing into paperwork, which will come at the proper time."[8]

These words reflect not only a natural prudence, but also the clarity with which Fr. Escrivá foresaw the juridical difficulties. His was the duty of finding for the Work, owing to its newness, a proper canonical form, and therefore of avoiding, insofar as possible, false steps. In January 1936 he returns to the same topic: "Undoubtedly all the indications point to the fact that, were I to ask the bishop for the first ecclesiastical approval of the Work, he would grant it." Then he explains the delay: "But it is a matter of so much importance that it must mature well. The Work of God has to exhibit a new form, and it would be easy to harm the way."[9]

Already in the earlier years he had suffered from the lack of understanding caused by the novelty of Opus Dei. Some called him deluded or even heretical, because he maintained that full sanctity

---

Archbishop of Seville, judged the situation recallinng those years when he was the Promotor of Justice of the diocese of Madrid, and took part in the first approval *in scriptis* of Opus Dei. This deposition, dated November 22, 1977, is kept in RHF, T-6182.

(*Translator's note.* This testimony has now been published in José María Bueno Monreal, *Testimonies to A Man of God: Blessed Josemaría Escrivá*, No. 1, London 1993.)

[8] *Intimate notes*, no. 1192.

[9] *Ibid.*, no. 1309. Cardinal Bueno Monreal in the cited deposition refers to the novelty of the apostolic work of Fr. Escrivá: "Those of us who knew him and who dealt with him more closely were familiar with the spirit and ultimate objective towards which he was driving. I knew how keenly Josemaría felt the desire to help laypeople seek their sanctification through the fulfilment of their civic, social and professional duties.This applied from the first moment. These themes cropped up again and again when we would be talking together. Josemaría spoke to me about how he saw with great clarity that the times we were living in were times in which it was necessary for the world to be sanctified from within: God calls all men and women to sanctify themselves and to assume their apostolic responsibility within the Church. That is to say, he spoke to me about what was to be enunciated later in the Second Vatican Council. And not only did he speak about these things, but he went on to make them happen through that characteristic pastoral work of his, so quiet, so humble and so unceasing."(RHF, T-6182).

(*Translator's note.* See *op. cit.*, note 7 of this chapter, page 2:32.)

could be sought not only in religious orders and congregations but also in the world.  Others accused him of trying to create a new state in the Church or even worse of seeking to destroy the religious state.  They failed to see that his effort and mission, as already pointed out, were aimed elsewhere.  Even among friends who helped him in particular ways, there were some who did not manage to understand the Work; this pained him very much.

This was the case, for example, of the diocesan Vicar General, Fr. Francisco Morán, with whom the founder maintained a most cordial relationship and who showered signs of appreciation upon Fr. Escrivá's apostolic work.  In one conversation on March 30, 1936, Fr. Josemaría, as was his habit, commented on the apostolic work in hand as well as some of his immediate projects, among others, the usefulness of enlarging the group of those dedicated to God in celibacy.  According to a report written by Fr. Escrivá the following day, Fr. Morán said: "These works usually end up becoming religious congregations. . . . It's clear that, in spite of the affection he has for us, he does not understand the Work," the founder noted, "I protested: Congregation, never.  Religious, no."[10]  A few weeks later on May 7 a similar exchange took place.  A marginal note to this account reflects that of March: "He doesn't get it, he doesn't get it."[11]  Thus did the founder receive a foretaste of the difficulties to come.

Soon after this the Spanish civil war broke out.  Like so many other priests, Fr. Josemaría spent several months hiding in various places in Madrid because of the virulent religious persecution which the war unleashed.  In December 1937 after a very painful odyssey, he reached the free zone of Spain and there fully resumed his priestly work.  His relentless activity allowed him to re-establish contact with many students he knew and in a special way with those who had committed themselves to Opus Dei.  Wartime nevertheless represented a brake on the Work's development.

When in late March 1939 Fr. Escrivá returned to Madrid, he was a whirlwind of apostolic activity: a new student residence in Madrid; trips to Valencia, Saragossa, Barcelona, Valladolid and other Spanish cities; new vocations of students and young professionals.  In addition, though more slowly, the work of the women's branch began again.  Fr. Josemaría again kept all the diocesan authorities informed.  He recorded minutely his personal conversations not only with the Vicars General of the diocese—including now Fr. Casimiro Morcillo—but also with the bishop himself.  Between the Bishop and Fr. Escrivá there soon arose a deep friendship and mutual affection.

---

[10] RHF, AVF-16.

[11] RHF, AVF-18.

Aware of this growing appreciation for his work, someone in 1939 recommended to the founder that he ask the bishop for written approval of the Work.[12] But the reasons for not being in a rush were still valid.  Fr. Escrivá's work had to continue being one of formation, spiritual direction, dealing with souls one by one, without yet seeking a legal framework.  As Cardinal Bueno Monreal says in his deposition, Opus Dei's founder "wanted these longings to sanctify the world to become a reality, not to be just a theory, that this message should take hold in the greatest possible number of people and afterwards be spread around, simply, without fanfare, with the efficacy of the leaven that disappears in the mass of the dough, each one sanctifying himself in his own particular milieu, in his job, in the exercise of his professional work.  And all this without *triumphalism* as later, from the time of the Vatican Council, we would come to call it. . . . Viewing in this way the Work and his pastoral activity, we readily understand why at that time any kind of juridical recognition would have been premature."[13]

Clearly, as Fr. Josemaría saw from the start, as the Work grew it would need some kind of organization and, therefore, a juridical structure.  We see this in some of the same writings which have already been cited as well as in comments by others.  Cardinal Bueno Monreal writes: "Josemaría knew that a moment would come in which the juridical approval of the Work would need to be applied for officially.  But he delayed taking that step.  He had a trained and clear legal mind and knew that an organized apostolic activity could not continue in the Church without canonical approval.  As I understand it, he had discussed this with the Bishop, who agreed with Josemaría in everything.  Don Leopoldo approved of Josemaría's quiet and humble way of acting.  Besides this, both Josemaría and the Patriarch, who understood very well the radically lay essence of the Work of God, knew that in the common law of the Church at that time there was no formula into which Opus Dei coud fit—that is, without doing violence to its nature.  For this reason they clearly appreciated that the juridical approval and sanction of the Work would have to await its moment and come from the Holy See."

## 2. The approval *in scriptis* of the Bishop of Madrid and its historical context

A series of dramatic events precipitated matters.  We have seen how the novelty of the pastoral phenomenon of Opus Dei provoked

---

[12] *Intimate notes*, no. 1607.

[13] With respect to this deposition, see note 7 of this chapter.

(*Translator's note.* See *op. cit.* at that note, pp. 2:32-34.)

suspicions and misunderstandings. These took on greater viru-
lence as the Work continued its apostolic growth. The vocation to
Opus Dei was censured as madness and even heresy, and those who
followed it were ignorant at best. The calumnies grew in volume,
soon degenerating into a vicious and systematic campaign. The
persecution was the more painful as it was provoked by those from
whom it was least to be expected: other Catholics, even some religious and people closely allied with them. Opus Dei members were
berated for exalting the laity at the expense of religious and priestly
vocations, for undermining the religious state and thus for embracing and propagating heresy. From this the critics passed on to
baseless accusations of the most varied kinds. Insinuations alter-
nated with open attacks, even from pulpits. Parents of Opus Dei
members were visited and told that their children were being de-
ceived and ran the risk of excommunication and even eternal con-
demnation, if they continued along this way. . . . Fr. Josemaría
suffered deeply, while maintaining peace and serenity which he
transmitted to his followers.[14] Since the bishop of Madrid knew the
Work and its founder well, he could therefore bear witness to the
falsity of these accusations. He intervened several times in this
way. He reached the conclusion that in order to cut short this
campaign, he himself, as the bishop of the diocese where the Work
had been born, must grant it a written approval. He sought to show
clearly, and backed by law, the appreciation the ecclesiastical hierarchy had for Opus Dei—support it could count on. He so informed Fr. Escrivá in March 1940, asking him to present the request
for approval with the necessary documentation.

The founder gratefully saw in this decision affection both for
himself and for the Work, even though he realized that canon law
lacked provisions for such a pastoral phenomenon. On June 21,
1940, Fr. Josemaría wrote, "We face the grave problem of *fitting*
Opus Dei into canon law."[15] Cardinal Bueno Monreal, who at the
time was the Promotor of Justice of the diocese, declares: "It was
necessary, therefore, to give juridical substance to the Work, and
Josemaría agreed to study the matter in order to find a solution.
This would of course be provisional, and one that would allow for
approval at the diocesan level, in expectation of the ultimate satisfactory solution which would in due course come from Rome."[16]

Fr. Josemaría discussed the matter with canon law experts, among
others with the aforementioned Promotor of Justice of the diocese.

---

[14] Some of the facts about this campaign can be seen in A. Vásquez de Prada, *op. cit.*
(chap. 1, note 1), pp. 222ff.

[15] *Intimate notes*, no. 1613.

[16] Cf. deposition described in note 7 of this chapter.

(*Translator's note.* See *op. cit.* at that note, p. 2:34.)

He concluded that the only viable solution at the time—although not the best for reasons to be seen later—was that of a pious union.

On February 14, 1941, the founder requested episcopal approval of Opus Dei as a pious union,[17] to which petition was annexed a brief *Reglamento* (by-laws) and five supplementary documents.[18] On March 25, 1941, the bishop of Madrid, through his Vicar, Casimiro Morcillo, told Blessed Josemaría that he had approved Opus Dei as a pious union with a decree dated March 19.[19]

In the document the bishop of Madrid-Alcalá expressed his satisfaction at "giving canonical approval to such an important work of zeal," and he beseeched the Lord, through the intercession of St. Joseph, "not to allow any of these great fruits to be lost." He also stated that Opus Dei, founded by Fr. Josemaría Escrivá de Balaguer, has "met with our good will and that of our Vicar General since 1928." He also says that the *Reglamento* had been carefully studied.[20]

---

[17] The text of this petition can be found in the Appendix, document no. 4. We point out that in the draft that served as the basis of his decree the Bishop of Madrid introduced a few modifications into the text written by the founder: concretely after the phrase "with the consent of the Vicar General," he inserted: "and the blessing of the Most Reverend Bishop and"; and in the *petition* he added: "leaving to the consideration and decision of Your Excellency the designation of the members of this Curia who are to know the regulations of Opus Dei, given the character of the same."

We point out, in addition, that from the time in which some recommended to Don Josemaría Escrivá that he request the diocesan approval—1939—and the time in which he began the process to obtain the written approval several months passed, a fact in which the founder of Opus Dei always saw a sign of his own clear awareness of the inadequacy of the juridical solutions that were possible at that time. (*Intimate notes*, no. 1609; *Letter*, December 29, 1947/February 14, 1966, no. 156).

[18] In the Appendix we present the *Reglamento* (no. 5) which contains a general description of Opus Dei. We will deal with its content and the content of the supplementary documents in subsequent pages.

[19] From the testimony of Casimiro Morcillo we know several details related to this approval. Among others, the decree was really written on March 24, 1941, then the feast of St. Gabriel, but to give greater joy to the founder it was dated March 19, the feast of St. Joseph to whom Fr. Escrivá had great devotion (See *Letter*, December 29, 1947/February 14, 1966, no. 157). The decree of the bishop of Madrid can be found in the Appendix, document no. 6.

[20] At the end of the decree of approval we read: "For the safekeeping of the 'Reglamento,' etc., what we say in a special decree will be observed." A special decree with the same date—which can be seen in the Appendix, document no. 7—which directs that "a discreet reserve" be exercised with respect to the documents, should be kept in the secret archive used for the most delicate matters in all dioceses (cf. CIC 1917, cc. 379-382 and CIC 1983, cc. 489-490). That the bishop considered this case sensitive is justified by the campaign of misunderstanding and calumny. In fact, Bishop Leopoldo in a letter of September 1, 1941, to the Coadjutor Abbot of the Monastery of Montserrat—the occasion and purpose of which we will see later—refers to the two decrees: "I personally wrote the decree of approval and I added another, not without consulting very prudent and authorized people, in which I ordained that the *Constitutions* should

The approval granted to Opus Dei was immediately known in ecclesiastical circles. Nevertheless, it did not silence the calumnies which had spread from Madrid to other cities. In Barcelona, where there were not even half a dozen members of Opus Dei, the persecution was particularly vehement. This prompted the Coadjutor Abbot of the Monastery of Montserrat, Aurelio María Escarré, to ask Bishop Eijo y Garay for information. Thus there began a correspondence between the two men which constitutes an invaluable source of information about the events of this period.[21]

On May 9, 1941, Abbot Escarré first wrote the Bishop of Madrid informing him about the slanders against Opus Dei and asking his opinion. Bishop Eijo y Garay answered him on May 24. Among other things he says: "I know about the agitation against Opus Dei arisen in Barcelona. . . . The sad thing is that people very dedicated to God are the instrument of this evil; of course it is *putantes se obsequium præstare Deo*." Then comes the main topic of the letter: "I know everything, because the *Opus*, from the time it was founded in 1928, is so much in the hands of the Church that the diocesan Ordinary, that is to say either the Vicar General or myself knows and, when necessary, directs all of its steps; both its cries as a newborn creature and its current groans resound in our ears and . . . in our hearts. Because, believe me, Most Reverend Father, the *Opus* is truly *Dei*, from its first idea and in all of its steps and works. . . . Yet nevertheless, it is good people who attack it. It would merit amazement, if the Lord did not have us already accustomed to see this same thing happen in many other works of His."[22]

---

be kept in a separate place. All of this was well thought out, and if I am not mistaken, correct; I had in mind only the service of our Holy Mother the Church and the glory of God."

[21] The originals of these letters are kept in the archives of the Abbey of Montserrat; a copy is found in RHF, D-3545.

[22] In the same letter, he adds burning praises of the founder of Opus Dei: "Doctor Escrivá is a model priest, chosen by God for the sanctification of many souls, humble, prudent, self-sacrificing, extremely obedient to his prelate, outstanding in intellect, of very solid doctrinal and spiritual formation, ardently zealous, an apostle of the Christian formation of young students, and with no other end or desire in mind than that of preparing for the service of our country and the service and defence of the Church a large number of intellectuals and professionals, who in the middle of the world are not only a leaven of holiness of life but also work with the soul of apostles.

"And in the mold of his spirit he has poured out his *Opus*. I know it, not by reference of others, but by my personal experience. The *men* of Opus Dei (I emphasize the word men, because among them even the young ones are men thanks to their recollection and the seriousness of their life) are traveling a safe way not only for the salvation of their souls but also to do great good to countless other souls."

More letters followed.  On June 21, 1941, Bishop Eijo y Garay dealt with one of the accusations against Opus Dei members:  their suppposed disaffection for religious orders and congregations.  "It is one of the greatest calumnies," he writes, "against *Opus Dei*; and I can guarantee you, Most Reverend Father, that it is pure calumny. How could they love the holy Church without loving also the religious state?"  He continues with words that witness to the secular character of Opus Dei, "They love it, they venerate and proclaim it a means of salvation for those called by God to it; but they do not feel called to this vocation, but rather to that of sanctifying themselves in the middle of the world and exercising in the world their apostolate.  This is what they feel and this is what they say, without implying in any way the slightest disrespect for the religious state; it is precisely him who teaches them how they are to live in the world in as holy a manner as if they were religious.  And they believe that, called to this kind of apostolate, if they are faithful, they will give more glory to God than if they were to turn a deaf ear to this vocation and were to become religious. . . .  Think, Most Reverend Father, that all of this storm has arisen after two or three young men who had wanted to become religious have preferred *Opus Dei* once they knew of it!"

On September 1 Bishop Eijo y Garay answered two earlier letters informing him of an intensified campaign and other details.  He wrote: "I can do no less than thank you for your kind interest in Opus Dei, for which I have such great esteem.  I am pained by what Your Reverence tells me: that the campaign has grown, if not in extension at least in intensity and in depth."  He reiterates his esteem: "It goes ahead because it walks united to the bishops, holding tightly to their hand and with no other desire than that of obeying them and of serving the Church; their motto and password and the order of every day is *Serviam!*"  He sadly mentions some facts that allow one to grasp, even over the distance of time, the violence of the persecution: "Tell me if this is not a most cruel persecution, to call this Work which Your Reverence knows and esteems and for which you are rightly so interested, masonry, a heretical sect . . ., den of iniquity where souls are lost without remedy; and its members, iconoclasts and hypnotized, persecutors of the Church and of the religious state, and so many other "niceties" of this kind; and to move the civil authorities against them and try to close their centers and to put the founder in jail and have him condemned in Rome; and the most tragic and painful of all, to sow weeds by all means, from the confessional to visits to the homes of the families of those who wish well of Opus Dei.  If this is not a most harsh persecution, what is?  Believe me, Most Reverend Father, the spirit of holy joy and peace, the charity and loving resignation with which the members of Opus Dei accept this persecution and kiss the hands of those who have raised it up, this is edifying and consoling. And this confirms me even more in what I said to Your Reverence before: that the *Opus* is truly *Dei*."

These texts reflect the environment of the time and the months which preceded it. While appreciation for Opus Dei was not lacking—the letters of Bishop Eijo y Garay bear witness to this and others could be mentioned as well—the organized campaign was very harsh. This was the context in which the first written diocesan approval was granted. We turn now to study its characteristics and juridical scope.

## 3. Charism, particular law and juridical form

Before analyzing the 1941 approval and the Work's configuration as outlined in the *Reglamento* and other documents presented for approval, let us look more extensively at the relationship between charism and law.

One of the characteristics of civil legislation is its dynamism: being adjusted time and again to the evolving requirements of society. Nearly every social change ordinarily brings with it changes in legislation. The dynamism of positive law derives from the living pursuit of the common good, the aim of every law.

Along with their traditional character, canonical laws also have a dynamism: developments and changes within the framework fixed by the foundational will of Jesus Christ. Even in ecclesial society, life often precedes changes in mutable structures or the birth of new structures so long as they do not contradict the Church's constitutional principles. Changes in the Church are not merely human; human and divine factors intertwine in incubating changes. As the Second Vatican Council reminds us,[23] the Holy Spirit in a thousand ways guides and animates history and shapes it with his gifts and charisms.

The living reality confronting the canonical system is enriched and diversified by the inclusion of these charisms. These divine gifts have spawned an array of activities, norms and structures. This regulating action of the Holy Spirit, as Professor Javier Hervada points out, does not take place at the juridical level, but at the level of supernatural life, which the law must take into account in extending to it the Church's imprint of legality.[24] We find on the one hand charisms and what derives immediately from them, and on the other the hierarchical magisterium, inspired by the Holy Spirit and thereby endowed with the capacity to discern charisms. And finally we have laws that ought to accommodate discerned charisms,

---

[23] See Dogmatic Constitution *Lumen Gentium*, no. 4.

[24] Cf. J. Hervada, "Sugerencias acerca de los componentes del Derecho," in *Ius Canonicum*, 6 (1966):93-94.

so that juridical structures adequately ratify them. The Church ought not only to respect charisms, but also to incorporate them into herself, and further their momentum.

Consequently, the importance of Opus Dei's *ius peculiare* or particular law is obvious for its proper juridical-canonical configuration. "The Work grew by God's power, and the ascetical phenomenon promoted by the Lord in 1928 became in fact universal," the founder wrote in 1961, looking back on the preceding 33 years. "With God's grace I elaborated, little by little, the norms of our *particular law*, measuring the Work as it grew."[25] Particular law is, then, the expression of the charism or, more exactly, the specification of what the charism requires. First, the charism is played out by experience, the living realization of the foundational divine gift; in that light Fr. Escrivá discerns in practice what fits the charism and what does not. We read in the same document that the particular law is "a law fitted to our spirit, to our asceticism and the needs of our specific apostolates."[26]

This reality, let us repeat it, is placed before the Church's juridical system with the concrete characteristics of that specific moment, the fruits of past studies and experiences that have progressively enriched that legislation. Historical-juridical development presupposes interaction, in which the legal system implies and evaluates social phenomenon born of history, but at the same time legislation is judged by that life. Legislation shows itself to be more effective as it configures itself to the developments history brings in its wake. Furthermore, the problem acquires special characteristics when it is situated in the field of canon law. Here the realities in play can or do transcend purely human experience, as in the case of the charisms and the movements or institutions that incarnate them. If the question is to avoid adversarial attitudes, special attention must be given to the action of the Holy Spirit in an ongoing challenge of discernment in the light of the deposit of revealed truth.[27]

Moreover, the importance the founder of Opus Dei gave to particular law stems from his keen consciousness of the novelty that Opus Dei represents in the history of the Church. He clearly perceived, in 1941 and later, a tension between the charism that defines

---

[25] *Letter*, January 25, 1961, no. 5. (emphasis added)

[26] *Letter*, January 25, 1961, no. 20.

[27] It is the hierarchy or the historical-ecclesial connection that we find clearly formulated in another text of the founder of Opus Dei: "First there is life, the lived pastoral phenomenon. Afterwards, comes the norm that usually arises out of custom. Finally comes the theological theory that develops with the lived phenomenon. And from the first moment, always, the vigilance of doctrine and of the way of acting so that neither life, nor the norm, nor the theory stray from the faith and moral teaching of Jesus Christ" (*Letter*, March 19, 1954, no. 9).

the Work and the canonical legislation in force at the time. Opus Dei simply did not fit into any traditional ascetical, pastoral or apostolic patterns. Hence he always strove to base everything on the charism, to underline and explain what the charism required in order to pry into the future and decide how to act today and now—something that on occasion was urgently necessary.

History waits for no man. By 1941 apostolic growth and other circumstances underscored the need to obtain a juridical framework for Opus Dei in a canonical system where there was no place for it. This led to that specific *modus operandi* that Msgr. Escrivá sometimes described as "giving in without giving up, with every intention of recovering" those concessions. He would accommodate himself to the legislation in force, when it seemed impossible to raise the question of its eventual reform. This going along with the legislation in force permitted taking steps forward. His was, however, a sincere accommodation without mental reservations; his deep sense of being a man of the Church prevented him from acting in any other way. Meanwhile, however, he remained fully faithful to the charism, affirming and proclaiming it in the very act whereby he accepted a less than adequate solution establishing, hence, a platform from which to go beyond the solution obtained.

The concept of particular law played an essential role here; it served as the fundamental lever with which to reach a final juridical framework. In fact, whenever one such situation arose, Opus Dei's founder took great pains to make sure that in the documents of approval or in the texts these documents sanctioned, the substantial nature of Opus Dei and its particular law were clearly expressed. Thus Opus Dei's fundamental norms would serve as the criteria for interpreting those derived from the general legislation, which Fr. Escrivá saw himself obliged to accept. The founder explained it himself in a 1961 *Letter* where he evoked some events of this juridical evolution. In accepting certain solutions "I felt compelled to make our *particular law* clear, so that if some day the general legislation were to be interpreted in a way foreign to the traits of our vocation, our particular law would be clearly sanctioned and in accord with the essential characteristics of our way."[28] This was an arduous task: on occasions it was not possible to avoid—because of the inadequacy of the law in force—having to accept foreign ele-

---

[28] *Letter*, January 25, 1961, no. 22. Preceding the paragraph quoted in the text the founder wrote: "In things of government, especially in a pastoral mission of souls, the most direct way is not always the straight line. Sometimes one must go around, zigzag, retrace one's steps, in order later to make a jump; to give in in accidental matters—with the intention of recovering them at the proper time—in order to save more substantial values.

"This way of acting, my children, is not hypocrisy, because one does not pretend to be what one is not; it is prudence, charity and even many times a duty of justice."

ments in non-essential matters. The founder points this out with reference to one of the later stages of the juridical development: "As the Work had been defined and approved, its *particular law* was in perfect agreement with the essence of our path, except in those things belonging to the state of perfection that I had to allow. We will rid ourselves of them when God presents us with the opportunity."[29]

This process entailed greater interior tension and efforts than it might seem. To endow a reality with a juridical configuration requires that it be analyzed and evaluated from the perspective of the legal categories then in force. How can it be adjusted to the applicable norms? If the juridical categories are fully adequate and adjustable to the reality being configured, the entity acquires a potential for its practical realization as legal implications are played out. But when the existing juridical categories cannot be accommodated completely to the entity seeking legal status, then the situation is clearly complicated. The pure and simple application of existing categories can transform and even adulterate that reality.

History presents us with more than one example of such dislocation, both in civil society and the Church. This explains the prudence that Msgr. Escrivá lived at each successive legal step. Ecclesiastical legislation did not afford proper channels for an adequate reception of Opus Dei; thus the process could be hazardous. Fr. Josemaría had to use all the available means to defend and authenticate the pristine and specific nature of Opus Dei.[30]

The particular law sought by Fr. Escrivá was certainly to contain juridical norms. However, it must also inseparably reflect extralegal realities: a spirit, certain spiritual means, specific consequences of a Christian vocation to be lived amid secular activities and situations. At each stage of the juridical process, the founder had to make sure the essential characteristics of Opus Dei's spirit were included in the appropriate documents. Henceforward, Opus Dei's specific reality was embodied within the concrete juridical figure adopted. This contributed to the interpretation and development of such figure. It was also a means for the law to be progres-

---

[29] *Letter*, January 25, 1961, no. 42.

[30] So reads a later letter: "The Lord continued to help us so that in our *particular law* everything would remain very clear. Law is not life, but if law is not in accordance with the living reality that it regulates, it suffocates the very life it is supposed to channel.

"Therefore it was not vain legalism that moved me to work untiringly so that everything was fixed in broad norms that accorded with our vocation; what moved me was the grave responsibility of making sure that this new phenomenon was set forth in the norms of our *particular law*, according to what God wanted." (*Letter*, January 25, 1961, no. 28).

sively adapted to the substantive reality it is supposed to serve, that is to say, to the charism and mission received from God. A 1952 *Letter* refers, in a metaphoric way, to what had been accomplished and what remained to be done: "My children, at that time it was not possible to obtain more. When one gathers water from a fresh, cascading spout, one must have the humility, wisdom and temperance of taking it little by little. One places only the edge of a glass under the source; if not, the water is lost, sacrificed to the water's wildness and to an overeagerness to drink."[31]

In 1941 the tension between charism and legislation was much less severe than in later years. The first diocesan approval took place at a relatively simple level, all things considered. Nevertheless, there was tension, with very concrete manifestations, which we will now study as we return to the thread of the story.

## 4. Opus Dei as a pious union

Why did the founder request that Opus Dei be approved first as a pious union? The answer couldn't be simpler: it was reached by a process of elimination. Cardinal Bueno Monreal recalls the conversations he held, as Promotor of Justice of the diocese of Madrid, with the founder: "He told me with great confidence about his thoughts, and he was happy that I gave him my opinions with all sincerity. He had already written the first statutes of the Work, contained in six brief documents: *Reglamento* (By-laws), *Régimen* (Government), *Orden* (Order), *Costumbres* (Customs), *Espíritu* (Spirit) and *Ceremonial* (Ceremonies). These writings detailed the spirit of Opus Dei. Beyond these documents—which were the way they were and could not be in any other way and about which I had nothing to say—was the question of the juridical classification the Work should have. I was well-informed on these matters, because that was my job in the diocese.

"Speaking with Josemaría, it became very clear to me that Opus Dei was not in any way a religious congregation. Josemaría never conceived of following that route: he manifestly rejected it and in no way did he pursue it. Thus it was not, nor could it be a religious congregation. The only remaining juridical figure in the canonical system of the time was that of lay associations. Among such it was also clear that Opus Dei could not be a third order nor a confraternity or sodality; thus there only remained the possibility of constituting it as a pious union."

"Since this had been a very narrow classification, inadequate to the Work, Josemaría did not like it. I could not say now whether he said so or I thought so myself later; but he clearly desired to abide

---

[31] *Letter*, December 12, 1952, no. 5.

strictly by the letter of the evangelical norm of prudence that discourages putting new wine in old wineskins."[32]

If the members of Opus Dei are not religious, the only viable way was that of the third part of the second book of the 1917 Code that deals with the ordinary lay faithful and their associations.[33] Among these associations the Code presented three different kinds: third orders, confraternities and pious unions. Opus Dei could not be a third order: "under the direction of some order and in conformity with its spirit" (c. 702). Nor could it be a confraternity or sodality dedicated to public worship: "erected for the embellishment of public worship" (c. 707 par. 2). There remained only the category of pious unions, an association with a variety of purposes: those compatible with the Code's very generic formula: "the practice of certain works of piety or charity" (c. 707 par. 1).[34]

Pious union therefore was the least unsuitable solution. The secular and lay character of Opus Dei was preserved: its members remained ordinary Christians, whose canonical and civil status did not change in any way. As the founder wrote in 1944, "With this first juridical step, Opus Dei members continued being ordinary faithful; the recognition of our apostolic work, by the legitimate authority of the Church, was accomplished in terms then appropriate to the stage of development we had achieved."[35]

The door was left open to new advances in this juridical direction; the category of pious union was broad enough for such development. Unlike other associations such as confraternities, pious unions could be erected or simply approved.[36] The form of ap-

---

[32] Deposition quoted in note 7 of this chapter.

[33] CIC 1917, cc. 684-725. One of the first canons offers a general perspective of the norms: "Associations distinct from religious institutes or societies of canons 487-681 can be established by the Church, either to promote a more perfect Christian life among their members, or to practice certain works of piety or charity, or finally for the embellishment of public worship" (c. 685).

[34] For further information regarding pious unions, see among others, S. De Angelis, *De Fidelium Associationibus*, I, Naples 1959, pp. 54ff; W. Onclin, "Principia Generalia de Fidelium Associationibus," in *La Sacra Congregatione del Concilio*, Vatican City 1964, pp. 512ff; E. Vromant & L. Bongaerts, *De fidelium associationibus*, Turin-Rome 1955, nos. 69ff, pp. 99ff.

[35] *Letter*, February 14, 1944, no. 6.

[36] Canon 686 par. 1 of the CIC 1917 established: "No association is recognized in the Church, which has not been erected or at least approved by legitimate ecclesiastical authority." And canon 708 specified: "Confraternities can be established only by a formal decree of erection; but for pious unions the approval of the Ordinary is sufficient, and after this is obtained, although they are not moral persons, they are nevertheless capable of obtaining spiritual favors and especially indulgences." *Erection* is usually defined as "an authentic act of ecclesiastical authority by which an association is formally constituted as a moral person, with all of the rights proper to an ecclesiastical moral person" (E. Vromant-L. Bongaerts, *op. cit.*, note 34 of this chapter, no. 7, p.

proval in Opus Dei's case was discussed by the founder and the
bishop of Madrid. They opted for that of simple approval. The
provisional character of the decision was thus highlighted in antici-
pation of future developments. Thus was achieved the practical
purpose for this intervention of the ecclesiastical authority on behalf of Opus Dei: public recognition of its existence by the bishop of
the diocese, manifestation of the appreciation and support of the
hierarchy and the proclamation that, in its nature, ends and norms
of life, there is nothing contrary to Church teachings.

What characteristics of Opus Dei can be gleaned from the documents Fr. Josemaría submitted with the request for approval? As
said before, these documents consisted of the *Reglamento*, complemented by other texts respectively entitled *Régimen*, *Orden*, *Costumbres*,
and *Ceremonial*. The interplay between these documents is clear:
the By-laws (*Reglamento*) offers a brief but general overview of Opus
Dei: its aims, the people who constitute it, and the agents of authority and other aspects required by the civil legislation then in force
in Spain. The other documents specify various points with regard
to forms of government, practices of piety, spirit, periodic gatherings for formation, and the like.

What most catches one's attention in these 1941 texts is doubtless their breadth of vision, not only from juridical and theological
perspectives, but from an historical one as well. While Opus Dei's
apostolate had spread to several Spanish cities, its membership was
still small: no more than 50 people. The documents presented for
approval look much further: beyond what already exists, into the
future, and this even in organizational terms. For example, they
foresee, in detail, a central governing body which is interdiocesan.
There will be a president—who is called simply Father, it being
prohibited to use any other form of address within the Work—his
office is for life" (*Régimen*, art. 14). To help him direct Opus Dei
there will be a "Senate, made up of the Secretary General, three
Vice Secretaries, and at least one Delegate for each Territory" (*Régimen*,
art. 15). There will also be an "Advisory Council" for the women
of Opus Dei, made up of "the Father and the General Secretary, and
three Vice Secretaries, and at least one Delegate for each Territory"
(*Régimen*, art. 24). The possibility of a Vice President is also contemplated (*Régimen*, art. 22). The Father will be assisted in his

19). Therefore it confers on associations juridical personality with the consequence of
perpetuity (c. 102), the right to possess and administer goods (c. 1495 par. 2), etc.
*Approval* in the meaning of c. 686 par. 1, on the other hand, is an act of jurisdiction of
the ecclesiastical authority which "does not constitute an association as a moral person, but gives it the right to exist and the capacity for receiving spiritual graces and
especially indulgences" (c. 708), (S. de Angelis, *op. cit.*, note 34 of this chapter, no. 20,
p. 8). It does not however originate the other effects.

spiritual life and material things by two *custodes* designated by the Father himself from a list of nine names of members presented by the Senate (*Régimen*, art. 19). Assemblies are also foreseen: ordinary, extraordinary and elective.

It also provides for dividing the apostolate according to territories, at the head of each would be a "Territorial Commission" made up of a "Counselor, a Defensor and three Secretaries," depending directly upon the Father and the Senate (*Régimen*, art. 27). Similarly there will be analogous "Territorial Advisory Councils" for the women (*Régimen*, art. 31). "In each Territory there will be at least one Center of Studies for the male members and another for the female members where they can receive the formation required by the apostolates" (*Régimen*, art. 39). "All the work of the Center of Studies will be carried out without removing members from their normal environment" (*Régimen*, art. 40).

What the bishop of Madrid-Alcalá approved at the time as a pious union was a then existent reality, but one that already pointed to future developments that in turn would ultimately require a different juridical formula. Not for long could Opus Dei remain at the diocesan level. The founder always thought in universal terms: while the Work might be just starting, he knew it was destined to grow and spread. Thus even the first steps must be taken with a view to this universality. Its juridical configuration as a pious union was obviously a provisional solution.

What characteristics of the vocation and spirit of Opus Dei are reflected in these texts? In an account dated January 9, 1943, whose purpose is to explain some of the historical background, the founder refers to the request presented to the bishop of Madrid in 1941: "I prepared the documentation the bishop asked for. First I included what was and would be the nucleus of our statutes: the *Reglamento*. Speaking with some of my children or with people who understand and love us, I have often explained that this *Reglamento*—two full pages, I might add—illuminates our whole path; it is a spotlight that, with the passage of time, will point out how our life will be regulated, just as the Lord made me see it in 1928."[37]

This *Reglamento*, especially the description of Opus Dei contained in the first article, evinces its essence: the call to radical discipleship of Jesus Christ—sanctity and apostolate—in the common circumstances of daily life. Here is the article in its entirety:

---

[37] RHF, AVF-28. As late as January 27, 1974, during a get-together with Opus Dei members studying in Rome, the founder evoked the *Reglamento* he had elaborated many years before: "Those who study law, when years have passed, will be able to follow that juridical light from the very first moment until the present, and will see that it has always been the same" (RHF-20163, p. 287).

"Paragraph 1. The Work of God—Opus Dei—is a Catholic association of men and of women, who, living in the middle of the world, seek Christian perfection, through sanctifying ordinary work. Convinced that man has been created *ut operaretur* (Gen 2:15), the members of Opus Dei commit themselves to continue with their professional work or its equivalent, even though theirs be a high economic or social position.[38]

"Paragraph 2. The means by which the members are to attain the supernatural end they set for themselves are: to lead an interior life of prayer and sacrifice, according to the norms and spirit approved by holy Church, and to discharge with maximum integrity their professional and social duties." ·

In this first legal text and in those to follow, Opus Dei is described as an institution made up of ordinary Christians, men and women, of various social conditions and civil states—celibate or married.[39] All are united by a common Christian pledge and by a real and effective commitment to each one's own occupation. It is by this commitment to their own profession or occupation that they belong to the society where they live. There is a great insistence on this last point. It is mentioned in the first article of the *Reglamento* three times: in the initial definition, the perfection or fullness of the Christian life is said to be sought "through the sanctification of ordinary work"; then it is emphasized that every member of Opus Dei, whatever his or her condition, must work, that is, have a profession or occupation; and finally in describing the means for achieving holiness members are said "to discharge their professional and social duties with maximum integrity."

Obviously Opus Dei members are not to form a group of world-shy people seeking mere personal perfection nor a group which

---

[38] The last part of this paragraph repeats a text from *Intimate notes*, January 20, 1934, which we have referred to before (cf. chapter 1, note 25).

[39] The first article of the *Reglamento* itself does not make this point precise. This is done, however, by the other documents. The one entitled *Régimen* (art. 2, paragraph 2) declares that "men and women, married and celibate," can be admitted as members.

To detail this point and to specify the form whereby the 1941 texts reproduce it, we must refer to the kinds of members described in the *Reglamento*, art. 2, and in *Régimen*, art. 2 and 3. Three kinds of members are distinguished: a) inscribed, men or women, celibate or married; b) supernumeraries, men or women but in any case celibate; and c) numeraries, designated from among the men or women previously admitted as supernumeraries to occupy positions of direction.

In speaking of various kinds of members, we are only trying to point out (see also note 3 of this chapter) different degrees of availability for the specific directive or apostolic tasks. Presupposed in everyone is the call to full holiness and apostolate in the middle of the world, the nucleus of the Work's spirit and the reason for its being. This was always the mind of Opus Dei's founder. We will speak about this and specifically of married members of Opus Dei more extensively in subsequent chapters.

from behind an institutional shelter pursues a limited apostolic goal. On the contrary, by divine vocation the members of Opus Dei are called to embrace the radical demands of baptism and to respond with new lights to the invitation to holiness and apostolate derived therefrom. Then each one, according to his state in life and retaining the condition and work he has in the world, seeks to be holy and apostolic which are inseparable qualities of any Christian way of life.

Thus the first article of the document *Régimen* states: "Opus Dei seeks the sanctification of its members and the salvation of souls." The *Reglamento* points out that, to achieve the "supernatural end they set for themselves," members of the Work are to "lead an interior life of prayer and sacrifice according to the norms and spirit approved by holy Church, and to discharge with maximum integrity their professional and social duties" (art. 1, paragraph 2). As ordinary Christians—and as expressed repeatedly elsewhere— "they fulfill all their civic duties and, at the same time, exercise all their rights" (*Espíritu*, no. 4). These activities are to be carried out in many different settings and environments, from public service to ordinary domestic work, shunning no upright and lawful occupation.[40]

Members of Opus Dei are not "to form a group" but "to open up like a fan," in varied directions, each striving to be where he lives a witness to Christ and a bearer of the Gospel's light (*Espíritu*, no. 26). Thus he or she brings it to others through friendship (*Espíritu*, nos. 7 and 40), doctrine (*Régimen*, art. 12, paragraph 2) and example (*Espíritu*, no. 50). The spiritual training that Opus Dei offers is addressed to all kinds of people of every class, as repeatedly stated in many passages of these documents (*Régimen*, articles 12, par. 2; 13, etc.). This classlessness is no obstacle to the particular importance given to apostolate with university students and the fostering of vocations from their ranks (*Régimen*, art. 12, par. 1), as we explained at the outset of this chapter.

Present in all social environments, Opus Dei members will ordinarily work on their own, according to their personal preferences. Occasionally, however, they may join with other citizens to promote apostolic initiatives in the various ways sanctioned by civil society, "adapting themselves always to the circumstances of place and time" (*Régimen*, art. 8, par. 2). In any case, as the first article of

---

[40] A year before Opus Dei's founder wrote in a *Letter*: "Light of the world, my children, living with naturalness on earth, the normal environment of our life; participating in all tasks, in all the noble activities of men; working side by side with them, in the occupation proper to each one; exercising our rights and fulfilling our duties, the same rights and duties our fellow citizens—equal to ourselves—have in the society where we live" (March 11, 1940, no. 9).

the *Reglamento* points out, they make their occupation the hinge of their sanctification and apostolate.[41]

Primacy is clearly given to personal apostolate.[42] This dispersal of personal initiatives in many environments has its parallel, in keeping with the systemic orientation mentioned in the previous article, in the description of Opus Dei as an institution whose fundamental purpose is not so much to elicit deeds as to form people (*Régimen*, art. 8, par. 1). This essential feature of Opus Dei is further ratified in the freedom and spontaneity with which each member acts in temporal matters. This personal pluralism dovetails with Fr. Escrivá's theological conviction that the Work was not his, and both lead to renouncing all institutional glory. This facet, alluded to in the previous chapter, is echoed in the 1941 documents: "We must gladly practice collective humility. May a false love for our supernatural undertaking never lead us to forget that Opus Dei's glory is to live without human glory: to pass unnoticed. *Deo omnis gloria!*" (*Espíritu*, no. 39). "It will never be possible to attribute to the Work the fame or merit of the activities of its members. All the glory is for God and in human things for other associations" (*Espíritu*, no. 10).[43]

## 5. Ordinary Christians and ordinary citizens

In the early texts just examined, Opus Dei is described in brief formulas in keeping with the style of a juridical document. It is an enterprise whose purpose is to foster among all Christians an awareness of the implications of baptismal grace, above all the need of sanctifying ordinary tasks. In many souls this awareness leads to a special divine vocation sanctioned by a stable, lasting and profound commitment. Amid the ordinary conditions and walks of life, a

---

[41] This possibility of a collective apostolate was foreseen—as we saw at the time—in the earliest texts of the founder and was manifested in the Academy DYA, set up in 1933, and in subsequent student residences. The activities of which we speak are activities of an apostolic character, different from the activities, associations or entities of another kind where in the use of their professional freedom members of Opus Dei could participate.

[42] "It can well be said, my children, that the greatest fruit of the work of Opus Dei is that obtained by its members personally, with an apostolate of example and of their loyal friendship with their colleagues" (Letter, March 11, 1940, no. 55).

[43] The Reglamento (art. 12 par. 2, 1) also prescribes that no propaganda be made of the Work as such; a norm which, obviously, does not apply to the different activities Opus Dei members may foster with other citizens, as in fact occurred with the Academy-residence DYA and subsequent activities.

As will be noticed from the paragraphs quoted in the text, the numbers of *Espíritu*—and something similar happens with the document called *Costumbres*, which complements it—are formed by brief and incisive sentences redolent of *The Way*, although logically they are descriptive, not hortatory, as in *The Way*.

person thus dedicates himself to seek holiness and help others to discover and live the same baptismal requirements that define the Christian vocation.

Moreover, this description fully reflects what Opus Dei was in fact and what it will continue to be, as we see in the letters from Madrid's Bishop to the Abbot of Montserrat, particularly that dated June 21, 1941.[44] The Bishop describes the growth of Opus Dei in the early 1940s. A group of university students had gathered around Fr. Josemaría. He dedicated himself intensely to their formation, "instilling in them a profound piety, a spirit of faithful fulfillment of their duty, and above all love for Holy Mother Church and devotion to its Hierarchy." The letter continues: "When the group became more numerous, a residence for students was established governed by the Father helped by some of the brighter and more fervent young men." The Work continued to grow and some of them wanted to "bind themselves to the Father in order to help him." Other centers were opened in various university cities where new vocations arose, closely followed by the founder, who likewise reinforced their pursuit of personal holiness and their desire to be apostolic.[45]

After describing the apostolic growth, the bishop mentions the Work that sustains it: "To preserve this spirit they needed organization, a family tie, to communicate among themselves, to support and encourage one another; where the number was sufficient, meetings dedicated to piety and study were deemed necessary. This organization and family is Opus Dei. . . . Its end (that of the Work and of each of its members) is the sanctification of each one in his occupation in the middle of the world, to work, to work always. This is the sense that *Opus* has: God put man in paradise *ut operaretur*.

---

[44] With regard to these letters see note 20 of this chapter.

[45] The letter reads thus: "The Work grew, and more in intensity than in extension; some of the better formed, convinced of the usefulness for the glory of God of an apostolate of this kind wanted to bind themselves to the Father in order to help him; those who finished their university studies and began to exercise their professions kept in touch with him; they owed to him what they most treasured: holiness of life and the desire to do good to souls, each one in his own place. Fully committed to these young men, the Father advised and encouraged them, while continuing to direct their lives. There arose the idea of opening residences and academies in other places, to extend to more students this fruitful work; and in various university cities (Barcelona, Valencia, etc.) they were established, under the direction of the Father and the care of those who had consecrated themselves to such a beautiful apostolate. The Ordinary of each of these places, without whose permission and blessing nothing has been done, just as here in Madrid, knew everything and applauded and blessed it.

"With the passage of years the Work bore fruit, as is very natural: those formed in it began spreading out all over Spain, more notable for the solidity of their formation than their number, inflamed with desires of serving God and with the supreme zeal of being useful to Holy Church."

The ideal of the Father and of his sons is to serve God working in a holy manner, each one in his own line of work, always focused on the defense and service of the Holy Church and with faithful and self-sacrificing submission to the Hierarchy, that is to say to the Pope and to their own Bishop." The description ends on the prayer life of Opus Dei members: "Very deep, very solid and very healthy." He adds: "In no way is it different from that of all faithful Christians, unless it be in the intensity of its cultivation."

The last sentence of the Bishop of Madrid ties in with the documents approved in 1941. Together they reflect another essential characteristic of Opus Dei's spirit: the call to intimacy with God, the source of Christian life, with all its consequences: prayer, spiritual life and personal commitment.

The *Reglamento's* first article expressly states that members of the Work must rely in their apostolate, above all, on "interior life of prayer"; article 2 describes the commitments entailed in the pledge to interior (or prayer) life, theologically consistent with the *esse* and *operari* of a Christian. The time devoted to prayer referred to in *Reglamento* is completed in the documents *Ordo* and *Ceremonial* with the mention of other practices of Christian life: reading the Gospel, personal dealings with Jesus Christ, holy Mass, eucharistic life, Marian piety. . . .

Opus Dei's founder did not conceive of these practices as something juxtaposed to life. Rather they are moments of light and depth, accommodated to the stuff of life, "as the glove fits the hand." Thus piety leads to an awareness of God's constant presence and to the desire to direct everything to God, who is at the core of all reality and behind every event. This spiritual program is reflected in *The Way*, a particularly vivid expression of Fr. Escrivá's preaching before and after 1940,[46] from which arises the desire to be "contemplatives in the middle of the world,"[47] without detriment to the members' secular condition. Their prayer life presupposes, enlivens and reaffirms their active presence in the world. Members of Opus Dei do not separate themselves from the world, not even temporarily. Rather they are ordinary Christians whose lives take on a new and definitive meaning when called by God to live the ordinary circumstances of daily life with Christian fullness.

---

[46] The first edition of *The Way* appeared in 1939—only two years before the approval of the Work as a pious union—as an elaboration of an earlier text called *Consideraciones espirituales*.

[47] "Contemplative souls in the middle of the world . . . wherever we greet the noise of the street and human activities—factory, university, farm, office, home—we find ourselves in a simple filial contemplation, a constant dialogue with God" (*Letter*, March 11, 1940, no. 15).

From the start the founder had presented to prospective members an ideal of full dedication, a commitment of the whole person translated into a stable bond with Opus Dei.[48] The 1941 documents express this in various ways. This commitment is not "something transitory." The "surrender to Jesus Christ" in the intimacy of each one's conscience is "definitive and complete" (*Espíritu*, no. 3). It translates juridically into a bond with Opus Dei. Speaking of those embracing celibacy, the commitment is made "for a determined period of time by virtue of what is called the *oblation*." Later the commitment is "perpetual, by virtue of what is called the *fidelity*" (*Régimen*, art. 4). Note there is no reference to vows or other sacred bonds in any of the documents approved in 1941.

Once again we find ourselves confronted with the same difficulty: How to reflect in a juridical text the reality of Opus Dei as a pastoral phenomenon which fosters a full commitment to holiness and apostolate in the world, each person in his (or her) own setting, without modifying one's state in life or social condition, being ordinary citizens and Christians? How are all its characteristics to be expressed, while at the same time avoiding any confusion with pastoral phenomena of a different nature, i.e., that of the religious orders and congregations or of institutions which in one way or another were considered their equivalent. At that time every invitation to holiness was reduced to this.

Fr. Josemaría was even aware of the danger of confusing the two pastoral phenomena, especially since the religious state had been well established for centuries, while that represented by Opus Dei was just taking its first steps. To equate the two phenomena, so distinct from one another, the founder thought, would undermine the charism of the foundation recently begun. Only the passage of time and apostolic growth would lead to the definitive solution. Experience would have to demonstrate the authenticity of the pastoral phenomenon engendered by Opus Dei: full Christian life in the middle of the world. To reach that final step, however, the earliest juridical texts must incorporate declarations that precluded any ambiguity or confusion with the religious.

The first paragraph of the document *Espíritu* declares that Opus Dei members "are not religious." There is no more authoritative commentary of this affirmation than the founder's texts, such as those mentioned in the preceding chapter. To these can be added the testimony of the Bishop of Madrid in the June 1941 letter to the Abbot of Montserrat. In fact, after referring to the need that Opus

---

[48] In 1934 he had written, for example: "Our dedication to God is not a *state of mind*, a passing situation, but is—in the intimacy of the conscience of each one—a definitive state to seek perfection in the middle of the world" (*Instruction*, April 1, 1934, no. 20).

Dei be constituted as "an organization and a family," he adds: "Indeed, the Founder has never intended to found a religious institute; I know this because he has always said it. . . . He has always wanted the organization born by the grace of God in his hands to be always made up of lay people and be for lay people, and that is how I have approved it in keeping with his opinion. . . . The ideal of the Father and his children is to serve God by working in a holy manner at one's own profession. . . . What he has set for himself is that they live in the holiest way possible but as lay people."

Finally, to make it clear that Opus Dei does not represent a dilution of the demands of authentic holiness—there is no second-class holiness—but rather a new form of full discipleship of Jesus Christ, the Bishop compares the two phenomena. He compares the new form to the traditional in order to emphasize the fullness of the lay call to holiness and its profound difference: "He (that is to say Fr. Josemaría Escrivá) impresses on them that they are to live in the world in as holy a fashion as if they were religious. And they believe that, called to this kind of apostolate, if they follow it they will give more glory to God than if by not heeding their vocation they were to become religious."[49]

The keen consciousness of promoting a way of holiness and apostolate for lay people, men and women who live in the world and receive God's call there, is manifested in other parts of the documents approved in 1941. Thus we find a whole series of declarations intended to underline the secularity of Opus Dei, while heading off any hypothetical attempts at reducing every phenomenon of Christian life to the figure of the religious state, considered as an ideal. (The mentality of the time and place was very inclined to this way of thinking.) For example number 14 of *Espíritu* clearly declares that "the members of the Work in their exterior appearance are indistinguishable from their professional or social peers. For this reason no uniform or distinctive mark will be allowed under any pretext." They must act in the same way as other citizens, their equals. To do otherwise would lessen the strength of their vocation as ordinary Christians.

Number 2 of this document interestingly enough, reinforces this concept with abundant particulars. "The buildings, furniture and environment of the centers where members carry out their apostolic work will never have a monastic appearance; nothing will be allowed, not even the smallest detail, that could liken the Work to a

---

[49] The founder on December 8, 1941, describes the call members of Opus Dei have received as "a vocation to acquire Christian perfection in the place where each person is, without having to retreat to a convent and without living a life similar to that of religious." A few lines further on: "And they will not seek a perfection which is inferior to that of the religious" (*Instruction*, Dec. 8, 1941, no. 70).

religious institute." It specifies that the centers and works of Opus Dei must always have "the tone and environment of the home of a Christian family," (*Espíritu*, no. 23) a comparison that is indeed appropriate.[50]

In an environment where practically every form of dedication was assimilated to the religious life or state, Fr. Josemaría found it necessary to recommend to Opus Dei members that they be very discreet with respect to their call so that their dedication, which is not public, nor ought it to be, in the way that that of the religious is, would remain in the realm of private life. "The members are advised not to speak to people outside the Work about their vocation, because it is something supernatural and ought to be something silent and modest" (*Reglamento*, art 12, par. 2, 3; the same idea is found in *Espíritu*, no. 10).

This discretion, he adds, is neither mystery nor secrecy,[51] but rather the naturalness of one who neither intends nor wants to be

---

[50] The founder constantly explained these ideas in the instruction he gave to his children both orally and in writing. Examples of this can be found in the following affirmations from a document of 1941:

- "You and I have felt a divine call . . . to seek in the street—in ordinary everyday professional work, both lay and secular—holiness, Christian perfection."

- "We come from the street, and we stay in the street."

- "Our way of acting is that of the first Christians . . . : they remained in the middle of the street among their fellow men . . .we must not be different in anything from our colleagues and fellow citizens."

- "Like the first Christians, we cannot have habits or ways of speech that smack of the convent; we must speak the same language as our colleagues."

- "Citizens among fellow citizens, our peers, we cannot dispense with the means other men of the world use in their polite fellowship." Then he refers to ways of dressing, social usage, use of material things, etc., and he sums up giving the reason: "Because we are not friars, nor can we be, since God has not given us their vocation" (*Instruction*, Dec. 8, 1941, nos. 5, 36, 80-81, 82, 87-88).

These and similar statements reflect the desire and need to underline the specific characteristics of each pastoral phenomenon; they do not cast aspersions on the religious state. Then and later the founder manifested always, in word and deed, a great appreciation for religious, as the biographies already quoted show. (See chapter 1, note 1.)

[51] These are expressions, as we said before, the founder liked to use in this context: they are reproduced textually in the documents of 1941. "Without mystery or secrecy, let us be discreet" (*Espíritu*, no. 58). Similarly in *The Way*, no 641: "Discretion is neither mystery nor secrecy. It is simply naturalness." With different words he expresses the same idea in a *Letter* from which we have already quoted. After reaffirming that the members of Opus Dei are "equal in everything to their fellow citizens, to their occupational or professional colleagues" and that they "act externally the same as other Christians," he writes: "It is not a question, therefore . . . of acting in this way as an apostolic tactic, nor of adopting unnecessary camouflages. . . . We have nothing to cover or hide: the spontaneity of our way of acting and of our conduct cannot be confused by anyone with secrecy" (*Letter*, March 11, 1940, nos. 56-58).

considered different from what he is: an ordinary Christian. This discretion is colored by the historical circumstances that called for it. The danger of being confused with religious was no mere possibility, but a reality. Fr. Escrivá wrote in 1941: "They look at us with the prejudice of believing that we are religious who hide our condition . . . a prejudice that is false from the start. . . . They do not realize that we are of the world without being worldly and that by our divine vocation we do not want to, nor can we, leave the world."[52]

Because it wasn't common, it was necessary to accentuate the naturalness and secularity that, as ordinary Christians, the members of Opus Dei must live. Fr. Josemaría explained this in the report of January 9, 1943: "I thought about this before the tabernacle, and I saw that it was necessary to proceed with great prudence—both supernatural and human—because the way opened by the Work is not easily understood by many with an ecclesiastical and religious mentality." After mentioning the external circumstances that required greater prudence, he continues: "It is never a question of secrecy or of secrets—something I have always abhorred and rejected. It is simply one more defense against our being confused with religious and against our houses—family homes where professional men live as ordinary citizens the same as others—being considered convents or religious houses." He added: "Our dedication to God is not public, unlike that of religious. They are phenomena distinct from one another. Thus I have been obliged to say that one should not speak of the Work with outsiders, that dedication to God in the Work should not be communicated to anyone, etc. Only those who race through these texts could think there is something secret; it is merely the care for a new creature, still in the maternal womb. In other words it is the secrecy of gestation, hidden from no one. Yet natural logic and discretion require that it not be brought into the open, lest the creature be lost."[53]

Secularity, naturalness, the need to affirm the Work's specific identity, a prudence of the first steps, plus a vivid awareness of the primacy of God's glory and the exclusion of any hint of self-affirmation and vanity (the personal and collective humility we spoke of before[54]): there we have the foundation of the norms of 1941. Neither then nor later did everyone understand this theological core,

---

[52] *Instruction*, December 8, 1941, no. 44.

[53] Declaration of the founder quoted in note 37 of this chapter.

[54] To the texts already cited we add another: "Let us be humble, let us seek only the glory of God. . . . Humility is the foundation of our life, a means and condition of effectiveness. Pride and vanity can make attractive the vocation of the party lantern

but that is a different story from the one we are dealing with here.[55] We repeat, then, what is essential: the value of these documents dating from 1941 as the first step in a juridical process, provisional by its very nature, but bearing witness to a consistent and determined effort to incarnate, in adequate canonical terms, a pastoral and spiritual phenomenon of holiness and apostolate in the midst of the world.

---

that shines and moves and is seen by everyone, but in reality it lasts only one night and it dies without leaving anything behind it.

"You should rather aspire to burn in a corner, like vigil lamps that accompany the tabernacle in the shadows of the oratory, so effective in God's eyes. Without making a show accompany men—your friends, your colleagues, your relatives, your brothers!—with your example, with your doctrine, with your work, with your serenity, and with your cheerfulness.

"*Vita vestra est abscondita cum Christo in Deo* (Col 3:3) live facing God, not facing men. This has always been and will always be the aspiration of the Work: to live without human glory. . . . This should also be the aspiration of each one of you, my children." (*Letter*, March 24, 1930, no. 20).

[55] With respect to subsequent developments, and, specifically, leaving behind the particular prudence necessary at the beginning, when the founder "erased from his dictionary" the word "discretion," we will deal at its proper time.

# Chapter IV

## *THE DIOCESAN ERECTION OF 1943*

1. The 14th of February, 1943
2. The diocesan erection of the Priestly Society of the Holy Cross and the first ordination of members of Opus Dei
3. The significance of the *nihil obstat* of the Holy See (October 11, 1943)
4. Characteristics of the new legal configuration
5. Evaluation of this stage of the legal *iter*

# Chapter IV

## THE DIOCESAN ERECTION OF 1943

### 1. The 14th of February, 1943

Without a doubt Opus Dei's approval in 1941 was a milestone in its juridical development but it was soon outgrown. In reality it was already insufficient from the start. For the founder and to a greater or less extent for all the protagonists of those events, the first approval was provisional, a necessary first step soon to be superseded, if Opus Dei were to grow and develop. Opus Dei continued to spread rapidly. In two short years the number of members had doubled, reaching a hundred. In Madrid a student residence with greater capacity and activity than previous ones opened its doors. The apostolate spread to other Spanish cities, where it took hold: Valencia, Valladolid, Saragossa, Barcelona. . . . Many bishops and other ecclesiastics continued to have a high regard for it.

The outlook for future expansion, even beyond Spain was encouraging. In 1935-36, Fr. Escrivá had thought of launching the Work beyond Spanish borders, specifically in Paris. The Spanish Civil War and shortly thereafter World War II, had delayed this growth. In 1943 the founder eagerly anticipated the day when with peace restored Opus Dei could spread to other countries.

This growth raised the question of how to make available to the members God sent to Opus Dei both a solid doctrinal grounding and the specific priestly attention they also needed. Priests were needed who were steeped in the Work's spirit and who could dedicate themselves completely to this growing pastoral task. From the first moment Fr. Josemaría saw that the realization of the Work implied the cooperation of lay people and priests. He had reached out to some priests, who even came to bind themselves in some way to the Work. But these clerical collaborators had not been for him a positive experience; he could not count on them.[1]

---

[1] Fr. Escrivá alludes to these events in the *Letter* of February 14, 1944: "In the first years of apostolic work I accepted the cooperation of a few priests, who showed their desire

Priests were needed "who knew well our specific ascetical spirit and our apostolic ways of working, those proper to us." They should "deeply love the lay character of our vocation and work with souls . . . who have been fed with the spirit that God has given to us, who have grown up in the Work." Finally "they can come only from the ranks of the lay members of the Work."[2]

This decision is reflected already in the documents presented for the 1941 approval. In article 3 of the *Reglamento* we read that "those who undertake ecclesiastical studies and become priests after being members of Opus Dei, do not for this reason cease to belong to the Work." And article 7 of the document *Régimen* says: "When this takes place the appropriate regulations will be set forth for the priest members."

These norms of 1941 were not something hypothetical; several lay members of Opus Dei were already engaged in the ecclesiastical studies required for priestly ordination. They were members of the Work whose vocation had been well tested. The founder had asked if they were freely willing to be priests. It hurt him to take this step, because he would no longer be able to count on their valuable lay contributions. Yet they were absolutely necessary for Opus Dei to flower. They followed a plan of studies approved by Madrid's bishop and were taught by some of the most qualified theologians and canonists found in Madrid at the time. It was not known when they would be ordained or with what ecclesiastical title. Yet things must move ahead; Fr. Escrivá was confident the Lord would make known the solution.[3]

---

of binding themselves to Opus Dei in some way. The Lord quickly made me see with all clarity that—while they were good, and even very good—they were not called to fulfill the mission that I have pointed out before. For this reason, in an early document, I ordered that for the time being—and I would say until when—they should limit themselves to administering the sacraments and to purely ecclesiastical functions. Nevertheless, since they did not manage to understand what the Lord was asking, especially in the specific apostolate of the women's branch... I soon had to do without them" (*Letter*, February 14, 1944, no. 9). While seeking a permanent solution, which we will see shortly in the text, he had recourse to some priests, not bound in any way to Opus Dei, to take care of confessions and other liturgical functions. From the beginning, Fr. Josemaría decided not to hear the confessions of Opus Dei members in order to respect fully the freedom of their consciences and to avoid any possible interference between the sacramental forum and the work of government.

[2] *Letter*, February 14, 1944, no. 10.

[3] The founder wrote, "It was necessary to go ahead in the juridical path of the Work in such a way as to make compatible the secular and lay nature of our Work with the ascription of the necessary priests, resolving in an adequate way the requirements that in the canonical system this ascription presupposed" (*Letter*, February 14, 1944, no. 11).

A later *Letter* expresses the problem: "Various solutions were presented to me for the almost immediate problem of the title of priestly ordination, and all of them were bad. The best one was suggested to me by Bishop Leopoldo: to create chaplaincies, so that these priests could in some way be ascribed to Opus Dei."[4] To understand how this proposal could be the best and yet still not solve the problem, let us briefly recall some aspects of the ecclesiastical legislation in force at that time.

According to the 1917 Code of Canon Law, every priest had to be ascribed to a diocese or a religious order or congregation, lest there be unattached, errant clerics.[5] This ascription did not engender the same effects in all cases, because it was interwoven with another canonical requirement, the "title" of ordination. This had to do with assuring that each cleric had a decent, lifelong source of support. Without this provision any ordination would be illicit and the exercise of inherent priestly powers prohibited.[6] For diocesan (secular) clerics, there were several possible titles,[7] one of which was that of patrimony or pension. Those ordained with this title were incardinated in a diocese, but they were obliged to assume functions entrusted to them by their bishop only when there existed a need (in fact a relatively serious one) and when not excused by some legitimate impediment. In principle this title allowed them to dedicate themselves in a stable way to other tasks.[8] On the other hand, those ordained with any of the other titles were subject to a greater or lesser degree to the local ordinary and were obliged to accept whatever ministry he entrusted to them.

From this we construe that Madrid's bishop, by suggesting that Opus Dei priests be ordained with the title of patrimony or pension (the category that allows for the creation of chaplaincies), presup-

---

[4] *Letter*, December 29, 1947/February 14, 1966, no. 159.

[5] CIC 1917, c. 111, par. 1.

[6] CIC 1917, cc. 974 and 968, par. 2.

[7] "For secular clerics the canonical title is the title of benefice and in its defect that of patrimony or pension." (CIC 1917, c. 979, par. 1) The title of benefice required the appointment to an office and benefice on receiving sacred orders, according to the benfice system, so rooted in history and at that time very much in force. The title of patrimony or pension required the possesssion of a personal capital sufficient to maintain oneself throughout life. Canon 981 established as supplementary titles two more: those of service of the diocese and of mission.

[8] CIC 1917, c. 128. See H. Jone, *Commentarium in Codicem Iuris Canonici*, I, Paderborn 1950, p. 137. The earlier teaching had affirmed that a person ordained with the title of patrimony was not obliged to the service of any specific church. Thus, according to Panormitano, "...patrimonium non ligat eum cum respectu illius non sit obligatus officiare certam ecclesiam sed tantum tenetur dicere officium non respectu patrimonii sed respectu sacri ordinis quem recipit." (*Commentaria in III librum Decretalium, De proeb. et dign. c. Tuis*, no. 7).

posed that the founder excluded as unfitting any titles of ordination proper to religious. Rather the bishop sought a formula along the lines of the secular clergy. In keeping with this, he offered to Fr. Escrivá, as a possible juridical solution, incardination in a diocese (undoubtedly that of Madrid) but with a title of ordination that would leave the new priest free from ministerial dependence upon the bishop. Such a priest would *de facto* depend on the founder of the Work.

Nevertheless, with a bit more leisure and reflection, the founder realized that this was not the way to go. As he explained in a *Letter*, this solution "entailed an enormous expense beyond reach, plus it solved nothing."[9] Costly, because sizable capital would have to be invested to guarantee the requisite yield. Neither did it solve anything canonically because priests so ordained would lack the complete juridical availability required to serve a universal apostolate. Neither would it provide for the necessary specific training according to the spirit of the Work. Blessed Josemaría saw this as crucial to carrying out this specific pastoral work, the reason for making these Opus Dei members priests.

A better formula must be found. The solution must combine the lay, secular character of Opus Dei with the availability of priests to serve an apostolate.

Then February 14, 1943 dawned. Fr. Josemaría was celebrating holy Mass in a center of Opus Dei's women's branch in Madrid. Suddenly, during the holy sacrifice a new light shown in his interior. Once again God had entered his life and marked out the way. "When I finished celebrating Mass I designed the seal of the Work, Christ's cross embracing the world, in the very heart of the world, and I could speak of the Priestly Society of the Holy Cross."[10]

The original vision of Opus Dei (Oct. 2, 1928) as an apostolic enterprise calling for lay people and priests to cooperate became more precise and complete. Fr. Escrivá now saw, with a clarity that confirmed the earlier lights, that God wanted there to be, as an integral part of Opus Dei, a priestly body to perpetuate Christ's actions, especially the Mass, which represents and makes present the supreme immolation of the cross. The cross must be inscribed in the world, reaching the four cardinal points, brought by each Christian with his life and work. To make this possible, so that ordinary Christians—with their common priesthood—might be one with Christ and make him present among men, they must be backed by like-minded sacred ministers, as instruments of Christ to communicate life and grace. Hence, as the Church is structured so also must Opus Dei be, in its own way.

---

[9] *Letter*, December 29, 1947/February 14, 1966, no. 159.

[10] RHF, 20159, p. 105.

## 2. The diocesan erection of the Priestly Society of the Holy Cross and the first ordination of members of Opus Dei

God had shown the way.  The earlier obscurity had been substantially overcome; many of the suggested hypotheses or solutions could be dismissed.  Yet one task remained: to express the God-given light in juridical terms permitted by the canon law in force at the time.  Fr. Josemaría Escrivá began to think.  The following day, February 15, he traveled to a city near Madrid where one of the first members of Opus Dei who had been Fr. Josemaría's closest collaborator since 1939, Alvaro del Portillo, was spending a few days studying together with two other members (José María Hernández de Garnica and José Luis Muzquiz.) (These three were the ones whom Fr. Escrivá was preparing to be the first priests to come from the lay members of Opus Dei.)  Fr. Josemaría explained to Alvaro del Portillo what had happened the previous day.  Both of them hastened back to Madrid to study the matter and to present a proposal to Bishop Leopoldo Eijo y Garay, the competent ecclesiastical authority.[11]

What aims was the founder trying to accommodate?  He sought the canonical  erection of a priestly group or body within the total pastoral phenomenon of Opus Dei, so he could count on priests, from the lay ranks of Opus Dei and formed according to its spirit, ascribed to the Work with no change in their secular condition.  They would answer to the President General for the exercise of their ministry: pastorally tending to the members of Opus Dei and cooperating with them in their apostolic endeavors.

But the 1917 Code of Canon Law permitted only ascription to a diocese or a religious institute.[12]  This arrangement was supplemented by other forms of linkage, by the juridical technique of equivalency *in iure*.  Thus prelatures and abbeys *nullius* could incardinate priests, since they were equivalent to dioceses, "unless by the nature of the matter or by the context of the phrase something else appears."[13]  Among the non-religious associations or societies, only some, the so-called Societies of common life without vows (title 17, book 2, CIC 1917) enjoyed the faculty of incardinating priests, if with the Holy See's approval this were established in their constitutions or granted to them by papal indult.  The Code made the governance of these institutes partially equivalent to that of religious institutes.[14]

---

[11] Cf. A. Vázquez de Prada, *op. cit.* (chapter 1, note 1), pp. 232-234.

[12] CIC 1917, c. 111, par. 1.

[13] CIC 1917, c. 215, par. 2.

[14] CIC 1917, cc. 673, par. 2, 675, etc.

With the light of February 14, Opus Dei's founder decided to take a new juridical step. He proposed to the ecclesiastical authority a formula he characterized as "the only viable solution within the framework of the present law. I am ready *to yield in the words*, so long as the document itself always affirms in a precise way the true substance of our way."[15]  The step would solve immediate problems, though still not totally satisfactory.

This solution was to be structured, in accordance with Madrid's bishop, within the broad boundaries offered by title 17 of book 2 of the Code then in force, which regulated Societies of common life without vows. This was the juridical figure to be used, albeit in an original manner.

The pastoral phenomenon that underlies Societies of common life and that characteristic of Opus Dei are not the same, as we have seen.[16]  Nevertheless, Opus Dei could avail itself of this form without prejudice to the secularity proper to it, thanks to the formal and explicit declaration that members of these societies are not religious.[17]

In choosing this solution for the sake of having priests, the founder did not see Opus Dei as such being transformed into a Society of common life. Rather as he explained in a 1944 *Letter* his idea was: "to transform a small nucleus of our Work, made up of priests and some laymen approaching ordination, into a Society of common life without vows, the Priestly Society of the Holy Cross."[18]

---

[15] *Letter*, February 14, 1944, no. 11.

[16] Under the heading of Societies of common life without vows were grouped a series of institutes which arose in the 17th century to carry out a specific apostolic activity (priestly apostolate, care for the sick, etc.) and based on the practice of common life. This characteristic, in some sense, made them similar to the religious. Nevertheless they were clearly different in other aspects. For example, the exclusion of public vows, although there existed the possibility that their members would individually make private vows. The Code of canon law, incorporating these societies in its systematic structure, adopted a system to reflect this reality: they were included within Book 2 but given a special Title (Title 17).

With regard to the Societies of common life without vows one can consult, with respect to their juridical regulation at that time, H. Rothoff, *Le droit des Sociétés sans voeux*, Brussels 1949. We must point out that the CIC of 1983 calls them "Societies of apostolic life" and accentuates, more strongly than did the 1917 Code, their differences from Religious institutes and other institutes of common life by the profession of the evangelical counsels, even though a partial equivalency in law is retained.

[17] Canon 673 of Title 17, Book 2, 1917 Code, begins: "Every society whether of men or women, whose members imitate the manner of life of religious by living in community under the government of superiors according to approved constitutions, but without being bound by the usual three public vows, is not properly a religious institute, nor can its members be properly designated by the name religious."

[18] *Letter*, February 14, 1944, no. 12.

The words reflect the balance and juridical refinement the solution entails. But before going on to examine in detail the solution to which the founder arrives, first let us describe the process of its canonical erection.

In November 1942 two members of Opus Dei—José Orlandis and Salvador Canals—began studying in Rome. Following the founder's indications, they also began to deal with some members of the Roman Curia to make the Work known to them. After having seen the possible solution, Fr. Josemaría sent Alvaro del Portillo to Rome in May 1943, so that, as Opus Dei's Secretary General he could initiate the necessary consultations with the Holy See. Alvaro del Portillo arrived in Rome with the founder's blessing, a letter from Bishop Eijo y Garay and the necessary documentation.

On June 4 he was received by Pope Pius XII, to whom he explained at length the nature of Opus Dei and its apostolates and answered many questions. He also met with Cardinal Maglione, the Secretary of State, and with other members of the Roman Curia. Owing to these conversations, among others, he saw that the proposed solution might be well received; and that consequently the request for the required *nihil obstat* for the erection of the Priestly Society of the Holy Cross as a Society of common life without vows could be presented to the Holy See. With this clear idea he returned to Madrid.[19]

On Pentecost 1943 the founder formally requested this erection of Madrid's bishop. In the petition he traces a brief history of Opus Dei from its founding in 1928, emphasizing the growth stemming in large part from its approval as a pious union. Having considered all things "before God and our conscience," he declares, with the desire "of better serving holy Mother Church," Opus Dei's erection as an "association of faithful who live in common without vows similar to those mentioned in cc. 673ff." will bring with it many advantages. It will bring about "a greater spreading of our spiritual activity and the members' better formation, both intellectual and spiritual." He then requests the diocesan erection of the Priestly Society of the Holy Cross. At the same time in accord with the norms and canonical practice of the time, he also submitted certain *Lineamenta generalia*, a general description of the institution whose erection is requested. There the solution is set forth, based on the distinction between the Priestly Society of the Holy Cross and the rest of the Work that retains the name of Opus Dei, a distinction but no separation.[20] On June 22, 1943, the bishop of Madrid wrote the

---

[19] Cf. F. Gondrand, *op. cit.* (chapter 1, note 1, pp. 190ff).

[20] The request made by Fr. Escrivá and the accompanying *Lineamenta* are reproduced in the Appendix of this study, nos. 8 and 9. Later we will comment on these *Lineamenta*. For now we merely point out they were elaborated from the documents approved by

Prefect of the Sacred Congregation for Religious, Cardinal Vincenzo La Puma, requesting the *nihil obstat* for this erection.[21] In his petition Bishop Eijo y Garay testifies that the founder had developed his apostolic work "with my total approval and blessing." Also the young men who had accompanied him in these first years "in all the works undertaken up to now have always done so in close communication with the diocesan authority, to which they have been subject with devotion as constant as it is filial." After emphasizing the development achieved by Opus Dei and mentioning its approval as a pious union in 1941, he adds: "The fruits already produced by the association and those it promises for the good of souls are that its founder and members vehemently desire to give it greater solidity and a higher canonical configuration, thinking above all in the more perfect Christian formation of the members and the perpetuity of the Work as well as its unity of action, lest it suffer harm in its extension and spread."[22]

The bishop highlighted the universal scope of the apostolate which Opus Dei aspires to carry out. Then, in conformity with the legislation in force, he requested the Holy See to grant a *venia* for the diocesan erection of the Priestly Society of the Holy Cross, in accordance with the *Lineamenta generalia* presented to him and now submitted to the Sacred Congregation for their eventual approval. "With filial spirit I publicly manifest the extraordinary importance of this initiative, the greatest usefulness of the fruits of holiness obtained so far and the hope of its growth with the granting of this grace, and therefore I express my ardent desire that it be granted the *nihil obstat*."

The Sacred Congregation promptly began to study the dossier. On July 16, Fr. Arcadio Larraona, C.M.F., consultor of the Congregation and a renowned canonist, sent Cardinal La Puma a report in the form of a letter. After praising the apostolate carried out by the Work, he gave his opinion that it is "most fitting, and I would even say necessary, to grant as soon as possible this Society, which has already produced such beautiful works, the juridical condition of a society of diocesan right, and I desire that it soon be raised to the rank of pontifical right, given the marvelous development achieved,

---

Bishop Eijo y Garay in 1941, particularly the *Régimen*. The *Reglamento* of Opus Dei approved in 1941 was also submitted by the bishop to the Holy See (Cf. Appendix, document no. 5).

[21] Although these Societies of common life without vows were not religious institutes, they depended on the Sacred Congregation for Religious; according to canons 674 and 492 and nos. 3-5 of the *Normæ* of the Sacred Congregation for Religious of March 6, 1921 (AAS, 13, 1921, pp. 312-319), previous permission of the Holy See was required for diocesan erection.

[22] The text of this petition can be found in the Appendix, document no. 10.

the great good that has been done and the wide range of the apostolate exercised even beyond Spain." In this document Larraona points out how this petition "was strongly formulated by the Most Reverend Bishop of Madrid, who praises the Work in the highest terms; as do other Spanish bishops, above all the Most Reverend Nuncio Archbishop Cicognani, who recommends the Work by writing, among other things: 'It goes without saying that the end the Work proposes for itself is highly worthy of praise and can be of great effectiveness and influence in intellectual and scholarly circles'."[23]

In some "descriptive notes," written by Fr. Siervo Goyeneche, C.M.F., for the Sacred Congregation for Religious, data on the spread of Opus Dei are presented. He adds: "The bishops of Spain are very favorable to this association, especially those of Barcelona, Zamora, Pamplona, the Archbishop of Valencia, etc., and principally Archbishop Gaetano Cicognani, the Nuncio in Spain." Fr. Goyeneche comments: "There does not exist either in Madrid or in Spain nor—unless I am mistaken—in the whole Church another society with the same purpose."[24]

The Sacred Congregation for Religious, in keeping with the norms approved by the pope in 1921[25] and its *modus operandi*, asked the bishop of Madrid, in a letter of August 4, 1943, about some points relative to possible extraordinary events in the founder's life and about the two branches, one for men and one for women, that make up the association Opus Dei.[26] The Bishop sent the requested information.[27] On August 24 the Congregation for Religious requested of the Holy Office its previous *nihil obstat*, required before the Sacred Congregation could grant its *venia* for the erection. This request encountered no difficulties. With a letter dated September 29, 1943, Msgr. Ottaviani communicated to the Secretary of the Congregation for Religious that the Holy Office decreed *Ex parte S. Officii nihil obstare*.[28] Finally, the Sacred Congregation for Religious on October 11, 1943, granted its *nihil obstat* for the diocesan erection.[29]

---

[23] A. Larraona, *Voto sulla Società Sacerdotale della Santa Croce*, Madrid 1943, in AGP, Sezione Giuridica, III/15015.

[24] These notes of Fr. Goyeneche can be found in the AGP, Sezione Giuridica, III/15017.

[25] These were quoted in note 21 of this chapter; nos. 3 and 4 are those that are applied.

[26] AGP, Sezione Giuridica, III/15018.

[27] Because of its biographical interest and because of the high esteem which Casimiro Morcillo, auxiliary bishop and Vicar General of the diocese of Madrid shows towards Josemaría Escrivá, we include in the Appendix, document no. 11, the *curriculum vitæ* of the founder.

[28] This can be seen in the Appendix, document no. 12.

[29] The letter communicating the *venia* of the Sacred Congregation for Religious is found in the Appendix, document no. 13.

On October 18, the feast of St. Luke, the bishop of Madrid told Fr. Escrivá that he had received a telegram from the Holy See that announced the granting of the *nihil obstat*. The founder made this known to the Opus Dei members then in Madrid; he also shared the news with the Nuncio, Archbishop Cicognani.[30] With the authorization once in hand the bishop of Madrid-Alcalá canonically erected the Priestly Society of the Holy Cross on December 8, 1943, feast of the Immaculate Conception, with the decree *Quindecim abhinc*.[31]

The title refers to the fifteen years passed since 1928, the year of its founding. In the body of the decree the bishop writes: "Divine assistance has constantly been with this pious institution from the beginning, as manifested principally by the number and quality of the young people—outstanding in their integrity and intellect—who have joined it, by the abundant fruits harvested everywhere, as well as by the sign of contradiction, which has always been the stamp of the works of God." He explains the motives of the erection (*motivatio facti*): "As the number of members of the Institution has increased, and as its scope of activity has spread in a marvelous manner, it has been seen that its purpose, constitution and method of action can no longer be retained within the framework of a simple Association, but require a broader and firmer organization, that of a true Ecclesiastical Society legitimately erected and constituted. Thus, at the same time that the different activities of the Institution will be better coordinated among themselves, the Institution itself will be more intimately united to the hierarchy, and it will obtain the necessary internal autonomy and the strength of a sanction not only from the local Ordinary, but also from the Apostolic See."

After setting forth the motives in law, the request of the *venia* for the erection, the granting of the *nihil obstat*, the faculties conferred by law in canons 674 and 492 par. 1, the decree states that the "until now praiseworthy Pious Association, which we have previously approved, we now erect and constitute as a true Society of Diocesan Right in accordance with Title 17, Book 2 of the Code of Canon Law, with the name of the Priestly Society of the Holy Cross."[32]

According to requirements of the Holy See in granting the *nihil obstat*, the president of the Priestly Society of the Holy Cross was to make his incorporation to this society before the bishop of Madrid

---

[30] RHF, 20167, pp. 914-915.

[31] The decree is found in the Appendix, document no. 14.

[32] The Decree of erection was published in the *Boletín Oficial del Obispado de Madrid-Alcalá* on April 15, 1944, pp. 170-171; and in *Ilustración del Clero*, 37 (1944):201-203. See also X. Ochoa, *Leges Ecclesiæ post Codicem Iuris Canonici editæ*, II, Rome 1969, no. 1780, col. 2231-2232. This last author puts it under the title or rubric of "1943 December 8—the Sacred Congregation for Religious—Ordinary of Madrid, Particular Decree," showing the double intervention of both Madrid's bishop and the Roman Curia.

or his delegate. Shortly after the erection, the founder was with the bishop, and the latter suddenly said to him that he had still not been incorporated into the Society. Fr. Josemaría remembered later that "I knelt down and I prayed by heart, stammering because of the emotion, the words we use for our Fidelity as found in our *Ceremonial*, which said nothing of vows, nor promises nor anything similar." Later the narrative says: "This seemed something natural to him as it did to me. Yet it was the first time that that venerable prelate, already on in years, had received the incorporation of a person who had constituted a nucleus of faithful to promote holiness and apostolate without their being vows or promises of any kind."[33]

On December 19, 1943, the Bishop of Madrid wrote to Msgr. Pasetto, Secretary of the Sacred Congregation for Religious, that the Priestly Society of the Holy Cross had been erected, including—in accordance with the norms of this Congregation from November 30, 1922—a copy of the decree of erection. He also communicated that the president of the Society had made his "perpetual fidelity" in his presence.[34]

The decree whereby the Priestly Society of the Holy Cross is erected states "So that said society may achieve more effectively the fruits to which it is ordained," *Constitutions* should be written in conformity with the "compendium of Statutes" sent to the Holy See, i.e., the *Lineamenta generalia*, upon which the *nihil obstat* was based. Madrid's bishop formally charged Fr. Josemaría with writing this text in the official document addressed to him regarding his perpetual incorporation into the new Society.[35]

Fr. Escrivá set about preparing the *Constitutions* of the Priestly Society of the Holy Cross. This document has three parts: the first (nos. 1-201) deals with the nature of the Society (its ends, members, incorporation, dismissal or departure of members, their obligations, some characteristics of its spirit and of the ascetical norms which are advised and recommended); the second part (nos. 202-309) describes how the Society is governed at three levels: general, regional and local; the third part (nos. 310-343) deals with Opus Dei, the object of the apostolic activities of the Priestly Society of the Holy Cross.

The *Constitutions* follow the outline of *Lineamenta*: the former's first two parts begin with and develop faithfully the description of the Priestly Society contained in *Lineamenta*; the third part repeats

---

[33] *Letter*, December 29, 1947/February 14, 1966, no. 87. See also in the Appendix, documents nos. 15 and 16, the formal communication addressed by the bishop to the president of the Priestly Society of the Holy Cross with respect to the act of incorporation he had to make and the formula to be utilized.

[34] See this document in the Appendix, no. 17.

[35] The texts of the documents quoted are found in App., nos. 14 and 15 respectively.

almost verbatim the description of Opus Dei sent as a supplementary text to those referred to in *Lineamenta*.[36] This was amplified by including other norms from documents sanctioned by Madrid's Bishop in 1941, when Opus Dei was approved as a Pious Union, as we have seen in the previous chapter.[37] The text of the *Constitutions* was sent by Fr. Josemaría to the bishop, who approved them by a decree dated January 25, 1944.[38]

While these events were taking place, the three members of Opus Dei who were slated and being prepared for the priesthood intensified their studies. The Holy See granted a dispensation from interstices and on May 20, 1944, they received the tonsure at the hands of Bishop Eijo y Garay in his private chapel; there they also received minor orders on May 21 and 23. They reached the subdiaconate on May 28 in an oratory of an Opus Dei center located on Lagasca Street (Madrid), thanks to Bishop Marcelino Olaechea, the bishop of Pamplona. On June 3 they were ordained to the diaconate in the seminary of Madrid by Bishop Casimiro Morcillo, the auxiliary bishop of the diocese.

On June 25 they were ordained priests in the bishop's chapel, the prelate himself conferring the orders. Immediately afterward they were received by the papal nuncio Archbishop Gaetano Cicognani. Opus Dei's founder did not attend the ceremonies. During the time of the ordination he celebrated Mass in an oratory of the center on Lagasca Street, offering the Mass for the new priests. Long before he had adopted a personal motto: "To hide myself and disappear, so that only Jesus shine."[39]

Thus began an important chapter in the Work's history: priests who came from Opus Dei itself and having as their priestly work the pastoral care of the members and their apostolic activities. A further step had been taken in fulfillment of the foundational charism, thanks to certain juridical formulas that, though provisional, made it possible and defended it.

## 3. The significance of the *nihil obstat* of the Holy See (October 11, 1943)

Many years later on October 11, 1964 (then the feast of the Divine Maternity of the Blessed Virgin Mary), the founder referred

[36] Let us recall—cf. note 20 of this chapter—that this complementary description of Opus Dei consists in the *Reglamento* of 1941. Both texts, that is, the *Lineamenta* and the *Reglamento*, are found in nos. 9 and 5 of the Appendix.

[37] We will deal more extensively with the content of the *Lineamenta* and also of the *Constitutions* of 1944 in the last part of this chapter.

[38] The text of this Decree is included in the Appendix, document no. 18.

[39] RHF, 20168, pp. 610-629. With respect to these events the biographies mentioned in note 1 of chapter 1 can also be consulted.

to these juridical steps in Opus Dei's development: "I have elsewhere reflected, my children, as I have called upon you to reflect,
that we have taken every step in Opus Dei's canonical evolution
under the protection of the Mother of God. As we celebrate now
her Divine Maternity, I remember—I cannot do less than recall—
that the first time the Holy See 'lay its hands upon' the Work was
on this feast so many years ago. . . . I did not know then the Mother
of God had interceded for this Work of God and that the first approval had been given."[40]

In this text Fr. Josemaría uses the expression "lay its hands
upon" and "approval." We have previously used various technical
terms for this papal intervention: *venia*, permission, authorization,
approval, *appositio manuum*, *nihil obstat*, etc. Before going on to a
more detailed description of the juridical figure adopted in 1943, let
us dwell on the significance of these technical expressions and on
the importance the founder gave to this intervention of the Roman
Curia.

When Fr. Escrivá decided to request the erection of the Priestly
Society of the Holy Cross as a Society of common life—with all the
peculiarities and safeguards indicated above and which we will
refer to later—he addressed himself to the appropriate ecclesiastical authority, that is, to the bishop of Madrid, who in turn requested from the Holy See the *nihil obstat* for this erection, in accordance with canons 674 and 492 par. 1 of the Code of Canon Law and
the norms of the Sacred Congregation for Religious of March 6,
1921. Norms three to five specify the points to be dealt with in this
consultation; the reply of the Holy See is given the name *permission*
(*licentia*) and establishes that its effect was *iam nihil obstabit* (there
was no obstacle) to founding a new society.[41] In addition a decree
of the Sacred Congregation for Religious of November 30, 1922, in
its number 7, categorized this intervention of the Roman Curia as a
*venia*.[42]

According to the norms and the decree referred to previously
the process for obtaining this *venia* or permission also determined
the praxis that the Roman Curia followed at that time and in fact
continues to follow today. In the Congregation for Religious this
procedure is known as obtaining the *nihil obstat* of the Holy See for
the diocesan erection of an institute.

In these procedural matters the Sacred Congregation for Religious did not grant the *venia erigendi* without first obtaining the
*nihil obstat* of the Holy Office. Before granting it, the latter office

---

[40] RHF, 20754, p. 8.

[41] AAS, 13 (1921), p. 313.

[42] AAS, 14 (1922), p. 645.

studied all of the material presented to verify that it contained no deviations from faith and morals. It thus signified approval of the ends, spirit, means and the like contained in the approved documents, in our case, in the *Lineamenta generalia* of the Priestly Society of the Holy Cross.

The final *nihil obstat* of the Sacred Congregation for Religious comprised in one single act the *venia* (permission or authorization), which opened the way for the bishop to exercise the juridical powers entrusted to him by the Law for the diocesan erection; it also implied the previous recognition and approval of the *Lineamenta generalia* presented with the request for the *nihil obstat*. For this reason one can speak of a first papal approval, not of the Society as such, but of the fundamental elements submitted to the judgment of the Holy See that later served as the basis for writing the *Constitutions*,[43] even though the act of erection in itself is diocesan.[44]

Every pontifical intervention—*appositio manuum*—entails either presenting a matter to the Pope, whereupon any lower jurisdiction ceases, or confirming the content of a document, privilege, etc., thus making any subsequent changes impossible.[45] In the specific case of the *nihil obstat* for the erection of a Society, the *appositio manuum* implies that in proceeding to erection everything submitted for the Holy See's *nihil obstat* must be carefully respected and faithfully observed.[46] The *appositio manuum* recognizes and approves the *Lineamenta*, an outline of the constitutions or statutes, whose content has to be respected by the Society and by the ordinary in writing and approving any subsequent constitutions or statutes.[47] Whence the bishop of Madrid both in the decree of erection and also in successive documents always refers to the compendium of the statutes or the *Lineamenta generalia* as the text to be observed.

---

[43] Thus the diocesan Curia of Madrid understood matters, when—after the *nihil obstat*—it issued a certificate of the *Lineamenta*: "The present 'Lineamenta Constitutionum' of the Priestly Society of the Holy Cross were approved by the Sacred Congregation for Religious on October 11, 1943, and are in conformity with the copy preserved in the archive of this diocese. Madrid, December 12, 1943. The Vicar General + Casimiro Morcillo, Auxiliary Bishop" (AGP Sezione Giuridica, III/15079).

[44] This intervention of the Roman Curia is categorized by E. Jombart as "the approval of the Holy See," and he defines its scope thus: "It endows the erection made by the Bishop with legitimacy, but it does not make it pontifical." (*Traité de Droit Canonique*, I, directed by R. Naz, Paris 1946, no. 810, p. 563).

[45] J. B. Rigantius, *Commentaria in regulas, constitutiones et ordinationes Cancellariæ apostolicæ*, Romæ 1744, reg. I, rubrica, nos. 78 & 81, p. 30.

[46] F. Muzzarelli, *Tractatus canonicus de congregationibus iuris diocesani*, Roma - Alba 1943, p. 32.

[47] See J. B. Ferreres, *Instituciones canónicas*, I, Barcelona 1920, no. 795, p. 380. The Code of 1917 in c. 495 § 2 *in fine*, established that when a Society of diocesan right goes to another diocese, its norms can only be changed with the consent of all of the Ordinaries

With the *nihil obstat* and *appositio manuum* of the Apostolic See a greater juridical stability is obtained, as the founder liked to say.[48] Thenceforth any modification of what was covered by the *nihil obstat* would require the intervention of the Holy See. Thus the foundational charism is defended by making possible deviations more difficult because of the Church's sanction supposed in its granting the *venia erigendi*.[49] Thus the bishop in the decree *Quindecim abhinc* of December 8, 1943, mentions, among other reasons advising diocesan erection, having consulted the Holy See. Thus "the necessary internal autonomy will be attained along with the firmness of a sanction not only of the local ordinary but also of the Apostolic See."[50]

The founder prized this papal sanction. In addition to the reasons already mentioned it represented support in the face of falsehoods spread and still spreading. Thus he remarked, on learning of the *nihil obstat*, to Opus Dei members then in Madrid. "Now I tell you, that while some out there—I forgive them and I love them—have said that the bishops have taken priestly faculties away from this sinner there has come now from Rome a telegram addressed to the bishop announcing that the Holy Father has given the *nihil obstat* to the Work and that he blesses us with his whole heart."[51]

## 4. Characteristics of the new legal configuration

The founder turned in 1943 to the sole viable solution according to the law in force at that time. He thus adapted Opus Dei to a juridical system not fully satisfactory. He was willing *"to yield in words, so long as the document itself always affirms, in a precise manner, the true substance of our way."*[52]

---

in whose dioceses it has houses "except for those things which in accordance with canon 492 § 1 were submitted to the Apostolic See." A. Larraona in his *Commentarium Codicis*, in "Commentarium pro religiosis," 5 (1924):330 speaks expressly of the *appositio manuum* for this papal intervention. F. Wernz - P. Vidal, *Ius Canonicum*, III, Romae, 62 (1933):61-62. See also c. 595 & 1 CIC 1983 which expressly says *"Apostolica Sedes manus apposuerit"*.

[48] See, for example, the text of October 11, 1964 which we have referred to above. Among many others he employed this expression in the *Letter* of December 29, 1947/ February 14, 1966, no. 2.

[49] Thus F. Muzzarelli, *op. cit.* (note 46 of this chapter), pp. 120-122; F. Capello, *Summa Iuris Canonici*, II, Romae 1934, no. 571, p. 132; A. Vermeersch - J. Creusen, *Epitome Iuris Canonici*, I, Mechliniae-Romae 1949, no. 601, p. 449; M. Conte A Coronata, *Compendium Iuris Canonici*, I, Taurini-Romae 1950, no. 883, p. 447 interpret the clause of canon 495 par. 2 of the CIC 1917 in the same sense.

[50] Cf. Appendix, document no. 14.

[51] RHF, 20163, p. 914.

[52] Text quoted in note 15 of this chapter.

Fr. Josemaría reached this conclusion with the light received on February 14, 1943 and after consulting not only the bishop of Madrid, but also outstanding churchmen conversant with canonical legislation and Opus Dei's characteristics. Among them were the auxiliary bishop of Madrid, Casimiro Morcillo; the promotor of justice of the diocese, José María Bueno Monreal; and the spiritual director of the seminary, José María García Lahiguera, also at the time Fr. Escrivá's confessor.[53]

Both Fr. Escrivá and Bishop Eijo y Garay realized the danger of a possible confusion with religious, despite the Code's clear affirmation that a Society of common life "is not properly a religious institute, nor can its members be properly designated by the name of religious."[54] In a handwritten memo dated February 28, 1943, the founder states: "Casimiro, Bueno and Lahiguera see perfectly well that there is no other way out than that of the establishment of this Priestly Society." He adds that in the juridical documents, in the opinion of these three ecclesiastics, "it will be possible to foresee and avoid, so far as possible, the inappropriate questions that Don Leopoldo pointed out and that we all see." Opus Dei members "cannot appear or be religious (we will not be, nor will we appear to be, because our spirit is different, even though we love the religious state)."[55]

In making use of title 17, Fr. Escrivá did not intend that Opus Dei, as such and in its totality, be transformed into a Society of common life (one of the fundamental aspects spelled out in the solution adopted). Only a small part of the Work, made up of priests and some laymen, would be erected as a Society of common life—the Priestly Society of the Holy Cross—to which would be intimately united, under the name of Opus Dei, the association of the faithful approved with this name in 1941, to which the members of the Priestly Society of the Holy Cross would continue to belong.

The central point of this new configuration consists in the recognition of a distinction between the Priestly Society of the Holy Cross and Opus Dei, but establishing at the same time vital and unbreakable relations between both. The Priestly Society of the Holy Cross presupposes the existence of Opus Dei, through which, in great part, it exercises its activity. At the same time Opus Dei, a work made up of men and women, can carry out its purposes thanks to the priestly attention, orientation and impulse it receives from the Priestly Society of the Holy Cross.

Let us examine, then, the fundamental characteristics of this juridical configuration, the result of inserting elements proper to

---

[53] RHF, EF-430228-1.

[54] CIC 1917, c. 673.

[55] RHF, EF-430228-1.

the Work's pastoral phenomena into the canonical system of Title 17, as they appear in the *Lineamenta generalia*, the object of the *nihil obstat* of the Holy See in 1943, and in the *Constitutions* approved by the bishop of Madrid in 1944.

a) The Priestly Society of the Holy Cross is prevalently (*prevalenter*) or preferentially (*præferenter*) clerical. It is comprised of two groups: priestly and lay. The priests come from the lay men of the Society and they receive their previous formation within the Society (*Lineamenta*, nos. 1 and 8; *Const.*, nos. 1, 2 and 8); they are called to holy orders by the President General, having heard his Council; and they are ordained *ad titulum Societatis* (*Lineamenta*, no. 10; *Const.*, nos. 56-61).

b) The two sections of the Priestly Society of the Holy Cross have the peculiarity of not forming separate classes, since the lay men—all of them celibate, coming from the association Opus Dei—are considered as in preparation for the priesthood (*Lineamenta*, no. 8; *Const.*, no. 10). Thus the existence of priests will not threaten the Work's unity but rather will reinforce the cooperation between priests and laity in its specific service to the Church.

c) The Priestly Society of the Holy Cross presupposes the existence of Opus Dei, since nobody can be received into the Society if he has not previously formed part of Opus Dei (*Lineamenta*, nos. 3 and 20; *Const.*, nos. 5, 310-312).

d) The purpose of the Priestly Society of the Holy Cross is described in the 1943 text with language that respects the requirements of the law in force and of the praxis of the Sacred Congregation for Religious for the approval of Institutes and Societies, while introducing some small changes.

These juridical norms required on the one hand that there be indicated a general purpose—common for all Institutes and Societies—as well as a specific one, proper to each Institute or Society which therefore should be explicated.[56] Thus we read: "The general aim is the sanctification of its members by the practice of the evangelical counsels and the observance of the *Constitutions* of the Society; the specific aim is to encourage intellectuals, and professionals, who exercise a leading role in civil society, to adhere to the precepts of Jesus Christ our Lord and even to his counsels" (*Lineamenta*, no. 2). The bishop's decree of erection of December 8, 1943, speaks of this specific aim, as do the *Lineamenta* in other sections. In its narrative part the decree of erection makes it clear that the members of the Institution founded by Fr. Josemaría Escrivá dedicate

---

[56] Cf A. Battandier, *Guide Canonique pour les constitutions des instituts à voeux simples,* Paris 1923, nos. 78ff, pp. 57ff; *Normæ* of March 6, 1921, *op. cit.* (note 21 of this chapter), nos. 4 & 13.

themselves to work with intellectuals and professionals "as a specific aim, *even though it is not the sole aim.*"[57]

With regard to the *Lineamenta*, various passages complete the formulation of this aim, while introducing a criterion that departs from that habitually followed by the Sacred Congregation for Religious with regard to Societies of common life. According to praxis, the members of these Societies carry out their apostolic activity through works proper to them, corresponding to the Society's very specific aim; in the *Lineamenta* the specific aim of the Priestly Society of the Holy Cross is described, on the other hand, in very broad terms:

- the spiritual formation of other members and the spiritual direction principally of intellectuals is entrusted to the priestly members (*Lineamenta*, no. 19);

- the lay members exercise their respective professional activities (*Lineamenta*, no. 19), which they do not give up (no. 3) and which quite naturally are varied; with the occasion of these tasks they carry out their apostolate (no. 19).[58]

The *Constitutions* regulate the specific end of the Society in terms similar to number 2 of the *Lineamenta* but with a specification proper to the decree of erection and the points of the *Lineamenta* quoted from previously: "to work *principally* so that intellectuals and professionals, leaders in civil society, adhere to the precepts of Jesus Christ our Lord, and even to his counsels; and that they put them into practice" (no. 3).[59]

e) Opus Dei retains its own features as an institution aiming to promote the fullness of Christian life in the world: holiness and apostolate among married and celibate persons of all professions or occupations, through the sanctification of work and the fulfillment of one's family, social and professional duties. It continues to be made up of two branches—for men and for women; it is governed

---

[57] Emphasis added.

[58] We should not lose sight of the fact that all of this refers to the aim of the Priestly Society of the Holy Cross, and not to the total pastoral phenomenon: the aim of Opus Dei, presented as inseparable from that of the Priestly Society of the Holy Cross, is, effectively, described—as we will underline shortly—according to earlier texts and in a simpler way, without distinguishing between the generic and specific end, and speaking without further distinctions of the pursuit of holiness and the exercise of apostolate in the middle of the world, each one in his own professional work.

It should be pointed out, in addition, that in this whole description of the ends, what we have said in the previous chapter has a bearing, that is, how at that time—as we pointed out and because of the causes which we spoke of there—the founder saw it was necessary to accentuate the work with students and intellectuals in order to guarantee in this way the solidity of the beginnings of the apostolate of Opus Dei and its consequent universal spread among people of all occupations and professions.

[59] Obviously, emphasis added.

by its own statutes; and it always counts on the priestly attention and spiritual direction given by the Priestly Society of the Holy Cross with which it forms an organic institutional unity.[60]

Together with these aspects, which spell out the relationship between the Priestly Society of the Holy Cross and Opus Dei,[61] the juridical solution adopted with the diocesan erection presented other peculiarities worth examining.

a) With respect to the Priestly Society of the Holy Cross common life is spoken of, (one of the requirements of title 17), but indicating that this concept is to be interpreted in a broad sense (*Lineamenta*, no. 1; *Constitutions*, no. 1). Common life is not to be considered when applying it to the Priestly Society of the Holy Cross in the strict sense of canonical common life proper to religious: living in the same house and the like,[62] but rather in a broader sense. As the founder explains, "This refers solely to our spirit and our particular law, never to the material fact of living under the same roof."[63]

b) The governance of the Society at its three levels—general, territorial and local—reproduces, with a few adaptations, the structure foreseen in the document *Régimen*, approved in 1941 by the bishop, to which we referred in the previous chapter. The text (*Lineamenta*, nos. 26-52; *Const.*, nos. 202-309) contains provisions for an inter-diocesan and international government, which, in one way or another, will remain the same throughout the juridical development of the Work.

c) Finally we underline that the *Lineamenta* refer explicitly to a life of prayer and other practices of Christian piety the members of the Priestly Society of the Holy Cross are to live (*Lineamenta*, no. 23;

---

[60] As we have already said (cf. note 20 of this chapter), the *Reglamento* of Opus Dei, approved by the Bishop in 1941 was sent to the Holy See as a complement to the project of the juridical scheme of the Priestly Society of the Holy Cross, so as to obtain the *nihil obstat* for its erection; the *Lineamenta* declared in turn (no. 20) that the norms by which Opus Dei is governed are maintained in full force in the new configuration. Along these lines, as we already pointed out (see note 36 of this chapter), the third part of the *Constitutions* repeats almost verbatim the text of the *Reglamento*.

[61] The depth of the relations between the Priestly Society of the Holy Cross and Opus Dei, underlined in these texts, explains the fact that even in juridical documents—the very decree of December 8, 1943—it could seem as though what is being erected into the Priestly Society were the whole preexisting pious union. But if these documents are read carefully, in the light of the *Lineamenta* to which they expressly refer, one can notice that what is erected is the Priestly Society of the Holy Cross, although this erection implied an erection and approval of Opus Dei as a work inseparable from the Priestly Society, and even more, without which this Society could not exist nor would it have a reason to exist.

[62] CIC 1917, cc. 487 and 594.

[63] *Letter*, February 14, 1944, no. 12.

*Const.*, nos. 157-162). These are identical to those the 1941 documents foresee for all Opus Dei members. These exercises of prayer
are not relegated to the margin of ordinary life. Rather they are to
burrow deep, while adjusted to one's personal and social circumstances; leading them to live as "contemplatives in the middle of
the world."[64]

We could comment on other points, but those chosen perhaps
provide a sufficient description of the general lines of the solution
adopted in 1943.[65] Despite the shared framework and some references to the "praxis" and law of Societies of common life without
vows (e.g., the topic of dismissal from the Society: *Lineamenta*, no.
18) required by the Code, the figure outlined in the *Lineamenta* and
the *Constitutions* clearly differs from the habitual type of institution
or Society of common life regulated by the *Codex* at the time. Thus
Fr. Larraona, in a letter to Cardinal La Puma for the concession of
the *nihil obstat*—quoted from previously—points out these peculiarities. He then justifies them, since it is a new institution adapted
to the needs of modern times.[66] Later documents and doctrine will

---

[64] Number 24 of the *Lineamenta* and the *Constitutions*, nos. 163-165, refer to the "brief
circle" provided for and already regulated in detail in the documents of 1941 (*Ordo*,
arts. 2-3, and *Ceremonial*, 8). It is not described in all of its parts. Because one of its
elements—it is not the most essential part—is compared with the traditional "chapter
of faults" of some religious institutes, inasmuch as the document is addressed to the
Sacred Congregation for the Religious, and adapts itself to that "praxis." This weekly
meeting (called "brief" in comparison with the monthly meeting or day of recollection)
comprises commentary on a passage of the Gospel; a talk or commentary on some
point of the ascetical spirit of Opus Dei; a brief examination of conscience; reading
from some spiritual book or a doctrinal talk; a period of get-together on apostolic
matters of Opus Dei; plus initial and final prayers. Following the examination of
conscience, members may if they desire "make mention of their faults—neither sins
nor matters of conscience—"(*Ceremonial loc. cit.*) This gathering is similar to those
common in some ordinary associations of faithful and quite different from the "chapter of faults," to which it can be compared only by virtue of the possible and not
obligatory manifestation of external faults against the statutes, to which we have referred. With regard to this chapter, its history and its nature, see P. Schmitz, *Chapitre
des Coulpes*, in *Dictionnaire de Spiritualité*, vol. II, Paris 1953, cols. 483-488.

[65] Apart from the advantages and disadvantages the present juridical configuration
presented, and those to which we will shortly refer, we find necessarily some elements
that do not affect either the essence or the spirit of the Work. By way of example we
point out no. 14 of the *Lineamenta* (*Const.*, no. 21). This establishes as a rule the exclusion of neophytes and those who do not have at least one Catholic parent. This impediment calls to mind those given in cc. 987, 1° and 6° and 542, 2° of the 1917 Code,
frequent in many juridical texts of the time, but which had no application in this case.
This norm is not found in the *Constitutions* from 1947 nor in any subsequent documents.

[66] A. Larraona, *Voto sulla Società Sacerdotale della Santa Croce*. Madrid, *op. cit.* (note 23
of this chapter). Fr. S. Goyeneche expresses himself in similar terms in the text we
will analyze in the following chapter.

echo these terms in categorizing the peculiar juridical configuration of 1943.[67]

## 5. Evaluation of this stage of the legal *iter*

The founder evokes this canonical stage in a *Letter* of January 25, 1961: "I have told you on another occasion how the Lord guided us, in 1943, causing us to take some steps that have been providential, in order to clothe the Work—a new creature—with ecclesiastical approvals *in scriptis*—necessary for the ordination of our priests and, without letting the slander some were hurling against Opus Dei harm our *way*."[68]

The canonical erection of the Priestly Society of the Holy Cross as a Society of common life without vows, composed of priests and some lay men preparing themselves for the priesthood, effectively resolved the problem of ordaining Opus Dei lay men *ad titulum Societatis*, with all of the advantages this brought with it. The founder in a *Letter* of February 14, 1944,[69] spoke of the need for these priests to tend to the apostolates of Opus Dei. Some priests will always be needed "to occupy some positions of government . . . a fundamental point in the very constitution of the Work," a characteristic "strictly necessary for the juridical figure that corresponds to our characteristics."[70] As Le Tourneau comments, one catches a glimpse that the founder is thinking of a structure where priests and lay people form a single reality, but where the principal positions of government—functions of ecclesiastical jurisdiction requiring holy orders—should be carried out by priests.[71]

Even as an institute of diocesan right the Priestly Society of the Holy Cross received a higher juridical standing than that of a pious union. It thereby enjoyed a certain autonomy and could count on priests ordained *ad titulum Societatis* for the service of all of the apostolates of the Work. This canonical solution, writes Fr. Escrivá,

---

[67] Thus G. Escudero, *Los Institutos Seculares*, Madrid 1954, p. 35, refers to it as a society "without common life and with very special characteristics." L. Gutiérrez Martín, "Nacimiento de los Institutos Seculares", in *Vida Religiosa*, 27 (1969):314 talks about "special characteristics". Both authors refer to the whole pastoral phenomena that is the Priestly Society of the Holy Cross with Opus Dei.

[68] *Letter*, January 25, 1961, no. 5.

[69] We point out that this *Letter*—dated, significantly on the anniversary of one of the foundational events—was written by Fr. Josemaría with the purpose of explaining the reasons that moved him to accept the new canonical form and the precautions that he had taken in order to safeguard the spirit of Opus Dei, as well as to make clear the provisional character of the solution reached, pointing out some of its fine points.

[70] *Letter*, February 14, 1944, no. 9.

[71] Cf. D. Le Tourneau, *What is Opus Dei, op. cit.* (chapter 2, note 22) pp. 56-57.

though "by its nature transitory," and destined to be "surpassed as soon as there is a different juridical path that allows it," is nevertheless "useful for some period of time." It endows the institution with a "juridical statute that will facilitate for some years the internal governance of the Work."[72]

Erecting a part of the pastoral phenomenon into a Society of common life, while keeping the rest under the name of Opus Dei as "a work *proper, united and inseparable*" to the Society, effectively preserves the traits Opus Dei had in 1941. The Work remains an association of the faithful, whose lay members *"continue being ordinary Christians,"*[73] while making possible the achievement of the goals mentioned.

Evaluating the formula adopted, the founder writes "it offers undeniable advantages." His words express his satisfaction with what has been accomplished, but he immediately refines them by saying, "even though I cannot hide from you . . .," which opens the way to examining the limits and difficulties this solution implied.[74]

These shortcomings were two. First, the relationship established between the Priestly Society of the Holy Cross and Opus Dei does not properly reflect the reality of the pastoral phenomenon. Opus Dei could be considered "a part of the Priestly Society of the Holy Cross, when the fact of the matter is that the Priestly Society of the Holy Cross is only a small part of the Work."[75]

Years later he puts it: "Opus Dei appeared as something secondary: as an association proper to and inseparable from the Priestly Society of the Holy Cross, when the fact of the matter is that none of these two parts of our Work is secondary. Both of them are principal."[76] The priests and lay people who are the protagonists of a single pastoral phenomenon, united in self-giving, are co-responsible for a single mission, to whose realization both actively contribute. The function of the ministerial priesthood consists in making present in the organism of the Work Christ's face and grace, mainly through the sacraments.

---

[72] *Letter*, February 14, 1944, nos. 12 and 13.

[73] *Letter*, February 14, 1944, no. 12. Further along he writes, "I repeat to you, my beloved children, that you continue being ordinary faithful, you continue in the state you had when the Lord called you to his Work." And, referring to what the Work gives to its members, he says: "The means to achieve Christian perfection in one's own state in life," which is translated into "the pledge of striving for personal sanctity and the exercise of apostolate in the middle of the world, which is something fitting for all souls without exception" (*Ibid.*, no. 14).

[74] *Ibid.*, no. 13.

[75] *Ibid.*, no. 17.

[76] *Letter*, December 29, 1947/February 14, 1966, no. 160.

The second shortcoming: even though the new juridical formula clarified that Opus Dei members were not religious,[77] the figure of Societies of common life was seen by most canonists as approaching the religious state. This formula, therefore, could sow confusion. The founder did all he could to stress the differences. For example, in requesting the erection of the Priestly Society of the Holy Cross in June 1943 and to underline the special characteristics of the juridical form submitted for approval, he did not refer to the canons that then regulated the Societies of common life without qualifications. Rather he interjected the phrase *ad instar*—with a resemblance—to indicate the existence of these special characteristics.[78]

Further he made a distinction with regard to the very concept of common life itself, the essential element by which they were assimilated to religious institutes. In the Priestly Society of the Holy Cross the concept of common life is to be understood "in a broad sense" (*Lineamenta*, no. 1; *Const.*, no. 1). He further underlined that its members "take no religious vows nor carry any external sign (on them or in their homes) which would remind one of religious" (*Lineamenta*, no. 6; *Const.* no. 7).

The founder spared no pains to reflect and safeguard in the best way possible Opus Dei's secularity. But the limitations of the juridical figure remained. In itself it was incapable of faithfully expressing the reality of Opus Dei. While the additional refinements managed to safeguard the substance, they did not achieve a fully satisfactory fit.[79] It was the "least inappropriate" solution from among the possible ones, the founder taught. In 1944 he wrote, "For the moment there is no better arrangement."[80] It was a question of taking a step forward, "yielding in the words, but without giving up as regards substance," to make growth in the apostolate possible and to facilitate in this way a better solution in the future. "Let's pray and live in a holy way," he added, "the spirit we have received from God, and he will give us the definitive juridical structure to preserve us faithful to our vocation and to render us effective in the tasks of our apostolate."[81]

---

[77] This applies also to those who make up the Priestly Society of the Holy Cross, since—as we have commented before—the members of Societies of the common life without vows are not religious (CIC 1917, c. 673).

[78] The text of this petition is to be found in the Appendix, document no. 8.

[79] In fact, in order to accommodate itself to the norms of Title 17 of the 1917 Code it was necessary, on occasions, to adopt a terminology which was not totally adequate. This is what explains, for example, the reference to evangelical counsels in some circumstances and documents in referring to the general end of the Priestly Society of the Holy Cross.

[80] *Letter*, February 14, 1944, no. 12.

[81] *Ibid.*

Summing up, Fr. Josemaría, at this moment of the juridical itinerary of Opus Dei, realized full well the provisional nature of the
formula; he considered it a milestone, a stage, but still a beginning
one in the canonical development and practical incarnation of the
universal nature the Work had from the beginning. The spread of
the apostolate of Opus Dei beyond the borders of Spain was, moreover, a project drawing close. Only three years later it would become a reality. But this places before us a new stage and new
juridical steps.

Part Three

PONTIFICAL APPROVALS
(1947 and 1950)

# Chapter V

## OPUS DEI AS A SECULAR INSTITUTE

1. The need for pontifical approval: requesting the *Decretum laudis*
2. The applicable law: Title 17 of the 1917 Code or a new juridical approach
3. The founder in Rome: the Apostolic Brief *Cum Societatis* (June 28, 1946) and the Letter *Brevis sane* in praise of the aim (August 13, 1946)
4. The "new forms" and the Roman Curia
5. The Apostolic Constitution *Provida Mater Ecclesia*: the new juridical figure of Secular Institutes

# Chapter V

## *OPUS DEI AS A SECULAR INSTITUTE*

### 1. The need for pontifical approval: requesting the *Decretum laudis*

The canonical erection of the Priestly Society of the Holy Cross on December 8, 1943, made possible, as we saw in the previous chapter, the ordination of the first three priests on June 25, 1944. It also provided for their stable ascription to the Society to minister to the members of Opus Dei and to their apostolic activities. With the decisive help of these priests the founder continued to encourage the Work's expansion, basing it on interior life and a solid training. In 1946 a second group of six priests was ordained, establishing a since unbroken annual tradition. The apostolic activities were thus well taken care of and progress was made possible.

Throughout 1945 Opus Dei continued expanding to different parts of Spain. In March Fr. Escrivá traveled to Andalusia to visit members in Seville and to study the possibility of opening a center in Granada. A few weeks later four members of Opus Dei went to Bilbao with the idea of opening a residence for college students as soon as possible. In early 1946 there was a stable apostolate of Opus Dei in the cities of Madrid, Barcelona, Saragossa, Valencia, Seville, Granada, Santiago de Compostela, Valladolid, Bilbao.

On three separate occasions in 1945—February, June and September—the founder also visited Portugal to prepare the way for apostolic work there and to meet with Cardinal Cerejeira and some other bishops of that country. Early in 1946 a member of the Work went to Coimbra and shortly thereafter was joined by two more. The presence in Rome of several Opus Dei members studying there since 1942 made the Work known not only to the Curia but also to other sectors of Italian society. The prospect of some Italians joining Opus Dei was near.

With the end of the Second World War more possibilities opened up. Thanks to the professional trips of some members to Germany, Belgium, Denmark, United States, France, England, Switzerland, . . .

the Work was being spoken of.  Fr. Josemaría soon sent members to Great Britain, Ireland and France.  Opus Dei's intrinsic universality, affirmed from day one, was becoming a reality.[1]

This expansion confirmed the rightness of the 1943 erection, which had resolved the problem of priestly attention to all the members of Opus Dei.  It also consolidated juridically its government structure and laid the foundation for an interdiocesan form of government and one of pontifical right.  It was but a matter of time and growth for this step to become appropriate.  This is what happened in the mid-1940s.[2]

The appropriateness of this pontifical status was rooted also in a foundational requirement: Opus Dei's universality and the profound commitment to the Church that always moved its founder. "Christ. Mary. The Pope," he had written in the important *Instruction* of March 1934.  "Have we not pointed out with these three words the loves that make up our Catholic faith?  Sincere and generous union with the bishops in communion with the Holy See, whom the Holy Spirit has placed to govern the Church of God (Acts 20:28). . . .  In these words our ideals are completely set forth."[3] How often he taught and repeated *Omnes cum Petro, ad Iesum per Mariam*.  How can there be Christian life without union with the Church, without therefore a deep, real communion with those established as the sign and reference point of unity?

An institution of universal scope, as is Opus Dei, spreading the pursuit of holiness and the exercise of apostolate to people of all conditions and occupations, must be strongly united to the Roman Pontiff.  In the *Letter* of February 14, 1944, Fr. Josemaría wrote: "We

---

[1] With regard to this expansion, see the biographical studies mentioned in chapter 1, note 1.

[2] In the February 14, 1944 *Letter* from which we have already quoted, the founder refers to these realities and needs, expressly mentioning the possibilities that *de iure* were opened with the diocesan erection: "We have already been established in many dioceses, and we must reach out to the whole world with our apostolate. This is a requirement of the universal heart God has given to his Work. The previous canonical approval we had was insufficient for this purpose. A pious union cannot have *de iure* an interdiocesan form of governance. *De facto* we did, because of the affection the bishops of all the dioceses where we were working felt for Opus Dei" (no. 13). Fr. Escrivá knew that this interdiocesan and worldwide form of governance could not be obtained with just a diocesan erection, but this was a necessary step to achieving it. Besides the advantages accruing from the diocesan erection considered in the previous chapter, the way was opened for attaining a pontifical form of government. Thus "our internal hierarchy may be universal and thus facilitate, in the service of the whole Church, the fulfillment of the divine program entrusted to us. We are not an enterprise born to remedy the spiritual needs of a single country or a specific age: I don't think it presumptuous to say Opus Dei will last so long as there are men on earth" (*Ibid.*).

[3] *Instruction*, March 19, 1934, nos. 31 & 34-35.

have always been very Roman: our spirit calls for a close union with the Roman Pontiff, the visible head of the universal Church. I have so much faith, so much confidence in the Church and in the Pope!" A few lines before he had said that from the Holy See must come "the supreme direction of our activity."[4] Only by a strong union with the Roman Pontiff, confirmed in deeds and juridically expressed, can Opus Dei discharge its proper mission: fostering among men and women of all countries and walks of life a Christian desire, a Catholic spirit and a sense of Church. Each consequently will serve the nation, community, and local church where he or she lives.[5]

So the founder in 1946 began to seek pontifical status. Beforehand he informed the diocesan authorities and obtained the support of many bishops who knew and appreciated the work of Opus Dei. Once again he sent to Rome Alvaro del Portillo, the General Secretary of Opus Dei, to initiate the process with the appropriate departments of the Roman Curia. On February 26, 1946, Don Alvaro del Portillo reached Rome.[6]

"What did I want?" the founder of Opus Dei would ask a few years later. "A place for the Work in the law of the Church, in accordance with the nature of our vocation and the requirements of our apostolic expansion; the full sanction by the magisterium of our supernatural way whereby the fundamental traits of our spiritual physiognomy would be clearly set forth."[7] Fr. del Portillo, following Fr. Escrivá's indications, established contact with salient persons of the Roman Curia, among others, Msgr. Montini, Substitute Secretary of State. Some of these prelates he had already spoken to

---

[4] *Letter*, February 14, 1944, no. 17.

[5] Along with the more specific ecclesial aspects—like the universal and particular nature of the Church, the search for an interdiocesan, centralized juridical solution of pontifical right—Fr. Escrivá often commented, mainly in the 40s, other consequences, even cultural, of catholicity, as a counterbalance to provincialism, and the small-town outlook of exaggerated nationalism so frequent in the first half of the century. "Don't have a 'small town' outlook. Enlarge your heart until it becomes universal—'catholic.' Don't fly like a barnyard hen when you can soar like an eagle. . . . To be 'Catholic' means to love our country and to let nobody surpass us in that love. And at the same time, it means to hold as our own the noble aspirations of all the other lands. How many glories of France are glories of mine! And in the same way, many things that make Germans proud—and Italians, British, Americans and Asians and Africans—are also sources of pride to me. Catholic! A great heart, an open mind" (*The Way*, nos. 7 & 525).

[6] A few years later Fr. Josemaría recalled: "We were not really happy with the new path on which we were (referring to the juridical statute obtained in 1943) instead of traveling a highway appropriate for the development of the Work. And I sent Alvaro again to Rome in February of last year" (*Letter*, December 29, 1947/February 14, 1966, no. 161).

[7] *Letter*, January 25, 1961, no. 18.

about Opus Dei in 1943; others he saw now for the first time.  He was received as cordially this time as on the earlier occasion.  Nevertheless, the outcome was not positive.[8]

Even at the risk of repeating ourselves, let us review the law then in force.

According to the 1917 Code, institutions with a universal and unified form of government depended on the Sacred Congregation for Religious and should be invested with the juridical form of Religious Institutes (cc. 487-672) or Societies of Common life without vows (cc. 673-681).[9]  Other associations were regulated by part three of book two under the heading of *de laicis* and fell under the competence of the Sacred Congregation of the Council.  These secular associations of the faithful had a local character.  Although they could be gathered together in confederations and unions, for the purpose of receiving indulgences, privileges, spiritual graces and ascetical directives (cc. 720-725), nevertheless, they could not juridically enjoy a universal and unified form of governance.[10]

During his 1943 stay in Rome Fr. del Portillo had realized, in many conversations with Vatican officials, that it was not possible to solve the question of the stable adscription of priests to the Work, nor to obtain a centralized and universal structure within the scope of the Sacred Congregation of the Council.[11]  Once again that path remained closed.[12]

---

[8] The founder of the Work has left a record of these events in his *Letter*, October 7, 1950, no. 18.

[9] With more precision it should be pointed out that the Congregation for Religious was competent not only with regard to Religious Institutes and Societies of Common Life, but also for Third Orders Secular (c. 251).  Third Orders were of solely diocesan right, except by apostolic privilege (c. 690), but they were ascribed to the Congregation for Religious because of their connection with the First Orders.  The other two institutions—Religious Institutes and Societies of Common Life—enjoyed, according to the character of each one, an autonomous form of internal governance, which could be raised to an interdiocesan and pontifical level.  The existence of a juridical form of governance of this kind, i.e., universal and pontifical, had been throughout the history of this Roman Congregation the principal criterion for establishing its competence.

[10] Cf. A. Larraona, "Unione gerarchica dei due cleri," in *Theologica*, (1961): 21, note 59; *Suore di Notre Dame du travail. Decreto di Lode e prima approvazione delle Costituzioni*, Roma 1943; S. De Angelis, *op. cit.* (chapter 3, note 34), pp. 15ff; F. Wernz-P. Vidal, *Ius Canonicum. III. De Religiosis*, Rome 1933, pp. 509ff, nos. 467ff; E. Vromant- L. Bongaerts, *op. cit.* (chapter 3, note 34), Louvain 1955, pp. 36ff.

[11] See c. 111 of the CIC 1917.  Also the previous chapter.

[12] In the course of conversations a highly placed member of the Roman Curia told Fr. del Portillo that "l'Opus Dei era giunto a Roma con un secolo di anticipo" (Opus Dei had come to Rome a century too soon).  Thus for the time being there was no possibility of its request being granted (*Letter*, October 7, 1950, no. 18).

At that time the 1917 Code of Canon Law was at its apex. After a period in Church history when a consensus had been reached that the old sources of legislation lacked the clarity and vitality to confront the grave and great questions facing the Church—missionary expansion, problems derived from secularism or the modernist crisis, etc.—the *Codex* was seen as the answer. It would foster the formation and improvement of the clergy to direct the ecclesiastical organization, while offering improved or new channels for pastoral action. This view was solidly grounded. But one must also recognize that, without doubting the Code's undeniable advantages, it was sometimes applied too rigidly. The traditional flexibility of Canon Law to welcome renewing and rejuvenating movements in the pastoral life of the Church was curtailed. Some even claimed that what was not regulated or recognized in the *Codex* could have no citizenship in the life of the Church. A phrase circulating in Rome and attributed to Cardinal Gasparri, Secretary of State until 1930 and principal mover of the new Code, had acquired the status of a maxim: *quod non est in Codice non est in mundo* what is not found in the Code does not exist in the world.[13]

In this context the founder could not wait for a reform of the Code to open an adequate juridical path for Opus Dei. His prudence and knowledge of history prompted him to foresee that decades might have to pass before this happened. Meanwhile the growth of Opus Dei urged him to win pontifical approval. Such a step would endow the institution with an interdiocesan and pontifical form of government; it would also represent praise and express recognition by the Holy See of Opus Dei's spirit and apostolate. The latter benefit was deemed necessary in the face of the misunderstandings of some who, despite the *nihil obstat* of October 11, 1943, persisted in their negative attitude.[14]

Fr. Josemaría then decided to forward his request for a universal form of government to the Sacred Congregation for Religious, the only congregation competent to authorize such a juridical form.

---

[13] See J. Hervada, "El nuevo Código de Derecho Canónico: visión de conjunto," in *Scripta Theologica*, 15 (1983):744. Similar expressions are found in A. Oberti, "Gli Istituti Secolari a vent'anni dal *Perfectæ caritatis*," in *Vita consacrata*, 21 (1985):444. With regard to the difficulties Cardinal Mercier had in obtaining approval of his "Priestly Fraternity" see J. I. Tellechea, "La 'Fraternidad Sacerdotal de amigos de Jesús' del Cardinal Mercier (1926-1951)," in *Revista española de Derecho Canónico*, 7 (1952):517-551.

[14] These misunderstandings did not restrain the development of Opus Dei nor did they breed feelings of bitterness in the founder. Rather he grew in awareness of the spiritual value of difficulties if received with faith in divine providence. In a *Letter* addressed to his children in 1945 he wrote: "In my country they pinch the first flowering of figs so that they sweeten and ripen more quickly. God our Lord, to make us more effective, has blessed us with the Cross" (*Letter*, May 6, 1945, no. 45).

It was necessary, therefore, to navigate within the least objection-able channel—Title 17 of Book two of the 1917 Code. The passage from a diocesan level to that of pontifical right was effected by the Congregation for Religious by means of a so-called *Decretum laudis*.[15] Thus the founder requested a "Decree of praise" for the Priestly Society of the Holy Cross, already erected as an institution of dioc-esan right on December 8, 1943, with the approval of a particular statute that would best guarantee the institution's nature. He sought "a less forced juridical formula than that of 1943 whereby the true nature of the Work would be better seen." Thus it would be seen that "the Priestly Society of the Holy Cross has as its purpose to serve the other members of Opus Dei."[16]

What were the specific advantages of the juridical formula the founder sought? In a few words the papal approval was sought for the Priestly Society of the Holy Cross *with* Opus Dei. The latter was to be configured not as a common association of the faithful but rather as forming a single reality with the Priestly Society. The distinction between the Priestly Society of the Holy Cross and Opus Dei would continue, but Opus Dei is to be conceived as an integral part of the Society, the whole comprising in effect one entity. Thus neither the lay members nor the priests who make up the Priestly Society of the Holy Cross would cease to belong to Opus Dei by reason of their incorporation into the Priestly Society. Opus Dei would consequently be governed by the same moderators or direc-tors governing the Society and exercising the same faculties both in this and in Opus Dei. Opus Dei would continue to be made up of two branches—one for men and another for women—with both celibate and married members moved by an apostolic vocation that leads them to seek their own sanctification and that of others in professional work, which is thus converted into a specific means of sanctification.

## 2. The applicable law: Title 17 of the 1917 Code or a new juridical approach

The sought-after statute, whose central points we have just sum-marized, would have to fit within the bounds of Title 17 of Book two, (the least inadequate of the possible configurations then avail-able) respecting at the same time Opus Dei's foundational charac-teristics. However, when Fr. Alvaro del Portillo reached Rome for a second time, new data and possibilities had arisen.

Already in 1943, on the occasion of Opus Dei's request for the *nihil obstat* of the Holy See for diocesan erection, Fr. Siervo Goyeneche,

---

[15] Cf. *Normæ* of the S.C. for Religious of March 6, 1921, *cit.* (chapter IV, note 21) no. 6.

[16] *Letter*, October 7, 1950, no. 18.

C.M.F., consultor and member of the commission for the approval of new institutes, had foreseen a new possibility. Writing on the Priestly Society of the Holy Cross and addressing himself to the Prefect of the Sacred Congregation for Religious, Cardinal La Puma, Goyeneche remarked: "We have before us one of those forms of modern institutions, to which Your Eminence referred in the juridical congress of 1934 and which continually knock at the doors of this Sacred Congregation. They seek a canonical sanction allowing them to work securely and fruitfully within the Church. Theirs are works of apostolate required by the new and always urgent needs of the present times."[17] Fr. Larraona, another consultor at the time, expressed himself in similar terms.[18]

With respect to the eventual canonical sanctioning of these "new forms of Christian life," as Cardinal La Puma had called them, there were two schools of thought in the Sacred Congregation for Religious. Some thought they could be fitted within the broad terms of Title 17 of Book Two. Others, on the other hand, opined that a new normative statute (though not yet formulated) was required as this "new form" could not fit in Title 17 of the 1917 Code. This divergence of opinions showed up in the Sacred Congregation's deliberations with respect to the Founder of Opus Dei's petition and influenced subsequent events.

There were those in the Congregation who thought a positive answer could not be given to Opus Dei's founder. In their eyes an institution of such special characteristics could not be accommodated in Title 17. Since no slot existed in the present law, Opus Dei would have to wait, joining the ranks of other institutions quite different from one another, yet all falling under the generic heading of "new forms."[19]

Others, such as Fr. Goyeneche, favored granting the *Decretum laudis* to the Priestly Society of the Holy Cross within the terms of Title 17. He considered it flexible enough to accommodate these new forms. In his *votum* of 1946 he affirms among other things:

a) Opus Dei "was the source of the present Society" and "is inseparable from it. . . . This *Opus Dei* was organized to teach the world sanctification and perfection of Christian life in the fulfillment of one's professional duties; from the beginning it embraced all the different classes of society, men, especially professionals,

---

[17] S. Goyeneche, *Voto sulla Società clericale della S. Croce (Madrid)*, 1943, in AGP, Sezione Giuridica, III/15135. The phrase of Cardinal La Puma to which Fr. Goyeneche refers in the text is to be found in V. La Puma, "Evoluzione del diritto dei religiosi da Pio IX a Pio XI," in *Acta Congressus Iuridici Internationalis, Romæ 1934*, IV, Rome 1937, p. 203.

[18] A. Larraona, *Voto sulla Società Sacerdotale della Santa Croce, Madrid, cit.* (chapter IV, note 23).

[19] AGP, Sezione Giuridica, IV/15524-1.

and also women. It was soon seen that it was necessary to give this organization, then acting as a pious union, a *directive* and *formative* body, from which arose the idea of the Priestly Society to incarnate the spirit and moderate all the activity of this vast institution by giving it unity." He adds that "a person who becomes a member of the Society does not for this reason cease to belong to Opus Dei. No one can be admitted in it without having carried out a long apprenticeship in Opus Dei." In the latter "there is room for everyone, men and women, and even married people, making up different categories."

b) He described the Priestly Society of the Holy Cross as "a *Society* that falls within the broad scope of Title 17 of Book Two of the Code of Canon Law and that avails itself of all the possibilities of action the aforesaid title offers. Effectively, the Priestly Society of the Holy Cross is one of those daring new forms of apostolate that responds to the needs of today, which, for the good of souls, in these times of ours the Lord has raised up in his Church."

c) "The Priestly Society of the Holy Cross is a clerical society, even more, priestly, though not precisely in the material sense of c. 488, no. 4, that is to say, because *plerique sodales sacerdotio augentur*. Rather, because, while the majority of its members are lay men, the government of the Society is principally in the hands of priests and because all the members can be called to the priesthood, when the need or the usefulness of the Society requires it. In addition all must live a priestly spirit."

d) "Nevertheless, bearing in mind the end of the Society, it is understood that *in fact* the majority of the members are and remain lay men, since only in this way will it be able to achieve that end."

e) "Summarily we can say that the Priestly Society of the Holy Cross achieves its apostolic aim by sanctifying and teaching how to sanctify professional work. For this reason the members, especially the lay men, are prepared to exercize, and in fact exercize, all civil professions to which they have the same access as their fellow citizens." He emphasizes that these lay men do not give up their profession when they become members of the Society; "thus the engineer, the professor, the physician and so on continue to exercize this work. An undertaking of this kind," he added, referring to the apostolate of the members of Opus Dei, "requires above all a profound religious and civil formation, which the Society outstandingly provides in its centers of study and formation."

f) He concludes by favoring the approval requested by the founder. He bases his opinion on the breadth he sees in Title 17. "A wide freedom of organization," he writes, "is given to attain the end. Generally everything is left to the constitutions (cf. cc. 675, 676 § 3, 677, 679, 682). Whenever the Code wishes to apply the law of Religious to these societies, it does so with a prudent breadth of criteria expressed in the accommodating and comprehensive formula *congrua congruis referendo* (cf. cc. 675, 681)." Then, referring to the Priestly Society of the Holy Cross, he adds, "It has taken full advantage of this freedom of organization in areas deemed fitting, according to the spirit of Canon Law, which evidently allows similar societies a freedom of movement required for the specific end pursued by each."[20]

In this situation of divided opinions two events had special importance for the juridical evolution of Opus Dei: the intervention of Fr. Larraona, Undersecretary of the Congregation for Religious, and the audience granted to Fr. Alvaro del Portillo by Pope Pius XII.

Fr. Larraona already knew of the Work from its being granted a *nihil obstat* for its diocesan erection. In subsequent conversations, Fr. del Portillo had informed him of Opus Dei's burgeoning apostolate and the urgent need to obtain a juridical configuration as a pontifical institution.[21] On April 3, 1946, Fr. del Portillo was received by Pope Pius XII to whom he spoke of his discussions with the Roman Curia and the obstacles standing in the way of finding an adequate legal configuration. He informed him as well of the expansion of Opus Dei since June 4, 1943, when he had first been received by his Holiness.[22]

What did the Opus Dei's Secretary General point out? To both the Pope and Fr. Larraona, Fr. del Portillo emphasized the breadth and special characteristics of the ascetical and pastoral phenomenon Opus Dei represented and the need to give it a full government of pontifical right which in substance is what the founder desired and was requesting. Similarly he stressed that in fact the institution is eminently lay. It is made up for the most part of lay people who, in the midst of the world and dedicated to their professional tasks, seek holiness and strive to bring to their friends and colleagues the conviction that they too can and ought to seek Christian perfection, each in his own circumstances. A profound and solid formation is required as well as careful spiritual attention. To that end some of them—only those pastorally necessary—are ordained priests in the Priestly Society of the Holy Cross. Their mission (besides occupying certain positions of government) is to contribute to the training and spiritual guidance of all the members of the Work. Forming one body, without different classes, lay man and priest pursue together the end proper to Opus Dei.

---

[20] S. Goyeneche, *Società Sacerdotale della Santa Croce*, Rome 1946, in AGP, Sezione Giuridica, IV/15529.

[21] AGP, Sezione Giuridica, IV/15524-1.

[22] AGP, Sezione Giuridica, IV/15524-2.

Throughout early 1946 letters of commendation from 60 bishops requesting papal approval of Opus Dei had reached the Holy See; among these were eight cardinals and all the Spanish archbishops.[23] These letters speak of the growth of an institution only 18 years old and of its close union with the ordinary hierarchy of the Church. They also bear witness to the results; Opus Dei was no mere hope, but a fruitful reality.

The Work's growth and supernatural vitality, plus its special characteristics and episcopal support, sparked some Curia officials to seek a suitable canonical status. Thus came about the diversity of opinions to which we have referred and Fr. Larraona's initiative. In his view Opus Dei's special traits could not be accommodated under Title 17, which in his opinion was not susceptible of such a broad interpretation. Nevertheless it might fit within a new framework being studied in the Congregation for Religious under his direction. He wished to give sufficient breadth to these norms so as to accommodate various institutions generically called for the present "new forms of Christian life." Thus Fr. Larraona intensified and accelerated the project.[24]

Aware that the Priestly Society of the Holy Cross had been erected as a diocesan Society under Title 17 of Book two, Pope Pius XII clearly understood that it was a new phenomenon. Duly informed also of Fr. Larraona's project, he took under advisement the founder's request and ordered the Sacred Congregation for Religious to examine more carefully the documents presented by Fr. Escrivá. It was to see if, in accordance with said project, the Priestly Society of the Holy Cross and Opus Dei could be granted the *Decretum laudis* as an institution of pontifical right—in essence what the founder was requesting. This examination should be carried out (the Holy Father also ordained) according to a new procedure, already elaborated and later to be incorporated in paragraph 3 of article 7 of the Apostolic Constitution *Provida Mater Ecclesia*.[25]

This examination soon began. Its first phase ended on June 8, 1946, with the Commission of consultors favorable in principle to granting a "decree of praise," in accordance with the criteria indicated by the Holy Father.[26]

---

[23] AGP, Sezione Giuridica, IV/15525. See *Primum Institutum*, § 3, in the Appendix, document no. 22.

[24] AGP, Sezione Giuridica, IV/15524-1

[25] AGP, Sezione Giuridica, IV/15524-3. See Decree *Primum Institutum* § 4 in the Appendix, document no. 22.

[26] The consultors who studied this question were Fr. Goyeneche, President of the Commission, Fr. Kramer, Fr. Sartori and the Secretary Msgr. Sposetti. See AGP, Sezione Giuridica, IV/15540.

## 3. The Founder in Rome: the Apostolic Brief *Cum Societatis* (June 28, 1946) and the Letter *Brevis sane* in praise of the aim (August 13, 1946)

This was significant progress, but it must be seen in context. The only thing thus far obtained was, in principle, the favorable opinion of the Commission of consultors. The question had still to be brought to a higher body of the Congregation for its study and approval. Thereupon it must be submitted to the supreme judgment of the Holy Father. A long path lay ahead, hardly exempt from obstacles. But this was not the overriding challenge. The true problem was the absence of legal norms, by virtue of which to grant Fr. Escrivá's request. The set of norms the consultors had in mind in studying the petition was still a project. As we shall see in the next section, the project had been initiated in the 1930s and was still being elaborated; it ran the risk of never being promulgated or at least of undergoing serious delays. For some the new framework would necessarily suppose a modification of the 1917 *Codex*. Like all codes, this one too came endowed with stability and permanence; consequently, such innovation was considered premature. Others opined that this new set of norms might undermine the state of perfection and even, by forfeiting some of its theological content, empty it of meaning.[27]

Fr. del Portillo, familiar with these circumstances, was also aware of how delicate the situation was. In a letter to the founder on June 10 he relays the news of the positive results of the Commission of consulters, conveyed to him by Fr. Goyeneche the previous day. He added that, in his judgment, Fr. Josemaría needed to travel to Rome to smoothe over the difficulties, expedite subsequent steps and obtain papal approval.[28]

Before writing this letter, Fr. del Portillo had deliberated and prayed more than usual, given the founder's precarious health in

---

[27] The commentary that accompanied the publication of the apostolic constitution *Provida Mater Ecclesia* in the *L'Osservatore Romano* of March 14, 1947, is significant: "It is not a question (even though it may be superfluous to say so it is good to recall) of considering the present time as more propitious for these new outpourings of grace and apostolate, as though earlier institutions productive of so much fruit now were fulfilling less important tasks or had fewer opportunities for expansion. On the contrary, it is a question of adding new precious stones to the crown of the Church, in such a way that it shines with greater intensity. It is not a question certainly of replacing the ancient with the new. The older Orders and the newer religious Congregations preserve integrally their tradition and their irreplaceable importance even today in the face of the most varied needs and demands of modern life; their function continues to be fully up to date with a life so full of merits that it should be considered one of the highest glories of the Catholic Church; they extend each day more in every sacred field their glorious palestras of generous souls and of heroes."

[28] AGP, Sezione Giuridica, IV/15664.

those months. In May 1944—coinciding with the reception of minor orders by the first three priests of the Work—Fr. Josemaría had been diagnosed as suffering from a very severe form of diabetes, which would worsen with time. In May 1946 he was examined by Dr. Rof Carballo. A few days later, when Fr. del Portillo's letter arrived, he consulted him about making the trip. The physician's opinion was negative: the development of the disease made the trip inadvisable; travel could exacerbate his condition and even prove fatal. Nevertheless the founder began to ready his personal papers to go to Rome. A second letter dated two days later reached him; Fr. del Portillo reaffirmed the need for his presence in the Eternal City.[29] That same morning the founder gathered together members of the General Council of Opus Dei in Madrid to inform them of the letters and to ask their opinion. The Council favored the trip, despite the illness. Fr. Josemaría replied: "I thank you; but I would have gone in any case. What has to be done, has to be done."[30] "Confronted by these difficulties," Fr. Escrivá later wrote, "I came to Rome with my soul fixed on my Mother the most holy Virgin and with a burning faith in God our Lord."[31] He went from Madrid to Barcelona. Along the way he visited Our Lady of the Pillar in Saragossa and the monastery of Montserrat. To her he entrusted his longing for a path to be open to fulfilling God's will as made known to him on October 2, 1928.

Once in Barcelona, he celebrated Mass in an Opus Dei Center. Beforehand he shared his worries and his confidence in the Lord with the members present. Some had earlier experienced persecution, still alive and especially virulent in Barcelona. He made his own the words Peter addressed to Christ: *Ecce nos reliquimus omnia et secuti sumus te, quid ergo erit nobis?* (Mt 19:27): What will happen to us who have left everything to follow you? "Lord," he exclaimed, "have you allowed me in good faith to deceive so many souls!? I have done everything only for your glory and *knowing* that it is your will! Is it possible that the Holy See tell us that we have come a century too soon? . . . I have never wanted to deceive anyone. I have had no other will than that of serving you. Will it then turn out that I am an impostor!?"[32]

His is an anxiety before a humanly dark horizon: unabated misunderstandings, the difficulties in Rome. . . . Yet he is vividly aware of his own responsibility. Still stronger is his firm hope that God who had wanted Opus Dei would overcome all the hindrances.

---

[29] AGP, Sezione Giuridica, IV/15665.

[30] RHF, 20165, p. 959.

[31] *Letter*, January 25, 1961, no. 18.

[32] RHF, 20164, p. 1561.

The founder of course was aware that it is the hierarchy, assisted by the Holy Spirit, who must judge the authenticity of different graces, charisms, and vocations with which God enriches his Church.  He felt the urgency of winning papal approval for the phenomenon of Christian life in the world that is Opus Dei.  The papacy must recognize the reality of its members' dedication, misunderstood by others, that of ordinary faithful, in their own state and occupation, and in the most unforeseen places and situations, who dedicate themselves to the fullness of Christian life by answering to the radical demands of sanctity and apostolate.  Such approval would invest the ascetical and pastoral phenomenon of Opus Dei with canonical authentication.  Such a framework would also serve as a channel and would afford it an adequate safeguard.

Years later the founder would write, "In that critical hour of the Work's history, in 1946, the legal question was particularly important.  A mistake then, a concession in something substantial, could give rise to irreparable damage.  I risked my soul, because I could not adulterate God's will.  You will understand my worries and sufferings.  But God—*adiutor meus et protector meus!* (Ps 39:18)—filled me with peace.  A great peace grounded in the certainty that Jesus Christ wanted his Work to be carried out."[33]  This conviction explains his trip and intense prayer.  On June 21, after celebrating Holy Mass and just before boarding the ship "J. J. Sister" for Genova, he visited another Marian shrine: the Basilica of Our Lady of Ransom, Patroness of Barcelona, to entrust to her the purpose of his trip.  Late, on June 22 the ship docked at Genova, where Fr. del Portillo awaited the founder.  Twenty-four hours later they reached Rome.[34]

Immediately Fr. Escrivá began visits to Vatican officials.  Again and again he spoke of the urgency of obtaining papal approval, along with achieving a universal form of governance.  Preparations were under way to begin apostolate in a stable way in Great Britain, Ireland and France and there was need for a juridical form of governance within a new normative framework to facilitate expansion and to respect the specific traits of the Work.

One of the persons Fr. Escrivá saw was Msgr. Montini, the *Sostituto* Secretary of State, who gave the founder a photograph of Pope Pius XII with a handwritten dedication: "To our beloved son Josemaría Escrivá de Balaguer, Founder of the Priestly Society of the Holy Cross and Opus Dei, with a special blessing.  June 28, 1946.  Pope Pius XII".  On July 16, feast of our Lady of Mt. Carmel, the Holy Father cordially received him in a private audience.

Shortly thereafter he was told the process would be suspended until autumn.  Fr. Josemaría decided then to return to Madrid,

---

[33] *Letter*, January 25, 1961, no. 6.

[34] For these events and those that follow see AGP, Sezione Giuridica, IV/15666.

reaching there on August 31. He did not leave Rome empty-handed; he brought with him two non-decisive but still important documents: the Apostolic Brief *Cum Societatis* and the Letter *Brevis sane* in praise of the aim.

By means of the Apostolic Brief *Cum Societatis* (dated June 28, 1946, feast of the Sacred Heart of Jesus) Pope Pius XII granted several indulgences to the members of the Priestly Society of the Holy Cross and Opus Dei.[35] In recent months Fr. del Portillo had obtained from the Sacred Penitentiary various faculties and indulgences. To them were now added new ones more solemnly granted, thanks to the Secretariat of State and the good offices of Msgr. Montini, "the first friendly hand I encountered in Rome," the founder would always remember with gratitude.[36]

The narrative part of the Apostolic Brief makes explicit mention of the apostolic fruits born of the Priestly Society of the Holy Cross and Opus Dei in so few years, owing to the founder's efforts: "Since the admirable work and the most fruitful labor of the Priestly Society of the Holy Cross and Opus Dei that our beloved son Josemaría Escrivá de Balaguer y Albás, Priest and Doctor, founded with so much generosity and directs with such prudence it is fitting that he be accompanied by our warm assent and our favorable will, it is pleasing with Us through these letters, by which we enrich it with spiritual gifts of indulgences to recall the very abundant fruits that for the glory of God and the good of souls the illustrious Founder has obtained in such a brief space of time with constant work and diligence."

The Apostolic Brief also reviews the path followed by the Priestly Society of the Holy Cross and Opus Dei; it expressly refers to the present breadth of its apostolate, which "with the favor of God not only spreads itself throughout Spain but also to far distant regions." Finally, it grants some indulgences of which those related to work directly bespeak the essence of the spirituality followed by members of the Work.[37] Those referring to the wooden cross (to be found in oratories of centers of Opus Dei) establish that indulgences can be earned by kissing it or praying before it some pious aspiration.

In 1940 the founder had already obtained indulgences from Madrid's bishop for kissing the cross.[38] To understand better the

[35] This document is in the Appendix, no. 19.

[36] RHF, 20115, p. 47.

[37] The apostolic Brief *Cum Societatis* makes express reference to intellectual work; the subsequent Brief, *Mirifice de Ecclesia*, of which we will speak in section 7 of this chapter extends these indulgences to manual tasks of all kinds.

[38] The document granting these indulgences of the Bishop of Madrid-Alcalá can be found in the Appendix, document no. 20.

scope of these indulgences—first diocesan and later papal—let us look at a bit of history. From the start Fr. Josemaría was greatly devoted to the Holy Cross. He introduced the custom of placing a wooden cross, without a corpus, in its oratories as a reminder that the Christian way is one of surrender, self-denial and sacrifice, as Fr. Josemaría wrote in *The Way*.[39]

Very soon, as early as 1934, this simple wooden cross was mis-interpreted by some people alleging scandal that it did not have a corpus. As if there weren't countless precedents.[40] Later, in Barcelona at the beginning, misunderstandings reached the unbelievable point of attributing to the symbolism of point 178 of *The Way* a macabre interpretation. Perhaps because the plain cross in the first center of the Work was quite large, some spread the tale that human sacri-fices were made thereon. Fr. Josemaría had the cross replaced with one so small it wouldn't even accommodate a newborn, Fr. Escrivá commented wryly.[41]

Such events help us to understand the special significance the founder always afterwards attributed to the Brief *Cum Societatis.*

---

[39] "Whenever you see a poor, wooden cross, alone, uncared-for, worthless . . . and without a corpus, don't forget that that cross is *your* cross—the everyday hidden cross, unattractive and unconsoling—the cross that is waiting for the corpus it lacks: and that corpus must be you."

"You ask me, 'Why that wooden cross?' And I quote from a letter: 'As I raise my eyes from the microscope, my sight comes to rest on the cross—black and empty. That cross without a corpus is a symbol; it has a meaning others won't see. And I, tired out and on the point of abandoning my work, once again bring my eyes close to the lens and continue. For that lonely cross is calling for a pair of shoulders to bear it" (*The Way*, nos. 178 & 277).

[40] The founder was also accused, with members of the Work, of "an iconoclastic orien-tation." The bishop of Madrid refers to this in his letter to the coadjutor abbot of Montserrat of June 21, 1941: "*Iconoclastic orientation!*—It would be laughable if it were not causing so many tears to mothers who believe that their sons are irremediably condemned soon after having been enchanted with the edifying life of piety they have seen born and consolidated in their children. All of them have their images—their crucifixes, their medals, the same we all have; they have as an obligation a picture of the Most Holy Virgin in their room and the precept of glancing at it lovingly whenever they enter or leave the room; there is nothing of an iconoclastic orientation at all. But some *spies* sent *ad hoc* to find out what was happening there were shocked at seeing a large wooden cross but without the body of our Lord Jesus Christ; a cross that reminds each member of the *Opus* that the cross awaits him, that he not pull back or deny letting himself be crucified out of love for the one who rose to the cross; and those who have seen this cross-invitation have had to see and have had to tell that at the foot of this cross there is a plaque that says that the Bishop grants 50 days of indulgence to those who lovingly and devoutly kiss this holy cross and address to it the enduring expressions of love which St. Andrew addressed to his, and those who divulge this must also spread this truth" (RHF, D-3545).

[41] RHF, 20165, pp. 756-757.

The papal document not only supported the whole of his apostolic work, but also answered the absurd misunderstandings that still had not ceased. Msgr. Montini, referring to these incidents and other hardships in 1946 wrote to the founder: "The Lord has allowed you to suffer from the beginning what other institutions suffer only after many years."[42] In fact, as a sign of filial gratitude to the pope, Fr. Escrivá had placed next to each of those wooden crosses an inscription: "His Holiness Pope Pius XII by the Apostolic Brief 'Cum Societatis' of June 28, 1946, graciously deigned to grant an indulgence of 500 days each time this wooden Cross is devoutly kissed, or a pious ejaculation is said before it."

The second document accompanying the founder was a letter praising Opus Dei's aims, *Brevis sane*, issued by the Sacred Congregation for Religious and dated August 13, 1946.[43]

The reasons that moved the founder insistently to request the *Decretum laudis* have already been set forth: to have an international structure, with the necessary internal autonomy, to foster the organic growth beyond diocesan and national borders and to obtain a papal sanction that would restrain the misunderstandings and persecutions that continued to beset Opus Dei. Both objectives would be obtained with a "decree of praise." But the inevitable delay in obtaining this decree led the Congregation to complement the expression of papal approval of the fruitful apostolic work of Opus Dei contained in the Brief *Cum Societatis*. Thus the founder on his return to Madrid should also bear an official document of the Sacred Congregation whose object would be to praise explicitly Opus Dei's purpose and apostolate, making express reference to the divine vocation of its members.

The idea arose of a "letter in praise of the purpose," a document that had not been given by the Holy See for some time. In the praxis of the Congregation this document was only given when a decree of praise could not be granted, but the institution was deemed worthy of this support and there were serious reasons for showing this. Its object is to encourage the institution to continue its activity and to develop, since as it declares, its purpose merits the approval of the Church.[44] The "Letter in praise of the purpose" granted to Opus Dei is signed by Cardinal Lavitrano, Prefect of the Sacred Congre-

---

[42] RHF, 21503, p. 380.

[43] Appendix, document no. 21.

[44] The document of praise of the aim, whether in the form of a letter or a decree, was one of the possible but not necessary steps within the procedure for the approval of Institutes by the Holy See. "Si institutum recenter erectum fuerit . . . laudatur finis seu scopus fundatoris, vel finis seu scopus instituti pro qualitate circumstantiarum" (A. Bizzarri, *Collectanea in usum Secretariæ Sacræ Congregationis Episcoporum et Regularium*,

gation and Msgr. Pasetto, its Secretary at that time.[45] The text says that in spite of the short time passed since the Sacred Congregation "gladly granted permission for the canonical erection of the Priestly Society of the Holy Cross and Opus Dei," abundant and authorized documents reach it that greatly praise and recommend the institution. These documents and testimonies verify what the Congregation itself had concluded "with regard to the sanctity, need and appropriateness of the purpose and apostolate" of the Priestly Society of the Holy Cross and Opus Dei.

It ends with a greeting to the President General and all the members of Opus Dei who carry out a vanguard apostolate both in the intellectual world as in all civil professions, "for the abundant fruits obtained, by the rapid growth achieved and for the good spirit that animates them." To the founder it addresses: "Continue with good spirit what you have begun with vigor, and may all of those continue faithfully with you, both men and women, who by divine vocation have joined or in the future join such a noble and holy Work."

## 4. The "new forms" and the Roman Curia

In early 1946, while studying Fr. Escrivá's request, the Roman Curia concluded that a pastoral phenomenon of such breadth, supernatural impulse and special characteristics as Opus Dei should be endowed with a universal form of governance. For this reason the Congregation for Religious resolved to expedite a set of regulations to embrace and regulate the broad range of initiatives, institutions and projects, more or less elaborated according to the different cases, that for some time had been designated as "new forms." Before continuing our consideration of the juridical development of Opus Dei, we should stop to examine the process, begun decades before, that culminated in 1947 with the promulgation of the Apos-

---

Rome 1863, p. 828) See also *Normæ secundum quas S. Congregatio Episcoporum et Regularium procedere solet in approbandis novis institutis votorum simplicium, June 28, 1901, nos. 1-7, 18-25;* J. B. Ferreres, *Instituciones canónicas,* I, Barcelona 1920, no. 798, p. 381; A. Battandier, *op. cit.* (chapter IV, note 56), no. 31, p. 21.

[45] Referring to this letter, the founder would later say: "The Lord brought it about that last year we obtained from the Holy See through the venerable Cardinal Lavitrano a document which has not been issued for more than a century: *the Letter or Decree in praise of the aim.*

"Doubtless they saw the need we had to have something in writing right away, in order to defend ourselves. The principal reason for obtaining some approval from Rome (even though for the moment it is not how we desire it) is none other than seeing ourselves so harshly persecuted. And thus we feel reinforced to spread the objective truth" (*Letter,* December 29, 1947/February 14, 1966, no. 167).

tolic Constitution *Provida Mater Ecclesia* and the creation of Secular Institutes.[46]

In the introduction *Provida Mater Ecclesia* sketches a panoramic view of the development of the canonical state of perfection throughout the history of the Church. "But the most benevolent Lord who, without exception of persons, invited once and again all the faithful to practice perfection in all places ordained with the advice of his admirable divine providence that also in the world deprived by so many vices above all in our days that there should have flourished and continue to flourish in a great number of select souls who burn not only with a desire of individual perfection but also of remaining in the world by a special vocation from God, that they may find the best and new forms of association carefully accommodated to the needs of the times that permit them to live a life magnificently adapted to acquiring Christian perfection."[*]

With the words "eminently good and new forms of association," Pope Pius XII evidently refers to those institutions that, while not common associations of the faithful nor religious institutes, are more or less assimilated to ones or the others to them. These had been called in the Roman Curia and in scholarly opinion "new forms of Christian life," "new forms of apostolate," "new forms of ecclesiastical associations," "new forms of perfection," "new forms of consecration," "new forms of religious life," or more simply, "new forms."

Some of these institutions though existing prior to 1917, were not recognized by the Code of Canon Law.[47] This pastoral phenom-

---

[46] We will not attempt here a detailed examination of this question but only an analysis of the general outlines. The bibliography regarding Secular Institutes is very extensive. We are only interested in those aspects that shed light on the juridical evolution of Opus Dei. The vast bibliography on Secular Institutes can be obtained by consulting: J. Beyer, "De Institutis Saecularibus, Bibliographia," in *Periodica de re morali, canonica, liturgica*, 52 (1963):239-259; A. Oberti, "Bibliografia", in *Gli Istituti Secolari: consacrazione, secolarità, apostolato*, Rome 1970, pp. 261-273; F. Morlot, "Bibliographia de Institutis Saecularibus," in *Commentarium pro Religiosis*, 54 (1973):231-297 and 354-362, 64 (1983):193-253; B. Bosatra, *Istituti Secolari e Teologia. La ricerca post-conciliare (1965-1978)*, Rome 1980, pp. XIII-XXIII; A. Oberti, "Nota bibliografica sugli Istituti Secolari," in M. Albertini and Y. Damiani, *Introduzione alla spiritualità degli Istituti Secolari*, Milan 1981, pp. 71-82.

[*] (*Translator's note*. See an official translation of the introduction to *Provida Mater Ecclesia* in Bouscaren, *Canon Law Digest*, Vol. 3.)

[47] In the last century and even before there had appeared associations of perfection and apostolate atypical with respect to the legislation in force at that time for the canonical states of perfection. They fundamentally lacked either common life or the religious habit or the three public vows or one of them. Some of them had received diocesan approval. Subsequently the decree *Ecclesia Catholica* of the Sacred Congregation of Bishops and Regulars, confirmed on August 11, 1889 by Pope Leo XIII (*ASS*, 23 (1890-1891):634-636), subjected them to the authority of the local ordinary and constituted them as pious associations of the faithful, without giving them the cat-

enon was the object of attention by canonical doctrine after the Code of 1917,[48] and it would be dealt with by the Holy See in the pontificate of Pius XI. Following the promulgation of the Code in 1917 these new institutions greatly developed in both number and geographic expansion; examples could be found in Germany, Austria, Belgium, France, Spain, Holland, Hungary, Italy, and so on.

If the number and variety of these new forms were great, no less various were the paths followed for their juridical recognition. Generally speaking, in the face of uncertainty as to which path to follow, they began their life as simply associations *de facto*, although some with the knowledge and blessing of diocesan authorities. Some were declared pious unions by means of diocesan approvals; others were established as sodalities with juridical personality of a local nature. Still others, having received the *nihil obstat* of the Holy See, were recognized as diocesan societies under Title 17, applied to

---

egory of religious orders or congregations (cf. A. Gambari, "Institutorum Saecularium et Congregationum Religiosarum evolutio comparata," in Various authors, *De Institutis Sæcularibus* I, Rome 1951, pp. 331-348.

When the work of codification began under Pope Pius X within the competency of the Sacred Congregation of Bishops and Regulars, besides religious orders and congregations, societies without public vows were also included. From among these societies with common life gave rise to Title 17 of Book Two of the Code of 1917, while the legislation was silent with regard to associations without common life (cf. S. Goyeneche, "Annotationes ad Const. Apost. 'Provida Mater Ecclesia'," in *Apollinaris*, 20 (1947):23-24).

As the result of an observation from the ecclesiastical province of Toulouse (France) to the draft canon of 528 of the schema of 1912—corresponding to c. 681 of the 1917 *Codex*—it seems the question of whether or not to regulate these "new forms" was discussed in the code commission. It was decided to leave to each case the determination of which norms of the common law should be applied or not applied to these institutions. (Cf. G. Escudero, *Los Institutos Seculares, su naturaleza y su derecho*, Madrid 1954, p. 31.)

[48] Among other writings of this period, we can cite: Ph. Maroto, "Consultationes," in *Commentarium pro Religiosis*, 5 (1924):342ff. and "Annotationes In S.C. de Religiosis - De consecratione virginum pro mulieribus in saeculo degentibus," in *Ibid.*, 7 (1927):154ff; J. Creusen, "Formes modernes de la vie religieuse," in *Revue des communautés religieuses*, 8 (1932):1ff. and "Societés religieuses," in *Ephemerides theologicæ lovanienses*, 11 (1934):780ff; M. Heimbucher, *Die Orden und Kongregationen der katholischen Kirche*, II, Paderborn 1934, pp. 632ff; P. Delatre, "Les filles du peuple," in *Revue des communautés religieuses*, 10 (1934):73ff; I. Mennessier, "Donation à Dieu et voeux de religion," in *La vie spirituelle. Suppl.*, 49 (1936):277ff; W. A. Stanton, *De Societatibus sive virorum sive mulierum in communi viventium sine votis*, Halifax 1936, pp. 88ff; V. La Puma, *op. cit.* (note 17 of this chapter); S. Goyeneche, "De votis simplicibus in fontibus et doctrina in ordine ad statum religiosum constituendum," in *Acta Congressus Iuridici Internationalis, Romæ 1934*, IV, Rome 1937, pp. 314-315; F. Wagner, "Neue Formen des gottgeweihten Lebensdienstes der Frau," in *Caritas*, 42 (1937):74ff; Ph. Hofmeister, "Die Rechtsverhältnisse der weltlichen Schwesternschaften," in *Archiv für katholisches Kirchenrecht*, 117 (1937):127ff; G. Dossetti, *Il concetto giuridico dello "status religiosus" in Sant'Ambrogio*, Milan 1940, pp. 2ff.

them extensively. Finally others, following an indication of Benedict XV, were configured as third orders *sui generis*, under the protection of religious orders. None of these solutions, nevertheless, was adequate, for many of these institutions as by the nature of their apostolate required a supra-diocesan form of government. They consequently knocked at various Vatican doors seeking new solutions. The papal reply, nonetheless, was being delayed (*dilata*), which is understandable since the problems presented by these "new forms" with regard to the possible juridical form of governance were complicated by uncertainty over which department of the Roman Curia was competent.

As just said, some of the foundations bent on spreading beyond strictly diocesan environments were configured as third orders *sui generis* under the protection of the great religious orders. This figure, however, did not give them an interdiocesan form of government with sufficient internal autonomy. For this reason, Pius XI, favorable to the development of these "new forms," advised that some of them in late 1924 give up their juridical dependence on religious orders and address themselves directly to the Roman Curia.[49]

Confronted by the great diversity of these institutions and the absence of any normative guidelines, the Roman Curia vacillated as to which office was competent: that of the Council or that for Religious.[50] In requesting approval these "new forms" addressed themselves indistinctly to one or the other congregation.[51] Generally speaking, the Congregation for Religious, except in exceptional cases, did not honor these petitions and sent them on many times to the Congregation of the Council where little by little a special section for these institutions was set up. This step offered a possible channel, but the legislation in force did not provide a way for these associations to obtain the supradiocesan form of government they sought.

Seeking to clarify their proper canonical status, Pope Pius XI, who had personally intervened in the study of some of these institutions, entrusted an in-depth study to the Congregation of the Council. In May 1938 with the authorization of Pius XI,[52] a meeting was held at Sankt Gallen (Switzerland), attended by representatives of 25 of these associations, predominantly lay. The assembly was presided by Fr. Agostino Gemelli, O.F.M., who later compiled

---

[49] Cf. L. Morosini Montevecchi - S. Sernagiotto di Casavecchia, *Breve storia degli Istituti Secolari*, Milan 1978, p. 18.

[50] With regard to the historical moment and those that follow, see A. Larraona, *Società di perfezione cristiana e di apostolato nel secolo* (pro manuscripto), Rome 1946, I, part 1, p. 19ff; cf. also L. Gutiérrez Martín, *op. cit.* (chapter IV, note 67), pp. 311ff.

[51] See for example J. I. Tellechea, *op. cit.* (note 13 of this chapter), pp. 540ff.

[52] S. Goyeneche, *Annotationes...*, *op. cit.* (note 47 of this chapter), p. 26.

a historical and canonical report entitled "Le associazioni di laici consacrati a Dio nel mondo" and addressed to the Congregation of the Council. Its receipt in 1939 fell within the first year of the pontificate of Pius XII.[53]

As early as 1932, the attitude of the Congregation for Religious towards these new forms had begun to change. In the fall of 1934 the secretary of this congregation, Archbishop La Puma, in the conference quoted from earlier,[54] showed himself in favor of the recognition of these new initiatives of Christian life.

Some years later the Sacred Congregation of the Holy Office in a letter of May 2, 1942, occasioned by a concrete case, solicited of the Sacred Congregation for Religious its opinion about these "new forms". The Sacred Congregation for Religious on July 27 of the same year gave a favorable reply, at the level of general principles, to the approval of these institutions, with due precautions. It communicated that it was studying how to unify criteria with regard to the norms applicable to these institutions. The Holy Office agreed with this reply.

The Congregation for Religious had dealt extensively with the question of the "new forms" as part of the study undertaken to grant the *Decretum laudis* to the Institute "Notre-Dame du Travail," which had been awaiting approval since 1937. Fr. Larraona wrote a lengthy *votum* (June 18, 1943) for the Commission of Consultors. Besides studying the singular characteristics of this institution, he related the question of new forms of perfection and apostolate in the world to current legislation. He favored their approval. The Consultors approved the general approach set forth in Fr. Larraona's paper. But the *plenarium* of Cardinals could not be celebrated because of the death of Cardinal La Puma, Prefect of the Congregation, on November 4, 1943. The Second World War offered further inconveniences.

Meanwhile, the Holy Office by reason of its specific competence had once again taken up the study of the question with a view to establishing some fundamental requirements for approving these institutions. It ended up drafting a set of normative guidelines. These were sent by the Holy Office to the Congregation for Religious on March 6, 1945, indicating that "it considers it proper that the Congregation [for Religious] complete the study of the question and dictate the dispositions it considers necessary in this matter." Consequently, the Congregation for Religious reviewed the work of the Holy Office and set about drawing up normative guidelines.

---

[53] It was published *pro manuscripto* in Assisi in 1939 with the title *Le associazioni di laici consacrati a Dio nel mondo.* It was later reproduced in the volume *Secolarità e vita consacrata*, Milan 1966, pp. 363-442.

[54] Cf note 17 of this chapter.

To finish the task, a new commission was appointed within the Congregation, made up of consultors from the Congregation for Religious and the Holy Office.[55]  This commission was presented with: a) a commented draft of a decree to be submitted for confirmation to the Holy Father for its publication, based largely on the project of the Holy Office;  b) an internal instruction for the use of the Congregation that essentially contained the conclusions of a general character contained in the *votum* of Fr. Larraona with regard to the Institute "Notre-Dame du Travail"; and c) procedural norms for approving these new institutions that would simplify the method observed until that time by the Congregation.

On May 11, 1945, this commission agreed to these norms duly corrected and expressed its desire that, once approved by the full congress (with the assistance of technical consultors but without passing through a plenum of cardinals), it could be submitted directly to the Roman Pontiff for promulgation as a Motu proprio. Moreover the commission entrusted Fr. Larraona with the execution of what had been agreed upon and the preparation of the definitive text.

## 5. The Apostolic Constitution *Provida Mater Ecclesia:* the new juridical figure of Secular Institutes

Such was the state of affairs when in 1946 Opus Dei requested in Rome approval as an institution of pontifical right.  Thus, work interrupted in May 1945 was resumed and even intensified to make available as soon as possible a proper juridical setting for pontifical approval of both Opus Dei and other institutions awaiting recognition.

New consultors were added, and Fr. Larraona finished his report in July 1946.[56]  The Sacred Congregation approved this report; after slight reworking, it was soon submitted to the Holy Father for his final decision.[57]

As the *pars narrativa* of the *Provida Mater Ecclesia* makes clear, Pope Pius XII, at whose command and under whose direction— *iussu ductuque nostro*—the Sacred Congregation for Religious had drawn up a juridical statute for these "new forms," sought expressly to give it his pontifical sanction in the most solemn way.  It was thus not to be a decree of the Sacred Congregation, but an apostolic

---

[55] This commission was presided by Msgr. Passetto, Secretary of the Congregation for Religious, and was made up of Fr. Larraona, undersecretary, and by the Revs. Goyeneche, C.M.F., Grendel, S.V.D., and Creusen, S.J., and technical assistant Msgr. Sposetti.

[56] This report includes the execution of the points agreed upon in the meeting of the Commission of May 11, 1945, various earlier and subsequent documents and the draft decree in its final version.

[57] AGP, Sezione Giuridica, IV/15666.

constitution. Dated February 2, 1947, it was published in the *Acta Apostolicæ Sedis* of March 29, 1947, with the title of *Apostolic Constitution "Provida Mater Ecclesia" on the Canonical States and Secular Institutes for acquiring Christian perfection*.[58] The same number of *Acta Apostolicæ Sedis* announced that a special commission for Secular Institutes had been established within the Congregation for Religious on March 25.[59]

The following year two further documents were published by the Holy See to complete the special legislation on Secular Institutes: the Motu proprio *Primo feliciter*, March 12, 1948,[60] and the Instruction *Cum Sanctissimus*, March 19, 1948.[61]

The Apostolic Constitution *Provida Mater Ecclesia* created a new juridical figure, that of Secular Institute. Its juridical treatment *extra Codicem* does not modify particular aspects of the 1917 Code, but it does complete them.[62] What are the principal characteristics of this figure? To elaborate this let us refer to the legislative part (*pars dispositiva*) of the apostolic constitution entitled the "*lex peculiaris* of Secular Institutes".[63]

The first article of the *lex peculiaris* defines Secular Institutes as "societies, whether clerical or lay, whose members, in order to attain Christian perfection and to exercise a full apostolate, profess the evangelical counsels in the world."

Therein are contained three fundamental points:

a) The secular condition of their members, of whom the article says they seek Christian perfection and exercise apostolate in the world. This characteristic was strongly emphasized in the Motu proprio *Primo feliciter*. Its second article declares that in these institutes there should shine forth what is their "proper and peculiar" character: the "*secular* character that is the root of their reason for being." This therefore should be reflected in all facets of their being and activity. The Motu proprio says: "Perfection must be 'exer-

---

[58] *AAS* 39 (1947):114-124.

[59] The Commission was made up by M. Suarez, O.P., J. Grendel, S.V.D., Agatangelo de Langasco, O.F.M., J. Creusen, S.I., S. Goyeneche, C.M.F., and Alvaro del Portillo, of Opus Dei, as Secretary. (*AAS* 39 (1947):131-132).

[60] *AAS* 40 (1948):283-286.

[61] *AAS* 40 (1948):293-297.

[62] The fact that this Constitution did not repeal any aspect of the Code legislation is set forth in the *pars narrativa*. It says the 1917 Code was intentionally silent with regard to these institutions "and left for future legislation what should be determined in their respect, since the matter was not yet sufficiently mature." It implies historical events, while presenting the new legal text as an attempt to fill a gap in the framework of Code legislation.

[63] We will complete the explanation with some references to the documents issued in 1948, i.e. the Motu proprio *Primo Feliciter* and the Instruction *Cum Sanctissimus*, designed precisely to explicate some aspects of *Provida Mater Ecclesia*.

cised and professed in the world'" and apostolate "must be exercised faithfully not only in the world (*in sæculo*), but also from the world (*ex sæculo*), and therefore in the professions, activities, forms, places and circumstances corresponding to this secular condition."

b) Members' profession of the evangelical counsels. The first article of the *lex peculiaris* establishes that "members, in order to attain Christian perfection and to exercise a full apostolate, profess the evangelical counsels in the world." The Motu proprio *Primo feliciter* in its introduction refers to the members of Secular Institutes as "souls hidden 'with Christ in God' (Col 3:3), who aspire to sanctity and consecrate themselves cheerfully to God for their whole life." They come to enlarge "the army of those who profess the evangelical counsels."

c) The full exercise of apostolate by its members. This dedication to apostolate, set forth in the first article of the *lex peculiaris*, says that members of these institutes, "in order to exercise a full apostolate, profess the evangelical counsels in the world." This is further clarified by *Primo feliciter*, which says, "the whole life of the members of Secular Institutes, dedicated to God by the profession of perfection, should be converted into an apostolate embracing the whole of life" (no. II). The Instruction *Cum Sanctissimus*, reviewing the characteristic features to be found in the associations that can be recognized as Secular Institutes, states: "it must clearly appear that it is truly a question of associations that propose a full consecration of life to perfection and apostolate" (no. 6).

Contrasting the genuine nature of this new juridical figure with other institutions, *Provida Mater Ecclesia* declares that "by law, and as a norm (*iure, ex regula*), [they] neither are nor can properly be called religious institutes (*Religiones*, cc. 487 and 488, no. 1) nor Societies of common life (c. 673 § 1)" (art. II, § 1 no. 1). The reason is: "they neither take the three public vows of religion (cc. 1308, § 1 and 488, no. 1), nor oblige their members to live common life, that is, to dwell under the same roof, according to the canons (cc. 487ff. and 673ff)" (art. II § 1). They belong, rather, to the genus of secular associations of the faithful. Though "they may be properly distinguished from other common associations of the faithful (part three, book two of the Code of Canon Law). [They] are rightly called institutes or Secular Institutes and are subject to the norms of this Apostolic Constitution" (art. I).

Let us complete our explanation by describing three more traits:

a) The importance their own constitutions have for each Secular Institute. Their function is even broader and more incisive than that attributed to the constitutions of Societies of common life without vows under Title 17 of the Code (*lex peculiaris*, art. II, § 2, no. 3).

b) The possibility of being granted an interdiocesan and universal form of government of pontifical right. This clearly sets them apart from other common Associations of the faithful (*lex peculiaris,* art. VII).

c) Another characteristic of this new association, different from the existing ones, is the possibility of clerical as well as lay Secular Institutes (*lex peculiaris,* art. I).

Finally, according to *Provida Mater Ecclesia,* all these institutes depend upon the Sacred Congregation for Religious (*lex peculiaris,* art. IV § 1). In turn the Motu proprio decrees that the juridical form of Secular Institute is obligatory for all the institutions that meet the requirements and elements prescribed in the apostolic constitution. They can no longer remain among the common Associations of the faithful (no. I). The Motu proprio completes this specification by establishing that "all the societies, from wherever they may proceed—even though they have received the approval of the ordinary of the place or papal approval—when it is seen that they meet the elements and requirements proper to Secular Institutes, must necessarily and immediately accommodate themselves to this new form according to the aforementioned norms (cf. no. I); and in order to maintain uniformity of direction, we have decreed that they precisely be assigned and subjected solely to the Sacred Congregation for Religious, where a special office has been set up for Secular Institutes" (no. V).

The apostolic constitution grants broad faculties to the Congregation to issue guidelines as need requires or experience advises, "for all or some of these institutes . . . whether reinterpreting the apostolic constitution (which constitutes the special law of all Secular Institutes: art. II, § 2, no. 1) or completing or applying it" (*lex peculiaris,* art. II, § 2, no. 2).[64]

## 6. The importance and limitations of the legislation of 1947-1948

At first glance this legislation displays an enormous breadth and even flexibility in many points left to the constitutions of each institute and to subsequent legislation. This is heightened by the admission in *Cum Sanctissimus* of the incomplete character of the norms of the *Provida Mater Ecclesia.* Until the process of evolution of all these institutes given a place under the apostolic constitution reaches its maturation, all parties are told to wait. What factors

---

[64] The Instruction Cum Sanctissimus, in its introduction indicates that the task entrusted to the Sacred Congregation for Religious should be wide-ranging. The norms in effect until then with regard to Secular Institutes are not yet "complete and definitive," even though, it adds, the task of completing them ought to be delayed "until a more opportune time so that the present evolution of these Institutes not be dangerously curtailed."

explain these characteristics of the normative guidelines promulgated by the *Provida Mater Ecclesia*?

The introduction of the apostolic constitution itself gives a double reason (negative and positive) for its promulgation: "in order to avoid the danger of the erection of new Institutes sometimes founded imprudently and without mature examination; . . . so that the Institutes that merit approval obtain a special juridical statute that corresponds aptly and fully to their nature, ends and circumstances." This observation is completed by the declaration that "Secular Institutes have multiplied silently and have taken many forms diverse from one another *(satis inter se diversas)*"; this idea is repeated in the *pars dispositiva* (art. II, § 2, no. 3) that speaks of the different "purposes, needs and circumstances *(non parum inter se diversis)* of each of the institutes."

Multiplicity, diversity, variety of inspirations and traits of these "new forms": these are realities for which the juridical figure of Secular Institute was created as a general framework within the law of the Church. The legislation responds not to a recent question, but to a reality making itself known for years. Thus, for example, Fr. Gemelli in his 1939 Report speaks of a perhaps excessively exuberant flowering of these institutions. Their "experiments and experiences are multiplied each day in all countries, and it cannot be said that all of them present the necessary guarantees of seriousness, solidity, or organization and apostolic effectiveness.

"Besides organizations more or less directly known by the hierarchy," Gemelli adds, "it is legitimate to suppose, owing to many evident signs, that there exist many others that for the present escape any knowledge or control. They have arisen out of the uncontrolled individual zeal of simple priests not invested with authority or mission. Perhaps it is not exaggerated to affirm that in practice in every city there is at least one priest who, having a large group of penitents, tries to form with them or with some of them an organization of persons consecrated to God in the world. This for many reasons can give rise to various difficulties and sometimes be the cause of serious harm.

"Therefore it seems fitting," Gemelli concludes, "to ask the Church to deign no longer to ignore completely these experiences, but rather to intervene and lead them to the field of its discipline, establishing some fundamental directives to authorize and recognize those institutes in conformity with them and that present a minimum of guarantees and requirements, while formally prohibiting all the others."[65]

---

[65] A. Gemelli, *op. cit.* (note 53 of this chapter), p. 57.

One of the *vota* presented to the Congregation for Religious in the last stage previous to the promulgation of *Provida Mater Ecclesia* referred extensively to this variety of institutions.[66] Besides the lack of common life in the material sense—the external and negative sign of all of these institutions—there are such differences among them as to distinguish "two types of institutions clearly different from one another":

1. Those institutions that can be categorized as "secular institutes of perfection," whose characteristics are:

a) "they want to be religious and to profess the three holy vows, even, if possible, public";

b) "the absence of common life is motivated solely by reasons of apostolate; it is simply a means; it has an instrumental significance and is not a form of life arising out of the internal needs of its program and spirituality";

c) their apostolic purpose is "to conquer the laity for God. . . . They wish to achieve this end in a certain sense from the outside, in circumstances different from those of lay people."

2. Those institutions, on the other hand, that can be designated as "secular institutes of apostolate," whose characteristics are:

a) "They can be distinguished from the former by their clear intention of not wanting to be religious, but of continuing to be lay people"; for this reason they can also be called "lay movements (which does not mean that priests cannot be members of them)";

b) For them "to continue living in the world is a necessity, a program, the form of life." They seek "Christian perfection with total dedication of themselves to the Lord (by means of chastity, apostolate, prayer and also poverty and obedience). . . . They think it is possible for lay people living in the world to achieve Christian perfection, *diligere Deum in omnibus et super omnia.*"

c) The apostolic ideal of these movements is also "to conquer the laity for God . . . but from within, continuing to be lay people both in their form of life and in their lay way of attaining Christian perfection. . . . apostolate in their own environment, according to the thought of Pius XI, in the sense that each lay environment (engineers, professors, doctors, workers, etc.) has its own apostles."

The *votum* affirms that the secular institute of perfection,"while using, always for apostolic reasons, its broad freedom from the juridical point of view, nevertheless, it has a certain inclination to the religious state . . . and uses the traditional terminology." On the other hand, the secular institutes of apostolate, still in "their initial and 'charismatic' state . . . lack those experiences offered by

---

[66] P. Dalos, *Le nuove forme delle consocietà ecclesiastiche,* 1946, in AGP, Sezione Giuridica, IV/15523.

earlier times and historical precedents . . . and their juridical terminology is quite different from the traditional one."

The author then goes on to suggest the appropriateness of regulating each type separately, a conclusion that seems to follow logically from his premises. Nevertheless, his reply, though with some
misgivings, is negative. His reason? "The time is not yet right" and
perhaps "too great an innovation could lead to confusion. . . . It is
not possible to do everything at once. For the present a common
regulation would be sufficient; it would not be necessary to draw
up several decrees, different norms for the different types of secular institutes. But, on the other hand, it would be highly necessary
and useful to point out there are two different types. Thus a clear
direction can be given for future development; and it would be
possible to avoid unfortunate interpretations and deviations both
in the official juridical field and in canonical literature."

With regard to the proposed decree, in strict consequence of
what he has already said, he proposes to avoid "excessively narrow, exact and general rules," which would make this set of guidelines "more inflexible than that for Societies of the common life
without vows." Moreover tight rules "would hinder the definitive
regulation" of Secular Institutes. He consequently proposes doing
what the Code did in Title 17, setting few juridical requirements
and allowing for ample breadth. Thus the institutes can be dealt
with case by case, while giving first importance to the constitutions
of each institute. "This minimum would suffice for the present, but
it would be necessary. Thus the direction and paths to be followed
for future development would be pointed out and the correctness of
this development would be assured." Meanwhile such a step would
create "an adequate juridical foundation to make possible a unity of
procedure, regulation and competent forum." It would also respect
their individual nature, make possible the recognition of all of them
and endow them with the appropriate internal autonomy and
interdiocesan form of government. All would likewise depend on
the Congregation for Religious, the only body competent in the law
in force at that time for granting this form of government. Thus
"not only any harmful delay, but also any premature solution" would
be avoided.

As evidenced by the tone of *Provida Mater Ecclesia*, the legisla-
tor, on the basis of this and other studies, opted for a single set of
normative guidelines embracing all the "new forms" described in
the *votum* to which we have referred. He did not, however, act on
the suggestion of expressly pointing out the existence of the two
diverse kinds of institutes that *votum* refers to. Rather, on the other
hand, a wide and even generic (in more than one point) set of norms
is established.

It can be said that the legislation promulgated—the apostolic constitution *Provida Mater Ecclesia*, plus the Motu proprio *Primo feliciter* and the Instruction *Cum Sanctissimus* while slightly differing among themselves—results from an attempt to harmonize and balance different factors and situations, even divergent ones. The new figure arises from a compromise between factors and situations which came to light while preparing a new set of norms. Its promulgation moreover was urgently desired so as not to delay further the recognition of institutions seeking a solution. This balancing act and compromise is visible in the establishment of a broad juridical framework capable of embracing the greatest number possible of "new forms," so different one from another. It is also evidenced in the provision for a future evolution implicit in the *lex peculiaris* (art. II, § 2, 2°) and expressly affirmed in the Instruction *Cum Sanctissimus*. The compromise is also reflected in many particulars that came out while drafting *Provida Mater Ecclesia* and reflected in one way or another in the resulting set of norms. We point out two: the name with which the institutions regulated are designated, and the formula established by the *lex peculiaris* that differentiates them from the religious (art. II, § 1, 1°).

The name—Institute or Secular Institute—was born of much hard work and study. The 1939 Report of Fr. Gemelli speaks in its very title of "associations of lay people consecrated to God in the world." In the draft of norms sent to the Holy Office by the Congregation for Religious on March 6, 1945, after making it clear that these institutions are not religious orders or congregations or the societies of canon 673, they are called Religious Unions. The Congregation for Religious, in rewriting these norms, and in the draft discussed and approved in a meeting of May 11, 1945, of the special commission created for this purpose, gave them the name of Religious Sodalities. This name was retained in the penultimate draft decree (art. 1), which Fr. Larraona, incorporating what the commission agreed upon on May 11, 1945, included in his report a year later.[67]

This report explains the thinking of that commission in these words: "The name of *Sodalitia religiosa* approved after mature discussion corresponds *canonically* quite well to the object under consideration. *Sodalitia* is a name that corresponds to the *secular* character of these societies. It is a name taken from the title *De laicis* (canon 707 § 1). *Religiosa* alludes to the similarity with religious institutes and societies of common life. Thus these *sodalities*, which as such are not religious institutes nor societies of common life but rather coincide in the genus with other secular sodalities, have their own characteristics. These features clearly distinguish them from

---

[67] A. Larraona, *Società...*, *cit.* (note 50 of this chapter), I, part 2a, p. 34.

ordinary sodalities, while pointing to their affinity with religious life. The categorization of *religiosa* does not destroy the concept of sodality, but modifies it in a notable way." Then it adds: "It has to be said that *part*, perhaps *not the greatest part*, of these sodality members do not like to have *commonly* applied to them the word *religious*, lest they be *externally* confused with religious, a confusion that could cause harm to their apostolates and deform them."[68] Although in its opinion this confusion should not arise, the report nevertheless proposes other names in case the Sacred Congregation should desire to take them into account.[69] Among these it mentions that of Secular Institute, which Fr. Larraona included in the definitive draft of the decree later approved by the Sacred Congregation.[70] It was subsequently included in the text of the apostolic constitution.[71]

---

[68] *Ibid.*, pp. 35-36.

[69] "Certainly, the article is sufficiently clear (ad profitenda *in sæculo*, ut ab *aliis* fidelium associationibus distinguantur) and what it says is reaffirmed in the following articles (see for example art. 2) that confusions should not be possible or probable. Nevertheless if it is wanted to take into consideration the psychology of some of these sodality members, other possible names could be discussed. We propose some: *Societates perfectionis christianæ* or *Societates perfectionis et apostolatus*.

*Congregationes sæculares* -it would be the *contrariorum eadem est ratio* in relation to the religious sodality, that is to say, in the latter case the word *Sodalitia* is taken from secular terminology, and the word *religiosa* alludes to the similarity with religious institutes, while in the former case the formula *congregationes sæculares*, the word *congregationes* is taken from religious terminology (canon 488, 2°), and on the other hand the word *sæculares* (in place of *religiosæ* canon 488, 2°) would clearly indicate that it is not a question of religious institutes. *Instituta sæcularia* (perfectionis et apostolatus). The word *Instituta* in the Code is not a technical one nor is it reserved to religious orders or congregations or to societies of common life. The *juridical* use in the period preceding the Code and also the common use after the Code usually adopts it to refer to religious orders and congregations and to societies of common life. Therefore, this word would contain an allusion to firmer juridical structures than those of *Societies* or *Sodalities* with some similarity to religious orders and congregations. By adding the word *sæcularia* clear distinction from religious institutes is affirmed. The word *sæcularia* could also be eliminated, because it is not strictly necessary and it would not fit well for those cases in which *exceptionally* these *institutes* can be recognized as religious institutes as is said in the Instruction" (*Ibid.*, pp. 36-37).

[70] In one of his Letters the founder of Opus Dei, referring to the many factors at play in the writing of *Provida Mater Ecclesia*, pointed out that because of these divergent factors a compromise formula had been adopted. As a revealing sign of this compromise he mentions the question of the name: "At first they wanted to call these new institutions *religious sodalities* with the deliberate intention of showing with the name the nature of the commitment: *sodality* is an allusion to the associations of the faithful; *religious*, to the state of perfection. Since I could not consent to this ambiguity, we opposed this nomenclature, and that of *Secular Institutes* was accepted instead" (*Letter*, December 29, 1947/February 14, 1966, no. 167).

[71] In the previously mentioned *votum* (cf. note 66 of this chapter), and referring to the laborious path traveled in the drafting stage, specifically with respect to the name, we

A second point that shows the diversity of factors and situations, even opposed to one another, that gave rise to the compromise formulas of *Provida Mater Ecclesia*, is contained in art. II of the *lex peculiaris*. It affirms that these Secular Institutes "by law, and as a norm, (*iure, ex regula*) neither are nor can properly be called religious institutes (*religiones*, canons 487 and 488, no. 1) nor societies of common life (canon 673, § 1)."

This norm is not easy to interpret. Its meaning and its scope can nevertheless be glimpsed in the commentary Fr. Larraona made shortly after the promulgation of *Provida Mater Ecclesia*. "It is said that Secular Institutes neither are nor can they be called religious institutes or societies of common life, *iure, ex regula*. Certainly, *by way of exception*, it has been granted sometime and it could be granted again that some societies having the form and figure of Secular Institutes and properly juridically ordered as such, nevertheless *by way of dispensation* are truly religious institutes and their vows are considered as truly public."[72] The norm that is the object of commentary is evidently the fruit of a compromise, allowing it to contain both types of Secular Institutes referred to before: those whose members did not want to be religious or equated to them,[73] as well as those who did desire to be religious, even though they lacked some of the requirements called for by the 1917 Code, particularly canonical common life.

The compromise is even clearer if we turn to the antecedents to this article of *Provida Mater Ecclesia*. The draft norms sent by the Holy Office to the Congregation for Religious on March 6, 1945, characterized the class "new form" with the simple affirmation: "such association, neither is a religious institute nor a society governed by canon 673." It included no formula of equivalency with

read: "It seems difficult to me that a more fitting name could have been found for these new forms than that of Secular Institute. It is to be hoped that now this name will not be changed again, although certain pressures have been felt. 'Quod bonum est tenete.'" Perhaps these pressures gave rise—manifesting once again the spirit of compromise—to mentioning in art. I institutes without adding the qualifying word "secular", which some people did not like and this, despite the fact that *Provida Mater Ecclesia* generally uses the name, Secular Institute.

[72] A. Larraona,"Constitutionis 'Provida Mater Ecclesia' Pars Altera seu Legis Peculiaris Institutorum saecularium exegetica, dogmatica, practica illustratio," in *Commentarium pro Religiosis*, 28 (1949):173.

[73] We have referred to the continual affirmation of Opus Dei's founder that its members are not nor can they be considered religious or anything equivalent to them. In a Letter of 1949 he wrote: "I never concealed from the Curia what was the spirit of the Work. I began by pointing out very clearly, even before we were approved as a society of common life: we do not want to be sacred persons. Only the priests are" (*Letter*, Dec. 8, 1949, no. 43). And in another Letter from 1950, referring to the months preceding the promulgation of *Provida Mater Ecclesia*, he says: "I could relate to you many specifics

religious institutes nor the phrase *iure ex regula*. Expressions that do imply comparison with religious, nevertheless, appear in the various stages of the norms drafted by the Congregation for Religious.[74] In the final draft of its writing every formula of equivalency disappears.[75] The expression *iure ex regula* is nevertheless approved and included in article II of the *lex peculiaris*: doubtless an ambiguous phrase, but one that at least underlines clearly the essential difference.

The above points sufficiently document the balancing act or compromise that characterizes the 1947-48 legislation regarding Secular Institutes. When *Provida Mater Ecclesia* was published the commentator in *L'Osservatore Romano* presents it as a "historical document in the internal life of the Church."[76] That it is, to be sure, since it affirms most solemnly the possibility of full holiness and Christian life in the world amid ordinary secular occupations.[77] Nevertheless, it needs to be pointed out that this prospect is largely seen through the lens of the religious vocation. The development is viewed as an adaptation or rapprochement of the religious state to the world, rather than affirming the Christian potential of the secular or lay condition in all of the consequences.[78]

---

of our filial struggle during these months: the effort we made so that members of Secular Institutes not be considered sacred persons, as some wanted, but ordinary faithful, which is what they are; my concern to make it clear that we were not, nor could we be, religious" (*Letter*, Oct. 7, 1950, no. 20).

[74] In successive drafts we find the following formulas of equivalency: *ad instar religiosorum* (draft of March-April 1945); *totaliter ad instar religiosorum* (decision of the special commission in its meeting of May 11, 1945); *ad instar quadamtenus religiosorum*; *totaliter ad instar quodammodo religiosorum*. (A. Larraona, *Società...*, *op. cit.* note 50 of this chapter)

[75] With occasion of the name we mentioned the reaction of some of the new forms to the term "religious," whether applied directly or by equivalency. The *votum* quoted before (cf. note 66 of this chapter) explains their objection: "It is not a question of an anti-religious sentiment, but simply of a natural defense." Their position rests on these points: "1. The dignity and importance of the religious state. 2. Outside of this state there are also other possibilities and forms of perfection, which the Holy Spirit raises up, always corresponding to the special needs of different times. 3. These other forms are not necessarily religious by reason of their tendency towards perfection; nor are they 'quasi' and not even 'ad instar'. All of these forms within the Mystical Body complement and help each other."

[76] *L'Osservatore Romano*, March 14, 1947, p. 1.

[77] In fact *Provida Mater Ecclesia* is one of the documents to which the Constitution *Lumen gentium* of the Second Vatican Council refers in note 40 as antecedents in the Magisterium of modern times to the solemn proclamation of the universal call to holiness the Council wished to make and to which it dedicates this number and the following ones of the Constitution on the Church.

[78] This focus is particularly obvious in the introductory part of *Provida Mater Ecclesia*, though it shows up also in the *lex peculiaris* and in the other documents of 1948: *Primo Feliciter* and *Cum Sanctissimus*.

## 7. Opus Dei, a Secular Institute of pontifical right

Returning to the thread of our story, we call to mind the months previous to the promulgation of *Provida Mater Ecclesia*. On November 8, 1946, Fr. Josemaría once again left Spain for Rome. As previously, he passed through Barcelona where he again entrusted to our Lady of Ransom the negotiations awaiting him in the Eternal City to win pontifical approval. During the months in Spain he encouraged the general growth of the apostolate; he had personally overseen the final training of six members of Opus Dei to be ordained to the priesthood on September 29; he readied the expansion of the Work to Great Britain, Ireland and France; and he began to study the spread of apostolate to the American continents.

Once in Rome, he resumed conversations with members of the Roman Curia to expedite a juridical framework suitable for papal approval of the Work. On December 6, 1946, he wrote Opus Dei members in Madrid: "All of our efforts are going very well, but too calmly."[79] Two days later on the feast of the Immaculate Conception he was received in audience by Pope Pius XII. On the 16th he wrote again to those in Madrid: "Do not forget that it has been during the octave of the feast of the Immaculate Conception that the *solution* in Rome began to jell."[80]

The founder had grasped the difficulties in writing *Provida Mater Ecclesia*; consequently he knew the final result would not be completely satisfactory.[81] The usefulness, or better said, the need, of obtaining a juridical statute of pontifical right was ever before his eyes. The reasons that prompted him in February 1946 to send Alvaro del Portillo to Rome continued to press[82] and had even taken on new urgency. Furthermore the Sacred Congregation showed itself not only ready but avid to grant approval to Opus Dei as soon as possible. Was this opportunity to be shunned just because in some points it was only possible to obtain something provisional?

The efforts continued. On February 2, 1947, Pope Pius XII gave his consent to the apostolic constitution *Provida Mater Ecclesia*. Thus a juridical framework was established within which it was possible to proceed to the pontifical approval of Opus Dei. On February 14 the "Congress" of the Sacred Congregation for Religious, presided

---

[79] RHF, EF-461206-2.

[80] RHF, EF-461216-1.

[81] In the Letter quoted from frequently, whose first date of writing is 1947, he comments that *Provida Mater Ecclesia* is "the result of an emergency situation where many different factors and opposing situations were present," which led "to the fact of reaching a compromise formula" (*Letter*, December 29, 1947/February 14, 1966, no. 167).

[82] See section 1 of this chapter.

by its Prefect, Cardinal Lavitrano, favorably voted on this proposal. The Roman Pontiff in an audience granted to Cardinal Lavitrano on February 24 ratified their opinion. Thus Opus Dei with the Priestly Society of the Holy Cross was approved as a Secular Institute of pontifical right together with its *constitutions*. The decision of Pius XII was formalized in the *Decretum laudis*, entitled *Primum Institutum* and dated February 24, 1947.[83]

The following day the founder wrote to his daughters in Madrid: "Give thanks to the Lord for so many good things: the *decretum laudis!*" He shows himself to be optimistic and hopeful as a result of the approval. Opus Dei was thus given its international charter. But he doesn't hide the need to take further steps along the juridical path: "With these blessings of the Church we will overcome all obstacles, which furthermore are inevitable. Everything will be solved with the passage of years."[84]

The Decree opens by describing the path traveled hitherto by Opus Dei from its founding on October 2, 1928.[85] Among other things it mentions the apostolic work carried out with the approval and blessing of the ecclesiastical authorities, first as an association *de facto*, then as a pious union (1941), even more recently as a society of diocesan right (1943).[86] It also points out (something uncommon in this kind of document: "After long delays and many trials Opus Dei as a true work of God (Acts 5:39), having overcome neither few nor small hardships, proceeding even from good people, has grown and consolidated itself."[87]

---

[83] This Decree can be found in the Appendix, document no. 22. Although well known to every canonist, we recall that, unlike the Letter of praise of the aim granted in August 1946, the *Decretum laudis* of 1947 refers not only to the worthiness of its aim, but also to the institution as such, which is approved as a Secular Institute endowing it with a universal form of government of pontifical right.

[84] RHF, EF-470225-1.

[85] " . . . die Angelis Custodibus sacra, II octobris anni a nostra reparata salute MDCCCCXXVIII, Operis Dei ima atque solida fundamenta iacta sunt" (Decree *Primum Institutum* § 3).

[86] Both when speaking of the 1941 approval and the 1943 erection the decree points to Opus Dei as the object of these two interventions on the part of the ecclesiastical authority, using the generic name of the whole pastoral phenomenon, that is Opus Dei. With regard to the scope of both steps in its juridical evolution, see chapters 3 and 4.

[87] The founder refers to these troubles in the *Letter* of 1947/1966 to emphasize, among other things, the influence they had on the juridical study then being carried out: "By this God-given means after a rigorous study much deeper than is usually carried out, the Holy See has given us the *appositio manuum*, permission first for the diocesan erection and afterwards, as I said before, the *Decretum laudis*, the Decree of praise." Earlier there is an even broader statement: "These contradictions have done us a lot of good: because they have made us adults at a time when others are young with little or no personality; because they have given us extraordinary means to suffer in the Lord's

The Decree points to the great development of Opus Dei in recent years that makes papal approval at this time appropriate: the extension of its work to various countries, its imminent establishment in America; the variety of professions found among its members: physicians, lawyers, architects, military personnel, researchers, artists, writers, professors, students; and the depth of the apostolic work all of them are carrying out with their colleagues.

After a brief historical review it states that, precisely when Opus Dei's founder was turning to the Holy See to request the Decree of praise, the apostolic constitution *Provida Mater Ecclesia* was in its last stages. In the light of this document, "The Institute Opus Dei and its constitutions were studied in the Sacred Congregation, particularly those aspects of its internal structure, organization, activities and common life (taken in the broad sense of the word) that seemed to be more complex and entailed some novelty. It was thereupon concluded that Opus Dei corresponded in an exemplary way to the figure of Secular Institute foreseen by the same Apostolic Constitution."[88]

The Decree then describes the juridical features of the new Institute that we will see the following section. It concludes by establishing that the Holy Father Pius XII, "by the present Decree in accordance with the Apostolic Constitution *Provida Mater Ecclesia* and with the Constitutions, reviewed and approved by the Sacred Congregation for Religious, praises and recognizes Opus Dei with the Priestly Society of the Holy Cross as a Secular Institute under the authority of a sole Superior General, whose office is *ad vitam* and it declares it of pontifical right, safeguarding the rights of bishops according to the terms of the same Apostolic Constitution."

The Constitutions are a redraft of those of diocesan right from 1944, modified in the ways that reflect the negotiations held in Rome since February 1946. They were further integrated to stress the unity of the pastoral phenomenon that is Opus Dei; they were revised again in the light of subsequent events, especially the terminology established by *Provida Mater Ecclesia*. Thus we have the

---

service and to mature spiritually; because they have shown even more that the Work is not done by men but by God." He adds these difficulties, "even though they have made us suffer and they may still make us suffer for years yet to come, have served to etch, to engrave in stone, all the specific characteristics of our spirit and our special way of doing apostolate" (*Letter*, December 29, 1947/February 14, 1966, no. 2).

[88] The Congregation for Religious referred to other Secular Institutes it approved in similar words. For example: "Quis igitur in his summis lineamentis non viderit perfectam imaginem Instituti Saecularis prout SSmus. D.N. Pius Pp. XII, feliciter regnans, in Const. Apostolica *Provida Mater Ecclesia* instituit et creavit?" (Decree of approval of the Teresian Institute June 29, 1951, no. 8 in X. Ochoa, *Leges Ecclesiæ...*, cit. -chapter IV, note 32-, II, Rome 1969, no. 2223, col. 2910) The Decree of approval of the Society of the Heart of Jesus of February 2, 1952, uses identical terms (see *Commentarium pro*

Constitutions of a single Secular Institute, called "The Priestly Society of the Holy Cross and Opus Dei." The Constitutions consist of 363 points, divided in three parts; they deal with the nature of the Institute (nos. 1-202), its government (nos. 203-314), and of Opus Dei as an apostolic activity of the Institute (nos. 315-365).[89]

We close this section with mention of a complementary, though lesser, document. In an Apostolic Brief Pope Pius XII granted abundant indulgences to Opus Dei members for their manual work. On March 31, 1947, the Procurator General of the Institute had requested the Sacred Apostolic Penitentiary to grant these indulgences. On June 30 the Sacred Penitentiary responded affirmatively and passed the matter to the Secretariat of State, because the decision had been reached to authorize the indulgences by means of an Apostolic Brief. On July 20, 1947, Pope Pius XII, by means of *Mirifice de Ecclesia*, granted a plenary indulgence (or a partial indulgence according to the cases) to the members of Opus Dei when they offered their manual work to God with some invocation or ejaculatory prayer.[90]

Besides granting the indulgences, the Brief contains other points worthy of note. The narrative part begins by confirming the praise made in the *Decretum laudis*. Opus Dei "in the heart of the Church itself has grown in a short space of time from a small sprout to a flowering tree, praised and once again worthy of praise because of the work of its founder and supreme Moderator, Our Domestic Prelate, beloved son José María Escrivá de Balaguer y Albás."[91]

Turning directly to the indulgences, *Mirifice de Ecclesia* emphasizes that "the reason, the essence and the special end of Opus Dei is to be found in becoming holy through ordinary work."[92] In under-

---

*Religiosis*, 36 (1957):47.) We have, in a word, a declaration that tends towards becoming a commonplace. It stems from the broad character of the legislation contained in *Provida Mater Ecclesia* and the consciousness it displays of accommodating diverse, even heterogeneous institutions.

[89] The first chapter of these Constitutions is found in the Appendix, document no. 23. There the principal characteristics, the nature and purpose of the Institute are described.

[90] This document is found in the Appendix, document no. 24.

[91] On April 22, 1947, the founder was named Domestic Prelate of His Holiness (cf. *AAS*, 39 (1947):245). In the Appendix, document no. 25 is found the letter of Msgr. Montini that accompanies the diploma of this appointment.

[92] Among the many texts dedicated to work (some already mentioned) we present one more. In 1954 the founder wrote: " . . . Man was created *ut operaretur*. Work is a means with which man participates in creation: and therefore, not only is it worthy, of whatever kind it may be, but it is an instrument for achieving human perfection—earthly perfection—and supernatural perfection. . . . So the professional vocation is not merely a part, but a principal part of our supernatural vocation. Professional work, with all its consequences of duties of state, obligations and social relations, is not only the

lining the nucleus of Opus Dei's spirit, the Brief mentions the earlier Brief *Cum Societatis* of June 1946. It had previously granted indulgences to Opus Dei members dedicated to intellectual tasks—a grant now extended to manual work.

Thus, as the Holy Father points out, his paternal care extends to all the members of the Institute, with special mention of those women who, having received a vocation to Opus Dei, dedicate themselves professionally to domestic work, marking out consequently the universal reach of this tenet of Opus Dei. "Work is intimately bound to the very essence of the spirituality proper to the members of Opus Dei," the founder will write a few years later; "the exercise of one's own profession or occupation, high or humble according to human criteria. For God the importance of any job depends on the supernatural qualities brought to its execution. Therefore, without taking anybody out of his place, we have come to ennoble all human occupations. We give them a divine meaning even to the most modest manual labor—*ut . . . operemini manibus vestris* (1 Thess 4:11): may you work with your hands—the same labor that our God Jesus Christ the Lord dedicated himself for many years." This was the reason, he adds, for which "I requested of the Holy See and obtained abundant indulgences for this work: *opera manuum nostrarum dirige super nos* (Ps 89:17): direct the work of our hands."[93]

It is no wonder, then, that Opus Dei's founder always showed special appreciation and gratitude for this document.

## 8. The juridical characteristics of Opus Dei in the 1947 documents

What traits ought to be emphasized in the 1947 documents? Above all we will scrutinize the single reality that has two names. The *Decretum laudis* opens: "The first Secular Institute, which immediately after the approval of the apostolic constitution *Provida Mater Ecclesia* . . . has merited the *Decretum laudis*, is the Priestly Society of the Holy Cross and Opus Dei, briefly called Opus Dei."

---

environment where members of Opus Dei must seek Christian perfection, but it is the means and the way they use to obtain it: *exibit homo ad opus suum* (Ps 103:23) each one to his own work, knowing that he has to sanctify his job, sanctify himself in that job and sanctify others with that job" *Letter*, May 31, 1954, nos. 17-18).

[93] Letter quoted in previous note, no. 18. He continues: "Opus Dei, *operatio Dei*, work of God, demands that its members work—*maledictus qui facit opus Domini fraudulenter* (Jer 48:10)—that each one have a profession or definite occupation—*munus publicum*— well known by all, because work is for all members of Opus Dei, I repeat, a means of sanctification and apostolic action. . . . An essential part of this work, the sanctification of ordinary work, which God has entrusted to us, is to do the work itself well, also with human perfection, the faithful fulfillment of all professional and social obligations."

Why a longer and abbreviated name? The founder always spoke of the Work or Opus Dei to refer to the pastoral phenomenon in its entirety: laity and priests, men and women, single and married. We recall that with the first diocesan approval—pious union (1941)—mention is made of "men and women, married and celibate" members. It was also foreseen that priests—necessary for the spiritual attention of other members—would have to come from its lay male ranks.

The hurdles to be surmounted to achieve the proper juridical regulation of such a broad pastoral phenomenon did not escape the knowledge of the founder. The most immediate and important was the ascription to Opus Dei of priests from among the lay members. Thanks to the light received on February 14, 1943, the canonical solution of this question was found, even though in a provisional juridical form, by the establishment of the Priestly Society of the Holy Cross as a society of diocesan right, according to Title 17 of the Code of Canon Law. To it was essentially linked, under the name of Opus Dei, an association of the faithful, made up of men and women, married and single, of various professions and social conditions. To it also belonged the members of the Priestly Society of the Holy Cross. This formula, allowing apostolic work to continue and spread, was no tailor-made suit; it brought its problems. Opus Dei, the fundamental pastoral phenomenon embracing at its deepest the Priestly Society of the Holy Cross, nevertheless appeared juridically as something secondary.[94]

The progress achieved in 1947 is of great importance. The Decree *Primum Institutum*, in its normative part, approves Opus Dei along with the Priestly Society of the Holy Cross (*Opus Dei cum Societate Sacerdotali Sanctæ Crucis*) as a single Secular Institute of pontifical right under the authority of a President General. This is why it calls it "the Priestly Society of the Holy Cross and Opus Dei, briefly called Opus Dei." The unity of the pastoral phenomenon is thus juridically expressed. This is reflected in the 1947 Constitutions. Number 1 establishes that the Institute is called the "Priestly Society of the Holy Cross and Opus Dei." In no. 5 it says, "the name Opus Dei belongs to the whole Institute" (*denominatio Operis Dei pertinet ad universum Institutum*).

Leaving a detailed analysis of these juridical texts for when we deal with the definitive approval,[95] we limit ourselves now to a brief review of *Primum Institutum* and the 1947 Constitutions.

---

[94] We dealt extensively with this in chapter 4.

[95] The 1950 *Constitutions* are a rewriting of those of 1947. Therefore to repeat the analysis would lead us to useless repetitions. We will leave this study for chapter 7, where as often as is necessary we will point out the changes introduced in comparison

Opus Dei is described as a Secular Institute "dedicated to acquiring Christian perfection in the world and to the exercise of the apostolate," in accordance with the apostolic constitution *Provida Mater Ecclesia*.[96] As noted earlier, this apostolic constitution, while exempting Secular Institutes from the law of religious,[97] declares that the principal source of their regulation would be their own constitutions. In the face of such a variety of institutional candidates to become secular institutes, this was a wise move. Of course the constitutions in each case would have to be prudently adapted to the general and special norms (the apostolic constitution and those the Sacred Congregation for Religious might lay down). "The ends, needs and circumstances of each of the Institutes differ not a little from one another (*non parum inter se diversis*)."[98] With *Primum Institutum* and the 1947 Constitutions, within the framework of the general law of Secular Institutes, the essential characteristics of Opus Dei's spirit and apostolate are recognized.

*Primum Institutum*, in keeping with the reality of Opus Dei, described it as largely composed of lay people, men and women, who form two branches (*Opus Dei ex duabus quasi sectionibus constat, virorum nempe et mulierum*).[99] In sketching some of the spiritual and apostolic traits of members, the *Decretum laudis* properly acknowledges the role of work: "The Institute constantly promotes the holiness of its members by the sanctification of ordinary work and the diligent and careful exercise of the occupation or the civic and public offices proper to each one."[100] The Constitutions repeatedly return to this essential feature; let us see but two references. Number 4 says Opus Dei inculcates in its members "the perfect fulfillment of their job-related tasks, including those carried out in civil service, wherein one is to seek perfection in his own state." The goals of sanctity and apostolate, we read in no. 317, "are obtained by sanctifying ordinary work and exercising one's professional calling or equivalent work; members never exempt themselves from working, because they seek sanctification by means of their work."

Following the Roman Curia's praxis, the Decree also describes a sample of apostolic activities, which, always in accordance with their lay condition, Opus Dei members may carry out. Of the men it says: "The specific apostolate of members of Opus Dei is exer-

---

with the text of 1947. The outline and general content of the 1947 Constitutions has been summarized in previous pages.

[96] *Primum Institutum* § 6; *1947 Constitutions* , no. 1.

[97] *Provida Mater Ecclesia*, art. II, § 1, 2°.

[98] *Ibid.*, § 2, no. 3.

[99] *Primum Institutum*, § 8; see also *1947 Constitutions*, nos. 337, 342, 347 and 348.

[100] *Primum Institutum*, § 6.

cised principally: by sanctifying one's occupation; by the example of a Christian life in one's social relations; by the religious and professional education of students, principally university students; by exemplary fidelity in the exercise of public offices; by spreading the doctrine of Catholic faith by word, writing and other means most appropriate for its propagation."[101] With respect to women it partially lists some apostolates analogous to those for men (oral and written Catholic propaganda, residences for students, schools) and others more appropriate to women: "fostering Christian modesty among women with the most appropriate means; fostering training centers for domestic service; taking charge of the domestic work of the Institute's centers in a completely autonomous locale, so that always with one single decree of erection there are generally speaking two separate centers of Opus Dei in each one of its domiciles."[102]

Coherent with the personal pursuit of holiness and the personal exercise of apostolate, the founder saw Opus Dei as a "great catechesis." It offers members and others who participate in its apostolate the best possible training in interior life and instruction in Church teaching, adapted to the background of each. The 1947 Decree declares that Opus Dei "seeks first of all the spiritual and apostolic training of its members; then, the members carry out apostolate as would any other citizen."[103] In the service of spiritual formation and the primacy of personal apostolate, the Institute "promotes and directs institutions and undertakings that offer intellectual and spiritual instruction, such as residences for students, retreat houses and others of this kind."[104]

In the context of one's job and the social and cultural activity of ordinary Christians essential to Opus Dei, *Primum Institutum* also refers to the freedom in temporal matters of Opus Dei members, one of the hallmarks of its spirit. "With regard to the professional activities of the members and the stances, be they social, political and the like, of each Opus Dei member, each one enjoys complete freedom within the limits of Catholic faith and morals. The Institute appropriates neither the professional work nor the social, economic, political activities of any of its members."[105] Elsewhere it

---

[101] *Ibid.*, § 9.

[102] Parallel descriptions are found in the 1947 Constitutions, nos. 345 & 359. We emphasize that these enumerations are not exhaustive but rather only by way of example. The apostolate of members of Opus Dei—as that of all lay people in general—cannot be reduced to a list of functions or tasks. All the facets of social, professional and family life can be apostolic; as Msgr. Escrivá liked to say, "a sea without shores." As we will see further on, as soon as it was possible, this listing was eliminated.

[103] *Primum Institutum*, § 9; similar words in *1947 Constitutions*, nos. 4 & 339.

[104] *1947 Constitutions*, no. 4.

[105] *Primum Institutum*, § 9.

adds, as with other ordinary citizens, "[members] strive to fulfill all their civic obligations and to exercise all their rights. When they carry out various apostolic activities, they always show the maximum reverence and respect for the civil laws of each region or country. . . ."[106]

Two more facets are of great import:

a) First, both in the *Decretum laudis* and in the 1947 Constitutions, the commitment to pursue full holiness in the world concomitant with the vocation to Opus Dei is clearly manifested. Thus, in accord with *Provida Mater Ecclesia*, a formula is used—one common at the time to all institutions the Church recognized as ways of striving for holiness—that identifies the generic end of the Institute as "the sanctification of its members, by keeping the evangelical counsels and observing its own special constitutions."[107] It then adds that the struggle for holiness takes place in the world (*in sæculo*), a point on which many texts insist.[108] "None of the members of the Priestly Society of the Holy Cross and Opus Dei are religious."[109] Besides the general declaration of *Provida Mater Ecclesia*,[110] the decree affirms that "they do not lead the common life of religious, nor do they profess religious vows, nor do they wear a religious habit."[111] The Decree continues: "Externally in all the things common to people of the world, so long as they do not detract from the state of perfection, they act as do their peers of the same social condition and calling."[112] For this reason, not being religious, the Constitutions repeat that neither their persons,[113] nor their houses,[114] are sacred. Neither are they to adopt any external manifestations displaying or implying a lack of naturalness proper to ordinary citizens.[115] Such naturalness also leads them to be personally and

---

[106] *Ibid.*, § 10. "The members, as ordinary citizens, fulfill their duties and exercise their rights." (*1947 Constitutions*, no. 82) and "they have the highest regard for the legitimate laws of civil society" (*1947 Constitutions*, no. 339).

[107] *Primum Institutum*, § 6; *1947 Constitutions*, no. 3.

[108] *Primum Institutum*, § 6; *1947 Constitutions*, no. 1.

[109] *Primum Institutum*, § 10.

[110] *Provida Mater Ecclesia*, art. II, § 1.

[111] *Primum Institutum*, § 10.

[112] *Ibid.*

[113] "The clerics wear the clerical garb common to the place where they live and the lay people dress as do the other members of their social class or profession" (*1947 Constitutions*, no. 7). Similarly *1947 Constitutions*, nos. 77 and 355.

[114] " . . . In their domiciles there is nothing of an external nature evocative of a religious house" (*1947 Constitutions*, no. 81).

[115] The Constitutions go on to say that the Institute "does not use any term by which to designate members" (*1947 Constitutions*, no. 88); " . . . membership in the Institute has no external manifestations" (*1947 Constitutions*, no. 89); "therefore no form of insignia

collectively humble.[116] May it be superfluous to point out that these prescriptions are no tactic or penetration scheme, but logically follow from the secular condition of Opus Dei members. In 1947 the founder commented on these passages of the *Decretum laudis* and the Constitutions: "Members of Opus Dei are not religious: they are ordinary Christians dedicated for life to serve the Church, according to the Constitutions approved by the Church; but without being religious . . . they dress as any other person of their social class, without anything strange, always within the norms of Christian morality . . . they are not religious without a habit: they do not wear a habit, because they are not religious."[117]

b) The second point relates to the article of *Provida Mater Ecclesia* that foresees either lay or clerical Secular Institutes.[118] The 1947 documents refer to the Priestly Society of the Holy Cross and Opus Dei, with the abbreviated name Opus Dei, as an Institute *prævalenter clericale*.[119] This did not detract from the fact that the reality of Opus Dei was—and is—that of an institution most of whose members are lay people. Thus the 1947 texts in referring to members speak fundamentally of lay people—men and women—ordinary citizens, etc., thus clarifying the characteristics of the pastoral phenomenon. For this reason the *Decretum laudis* itself contains the following crucial declaration: "Opus Dei, even though by the ordinary condition of its members, seems to be a lay Secular Institute (canons 488, no. 4; 673, § 2; *Provida Mater Ecclesia*, art. I), nevertheless, because of the Priestly Society of the Holy Cross, which completely informs it, is defined expressly in the Constitutions (no. 2) as a prevalently clerical Institute, juridically equivalent to clerical Institutes."[120] Thereupon the decree declares that Opus Dei is made up of two branches, one for men, the other for women, each with its own organizational structure, united only in the President General or in his delegates; and in each region in the person of the Regional Counselor.[121]

---

is allowed that would separate members from their fellow citizens whether clerics or lay people" (*1947 Constitutions*, no. 90).

[116] "All love and foster humility, not only personal but also collective; thus they never seek glory for the Institute but rather they have well engraved in their souls that the greatest glory of our Institution is to live without human glory" (*1947 Constitutions*, no. 108).

[117] AGP, Sezione Giuridica, IV/15528.

[118] *Provida Mater Ecclesia*, art. I.

[119] *Primum Institutum*, § 7; *1947 Constitutions*, no. 2.

[120] *Primum Institutum*, § 7.

[121] *Ibid.*, § 8.

By the designation of the Institute as *prævalenter clericale*, juridically equivalent to clerical Institutes—*juridice clericalibus Institutis æquiparandum*—the organic unity of the pastoral phenomenon and the necessary internal autonomy are guaranteed in law. Opus Dei was likewise guaranteed the requisite priestly attention with the ascription to the Institute of priests proceeding from its lay members. This is no inconsiderable facet, rather a fundamental aspect of the charism the defense of which constitutes a constant objective along the juridical evolution of Opus Dei. To eliminate any doubt as to whether this equivalence of Opus Dei to clerical Institutes applied to the whole Institute, including the women's branch, as well as to the scope of this equivalence, Opus Dei's Procurator General presented this question to the Holy See. On August 7, 1947, the Sacred Congregation for Religious declared itself in agreement with the Procurator's statement. Namely, since "our whole Institute, that is, the Priestly Society of the Holy Cross and Opus Dei *'juridice clericalibus Institutis æquiparandum esse'*", canons 618 § 2 and 512 § 2, no. 2, i.e. the precepts of the Code regulating the competency of local ordinaries with respect to clerical Institutes of pontifical right, should be applied to the whole Institute.[122]

Besides assuring the organic unity of Opus Dei, this setup guaranteed its union with papal and episcopal authority. Relevantly the *Decretum laudis* states: "All the members of Opus Dei manifest always and in everything a great love, reverence and obedience for ecclesiastical superiors, bearing in mind that in the Church there is only one hierarchy of divine right, made up of the Roman Pontiff and the bishops, whom the Holy Spirit has given to govern the Church of God. Consequently all have well engraved in their souls that the internal hierarchy is completely consecrated to serving the hierarchy of the Church."[123] In the Constitutions these same expressions are found word for word.[124] It is further established that "members of the Institute are obliged humbly to obey the Superiors in everything pertaining to the end of the Institute. This obligation of obedience binds all of our members with a strong and sweet bond first of all in everything having to do with the Roman Pontiff, then of all the Superiors. They are submitted to the local Ordinaries, according to the common law, and they will show for them the greatest reverence and love, sentiments they should also foster unstintingly among all others."[125]

---

[122] This rescript is found in the Appendix, document no. 26.

[123] *Primum Institutum*, § 10.

[124] *1947 Constitutions*, nos. 87 and 332.

[125] *1947 Constitutions*, no. 62.

Our panoramic view of the 1947 documents is concluded. Nevertheless it may be beneficial to evaluate the whole configuration of Opus Dei as a Secular Institute in the texts of this date. The advantages of this step in the juridical development of Opus Dei are these: papal approval whereby the Church recognizes Opus Dei as a way of holiness and apostolate amid the world, in the ordinary circumstances of life, work, commitments, duties and rights; an interdiocesan (international) juridical statute that expedites a universal apostolic expansion; consolidation of the unity of the single pastoral phenomenon that is the Work; equating Opus Dei with clerical Institutes of pontifical right, thereby guaranteeing the necessary internal autonomy and priestly attention, while endowing the President General with certain faculties that juridically assure the Work's unity, with a single government embracing everyone incorporated in Opus Dei: priests and lay people, men and women.

The juridical solution of 1947, nonetheless, also came with limitations and shortcomings. The founder of Opus Dei usually pointed out two: 1) In accordance with *Provida Mater Ecclesia*, Opus Dei remained dependent upon the Sacred Congregation for Religious, which in time would lead to confusion. 2) The application of this legislation set Opus Dei in the context of the states of perfection, something foreign to its spiritual reality.[126] Certainly *Provida Mater Ecclesia* declares that members of Secular Institutes are not religious, and the Decree *Primum Institutum* and the 1947 Constitutions reaffirm this with regard to Opus Dei. No less certain also is the fact that the figure of Secular Institutes is a significant step forward over the Society of common life, then organized *ad instar religiosorum*. Its advantages explain why the founder reached out to this figure created in 1947.

A better "fit," however, is no reason to forfeit a best fit. In truth, the serious ambiguities of *Provida Mater Ecclesia* reflected its unwieldy breadth, as pointed out earlier. The founder emphasized this from the very start.[127] This ambiguity was bound to affect the texts as they related to Opus Dei, even though Msgr. Escrivá made every effort to avoid negative repercussions—or at least to counterbalance them.

---

[126] With regard to dependence upon the Sacred Congregation for Religious, he wrote: "with this dependence we can foresee not a few dangers for the future" (*Letter*, December 29, 1947/February 14, 1966, no. 167). In the same Letter he refers also to the second difficulty, as we will see in note 128 of this chapter.

[127] See section 6 of this chapter. A paragraph from a *Letter* previously cited: "The juridical statute obtained with *Provida Mater Ecclesia*, a document resulting from an emergency situation, where very diverse factors and opposing situations have come together, has led to a compromise formula. . . ." Later he adds this Apostolic Constitution "is—as a fruit born of compromise—obscure, but opportune and necessary. . . ." Still later: "In any case, it seems that, for the moment and related to us, it has been

It should be noted that in the *Constitutions* of the Priestly Society of the Holy Cross and Opus Dei approved in 1947 frequent mention is made not only of "Christian perfection," "sanctification," "dedication," "progress in spiritual life," etc., but also of "evangelical counsels" or other expressions common in the religious literature with respect to the states of perfection. But nowhere does the formula of "state of perfection" as such appear. It does say, on the other hand, in no. 4 of the Constitutions, that the Institute fosters in its members "the perfect fulfillment of their professional tasks," adding "it is in them that they must seek perfection of their own state": *quibus perfectio proprii status est prosequenda.* Number 322 declares that, to be admitted in Opus Dei, the candidate is required to "strive for his own sanctification by means of the observance of the evangelical counsels according to his own state": *per observantiam consiliorum evangelicorum proprio statui conformium.* Throughout, the 1947 documents stress that Opus Dei members should sanctify themselves and be apostolic according to their own occupation and in their own walk in life.[128]

The need to accept the context of the states of perfection as required by the guidelines for Secular Institutes, while affirming that Opus Dei members seek sanctity, Christian perfection, without

---

established that members of Secular Institutes are not religious nor sacred persons; and that, even though they make a consecration to God—which we call dedication—they continue being *sæculares*, ordinary *sæculares*, i.e., lay people (if they are not priests) ordinary citizens. And they belong to the genus and body of Associations of the faithful" (*Letter*, December 29, 1947/February 14, 1966, nos. 167 & 181). See also note 75 of this chapter.

[128] The contrast between both formulas—"state of perfection" and "sanctification in one's own state"—will henceforth be constant in the writings of the founder of Opus Dei. We mention, for now, only a few texts taken from the *Letter* from which we have been quoting: "We have never thought of belonging to the *state of perfection*. On the contrary: we have always preached and tried to practice that each one must seek *Christian perfection*, in the middle of the world and *in the state proper to him* . . . by the fact of belonging to the Work, *one does not change his or her state in life*; each one continues in the state he had . . . each one in his own state, in his own occupation, in his own intellectual or manual profession, in his own civil and public life . . . the members of the Work *seek Christian perfection in their own state and in the exercise of their own proper profession or occupation in the middle of the world* . . . [in the Work] "there is no change of state [and therefore] no external manifestation to signify a juridical change in the members of Opus Dei in their social life because the only change is exclusively spiritual and private. It is a light enkindled in the soul, a fire that burns more and more, a generous correspondence to the abundant and special grace of God" (*Letter*, December 29, 1947/February 14, 1966, nos. 84, 92, 151, 167, 171; the underlining is the author's). The statements with regard to "not changing one's place" were quite frequent many years before in *Consideraciones espirituales* and in *The Way*, from a different perspective, but they largely coincide with that of the meaning of these years (see, for example, *The Way*, nos. 832 & 837); for a commentary on these points see P. Rodríguez, "Vocación, trabajo, contemplación," *cit.* (chapter II, note 49), pp. 97ff).

changing their state, discharging their occupations amid the world and secular circumstances is fraught with potential friction. No wonder then that in a single 1947 document are found, as the founder will say, "affirmations that have obliged me to accept or concede, and others diametrically opposed to what seemed to be conceded. . . . It's not as though I said one thing and wrote another, no. Everything was in writing, so that each one of the consultors, of the employees, of the prelates who intervened, could see the sincerity of my concessions and of my contrary affirmations. . . . I realize the law is not made for a particular case: it has to do with the common good. Owing to this, it was reasonable we should make concessions, while trying to show that our particular case within the general law was resolved without altering anything essential in the nature of the Work, so far as this was possible."[129]

It goes without saying that all of this pointed to an unstable situation open to further changes. Even more, profound changes in the environment were to come and a maturing of ideas. This in fact is what happened in successive years. The process passes through a new approval Opus Dei received in 1950 and culminates beginning in the 1960s.

---

[129] *Letter*, December 29, 1947/February 14, 1966, no. 168.

# Chapter VI

## PREPARATIONS FOR A NEW PONTIFICAL APPROVAL

# Chapter VI

## PREPARATIONS FOR
## A NEW PONTIFICAL APPROVAL

### 1. Opus Dei before the new approval of the Holy See

Little more than three years passed between the Decree of Praise (February 24, 1947) and Opus Dei's definitive approval on June 16, 1950. Then the Holy See, by means of the Decree *Primum inter*, completed its recognition of the Work of God as a Secular Institute of pontifical right in conformity with article VII, paragraph 3, of the Apostolic Constitution *Provida Mater Ecclesia*.[1] In such a short period of time, Opus Dei had grown significantly, thanks to the tenacious energy of the founder, who was likewise engaged at the Holy See furthering the Work's juridical development. Opus Dei's growth was manifested in the number of members, the territorial extension of its apostolate and the formation of an organizational structure required to accommodate this expansion.[2]

With respect to the number of members, in 1946 there were 268 (239 in the men's branch and 29 in the women's). Early in 1950 they totaled 2945 (2404 men and 550 women).[3] In 1946 when the founder

---

[1] Once having obtained the *Decretum laudis*, Institutes and Societies subject to the Congregation for Religious could receive a new decree of approval from the Holy See. This new approval was called definitive approval, because, once granted, it did not have to be renewed. This definitive approval of the Institute coincided with an approval, also definitive, of its constitutions or statutes.

[2] This is pointed out in the Decree *Primum inter* extending definitive approval; in its second paragraph referring to the growth in the number of members it says: "ita, Dei benignitate, multiplicatus fuit, ut parvum granum sinapis in dominico agro seminatum, quasi in magnam arborem mirum in modum creverit" (the complete text is found in the Appendix, document no. 31).

[3] These and other data cited later are for the most part taken from the Report on the state or situation of Opus Dei presented by its founder to the Holy See, when request-

came to Rome there were four priests in Opus Dei, by 1950 there were 23. Meanwhile another 46 members of the Work were preparing for ordination; of these, 11 were completing their ecclesiastical studies in several pontifical universities in Rome.

Opus Dei first expanded outside of Spain with Msgr. Escrivá's trips to Portugal in 1945, followed in 1946 by the start of apostolate there in a stable way. The same year saw apostolic activity begin in Great Britain, Italy, Ireland and France. In April 1948 several members traveled for some months throughout North and South America to study the possibiliies for Opus Dei to establish itself in the New World. On their return the founder decided to launch apostolate in a stable manner in 1949 in both Mexico and the United States. In 1950 work began in Chile and Argentina.[4]

By June 1950 there were more than 100 centers of Opus Dei distributed through various countries of Europe, America and Africa.[5] This quadrupled the number of those in existence in 1946. The territorial divisions foreseen in the statutes of the pious union of 1941 (*Régimen*, art. 27f), and later in the 1947 *Constitutions* (no. 276) had become a reality by 1950. The 1947 *Constitutions* called for a single kind of territorial division called a Region. To expedite further growth, in 1948 the founder requested of the Holy See that, besides Regions (which normally comprise all the centers in a country), there also be other divisions: on the one hand, Quasi-Regions and Delegations dependent upon the President General (divisions lacking some of the elements required for a Region, but soon to become one); and, on the other, Delegations dependent on the Regional Counselor (territorial divisions within a Region as apostolic growth demanded it). The Holy See agreed to this petition on October 25, 1948.[6] Thus the progressive consolidation of the governing structure was achieved. In mid-1950 Opus Dei was distrib-

---

ing the definitive approval in 1950 (AGP, Sezione Giuridica, V/15532). To understand the difference in the development between the men's branch and the women's branch, one must bear in mind that the apostolate which Msgr. Escrivá directed towards the development of the women's branch began in the 1930s but was cut short by the Spanish Civil War (1936-1939). Msgr. Escrivá had to begin again practically from zero in 1939. About these events see S. Bernal, *op. cit.* (chapter I, note 1), pp. 135-142; F. Gondrand, *op. cit.* (chapter I, note 1), pp. 73-74, 92-93, 167-168; A. Vázquez de Prada, *op. cit.* (chapter I, note 1), pp. 131-132, 206-207.

[4] See S. Bernal, *op. cit.* (chapter I, note 1), pp. 299-301; F. Gondrand, *op. cit.* (chapter I, note 1), pp. 215-216 and 223.

[5] *Primum inter*, § 2.

[6] This rescript is found in the Appendix, document no. 27. At this time Msgr. Escrivá also wrote to the Holy See to define further other aspects of the government of Opus Dei that the expansion of the Work and the experience made him see as appropriate. Thus, for example, with respect to overall government, he requested the help of a priest (the central Priest Secretary) who would help the President General in directing

uted into the following territorial divisions: the Region of Spain (comprising also the Spanish possessions of Africa and recent centers in France and Ireland); the Quasi-Regions of Portugal, Italy, Mexico and the United States; and the Delegations of England, Argentina and Chile.

To provide for the doctrinal and theological training of Opus Dei's new members, Centers of Study were also established. There members could be educated and formed without having to separate themselves from their workaday environments. By 1950 the men's branch had seven of these Centers (and eight more in the preparation stage); the women's branch had four. All the professors of these Centers were required to hold doctorates in their respective subject matters; some, concurrently, were university professors of these subjects or held analogous positions in civil universities.

These few facts (but a few brush strokes in fact, with the coldness inherent to statistics) bear witness to Opus Dei's growing maturity, particularly if we bear in mind the wide-ranging professions and occupations its members were engaged in.

## 2. Marriage, a christian vocation

Opus Dei's development in these years is reflected in the spread of its apostolic work but in other ways as well. Beginning in 1947 the founder, with pontifical approval in hand, could take some steps to incarnate more fully the foundational charism. He had perceived these dimensions at the very start, but so far had been able to give them only partial expression.

In 1928 Msgr. Escrivá saw Opus Dei reaching people of all ages and walks of life: young and old, single and married, men and women, laborers and professionals. His priestly concern sought to reach all and sundry. Very soon he realized he must concentrate, for some years, on university students. Promoting vocations among those who would commit themselves to apostolic celibacy would lay the foundation for other apostolic endeavors.

*The Way*, written precisely in and for those years, discloses one of the dimensions: "Do you laugh because I tell you that you have a 'vocation to marriage?' Well you have just that, a vocation. Commend yourself to St. Raphael that he may keep you pure as he did Tobias, until the end of the way."[7]

---

the women's branch; so also the creation of an analogous position (the regional Priest Secretary) for each of the Regions. He also requested adding a Secretary to complete the government of the territorial Commissions. These and other similar requests were approved by a rescript of the Holy See on January 27, 1949. (It is found in the Appendix, document no. 28.)

[7] *The Way*, no. 27.

These are not mere words or a simple declaration of principles. Particularly during the '40s, Msgr. Escrivá spiritually tended to many people whom he saw God was calling to marriage and to others already married. Entrusting the former to St. Raphael and the latter to St. Gabriel, he tried to open new horizons of sanctity to them, vistas of a full Christian life and apostolate. This was the case of Professor Víctor García Hoz, who regularly went to confession with Fr. Josemaría, who told him one day in 1941: "God is calling you to paths of contemplation." Married, with children, teaching and doing research in the University of Madrid, García Hoz was astonished. "In those years it was almost inconceivable that a married man," he said, writing of himself, "should be encouraged to strive for contemplation as something that he had to achieve."[8] The founder spoke to García Hoz and others of the prospect of formally joining Opus Dei when the right channel had been opened. Meanwhile he told them "begin to live the Norms and Customs of the Work without any actual bond with it."[9]

This way of acting is very telling. It shows Msgr. Escrivá's keen awareness of what steps to take to ratify Opus Dei's basic message. Juridically, since 1941 Opus Dei had been a simple pious union that could admit both single and married people without any problem. Rather, the challenge was theological: the founder was not inviting people to partial decisions or halfway commitments, but to a full, radical decision to lead a Christian life. Back in the '40s the idea of tending to sanctity in marriage was far from universal acceptance. Still less so as part of an institution whose purpose was to foster unconditional Christian perfection precisely in the world (of all places!) The universal call to holiness was not yet common doctrine then and thus was not echoed in pastoral practice. The founder was aware of it and concious that he could not take the appropriate steps to welcome spouses so long as the necessary juridical recognition had not been extended. He felt bound to seek express Church acknowledgement that Opus Dei was a true way to Christian perfection, holiness, for ordinary people, both single and married. Con-

---

[8] See S. Bernal, op. cit. (chapter I, note 1) p. 111. Professor García Hoz himself tells how in the early 1940s Msgr. Escrivá specified these paths of contemplation: "I realized the exquisite respect that the Father had for my opinions, work and professional aspirations. His constant concern was that I manage to live in God's presence continually, offering all my work, joys and difficulties to God, purifying my intention as often as necessary so that God's service and glory become my dominant motive. I should also take care of the details of whatever task and try to work well and finish things so as to offer something worthy to God. He also fanned my idealism in my professional work, the principal means of sanctification God had placed within my reach. I should also love my wife and my children each day more and more" (Deposition of Víctor García Hoz, July 15, 1975, in RHF, T-1138).

[9] V. García Hoz, loc. cit.

scious of the radical demands of baptism, both can seek to live them in ordinary, secular settings and spread them among their relatives, friends and colleagues. Meanwhile, with married people and with those in whom he detected signs of a marital vocation, Msgr. Escrivá limited himself to present these radical demands at an ascetical or spiritual level, without any formal membership in Opus Dei that would have to await the proper moment.

The 1947 *Constitutions*, describing the category of members, which includes married persons, focuses the topic in strictly spiritual terms. The charter reads: "Such members strive to live the spirit and apostolate of the Institution, without being incorporated into it by a juridical bond."[10]

Various texts from the same document reflect the depth of this spiritual decision. For example, married persons must also endeavor "to seek their own sanctification by the observance of the evangelical counsels in a way appropriate to their proper state (*proprio statui*)."[11] Here too, though generically, it is seen that a vocation to Opus Dei does not create a state, but that each sanctifies himself in the state already his in secular society.

There has also been a very significant change in terminology. As will be recalled, the 1941 texts, in speaking of different possibilities of dedication in keeping with personal circumstances, envision three. Numerary members are celibate and capable of dedicating themselves to tasks of government and formation; supernumeraries, also celibate, enjoy less freedom to commit themselves to these functions; finally, inscribed members, who can be either celibate or married.[12] In the 1947 *Constitutions* the term numeraries applies to those who with a celibate commitment are available for tasks of government and formation, while all other members are called supernumeraries.[13] It expressly says that married people can unite themselves to Opus Dei, but with no formal juridical link to the Institute.[14] Their intimate relationship with the Work, the reality of a profound spiritual commitment, a decision of total dedication, is reinforced,[15] al-

[10] 1947 *Constitutions*, no. 342, 3; see also in the same sense no. 347, 3.

[11] 1947 *Constitutions*, no. 322, 2.

[12] Cf. chapter III. The 1944 Constitutions retain the terminology of 1941.

[13] The name Inscribed members is retained in the text of 1947, but its meaning is changed. It describes those members of Opus Dei bound to it with a celibate commitment and with a special dedication to internal tasks of government or formation, owing to their personal aptitudes and work.

[14] 1947 *Constitutions*, no. 342.

[15] In a letter written on December 18, 1947 Msgr. Escrivá indicated that married persons or people with a vocation to marriage in contact with Opus Dei should be coura-

though the canon law of the day was not prepared to recognize it explicitly.[16]

The content and scope of the steps taken in this respect by Opus Dei's founder up to February 1947 come into sharper focus, if we study his actions subsequent to that approval. After the summer of 1947 he devoted himself particularly to some married persons who for some time had been seeking his spiritual guidance and to whom he had mentioned the possibility of binding themselves formally to Opus Dei. "You will be," he wrote to some of them on January 1, 1948, "the seed of thousands and thousands of brothers of yours, who will come sooner than we think."[17] Meanwhile, he reflected on the way to transform their ascetical bond with the Institute into a juridical one, thus making it a clear and explicit expression of their vocational commitment. On January 11, 1948, he reached a decision. On February 2 he addressed himself to the Holy Father requesting the approval of a statute to be added to the 1947 *Constitutions*. Its purpose would be juridically to incorporate into the Institute members other than numeraries, be they single or married, of any background or occupation. In the letter formulating this request Msgr. Escrivá stressed it was a question of putting into effect something foreseen from the start: *iam a prima ipsius Instituti delineatione*.[18] A month and a half later the Sacred Congregation for Religious in a letter signed by the Secretary, Archbishop Pasetto, and authenticated by the Undersecretary, Fr. Arcadio Larraona, approved the statute submitted.

This statute established that in the numbers of the 1947 *Constitutions* that speak of members of the Institute with a juridical bond (numeraries) a reference be made also to supernumerary members. It further specifies that these members "dedicate themselves partially to the service of the Institute and they employ as means of sanctification and apostolate their own family and occupations or work . . . they live the same spirit and, according to their individual possibilities, the same customs as the numerary members; although

---

geously confronted with the prospect of a full Christian life: "We cannot lose sight of the fact that they are not *signing up* for a particular association but answering a supernatural *vocation* to a life of perfection and apostolate. To be a supernumerary is a great grace of God!" (RHF, EF-471218-1)

[16] It is said in the text that canon law was not yet ready to receive this full vocational commitment, because, although *Provida Mater Ecclesia* implicitly allowed in article III § 2 the possibility of members *lato sensu*, its scope was only made more explicit by the Instruction *Cum Sanctissimus* (no. 7a). It was published after the events dealt with in these and successive paragraphs.

[17] RHF, EF-480101-1.

[18] This request is found in the Appendix, document no. 29.

they are to be entrusted only with tasks compatible with their natural family and civil obligations."[19]

At the end of September 1948, taking advantage of a trip to Spain, Msgr. Escrivá met at a conference center close to Madrid with 18 people who had been connected to the apostolates of Opus Dei for some time. Some had already juridically bound themselves to the Institute in preceding months. In meditations, talks and conversations he explained facets of Opus Dei's spirit, showing how it is to be incarnated in married and professional life. To those uncommitted to Opus Dei he suggested they maturely and serenely pray to discover if God was calling them to appropriate this spirit by binding themselves stably to the Institute. The response was unanimously positive.[20]

The apostolate of the supernumerary members of Opus Dei was thus not only juridically recognized but also launched in a practical way. On September 8, 1949, the founder received a rescript from the Holy See that particularized and completed the statute of March 18, 1948. Thus, within the category of supernumerary members (those who because of permanent circumstances of a personal, family or professional nature, cannot make themselves fully available for tasks of formation and direction) there can also be people who commit themselves to lead a celibate life as the numeraries. Because they require a specific training and pastoral attention, they are to be called internal supernumeraries (to distinguish them from supernumeraries with a matrimonial vocation).[21]

The importance, canonical as well as theological and spiritual, of these developments, is obvious. They reflect more fully the pastoral phenomenon of sanctifying the diversity of human situations to which Opus Dei was slated from the beginning. Then too the implications of the universal call to sanctity are emphasized. Consequently something of a juridical, canonical nature is likewise determined: the vocation to Opus Dei does not originate a new state in life, but rather leads one to sanctify one's own secular state and conditions. In successive stages we will see how the founder mines the rich lode of broadening membership possibilities—something simple in form but truly revolutionary in its implications. The new step further spurred growth in Opus Dei's apostolates. Of the 2404

---

[19] *Constitutionibus Operis Dei Addenda,* March 18, 1948 (AGP, Sezione Giuridica, V/15506). We point out that with this document the Sacred Congregation approved not only this article, but also other modifications of the 1947 *Constitutions,* specifically an addition to no. 1, whose importance we will see in the following chapter.

[20] RIIF, T-2769.

[21] This rescript is found in the Appendix, document no. 30.

members of the men's branch and the 550 of the women's branch early in 1950, 519 were male supernumeraries and 163 were female.[22]

## 3. Developments of the normative framework

The years after 1947 witness not only Opus Dei's growth, but also some developments in the legislation concerning secular institutes. They correspond to questions raised by the new Institutes. Considering these documents and ideas will help us interpret some aspects of the 1950 Decree of approval and other texts of that year. They are the immediate prelude to a further evolutionary process whose consequences will be evident later on.

The promulgation of *Provida Mater Ecclesia* evoked keen interest in many environments and institutions. In the months following the appearance of the Apostolic Constitution numerous petitions for the *nihil obstat* previous to the diocesan erection of secular institutes reached the Sacred Congregation for Religious, the only papal office competent in this matter according to the legal text. This influx of petitions, some from associations with little or nothing to do with the spirit and letter of *Provida Mater Ecclesia*, plus reactions to this document in various sectors, moved the Roman Pontiff on March 12, 1948 to promulgate the Motu proprio *Primo feliciter* which we referred to in the previous chapter.

In the final paragraphs of the narrative part of *Provida Mater Ecclesia*, Pius XII addressed himself to the Sacred Congregation for Religious, entrusting it with "all the necessary and appropriate faculties for carrying out this apostolic constitution." In its normative section, he empowered this Congregation to dictate necessary regulations, "according to the requirements of all or some of these Institutes interpreting the apostolic constitution, whether completing it or applying it."[23] The scope of the competency and faculties granted to the Congregation was given practical effect in the issuing of many regulations: the Instruction *Cum Sanctissimus*, March 19, 1948, applicable to all secular institutes; the Constitutions of each Institute, whose approval rested with the Congregation, which applied the few brief norms of the *lex peculiaris*, *Primo feliciter* and *Cum Sanctissimus* "to the goals, needs and circumstances diverse among themselves" of each Institute.[24]

---

[22] Data from the report mentioned in note 3 of this chapter.

[23] *Provida Mater Ecclesia*, art. II, § 2, no. 2. Article IV, § 1 entrusted competency over secular institutes to the Sacred Congregation for Religious; it was competent specifically to grant the previous permission for the erection of a secular institute (articles V and VI), and also the judgment on whether to grant the decree of praise and definitive approval (art. VII) and for the hierarchical ordering of the internal governance of these Institutes (art.IX).

[24] *Provida Mater Ecclesia*, art. II, § 2, 3.

The Congregation was cognizant of the radical novelty of these institutions with their apostolate of a secular style and tone in the most diverse environments. It took them under its responsibility and exercised its exclusive competence by means of declarations. On the basis of specific consultations it laid down criteria on particular questions; these pronouncements coalesced into a general orientation for all these institutions. Thus the Congregation developed its own jurisprudence: the official expression of its authentic mind. Little by little its official praxis in relation to secular institutes arose. Some of these declarations, resolutions and jurisprudential criteria, from the first years of secular institutes, were published in the review *Commentarium pro Religiosis*.[25] This made them more widely known. In fact they were considered by the Congregation and scholars[26] to be universal juridical developments of the normative framework set up by *Provida Mater Ecclesia*.

Although we are not making a complete analysis of secular institutes nor therefore of these documents and criteria, nevertheless it seems appropriate to point to aspects of special interest. Here we limit ourselves to listing these aspects with only indispensable comments and data.

a) *Primo feliciter* (no. II), as seen, gives particular emphasis to secularity, the essential purpose of this new juridical figure: "It

---

[25] Cf. *Commentarium pro Religiosis*, 28 (1949):292-345, where this material is presented in two sections: one dedicated to declarations and rescripts (pp. 292-307) and the other to jurisprudence (pp. 308-345).

The Sacred Congregation had a special interest in spreading these declarations and jurisprudential criteria, and so the same magazine published a special volume *De Institutis Sæcularibus*, Rome 1951, where the same two sections are retained. In the first section, "Decreta, Rescripta, Formulae (authenticae resolutiones S.C. de Religiosis)," pp. 182ff, the declarations and resolutions issued in response to five specific questions are reproduced, along with the annotations and commentaries of Fr. Fuertes and Fr. Larraona, at the time the Undersecretary of the Congregation. The first of these consultations was from 1947 and the most recent from 1949. One was presented by the Misioneras de la Realeza de Nuestro Señor Jesucristo; the other by the Instituto de los Siervos de la Santa Iglesia; and the three others by then Procurator General of Opus Dei, Fr. Alvaro del Portillo. Del Portillo at the time was also Secretary of the Special Commission created within the Congregation to study all matters having to do with secular institutes and to oversee their development (see chapter 5, note 59). The second section is entitled "Iurisprudentiae pro Institutis saecularibus hucusque conditae summa lineamenta," pp. 198ff, under the direction of Fr. Larraona and Fr. Gutiérrez. It published in systematic form the jurisprudential criteria and the praxis followed by the Congregation in studying questions pertinent to these Institutes, even though the said praxis in some cases had not been put in writing.

With respect to these two sections the contents of *Commentarium pro Religiosis* and that of the 1951 volume (*De Institutis Sæcularibus*) is the same. For this reason we will quote from the *Commentarium* since it is more available.

[26] See for example J. Beyer, *Les Instituts Séculiers*, Bruges 1954, pp. 273ff; G. Escudero, *Los Institutos Seculares . . ., cit.* (chapter V, note 47), pp. 82ff.

should always be kept in mind that in all of these Institutes their proper and special character must shine forth, that is to say, their secular character, wherein is rooted the very reason for their existence . . . the apostolate of secular institutes must be exercised faithfully not only in the world (in sæculo), but as it were from the world (ex sæculo), and therefore in the professions, activities, forms, places and circumstances corresponding to this secular condition."[27] Consequently, the Motu proprio (no. III) reiterates that the law concerning religious cannot be applied to these Institutes: "Secular institutes are not bound by dispositions that refer to the canonical discipline of the religious state, nor in general should religious legislation be applied to them, in accordance with the Apostolic Constitution *Provida Mater Ecclesia* (art. II, § 1)."[28] In sum the Holy Father highlights the great distance between religious life and the secular life proper to members of these new Institutes.

b) With respect to members of these secular institutes *Provida Mater Ecclesia* implicitly allows for a diversity of members. In establishing the requirements to be met by possible members, it adds, incidentally, that these demands fall on "members in the most strict meaning of the word": *ut membra strictiore sensu sumpta*.[29] *Cum Sanctissimus* develops this point by distinguishing between members in the strictest sense (those who profess "the three general evangelical counsels in one of the various forms which the apostolic constitution allows") and others in a less strict sense or wider sense. "Others can be admitted as members in a wider sense (*ut membra latiore sensu accepta)* and enrolled in the body of the association with a greater or less forcefulness or intensity, as members who aspire for evangelical perfection and strive to live it within their own state (*in propria conditione*), even though they do not embrace nor can they embrace each one of the evangelical counsels to the highest degree."[30] These members *lato sensu* are obviously no mere external collaborators of the secular institute,[31] but rather true members of

---

[27] There has been a certain amount of doctrinal controversy with regard to the origins of the texts of the *Primo feliciter* and the *Cum Sanctissimus* and their relations to the *Provida Mater Ecclesia*. The present state of the sources does not allow us to resolve this controversy completely. Nevertheless it seems clear that it is not proper to speak of them as counterpoised to the apostolic constitution; the decision to issue them and their specific contents resulted from a confluence of diverse influences.

[28] The same stance is found in *Cum Sanctissimus*, no. 8.

[29] *Provida Mater Ecclesia* , art. III, § 2.

[30] *Cum Sanctissimus*, no. 7 a).

[31] The implicit reference that is made in *Provida Mater Ecclesia* to members in the broader sense was interpreted by some as the possibility that the Institute could count on some people to help and collaborate with it without belonging to the Institute as such. For example J. Creusen, S.J., in "Les Instituts séculiers," *Revue des Communautés Religieuses*, 19 (1947):84.

the body of the association with a juridical bond according to the features determined by the constitutions of each Institute.[32] Among these members there is no apparent reason why there cannot be included married persons.[33]

c) With regard to the obligatory nature of the bonds (lex peculiaris, art. III), the Sacred Congregation issued a Declaration in Plenary Session (May 19, 1949) that substantially affirmed that the obligations arising from these bonds cannot be considered by themselves slight but rather grave. "In each case the obligation should be considered grave solely when the matter is certainly grave according to the constitutions and in accordance with the common teaching with regard to like or similar bonds." It later says: "The nature of the bonds assumed in each Institute and the reason for which they oblige—that is to say, if only out of justice and fidelity or also out of the virtue of religion—will be determined by deduction from the constitutions, and that this should be determined with all care together with the formula of consecration and incorporation by which these bonds are expressed." Its important conclusion: "Even when the obligation procceds explicitly from the virtue of religion, one should not attribute the malice of sacrilege to the violation of these bonds, because it is a question of bonds or vows that, although they are not completely private, nevertheless cannot either ex regula nor from the strict and specific meaning be called public, nor do they imply a public consecration of the person."[34]

d) Secularity, naturalness, discretion and reserve, clearly related concepts, are the object of a rescript of the Sacred Congregation dated July 24, 1947. In reply to a question presented to it, the Congregation declared that the discretion or reserve that secular institutes could live with respect to their houses, works and members, in keeping with their own constitutions or with the character approved for each Institute, should be maintained also by the diocesan ordinaries and other ecclesiastical authorities who know these matters ex officio, with respect to those persons who have no right to know these facts.

A first reading of this rescript betrays the strong need perceived by most authors and the Congregation itself for discretion during those first years of application of Provida Mater Ecclesia. Thus they

---

[32] Cum Sanctissimus, no. 3, in fine.

[33] Cum Sanctissimus bears the date of March 19, 1948, and the approval by the Congregation for Religious of the possibility of admitting married persons with a formal bond of incorporation to Opus Dei as members making up the body of the Institute bears the date of March 18, 1948 (see footnote 2 of this chapter).

[34] Cf. Commentarium pro Religiosis, 28 (1949):292-293; the commentary of Fr. Fuertes continues to p. 298. This reply answers questions raised by the Misioneras de la Realeza de Nuestro Señor Jesucristo.

would safeguard their secular character. The semi-official commentary by Fr. Larraona accompanying this resolution allows us to see
that it aspires to apply to a broad and complex context.[35] *Provida
Mater Ecclesia* offered a juridical framework for widely different
institutions. Some had arisen in countries where persecution was
taking place; others under the wing of religious orders; still others
sought presence in particular environments or sectors of society.
Some such institutes had been living, even for decades, as associations *de facto*, the fruit of the zeal of particular priests or religious,
though occasionally with the express approval of diocesan authority. Some others had adopted the form of common associations of
the faithful although the life of complete and stable dedication of
their members overflowed the juridical framework in force at the
time for these associations. Once *Provida Mater Ecclesia* had been
promulgated, some already existing institutions were reluctant to
make use of its norms, despite their breadth. Reasons varied. Its
directives signified for some a certain elevation and public recognition that contrasted with their previous existence as associations *de
facto* whereby dedicated members remained anonymous. Others
saw no need to acquire a distinct personality. Then too there were
those who did not want to submit themselves to the Congregation
for Religious for one reason or another, etc..

In this context the Congregation understandably tried to urge
the application of the recent legislation, while holding out sufficient
guarantees to dissipate hesitations or fear. This can be inferred
from the commentary by Fr. Larraona to the rescript just mentioned,
although he sees the criteria as having a general application (he
often insists on this point). On the one hand, in the wake of *Provida
Mater Ecclesia*, he echoes the need to submit to ecclesiastical authority, reaffirming the general prohibition of clandestine or secret societies.[36] On the other hand, he offers to institutions wary of juridical recognition the guarantee that ecclesiastical authorities will keep
a due reserve in accordance with what is approved for each Institute by the Holy See or by the diocesan authority, according to the
case. Church authorities could consider reserve necessary in some
cases and fitting in others to preserve early on the non-public character of the members' dedication to perfection and apostolate and

---

[35] See the comments in *Commentarium pro Religiosis*, 28 (1949):298-300. The question
which gave rise to the rescript of the Congregation and to the subsequent commentary
by Fr. Larraona had been formulated by Fr. Alvaro del Portillo.

[36] Cf. canon 684 of the CIC of 1917. In this regard the Decree *Ecclesia catholica* of the
Sacred Congregation of Bishops and Regulars, July 11, 1889, is significant. It demands
that new forms of the life of perfection arisen in times of persecution, submit completely to the bishop, and it prohibits their clandestine character. (*ASS* 23 (1890-1891):634-
636).

thus to avoid confusion with those pledged to a public state of perfection, i.e., the religious.

e) With regard to the breadth of application of *Provida Mater Ecclesia*, the Motu proprio *Primo feliciter* and the Instruction *Cum Sanctissimus* establish an obligatory recourse to the norms of the Apostolic Constitution by every institution corresponding to its elements and requirements. Thus *Primo feliciter* in its no. I decrees: "Societies of clerics or lay people professing Christian perfection in the world and seeming to possess fully and certainly the elements and requirements prescribed in the Apostolic Constitution *Provida Mater Ecclesia* under no pretext ought nor may they remain among the common Associations of the faithful (canons 684-725), but must necessarily be accommodated and raised to the nature and form proper to secular institutes, which corresponds perfectly to their special character and needs." In no. V it returns to this topic, while concluding: "To maintain unity of direction, [these Institutes] will be assigned and subject solely to the Sacred Congregation for Religious, where a special office has been created for these secular institutes." The compulsory character, not merely facultative, of the norms defining the traits of this new figure, plus the consequent need to submit in their governance to the exclusive competence of the Sacred Congregation for Religious, were reaffirmed by the Instruction *Cum Sanctissimus* in no. 2.

f) Regarding how these Secular Institutes are to be governed and their possible supradiocesan character, *Primo Feliciter*, in no. IV, describes and ponders the various forms the constitutions and government of these institutions may take. "A hierarchical, interdiocesan, universal constitution can be applied to secular institutes." The Motu proprio weighs the advantages of an international governance: "Undoubtedly this application will give them internal vigor and a wider and more effective influence and firmness." Nevertheless, "in this ordering, which has to be adapted to each one of the institutes, there should be borne in mind the nature of the end pursued by the institute and the greater or lesser scope of the designs of its expansion, its degree of evolution and maturity, the circumstances in which it finds itself and similar factors." This does not mean that "those Institutes founded on a confederational basis that wish to retain and foster moderately their local character," are to be rejected, so long as they are informed by "the sense of catholicity of the Church."

One of the reasons for the Holy See's intervention in regulating these new secular institutes of perfection and apostolate, as already seen in the previous chapter, was the appropriateness of a hierarchically organized internal form of governance. In many cases, given the Institute's nature or expansion, the indicated structure should be of an interdiocesan and universal nature—something impossible under the form of common associations of the faithful.

To meet this need, *Provida Mater Ecclesia*, speaking in its narrative part about how these new forms of Christian life are to be governed, established they could be of diocesan right (*lex peculiaris*, arts. V-VI) or of pontifical right (art. VII). Article IX reaffirms: "The internal government of secular institutes may be arranged hierarchically after the manner of the government of religious institutes and societies of common life, due allowances being made in the judgment of the same Sacred Congregation for the respective differences and taking into account the nature, ends and circumstances of the Institutes themselves." *Primo feliciter* took a further step, since, without excluding the possibility of exclusively diocesan Institutes, it in fact recommended an interdiocesan and universal government, because this fosters "internal strength and a wider and more effective influence and firmness" (no. IV).

The Holy See's previous permission is required for the diocesan erection of an Institute (*lex peculiaris*, art. VI, § 1). Number 5 of *Cum Sanctissimus* establishes conditions before requesting permission for this erection of the Holy See. "These new consociations until they shall have proved themselves sufficiently, should be retained and exercised under the paternal hand and guardianship of the diocesan authority, first as mere associations existing in fact rather than *de iure*, and then, not in one leap but gradually and by degrees, should be developed under some form of associations of the faithful, such as Pious Unions, Sodalities, Confraternities, as may seem appropriate according to the case." The local ordinary, says the Instruction, must be very prudent in this previous phase, exercising vigilant care, lest anything be permitted, either internally or externally, that exceeds their present condition and seems to belong specifically to secular institutes. Especially to be avoided are things that, were permission denied to erect the society as a secular institute, could not easily be taken away or undone and would seem a *fait accompli* putting moral pressure to grant the erection (*Cum Sanctissimus*, no. 6).[37]

Institutes of diocesan right must obtain approval or a decree of praise from the Holy See before becoming Institutes of pontifical right according to the judgment of the Sacred Congregation for Religious, (*lex peculiaris*, art. VII, § 1 and 2). Being of pontifical right makes it possible to have a centralized organizational structure with several levels of government—general or supreme, intermediate or regional, and local—similar to other institutions dependent upon the Sacred Congregation for Religious (*lex peculiaris*, art. IX). But, as Fr. Larraona

---

[37] In no. 28 (1949) of the *Commentarium pro Religiosis*, various criteria of the praxis and jurisprudence of the Sacred Congregation for Religious with regard to diocesan erection are given on pp. 300-303, (answering questions presented by the Institute Los Siervos de la Santa Iglesia) and pp. 317-319.

commented, with the logical adaptation made by the Sacred Congregation, that is to say, not literally applying the law of religious, but *congrua congruis referendo*, bearing in mind the special nature of these qualified associations of the faithful.[38]

g) *Provida Mater Ecclesia*, in article VIII of the *lex peculiaris*, established criteria regarding the submission of these Institutes to the local ordinary: "Secular institutes, besides being subject to their own laws if they have any or if any be established in the future, are subject to the local ordinaries, according to the law which is in effect for non-exempt congregations and societies of common life."[39] After 1947 a question with respect to the intervention of the local ordinary in the erection of centers of these Institutes was raised. The Sacred Congregation again invoked *congrua congruis referendo*: that is, bearing in mind the criteria just mentioned and the dispositions of the Code relating to other institutes and societies submitted to its competence.

The grouping together of members of these Institutes under the authority of a moderator—something different from a religious house—has rather a more personal than territorial character. Members may not require a building or a material place and can live dispersed, even in different cities. Consequently they are better designated by such terms as center, group, union or other similar terms. Furthermore it is necessary to distinguish between centers properly so-called (those juridically erected) and the simple fact that some members of an Institute coincide in the same city and house, without the aforementioned juridical relevance. This distinction is relevant to the rights enjoyed (oratory, reservation of the blessed Sacrament, etc.); and to the requirements for their establishment.

The latter was made more precise by the Congregation on August 8, 1949, when it declared the permission of the diocesan bishop is required to erect a center, but not for individual members to live together in a city or a place, whether individually or severally. Neither do they need special permission to be able as simple faithful to carry out an individual and personal apostolate—only for corporate apostolate of the Institute is it needed. Similarly the

---

[38] "The ordering of the government of these Institutes *ad instar* of the government of religious institutes should not be done literally, but *congrua congruis referendo*, under the guidance of the Sacred Congregation for Religious, which, according to the criteria three times repeated in the Constitution (art. VI, § 1; art. VII, § 2; art. IX), can help with its intervention, especially in those doubtful questions; and, *ex officio*, according to its prudence, *ought* to orient the teaching and, what is more, resolve *in practice* the questions and to fix a sure path in ordering the particular law of the Institutes." (A. Larraona, *Constitutionis . . ., cit.* -chapter V, note 72-, p. 252).

[39] A commentary on this article can be found in *Commentarium pro Religiosis*, 28 (1949):321.

Congregation for Religious declared (August 1, 1949) that, in order to grant permission, when necessary, the local ordinary can request the decree of approval of the Institute and its constitutions, a summary of the latter approved by the Holy See, and if desired, a report on the privileges the Institute has obtained with respect to those things that the common law subjects to the local ordinary.[40]

Overall, the normative developments dealt with in the preceding paragraph reveal some fundamental concerns. For example: the desire of coordinating the competence of the local ordinary with the autonomy necessary for each Institute and with the broad faculties entrusted to the Congregation for Religious. Perhaps more important: the search for criteria to orient the task of adequately regulating the questions raised by the life of these new Institutions.

It is easy to intuit the complexity and risks attendant on finding solutions. On the one hand, the Congregation was conscious of the novelty of secular institutes, especially some of them; their novelty had justified the promulgation of *Provida Mater Ecclesia*. On the other, it was inevitable that searching for solutions would lead, as a source of inspiration, to models and solutions already coined. That the Apostolic Constitution had placed secular institutes in the context of states of perfection made it that much easier to seek these parameters in religious life. Yet, all the while, as the already quoted texts repeatedly affirm, it was not possible merely to transplant tried terms and solutions. All must proceed *congrua congruis referendo*. Therefore, building on what could be described as the common Christian life, it was a question of how to make more precise the defining note of secular institutes, even in the same legal text: their very secularity. This challenge would require uncommon juridical and spiritual acumen and an equilibrium far from easy to maintain. Very diverse were the institutions that had prompted the promulgation of *Provida Mater Ecclesia*. No less diverse were the scholarly interpretations of doctrinal commentaries on this new figure. To the latter topic we now turn.

## 4. First doctrinal discussions

Different scholarly interpretations soon arose around the personality of secular institute, in part as a consequence of the very same breadth and ambiguity of the legal texts.[41] Their disputes af-

---

[40] Cf. *Commentarium pro Religiosis*, 28 (1949):303-307 (these criteria are established by the Congregation in response to questions addressed to it by Fr. Alvaro del Portillo). In the summary of jurisprudence of this issue of the review, the same topic is treated, with analogous criteria (pp. 316 & 320).

[41] A. Oberti, referring to the charism proper to secular institutes, writes that the first recognition by the Apostolic Constitution *Provida Mater Ecclesia* was truly "a partial

fected, more or less according to the case, first the practical applications made by the Congregation for Religious and later, subsequent magisterial and legislative developments.

In a note published in 1964 Fr. W. Peters made a balance of the relevant literature published till then. Affirming that *Provida Mater Ecclesia* "is not sufficiently clear," he adds: "This is so not only because of what was written between 1947 and 1950; in the years 1957-1960 this question continued to be sharply debated." Owing to the "ambiguity" of the Apostolic Constitution and *Primo feliciter* and *Cum Sanctissimus*, two schools or lines of interpretation could be identified: "On the one hand, there were those who take as their point of departure the fact that a secular institute is described as a state of perfection and thus equivalent to a religious order or congregation. On the other hand, we find those who accentuate the secular character as the essential element and therefore highlight the difference."[42]

We can use this division as a point of departure, even though it obviously needs to be refined. In any case in the first years—those that now concern us—discussion revolved around two axes: the nature of the vows to be taken by members of secular institutes; and the relationship between these new Institutes and the state of perfection. Proponents of contrary opinions had recourse to different legal texts in support of their respective positions.[43]

*Provida Mater Ecclesia* establishes expressly that secular institutes "do not admit the three public vows of religion" (cc. 1308, § 1, and 488, no. 1).[44] Commenting on these words already in 1947, authors disagreed as to the scope of the vows or promises pronounced in secular institutes. Thus, Fr. Siervo Goyeneche declared that, while these vows are private, nevertheless they give rise to true juridical effects.[45] Fr. Creusen, also in 1947, recognized that vows taken in these Institutes are private, but the Holy See can grant to

---

recognition and in a certain sense an ambiguous one. The charism is received not from the point of view of the lay nature of those who live it—which is what constitutes a fundamental novelty for ecclesial life—but, rather, from the point of view of the apparent similarity that they demonstrate with religious because of their consecration." ("*La vita consacrata secolare e il nuovo rapporto Chiesa-mondo,*" in *Vita consacrata,* 21 (1985):513.)

[42] W. Peters, S.J., "*Het Lekeninstituut.- Nog steeds niet voldoende klaarheid,*" in *Tijdschrift voor Geestelijk Leven,* 9 (1964):648-654.

[43] A summary of this discussion is found in G. Escudero, "*De natura Institutorum Saecularium.- Scribendi occasio et distinctio quaestionum,*" in *Commentarium pro Religiosis,* 32 (1953):72-93.

[44] *Provida Mater Ecclesia,* art. II, § 1.

[45] S. Goyeneche, Adnotationes ad Constitutionem Apostolicam *Provida Mater Ecclesia,* in *Apollinaris,* 20 (1947):31.

some the benefit of an official recognition of their vows.[46] In 1948 he broadened his opinion when he averred that nobody could prevent these vows in secular institutes from being public. It suffices to distinguish them carefully from "vows of religion"; he further commented that the Congregation has already recognized public vows in the case of one secular institute.[47]

In his 1947 study on secular institutes Salvador Canals stressed the difference between these vows and public ones: "It is taken for granted that vows, if they exist, are not public, that is, received by the Church (canon 1308, § 1)." He continued: "But neither are these vows absolutely private, that is to say, such that the Church in the external forum not only does not receive them but ignores them, just as it excludes from this forum vows pronounced in the internal forum, remitting them when necessary to the Sacred Penitentiary (for dispensation, commutation, etc., canon 1308, § 1). Consequently, they are vows that the Church acknowledges and regulates via each Institute's constitutions and to which it attributes effects with regard to the Institute: for government, for dismissal in the case of failure to fulfill them, etc. Therefore it can be affirmed that the Church welcomes and presupposes them in some way, even though it does not receive them."[48]

In 1949 Fr. Larraona concluded that the vows should be called private, inasmuch as they are not received by the Church, but insofar as they have effects in the external forum and are equivalent in many respects to public vows they can be canonically referred to as semi-public.[49] In 1950 Fr. Anastasio Gutiérrez maintained a similar opinion; he calls them "semi-public," "private recognized" or "social".[50] Fr. Alvaro del Portillo also in 1950 speaks of "private recognized vows."[51]

That same year Fr. Creusen again dealt with the matter: "A still debated point among canonists is the character of the vows pronounced in secular institutes. They cannot be called entirely 'pri-

[46] J. Creusen, S.J., "Les Instituts séculiers", cit. (note 31 of this chapter), pp. 85-86.

[47] J. Creusen, S.J., "Les Instituts séculiers," in Revue des Communautés Religieuses, 20 (1948):171-173. A similar opinion was expressed by this author in Periodica de re morali, canonica, liturgica, 37 (1948):270.

[48] S. Canals, "Los Institutos seculares de perfección y apostolado," in Revista Española de Derecho Canónico, 3 (1947):855.

[49] A. Larraona, "Constitutionis . . .", cit. (chapter V, note 72), pp. 167-168.

[50] A. Gutiérrez, "Doctrina generalis theologica et iuridica de statu perfectionis evangelicae et comparatio inter eiusdem diversos gradus ab Ecclesia iuridice ordinatos," in Commentarium pro Religiosis, 29 (1950):83 and 115.

[51] A. del Portillo, "Constitutio, formae diversae, institutio, regimen, apostolatus Institutorum saecularium," in Acta et Documenta Congressus generalis de Statibus perfectionis (Romæ, 1950), II, Rome 1952, pp. 292 and 293.

vate,' since the Holy See recognizes and regulates them in a certain way.  If called 'public,' there is the danger of confusing them with the vows of religious."[52]

The root of the debate clearly puts in play the very substance of the new Institute.  The declaration of the Congregation for Religious of May 19, 1948, thus takes on special importance, a decree seen in the previous section.  This declaration addresses the problem debated by scholars as to whether the violation of obligations assumed by members in the strict sense (*stricto sensu*) of secular institutes constitutes a sacrilege.  Number 5 of the declaration expressly affirms that the bonds or vows "even though they are not wholly private, nevertheless they can not, neither *ex regula* nor in a strict and specific sense, be called public, nor do they imply a public consecration of the person."

The Congregation does not adopt any of the technical terms then circulating, but emphasizes that the vows or promises pronounced in secular institutes are not public, nor do they transform those pronouncing them into sacred persons.  The distinction between secular institutes and religious communities is thus reaffirmed.

Closely tied to this discussion is another question raised in the first years: do secular institutes constitute a form of the historical evolution of the religious state or not.  The authors were divided; let us quote some as representative of the various viewpoints.

Some affirmed that secular institutes have joined states of perfection, the religious state and societies of common life without vows, as a third canonical state of perfection.  Strictly speaking they distinguished three distinct species or grades of the state of perfection.  They thus ranked the religious state as the first and in a certain way the model of the others, because it is the complete state of perfection to which the others refer or approach.[53]  Some authors even saw no reason why the name of religious should not apply to persons forming part of the second and third grades of the state of perfection.[54]

---

[52] J. Creusen, "Les Instituts séculiers," in *Revue des Communautés Religieuses*, 22 (1950):30.

[53] Cf. J. Creusen, "Les Instituts séculiers," *cit.* (note 31 of this chapter), pp. 57-88, especially pp. 74-75; and in *Revue des Communautés Religieuses*, 20 (1948):136-139; E. Jombart, S.J., "Un nouvel etat de perfection," in *Revue d'ascétique et de mystique*, 24 (1948):270-272; E. Bergh, S.J., "Les Instituts séculiers," in *Nouvelle Revue Théologique*, 70 (1948):1052 and 1061; P. Capobianco, O.M.F., in *Acta et Documenta Congressus generalis de statibus perfectionis (Romæ, 1950)*, I, Rome 1952, p. 517.

[54] Thus, for example, P. Bergh in an article on the International Congress of the States of Perfection, celebrated in Rome in 1950, wrote: "Whenever we use the word 'religious,' it should always be understood as applied to all souls consecrated to God in the three states of perfection: orders and congregations, societies of common life without public vows, secular institutes" (*Revue des Communautés religieuses*, 23, (1951):24). For his part, H. U. von Balthasar (*Der Laie und der Ordensstand*, Freiburg 1949, p. 2, note 1)

Another group of authors underlined the institutional features of this new figure in contrast with the religious, accenting the three definitional affirmations of secular institutes: a) they are associations of the faithful, although a qualified species thereof, with a proper name and juridical government; b) they constitute a state of perfection distinct from the religious state: a secular state of perfection; c) their members do not lose their lay or clerical condition by being incorporated into the Institute.

This scholarly group distinguished between the canonical state and the juridical state of perfection. An important representative of this line of thought, Fr. Larraona explained in 1954 at some length: "Secular institutes are not comprised within the canonical states of perfection in the strict sense." He further stated that by canonical state in the strict sense should be understood that which lays "the foundation for the classes of ecclesiastical persons and the states of canonical life," that is to say, the clerical state, the religious state and the lay state. In sum: any situation, commitment, bond and so on that does not give rise to a new personality or a change of state in the Church could not be characterized as a canonical state.

Having set this foundation, Fr. Larraona then examined the three institutional modes of seeking Christian perfection: "There are three juridical forms of life of perfection: the religious life, with totally public vows and an internal hierarchy; the societies without public vows, made the equivalent of religious in everything related to juridical organization, some of the religious and/or clerical obligations, etc.; and secular institutes, which should not be placed in the second part of the Code of Canon Law dealing with religious, but in the third part dealing with the laity, because they form the first class of associations of lay people. They have a point of contact with the two states: religious and lay. In part the legislation of lay societies is applied to them. They form a unity of state with the religious in the theological field, but not in the juridical field. Juridically, religious, by the fact of being religious, form a special state. On the other hand, the members of secular institutes are lay people or clergy without anything more: their canonical state is not changed by the mere fact of belonging to a secular institute."[55]

---

applies the term "religious state" also to members of secular institutes, although he does give it a broad meaning. A. M. Henry, in "Le laïcat et l'état religieux," in *Supplément de la vie spirituelle*, 11 (1949):333 follows this same opinion.

[55] A. Larraona, in *Actas del Congreso de los estados de perfección de la Argentina, Bolivia, Chile, Paraguay y Uruguay*, Buenos Aires 1954, p. 159. The terminology that distinguishes between the canonical and the juridical state of perfection had been proposed by Larraona in 1949 (cf. "Constitutionis . . .", *cit.*, chapter V, note 72, p. 60). It was used in the same sense by other authors, as for example: A. Gutiérrez, "Commentarium in Motu Proprio *Primo feliciter* Pii Pp. XII et Instructionem S. C. de Religiosis *Cum*

The distinction between juridical and canonical state was criticized by some who claimed that in the Church's legal system there was no way to distinguish between juridical and canonical. Thus every state of perfection—even that of secular institutes—ought to be characterized as a canonical state of perfection. In one case someone affirmed that even such terminology ought to be rejected, since it could easily lead to confusion.[56] Yet the problem was not terminological, but more fundamental. The heart of the question lay in what these terms with greater or less success sought to defend. Do members of secular institutes constitute a contemporary version of the religious state or on the contrary are they to be located in a different line of development? One of the writers who most opposed this terminological distinction was C. Lauwers. The whole state of perfection, he affirmed, has to be religious. Thus secular institutes ought to be called a canonical state in the sense that they must be ascribed to the second of the states mentioned in canon 107 of the 1917 Code. The term "religious" of that canon should not be restricted to religious properly speaking, that is to say, those mentioned in canons 487 and 488. Rather it should be extended to all those belonging to any of the states of perfection authentically recognized by the Church and introduced by *Provida Mater Ecclesia* and, therefore, also to the members of secular institutes.[57]

In 1951 A. del Portillo wrote that before *Provida Mater Ecclesia*, the *status perfectionis adquirendæ* was deemed synonymous with the religious state. Thanks to the Apostolic Constitution, one now speaks of a new, complete state of perfection, with the existence of a "special vocation from God," whereby none of its members are religious, as *Provida Mater Ecclesia* declares (art. II, § 1). Members of secular institutes, he continues, remain before Canon Law clerics or

*Sanctissimus*, "in *Commentarium pro Religiosis*, 28 (1949):281-282 and "Doctrina generalis . . .", *cit.* (note 50 of this chapter), pp. 111-115; G. Escudero, "De natura Institutorum . . .", *cit.* (note 43 of this chapter), pp. 76 and 77; S. Canals, "Los Institutos Seculares de perfección . . .," *cit.* (note 48 of this chapter), pp. 859ff.

[56] Cf. J. Beyer, *Les Instituts Séculiers*, *cit.* (note 26 of this chapter), pp. 289-297.

[57] Cf. C. Lauwers, "Societates sine votis et status canonicus perfectionis," in *Ephemerides theologicæ Lovanienses*, 28 (1952):215ff. In a subsequent monograph dedicated to this topic, J. M. Setién summarized the discussions on this subject. But he maintained—contrary to the preceding author and those agreeing with him—that vows and promises emitted in secular institutes are strictly private, a character according perfectly with the state they bring about: a canonical, secular state of perfection of private law; the characteristic of these Institutes, he affirms, "is in the fact that they establish a state of perfection outside of the religious state and within the secular world without altering the condition of cleric or laity one previously had." (*Naturaleza jurídica del estado de perfección en los Institutos Seculares*, Rome 1957, p. 145; in general see the whole chapter, pp. 125-160).

laity according to their proper condition; their total consecration to God does not modify their respective canonical personality (cf. CIC, c. 107, *Provida Mater Ecclesia*, art. II, § 1; *Primo Feliciter*, nos. II & III).[58]   In a Congress held in 1950 he had stated of the members of those Institutes that "their consecration to the Church is not canonical—albeit juridical—but rather ascetical."[59]

Similar expressions are to be found in the *Annuario Pontificio* of that period.  Describing the new figure of secular institute, it affirms that their members "profess the state of perfection, but not the canonical state, which is proper to religious."  Relating to the practice of the evangelical counsels, it points out "they do not make public vows, in the sense considered by the Code of Canon Law, but private vows with equivalent moral bonds."  Explaining the name of secular institute, it adds: "With the name of *secular* it has been desired to stress that persons professing this new state of perfection do not change the social condition they had in the world; therefore after their consecration to God they continue as clerics or lay people, according to the character they have, with all the juridical and practical consequences deriving therefrom".[60]

The presuppositions of this question point in the basic direction of ecclesiology and spiritual theology.  This becomes more manifest with time, as we shall see.

## 5. A conference of the Founder

Let us now deal with a conference given by Msgr. Escrivá towards the end of 1948.  The founder of Opus Dei did not enter into particular aspects of the questions being debated; rather he spoke at a different level.  Through his words, nevertheless, he evinces familiarity with these debates, while his is a witness of no little value.

The conference was delivered in Madrid on December 17, 1948, at the headquarters of a noted lay association in Spain: the Asociación Católica Nacional de Propagandistas.  Under the title, "The Apostolic Constitution *Provida Mater Ecclesia* and Opus Dei",[61]  Msgr. Escrivá, besides succinctly presenting the papal documents regarding secular institutes, set forth the characteristic notes of Opus Dei as a secular institute of pontifical right.

---

[58] A. Del Portillo, "Istituti Secolari," in *Enciclopedia Cattolica*, VII, Florence-Rome 1951, p. 354.

[59] A. Del Portillo, "Constitutio, formae diversae . . .", *cit.* (note 51 of this chapter), p. 290.

[60] *Annuario Pontificio* (1951):793.

[61] J. Escrivá de Balaguer, "La Constitución apostólica *Provida Mater Ecclesia* y el Opus Dei": this conference was published in the *Boletín de los Propagandistas* (no. 427, January 15, 1949) and also in a separate edition, Madrid 1949, from which we quote.

He first professed faith in God's lordship over history, or better still, in the Holy Spirit's presence and action in the Christian community: "The Church, living body that it is, shows its vitality with the immanent movement animating it. Often this movement is something more than a mere adaptation to the environment: we see God intervening in it with a positive and lordly impetus. The Church, led by the Holy Spirit, does not pass through the world as along an obstacle course, trying to avoid barriers or exploring paths of least resistance. Rather she treads the earth with a firm and sure step, opening herself the way."[62] The fruit of the Spirit's action is holiness in the Church and the successive appearance of initiatives leading to the fulness of Christian life.

He reviewed historically how various forms of fostering perfection and apostolate had opened up paths in the Church: "both in a contemplative life dedicated to prayer and sacrifice, and in an active life dedicated to remedying from outside of the world the evils and needs of the world."[63] Commenting on *Provida Mater Ecclesia*, he said: "There arises now in the house of the Father, 'in which there are many mansions' (Jn 14:2), a new form of life of perfection whose members are not religious. . . . Now it is from the world itself that these apostles arise who dare to sanctify all ordinary activities of men."[64]

The second part of the conference dealt with Opus Dei as a secular institute. Msgr. Escrivá pointed out some of its fundamental characteristics; a sample:

"Opus Dei embraces Christians of all classes, men and women, single and married, who being in the world, or rather, being of the world—because they are ordinary lay people—aspire, by a divine vocation, to strive for evangelical perfection and to bring Christ's light to all men and women within their own environment, by means of sanctifying ordinary work."[65]

"The Institute provides the means of sanctification, it gives its members a solid religious formation required for acting in the world: above all, it sows in them the necessary interior life to be apostles in their own environment."[66]

"One who cannot go beyond the classic molds of perfection will not understand the structure of the Work. The members of Opus Dei are not religious—to give an example—who, full of holy zeal,

---

[62] *Ibid.*, p. 7.

[63] *Ibid.*, p. 16.

[64] *Ibid.*, pp. 16-17.

[65] *Ibid.*, pp. 18-19.

[66] *Ibid.*, pp. 19-20.

exercise the professions of lawyer or doctor or engineers, etc. Rather they are simply lawyers, doctors, engineers, etc., with all their professional idealism and their characteristic features, for whom their profession itself, and naturally all of life, takes on a full meaning rich in consequences when completely oriented towards God and saving souls. This character conditions and explains their way of acting; i.e., the fullest and most absolute naturalness, because their ways of life and their professions are natural. . . . Because they are not different or strange, they have sometimes seemed so to those who insist upon including them in the traditional and worthy forms of Christian perfection.[67]

"Its ends [those of Opus Dei] are clear and precise: to seek the evangelical perfection of its members by means of sanctifying ordinary work, in the most varied fields of human activity. These members themselves, each with his own personality, neither lost nor forfeited, act in the world on their own personal and exclusive responsibility. To this end they enjoy complete professional freedom since Opus Dei does not enter into these questions."[68]

These are rich texts. While the founder does not directly enter into the debates then taking place, their meaning is obvious. This conference, plus other writings of Msgr. Escrivá, represent a decisive point of reference for judging and evaluating Opus Dei's juridical development to which we return now.

## 6. Steps taken for the new approval

A few weeks after this conference Opus Dei's founder was received in audience by Pope Pius XII on January 28, 1949. He informed the Holy Father of the Work's growth in these last years and its expanding apostolate.[69] A few days later he returned to Spain to spend two months giving encouragement to the apostolates in that country. The following summer he visited various cities in southern Italy to lay foundations for initiating apostolate in a stable way in that area. The same purpose took him in the fall to cities in northern Italy and then to Austria and southern Germany. All the while he was readying the documentation to request definitive approval of Opus Dei, with the active cooperation of Fr. Alvaro del Portillo. This would complete and further define and confirm the approval obtained in 1947.[70]

---

[67] *Ibid.*, p. 20.

[68] *Ibid.*, p. 21.

[69] Cf. *L'Osservatore Romano*, January 29 and February 5, 1949.

[70] F. Gondrand, *op. cit.* (chapter I, note 1), pp. 229ff.

In a Letter of December 8, 1949, Msgr. Escrivá explained his state of soul before the new juridical step about to be taken. "I have reminded the Lord: *sub umbra alarum tuarum protege nos* (Ps 16:8): we need all this grace, all this help of our Lord, because we must present the Work in accordance with *Provida Mater Ecclesia*. They will scrutinize our dossier as they did for the *Decretum laudis*; if not, we will not pass." He added, "We have prepared the documents under the strict obligation in conscience of unambiguously determining the special traits of Opus Dei." He concluded: "Without departing from the truth we must show our way of acting before the Roman Curia in this way: always obeying, affirming the spirit of the Work, in order to defend it; giving in without giving up, intent on recovering any concessions later."[71]

On December 25, 1949, Pope Pius XII solemnly inaugurated the jubilee year he had proclaimed. On January 1, 1950, Msgr. Escrivá, accompanied by three Opus Dei members, went to St. Peter's to earn the holy year indulgence. He also carried in his heart two crucial petitions: to spur on further the apostolic work of Opus Dei and the Work's definitive approval by the Holy See.[72]

Msgr. Escrivá felt constrained to take this new step—for him so important—in the juridical evolution of the Work.[73] He had sought in 1947 the Holy See's approval for a new pastoral phenomenon, forging ahead, as happens in similar cases, in the face of difficulties and misunderstanding. The 1947 approval and the universal form of government that came with it efficaciously aided Opus Dei's growth and expansion. But the misunderstandings did not cease. Msgr. Escrivá writes in a Letter already quoted from: "From the end of 1947—when we thought they would be silent!—even more serious calumnies, more constant and more organized, have been raised against us."[74] The very same papal approval, the favorable reception accorded Opus Dei in the Roman Curia and in so many corners of the world, the great number of vocations, were all paradoxically accompanied by a smear campaign in Spain and later in Italy.

---

[71] *Letter*, December 8, 1949, no. 18.

[72] F. Gondrand, *op. cit.* (chapter I, note 1), pp. 232-233.

[73] From the *Decretum laudis* (February 24, 1947) to the decree of definitive approval (June 16, 1950) little more than three years passed: a relatively short space of time for the Roman Curia.

[74] *Letter*, December 8, 1949, no. 4. When he refers to these misunderstandings, he does not fail to speak also of the esteem so many people show for Opus Dei. Thus, in a 1950 Letter, making a balance of the previous years he says: "Together with many souls who in knowing Opus Dei become enamored of us and help us generously, there have not been lacking some—thinking *obsequium se præslure Deo* (Jn 16:2)—who insist with incredible perseverance in hindering the growth and work of our Opus Dei" (October 7, 1950, no. 10).

Some even visited parents of members and others taking part in its apostolate to warn them against the dangers their children ran of eternal damnation. They claimed the pontifical sanction of Opus Dei was provisional and would not lead to definitive approval.

No wonder then that the founder sought to obtain as soon as possible this new and definitive approval. Such a step would give greater stability to the legal structure of Opus Dei, integrating the declarations and rescripts obtained from the Holy See subsequent to the *Decretum laudis* in a single unified body. It would also signify a final papal commendation of the institution, with full recognition on the part of the Church that Opus Dei is a true path to holiness. Msgr. Escrivá wrote in the same Letter: "Since then [after evoking the foundational year of 1928] so much water has passed under the bridges of the Tiber. God has helped us greatly, he has increased our work: vocations, the formation of my children, apostolates, expansion. He has also allowed not a few hardships to arise. . . . The definitive approval will give us, my daughters and sons, a new stability, a new weapon of defense, a more propitious environment for our apostolic work. It will once again set the principal foundations of the Work: secularity, sanctification of work, our being ordinary citizens and, above all, especially in the spiritual dimension, the conviction that we are God's children."[75]

The discussions began on February 11, 1950 in accordance with the applicable norms.[76] A lengthy report was presented to the Holy See on the present state of the Institution signed by the President General and members of his Council. It conveys in great detail substantive data regarding the extension of Opus Dei, its territorial divisions, the number of centers and members.[77] Above all it contains the *Constitutions* for their definitive approval.

The *Constitutions* approved in 1947 comprise 363 numbers. In the draft elaborated for definitive approval the text has grown to 456. Besides those approved in 1947, new ones reflect the prescriptions of the different rescripts the founder had obtained from the Sacred Congregation for Religious during the years 1947-50.[78] There are also new numbers (or revised ones) relative to the fulfillment of the *Constitutions*: government (giving greater scope in directing the Institute to the councils, advisory boards and commissions), etc.

---

[75] *Letter*, December 8, 1949, nos. 1 & 19.

[76] That is to say, the *Normæ* of the Sacred Congregation for Religious of March 6, 1921, *cit.* (chapter IV, note 21), nos. 10 & 20c, to which article VII, § 2 of *Provida Mater Ecclesia* makes reference.

[77] From this report (AGP, Sezione Giuridica, V/15532) are taken some of the data on the expansion of Opus Dei included at the beginning of this chapter.

[78] Those already commented on in sections 1 & 2 of this chapter.

Furthermore the whole text has been reorganized: in place of the three parts and 19 chapters of the 1947 version, there are now four parts and 20 chapters.[79]

The request for definitive approval was supported by 110 prelates who sent their letters of recommendation to the Holy See. Among these were 12 cardinals and 26 archbishops. These prelates came from 17 countries.[80] The Congregation for Religious began its study of the founder's request. To the documentation presented was added—as was the practice of the Congregation—the opinion (*votum*) of one of the consultors. The person designated was Fr. Suarez, the Master General of the Dominicans, who declared himself favorable to the approval. Various sessions of the relevant body met several times in regular sessions under the presidency of Fr. Larraona, the Undersecretary of the Congregation.[81] Having attentively studied all the documents presented, the commission unanimously approved granting the definitive approval.[82]

Its opinion was brought before the *plenum* of the Congregation on April 1, 1950, under the presidency of Cardinal Lavitrano, Prefect of the Congregation; and in the presence of Archbishop Pasetto, Secretary; Fr. Larraona, Undersecretary; and other officials of the Congregation, plus the consultors who had made up the commission. They accepted the opinion favorable to the definitive approval of the Institute. But with regard to the *Constitutions* it ordained further study of some questions, "which seemed to present certain difficulties, given the novelty of these Institutes and hearing for this purpose the founder of Opus Dei."[83]

---

[79] AGP, Sezione Giuridica, V/15845.

[80] AGP, Sezione Giuridica, V/15860 and *Primum inter*, § 3 (This decree is found in the Appendix, document no. 31.)

[81] The following consultors of the Congregation composed this commission: Fr. Agatangelo de Langasco, O.F.M. Cap.; Fr. José Grendel, S.V.D.; and the officials of the Congregation, Fr. Elio Gambari, S.M.M. and Fr. Anastasio Gutiérrez, C.M.F. (AGP, Sezione Giuridica, V/15934).

[82] The very decree of definitive approval summarizes this phase of study in the following words: " . . . res, in Commissione Consultorum semel iterumque discussa atque ad trutinam revocata, cum Consultores omnes expostulatae concessioni favissent, ad Congressum plenum die I aprilis labentis anni Maximi Iubilaei, MDCCCCL, relata fuit" (*Primum inter*, § 4).

[83] Thus the very decree of approval says: "Congressus plenus, precibus meritissimi Conditoris Operis Dei aures praebens, concessionem approbationis definitivae decrevit. Ipse Congressus, praeside Em.mo Sacrae Congregationis Cardinali Praefecto, voluit etiam, relate ad Constitutiones, ut quae Institutorum novitate difficultatem quamdam offerre viderentur, audito Rev.mo Patre Domino Fundatore Operis Dei, ex allatis ab ipso declarationibus ac commentariis, a Commissione Consultorum dilucidarentur." (Decree *Primum inter*, § 5)

So, the *Congressus Plenarius* of April 1 ended in a delay: *dilata donec compleantur acta.*[84] During those days an event took place that highlighted—even though merely by way of example—the challenge of understanding the call to sanctity and a commitment to Christian life by lay people to whom logically, the exercise of any decent profession was open. In the *Acta Apostolicæ Sedis* of May 1, 1950, a decree was published of the Sacred Congregation of the Council dated March 22, 1950, that reaffirmed the prohibition of the exercise of business by clerics (CIC 1917, canon 142), religious (CIC, canon 592) and members of societies of the common life (CIC 1917, canon 679). Neither excepted are "the members of the recently established secular institutes." To the violation of this prohibition was added an excommunication *latæ sententiæ*, especially reserved to the Holy See, plus other penalties.[85] This decree seems inspired in a teaching mentioned earlier that tended to equate secular institutes and their members with religious orders and congregations and those who belonged to these. Thus the Congregation adopted a criterion different from that of the Congregation for Religious, which had reaffirmed its position in the direct declaration of May 19, 1949 already commented upon.[86] Doubtless such actions contributed to the worry and work of one who like Opus Dei's founder found himself walking a tightrope.

On May 3, 1950, Msgr. Escrivá gave the Congregation for Religious a detailed written statement that probably shortened the delay begun on April 1.[87] He first manifests a desire to make "some clarifications that in his modest opinion would be useful to keep in mind in proceeding with the study and approval of the Institute. . . . In formulating these suggestions *coram Domino*, the person who writes desires above all to fulfill a duty of conscience and, secondly, to make available to this Congregation elements that can better enlighten some points of the *Constitutions*, citing to this effect the proof of time and the confirmation of experience." The founder sought not only to respond to specific questions but also to offer some fundamental considerations. We cite only the principal ones.

---

[84] AGP, Sezione Giuridica, V/15934.

[85] " . . . Clerici et Religiosi omnes ritus latini de quibus in canonibus 487-681, ne exceptis quidem recentium Institutorum saecularium sodalibus, per se vel per alios, mercaturam seu negotiationem cuiusvis generis, etiam argentariam, exercentes, sive in propriam sive in aliorum utilitatem, contra praescriptum can. 142, utpote huius criminis rei, excommunicationem latae sententiae Apostolicae Sedi speciali modo reservatam incurrant, et si casus ferat, degradationis quoque poena plectantur. Superiores vero qui eadem delicta, pro munere suo ac facultate, non impediverint, destituendi sunt ab officio et inhabiles declarandi ad quodlibet regiminis et administrationis munus" (Decree *Pluribus ex documentis*, March 22, 1950, in *AAS* 42 (1950):330-331).

[86] Cf. sections 3 & 4 of this chapter.

[87] RHF, EF-500503-1.

a) He observes that in scrutinizing the norms of Opus Dei all recourse to criteria, praxis or comparisons appropriate to a religious institute but not to Opus Dei should be avoided.  Such a misstep might endanger, even contradict, the foundational charism: "I should like to call the attention of the Sacred Congregation to a general question: one that is as it were a question of principle. Particularly, the criteria to be followed in judging the *Constitutions* and the spirit of a secular institute cannot be the same as those used to pass judgment on a religious congregation.  In fact they represent two different phenomena, both in the legal area as well as in the exterior aspects of social, professional and apostolic life."

b) He also points out the extension of Opus Dei and how the same spirit and norms "are lived equally in European and American countries as well as in Africa, and obtain in all places the same fruits of sanctity and apostolate."  There results a great unity, since the members of Opus Dei "are truly *cor unum et anima una*, both in the spirit animating them and the government to which they are subject and in the fruits of apostolate they gather."  A proof of this unity is that the Congregation has been spared "any complaint or protest of the members of the Institute against the internal hierarchy or the spirit of the Institute."  He forcefully points out "this unity is shown clearly in the cooperation, mutual understanding and union existing between clerics and laity within the Institute, both in the field of government, as in those of training members and apostolate."

c) Regarding possible changes in the *Constitutions*, he claims it would be extremely painful to Opus Dei members if some norm were to modify those things that, "having been lived with great fervor in the Institute," are considered by all as "a means of personal sanctification, of unity within the Institute and of effectiveness in serving Holy Church."  Finally he asks the Congregation that, if fitting, he be informed, "as has been done with other Institutes, of possible corrections and observations of the Most Reverend Commission, before they are passed on to the *Congressus Plenarius.*"

This thoughtful text, both confident and serious, reveals Msgr. Escrivá's deep consciousness of his responsibility as founder.  By command of the Cardinal Prefect he was consequently informed of the observations made on the *Constitutions* by the commission of consultors.  He was also invited to explain some questions and to give further information with regard to others so that everything could be properly weighed.

On June 2, 1950, he sent a written report to the Congregation. Among other things,[88] it dealt with the following principles:

---

[88] Further on we refer to other elements of this writing. It is found in RHF, EF-500602-1.

a) The first refers to the juridical equating of Opus Dei with clerical institutes so that it could be granted the capability of an internal organization necessary for its apostolic development. This equivalency had already been recognized by the Holy See in approving the 1947 *Constitutions* and confirmed in 1950 by a rescript of the Congregation for Religious. However, some difficulties had arisen from the fact that most members are lay people. Responding to these questions, Msgr. Escrivá declares: "We wanted to make use of the modern teaching beyond that of the Code with regard to secular institutes," according to which secular institutes, where neither the majority nor even many members are priests, can be recognized *iuxta modum* as clerical, so long as the supreme and intermediate government in whole or in part is reserved to priests.[89] He details some traits of the theological and spiritual formation received by numeraries, from whom the priests of Opus Dei come. "Both in the general government, as in the intermediate or provincial, the most important offices are entrusted to priests, specifically, that of President General, Secretary General, Procurator General, Central Secretary, Counselor and Regional Secretary." Finally, "without wanting in this to force the hand in the least of the Most Reverend Commission," he feels bound in conscience to indicate that on four occasions "the aforementioned equivalency has been granted by the Holy See to our Institute."[90]

b) The second question refers to admitting as members of the Institute married persons or those with a vocation to marriage. This prospect appeared doubtful to some consultors. Yet this is not a new matter, since it had been approved by the Congregation in its rescript of March 18, 1948.[91] In order not to go backwards in this important matter, he recurs to the distinction between members *stricto sensu* and *lato sensu* established by *Provida Mater Ecclesia* and confirmed and specified by *Cum Sanctissimus*: "We point out to the Most Reverend Commission that, in our opinion, the mind of the *Provida Mater Ecclesia* with regard to members *lato sensu* of secular institutes seems clear. Considered members *lato sensu* are those who have a certain consecration of life and a certain bond with the Institute, even though they lack some of the conditions required by article III of the Apostolic Constitution for members *stricto sensu*."

c) The third problem affected the professional work of the members and derived from a misunderstanding of the lay Christian condition. The founder took this opportunity to address the Congrega-

---

[89] This is the teaching maintained in *Commentarium pro Religiosis*, 28 (1949):315.

[90] These 4 occasions are: a) the granting of the *nihil obstat* in 1943 (*Lineamenta*, no. 1); b) the 1947 *Constitutions*, no. 2; c) the Decree *Primum Institutum*, § 9; d) the rescript of the Sacred Congregation for Religious 6649/47 of July 7, 1947.

[91] See sections 2 and 3 of this chapter.

tion in an official way, asking that there be added to number 15 of the *Constitutions* recognition of the members' professional freedom. Thus the *Constitutions* would expressly affirm something already implied in the earlier edition: members of Opus Dei, ordinary Christians that they are, "can also dedicate themselves to business and financial endeavors."[92] Thus did Msgr. Escrivá confront, indirectly and delicately while clearly and firmly, the contention of the Congregation of the Council whereby the exercise of business activities was prohibited to members of secular institutes.

Obviously, this is no little matter, but a general principle: to admit that an Opus Dei member could be prohibited from exercising an honest line of work—be it business, law, agriculture, mining or whatever—would be to question its lay and secular condition. Thus the founder argued that the decree to be published expressly mention these activities. This is one of the "filial contentions" with the Holy See that Msgr. Escrivá refers to in some Letters.[93] The founder firmly emphasized the essential feature of sanctifying ordinary work—that each member has—with full freedom and personal responsibility. In fact, as seen, this basic aspect of Opus Dei had been recognized in various documents of approval or of praise.[94] In the conference Msgr. Escrivá gave in Madrid in 1948 he reiterated variously that what is specific to the members of Opus Dei is sanctifying their ordinary work, profession or job, without excluding any human endeavors. Financial involvement, among others, is explicitly mentioned to stress the freedom Opus Dei members enjoy in this as in other fields: "With regard to professional work and social, political views, each of the members of Opus Dei, within the

---

[92] Number 15 of the draft *Constitutions* presented on February 11, 1950—which corresponds to no. 17 of the 1947 *Constitutions*—says as follows: "Sodales vero officia seu munera sive publicae rei administrationis, sive docendi in universitatibus vel Institutis civilibus, aut etiam professiones privatas advocatorum, medicorum et alias similes assumunt vel retinent. Quarum . . ." - It is in this text that the founder asks there be included a reference to the exercise of business and financial activities: " . . . medicorum aliasve similes assumunt vel retinent: *aut etiam commercio vel rebus nummariis operam navant.* Quarum . . .".

[93] For example, in a *Letter* dated October 1950 he refers not to the events cited in the text but to the months preceding the promulgation of *Provida Mater Ecclesia* and the consequent granting of the decree of praise to Opus Dei: "I could tell you many details of our filial contention during these months: the effort made so that members of secular institutes be not considered sacred persons as some have wanted, but ordinary citizens, ordinary faithful, which is what they are; my desire that it be clear that we are not nor can we be religious; the need that their way to any upright work or noble human task not be blocked" (*Letter*, October 7, 1950, no. 20).

[94] Among many other texts, one can see the *Reglamento* of 1941 (art. 1); the *Lineamenta* of the Priestly Society of the Holy Cross of 1943 (no. 3) and the *Constitutions* (nos. 4, 310, 312, 336, etc.); the Decree *Primum Institutum*, §§ 3, 6 and 9; 1947 *Constitutions*, (nos. 4, 17, 315, 317, 345, etc.); the Apostolic Brief *Mirifice de Ecclesia* of 1947.

limits of Catholic faith and moral teaching, is completely free. Therefore the Institute assumes no responsibility for the professional, social, political or financial undertakings of its members."[95]

d) Finally we mention that in this June 1950 document the founder seeks to add a statute to the draft of the *Constitutions* entitled "Statuto riguardante i Sodali Sacerdoti diocesani della Società Sacerdotale della Santa Croce." Here is a matter not of reaffirming something already recognized in the earlier juridical texts but of raising a new question. For this reason and given its importance, let us interrupt our study to dwell on its fundamental idea: the abiding concern of the founder for priests, especially diocesan priests.

## 7. With the occasion of a "dilata": helping diocesan priests in their path towards sanctity

On October 2, 1928, Fr. Josemaría saw Opus Dei composed of lay people and priests. In spreading the God-given message, he turned not only to young men and older professionals, but also to some priests incardinated in dioceses. He invited these latter to cooperate in the apostolate and to bind themselves in some way to the Work. Nevertheless, he soon realized that the novelty of Opus Dei's spirit required priests formed from the start in its spirit. They would come from the lay ranks of Opus Dei and would dedicate themselves completely to its pastoral and apostolic work. He worked in this direction until, with the lights received on February 14, 1943, he requested from Madrid's bishop the erection of the Priestly Society of the Holy Cross. As we know, after the granting of the *nihil obstat* of the Holy See, this took place on December 8, 1943, providing for the ensuing ordination of members of Opus Dei.[96]

Nevertheless Msgr. Escrivá did not give up his work with diocesan priests. The years he spent in the seminary of Logroño and later in the diocese of Saragossa had etched on his soul a profound appreciation for "my brother priests." He empathized with their concerns, problems, needs and virtues. His subsequent experience in Madrid, his friendship with priests with many of whom he lived in the capital and his work of spiritual direction with a good number of them reinforced these desires. At the request of many bishops throughout Spain and moved by his passion for holy priests, during the forties he dedicated much time to preaching retreats and

---

[95] These words, an almost textual reproduction of § 9 of *Primum Institutum*, were repeated literally in the draft *Constitutions* presented in February 1950 and from there they were included in subsequent juridical texts.

[96] See chapter IV.

spiritually guiding priests and seminarians, one by one. Thousands of priests received his spiritual encouragement, until he moved to Rome.[97] To all he stressed the need to be saints in the normal activities of the priesthood.[98]

By extensively working with priests he could reawaken their desires of holiness, while giving them a chance to air their problems and to receive fraternal help. He also realized that the spirit of Opus Dei—sanctifying oneself in one's state in life, taking occasion of the incidents of daily living—represented to them light and encouragement to help them live better their priestly vocation to serve their diocese and to fulfill their pastoral tasks.

When in 1946 he moved to Rome, his solidarity with and concern for priests did not wane. In 1948 and 1949 these sentiments intensified; he felt called to extend the light and energy God had communicated to him to diocesan priests. But how to do it? After prayerfully considering the question at length, he concluded it would be necessary to begin a new foundation to help diocesan priests. If necessary, he was also resolved to leave Opus Dei. Msgr. Escrivá was convinced that if God required this sacrifice, divine providence would surely take care of the Work, into which hitherto, at God's behest, he had put all his soul and life. He spoke about this prospect with some members of the Roman Curia, who were favorable. He even told Opus Dei's General Council and his sister Carmen

---

[97] Specifically, between June 1939 and the end of 1942 he preached 20 retreats for seminarians and secular priests of Madrid, Valencia, Avila, Pamplona, Vitoria, León, Lérida, Segovia, etc. To these should be added those he preached to religious communities: the Hieronymites of Parral, the Augustinians of El Escorial, the Piarists of the Colegio de San José de Calasanz de Madrid, etc. For more information see the biographies of Bernal, Gondrand, etc., referred to in note 1 of chapter I.

[98] Among many testimonies in the RHF, we quote the words of Most Rev. Pedro Cantero, who was the Archbishop of Saragossa and who knew Msgr. Escrivá from the first years of the foundation of Opus Dei. The love the founder of Opus Dei had for priests "deserves a separate chapter: for him helping priests was to work in the most important and crucial field of the Church: it was to work in the very heart of pastoral ministry. He was conscious of the pastoral transcendence and repercussions to follow from a priest deciding to follow resolutely a way of holiness and to offer himself as a generous holocaust. When he was younger—recently ordained—he sought to attract to himself priests with the object of stirring up their desire for everything God asked of them, helping them with his priestly prayers and giving them, on the other hand, all the extraordinary spirit of his interior life. He knew how to do this with great refinement, as though it were he who was learning. I remember that when he spoke to priests or gave them spiritual direction he used to say with simplicity and humility that it was like 'selling honey to the beekeeper,' but he sold it and with great profit for those who listened to him" (Deposition of Most Rev. Pedro Cantero Cuadrado, September 12, 1976, in RHF, T-4391).

(*Translator's note*. This testimony has now been published in P. Cantero Cuadrado, *Josemaría Escrivá de Balaguer: un hombre de Dios*, Madrid 1992, pp. 50-51.)

and brother Santiago of his decision to dedicate himself entirely to this new foundation.[99]

Such were matters in 1950 when discussions began for a new pontifical approval. On March 28 of that year the founder celebrated his silver jubilee as a priest. Four days later when all signs portended that the *Congressus* of the Sacred Congregation for Religious was to vote in favor of the definitive approval of Opus Dei as a secular institute, the delay referred to earlier came about. This *dilata* ("wait"), painful in itself, proved providential. In the weeks following the founder saw that, within the pastoral phenomenon proper to the Work, a place could also be made for priests incardinated in dioceses, who could be admitted as members of the Priestly Society of the Holy Cross. A new foundation, therefore, was not necessary, nor did God require of him the sacrifice of leaving Opus Dei.

We have a 1951 Letter where, after alluding to these events and to the willingness of his soul to fulfill God's will, he states: "But God did not so wish it, and he freed me, with his merciful hand, as affectionate as any father, from the truly great sacrifice I was preparing to make by leaving Opus Dei. In an unofficial way I had made known my intention to the Holy See . . . but afterwards I saw clearly that a new foundation, a new association, was unnecessary, since there was room within Opus Dei for diocesan priests."[100] If Opus Dei members must seek sanctification in the ordinary setting of work, doing their best, then priests too, without leaving their place, their status as members of the presbyterate of a diocese, can and ought to sanctify themselves in the exercise of their priestly ministry. They will carry it out with full dedication and fully united to their ordinary, with the stimulus and spiritual help they receive from Opus Dei aimed at fulfilling their very duties.

All of this was conveyed in the document addressed on June 2, 1950, to the Sacred Congregation for Religious whose examination we have interrupted. In this text Msgr. Escrivá succinctly sets forth the problem and how, once the juridical solution was perceived, he made known to Fr. Larraona, in his capacity as Undersecretary of the Congregation, his desire of making it possible for priests incardinated in a diocese to belong to the Priestly Society of the

---

[99] The present Vicar General of the Prelature of Opus Dei, Msgr. Echevarría, reflected on this state of mind of the founder and his collaborators at the time: "I imagined the profound sorrow that this would cause them, even though they understood the apostolic need for this new foundation. But, above all, one is impressed by the heroism with which Msgr. Escrivá was always ready to respond to what God asked of him and even, if this were the case, to abandon the Work, that had been born in his hands with so much prayer and sacrifice" (J. Echevarría, "La fraternidad sacerdotal en la vida de Mons. Escrivá de Balaguer," in *Palabra*, 239, June 1985, p. 25).

[100] *Letter*, December 24, 1951, no. 3.

Holy Cross and how their incorporation might be effected. He pointed out later that Fr. Larraona concurred with the solution. He further suggested that, taking advantage of this delay, the statute might be officially presented with the request that it be included in the *Constitutions*.

In the months that passed from the start of the discussions for the definitive approval, not only had studies been made and difficulties resolved, but steps had been taken, ones of undeniable moment. We are thus on the threshold of a pontifical approval that will be decisive from many points of view. But the consideration of this event and the examination of the 1950 *Constitutions* is left for another chapter.

# Chapter VII

## THE PONTIFICAL APPROVAL OF 1950

1. The Decree *Primum inter* (June 16, 1950) and the Constitutions of 1950
2. The spirit of Opus Dei in the documents of 1950
3. The Constitutions of 1950 and the unity of the pastoral phenomenon of Opus Dei:

   a) The aim of the Institute

   b) Diversity of members and unity of vocation
4. The configuration of the bond
5. With the naturalness of ordinary Christians
6. Description of apostolic activity

# Chapter VII

## *THE PONTIFICAL APPROVAL OF 1950*

### 1. The Decree *Primum inter* (June 16, 1950) and the Constitutions of 1950

In the first days of June 1950 the Commission of Consultors, entrusted with giving their opinion on the definitive approval of Opus Dei, began their deliberations. During the first fortnight of June they rigorously studied the texts presented, evaluated the development achieved by Opus Dei, and examined the *Constitutions* again. Of special interest were the features that represented greater novelty, given the information, observations, and proposals presented by the President General of Opus Dei.[1] Finally on June 22 the Commission satisfactorily concluded the new examination, and all its members expressed themselves favorable to granting the definitive approval of Opus Dei and its *Constitutions*.

This opinion of the Commission was ratified by Cardinal Lavitrano, the Prefect of the Sacred Congregation for Religious, on June 28, 1950. Using special faculties granted him by the Roman Pontiff with occasion of the jubilee year, he ordained that the decree of definitive approval—which begins with the words *Primum inter*—be dated June 16, the feast of the Sacred Heart of Jesus, in keeping with the express desire of Msgr. Escrivá.[2]

*Primum inter* is a solemn text of considerable length: it's 45 paragraphs make it three times longer than that of the 1947 decree of praise.[3] It begins, as usual, with some historical data, and then moves on to a detailed exposition of the characteristics of the Institute. It ends with the appropriate formula of approval, signed by Cardinal Lavitrano and Archbishop Pasetto as the Prefect and Sec-

---

[1] "Post satis longum rerum omnium examen, quae ratione novitatis peculiarem difficultatem prae se ferebant, Constitutiones accurate in singulis fixae ac definitae fuerunt" (Decree *Primum inter*, § 6).

[2] AGP, Sezione Giuridica, V/15934.

[3] The complete text of the decree is given in the Appendix, document no. 31.

retary respectively of the pontifical Congregation. "Having carefully considered and studied under all of its aspects everything
having to do with the Institute and *Constitutions* of Opus Dei and
the Priestly Society of the Holy Cross and having found everything
clear and solid, the Sacred Congregation for Religious, in use of the
special faculties granted to it with the occasion of the jubilee year
by his Holiness Pope Pius XII, in his name and with his authority,
has decreed to establish the following:

"1.- The Institute named the *Priestly Society of the Holy Cross and
Opus Dei* is definitively approved and confirmed as a secular insti-
tute in accordance with the Apostolic Constitution *Provida Mater
Ecclesia*";

"2.- The *Constitutions* of the Secular Institute *Priestly Society of
the Holy Cross and Opus Dei* are approved as they appear in the text
whose original copy is preserved in the archives of the Sacred Congregation."[4]

In the introduction both the international extension of Opus Dei
and the novelty it represents are twice emphasized to justify the
length of the text: *ne dubium quodlibet in posterum remaneat*: "so that
there never be any doubt" about the nature and government of
Opus Dei. Given the special theological and pastoral phenomenon
which it entails, the decree sets forth and comments on some of its
fundamental characteristics.[5] The decree then presents a detailed
panorama of Opus Dei: its nature (§§ 7-9); general organization (§§
10-17); apostolate (§§ 18-26); spirit (§§ 27-33); the formation it gives
its members (§§ 34-39); and finally its form of government (§§ 40-
44).

In more than one aspect the *Constitutions* approved by the Decree *Primum inter* are not only a milestone but also in a certain sense
a consolidation of the juridical path of Opus Dei. The maturity
achieved by the Work in 1950 was rooted not only in its expanded
apostolic activity but also in the fundamental advances whose sanction Msgr. Escrivá had obtained since the pontifical approval of
1947. The Holy See had approved membership in Opus Dei of
persons from the most varied social conditions, including those
married or at least with a vocation to marriage. Thus was clearly
highlighted the pastoral phenomenon of sanctifying the most varied human realities to which Opus Dei considered itself called from
the very start. The project Msgr. Escrivá presented to the Holy See
in February 1950 for approval included this expanded membership
and other steps achieved since 1947. It was completed with the text
regarding diocesan priests presented by the founder on June 2, 1950.
The whole text reflected the institutional development to that time.

---

[4] Decree *Primum inter*, § 45.

[5] *Ibid.*, §§ 5 and 6.

The *Constitutions* comprise 479 numbers divided into four parts and 20 chapters. The first part—*De Instituti natura et membris* (nos. 1-125)—deals with the nature of the Institute and its members (incorporation, separation, etc.); the second part—*De vita sodalium in Instituto* (nos. 126-292)—concerns the obligations, the formation, the customs, spirit, practices of piety, etc., of members; the third part—*De Instituti regimine* (nos. 293-436)—articulates the form of government at different levels: general, regional and local; finally the fourth part—*De Sectione mulierum* (nos. 437-479)—is dedicated to particular aspects of the women's branch while making reference to other parts of the approved text in common matters.[6]

In approving the official text of the *Constitutions* the Sacred Congregation addressed to Msgr. Escrivá in his capacity as founder, an important and significant document signed by the Secretary, Archbishop Pasetto, and dated August 2, 1950. This granted him "special faculties *vita durante*." "You and your Council are gladly granted the faculty of proposing whatever changes, declarations and complements for whatever reason may seem opportune or useful for the evolution and needs of the Institute and its extension and the intensity of its so singular and eminent apostolate."[7]

With the 1950 documents—the decree of approval and the *Constitutions*—the preceding steps are consolidated and new ones taken that better reflect the richness of the foundational charism. They lead us to affirm, as we have done before, that a stage is hereby closed. Much distance remains to reach a juridical solution fully accommodated to this charism; in subsequent stages the founder will invoke the special faculties of the document of August 2, 1950. But further evolution does not lessen the value of the decree of June 1950 nor the text of the *Constitutions* approved by this decree.

## 2. The spirit of Opus Dei in the documents of 1950

We begin our examination of *Primum inter* and the 1950 *Constitutions* with the primary and fundamental reality that endows both canonical texts with soul and meaning: Opus Dei's spirit. Reasons of a general character prompt this step, but also others related to the juridical development of Opus Dei and relevant to the historical moment before us. We refer to the founder's permanent desire to make Opus Dei's spirit stand out clearly in juridical documents so as to serve as an hermeneutical criteria for their correct understanding. This is especially the case when the juridical texts do not fully accord with the foundational charism, as continued to be the case.[8]

---

[6] The first chapter of the *Constitutions* is found in the Appendix, document no. 32.

[7] See this document in the Appendix, no. 33.

[8] This point has been extensively covered in section 3 of chapter III.

This is what Msgr. Escrivá had done in 1941 and 1943-1944, as
we have seen before.  When Opus Dei received papal approvals as
a secular institute (1947 and 1950), not only did he not renounce his
former way of acting but he reinforced it.  The juridical figures
adopted up to then were not completely satisfactory, since they
implied an accommodation in some points to features proper to the
states of perfection and were thus foreign to Opus Dei.  These ac-
commodations or concessions must therefore be counterbalanced
by declarations of its spirit that afford an adequate point of reference.  This was the more essential, the more important and solemn
were the approvals.

For this reason in 1947, besides dedicating a whole chapter of
the *Constitutions* (Chapter VIII) to the spirit of Opus Dei and diverse declarations throughout the articles of the *Constitutions*,[9] the
founder made sure the *Decretum laudis* included some paragraphs
on the spirit of Opus Dei.  He acted in the same way again in 1950,
with respect both to the *Constitutions*, where he kept the texts referring to this spirit, and to the Decree *Primum inter*.  In the latter he
sought and achieved the inclusion of a whole section based on his
explanations and texts that reflect the foundational charism.[10]  It is
this section of the decree of approval we are now going to examine.
We will supplement it occasionally with quotations from the *Constitutions* and from a 1961 *Letter*, where Msgr. Escrivá comments precisely on this text, while underlining essentials of Opus Dei's spirit.[11]

In the 1961 *Letter* he comments: "Our *particular law*, approved
by the Decree *Primum inter*, retains in all its vigor what is the hinge
of the pastoral phenomenon of Opus Dei: ordinary work, profession or job, sanctified and sanctifying."[12]  *Primum inter*, much before
its section specifically dedicated to spirit, declares in initial paragraphs referring to Opus Dei's nature and aims: its members seek
sanctity and apostolate "through the exercise of moral and christian

---

[9] In this chapter and in other numbers of the 1947 *Constitutions*, Msgr. Escrivá repeats
with a few additions or editorial retouches texts that come from the documents of 1941
and, especially, from that called *Spirit*, which we studied before.

[10] In the *Letter* of December 29, 1947/February 14, 1966, no. 171, he writes: "I saw to it
that included in our *Reglamentos* were the Customs, the spirit, the mortifications, the
way of praying, etc. They told me that was not juridical, that things were not done this
way anymore, that it was not the custom. I answered that because it is something new,
it should be done. And this we achieved." And in another *Letter* dated 1952, he insists:
"We managed to skirt the obscurities existent in the legislation by obtaining—after a
filial complaint—in our *particular law*, along with the technical language required by
the positive law of secular institutes, the inclusion of fundamental points of our spirit
and asceticism; the particularities of our aim and the specific characteristics of how we
carry out our mission" (*Letter*, December 12, 1952, no. 4).

[11] *Letter*, January 25, 1961, nos. 32-41.

[12] *Ibid.*, no. 34.

virtues and especially by means of sanctifying ordinary daily professional work."[13] This is the work accompanying the normal human
condition that the members of Opus Dei do not give up for their
vocation.   But rather they take it up with renewed determination
and conviction, because they see, in the light of supernatural faith,
that in that very work they are to ratify their destiny and mission as
Christians.[14]

Linked to work, is secularity, a fundamental quality of the spiritual makeup of members of Opus Dei.  It is to be understood from
the perspective of faith.  Thus the conditions, desires and obligations proper to ordinary life are not a mere sociological datum, but
a dimension of one's very own personal supernatural vocation. The
calling is not juxtaposed alongside human existence, but is found at
its heart, endowing it with full meaning.

The 1961 *Letter* is unambiguous.  Opus Dei's asceticism rests on
professional work carried out in the middle of the world, the founder
writes; from this there derives, as "an essential and correlative requirement," secularity, i.e., a way of being and of acting consistent
with the "fully lay condition of the members."  In a word it is a style
of life—including spiritual life—that connotes and presupposes living in and being in the world.  "This full secularity of the ascetical
and pastoral phenomenon of Opus Dei," the *Letter* continues, "is
not simply a conception of positive juridical law, nor a merely external note or tactic for obtaining a certain apostolic effectiveness.
Rather it is a reality consubstantial with the *raison d'être* of our
vocation.  Secularity surpasses and transcends every norm of positive law in order to insert itself in the very heart of our vocation of
work and apostolate."[15]

Precisely because of this, Msgr. Escrivá concludes, secularity is
a reality of a general scope "that infuses all our apostolic way of
acting, both individually and collectively."[16]  And, consequently (we
ourselves can add), it reaches into every corner of the spiritual physiognomy, bringing about a new synthesis in relation with the secular
form of being.

---

[13] Decree *Primum inter*, § 7.

[14] This is what is indicated by the *Constitutions* in declaring that the proper aim of Opus
Dei—the spreading of sanctity and apostolate in the middle of the world—is obtained
"by the sanctification of ordinary work and by the exercise of the professional task or
equivalent work, which the members do not abandon, because they seek sanctification
by means of this work" (no. 4, § 1). The words used by this text of 1950 are almost the
same as those of the *Reglamento* of 1941, an echo in turn—as will be recalled—of the
notes of the founder in the 1930s.

[15] *Letter*, January 25, 1961, no. 35.

[16] *Ibid*.

No wonder then that the first paragraph of *Primum inter*'s section devoted to describing the spirit of the Work speaks of unity of life. This term refers to the harmonious unification of many dimensions: spiritual no less than secular or temporal. "The Institute presents a double aspect, ascetical and apostolic, which correspond fully to, while intrinsically and harmoniously united and infused with, the secular character of Opus Dei. This secular character thus always motivates and necessarily brings with it a solid and simple unity of life."[17]

Nor need we say that such unification presupposes a center to which all the different dimensions are referred. The decree then refers to this very core: God, or more concretely the reality of God as revealed in Jesus Christ. At the center is a God who paternally loves each and every man and woman as his children. They are to have a deep sense of their divine filiation, as Msgr. Escrivá used to say. "The solid foundation upon which everything in Opus Dei is based and the fruitful root enlivening everything is a humble and sincere sense of divine filiation in Christ Jesus." The decree links everything to the gift of piety, "by which one sweetly believes in the paternal charity God has for us (1 Jn 4:16) and which leads us to see Christ our Lord, God and Man, as our first-born brother, full of unspeakable goodness."[18]

Apropos of the gift of piety, the same paragraph echoes the Pauline passage: *pietas ad omnia utilis est* (1 Tim 4:8). The reference is not merely rhetorical, but expresses a profound reality which the decree immediately indicates: "The oft-savored sense of divine paternity, of adoptive filiation and of fraternity in Jesus Christ, engenders as natural fruits in Opus Dei, love for contemplation and a spirit of prayer (Zac 12:10), a zeal and hunger for interior life, filial trust in the paternal providence, and a serene and cheerful abandonment to the divine will."[19] The enumeration could be completed by recourse, not only to various writings of the founder, but even to other paragraphs of the decree itself. Also related to divine filiation are several other characteristics, such as fraternity and spirit of service,[20] or magnanimity and daring. One ought to confront the world with an open and constructive spirit, relying on the certain

---

[17] Decree *Primum inter*, § 27. Here as in successive paragraphs the decree merely repeats—on occasions literally—teachings and texts of Opus Dei's founder.

[18] Decree *Primum inter*, § 28.

[19] *Ibid.* The decree continues to speak of the life of prayer and the norms of piety and other ascetical practices in §§ 29, 31 and 33.

[20] *Ibid.*, §§ 28 and 30.

loving help of a Creator who has drawn all things out of nothing, has set us to live among them and has sent us to them.[21]

The decree does not limit itself to describing unity of life; it points out how it is to be achieved: "the need and as it were the supernatural instinct to purify all actions, to raise them to the order of grace, to sanctify them and to turn them into occasions of apostolate."[22] Later it returns to this theme, though with other terms: those of imitation. "In Opus Dei the renewed sense of divine filiation in Christ Jesus leads necessarily to, and is translated in practice by, an ardent desire and sincere effort, tender yet profound, of imitating God as his beloved children (Eph 5:1). Similar to Christ the only-begotten of the Father and first-born of many brothers who is the way and model in everything, one submits his life fully and completely to whatever is required by christian perfection (Rom 8:29), precisely in the world and in each one's profession."[23]

In these texts we find, with various words and contexts, a radical focus. Beginning with divine filiation, a member is to raise created reality, in all of its dimensions, incorporating it into an intimate relationship between himself and God. An immediate consequence follows: the perception of human life, in all its circumstances, ordinary and secular, as the setting for an encounter with God. One is called to show love through deeds, to transmit to his peers the faith and the love thanks to which his life has acquired full meaning (i.e., apostolate). This overflow will always respect the structure and laws of created reality, without doing them violence. Rather they are to be vivified from within, as the decree says, alluding to a capital point: the connection between Christian and human virtues. "From this [supernatural instinct to raise everything to the order of communion with God] stems great care for moral virtues, an integral education, a worthy and noble social life: "All things are yours and you are Christ's" (1 Cor 3:23; Phil 3:8). In summary: the spirit of Opus Dei is supernatural, sincere and profound, simple, perfectly assimilable until it becomes connatural. Then its spirit penetrates and purifies everything; without deforming them, it transforms all things into an authentic reality of sanctification and apostolate: "you are Christ's" and following the example of Christ and with Christ, of God (Phil, *ibid.*)."[24]

---

[21] *Ibid.*, § 27 and the paragraph which we will soon reproduce in the text; this theological background of magnanimity explains its intimate relationship with humility of which the decree speaks in paragraph 28.

[22] Decree *Primum inter*, § 30.

[23] *Ibid.*, § 32.

[24] *Ibid.*, § 30.

It would be possible to derive many conclusions or consequences from this synopsis of some of the key elements of Opus Dei's spirit. We will mention only three, since they are highlighted in the 1950 texts. First, what Msgr. Escrivá often referred to as "care for little things." Attention to detail and daily actions, in themselves apparently unimportant, take on a profound meaning for those who, living their faith, are conscious of being the object of God's constant and loving gaze. This is an early teaching of the founder, as seen in the long pertinent chapter in *The Way*[25] to which he made explicit reference in the 1950 *Constitutions*: "The members of Opus Dei must also bring the greatest possible diligence to life's many little things, because what is proper to our vocation is the sanctification of ordinary work. Life does not always present us with big things; on the other hand there are always little things where it is possible to manifest with perseverance our love for Jesus Christ."[26]

A second essential feature is apostolic zeal or sense: the consciousness of mission arising from knowing oneself to be God's child and called to imitate and follow Jesus Christ. Like him, they are to announce to all men the love of God the Father and to offer up their life for the salvation of the world. The Decree *Primum inter* dedicates a section to apostolate to which we will refer more fully later. For now it suffices to point out that early on the document, in speaking of the Institute's aim, underlines the apostolic dimension proper to the spirit of Opus Dei.[27] Moreover, the first paragraph of the section on the apostolic activity emphasizes how apostolate takes place in a natural and spontaneous way within the total context of the life of Opus Dei members in accordance with the general principle of unity of life. This paragraph reads as follows: "The members of Opus Dei, by a special vocation from God, live in the world (*in sæculo*): clothed and living like the others, they exercise their apostolate by taking occasion of this very world (*veluti ex sæculo ipso*)."[28]

A third characteristic to be pointed out is mentioned by Msgr. Escrivá in the 1961 *Letter*. Secularity is manifested, he writes, "in the capital importance given in Opus Dei's spirit to the personal freedom of the members, their autonomy in everything that has to do with the temporal order. . . . The continual exercise of freedom, wherein the members of Opus Dei are formed, is at the basis of our

---

[25] *The Way*, nos. 813-830.

[26] 1950 *Constitutions*, no. 230. (In the present chapter we will mention on occasions both the *Constitutions* of 1950 and those of 1947. To avoid confusion we will always mention in the note the date of the *Constitutions* being quoted.)

[27] Decree *Primum inter*, § 8.

[28] *Ibid.*, § 18.

asceticism. It is something connatural and intimately united to the secular condition of my children, and to what is the hinge of our vocation and the specific mode of our full dedication."[29]

The 1950 decree of approval speaks at length of this freedom, though not in the section dedicated to spirit. Rather it is featured in the part dealing with apostolate. "In all things related to their own profession and secular condition or in some way referring to them, the members work and act the same as other citizens. They cannot force the Church nor the Institute to answer juridically or morally for their actions or their works. They exercise all legitimate civil occupations with the greatest perfection possible. Even though these tasks be profane, they strive ardently to sanctify them, by frequently renewing their intention, by fervently exercising interior life, by a cheerful and continuous spirit of self-denial and by a self-sacrificing effort of constant work, to the end that it be perfect in all aspects."[30]

The following paragraph continues: "They [the members] respect civil laws and strive to fulfill faithfully and conscientiously their civic duties. Under no pretext do they try to avoid just laws and the obligations deriving therefrom. Similarly they demand that their civil and political rights be respected, without imprudently excepting any, and they are obliged to exercise them with a tenacious spirit on behalf of the common good. Opus Dei does not impose upon its members any particular political opinion. It requires of all, nevertheless, a full and sincere fidelity to civil authority, in conformity with personal conscience and obedience in those things that the state has the right to demand of them."[31]

In the aforementioned 1961 *Letter* the founder comments: "The members of the Work enjoy the same personal freedom as other Catholic faithful, the same as their fellow citizens. And their divine vocation, harmoniously impregnating their lay condition, leads them to serve society faithfully, to foster the common temporal good, generously contributing and building a just and ordered society. . . . With this moral and ascetical foundation Opus Dei members work in their temporal activities without implicating either the Church or the Work, because they do not rely either on the Church or the Work to carry out these activities. . . . Any professional successes will be theirs and theirs also will be any possible mistakes." He concludes, "My children, we must always defend the blessed free-

---

[29] *Letter*, January 25, 1961, no. 37.

[30] Decree *Primum inter*, § 19.

[31] *Ibid.*, § 20. With respect to freedom in temporal matters the 1950 *Constitutions* speak in nos. 183, 202-203.

dom that makes possible the formation of adult Christians who know how to assume loyal responsibility for their actions."[32]

## 3. The Constitutions of 1950 and the unity of the pastoral phenomenon of Opus Dei

In our analysis of the 1950 documents, we now go from considering the spirit to studying the juridical configuration properly speaking. We address our attention above all to the general characteristics that, in keeping with these texts, Opus Dei presents. In these documents the founder managed to reflect the unity of the pastoral phenomenon represented by Opus Dei with much greater perfection than in earlier stages, as much as the moment allowed.

In 1941 Opus Dei obtained diocesan approval as a pious union. In chapter III we saw how this juridical formula, in itself, was the most appropriate among those feasible for the incipient development then achieved by Opus Dei. Its members were recognized as simple faithful and ordinary citizens, and the solution offered sufficient breadth to accommodate future stages and specifications.

In 1943 in order to go forward with the ordination of priests to serve Opus Dei's apostolates, Msgr. Escrivá obtained from Madrid's Bishop the erection of the Priestly Society of the Holy Cross. In this document first place is given to this new priestly body, while Opus Dei, as the pastoral phenomenon of Christian life amid the world, is relegated in a certain way to second place. In all the documents of this time Opus Dei and the Priestly Society of the Holy Cross formally appear as distinct institutions, although intimately and essentially bound together.

This intimate connection is underlined in the 1944 *Constitutions* of diocesan right, approved by the bishop, by the inclusion in a single normative text of the development of the *Lineamenta* of the Priestly Society of the Holy Cross and the particular statutes of Opus Dei. They still appear as two entities, but the treatment in a

---

[32] Letter, January 25, 1961, nos. 39-40. This is the proper context for understanding a prescription of the 1950 Constitutions not always well understood by those who abstract it from the spirit and practice of Opus Dei. Referring to members definitively incorporated into Opus Dei, it establishes that they bind themselves with an oath to seek advice with respect to professional matters that for some reason (because they imply important changes in place of residence or the way of living of the person involved or present aspects that affect ethical conduct, etc.) have a particular importance (1950 Constitutions, no. 58, art. 3°). We will deal with this oath, its true scope and meaning, as well as with its suppression in 1969 at a later moment (chapter IX). We point out now solely that it presupposes—as we have just said—a context of professional freedom, without derogating from this freedom in any way. Members of Opus Dei have always had full freedom to evaluate the advice they receive and to decide according to one meaning or another in accordance with their own conscience and with their own personal judgments or opinions. In fact and by law this commitment obliges one to seek advice; the advice is never a command.

single text emphasizes the unity of the underlying pastoral phenomenon.

The 1944 *Constitutions* were touched up, but without modifying the general structure. They became, in keeping with applicable canons, the starting point for the discussions begun in February 1946. This negotiation aimed at moving from diocesan to pontifical status. They culminated in the approval of the Priestly Society of the Holy Cross and Opus Dei as a secular institute of pontifical right on February 24, 1947. In the 1946 draft it is said that Opus Dei "is not an association after the fashion of pious associations, separate from the Priestly Society of the Holy Cross." Rather it forms "an internal association" of this Society, with which it "constitutes a *quid unum* and from which it is inseparable."[33] This strict union was emphasized in the discussions undertaken with the Holy See in the months preceding the promulgation of the Apostolic Constitution *Provida Mater Ecclesia*. The Sacred Congregation for Religious, in the studies previous to granting the *Decretum laudis*, names the Institution founded by Msgr. Escrivá as "Priestly Society of the Holy Cross and Opus Dei."[34] Analogously, Pope Pius XII, in his Apostolic Brief *Cum Sanctissimus* (June 28, 1946), and the Congregation for Religious in the letter *Brevis sane* praising its purposes (August 13, 1946), continue to use the same name of "Priestly Society of the Holy Cross and Opus Dei," implying thus a single institution.[35]

We come now to the 1947 *Constitutions*, which, in continuity with all preceding documents and interventions, have for their title *Constitutiones Societatis Sacerdotalis Sanctæ Crucis et Operis Dei*. No longer do they speak as in 1944 first of the Priestly Society and then of Opus Dei. Rather from the start reference is made to the one pastoral phenomenon of sanctity and apostolate in the middle of the world that constitutes Opus Dei. But even here in the development of the normative text a totally adequate structuring is not achieved.[36] In any case, these *Constitutions* stress that what is being approved is a single Institute, whose name is "Priestly Society of the Holy Cross and Opus Dei."[37] They further define that "the

---

[33] Draft of *Constitutions* of 1946, nos. 4, 5, 312-314.

[34] AGP, Sezione Giuridica, IV/15540 and 15530.

[35] These documents were dealt with in chapter V, section 3 and can be found in the Appendix, document nos. 19 and 21.

[36] In fact, after some references to the integrity of the pastoral phenomenon contained in the first chapter of the *Constitutions*, attention is focused on the nature and government of the Priestly Society of the Holy Cross (to which the rest of the first part and all of the second is dedicated) and then in the third part the totality of Opus Dei once again is described.

[37] 1947 *Constitutions*, no. 1.

name Opus Dei belongs to the whole Institute."[38]  Fostering Christian life in the world by lay people, ordinary Christians who have taken upon themselves the consciousness of their vocation, becomes paramount, while the Priestly Society of the Holy Cross tends to become ever more clearly in these juridical texts a priestly body at the service of a single pastoral phenomenon.[39]

The Decree *Primum Institutum* had employed in the beginning of its *pars narrativa* an expression worthy of note: *Societas Sacerdotalis Sanctæ Crucis et Operis Dei, breviato autem nomine Opus Dei.*[40] This important formula in its simplicity expresses in a comprehensive way the Work's single pastoral phenomenon.  Doubtless for this reason, the founder requested and obtained from the Holy See in 1948 that this brief formula be included, "with the abbreviated name, Opus Dei" in no. 1 of the 1947 *Constitutions.*[41]

These passages flow into the 1950 *Constitutions* which begin thus: "The Institute, which has for its name Priestly Society of the Holy Cross and Opus Dei, and, with the abbreviated name, Opus Dei, is a secular institute dedicated to seeking Christian perfection in the middle of the world and exercising apostolate.  The name Opus Dei corresponds to the whole Institute.  Within it is a group of members, called the Priestly Society of the Holy Cross, which is made up of the priests of the Institute and some laymen who, in the judgment of the Father, are considered more especially prepared for priestly ordination."

We are in the presence not only of a single Institute, as was the case with earlier texts but of a single description.  The document from the start situates us before a unity: a single pastoral phenomenon endowed with a juridical configuration, Opus Dei.  Moreover this oneness is reflected not only by the name and some general declarations but also by the systematic ordering of the text.

In the 1950 *Constitutions* Msgr. Escrivá gathered and incorporated the modifications and completions to the statutory text approved by the Congregation for Religious between 1947 and 1950.

---

[38] 1947 *Constitutions*, no. 5.

[39] The Decree of Approval *Primum Institutum* (February 24, 1947), and the Apostolic Brief *Mirifice de Ecclesia* (July 20, 1947), and the rescript of the Sacred Congregation for Religious of August 7, 1947, with regard to the clerical nature of the Institute refer to a single secular institute whose name is "the Priestly Society of the Holy Cross and Opus Dei." We have dealt with these documents in chapter 5, and they can be seen in the Appendix, document nos. 22, 24, and 26.

[40] Decree *Primum Institutum*, § 1.

[41] *Constitutionibus Operis Dei Addenda* (February 18, 1948) in AGP, Sezione Giuridica, V/15506. Thus no. 1 of the 1947 *Constitutions* came to read as follows: "Institutum, cui titulus Societas Sacerdotalis Sanctae Crucis et Opus Dei, breviato autem nomine Opus Dei, est . . ." (The initial capital chapter of these *Constitutions* is found in the Appendix, no. 23.)

The net result is a reorganization of the whole text. The result retains the content included in the 1947 *Constitutions* (plus the completions just mentioned). As we have seen, there are four parts: nature and members of the Institute (I); life of members of the Institute (II); government of the Institute (III); and women's branch (IV).[42] This simple enunciation of the parts compared with those of the 1947 *Constitutions* shows the progress made in reaffirming the unity of the pastoral phenomenon.

The 1950 *Constitutions* contain in their first part a structured and unitary description of the totality of the pastoral phenomenon. The language of no. 64 from the beginning of chapter V in part II entitled "the Priestly Society of the Holy Cross" is very significant. "The Priestly Society of the Holy Cross, which is dealt with in no. 1, being *aliquid intrinsecum* to Opus Dei, has the same superiors who exercise in the Priestly Society the same faculties that they enjoy in Opus Dei." The concern to obtain an adequate juridical formulation of the one pastoral phenomenon, overcoming the limits of the figure obtained in 1943, led the founder in subsequent years to bring it about that the name or title of this Institute, Priestly Society of the Holy Cross and Opus Dei, appear as a *quid unum*. He reiterates in successive legal texts that Opus Dei is an *instrumentum proprium*, a *modus specificus* of apostolic action, a *quid unum* or an *aliquid intrinsecum* of the Priestly Society of the Holy Cross. Deficient formulas all, but at least they presupposed and affirmed the unity. This form of speaking had been present in the 1947 *Constitutions* in whose no. 337 we read: "Being Opus Dei something intrinsic (*aliquid intrinsecum*) of the Priestly Society of the Holy Cross, it has the

---

[42] Part III ("Government of the Institute") is substantially the same as part II of the *Constitutions* of 1947 with the introduction of the rescripts of October 25, 1948, and of January 27, 1949, to which we have referred in section 1 of the previous chapter. Part II—"life of members of the Institute"—repeats chapters V-XI of part I of 1947. Chapters I-IV and XII and XIII of part I of 1947 become now part I of 1950—"nature and members of the Institute"—including the content of "Appendix to the Constitutions of Opus Dei" from March 18, 1948, as well as the rescript of September 8, 1949, and the "Statute of the diocesan priest members of the Priestly Society of the Holy Cross" of June 2, 1950—of which we have spoken in sections 2, 6 and 7 of the previous chapter. To this part I of 1950 are brought also many of the texts which in 1947 were found in part III—"Opus Dei"—in such a way that the former part III disappears almost completely, there remaining only two brief chapters which become part IV of 1950—"women's branch." It gathers together some peculiarities and specific aspects of their apostolate and government, referring to other parts of the text for the general norms. At the beginning of the *Constitutions* of 1950 mention is made of this section, in no. 13, where, after saying that the Institute is made up of clerics and laity, it adds that "there is also in the Institute a section for women which will be dealt with especially in part IV of these Constitutions." In no. 438—the second of this part IV—it states "what is established in these Constitutions holds also *pari iure* for the women, unless by the content of the language or by the nature of things something else is clear, or in this part of the Constitutions special prescriptions are explicitly established."

same major Superiors who exercise in Opus Dei the same faculties as in the Society." If we now reread no. 64 of the 1950 *Constitutions* recently quoted, we will see how things have literally been turned on their head with respect to the 1943 and successive texts. No longer is a part (the Priestly Society of the Holy Cross) put first, over the whole pastoral phenomenon. Rather Opus Dei, the effective promotion of sanctity in the middle of the world by the work of ordinary Christians, is the whole, a total unity, in whose interior there works a priestly body seconding the work carried out by the whole Institute.

Progress is even clearer if we note that this affirmation of institutional unity is parallel to the achievement of a juridical formula more adequate to the pastoral phenomenon in its full expansion. It is now possible to sanction the unfolding of the virtualities inherent in the foundational charism, which had been achieved since 1947. Then Msgr. Escrivá had judged that the time had come to consider ended the historical period begun in the years 1932-1933. Over the past decade and a half he had concentrated his apostolic activity on university students. The authorization granted by the Holy See in 1948 and 1949 to admit to membership in the Institute (i.e., with a juridical bond) men and women, single or married, of whatever profession, class or social condition, had its repercussions. The apostolate was broadened. This becomes embodied in the texts of the 1950 documents—Decree *Primum inter* and *Constitutions*—where Opus Dei is said to be a way of sanctity and apostolate in the middle of the world without limits of any kind, open therefore to men and women of whatever condition.

This broadening of the description and definition of Opus Dei manifests itself in different directions. Let's look at two: a) the purpose of the Institute and b) the diversity of members in a unity of vocation.

a) *The aim of the Institute*

Msgr. Escrivá had never conceived Opus Dei as an institution with a limited or restricted scope to which one might adhere by committing only a part of one's life. Rather he always saw it as a spiritual and apostolic work born of God's express will and affecting the whole person.[43]

In Opus Dei's first juridical statute this characteristic is forcefully set forth. In the 1941 *Reglamento* the aim of Opus Dei is expressed with extraordinary breadth. Opus Dei, this initial article affirms, is formed by "men and women who, in the middle of the world, seek Christian perfection by sanctifying ordinary work." In

---

[43] See the first two chapters, especially section 5, of chapter I.

even wider terms the document *Régimen* declares that "Opus Dei seeks the sanctification of its members and the salvation of souls."[44]

In 1943 when Msgr. Escrivá deemed it necessary to request the diocesan erection of the Priestly Society of the Holy Cross he had to adapt himself to the requirements and practice of the Congregation for Religious. This *praxis* required the definition of both a general and specific aim. This explains why the 1944 *Constitutions* (incorporating the *Lineamenta* of 1943 and what was established in the Decree of erection of December 8 of the same year) describe the specific aim of the Priestly Society of the Holy Cross to be an apostolic work especially directed to intellectuals. Yet the aim of Opus Dei—presented, let us not forget, as a reality inseparable from the Priestly Society of the Holy Cross—is described with the same breadth as in the text of 1941.[45] In the 1947 documents a step forward is made in formulating the aim. In accordance with the praxis in force one still speaks of a generic aim—the pursuit of holiness—and then of an aim denominated as special (identical to what is mentioned in the 1944 *Constitutions* as the "specific aim."[46] The Decree *Primum Institutum* establishes, that this special aim—work with intellectuals—is "intimately, intrinsically and perpetually united to the generic aim and to the spirit of the Institute." Yet it immediately adds that the "Institute constantly promotes sanctity of its members, through the sanctification of ordinary work and the diligent and careful exercise of professional offices or civil or public offices proper to each one."[47] The *Constitutions*, in turn, expand the panorama by affirming that the work of Opus Dei extends "to all classes of civil society." It seeks "the sanctification of its members and the salvation of souls," which is "achieved by means of the sanctification of ordinary work" and "the maximum fidelity in the fulfillment of the social activity or profession proper to each one."[48]

We find a clear formulation of the aim of Opus Dei as a unitary pastoral phenomenon in a document issued outside of the scope of the Congregation for Religious and, therefore, not conditioned by its praxis. This is the case of the Apostolic Brief *Mirifice de Ecclesia*, of July 20, 1947, where the "reason, essence and peculiar aim of Opus Dei lies in acquiring sanctity through ordinary work," is highlighted.[49]

---

[44] *Reglamento*, art. 1; *Régimen*, art 1. See in general section 4 of chapter III.

[45] See what was set forth at length in chapter IV, section 4.

[46] Decree *Primum Institutum*, § 6; 1947 *Constitutions*, no. 3. With regard to the description of the aim in the text of 1947, some commentaries have already been made in chapter V, section 8.

[47] Decree *Primum Institutum*, § 6; also 1947 *Constitutions*, no. 4.

[48] 1947 *Constitutions*, nos. 5 and 317

[49] We spoke of this document in chapter V, section 7. We recall that it can be consulted in the Appendix, document no. 24.

In 1950 it was not yet possible to abandon completely the terminology of generic and specific aim (which will disappear in subsequent periods). But it was possible to modify it and come close to surpassing it. The Decree *Primum inter* and the *Constitutions* of that date no longer speak of two aims, but of a single aim (though two aspects are distinguished: the generic and the special or specific).

The single aim with its two aspects is referred to in no. 3 of the *Constitutions* and in paragraph 8 of the Decree *Primum inter*. The generic aspect is formulated in the decree with a denser description than that employed in earlier texts: "to seek with all their might the glory of God . . . and sanctification in the middle of the world of its members." The 1950 *Constitutions* use, with regard to the generic aspect, expressions analogous to those of earlier texts, but they represent a strong step forward in another sense. What was said in the 1947 *Constitutions* in several numbers, even in closely connected ones, of the general aim is expressed now in a single text. Intellectually distinguishable aspects which in fact are but facets of a single-minded pursuit of a single aim are unified: "to work with dedication so that the so called intellectuals . . . may adhere to the precepts of our Lord Jesus Christ and reflect them in practice; to promote and spread the life of perfection in the world among all classes of civil society, and to form men and women for the exercise of apostolate in the middle of the world."[50]

The reaffirmation of unity in defining the aims has its consequences, as is logical, in the exposition of the means. Thus the 1947 *Constitutions*, after speaking in no. 3 of the apostolate among intellectuals as a special aim, says in the following number that to obtain these objectives "an exquisite cultivation of the spirit," is required of members "not only in the duties of piety but also in the fields of knowledge, both ecclesiastical and profane." Yet in other numbers the panorama is broadened. The 1950 *Constitutions*, in a manner parallel to the presentation of a unitary aim, open the description of means with a broad and general reference to work, in its various and multiple manifestations: "This aim is obtained by the exercise of the professional task or equivalent work, which the members do not abandon, because they seek sanctification by means of this work."[51] Only later and in a second paragraph introduced by *propterea* (in addition and in consequence) do they speak of other means and tasks ordained to this end. In this text are gathered the urgency of

---

[50] 1950 *Constitutions*, no. 3 § 2. In the Decree *Primum inter*, § 8, this aspect of the aim is described with the same words calling it "the special aspect," of which it says that it is "arcte atque intrinsece cum sanctificatione atque spiritu Instituti perpetuo coniunctus (Jn 17:19)."

[51] 1950 *Constitutions*, no. 4 § 1. This text comes from the third part—no. 317—of the *Constitutions* of 1947 and, in the last instance, from article 1 of the *Reglamento* of 1941 which gathered notes of Msgr. Escrivá from the 1930s.

an "exquisite cultivation of the spirit, not only in the duties of piety but also in those of knowledge, both ecclesiastical and profane," and the invitation to a "perfect fulfillment of professional and social tasks." Then it adds, "They must seek perfection proper to their own state." Education or cultivation of the soul becomes hence an essential element to the adequate realization of the work each must carry out, without excluding any honest task.[52]

The text, further, gives examples of some apostolic tasks of a formative character: "It promotes and directs institutions and works that offer intellectual and spiritual formation, such as houses and student residences, houses of spiritual retreat and analogous institutions."[53] The passage ends by connecting every possible means with what is the basic, characteristic reality of Opus Dei: sanctifying ordinary work. That goal calls for "a life of prayer and of sacrifice" and "the maximum fidelity to the fulfillment of the social and professional activity of each one."[54]

In synthesis, accommodating himself to the praxis of the Sacred Congregation, Msgr. Escrivá adapted himself, first in 1943, to the distinction between the generic and specific aims and to the specification of various tasks to achieve both. Throughout he was conscious of the fact that this way of speaking did not adequately express the spirit and experience proper to Opus Dei. Any transition from a generic sanctity to specific tasks that channel apostolic action is foreign to its collective life. Nor is there a gap between a particular apostolic task and a subsequent rooting in sanctity as the foundation for that action. Rather, by virtue of a unified experience, all the implications of the Christian vocation are engaged. Fusing the two aims—generic and specific—into a single aim with two aspects and reuniting the means, as we have just seen in the 1950 documents, constitutes, in this sense, a great step forward in the juridical expression of both the foundational charism and the single pastoral phenomenon issuing therefrom.

b) *Diversity of members and unity of vocation*

Consistent with this presentation of the aim, the Decree *Primum inter* and the 1950 *Constitutions* mention the existence of a variety of members, in keeping with a greater or lesser availability mandated by personal circumstances. In all cases, however, there is but one

---

[52] The text quotes expressly work in the public administration, as in other places (1950 *Constitutions*, no. 15). It speaks also of business and financial activities; about the reasons for this being mentioned we recall what was said in section 6 of chapter VI. With respect to the evaluation of the intellect and intellectual formation present also in the text, we refer to what was said in section 5 of chapter I.

[53] 1950 *Constitutions*, no. 4 § 2.

[54] 1950 *Constitutions*, no. 4 § 3. This text comes from no. 317 of the 1947 *Constitutions*, which reproduces in turn almost textually expressions from the 1941 documents. These expressions echo the constant preaching of the Founder.

spirit, one aim, and one government.  The ensuing picture is as follows:

a) Numeraries, men or women who assume a commitment of celibacy and usually live in Centers of Opus Dei; they are thus fully available to dedicate themselves to forming other members or to directing apostolic undertakings.[55]  Described as members in the strict sense, in accordance with the legislative terminology on secular institutes, they may, like any other citizen, exercise the most varied occupations—from public administration to university teaching, law, medicine, business, and so on—where they strive to give a Christian presence and witness.  Men members must pursue university or equivalent higher studies, plus the completion of ecclesiastical studies at a superior level.[56]  From among these some may be called to the priesthood to serve, mainly, the apostolates proper to Opus Dei.[57]  Among the numeraries of the women's branch some are called numerary assistants, who dedicate themselves to manual work or domestic service in Centers of Opus Dei.[58]

b) Oblates or associates,[59]  men or women who, though perhaps not possessing all of the requirements demanded for numeraries commit themselves to celibacy, make themselves available for appropriate apostolic tasks.  They also must be able to dedicate themselves to any honest profession or work, while they reside, ordinarily, with their families or in places in keeping with their work and condition that they consider most appropriate.[60]

---

[55] With regard to numeraries in general, see the Decree *Primum inter*, §§ 15 and 16; 1950 *Constitutions*, nos. 15, 16, 18.

[56] Decree *Primum inter*, §§ 14 and 35; 1950 *Constitutions*, nos. 35, 134 § 2, and 135.

[57] With regard to numerary priests see Decree *Primum inter*, §§ 12 and 13, 39; 1950 *Constitutions*, nos. 14, 65 and 66, 139-142 and 273.

[58] With regard to numeraries of the women's branch in particular, Decree *Primum inter*, § 16; 1950 *Constitutions*, nos. 440, 442-444 and 446.

[59] We stress that oblates (associates), in the rescript of September 8, 1949, received the name of internal supernumeraries, as another type within the general category of supernumeraries, which the Holy See had approved March 18, 1948 (see section 2 of the previous chapter and the Appendix, document no. 30).  They were included with this name, internal supernumeraries, by the founder in the draft of the *Constitutions* presented for approval in 1950.  Nevertheless in the final phase of the negotiations for the approval of this draft, it was suggested to the founder by the Sacred Congregation that the name be changed from internal supernumerary to that of oblate. Msgr. Escrivá thought it proper to accept this suggestion and with this name they appear, therefore, in the 1950 *Constitutions*.  Nevertheless, in the 1960s he changed this name to associate, in accordance with a general criterion he always tried to hold.  Namely, to avoid terms that could evoke the monastic religious spirit or experience, and to use on the other hand expressions that proceed from the common Christian language or secular environments.  Hereinafter we will only use this final term.

[60] Decree *Primum inter*, §§ 15 and 16; 1950 *Constitutions*, nos. 25, 41 and 440.

c) Supernumeraries, men or women, single or married, who, moved by an apostolic vocation and a desire for perfection, dedicate themselves with all their strength to pursue "perfection in their own state in life." They "employ as means of sanctification and apostolate their own family occupations and professions." They also "live the same spirit and, according to their possibilities, the same customs as the numerary numbers though they may only be entrusted with tasks compatible with the obligations arising from their natural family and place in civil society."[61]

d) Finally, cooperators may be affiliated without being juridically incorporated to the Institute as members. They cooperate with their prayer, their alms and, according to their circumstances, with their work, in the apostolates of Opus Dei. They likewise participate in its spiritual goods.[62] Non-Catholics and even non-Christians can be received as cooperators.[63]

Considering the panorama marked out by the texts just seen, plus the possibility of receiving in the Priestly Society of the Holy Cross priests incardinated in their own dioceses, we see that Opus Dei's founder managed to incarnate, with the wholeness and rigor of juridical norms, the breadth of the pastoral phenomenon that characterizes Opus Dei according to its proper charism. Thus Christians of every social condition consciously accept their call to holiness and apostolate precisely in and through their ordinary work and other circumstances proper to their walk in life.[64]

---

[61] Decree *Primum inter*, §§ 15 and 16; 1950 *Constitutions*, nos. 26-28, 41-45 and 440.

[62] 1950 *Constitutions*, nos. 16,29,43,145 and 440

[63] 1950 *Constitutions*, no. 29. The possibility of connecting non-Catholics—Christians or not—to the Institute as cooperators was one of the things Msgr. Escrivá obtained with the approval of 1950, after some insistence with the Roman Curia. In 1948 he asked the Holy See for this; they replied they had never before received such a petition and that they could not give permission. After some months he insisted in the petition, and they answered with a *dilata* [delay]. Finally it was included in the draft of the *Constitutions* approved on June 16, 1950: thus Opus Dei became the first Catholic institution with this possibility. The founder repeatedly referred to this, because he always gave to the apostolate *ad fidem*, wrapped in fraternity, truth and understanding, as he usually called it, a special preference. "With the approval of the Holy See in 1950," he wrote sometime later, "the Work admits among its cooperators also non-Catholics and even non-Christians. What was a reality of spirit and fact has been sanctioned by the Holy Father. . . . Protestants from different denominations, Hebrews, Moslems, pagans, go from developing a noble friendship with a daughter or son of mine to participating in the works of apostolate" (*Letter*, December 12, 1952, no. 33). (Among other texts, see for example *Conversations*, nos. 22 § 44; other data are found in K. Steiner, *Ecumenismo* in *Cristianos corrientes. Textos sobre el Opus Dei*, Madrid 1970, pp. 91-97.)

[64] Msgr. Escrivá, in the conference he delivered in Madrid in December 1948 thus described the pastoral phenomenon of Opus Dei: "Opus Dei joins together Christians of all social classes, men and women, married and single who being in the middle of the world, or better still, who being from the world—because they are ordinary lay

To achieve a variety of members Msgr. Escrivá made use of a distinction between members in a strict sense and those in a less strict sense included in the Apostolic Constitution *Provida Mater Ecclesia* (art. III) and subsequently developed as we have already pointed out by the Instruction *Cum Sanctissimus* (no. 7). He interpreted and applied it in ways appropriate to the reality of Opus Dei. It should be noted that this distinction implies—not a greater or less fullness of dedication, nor a greater or less disposition before God or the proper aim of Opus Dei (sanctity and apostolate in the middle of the world)—but a greater or less possibility of participating in governing the institution or forming other members or such like.

This is clearly affirmed in the *Constitutions*, which indicate points to be covered with whoever seeks admission as a supernumerary in Opus Dei. It is prescribed that "it be made known to the supernumeraries that the classes (of members) have no other purpose than that of instructing each of the members on his own obligations and occupations in accordance with the dispositions of his soul, the circumstances of his life and the special vocation received from God. Nevertheless all the members are equally committed to tend toward perfection in their own state and to cooperate, each according to his ability, to spreading Christ's Kingdom."[65]

Earlier the *Constitutions* had indicated that all of the members—not only the numeraries, but also the associates and supernumeraries—join Opus Dei by virtue of a divine vocation.[66] Incorporation into Opus Dei is not the result of a simple decision to cooperate in a worthy task—a decision doubtless praiseworthy, but not one that includes the totality of a person. It is a vocational phenomenon: seeing oneself before a God inviting us to respond completely from the very depths of our being to the love which he offers us and to incarnate this conviction in the large and small realities of daily life. From this follows a single vocation compatible with a diversity of circumstances; or better still, carried out in and through the most diverse of situations.

This implies—let us not forget we are talking always of secular circumstances—to recognize and to foster fully the Christian value of human realities. Its proclamation was one of the fundamental roles of Msgr. Escrivá throughout the whole of the foundational

---

people—aspire, out of a divine vocation, to achieve evangelical perfection and to bear the light of Christ to all men within their own environment, by means of sanctifying ordinary work"(*cit*. chapter VI, note 61), pp. 18-19. See also section 5 of the previous chapter.

[65] 1950 *Constitutions*, no. 44 § 2.

[66] 1950 *Constitutions*, no. 25 § 1, for the associates; no. 26, for the supernumeraries.

process.  It extends also into the late '40s and early '50s, when the matter presented new facets with respect to Opus Dei's canonical evolution.

If it had already been difficult for the Church to recognize, in approving Opus Dei at its different steps, that people living in the world, being single and carrying out their professional work, could dedicate themselves entirely to seeking holiness and exercising apostolate, it was still more difficult to admit that people, like the supernumeraries, in the married state, could do the same.  This possibility entailed a great novelty, something that seemed revolutionary.  No wonder then that the prospect defied easy understanding.  The founder of Opus Dei was well aware of this, and so he acted with great prudence and supernatural outlook, while displaying no little tenacity to achieve its recognition.

On March 18, 1948, the Sacred Congregation for Religious had approved, as we pointed out in the previous chapter, the texts and criteria relative to the supernumerary members of Opus Dei. Yet in its study of the draft of the 1950 *Constitutions*, the corresponding Commission balked at including these texts and so they asked for clarifications from Msgr. Escrivá.  He answered the objections in a writing addressed to the Sacred Congregation on June 2, 1950, as we have already shown.[67]

We can not be surprised that in *Letters* of these years Msgr. Escrivá refers again to the difficulties he encountered in winning acceptance of all the implications of the universal call to holiness.[68] Neither can we wonder why in the 1950 *Constitutions* he included throughout the text brief but significant phrases with the same meaning.  Thus for example, of the associates it is said that they employ

---

[67] For a more extensive reference to these difficulties and to the founder's answer, see section 6 of the previous chapter.

[68] We quote from a text by way of example: "Our way of acting is shocking: I can see it, they do not understand.  They ask how you are going to seek holiness in the middle of the world in all the crossroads of life.  They think that sanctity is sought only in the quietness of the monastery, in the silence of the corner of a church, in the recollection of the convent, in the loneliness of the cloister" (*Letter*, December 29, 1947/February 14, 1966, no. 106).  In another *Letter* with a sense of humor he comments: "A mentality accustomed to join directly together sanctity, apostolate and religious life finds it difficult to understand what is obvious.  If a professional man or woman who has interior life and feels the urgency of apostolic zeal is called a friar; a mother of a family with many children, cheerful, self-sacrificing, hard-working and apostolic, they will say that she is a nun. . . . With patience and faithful perseverance we must undo this confusion.  The witness of the life of so many daughters and sons of mine and the continual preaching of the spirit we have received from the Lord will clarify ideas. There will come a time when all will see as the most natural thing in the world what for so many years we have been making the effort to live and to preach" (*Letter*, December 12, 1952, no. 16).

"the same ascetical means" as the numeraries.[69]   A little further with respect to supernumeraries it is said (as we have already seen) "they live the same spirit, and according to their possibilities, the same customs as the numerary members."[70]   One can distinguish between members in a strict sense and members in a less strict sense, but this distinction, without denying its importance at the juridical level, does not give rise to different vocations: all members are called to live the same spirit and to strive for the same aim, shared completely by all of them.

This is the oft-reiterated teaching of Msgr. Escrivá, in writings contemporaneous with the 1950 *Constitutions*, as well as in writings dated before and after it.   "I have always pointed out that in the Work there is but one single vocation," he wrote in a 1951 *Letter*.[71] And in the *Letter* from which we have quoted so often that he started in 1947 and completed in 1966: "In the Work, it is clear, there is only one vocation for everyone and, therefore, one single class.   The different terms applied to the members of our supernatural family serve to explain, with a single word, up to what point they dedicate themselves to serving souls as children of God in Opus Dei, involving themselves in specific apostolic or formative tasks, having in mind their personal circumstances, even though the vocation of all is one and the same."[72]   On other occasions from a perspective that is not juridical but ascetical, the founder sometimes expressed this teaching by recurring to one of the graphic phrases strewn so often throughout his preaching: the comparison with large families whose members feed themselves from a single cooking pot.   "*We*," he expresses for example in a *Letter* dated 1957, "*are a healthy family, and therefore we have only one pot.*   Only in families where there are sick people must different meals be prepared.   We have a single meal, a single pot: we must say to all the same things, because *Opus Dei is for souls*, and souls have the same possibility of sanctifying themselves with the Work's spirit and norms of life.

"Nevertheless, it is true that my children are engaged in many different activities; that among them there are people of various cultures and ages and different states in life—some single, others married, some widows, others priests—and it is true that not all have the same temperament.   For this reason my children charged with forming others should do as mothers do when moved by a practical sense: they try to accommodate the common pot to the

---

[69] 1950 *Constitutions*, no. 25 § 2; see also Decree *Primum inter*, § 15.

[70] 1950 *Constitutions*, no. 27 § 2.

[71] *Letter*, December 24, 1951, no. 137.

[72] *Letter*, December 29, 1947/February 14, 1966, no. 107.

specific needs of each one. . . . But the pot is the same."[73] A single spirit, the same consciousness of being God's children, the same call to holiness, the same ascetical means that inform and vivify a host of different circumstances, adapting themselves to these circumstances not awkwardly or mechanically, but in a vital and spontaneous way. What Opus Dei invites men and women to do is none other than for each to sanctify his own state in life, the personal circumstances of his very life.

## 4. The configuration of the bond

The central message of Opus Dei—the call to a full dedication in different secular circumstances—leads us to one of the questions that concerned Opus Dei's founder for an important period of time: How to express this call to an earnest discipleship of Christ, with its consequent commitment between Opus Dei and each of its members in a fully adequate manner? How to do so, moreover, without recourse to terms or juridical expressions that could imply an assimilation to the religious state? Earlier this century that state was almost universally considered the ideal form or complete manifestation of the determination to become a saint.

In this important step in the juridical development of Opus Dei, presupposed by the approvals of 1947 and 1950, Msgr. Escrivá was not able to formulate the reality of dedication in a satisfactory way. Vows, especially those of poverty, chastity and obedience, could not be prescinded from, according to the classical theological trilogy of the state of perfection. Those sacred links were inevitable, if we bear in mind that *Próvida Mater Ecclesia* considered secular institutes to be a variant of the state of perfection. However nuanced, the traditional evangelical counsels, sealed with a sacred bond, were required of these Institutes' members. The apostolic constitution did no more than reflect the theology and canon law of the time in equating the fullness of dedication with the religious life or with

---

[73] Letter, November 29, 1957, no. 57. Texts could be multiplied; we cite only two more: "Our Work, my children, is a healthy family because we all aspire—faithful to the common vocation to Opus Dei we have received, the same both for laymen and for priests—to the holiness proper to the Christian vocation. A healthy family does not need more than one soup pot—nobody has special diets—because in a family with a sick person special meals must be prepared. For the spiritual life of the members of Opus Dei we have only one food, one spirit: one pot (Letter, February 2, 1945, no. 10). "Do not forget my children that this end, this spirit, these specific means are the same for all the members of the Work. I usually tell you that in the Work there is only one pot, and that all put their spoon into this single pot, all, whatever their state or circumstances of life in the world—single, married or widowed, priest or layman—all, with the same spirit, with the same specific apostolates, with identical means to achieve the aim. All in a full dedication, each one according to his circumstances, each one according to the gift received from God" (Letter, January 25, 1961, no. 55).

institutions equivalent to the religious.  Neither did it attribute the capacity of incardinating or ascribing priests to any entities other than jurisdictional structures of a territorial nature or religious institutes where one professes the evangelical counsels with a sacred bond (or societies equated with religious).  Only after this equation had been surpassed—decades later—was the way opened to other formulas.

At this crucial crossroads, even at the risk of repeating ourselves, might it not be appropriate to summarize the fundamental data that allow us to situate and evaluate the solution adopted? These are substantially three:

a) From the start the founder summons people to acknowledge the reality of God, who calls and invites one and all fully to a life of Christian faith in a radical and definite way, by means of a profound and decisive commitment of one's whole life, in the middle of the world, amid circumstances of the common human condition.

b) Also from the foundation's beginnings he affirms that this dedication, this commitment, "is not a *state of mind*, a passing situation; rather it is—in the intimacy of the conscience of each one—a definitive state for seeking perfection in the middle of the world."[74] This commitment translates into a stable bond with Opus Dei.

c) Finally, from 1928 on, he proclaims with absolute clarity that members of Opus Dei are ordinary Christians seeking sanctity amid the world in keeping with their secular condition.  Thus anything smacking of equivalence to the religious state must be avoided; otherwise the nature of the specific vocation received would be undermined.[75]

These coordinates demarcate the problem that confronted Msgr. Escrivá and help us to understand the concrete manner in which it arose.  It could be summarized thus: How to formalize the ideal of complete dedication, claiming as it does a commitment of the whole person to follow Christ by practicing all the Christian virtues in the world, and translated into a stable bond with Opus Dei?  From the first a negative criterion held sway: to avoid, as said above, anything that did or could imply an equivalence with religious.  But a positive formula was not easy to find in the first years.  The founder decided to act in the beginning without any formalization.  Those who responded to his personal invitation consciously committed themselves to lead a Christian life with an all-out dedication.  Early

---

[74] These words of the founder—previously quoted—come from the *Instruction* of April 1, 1934, no. 20.

[75] With regard to these extremes and some of their derivatives see what is said in chapter II.

on nothing more seemed necessary.[76] This decision was parallel to that of not yet having recourse to any approval *in scriptis*.

But with time and growth, around 1934 some of those who had answered the founder's call were made uneasy by certain people who claimed their dedication had no value and their way of life no stability. Circumstances, environment, meddling by these persons, some priests, led Fr. Escrivá to allow Opus Dei members to make private vows, without external manifestations (just as any Christian could and in fact not a few did at that time). Why? To facilitate, "for psychological reasons," he would say, an awareness of dedication for those coming to Opus Dei.[77] At the same time he established that the bond between the members and Opus Dei should consist in a simple manifestation of the willingness to commit one's life to the pursuit of holiness and the exercise of apostolate. Thus it was defined, when the founder, at the advice of the bishop of Madrid-Alcalá, presented documentation for the approval *in scriptis*. This ideal of full dedication requiring a commitment of the whole person—"dedication to Jesus Christ . . . not in a passing way," but rather "definitive,"—calls for a bond with Opus Dei expressed in a simple formula, with no reference to vows or other sacred bonds. Neither are such mentioned in any of the documents approved at that time.[78]

There is a clear distinction, even separation, between the bond with Opus Dei, formalized as we have just said, and the profession

---

[76] The founder dedicated his efforts in those early years to helping people to be consciously aware of this call, of this invitation—this gift of God—and of the commitment acquired. He wrote: "My task was to get those who felt themselves called to dedicate themselves to the Lord with this gift, to understand the effort, the engagement they were entering upon, the *commitment* they were acquiring" (*Letter*, December 29, 1947/February 14, 1966, no. 89).

[77] Years later Msgr. Escrivá referred to these events in a *Letter*: "I was thinking that these citizens, members of Opus Dei, should not make vows or promises. Then circumstances obliged me *to give in, but not to give up*—only for a time—and hence to allow that my children make private vows, *most private*, with no external manifestation: like any Catholic can." Later in the same document he says: "These most private vows, never received by the Work's directors, took nothing away from our secularity and gave my children in those moments when I did not want to use the word *vocation*, a psychological weapon, as I told you before, interiorly, whereby to reject the bad advice they were receiving" (*Letter*, December 29, 1947/February 14, 1966, nos. 84 and 180).

[78] The formula for the definitive incorporation to Opus Dei is found in the document *Ceremonial* of 1941 and reads as follows: "Domine Jesu: suscipe me tibi in servum sempiternum (ancillam sempiternam) Operis Dei, in obsequium et sacrificium laudis perpetuae: voluntarie et in aeternum meipsum (meipsam), cum omnibus viribus et affectibus meis, quanto intimius valeo, offero."

"Et intercedente beata et gloriosa Maria semper Virgine, cum beato Joseph, beatis Archangelis Michaele, Gabriele et Raphaele, ac beatis Apostolis tuis Petro, Paulo et

of private vows, with no external manifestation, limited to the intimacy of conscience of each one. In the early foundational years members of Opus Dei in the face of critics (or worse) could always have the clearest of consciences that their commitment to God was one of full dedication. Their private vows—we underline this character once again—were vows Opus Dei as such did not receive and even ignored.[79]

This solution, fully provisional in the eyes of the founder, was ·also insufficient, though for different reasons, in the view of those who examined the statutes of Opus Dei with a view to successive approvals. To a greater or less degree they were heirs to the theology and canon law of the time. They thus had no reason not to identify fullness of dedication and vocational commitment with *profession* of the evangelical counsels by means of vows or other sacred bonds. In a word theirs was the mentality of *consecration*.

This long-standing mentality is echoed in the constitution *Provida Mater Ecclesia*, in various passages of its narrative part and its statutory part (the *lex peculiaris* of secular institutes). It speaks specifically in article III of *consecration* and *profession* of Christian perfection by means of vows or other sacred bonds. To skirt erroneous interpretations regarding the entity and juridical effects of these vows and the profession of the evangelical counsels, it also states these counsels must be lived *in sæculo*—in the world;[80]   the vows

---

Joanne, et omnibus Angelis Custodibus, da, Domine, pacem in diebus meis: ut ope tuae misericordiae adjutus (adjuta), adimplere possim tuam sanctissimam voluntatem. Amen."

This formula analogous to that which Msgr. Escrivá himself used before the bishop of Madrid (Appendix, document no. 16) has been maintained unaltered throughout the whole juridical evolution as the expression of the unvaried criteria of the founder.

[79] This point would be constantly repeated by Msgr. Escrivá in his oral and written teaching. We quote from some texts. "Our life, therefore, is a divine commitment . . . that helps us to live, not the vows of the religious, but the Christian virtues" (*Letter*, March 11, 1940, no. 10). "We are interested in all virtues . . . we are not interested, on the other hand, in promises, or vows, even though they are theologically worthy of all respect, and with much more respect we see them in others: if members of Opus Dei personally make promises or vows, these vows and these promises are a particular devotion that they may have, something of the conscience of each one: the Work ignores them" (*Instruction*, Dec. 8, 1941, no. 86). "Vows—when they exist—are something of the private devotion of each one. They are not, nor can they ever be, a juridical or canonical manifestation of our dedication to the service of souls: with all sincerity I tell you that God has not wanted them for the Work. To achieve Christian perfection, the only thing Opus Dei asks of us are virtues. For this reason you have heard me say constantly that I am not interested in vows, even though I have a great esteem for them, an attitude theology teaches me to have" (*Letter*, Feb. 14, 1944, no. 14).

[80] *Provida Mater Ecclesia*, art. I.

made in these institutes are not the three public vows of religion.[81] This is no little novelty and certainly worthy of consideration.

For Opus Dei, therefore, to adapt itself to the *magna carta* of secular institutes, provision would have to be made in its *Constitutions* for vows or analogous bonds. Yet the common legal text allowed this to be done without implying assimilation to religious or equivalent institutions. In fact, in the 1947 *Constitutions* vows are mentioned, even though Msgr. Escrivá took all possible precautions within the norms and praxis in force to clarify the scope of these bonds for Opus Dei members. Thus it says members do not make religious vows,[82] but only private vows.[83] Thus the important criteria mentioned before are reaffirmed, according to which incorporation to the Institute is accomplished not by vows, but by formulas employed in Opus Dei from the very start.[84] Recourse is also had to expressions that, at least grammatically, make clear the distinction of one and the other moment, that is to say, between incorporation and vows: *incorporatio secum fert vota, incorporationi adnexum est votum privatum*, etc.[85]

Shortly after the approval granted to Opus Dei in 1947 there arose doctrinal discussions whether secular institutes constituted an evolutionary form of the religious state, that is to say, a third species or degree within the canonical state of perfection whose model is the religious. Or, on the contrary, were they in effect associations of the faithful characterized by a special state of perfection—secular—different from the canonical state proper to religious? This topic is closely connected to the debate about the nature of vows in secular institutes. Supporters of the first opinion tend to affirm there is nothing opposed to characterizing these vows as public. Those who adopt the second position energetically reject this possibility and have recourse to other characterizations, speaking of private vows, private recognized vows, social vows, etc. According to the first opinion it is difficult to maintain that their members do not change their state in life as by the public vows they would become religious, in the sense of canon 107 of the 1917 Code. According to the second opinion it is possible to maintain, on the contrary, that members of secular institutes do not change their

---

[81] *Ibid.*, art. II, § 1.

[82] *Primum Institutum*, § 10; 1947 *Constitutions*, no. 7.

[83] 1947 *Constitutions*, nos. 40, 63, 72, 78, 182 and 324.

[84] Incorporation is spoken of in the 1947 *Constitutions*—without any mention of vows—in nos. 12, 35-39, 323, 342, 343, 347, 357 and 360.

[85] These and analogous expressions are used in the numbers quoted in note 83 of this chapter. There is not found in these documents any formula for the making of these vows.

state but continue being clerics or lay people, in accordance with canon 107.[86]

While these discussions were taking place, Msgr. Escrivá stuck to his position, as we have described. Thus in the already-cited conference given in Madrid in December 1948, while explaining the characteristic notes of Opus Dei as a secular institute, he noted that its members take vows. In the next breath he clarifies that these are "private vows, like those any other Catholic could make."[87] With still greater emphasis he addresses Opus Dei members in a 1949 Letter. Affirming members of the Work are "common ordinary Christians," he added: "without it being necessary to make any vows in order to feel ourselves bound to Opus Dei, since the Work never receives the vows that like any other Christian its members may make." And he concludes: "I add that it is my desire that they not make any."[88]

During these days the documentation necessary for the new papal approval was completed. In the draft of the *Constitutions* presented to the Congregation for Religious, Msgr. Escrivá, with respect to incorporation to the Institute and the formalization of the corresponding bond, adhered to the same principles and used the same texts as in the 1947 *Constitutions*. The project was submitted to the appropriate commission of the Congregation for Religious; it in turn proposed various modifications (approved by the Sacred Congregation on June 28, 1950), some of which referred to the vows.

The most important modification (and that on which the others depended) had to do with no. 53 of the draft as written by the founder: "1. For numeraries incorporation into the Institute, made by the Oblation, brings with it the making of private vows of poverty, chastity and obedience; 2. These vows are private and only the Father may dispense from them."[89] The commission proposed that the second paragraph read as follows: "These social vows, even though they are not public according to law (canon 1308 § 1), are nevertheless recognized by the Church, by which they come to be called private recognized vows. These vows cease in the case of dismissal or of the dispensation of the bond by which the numerary was bound to the Institute, granted by the Holy See or by the Fa-

---

[86] We referred to this question in the previous chapter in sections 3 and 4. Note that the Sacred Congregation for Religious intervened in an indirect way in this controversy with its declaration of May 19, 1949, whereby it reaffirmed they are not public vows and therefore they do not imply a public consecration of the person nor is their violation a sacrilege.

[87] J. Escrivá de Balaguer, "La Constitución Apostólica *Provida Mater Ecclesia* y el Opus Dei", *cit.* (chapter VI, note 61), p. 19.

[88] *Letter*, December 8, 1949, no. 64.

[89] Draft of the *Constitutions* of 1950, no. 53 in AGP, Sezione Giuridica, V/15845.

ther, according to the circumstances."[90] In the definitive text of the *Constitutions* approved by the Sacred Congregation this latter version was upheld.[91]

Other slight changes were introduced at the last minute by the Sacred Congregation. For example, no. 61, which refers to vows made by the supernumeraries. The draft of the *Constitutions* said that "these vows are completely (*penitus*) private,"[92] wording accepted by the commission.[93] However, the definitive text reads: "these vows are private, but accepted and recognized by the Institute."[94]

In summary, the text of the 1950 *Constitutions*, approved by the Decree *Primum inter*, keeps the distinction found in the 1947 *Constitutions* between incorporation to the Institute, made in the way traditional in Opus Dei, and the vows.[95] Of the latter it is expressly said that they are not religious vows,[96] but are called, with a new terminology, private recognized vows or social vows,[97] while emphasizing they are not public vows.[98]

This terminology—recognized or social vows—refers once again to the doctrinal discussions of the years 1947 and following. Some put in doubt the private character of the vows made by members of secular institutes, alleging their effects are not only moral but juridical as well. They reasoned that since the vows were presupposed by incorporation to the Institute (and in some Institutes even served as the very bond of incorporation), the vows were as public as the secular institute. Others pointed out the error implicit in identifying juridical effects with publicness: vows, promises or oaths that can be made by any Christian do not become public just because they entail some juridical effects. They are public rather only when made before someone constituted in authority who represents the Church and receives them in its name in such a way that the making of vows brings with it a public consecration and a change in canonical status.

To clarify the matter, some advocates of the second interpretation proposed these vows be called "recognized" or "social" vows,

---

[90] AGP, Sezione Giuridica, V/15936.

[91] 1950 *Constitutions*, no. 53.

[92] Draft of *Constitutions* of 1950, no. 61, in AGP, Sezione Giuridica, V/15845.

[93] *Votum* of the Commission, in AGP, Sezione Giuridica, V/15936.

[94] 1950 *Constitutions*, no. 61 § 2.

[95] See, for example, 1950 *Constitutions*, nos. 49-52, 80, 438 and 446.

[96] 1950 *Constitutions*, no. 5.

[97] 1950 *Constitutions*, nos. 53, 56, 148 and 161. The Decree *Primum inter* also refers in § 7 to these vows as "social or private recognized."

[98] 1950 *Constitutions*, no. 53.

in recognition of the fact that, while private, they nevertheless produce juridical effects with respect to a society or institute. Lest in one way or another the vows be characterized as public, some Opus Dei members, as pointed out, utilized this new terminology, but emphasizing all the while that these vows did not bring about a change in status for the persons in question.[99]

For his part, Msgr. Escrivá wrote in a 1951 *Letter*: "I want to insist on the fact that the vocation to Opus Dei is not another way of professing the evangelical counsels." Then he adds: "I repeat to you, my children, in the Work we require virtues, not vows, which interest us not at all." He refers to the earliest days when "the vows taken were very private and not recognized by the Work." Then: "Before the persecution we underwent, in order to obtain pontifical approval, I had no remedy other than *to give in, but with every intention of winning it back.*" He continues: "For this reason I had to accept in our *ius peculiare* private or social or recognized vows." He explains: "I understood that these commitments were known—not accepted or received—by the Work and for this they could also be called social, though an unusual word to characterize vows."[100] It should be pointed out—since it leads us to the heart of the problem pointed out at the beginning—that the reiterated declarations of Msgr. Escrivá that he did not desire vows, that Opus Dei was not interested in vows, but in virtues, were always accompanied by the affirmation that the dedication of Opus Dei members was a full and total dedication. He had always stated this from the beginning and repeated it in the 1941 juridical texts and those of the following years; he reiterated this in many other writings, as, for example, the 1949 *Letter* to which we have often referred: "We must live, therefore, in a permanent stable way the life of sanctifying grace in its

---

[99] In the *Annuario Pontificio* (p. 793) of 1951 these vows are described—as we pointed out in section 4 of the previous chapter—with three fundamental statements: a) the state of perfection of secular institutes is not a canonical state, i.e. that proper to religious; b) their members do not make public vows in the sense of the Code of Canon Law, but private vows, with equivalent moral bonds; and c) their members do not change the social condition they had in the world; for which reason they continue being clerics or lay people with all of the consequent juridical and practical consequences. This categorization of the vows as private is maintained in the *Annuario* until 1960, when they begin to be called "private recognized or social" (cf. *Annuario Pontificio*, (1960):1529).

[100] *Letter*, Dec. 24, 1951, nos. 27 and 65. Alluding to the terminology employed in the *Constitutions* of 1950 he would write some years later: "The very characterization which was given to these commitments in the first jurisprudence on secular institutes—they were called *social* or *private recognized*—was an expression that had to be coined, as a lesser evil, so that it remain clear that there was a difference from the vows of religious. Likewise the consequences that, in what has to do with incorporation to the Work, these commitments had were thus affirmed" (*Letter*, January 25, 1961, no. 57).

fullness . . . and give ourselves completely to Jesus Christ so as to help him save the whole world . . . in a climate of persevering heroism and complete dedication."[101]  It was on that very point, his proclamation of a radical Christianity in the world, that arose the difficulties to which he alluded in that Letter: "We are . . . in a full theological and juridical campaign to win acceptance from churchmen for our vocation just as it is," because "our vocation is not, as some have erroneously said, a species of second-rate dedication."[102] It was no less than the universal call to sanctity that Msgr. Escrivá was defending, while trying to make the law echo this, even though initially with a few concessions: "For the moment it is very clear," he affirms in the same 1949 Letter, "that the Roman Curia will not recognize a spiritual commitment of this kind, without being linked to a vow or promise of some kind."[103]

In sum: in 1947 the founder, in order to obtain pontifical approval, had to accept sacred vows as required by the Apostolic Constitution *Provida Mater Ecclesia*.  In 1950 he saw himself obliged to continue this compromise and to accept also the categorization of these vows as "private recognized or social vows."  His intention? "Conceder, sin ceder, con ánimo de recuperar," (to give in, without giving up, eager to win back).  This principle has been mentioned several times and reappears in the 1951 *Letter* dealing directly with this topic.  "It was a concession, I insist, but eager to win it back."

---

[101] *Letter*, December 8, 1949, no. 34.

[102] *Letter*, December 8, 1949, no. 95.  In another *Letter* he expresses himself in similar terms: "Sanctity, then, but first class sanctity—you understand me, since sanctity is only one thing—with all of its consequences."  Earlier on he said: "What we have preached since 1928 is that sanctity is not reserved for a few and that our Lord wants all of his children to be saints: *estote ergo vos perfecti, sicut et Pater vester cælestis perfectus est* (Mt 5:48). The Lord has raised up his Opus Dei to make this desire of his a reality and to use as a witness, as a proof of his divine truth, the dedicated lives of men and women who commit themselves with all their strength to seek Christian perfection in all states of life, in all honest temporal activities, in the middle of the world.

"For this reason we have sought to live from the beginning the virtue essential to every Christian life, the *vinculum perfectionis* (Col 3:14), charity; and together with it, the other theological virtues and all the supernatural and human virtues: and thus we live also poverty, obedience and chastity, which are means—along with the other virtues—for achieving Christian perfection in the world, something our divine vocation requires of us" (*Letter*, October 7, 1950, nos. 27 and 22).

[103] *Letter*, December 8, 1949, no. 25.  To what the founder wanted and understood by the expression or formalization of this commitment, the 1951 *Letter* refers extensively, describing it as a "contract full of good will, by virtue of which, with God's grace and desirous of doing good, with the nobility and loyalty of soul the men and women members of the Work dedicate themselves to practice the Christian virtues personally and corporately, according to our specific spirit, with the constant manifestations of an apostolic drive" (*Letter*, December 24, 1951, no. 65).

He continued: "Pray, my children, so that soon the way will be opened for our returning to the beginning, without there having to be in our *particular law* anything with regard to vows, which we ought not to make and which we are not interested in." He then adds, "only incorporation will be spoken of."[104]

## 5. With the naturalness of ordinary Christians

The orientation proper to the spiritual theology and canon law of the time forced Msgr. Escrivá to accept vows, concretely social vows, with the limitations and precautions which we have indicated. It also obliged him to deal at length, in the section of the 1947 and 1950 *Constitutions* descriptive of the life of the members, with the triad of evangelical counsels. About these three virtues two stances were possible. To base a state of life on the profession of these counsels. Or, on the other hand, to pursue holiness so resolutely and amply that it vivifies every state and condition of human life and calls for all virtues. In the latter case one begins with life itself, seen first in God's orbit; then one discovers that life in each of its concrete settings can and should be the place where one encounters God and practices the virtues, those three and all the others. It is this second focus that Msgr. Escrivá advanced in his habitual preaching and writings.[105]

Among the juridical texts that mirror this second approach are those of 1941, as well as the exposition of the spirit and activity that Opus Dei carries out found in the Decree *Primum inter* (with some limitations). It is found also—though more limited by the praxis of the Sacred Congregation—in the *Constitutions* of 1947 and 1950. The part that speaks about the members' life opens with a chapter on formation; then follows one devoted to the obligations ensuing from poverty, chastity and obedience; and, finally, one describing their spirit. Both in the Decree *Primum inter*, and in the *Constitutions*, the three evangelical counsels are situated in a context that transcends them and points in the direction of sanctifying ordinary life.

Msgr. Escrivá spoke and preached many times about poverty, chastity and obedience, both separately as well as considering them all together. He recognized in these virtues, in keeping with a broad Christian tradition, a particularly significant expression of

---

[104] Letter, December 24, 1951, no. 65.

[105] It is what we find, for example, in *The Way*, as its index clearly shows; for more detailed analysis see P. Rodríguez, "Camino y la espiritualidad del Opus Dei," in *Teología Espiritual*, 9 (1965):213-245 (included in *Vocación, trabajo, contemplación, cit.*, chap. II, note 49, pp. 85-122) and R. Gómez-Pérez, "Encontrarse siendo cristiano," in W. Blanck-R. Gómez Pérez, *Doctrina y vida*, Madrid 1971, pp. 71ff.

the need for the detachment, self-dominion and availability that every Christian must live. But he never gave the impression that these three virtues could constitute as it were a characterization of the spirit of Opus Dei. Thus there appear in his writings expressions, not free from a certain polemical tone, that affirm that Opus Dei members should live not only the virtues proper to the three evangelical counsels, but the ensemble of all human and Christian virtues. We read, for example, in the already quoted 1951 *Letter*: "The vocation to Opus Dei is not another mode of professing the evangelical counsels. By that call God expressly wants my children ever to strive to renew in their conduct—without any ceremony of consecration—the promises they made at baptism. They are to exert themselves to be sincere, totally loyal to Christ's teachings without limiting themselves to living the three counsels proper to the so-called state of perfection, certainly neither the only virtues nor the principal ones. Rather they aspire to the entirety of Christian life amid the hubbub of the street."[106]

The bond with Opus Dei, he affirms in a December 1949 *Letter*, "obliges us to form ourselves well, conscientiously, throughout our lifetime, using all of the general means of the Church and the specific ones of the Work. In this way we will practice the theological and cardinal virtues in the world and become contemplative souls, constantly united to God, in continuous prayer; serving our holy Mother the Church and all souls in a secular way, without departing from the setting where God has placed each one of us on earth."[107] In another *Letter* he insists: "The vocation *does not take us out of our place*, from the social circumstances that are ours in the world. In the eyes of neither the Church nor the world do we make a profession other than the one that our peers and fellow Christians made: we fulfill all of our duties as responsible Catholics and exercise the obligations and rights of ordinary citizens."[108]

This fundamental focus is reflected in the Decree *Primum inter*, and in the 1950 *Constitutions*, where there are many declarations to the effect that the members of Opus Dei are neither religious nor should they allow anything in their way of acting or in their dwellings to evoke a religious order or institute.[109] This fact becomes more significant, if we bear in mind that *Provida Mater Ecclesia* had already said as much. Msgr. Escrivá is not content to have the law affirm this generically; rather, conscious of the import of the matter

---

[106] *Letter*, December 24, 1951, no. 27.

[107] *Letter*, December 8, 1949, no. 26.

[108] *Letter*, May 6, 1945, no. 10.

[109] Decree *Primum inter*, §§ 7, 18 and 19; 1950 *Constitutions*, nos. 5, 182 and 192.

no less than the active resistance of so many environments,[110]  he wants it repeated and underlined especially in Opus Dei's very own particular law.

It is telling that in the first chapter of the *Constitutions* and in the number immediately following (a text designed to point out from the very beginning that Opus Dei members are not religious), Msgr. Escrivá includes what from the beginning he called *collective humility*. "Opus Dei professes collective humility, and consequently will not publish magazines or any other publications bearing the name of the Work, unless it is for the use of its members.  Its members will not use any distinctive insignia, and will be prudent when speaking of the Work to people not belonging to it, since their way of acting should be simple and not call attention to itself.  Neither will Opus Dei participate, ordinarily, in social acts or be represented in them."[111]

The teaching on collective humility represents nothing new, since it was included in the 1941 *Reglamento* and the 1947 *Constitutions*.[112] The novelty in the 1950 *Constitutions* is that not only are earlier texts substantially retained,[113] but also included is an extensive descrip-

---

[110] He alludes to the problem in the various writings, which gloss various features of the environment of the 1940s and '50s.  We cite a few relevant texts.

First from the *Letter* of May 6, 1945: "Bear in mind, my daughters and my sons, that time will have to pass before some minds understand that we have not come to trample down what already exists: we value, we venerate and we love with all our heart the religious state.  But we have the mission of saying things in a different way and of doing them in a different way . . . . You cannot forget that till now it has been said at least with deeds—and many times in theory also—that the perfection of Christian life is essentially and exclusively in the religious state, to the point that some have warned Christians living in the world of the many dangers they run, even the risk of eternal salvation . . . . They fail to realize that the providence of God, always a most loving Father, wants others to be in the world and that 'all men should be saved and come to the knowledge of the truth' (1 Tim 2:4)" (*Letter*, May 6, 1945, no. 8).

A second from a *Letter* of December 24, 1951: "In the face of my insistence they admit that we are not religious, but they obstinately insist on seeing us assimilated to religious.  They fail to see how their erroneous idea contradicts the very reality of our vocation" (*Letter*, December 24, 1951, no. 27)  In another writing from the same time and with very similar words, he says: "Beyond all the juridical discussions [discussions regarding the concept of the state of perfection] is the living reality of our vocation with its very own ascetical characteristics and its very own specific purposes, which do not allow the Work to be classified as a pastoral phenomenon within the historical evolution of the life of perfection, but as a phenomenon *sui generis* within the lay apostolate.

"Things being as clear as they are, nevertheless there are people who insist on considering us like religious" (*Letter*, September 7, 1950, nos. 25 & 26).

[111] 1950 *Constitutions*, no. 6.

[112] See section of chapter III and section 8 of chapter V.

[113] 1950 *Constitutions*, nos. 189-192, 210 & 219.

tion of the institution's general features. Since this overview immediately follows the number where the secular condition of the members is established, it would seem to imply that the very entity
arises from secularity.

Considering all the texts referring to this topic, we can summarize their contents as follows:

a) It is forbidden for members to use insignias or employ language or collective terms distinguishing them from the rest of ordinary Christians.

b) It is established that Opus Dei ordinarily does not participate
in group activities nor have its own publications.

c) It is recommended, above all to those recently admitted, that
in dealing with people not of the Work they speak discreetly of
their own vocation, even establishing that, before manifesting their
membership in Opus Dei, they should consult with their own director.

More important than the simple enunciation of these criteria is
what they stem from and what gives them meaning. As said before,[114] this *modus operandi*, in Msgr. Escrivá's mind and action and
in the life of Opus Dei, depends on three different factors: a) *Juridi-
cal-institutional*: members should always act in ways consistent with
the condition of ordinary citizens and ordinary Christians, with no
insignias, distinctive marks, signs, dress or usages improper to a
secular style and mode of acting.[115] b) *Ascetical*: humility moves one
to a conscious awareness in faith of the absolute primacy of God
and therefore to avoid any vainglory, lest all honor and praise be
denied to God himself.[116] c) *Prudential*: one must adapt to circum-

---

[114] See section 2, "Personal freedom secularity and responsibility," of chapter II and
section 5, "Ordinary Christians and ordinary citizens," of chapter III.

[115] This is the aspect Msgr. Escrivá highlighted, e.g., in the 1948 conference to which we
have referred: "Because [the members of Opus Dei] are not strange, they have at times
perhaps appeared to be so to those who are bound and determined on including them
in the traditional and praiseworthy forms of perfection. . . . We have converted Christianity into a special manner of life, and occasionally a feeble one at that, instead of
simply living it, as our life; and for this reason we are surprised when there are some
who simply want to be Christians and nothing more, although nothing less either.
Thus Opus Dei is not a secret organization. It is a society like any other, which from
the beginning has had both religious and civil personality. Its purposes are clear and
precise: to seek the evangelical perfection of its members by means of the sanctification of ordinary work, in the most varied fields of human activity" (J. Escrivá de
Balaguer, *La Constitución Apostólica "Provida Mater Ecclesia" y el Opus Dei, cit.* chap. VI,
note 61, pp. 20-21). It is here necessary to insist once again on the considerable teaching of the founder on naturalness, which has been covered earlier.

[116] In this context we quote another text taken from a 1951 *Letter*: "Apart from personal
humility, absolutely necessary for all the faithful, and even more for those who, simple
faithful like all the others, aspire, like us, with a most free commitment to incarnate a
life of consistent Christianity, I have inculcated in your minds and gathered in our

stances, whether individual (for example, the recommendation addressed to recent vocations) or collective (as might be and was in fact, the novelty of the pastoral phenomenon). The need is relatively constant to take precautions, lest Opus Dei be confused with or reduced to other forms of life, thus ignoring and vitiating its specific charism and contribution.

We are not here dealing with secrecy (something absolutely forbidden),[117] but rather with criteria of an ethical and spiritual nature.[118] These can and ought at every step to have specific concrete manifestations, because they represent an underlying orientation susceptible of various applications in the light of prudence. In the early years a "secret of gestation" not hidden from anyone was necessary, of which some contemporary texts speak.[119] While the juridical evolution attained in 1950 supposed changed circumstances, a particular prudence or reserve was still advisable.

Obviously the creation of secular institutes implied a conceptual clarification, albeit limited. This figure was not only new but in these first years, as we have seen, was beset by a certain ambiguity and exposed to different interpretations. Thus, would it not be imprudent to manifest one's commitment to live a fully Christian life to others, especially those steeped in traditional ways? Such

---

*Ordinationes,* in our *Ius peculiare,* from the beginning, the continuous and indispensable urgency of loving and practicing collective humility. This *collective humility,* which is so pleasing to God, frees us from an exaggerated *esprit de corps,* from fanaticism, from forming cliques. It helps us to judge justly because love for our supernatural family, which does not exclude love for all the things created by God, will never be an obstacle to us from living as just men; and we reject the idea that what we do is good just because we do it; and what others do therefore is mediocre or bad.

"The Lord accepts as a pleasant offering our collective humility" (*Letter,* December 24, 1951, no. 42).

[117] "Discretion is not mystery nor secrecy. It is simply, naturalness," Msgr. Escrivá says in *The Way* (no. 641). Paraphrasing this point, the founder writes in 1943: "From the beginning of the Work I have said to you that we do not need any secret. Our discreet reserve about intimate matters of the conscience of each one, if then more necessary, is something we will always live with naturalness.

"But—I insist—without secrecy or secrets, which we do not need and which do not please us" (*Letter,* May 31, 1943, no. 44). Other texts can be consulted in the sections mentioned in note 114 of this chapter.

[118] The chapter from *The Way* dedicated to discretion (nos. 639-656) is very illuminating in this respect; see also nos. 379, 380, 410, 491, 499, 839, 840, 846, 848, 970, 972, 986. For an analysis of these points see P. Rodríguez, "Camino y la espiritualidad del Opus Dei," *cit.* (note 105 of this chapter), pp. 116-118.

[119] See section 5 of chapter III. Referring to naturalness, the founder said: "The simple and natural way of living our vocation is complemented perfectly with a sensible supernatural discretion, which the efficacy of our work and above all, personal and collective humility require: especially now, in these first moments of the Work, delicate hours of gestation" (*Letter,* March 11, 1940, no. 59).

would likely consider Opus Dei members to be "religious without a habit," instead of ordinary Christians bent on living in a way consistent with their faith in any and all secular settings. In this context naturalness—each one acting conformably to what one is—required paradoxically acting with caution and a special prudence in speaking of Opus Dei and one's personal relationship with it. This way required to guarantee, in as much as possible, that his words and deeds would be properly understood. In number 191 of the 1950 *Constitutions* the founder recommended this discretion, which is prudence and naturalness: "This collective humility will prompt our members to lead the life they have dedicated to God with a certain discretion, most suitable for the desired fruitfulness of the apostolate." Yet "with fortitude of spirit we absolutely avoid secrecy and clandestinity, since we are moved solely by humility to preserve this discretion, plus a greater and more fruitful effectiveness in the apostolate."[120]

Years later, when the apostolic work of Opus Dei was more developed and widespread, thus showing many more people the specific features of a vocation to the Work,[121] the circumstances had indeed changed. Then too consciousness of the universal call to holiness had spread throughout the Church, thus ending the equation of a commitment to a full Christian life with the religious state. At that point Msgr. Escrivá not only declared in disuse and totally superseded some of the consequences of criteria previously indicated but claimed "he had erased the word discretion from his dictionary."[122] Each member of Opus Dei no less than Opus Dei as

---

[120] After what we have just said it may seem unnecessary, but we still point out that both the Decree *Primum inter* and the *Constitutions* of 1950—analogous to the documents of 1947—clearly show that the activity of Opus Dei and of its members is carried out always with a maximum respect for civil laws (Decree *Primum inter*, § 20; 1950 *Constitutions*, nos. 7, 183 & 194).

[121] In the *Letter* of 1952 Msgr. Escrivá, after pointing out that "the knowledge of the reality of our life will make our spirit understood, along with the secular condition of our way," adds: "the most sensible thing is that it be . . . the daily witness of your apostolic effort and your simple task that teaches people the truth of our vocation." Then it is necessary, he continues "to give doctrine, in an understandable way, with concrete examples, about the reality of our way and secular way of being. . . . This apostolate, done with continuity and with a gift of tongues, will help along the external circumstances, the social environment—both among ecclesiastics and in civil life—until a collective consciousness is created. Then it will be considered the most natural thing in the world to find what we affirm" (*Letter*, December 12, 1952, nos. 18, 21 & 22.).

[122] Among other declarations we quote a letter written by Msgr. Escrivá on November 21, 1966: "I was amused for a while with the erroneous idea of discretion that some people have. Some, who have not *grasped* that we are *the same* as other citizens—we are not *like* them, we are their *equals*—think that we are living a fiction . . . because we do not carry a placard on our shoulders or a Christ on a banner. Others reason the

a whole ought to be humble, staving off any temptations to pride or vainglory, while eschewing any attitude, use or conduct that detracts from secularity, however legitimate it might be in a religious spirituality. But now there is no reason to adopt particular precautions in referring to Opus Dei; the sole criterion of naturalness, the witness of what each one is, suffices in the current climate. Precautions that earlier were necessary would in the current context be not only useless but counterproductive.[123]

## 6. Description of apostolic activity

The Decree *Primum inter* and the *Constitutions* of 1950 are not limited to the points we have analyzed. The same as earlier juridical texts, they deal also with a wide range of questions: those necessary to describe the Institute's features and to orient its life and activity. Some of these, such as requirements for admission or time intervals for incorporation, while important in themselves are not relevant to this stage of the juridical development. Take for another example, formation, presented and described as necessary for carrying out apostolate in the world, in and through professional work.[124] Or the role of prayer and a life of piety as the crucible for unity of life that leads to filling the minutiae of daily life with Christian and theological meaning.[125] It does not, however, seem necessary to study such matters at length here.

---

same as they did 40 years ago when discretion—which could not be more indiscreet—led us to bear the weight of the gestation of the Work as a mother guards in her womb the new creature: where is the secret, if *that* was a secret shouted out loud? And now? I do not want to hear people speak of discretion: it is better to say and to do things *with naturalness*, far from the way of thinking of *both mentalities*. Comedy does not fit us; we have lived with *naturalness* and we will always live with naturalness because this is our spirit: sincere and genuine." (RHF, EF-661121-2) We add that this letter, although written in a very personal tone, was destined to be made known to all the members of Opus Dei and this in fact happened.

[123] In an interview with *Le Figaro* on May 16, 1966, Msgr. Escrivá said: "Ever since 1928 my preaching has been that sanctity is not something reserved for a privileged few and that all the ways of the earth can be divine. The reason is that the spirituality of Opus Dei is based on the sanctification of ordinary work. . . . To proclaim and to teach how to practice this doctrine I have never needed anything secret. The members of the Work detest secrecy because they are ordinary faithful, the same as anyone else. They do not change their status when they join Opus Dei. It would be repulsive for them to carry a sign on their backs that said, 'Let it be known that I am dedicated to the service of God.' That would be neither lay nor secular. But those who associate with members of Opus Dei and are acquainted with them realize that they belong to the Work, for, even if they do not publicize their membership, neither do they hide it" (*Conversations*, no. 34). See also *Conversations*, nos. 30, 40, 64-66.

[124] 1950 *Constitutions*, nos. 126ff. The Decree *Primum inter* deals with formation and the incorporation of members of Opus Dei in §§ 34-39.

[125] 1950 *Constitutions*, nos. 234ff.

There is a question, however, we must deal with here: the description the 1950 documents give of the apostolic activity of Opus Dei members. We find expository systematic developments in the 1950 texts, cited extensively before, regarding the spirit, the unity of the pastoral phenomenon and, above all, the description of Opus Dei's specific purpose. These features will have their repercussions at the moment of describing apostolic action; it could not be otherwise, since between end and action there exists a tight nexus.

In the first part of our study we dealt extensively with apostolic activity according to the foundational charism of Opus Dei.[126] Let us now recall that from the foundation's dawn Msgr. Escrivá taught in a direct, clear and precise fashion that all men can and ought to aspire to sanctity, seconding the particular will God has for each of them. Sanctity and apostolate, intimacy with God and making known God's love for all men, are inextricably intertwined. And the marrow of Opus Dei's specific message is that this love for God and mankind is to be kindled in and through one's occupation and the ordinary human condition.

These core ideas were ever on the founder's lips. Among other texts there is one that despite its length seems an appropriate portal to the juridical texts we will see later. Again we draw on a *Letter* of March 1940: "If the Son of God became man and died on a cross, it was so that all of us men might become one thing with him and with the Father (Cf. Jn 17:22). All of us, therefore, are called to form part of this divine unity. With priestly soul, making the Holy Mass the center of our interior life,[127] we seek to be with Jesus, between God and men. . . . Our union with Christ gives us an awareness of being co-redeemers of the world with him, to helping make all souls partakers of the fruits of his passion, so that they may thus know and follow the way of salvation leading to the Father." In every moment, even "in the middle of the occupations of the world. United to Christ by prayer and mortification in our daily work, in the thousand human circumstances of our simple life as ordinary Christians, we will act out the marvel of placing all things at the feet of the Lord, raised upon the cross where he let himself be nailed out of such great love for the world and mankind.

"And thus working simply and loving God in the tasks that make up our profession or other occupation, the same one we had been carrying out when he sought us out, we fulfill the apostle's

---

[126] See especially section 5 of chapter I and sections 3 & 4 of chapter II.

[127] He refers to the Holy Mass in addition in no. 34 of the document *De Spiritu* from 1941: "The Holy Mass is the center of the spiritual life of the members," repeated almost textually in the *Constitutions* of 1947 (no. 104) and in the *Constitutions* of 1950: "The root and the center of the spiritual life of the members is the Holy Sacrifice of the Mass" (no. 206).

role by putting Christ at the summit, in the heart, of all human endeavors. No honest activity is excluded from the scope of our work, which then becomes the manifestation of Christ's redemptive love. . . . Again I tell you, my children: God has called us—each in his own state in life and in the exercise of his own profession or occupation—so that we sanctify ourselves in work, besides sanctifying that work and sanctifying others with our work."[128]

Work professionally carried out in the workaday world reveals itself once again as the pivot of the spiritual and ascetical life of Opus Dei members. It is no wonder, then, that apostolate comes to be seen, not as another activity added on from outside, but as an intrinsic dimension of all of one's existence, an interior capacity or leaning converting deeds into service. One consequently avails himself of all his tasks to draw all others closer to God. The doctrine on unity of life, seen before as a requirement of the Work's spirit, reappears here. So does that of a single aim: not a generic aim and a specific aim but rather one rich end. Namely, to know oneself called by God to redeem ordinary life and, by doing so, to disclose to others that they too are thus called to encounter God.

If Opus Dei's purpose is to show people of all classes and social conditions that they can and ought to seek God in the midst of the world, the next logical question is how. Thus the 1950 *Constitutions*, in the section following "purpose" and echoing almost verbatim the 1941 *Reglamento*, state that the aim is achieved "by sanctifying ordinary work in the exercise of one's profession or equivalent work, which they do not give up because they seek holiness by means of this work."[129] Later we read: "what is proper to our vocation is the sanctification of ordinary work."[130]

The Decree *Primum inter* expresses itself in similar terms early in the third part that speaks of apostolic works. Though quoted earlier, it bears repetition: "They practice all honest civil professions with maximum perfection, and, though their work be profane, they strive ardently to sanctify it by frequently rectifying their intention, by a fervent cultivation of interior life, by cheerful and continual self-denial and by the self-sacrificing effort of constant work, so that their work may be perfect in all aspects."[131]

If in 1947 and 1950 Opus Dei's founder had been free to be guided solely by his own ideas and preferences, his description of apostolate-through-work would probably have stopped there. Or

---

[128] *Letter*, March 11, 1940, nos. 11-13.

[129] 1950 *Constitutions*, no. 4 § 1.

[130] 1950 *Constitutions*, no. 230.

[131] Decree *Primum inter*, § 19.

he could have emphasized that every upright human task is meant to be apostolic.[132]   Or he may have explained with detail—as he frequently did in his preaching—what apostolate in and through work implies: example, witness, service, mutual trust, bringing Christian inspiration to environments, structures, etc.[133] Nevertheless, in 1950 it was not yet given to him to act in this way, since he had to accommodate himself to the praxis of the Sacred Congregation.  It required that the *Constitutions* of secular institutes submitted to them for their approval list all specific activities and undertakings. Thus the 1950 *Constitutions* skillfully devote several numbers to a gamut of possible apostolic activities.[134] The breadth of the description, its tone and its relation to other fundamental affirmations clearly manifest it is a non-exhaustive enumeration by way of examples. Everything points to the central core: sanctifying one's self and sanctifying others in the workplace.  This is what makes Opus Dei's apostolate in words of the founder "a shoreless sea."[135]

Consistent with this ideal of living Christianity fully in and through work, the founder also called Opus Dei "one great work of catechesis": its foremost work is integral formation, imparting to its members and those who approach Opus Dei a formation enabling them to shoulder their tasks and occupations as Christ would. Msgr.

---

[132] This was the decisive point—in which are implicit both the affirmation of the secular condition of the members of Opus Dei as well as the recognition of the Christian value of earthly realities—which led him, as pointed out in the previous chapter, to complain to the Congregation of the Council for having prohibited the practice of business to members of secular institutes. It was for this reason that he proposed that there be included in the *Constitutions* of 1950 an explicit mention of financial and commercial activities, plus those there already: educational, political, administrative, etc. (This mention is found, as already said, in no. 15 of the *Constitutions*.) The phrase "all honest civil professions," with which the recently quoted paragraph of the Decree *Primum inter* begins, is also meaningful.

[133] For a commentary on this teaching consult J. L. Illanes, "La santificación del trabajo," *op. cit.* (chapter II, note 41): P. Rodríguez, "Vocación, trabajo, contemplación," *op. cit.* (chapter II, note 49); L. Alonso, "La vocación apostólica del cristiano en la enseñanza de Mons. Escrivá de Balaguer," in Various authors, *Mons. Josemaría Escrivá de Balaguer y el Opus Dei, op. cit.,* (chap. I, note 3), pp. 229-292.

[134] 1950 *Constitutions,* nos. 18 and 444. These texts list a number of activities in accord with their lay condition that the numeraries can develop. The Decree *Primum inter,* §§ 24 and 26, offers a similar panorama, adding it does not exhaust the possibilities. Most of these tasks are included in the documents of 1947 studied before.

[135] In a 1949 *Letter*: "The apostolate of Opus Dei is intensified and spreads until it becomes—how many times have I repeated this—a sea without shores, a marvelous universal reality.  For this reason we did not want to accept any other name than that of Opus Dei, lest the field of our apostolic work appear restricted.   Our apostolate must always be carried out through every clean human activity, whatever the circumstances of place and of time" (*Letter,* December 8, 1949, no. 6).

Escrivá affirmed this from the very start,[136] reiterating it thousands of times in his preaching and *Letters*.[137] It is also declared in juridical texts from the earliest years. The 1950 *Constitutions* also reflect this reality: "As a general norm, Opus Dei does not have a specific way of external collective action. Above all it addresses the spiritual and apostolic formation of the members. These carry out apostolate by means of their public tasks and positions or by means of various established associations as the circumstances of time and place make advisable, always with complete respect for the laws of each country."[138]

Suffice it to say that the accent falls on the individual work each member can and ought to carry out with personal freedom and responsibility in the sphere of his work. That is the fundamental fruit of Opus Dei.[139]

---

[136] "We are and will always be a great catechesis." (*Intimate notes*, no. 548; the text dates from January 6, 1932.)

[137] By way of example, some more paragraphs from the *Letter* of 1949: "If we are to tend towards sanctity in our life as ordinary Christians and to practice apostolate in the form which our call to Opus Dei requires of us, we have an absolute need for a specific continual formation, so long as we are on earth." An essential part of this formation is to learn "that professional work of any kind ought always to be sanctified and sanctifying." Some aspects of this formation: "Each of the members of the Work has a specific formation that corresponds to his profession or occupation, to the work he performs the same as his colleagues in the world. And this formation is acquired where all other citizens acquire it.

"The members of Opus Dei also receive a common formation: a scholarly familiarity with the dogmatic teachings of the Church, with morality, liturgy, law and history of the Church; knowledge of the spirit, customs, history, juridical life of the Work; the study of the apostolic modes proper to the members of Opus Dei. And all of this formation has five aspects: human, spiritual, apostolic, religious-doctrinal and professional." He concludes: this formation "tends to make it possible for each person, in his walk in life and in his occupation or profession, to be a man or woman capable of doing good, a Christian" (*Letter*, December 8, 1949, nos. 83, 87 & 89).

[138] 1950 *Constitutions*, no. 7. This number, which has parallels in §§ 21-22 of the Decree *Primum inter*, reproduces nearly literally no. 339 of the *Constitutions* of 1947, which in turn echoes the documents of 1941, already quoted and analyzed.

[139] At the risk of repetition, some more relevant texts: One comes from the *Letter* of 1940 from which we have already quoted: "It can well be said, my children, that the greatest fruit of the work of Opus Dei is what its members *personally* obtain, with their apostolate of example and loyal friendship with their professional colleagues" (*Letter*, March 11, 1940, no. 55.). The *Letter* of 1949: "The most effective of the apostolic works Opus Dei carries out is that which each member does in the environment of his work or in the position he occupies because of social circumstances."

"This work cannot fail to be spontaneous: each one is alone and has to turn to the light of the Church's teaching, the formation received, God's grace which they implore and their own common sense" (*Letter*, December 8, 1949, no. 69).

*Primum inter* states, "The members of Opus Dei act and work more in an individual manner than corporatively."[140] However, this does not preclude that members individually or with other persons undertake activities with an apostolic character and purpose, for which Opus Dei as a corporation takes moral responsibility with regard to the doctrinal and apostolic dimension. This possibility was foreseen, as pointed out, in earlier documents and texts and had been put into practice: the Academy DYA in 1933, student residences established in Madrid and other cities from 1939 on. . . . Till 1950 these undertakings had been few and similar: student residences and retreat conference centers, almost exclusively. By 1950, with the continued growth of the Work, other collective ventures were foreseen: schools, universities, medical dispensaries and other charitable institutions, vocational training for workers and farm laborers and so on. Many of these came into being during the '50s or somewhat later. Msgr. Escrivá had often pointed out—not only at the start—the appropriateness of establishing some of these institutions as they would be important milestones in the Work's development. Nonetheless, he always insisted these corporate works would be few, since what is proper to Opus Dei is not fostering group activities, but forming people, one by one.[141]

That these corporative apostolic activities are less than primary explains the brevity of their norms in the 1950 documents. These rules serve merely to suggest possibilities as found listed in *Primum inter* or the *Constitutions* as mere examples.[142] They also establish a few general criteria derived from the very nature of Opus Dei. These undertakings, always carried out with strict respect for civil laws, are to have a civil, not ecclesiastical, character; they are the professional activities of ordinary citizens who exercise their normal rights and responsibilities.[143] In number 9 of the 1950 *Constitu-*

---

[140] Decree *Primum inter*, § 21.

[141] "Corporate works, educational or other," the founder wrote, "will always be relatively few and are never an end for the Work: they are a means. I measure the effectiveness of these works by the holiness attained by those who work in them: holiness achieved—I repeat yet again—by sanctifying ordinary work, making it the occasion of one's own sanctity and apostolate" (*Letter*, May 31, 1954, no. 34).

[142] These lists enumerate—and the fact closely connects with the fundamentally formative nature of the apostolic work of Opus Dei—largely tasks of formation and education: instructional centers for different social groups; houses for spiritual retreats and religious instruction; residences for university students; training centers for workers or farm laborers; youth and artistic and cultural clubs; home economics centers, etc.

[143] In his *Letters* Msgr. Escrivá describes corporate works. A few paragraphs from the *Letter* of December 1952: "My daughters and sons, imagine how much work lies before us, the good that can be done for the Church and the world with each one's own work

*tions* these group apostolic activities are seen from the perspective of the legal and economic support required by each.  The terminology used (though not for the first time) speaks of auxiliary societies, establishing there and in subsequent numbers their dependence on the Institute to ensure that they remain faithful to the apostolic purpose that alone led to the establishment of these organizations of a civil nature.[144]

In summary, the 1950 documents show that the apostolic work of Opus Dei accords with its original features.  Spiritual and apostolic instruction and training are the prerequisites for any activity pretending to be coherent with Christian faith.  These texts also underline the value of an exact and faithful fulfillment of one's professional commitments and duties, the primacy of personal apostolate and the need for positive efforts to spread Christianity, whether by witness, example and word, in an environment of friendship and trust, amid work and the affairs of daily life.[145]

---

and the works of apostolate we develop along with other citizens and within the framework of civil legislation.

"One first result of the lay spirituality of Opus Dei, nothing if not secular, is that corporate works of apostolate are also fully lay ventures.  The Work is responsible for the authentic human and Christian orientation of the initiative itself, but the task is not a *religious* work, nor an *ecclesiastical* work, nor one officially Catholic.

"They are works where some men and women discharge their professional work.  Thanks to that work and to the spirit whereby they sanctify that work, they perform a benefit to civil society and souls.  Works, therefore, open to everybody; tasks where the efforts of many come together; fruits of the free initiative of some citizens or their cooperation in official programs moved only by a common desire of Christian service.

"The activity of my daughters and sons in these corporate works is always, as I said before, professional with a human content specific to the nature of that work: be it scientific, educational, social, cultural, etc.  All work for a child of God in his Work is also from a supernatural point of view a way to sanctification and an occasion  for doing good to souls" (*Letter*, December 12, 1952, no. 30)

See other explanations in *Conversations*, nos. 18, 27, 31, 51, 71, and 84.

[144] Although this situates us later than 1950—a topic that reappears in chapter IX—we point out that later the founder decided to suppress the figure of auxiliary societies, to underline even more clearly that the apostolic activities to which they refer are carried out by ordinary citizens, who, like those who promoted them, also accept full responsibility for their maintenance and continuity.

To avoid misunderstandings, it should be noticed also that these auxilliary societies, foreseen in the 1950 *Constitutions* and in earlier texts as a source of support for apostolic undertakings, should be distinguished clearly from those financial activities Opus Dei members may effect in use of their professional freedom.  These activities, as the *Constitutions* and other writings of the founder point out, are carried out by these persons in full exercise of their personal autonomy, without any dependence on the directors of Opus Dei.  They must answer solely to their own conscience, to the owners or trustees of these activities and to civil society.

[145] Besides the texts already quoted from, references are made to this topic in nos. 202-205, 212-214, 222, 229-230 of the 1950 Constitutions, and §§ 18-23 of *Primum inter.*

## 7. Government of Opus Dei. The place of priests and lay people in the overall structure of the Work

a) *The organizational structure of government*

Although briefly, let us see how Opus Dei is organized in the 1950 *Constitutions*.[146]

Opus Dei's governance is established at three levels: general (universal), regional and local. This arrangement already appeared in the 1941 documents, from which it passed to subsequent juridical texts. The first level—general—has to do with the whole of Opus Dei; the second—regional—with the members and activities within a territorial circumscription (which may, in turn, be comprised of quasi-regions or delegations); the third—local—has to do with individual centers.[147] Opus Dei is governed by the President General, who is also called the Father. He is helped by two Councils, corresponding to the two branches; among the members of these Councils are to be found the Vice-President (if needed), the Secretary General, the Procurator General, the Central Priest Secretary, and at least one Delegate from each region for each branch.[148] At the head of each regional jurisdiction is found a Commission, for the men's branch, presided by a priest, the Regional Counselor. For the women's branch there exists a similar governing body, again presided by the Counselor, who with the help of another priest acts *nomine et vice Patris* (in the name and place of the Father). They oversee everything to do with the apostolic work within their circumscription; they take special care of the spiritual and doctrinal formation of the members, for which they count on a duly erected center of studies.[149]

Finally, the local level consists of Centers, defined not so much by a territory as by the members who make them up. In charge is a Director, assisted by at least two other persons. The canonical erection of the domicile of the Centers corresponds to Opus Dei's Directors, but the previous concurrence of the local Ordinary is required, given preferentially in writing.[150]

---

[146] The form of government is described in the 3rd and 4th parts of the *Constitutions*, nos. 293-436; 450-479, although there are also references in other numbers. *Primum inter* dedicates section VI, (§§ 40-44) to this; there are also references in other places, especially in §§ 10ff. In general lines, these texts reproduce those of 1947, with the completions and improvements sanctioned by experience, some of which had been approved by the Holy See in rescripts, to which we made reference in the previous chapter.

[147] 1950 *Constitutions*, nos. 293, 378, 398, 402.

[148] 1950 *Constitutions*, nos. 293-377; 450-460.

[149] 1950 *Constitutions*, nos. 378-402; 461-471.

[150] 1950 *Constitutions*, nos. 403-424; 472-474.

To complete this brief description reference should also be made to the Institute's various assemblies. Ordinary General Congresses are called periodically to study the development of the Institute, to appoint members of the various Councils, to propose the spread of apostolic work to new places, and the like. Elective Congresses provide for the office of President General when vacant. In addition, extraordinary Congresses can be called when special circumstances so warrant them.[151] In second place are either General or Regional Work Weeks, called to review various experiences in different Regions or apostolates; they also can be ordinary or extraordinary.[152]

b) *The cooperation of priests and lay people in Opus Dei*

The description just made was deliberately brief and schematic: a few points of reference. We cannot allow our attention to be distracted from the question in hand: understanding the juridical evolution of Opus Dei. We are not interested so much in the particulars of how Opus Dei is governed as in the principles that inspire it. Here, specifically, let us see how both the governance and apostolic activity of Opus Dei integrate laity and priests, the common priesthood and the ministerial priesthood. Without entering now into further theological reflections,[153] let us see how this interconnection is reflected in the 1950 documents.

The texts of the *Constitutions* and the Decree *Primum inter* presuppose and describe Opus Dei as a reality made up largely by lay people. At the same time emphasis is placed—from the very first number of the *Constitutions*—on the fact that Opus Dei priests have a very definite role in the organization. Their presence is not supererogatory or optional, nor even convenient; they are required by the foundational charism itself.

The *Constitutions* distill the early experience that led Msgr. Escrivá to see the need for priests coming from among the lay members of Opus Dei. Consequently the *Constitutions* deal extensively with the process of their selection, formation, etc.[154]

---

[151] 1950 *Constitutions*, nos. 304-326; 451. Mention of these Congresses is also made in the Decree *Primum inter*, § 43. In chapter IX we will refer concretely and more extensively to a special general Congress begun in 1969, which has great importance for the juridical path of Opus Dei.

[152] 1950 *Constitutions*, nos. 425-436; 477-479. See also *Primum inter*, § 44.

[153] Some considerations on this matter, taking into consideration the teaching of the founder, are found in P. Rodríguez, "Sacerdocio ministerial y sacerdocio común en la estructura de la Iglesia," in *Romana. Bolletino della Prelatura della Santa Croce e Opus Dei*, 4 (1987):162-176.

[154] 1950 *Constitutions*, nos. 13, § 1; 14, 65-68, 129, 151, 273. In the following pages we will refer only to these priests. (We will deal with the possibility of priests incardinated in dioceses being admitted as members of the Priestly Society of the Holy Cross and its form of government in the following section.)

Number 13 establishes that "Opus Dei is made up of priests and laity, who in no way constitute separate classes in the sense of the law regarding religious." It adds, "the passage from the lay to the clerical state is not forbidden; rather, on the contrary, it is fully approved." This lay condition is a prerequisite for there to be priests in the Work. "It is from the lay state that the priests come and in that state they are prepared." Later, numbers 129 and 273 establish the conditions for Opus Dei lay members to receive Holy Orders. They regulate what studies are to be carried out. They establish that "only those are promoted to Holy Orders whom the President General recognizes as endowed with an ecclesiastical vocation and whom he judges are necessary and appropriate for the Institute and its apostolates."[155] The title of ordination is "the Priestly Society of the Holy Cross." "When they receive the clerical tonsure they are ascribed to the Society and at the disposal of the President for their first and subsequent assignment to a Region of the Institute."[156] Such priests, plus some lay men more especially disposed to reach the priesthood, form within Opus Dei a social body which is called the Priestly Society of the Holy Cross.[157]

Having confirmed the existence of priests and lay people, the *Constitutions* insist above all on certain norms and criteria that express the heart of their mutual relationship: unity and harmonious cooperation. First of all, unity, because Opus Dei is not a clerical association or body that enlists some lay people to collaborate in its mission, nor is it a lay group that uses some priests as advisors or chaplains. Rather Opus Dei is a reality of Christian life that presupposes and implies both lay as well as priestly and ministerial activities. Msgr. Escrivá insisted forcefully on this point, clearly conscious of its foundational importance, which he seeks to ensure by regulating details, some of which are minute but truly significant.

From the start he stipulated that in the Work there should be priests and laity; he also insisted that apostolic work be carried out through a mutual and deep cooperation between both. On the other hand, he often told priests that they ought not to act as though lay people, for that very fact, were subordinate to them. Rather they should avoid anything that could be interpreted as letting them-

---

[155] 1950 *Constitutions*, no. 273. The ordination of priests from among the lay ranks of Opus Dei is carried out (see also no. 279) to serve the apostolates of Opus Dei. Of course their cooperation in other tasks is not excluded, so long as they are compatible with their principal function. The *Constitutions*, in nos. 139-142 and 273-279, deal more extensively with the formation of these priests, and the special centers in which this formation is given.

[156] 1950 *Constitutions*, nos. 276 & 68. See also, 1947 *Constitutions*, nos. 59 & 60.

[157] 1950 *Constitutions*, no. 1 and *Primum inter*, § 13.

selves be unnecessarily served by the laity.[158]  At other times he highlighted that all, priests and laity, are equally called to the fullness of holiness.[159]  Msgr. Escrivá also underlined that in Opus Dei the call to the priesthood is not considered as raising one up to a higher level; rather it is an invitation to service.  Moreover, full freedom exists to accept or not this priestly call.[160]

---

[158] "In Opus Dei we are all equal to each other, although we have a due veneration for the priesthood.  Within the Work we are all the same, there are not categories that distinguish and separate priests and lay people into two classes.  This marvelous characteristic of the unity of our Family leads us to live the teaching of the Apostle: *multi unum corpus sumus in Christo, singuli autem alter alterius membra* (Rom 12:5): we, being many, are one body in Christ, but each member is at the service of all the other members.

"All of you should serve, my children, serving one another, as well-lived fraternity requires, but the priests must not tolerate their lay brothers serving them unnecessarily.  We priests in the Work are the slaves of the others, following the example of the Lord—who did not come to be served but to serve: *non venit ministrari, sed ministrare* (Mt 20:28).  We must know how to put our hearts on the floor so that the others may walk softly.  For this reason, to let yourselves be served without necessity by your lay brothers is something that goes against the very essence of the spirit of Opus Dei" (*Letter*, February 2, 1945, no. 20).  This criterion he repeats in almost the same words in another *Letter* dated ten years later: "In the Work we all make up one single class: the priests will not allow their brothers who are laymen to perform unnecessary services for them" (*Letter*, March 28, 1955, no. 10).

[159] "We understand, with the whole of ecclesiastical tradition," Msgr. Escrivá affirms in a *Letter*, "that the priesthood demands—because of the sacred functions pertaining to it—something more than an honest life: it requires a holy life in those who discharge it. . . . But without in any way diminishing the importance and dignity of the priesthood, our spirit leads us to teach . . . how great also is the dignity of the Christian vocation. . . . If a priest is called by his ministry to consecrate the bread of heaven, it is not only to him that the gospel words have been spoken: 'Blessed is he who eats bread in the kingdom of God' (Lk 13:15).  All souls, without exception, are called by baptism to participate in the banquet of the great King, Jesus Christ.  To each one of them we must say: *amice, ascende superius* (Lk 14:10), aspire to participate in the banquet, do not forget your great dignity;  look to Christ whom you ought to imitate who says to all souls: *ecce prandium meum paravi*: my banquet is prepared; *venite ad nuptias*: come to the wedding (Mt 22:4)."  Then he adds: "While the states corresponding to priest and layman are distinct—as a consequence of the diversity of their respective tasks or ministries—in them there is a sole and common condition of Christians. . . . As a requirement of their common Christian vocation—as something demanded by their baptism—the priest and the lay man or woman ought to aspire equally to holiness, which is a participation in the divine life.  The holiness to which they are called is not greater in the priest than in the lay person: because the lay man or woman is no second-class Christian."  Then he concludes: "In the eyes of our Father God we are all children of equal condition.  Whatever may be the service or the ministry assigned to each of us: little children all, for whom—precisely because of their littleness—the kingdom of heaven has been reserved (Mt 19:14)" (*Letter*, February 2, 1945, nos. 4, 5 & 8).

[160] He writes, "I do not doubt that my sons, who, according to the needs of the Work, are called to the priesthood, will always consider this call a great honor and a great

In a word, the priesthood exists and is absolutely essential to Opus Dei—as it is to the whole Church—for sacramental reasons. It is not a state wherein the cleric, supposedly called to a higher level of holiness, allows the rest of the Christian community to partake of his perfection. The priesthood, rather, is an instrument Christ uses to sanctify his body, composed of living members who enrich and edify one another. The action of a priest consequently presupposes a strong sense of his role to be a servant, even when discharging functions of government. He must be no less aware of the value and specificity of the lay vocation.[161] The reverse is also true: the functioning of the lay man or woman connotes the necessary role of the priest. In helping others to draw closer to Jesus Christ, there comes a moment when we encounter the "sacramental wall," which only a priest can surmount.[162]

The 1950 juridical documents, having in mind this spiritual and theological foundation, speak to us of the importance that, as in every ecclesial community, the priesthood, specifically the presbyteral group called the Priestly Society of the Holy Cross, has in Opus Dei. By preaching the word of God, administering the sacraments and carrying out functions of ecclesiastical government reserved to clerics, the priesthood vivifies and informs the whole social body of Opus Dei.[163] The life-giving mission performed by the ministerial priest-

---

reason for joy. . . . All of you know well that nobody in the Work has either the right or the duty to receive priestly orders." For this reason, the call to the priesthood "does not oblige anyone: his is the most complete freedom. In the Work there will always be a need for many saintly and learned lay people. Thus your freedom fully remains until the moment of receiving ordination, and you will not displease me if you do not want to be ordained" (*Letter*, March 28, 1955, nos. 40-42).

[161] The priests in Opus Dei "will be the support and the sap of the work of their lay brothers, in whom they will foster a *healthy anti-clericalism*; the lay members of Opus Dei are not trained to be sacristans, but—with maximum fidelity to the Church and to the Pope—they go about their business on their own, with personal freedom and responsibility" (*Letter*, February 2, 1945, no. 28). With regard to "healthy anti-clericalism," or "a good anti-clericalism," Msgr. Escrivá has explained himself on several occasions; see, for example, *Conversations*, no. 47.

[162] The metaphor of "sacramental wall" was employed by Msgr. Escrivá on many occasions. "It is necessary that in the Work the salt of the priesthood not be lacking," he writes, for example, in a *Letter* from 1945. He continues, "Is the priesthood *saltier* than the lay condition? Well I will tell you: as members of Opus Dei, the same grace, the same salt; but the lay person can not administer sacraments. . . . And when we reach the sacramental wall, the priest is necessary" (*Letter*, February 2, 1945, no. 24). Elsewhere: "When we reach the need for the sacrament—which you have heard me call the *sacramental wall*—the priest becomes absolutely necessary" (*Letter*, March 28, 1955, no. 33). Without the cooperation of a priest, the laity's apostolic work is "incomplete," "maimed," "imperfect" (*Letter*, February 2, 1945, no. 28; *Letter*, March 28, 1955, no. 39).

[163] 1950 *Constitutions*, nos. 1 and 2; Decree *Primum inter*, §§ 9, 12-14.

hood also implies that the principal positions of government at the general and regional levels are reserved to clerics.[164]  Whence the justification that "the whole body of Opus Dei be equated to true clerical institutes, in accordance solely with what is established in these constitutions and in the special prescriptions or indults of the Holy See, which have been or will be granted to the Institute."[165]

All the members who make up the Institute—men, women; single, married; priests, lay people—carry out, in intimate unity of mind and heart, according to the role proper to each, the purpose that defines Opus Dei: seeking Christian perfection and echoing the call to holiness and apostolate in the middle of the world.  There is a real and sincere cooperation between lay people and priests in the development of this mission.  Each acts in the way and place proper to him or her, both in the Church and in the world, while treasuring the essential contribution of their complementary roles.

The presence and action of the ministerial priesthood has repercussions, furthermore, in the spiritual make-up or tenor of the whole Work and in each of its members.  It vividly manifests that the priestly dimension is essential to Christian life as a whole; whence "all the members of our Work have a priestly soul and practice the priestly virtues."[166]

This fact—and it is good to emphasize it—is perfectly coordinated with all lay aspects and dimensions.  Not only are most members of Opus Dei lay people, but they also sit on collegial governing bodies (as described by the 1950 Constitutions[167] that recapitulate earlier norms), even though major positions are reserved to clerics.  Opus Dei priests know full well they are ordained to serve, specifically, to activate the Christian personality—interior life and apostolate—of their lay brothers and sisters.  All of these facts finally endow the spirit and activity of Opus Dei with lay experience

---

[164] These positions, besides that of President General (and the Vice President, if there is one) are: a) at the general level that of Secretary General, Procurator General and Central Priest Secretary (1950 Constitutions, nos. 351-353, 452) and b) at the regional level, the Regional Counselor and the Regional Priest Secretary (1950 Constitutions, nos. 381, 384 & 463).

[165] 1950 Constitutions, no. 2; the Decree Primum inter, §§ 9, 12-13 express this in a similar manner.  This equating of Opus Dei as a secular institute with clerical institutes has been dealt in chapter V, section 8 and in chapter VI, section 6.  We also pointed out the precept of the Constitutions that given the lay condition of the majority of the members of Opus Dei, the juridical equivalency of Opus Dei to clerical institutes does not imply that "the lay members individually enjoy the rights and privileges of clerics, nor that they are subject in any moment to the obligations proper to them" (1950 Constitutions, no. 2; in the same sense, see Primum inter, § 9).

[166] Letter, February 2, 1945, no. 10.

[167] See the places quoted at the beginning of this section.

and sensitivity, to such an extent that Msgr. Escrivá could speak of Opus Dei's "lay mentality."

Occasionally he used this expression in isolated ways, but many other times in union with the aforementioned priestly soul. Their being joined is the key to effectiveness: "If the work of Opus Dei is eminently lay, and if, meanwhile, the priesthood informs the whole of Opus Dei with its spirit; if the work of lay people and that of priests complement one another and mutually benefit each other, our vocation requires that all members of the Work manifest this intimate union between the two elements in such a way that each is to have a *truly priestly* soul and a *fully lay mentality.*"[168]

c) *The President General*

The Decree *Primum inter*, in dealing with how the Institute is governed, emphasizes the decisive function of the President General. It expressly declares that whatever refers to his authority, reflected in a wide range of attributes and faculties, was diligently examined, first in various sessions of the Commission of consultors, then in the plenary congresses of the Congregation and finally approved by the Sacred Congregation after having been submitted to the Roman Pontiff, especially the most important aspects.[169]

The office of President General is *ad vitam* (for life).[170] He is elected at an elective general Congress, made up of members from the various nations or regions where Opus Dei carries out its apostolic work.[171] The election is communicated to the Holy See.[172]

The president governs the whole Institute with a power called "ordinary, social, of governance and dominative." Empowered to issue individual precepts and impose sanctions, he can also give "common precepts" and "ordain everything he judges necessary or fitting for the right governance of the Institute."[173] He is charged in a special way to make sure "the *Constitutions* are carefully observed and to foster the execution of whatever is ordained by the Holy See

---

[168] *Letter*, March 28, 1955, no. 3. With regard to the expressions "priestly soul" and "lay mentality" see the quotations presented and commented on in L. Alonso, "La vocación apostólica del cristiano," in Various authors, *Mons. Josemaría Escrivá de Balaguer y el Opus Dei, op. cit.* (chap. I, note 3), pp. 239-241 and 244-246; and M. M. Otero, "El alma sacerdotal del cristiano," in the same work, pp. 293-319, and particularly pp. 304-317.

[169] Decree *Primum inter*, § 42.

[170] 1950 *Constitutions*, nos. 298 and 303; *Primum inter*, § 42. The qualifications necessary for being elected President General are given in nos. 300-302.

[171] 1950 *Constitutions*, no. 304. The designation of electors is dealt with in nos. 22-24; with respect to other aspects of the elective process, see nos. 305ff.

[172] 1950 *Constitutions*, no. 322.

[173] 1950 *Constitutions*, nos. 299, 314, 328, 329.

and affects the members." It is also of his competence to dispense from the *Constitutions*, in matters of some importance that are susceptible of dispensation, especially if the matter concerns the whole Institute.[174]

With regard to the organization's structure and its positions of government and direction, the President General may erect, modify and suppress the various jurisdictions of the Institute.[175] He may visit them directly or through delegates.[176] He also may call and preside, personally or by a delegate, any assemblies, whose conclusions nevertheless have no normative force without his approval.[177] No one can occupy a position of government or direction, even at the local level, without his express consent.[178]

Everything to do with formation—doctrinal, spiritual, ascetic and apostolic—of all the members corresponds also to the President General.[179] He may erect regional centers of studies and special centers where Opus Dei members are readied for the priesthood; his is the right to appoint directors and professors for these centers.[180] Further, he sees to it that regional centers of studies are adequate to achieve effectively their formative purpose.[181]

Regarding priests, as already pointed out, he judges which members are to be called to the priesthood; he decrees their promotion to Holy Orders.[182] He grants the dimissory letters.[183] He verifies that canonical prescriptions for ordination are fulfilled.[184] He evaluates the need and opportuneness of ordaining priests for the Institute and its apostolates.[185] Once ordained, he assigns them to the various jurisdictions[186] and gives them ministerial faculties to hear the confessions of those belonging to the Institute, including people

---

[174] 1950 *Constitutions*, nos. 329 and 177.

[175] 1950 *Constitutions*, nos. 358 § 2; 378; 399 § 2; 400 § 2; 401 § 1 and 402 § 1.

[176] 1950 *Constitutions*, nos. 334-339.

[177] 1950 *Constitutions*, nos. 427, 429, 433, 477 and 479.

[178] 1950 *Constitutions*, no. 297.

[179] Chapter I of part II (nos. 126-146) of the *Constitutions* deals with this topic.

[180] 1950 *Constitutions*, nos. 132 & 139.

[181] 1950 *Constitutions*, no. 330.

[182] 1950 *Constitutions*, nos. 273 & 275.

[183] 1950 *Constitutions*, no. 277. See also 1947 *Constitutions*, no. 60.

[184] 1950 *Constitutions*, no. 330.

[185] 1950 *Constitutions*, no. 273.

[186] 1950 *Constitutions*, no. 68.

residing in its centers.[187] He also grants permission to accept ecclesiastical offices and to receive Mass stipends.[188]

This broad picture of faculties, here summarily outlined, documents the primacy of the President General and justifies the close study to which this juridical figure of the President General was subjected prior to the definitive approval of 1950. It is certainly an office with strong characteristics. It was hence normal that the Holy See wanted to evaluate how the office is rooted in the global reality of Opus Dei.

## 8. The admission of priests from dioceses in the Priestly Society of the Holy Cross

In the previous chapter we saw how Msgr. Escrivá wanted to extend the God-given light and energy he had perceived to priests incardinated in dioceses. In spring 1950 God made him understand how within the spiritual, apostolic and pastoral phenomenon of Opus Dei such priests could find a place, as members of the Priestly Society of the Holy Cross. Thus the founder on June 2 sent a letter to the Sacred Congregation for Religious; among other topics he proposed some new points for the *Constitutions*. Specifically, they ended up as numbers 72-89 of the *Constitutions* as approved by the Decree *Primum inter*; which also mentioned this topic in paragraph 17. These points supplement those already in the draft *Constitutions* submitted early in 1950, which establish the Priestly Society of the Holy Cross as a priestly group of the Institute. They all make up chapter five of the *Constitutions* as finally approved (nos. 64-96). Let us examine this chapter.

With regard to its members the Priestly Society of the Holy Cross is made up:

a) On the one hand by those numerary members of Opus Dei who have received Holy Orders or who are in a special preparation to receive them.[189] These are those members of the Institute who, called by the President General, are ordained with the title of "Priestly Society of the Holy Cross."[190]

---

[187] By rescript of the Sacred Congregation dated April 16, 1947 the delegated and subdelegatable faculty *ad normam iuris* of hearing sacramental confessions of all members of the Institute, including also the persons who reside in its centers, was granted to the President General. This faculty was confirmed by a rescript of the same Congregation dated June 20, 1950—granted along with the definitive approval—which states that this faculty can be subdelegated by the Regional Counselors with the consent of the President General. The literal sense of this rescript can be seen in the Appendix, document no. 34.

[188] 1950 *Constitutions*, nos. 14 § 4 and 10 respectively

[189] 1950 *Constitutions*, nos. 1 and 65-71.

[190] 1950 *Constitutions*, no. 276.

b) In addition by those priests, or at least clerics ordained *in sacris*, who are incardinated in dioceses and ask to be admitted to the Priestly Society of the Holy Cross, either as oblates (associates) or as supernumeraries, and are duly received in the Society.[191]

Diocesan priests join the Priestly Society of the Holy Cross for the same purpose as any other member of Opus Dei: to find help and encouragement in seeking Christian perfection, sanctity; they seek to do so according to Opus Dei's spirit and through its ascetical means—therefore, in and through the exercise of their ministry. In explanation Msgr. Escrivá wrote: "If it is possible to speak this way, for priests *their professional work*, wherein they are to sanctify themselves and wherewith they are to sanctify others, is the ministerial priesthood of the Bread and of the Word."[192]

It is essential for someone called to Opus Dei to stay in the place and state he occupies in the Church and in civil society. Therefore, a member of the Priestly Society of the Holy Cross does not alter or abandon his vocation as a diocesan priest; rather he recommits himself to follow it, with all its consequences, seeking at whatever cost Christian perfection, holiness. This commitment to sanctify one's life implies, for these priests, a yet deeper response to the demands of holiness and apostolate rooted first in baptism and secondly in priestly ordination. In full conformity with their diocesan condition, they receive from Opus Dei spiritual help and above all a spirit that leads them to value daily life, discovering there a constant summons to find God and to love and serve all souls.

Taking for granted the overall complexion of Opus Dei's spirit and ascetical life, applicable also to these priests,[193] the relevant points of the *Constitutions* particularly stress some consequences for diocesan priests. Two aspects especially merit comment.

a) Union with one's own bishop: The admission of a cleric to the Priestly Society of the Holy Cross "does not affect in any way his diocesan condition nor the full subjection owed to their Ordinaries; even more, in many aspects this is reinforced."[194] The spirit of Opus Dei leads to sanctify one's life with all that this implies; now the life of a diocesan priest implies primarily union with the diocese and

---

[191] 1950 *Constitutions*, nos. 72-73; 76-77. According to this legislation students in seminaries before being ordained *in sacris*, could only be considered as aspirants. With respect to the name associates, we refer to what has already been said in note 59 of this chapter.

[192] *Letter*, December 24, 1951, no. 148.

[193] In nos. 78-80 and 87-89 of the 1950 *Constitutions* we read that the juridical bonds and ascetical obligations of members of the Priestly Society of the Holy Cross are assimilated to the general norms of the same *Constitutions* with regard to these topics, *congrua congruis referendo et dummodo dignitati sacerdotali conveniant* (no. 89).

[194] 1950 *Constitutions*, no. 73.

with the one who governs it. Consequently, these priests are not to be given tasks that could hinder their diocesan ministry (in some cases — if tasks are to be entrusted —they ask the bishop's permission).[195] Moreover, the spiritual help Opus Dei gives them will always be prompted by the principle of *nihil sine Episcopo*.[196] They are hence encouraged both to be personally united to the Bishop and to foster this disposition in all their brother priests.[197]

b) Union with other diocesan priests. "They should not want to stand out in any way from their brother priests; they must make a greater effort to be united with all of them. . . . They must be filled with such fraternal charity that they radically avoid any hint of division; among all priests without exception they foster the greatest unity," even more, common life, if such were the bishop's desire.[198] The founder wrote that just as numerary priests are ordained "to work in the specific apostolates of the Work," associate and supernumerary priests "have as their aim to sanctify themselves in their diocesan ministry, while the Work makes available to them appropriate spiritual help." He adds: "Very special features of our spirit are the union of these priest sons of mine with their own bishop, whom they always venerate without ever criticizing him; their love for the diocese, for the seminary and diocesan initiatives; and their fidelity to the positions entrusted to them."[199]

---

[195] 1950 *Constitutions*, no. 79, § 1.

[196] 1950 *Constitutions*, no. 75, 1. *Nihil sine Episcopo* is the general principle of the juridical statute of these priests, the sure criterion for the spirit that should animate them and the directive norm for all of their priestly activity (no. 79, § 1 and § 8). It is therefore not only a principle of the personal spiritual direction that these priests receive in the Priestly Society of the Holy Cross—direction that ought to confirm and reinforce the collective spiritual direction the Bishop gives—but also a juridical norm incumbent upon the moderators of the Institute: "It should be absolutely and carefully avoided that with respect to these priests a special internal hierarchy proper to the Institute be created. The only thing that is sought and ought to be is: to improve the priestly life as the fruit of a diligent fidelity in their interior life, a tenacious and constant effort in their own formation, and an availability of spirit, criteria and apostolic zeal" (no. 82, § 1; in the same line see, nos. 82 § 2 and 84).

[197] 1950 *Constitutions*, no. 74.

[198] 1950 *Constitutions*, nos. 74; 75, 3 and 4. The rest of the points of this chapter are dedicated to details of practical organization or deal with priests named cooperators of the Priestly Society of the Holy Cross or who, with their priestly work, cooperate in some way with the apostolates of Opus Dei; it does not seem necessary to spend time on these points.

[199] *Letter*, December 24, 1951, no. 147. In another *Letter* dated in 1955, he comments again on these characteristics of the spirit to be lived by priests incardinated in dioceses who join the Priestly Society of the Holy Cross: "Because of their vocation to the Work, they confirm and reinforce their love for their own diocese and the veneration, affection and obedience they have for their Bishop. From the spiritual and psychological point of view there can only be in the souls of these sons of mine a confirmation of their cheerful and self-denying ministry in the service of the diocese to which they

## 9. Towards an evaluation of this stage of the legal *iter*

"The definitive approval, my children," the founder wrote in a *Letter* of December 1949, "will give us new stability, a weapon of defense, greater facility for our apostolic work; it will set down once again the fundamental principles of the Work: secularity, sanctification of work, the fact that we are ordinary citizens, and above all, especially in the spiritual aspect, our conviction that we are God's children."[200] In another *Letter*, a year following the 1950 pontifical documents, he states: "Although not a few difficulties are foreseen, the good expected from the definitive approval is great. . . . We have taken not just another step, but rather a good leap forward."[201] The better to evaluate this affirmation of Msgr. Escrivá, let us summarize some of the milestones of the juridical development Opus Dei has undergone up to this pontifical approval.

To obtain in 1941 the first written juridical approval, Msgr. Escrivá fashioned a text that went much beyond the entity's immediate needs. The documents describe not a simple diocesan pious union, but rather an enterprise of universal scope, open to all kinds of people—men and women, single and married. Opus Dei will not only need priests, but will prove capable of promoting from within itself priestly vocations to serve the apostolates it desires to carry out. When he presented these texts to Madrid's bishop the founder of Opus Dei was fully aware of the gap between the smallness of what the Work was in fact and the breadth of the panorama described by the documents. No less was he familiar with a host of theological and juridical problems raised by the Work. How to open a canonical path for a reality such as what Opus Dei implied? How to find a juridical formula that would allow the institution to have its own priests? How to articulate a stable juridical bond with married members such that their call to Christian perfection and their fidelity to what the marriage vocation required would be both affirmed? Conscious of these and other problems, he was not held back in drawing up the documents, loose ends and all, for he sought to reflect the breadth of the pastoral phenomenon Opus Dei was destined to bring about.

In the next few years Msgr. Escrivá had to confront ever more urgently these problems, especially those derived from the need for Opus Dei priests. On February 14, 1943, the answer was given to him, and he immediately requested the diocesan erection of the Priestly Society of the Holy Cross as a society of common life with-

---

belong and the service of all souls, in addition to a filial submission to the diocesan ordinary" (*Letter*, March 28, 1955, no. 45).

[200] *Letter*, December 8, 1949, no. 19.

[201] *Letter*, December 24, 1951, no. 295.

out vows.  This step, undeniably advantageous, since it resolved
the priest problem, was still flawed: the juridical formula of a society of common life did not adequately fit the secular life and apostolate
of Opus Dei.  Besides, this institutionalization gave prominence to
a part — the Priestly Society of the Holy Cross — rather than to the
whole.  For Msgr. Escrivá priests were meant to be a part serving
the whole: Opus Dei as a pastoral phenomenon inducing holiness in
the world, among people of all social conditions.  But in fact no
other way was open, if the Work was to be able to count on its own
priests and to lay the foundations for the growth of the Work, not
to mention the progressive development of the rich foundational
charism.

If we consider subsequent events, we can see that beginning in
1943 Msgr. Escrivá took very definite steps.  Using what had already been achieved as a platform, he was able, little by little, to
adjust the juridical configuration to the reality of the pastoral phenomenon.  The moves were also consistent with his plan to win
back, at the proper time, earlier concessions and to explicate what
was yet inchoate.  Such is what happened with the 1944 diocesan
*Constitutions*: they are the *Constitutions* of the Priestly Society of the
Holy Cross, though they include a broad description of Opus Dei.
The Work, the whole pastoral phenomenon, is thus described in the
constitutional text the bishop approved.  The overall unity is not
perfectly expressed, but an important step forward is taken towards its affirmation.

Unity, though major, nevertheless, was not the sole problem.  If
the Work was to be true to its mission, it must go beyond the
diocesan level also transcending the diocesan sphere and thereby
become universal.  Also needed from the Holy See was approval of
its charism together with an interdiocesan or universal juridical
personality.  This Roman step was made more urgent by widespread misunderstandings that questioned the legitimacy of the
foundational charism and gave rise to serious slander.  The petition
the founder sent to Rome in 1946 crossed paths with studies and
projects already under way.  Opus Dei thus became entangled with
other factors and realities in the process leading to the Apostolic
Constitution *Provida Mater Ecclesia*.  The figure of secular institutes
offered a new but still insufficient juridical path to Opus Dei.  The
*Constitutions* approved in 1947 clearly established the secularity
and unity of Opus Dei: a single pastoral phenomenon requiring a
single Institute.  Yet the systematic ordering of the document did
not reflect in each and every part this unity.

Once the pontifical approval was obtained, Msgr. Escrivá lost
no time: the months following February 1947 saw a series of petitions to the Holy See expanding upon and sometimes improving
what had already been achieved.  Everything culminated in the

definitive approval on June 16, 1950.  Throughout this chapter and the one before we have followed this story and pointed out the advances sanctioned by the 1950 approval.  Let's recall some: a) The oneness of the pastoral phenomenon is reaffirmed, thanks to seeing the Institute as a single reality, in whose interior works a priestly body.  Sanctity and apostolate in the world is obtained by an intimate and fruitful cooperation of the clergy and the laity.   b) The possibility of admitting married persons, of all walks and settings, as members (not merely as collaborators or cooperators) is institutionalized as well as the possibility of admitting priests incardinated in dioceses in the Priestly Society of the Holy Cross.  By broadening its welcome, the pastoral phenomenon of the Work attains a fuller development of the potentialities inherent in the original foundational charism.   c) Also proclaimed is the ordinary lay condition of most members of the Work.  Simultaneously the equivalency of Opus Dei with clerical institutes of pontifical right is reiterated, a matter of great juridical moment, for it guarantees an interdiocesan form of government, necessary internal autonomy and juridical means for adequate priestly attention.  d) Broad faculties for the President General are also authorized, a measure carefully studied and expressly approved by the Roman Pontiff.  Thus is assured juridically the cohesion of the pastoral phenomenon with a unified government of all incorporated in Opus Dei: priests and lay people, men and women, married and celibate.

But the greatest achievement brought about by the pontifical approval of June 16, 1950, is the definitive recognition by the Church that Opus Dei is a true way to sanctity and apostolate.  Thus is ratified the mission whereby all kinds of people, moved by a special divine call, stably commit themselves to live an integral Christian life in the middle of the world, in their jobs and other circumstances proper to secular, lay life.  Thus they spread among their peers the universal call to faith, Christian perfection, apostolate.  Thus the Christian and ecclesial value of Opus Dei's foundational charism is definitively recognized.[202]

All of this prompts us to understand better why the founder could say in the 1951 *Letter* that the approval of June 1950 does not constitute, in its juridical history, simply "another step, but rather a good leap forward."  That's also why we, in examining and com-

---

[202] The approval of 1950 is a definitive juridical approval, that is to say, it does not require any more approvals.  The studies and earlier steps taken by the Holy See have reached a judgment which makes reconsideration unnecessary.  It admits of course that future improvements or changes may be introduced in the juridical text, as recognized by the letter quoted earlier which the Sacred Congregation for Religious addressed to the founder of Opus Dei on August 2, 1950. (See Appendix, document no. 33.)

menting on the Decree *Primum inter* and the 1950 *Constitutions*, said that with these documents a stage is closed.

Decisive steps have been taken, but much distance must still be trod in the juridical *iter* of Opus Dei. And, above all, the capstone. In this period of papal approvals (1947-1950) Msgr. Escrivá vividly experienced the tension between charism and law, to which are dedicated some initial chapters of this study.[203] He knew how to avail himself of everything offered—new formulations, the legislative breadth of secular institutes. Yet he was no less aware that this legislation was not coterminous with the foundational charism.[204] Msgr. Escrivá felt urged to obtain for Opus Dei the Holy See's approval and the juridical means to facilitate its development. In all this he appealed to the prudential criterion: "to give in, without giving up, eager to win it back." He evokes this maxim in an oft-quoted Letter of December 1949: "In conscience we cannot fail to go ahead: trying to avoid any compromise; that is to say, we concede without giving anything up. Putting it in God's hands who writes straight with crooked lines, he will bring us to the final goal."[205]

In summary, the unsuitable elements of the 1950 solution—"the compromise," "the concessions"—lead us back to two items pointed out in evaluating the 1947 approval as a secular institute: dependence on the Congregation for Religious and placing the figure of secular institute within the framework of the states of perfection. No matter how broadened, this state remained other-worldly. Since we have dealt extensively with this, no further explanations are needed. However, let us just point out that this ill-fitting suit could not be superseded without a new theological and canonical focus. A new stage thus begins.

From the vantage point of 1950, given the reality of Opus Dei and the juridical-theological mindset then prevalent, one could see

---

[203] Cf. section 3 of chapter III.

[204] He was conscious that this was an inadequate situation. Referring to the petition he was about to make to the Vatican for the definitive approval, he writes in the aforementioned Letter of 1949: "In taking this step I feel a great concern" (*Letter*, December 8, 1949, no. 20). In 1950 after referring to the legislation for secular institutes that "it allows, although in a very forced way and with ambiguities, for fundamental elements of our vocation," he declared that "Nevertheless, there was no other way: either we accepted everything or we continued without a path on which to tread." For this reason, he continues, "I accepted the fact that along with the essential parts that correspond to our spirit and way of being, there appear others that do not fit us. . . . If this solution had difficulties, it was better to save what was essential, even though some points could not be well adapted to our way" (*Letter*, October 7, 1950, nos. 20-21). Summing things up: "We have accepted with sacrifice an unavoidable compromise that does not eclipse, however, the joy of having finally obtained a juridical path for our life." (*Letter*, October 7, 1950, no. 20).

[205] *Letter*, December 8, 1949, no. 16.

the juridical form adopted could not be maintained and, sooner or later, latent problems would come to the fore.  More difficult was it, on the other hand, to foresee when this would happen.  In fact, as we shall see, these incongruities soon arose, ushering in the final stage of Opus Dei's juridical development.

We conclude by again quoting from the founder.  Writing in 1961, he contemplates the path traveled to 1950 and what still remained, while expressing his gratitude to God and his utmost trust.  "In the midst of these historical circumstances God has guided us, step by step, with his loving providence: *misericordiam et iudicium cantabo tibi, Domine* (Ps 100:1): Lord, I will praise your mercy and your justice forever.  He lent us his fortitude so that we stick to our way.  He fed us, lest we grow faint in the face of hardships: *surge, comede: grandis enim tibi restat via!* (3 Kings 29:7): feed yourself with my Will because you have a long way to go.

"It seemed as though God our Father was looking upon his Work—a new creature—and addressing it in the words of St. Paul to Timothy: *nemo adolescentiam tuam contemnat, sed exemplum esto fidelium in verbo, in conversatione, in caritate, in fide, in castitate* (1 Tim 4:12): let no one despise your youth—your newness—but set the believers an example in speech and conduct, in love, in faith, in purity.  With virtues, my children: virtues are the important thing, the first thing God asks us: all the theological virtues and all the cardinal virtues.

"This is what the divine Spirit advises us, this is what the breadth of divine love inspires, because *hoc enim faciens, et teipsum salvum facies, et eos qui te audiunt* (1 Tim 4:16): for by so doing you will reach holiness and lead your hearers towards holiness.

"With these God-given helps, which were lights, consolations, roses and thorns, we have obtained the approval of the Work, within a broad juridical framework, with well-defined specific characteristics, with its specific ascetical practices and its character, fully lay, secular, repeatedly confirmed.  For this, the most important thing, my children, we had to tolerate the other obscure meanings and inadequacies."[206]  These obscure meanings and inadequacies will bring about events in the years subsequent to 1950 that will lead to new solutions.

---

[206] *Letter*, January 25, 1961, nos. 58-59.

Part Four

TOWARDS A DEFINITIVE
LEGAL SOLUTION

# Chapter VIII

## *IN SEARCH OF NEW WAYS*

# Chapter VIII

## IN SEARCH OF NEW WAYS

### 1. Opus Dei after the pontifical approval of 1950

The pontifical approval of 1950 represented new encouragement for the work of Opus Dei the world over.[1] The apostolic work begun during the second half of the '40s in Portugal, Great Britain, Italy, Ireland and France, soon reached other European countries: Germany (1952), Switzerland (1956), Austria (1957), Holland (1960), Belgium (1965). A trip to the New World by some members of Opus Dei in 1948 spurred the beginning of apostolic work in Mexico, the United States, Chile and Argentina. Later it spread to Venezuela and Colombia (1951), Peru and Guatemala (1953), Ecuador (1954), Uruguay (1956), Brazil and Canada (1957), El Salvador (1958), Costa Rica (1959), Paraguay (1962). . . . At the end of the '50s the apostolate leapt to new continents and cultures: in 1958 apostolic work began in Kenya and Japan. These were followed by Australia (1963), Philippines (1964), Nigeria (1965).

This geographical expansion was accompanied and made possible by the incorporation to Opus Dei of new members, not only in Spain. The 2954 members (23 priests) at the time of requesting approval in 1950, had become ten years later 30,353 of whom 307 were priests.[2]

On June 29, 1948, when the worldwide expansion of Opus Dei was still beginning, Msgr. Escrivá made Rome his place of residence. There he also erected the Roman College of the Holy Cross, as an international center of formation, where members of the men's

---

[1] With regard to the expansion of Opus Dei in these years an overview is found in the biographical works quoted in note 1 of chapter I; other data are taken from the AGP Sezione "Fondazioni."

[2] The figure of 307 refers to priests who have come from among the lay men of Opus Dei; it does not include the priests incardinated in dioceses, members of the Priestly Society of the Holy Cross. In the figure of 30,353 are included members of both branches, both married and single.

branch of Opus Dei would be trained.[3] On December 12, 1953, he erected the Roman College of Holy Mary, a similar center of the women's branch.[4] These centers developed rapidly. By the mid-fifties, the composition of the Roman College of the Holy Cross was truly international; and shortly thereafter so was the Roman College of Holy Mary.

During the first years of expansion in Spain Msgr. Escrivá often traveled to various cities, to launch the beginnings or later to encourage and orient it. The same was true later in Portugal. In moving to Rome, he continued the same custom. From the late '40s, he crisscrossed Europe to learn about new places, visit bishops and other ecclesiastical authorities and spend time with the pioneering members of Opus Dei.[5] In 1958 he went to London, a city to which he returned the following summers, and from which he also traveled to Ireland. In August 1959 an editor of *The Times* (London) interviewed Msgr. Escrivá, which was the basis for a literary portrait, published on the 20th in the section "People to watch."[6] The growth of Opus Dei was not passing unnoticed beyond the Church. In fact, many people were taking notice of Msgr. Escrivá and Opus Dei. Some did not completely understand it; others were mistaken with respect to its nature; most people, however, voiced respect, admiration and appreciation in its regard.

By the early 1960s Opus Dei had ceased to be a conjecture, a promise or even an incipient apostolate; it had become a worldwide reality. The confidence signified by the 1950 papal approval, the Church's supreme authority sanctioning the spirit and specific apostolic message of Opus Dei, plus having a solid juridical foundation that facilitated the expansion, had not been misplaced. The expansion did take place in a very short period.

The joy this brought the founder was sometimes dimmed by continued slanders and libels. These misunderstandings did not cease with the definitive papal approval.[7] In fact they spread to

---

[3] The formal document by which the Roman College of the Holy Cross was erected is in the Appendix, document no. 35.

[4] The document of the erection of this center is in the Appendix, document no. 36.

[5] Besides the trip in the fall of 1949, in April and May 1955 he traveled through the north of Italy, Switzerland, Germany and Austria; in November and December of the same year he visited France, Belgium, Holland, Germany, Switzerland and Austria; in June 1956 and August-September 1957, once again he was in various European countries.

[6] This correspondent of *The Times* concluded his literary portrait with the following words: "The achievement of Msgr. Escrivá is to have formed a corporate entity of mature men, of many nations, inspired by principles at once novel and elementary."

[7] The founder wrote in a *Letter* of 1951: "I thought that, once the definitive approval had been obtained, plus direct dependence on the Roman Pontiff, those who had at-

Italy, with similar results: letters and visits to families of Opus Dei members to disquiet them with regard to their children's vocations. Understandably this situation caused suffering to Msgr. Escrivá, who again sought supernatural help: on May 14, 1951, he consecrated the families of the members to the Holy Family, seeking thus to put an end to this tribulation.[8] These barbs and others of the same kind also reached the Roman Curia, giving rise to events we now relate.

During the summer of 1951 Msgr. Escrivá felt uneasy. Though he had no hard facts or information, he sensed something was happening, a grave threat to Opus Dei. As the days passed, this foreboding became even more acute. He visited the Marian shrine of Loreto to place all his worries in the hands of the most holy Virgin. He did so on August 15, 1951, and consecrated Opus Dei to Mary's most sweet heart. In the following months, information reached him, confirming to him that his fears were not unfounded. Among other sources were several comments of Cardinal Schuster, the Archbishop of Milan, to two members of Opus Dei which reached him. They were told to transmit to Msgr. Escrivá this message: a grave persecution was coming upon the Work and its founder. In a subsequent conversation on January 15, 1952, the Archbishop was even more explicit: "Tell him to remember his countryman St. Joseph of Calasanz and also St. Alphonse Mary de Liguori and to get moving."[9]

For anyone conversant with Church history the warning was clear: both founders had been, in one way or another separated from the institutions they had founded, left to contemplate subsequent crises and schisms. Such was the plot hatched by some people: that Opus Dei be split into two different institutions—one for men and another for women—and that the founder be removed from both.[10] Learning of these ploys was a great blow to Msgr. Escrivá. The attempt in itself, the false accusations on which it was based, the lack of an opportunity to clarify things and defend himself, all this caused him intense suffering.

He also understood that he had to act quickly, as Cardinal Schuster had suggested, because the operation seemed to be quite far ad-

---

tacked us would leave us in peace. But I was mistaken" (*Letter*, December 24, 1951, no. 229).

[8] *Letter*, December 24, 1951, no. 260; RHF 20154, p. 51; with regard to these events and those that followed see F. Gondrand, *op. cit.* (chapter I, note 1), pp. 238-240; A. Vázquez de Prada, *op. cit.* (chapter I, note 1), pp. 259-267; P. Berglar, *op. cit.* (chapter I, note 1), pp. 240-241.

[9] RHF, T-3360. In *Letter*, Jan. 25, 1961, nos. 44-45, Msgr. Escrivá recounts these events and the following ones.

[10] AGP, Sezione "Fondazioni", Italia VI, doc. 1-4.

vanced. The gravity of the situation and the way it had been carried out left but one option: to turn directly to the Pope in his defense. Meanwhile, on February 24, 1952, Cardinal Tedeschini had taken possession as Cardinal Protector of Opus Dei.[11] Shortly thereafter, Msgr. Escrivá gave him a letter, dated March 12, to be given to the Pope. In the letter in a respectful but firm tone, he said he was aware of what some people were trying to do; he asked that the whole secret process be ended; and he defended the right of Opus Dei to continue to live according to the norms repeatedly approved by the Holy See. Referring to the institutional unity of Opus Dei, he pointed out his surprise and sorrow that some people wanted to reopen a question that had been so profoundly studied, examined and decided upon, in approving the whole organizational structure of Opus Dei in previous years.[12] The letter, which Fr. Alvaro del Portillo also signed, was presented to the Pope by Cardinal Tedeschini in an audience on March 18. Upon reading it, Pius XII said that there was nothing to fear, since absolutely nothing would happen. The whole matter was resolved and everything ceased because of the direct intervention of the Pope.[13]

On October 2, 1953 the 25th anniversary of Opus Dei's founding was celebrated. In December 1952 Msgr. Escrivá had written a letter looking forward to this date.[14] Early in September 1953, the founder once again felt the need to disclose what this commemoration meant in his children's life of faithful dedication to the service of the Church.[15]

---

[11] The Cardinal Protector—a figure provided for in the CIC 1917, c. 499 § 2—was named by the Holy See. His function had been reduced in the Code then in force to that of promoting the good of the Institute with his advice and patronage. This figure was suppressed on April 28, 1964 with a notification of the Secretary of State to the Cardinal Dean of the S. College of Cardinals (cf X. Ochoa, *Leges Ecclesiæ post Codicem iuris canonici editæ*, III, Rome 1972, no. 3185, col. 4490).

[12] RHF, EF-520312t-1.

[13] RHF, T-3360. We will turn in section 3 of this chapter to the importance of these events in the juridical evolution of Opus Dei.

[14] "Within the year soon to begin, we will celebrate the silver jubilee of our Work. And we will celebrate it in our style, in a family celebration, without making noise: in each house, in each center, in each home, wherever a son or daughter of God in his Opus Dei lives, there will be youthful rejoicing, the supernatural outlook of our Way. . . . And there should also be a renewal of fidelity to the divine call, so as to be in the midst of the world sowers of joy and peace" (RHF, EF-521200-1).

[15] Msgr. Escrivá declared in his letter: "I write you these lines so that all of you—sons and daughters of God in his Work—prepare yourselves to celebrate this day not only in a traditional act of thanksgiving, but also with a joyful renewal of your dedication to the service of souls, each day more filially united to the Church and to the Pope." And further along he says that "the heroism of your ordinary life, without display, will be the most normal way of solemnizing this silver jubilee according to our spirit" (RHF, EF-530908-1).

Cardinal Tedeschini, as Protector of Opus Dei, transmitted to the founder the papal blessing for this anniversary, confirmed by a telegram from Msgr. Montini. On this occasion, some ecclesiastical personages manifested their sentiments of appreciation and congratulation. One of these was Cardinal Tedeschini himself. Recalling that he had been the nuncio in Spain (1921-1936) during Opus Dei's infancy, he stresses the importance of the theological and pastoral phenomenon of Opus Dei, in an affectionate and rhetorical tone that echoes the usages of the time: "The proximity of the feast of October 2nd brings to me great joy, as it evokes the event which is so engraved in our hearts. . . . The completion of twenty-five years from the foundation of an Institute rarely calls attention, and even less arouses interest, since twenty-five years are barely time for beginning and never for great progress. Opus Dei, with the Priestly Society of the Holy Cross, was born, on the other hand, great and mature, because of the inspired opportuneness of the idea, hidden before in the desire of the times, and entrusted now by God to the priestly strength and personal prestige of its eminent Founder."[16]

Cardinal Valeri, Prefect of the Sacred Congregation for Religious, wrote: "The Sacred Congregation for Religious, which because of its competence, has had to follow closely the development and expansion of the flowering Work and has been the organ of the Holy See for granting the successive approvals obtained by the Institute, takes cordial delight with Your Excellency and with the members of both branches, for men—priests and laity—and women, in this happy commemoration; with all of the members numeraries, Oblates and supernumeraries; with the diocesan priests of the Priestly Society of the Holy Cross: that is to say, with all who make up the agile and compact organism, the strong and ordered militia—acies ordinata—of Opus Dei." Later: "The Sacred Congregation desires the happy continuation of the rapid numerical growth and its fortunate spread, as well as that solid individual ascetical, cultural, professional and apostolic formation which begins on solid foundations and continues afterwards uninterrupted throughout life."[17]

Cardinal Pizzardo, at the time Secretary of the Supreme Congregation of the Holy Office, and later Prefect of the Sacred Congregation of Seminaries and Universities, spoke of "the wise ordering of the Constitutions of the Institute, especially in what has to do with the healthy and profound formation of the members, both university students and younger, not only of human knowledge and professional studies, but of ecclesiastical ones. . . . To unite the so-called profane disciplines with the ecclesiastical ones, while in-

---

[16] The complete text is in the Appendix, document no. 37.

[17] This letter is also in the Appendix, document no. 38.

tegrating and completing them mutually, is the Institute's members' most effective weapon for their apostolic action, and raises their souls towards the Lord of all knowledge." Declaring optimal the doctrinal-religious formation of all the lay and priestly members, he delights "in all the initiatives promoted by Opus Dei in the field of studies," while joyfully taking cognizance of "the admirable spread of the Work in the world, the abundance of select vocations, and the consoling apostolic fruits gathered up until now."[18]

These and other declarations expressing appreciation for the work of Opus Dei parallel a series of events that evince a clear consciousness of the apostolic promise and betoken the confidence of the Holy See.

Early in 1956, Archbishop Samoré, Secretary of the Sacred Congregation for External Affairs, communicated to Msgr. Escrivá that Pius XII wanted to entrust Opus Dei with a Prelature *nullius*. On April 12, 1957, the Holy See withdrew from the Archdiocese of Lima the Andean provinces of Yauyos and Huarochiri to establish the new Prelature *nullius* of Yauyos, as suffragan of the Archdiocese of Lima. On the same day Msgr. Ignacio María de Orbegozo, a priest of Opus Dei, was named prelate.[19] To emphasize the high esteem in which Opus Dei was held, Samoré communicated the news in an act celebrated in Opus Dei's headquarters in Rome.[20]

A few years earlier, in October 1952, thanks to a personal initiative of the founder, a university had been started in Pamplona, Spain. By 1959 its development was such that it deserved to be recognized officially as a university.[21] Cardinal Tardini told Msgr. Escrivá of the desire of Pope John XXIII that the then-named Estudio General de Navarra be established as a university.[22] On August 6,

---

[18] This letter is also in the Appendix, document no. 39. Reproducing these and other declarations of appreciation as well as a selection of texts from the documents of approval, a volume was published (*Opus Dei, 2-X-1928/2-X-1953*, Madrid 1953) and widely distributed.

[19] *AAS* 49 (1957):881-883. Msgr. Orbegozo was consecrated titular bishop of Ariasso in 1963. He headed the prelature until 1968, when he was named bishop of Chiclayo. He was replaced by Bishop Sánchez Moreno, also a priest of Opus Dei, who had been since 1961 titular bishop of Nilopolis and auxiliary of Chiclayo.

The two provinces of Yauyos and Huarochiri occupy a broad territory in one of the most rugged and impoverished areas of the Peruvian sierra. A few years later, in 1962, the Holy See added to the Prelature of Yauyos the province of Cañete, which until then had belonged to the Archdiocese of Lima. Thus the Prelature attained a total extension of 15,506 sq. km. (*AAS* 54 (1962):735-737).

[20] RHF, 20519, pp. 16ff.

[21] In 1959 it comprised the schools of law, medicine, nursing, history and sciences, and with institutes of journalism, business, and canon law.

[22] AGP, Sezione Giuridica "Fondazioni," Universidad de Navarra, I and II.

1960, the Holy See, with the Decree *Erudiendæ*, recognized this educational center as a university.[23] Shortly thereafter, on October 15, by decree of the Sacred Congregation of Seminaries and Universities, Msgr. Escrivá was named chancellor of the University of Navarra.[24]

The establishment of the University of Navarre saw the founder of Opus Dei meet, for the first time, with huge numbers of people. The solemn ceremony in which the University of Navarre was proclaimed took place on October 25, 1960. Before this the University of Saragossa conferred on Msgr. Escrivá an honorary degree of Doctor of Philosophy and Letters.[25] The city of Pamplona, in turn, named him an adopted son, by an agreement of the municipal corporation dated October 5, 1960. Thus it was necessary for him to make a trip which began in the middle of October and which ended on the 26th of that month. During the trip the founder visited Madrid, Saragossa and Pamplona.[26] The news of the visit spread widely. In churches, meeting halls, streets and squares, heterogeneous groups of people gathered to greet Msgr. Escrivá with outpourings of affection. These multitudinous events put the founder's humility to a test. He had always fled from anything that smacked of calling attention to himself, but at the same time they were a

---

[23] *AAS* 51 (1960):988-990. The Estudio General de Navarra had begun its activity linked to the state University of Saragossa. On September 8, 1962, it obtained from the Spanish government full recognition of the civil effects of its studies and degrees, after the signing of an agreement between the Holy See and the Spanish government with regard to universities of civil studies (April 5, 1962). With respect to this agreement, see A. de Fuenmayor, *El convenio entre la Santa Sede y España sobre Universidades de estudios civiles*, Pamplona 1966.

[24] RHF, D-15102. Shortly before, Msgr. Escrivá was named an honorary member of the Roman Pontifical Theological Academy (Dec. 19, 1955) (RHF, D-15099), and a Consulter of the Sacred Congregation of Seminaries and Universities (July 23, 1957) (RHF, D-15101); a few months after his appointment as chancellor, he was made a Consultor of the Pontifical Commission for the Authentic Interpretation of the Code of Canon Law (March 21, 1961) (RHF, D-15103).

[25] The *Boletín Oficial del Estado*, May 28, 1960, published an order of the Ministry of Education, April 21, 1960, by which, in view of the petition of the Faculty of Philosophy and Letters and the favorable opinion of the Rector of the University of Saragossa, it authorized granting to Msgr. Escrivá the degree of Doctor in Philosophy and Letters, *honoris causa*.

[26] With regard to these events information is found in P. Berglar, F. Gondrand and A. Vázquez de Prada (*cit.* in note 1 of chapter I). In addition a lengthy report of his stay in Spain by J. L. Albertos, "La gran jornada universitaria de Navarra," in *Nuestro Tiempo*, 7 (1960):610-628, and in *El Estudio General de Navarra, Universidad Católica*, Madrid 1961, a volume edited by the University of Navarre. With regard to the academic ceremony in Saragossa, see the review of the Secretariat of Publications of the University of Saragossa *Universidad. Revista de Cultura y Vida Universitaria*, 37 (1960): 26-31. With regard to the trip in general, RHF, 20541, pp. 18-36; and 20589, pp. 186-205.

source of great joy. The great crowds he had glimpsed on October 2, 1928, had become a reality; the seed sown by God in his mind and heart on that day had borne tangible fruit. One needed but to open his eyes to see the widest variety of people: men and women, young and old, intellectuals and workers, single and married, priests and lay people, all united by the same Christian ideal.

In Madrid on October 17 he had this experience for the first time as he entered the church of St. Michael, where he was about to celebrate Mass. He was moved on seeing the overflowing congregation. His homily began: "Be seated . . . those of you who can. I want to say a few words to you in this Madrid church, where I had the joy of celebrating my first Mass in this city. God brought me here with the inklings of our Work. I could not dream then that I would see this church filled with souls who love Jesus Christ so much. I am truly moved." Then he spoke of Opus Dei's spreading to Europe and America and its beginnings in Africa and Asia.[27]

Another multitudinous event, though of different traits, is the last to which we refer in this brief panoramic description of the growth achieved by Opus Dei by the beginning of the 1960s. We turn to the inauguration of an undertaking of a social nature that Pope John XXIII had entrusted to Opus Dei in a district of Rome called the Tiburtino.[28] It took place on November 21, 1965, during the fourth and last session of the Second Vatican Council. The act was invested with special solemnity since it was presided over by his holiness Pope Paul VI, accompanied by eight cardinals, many archbishops and bishops then in Rome for the Council, as well as many other noted figures.

---

[27] These same perspectives of universality were present, though with academic tones, on October 25, in the address which he gave at the solemn university celebration in Pamplona. Present were: the university faculty, representatives of other universities, of the municipal government of Pamplona, the nuncio in Spain, Msgr. Antoniutti, the Minister of Justice, Antonio Iturmendi, the official representative of the Spanish head of State, and various civil and ecclesiastical figures, among them a third part of the Spanish episcopate. "This Catholic character, that is to say, universal, is the distinctive note of the Estudio General de Navarra, to which the Church has entrusted a cultural and apostolic work, which, while rooted and carried out on the soil of Spain, reaches out, by the purpose to which it is dedicated, beyond the strict frontiers of one country. In the horizon of this work are found the countries of the American continent united by old traditions and young countries recently established, without forgetting those other ancient nations to which the light of faith reached and which the Church also dedicates its most solicitous concern."

[28] With the occasion of the 80th birthday of Pius XII in 1956 a collection was taken up throughout the Catholic world. Pius XII decided that this money should be destined to a social work, but his death occurred before a specific recipient could be determined. It was John XXIII who, in the early months of his pontificate, decided that it should be dedicated to a work of this type in one of the working areas of Rome, and he entrusted it to Opus Dei.

Msgr. Escrivá expressed his veneration for the Holy Father and presented to him the undertaking being inaugurated. His relevant topic was the human and Christian value of work. "Opus Dei has received with special thanks the pleasant charge of fostering the professional, human and Christian development of young workers. This is so not only because Opus Dei wants to serve the Church as the Church wants to be served, as I am in the habit of saying, but also because the task entrusted to it corresponds perfectly to the spiritual and apostolic features of our Work. Opus Dei, both in the training of its members as in the practice of its apostolates, has for its foundation the sanctification of the life's work of each person." Persons frequenting the center's classrooms will "learn that work sanctified and sanctifying is an essential part of the vocation of a responsible Christian, who is conscious of his high dignity. He knows besides that he has the duty to sanctify himself and to spread the kingdom of God precisely *in* his work and *by means of* his work, building up the earthly city." This will be learned in "an atmosphere of freedom where all feel themselves to be brothers, far from the bitterness born of loneliness or indifference."[29]

The events and texts just referred to depart from the strictly juridical, the subject of this book. Nevertheless, we mention them to evoke the panorama Opus Dei presented in the 1960s, and its apostolic echoes. They constitute a framework for evaluating the more directly juridical aspects we are now to consider.

## 2. The first years of secular institutes: heterogeneity and clarification.

Let us begin by referring to a process begun in the '50s that became more accentuated in the following decade: the complex evolution of secular institutes.

One of the scholars who paid great attention to this figure is Armando Oberti. He described the work of preparing for the international congress celebrated by secular institutes in 1970. The documentation sought and gathered reveals a broad range of orientations. "Some institutes," writes Oberti, "are secular in name only, but organized in such a way as to placate the theologians and canonists who insist on including secular institutes in the great family of the *religious*." In others the concept of consecration was reelaborated in terms that "seem to empty it of the radical commitment that has

---

[29] *L'Osservatore Romano* of the following day (Nov. 22-23, 1965) dedicated its first two pages to the solemn acts taken place at the Tiburtino. It carried in its entirety the homily given by the Pope as well as extensive passages from the address of Msgr. Escrivá, as well as other chronicles and commentaries. Even fuller documentation is found in RHF, 20571, pp. 19-38.

traditionally been considered part of this reality."[30] In a subsequent work Oberti claimed this situation gave rise to serious questions. Not only is there a "pluralism of secular institutes," but also a "radical heterogeneity," as a consequence of the diverse theological concepts affecting this figure.[31]

How did such a situation arise? What were its roots? We must return to *Provida Mater Ecclesia* itself, a broad charter capable of embracing a variety of institutes. The heterogeneity that existed among the new forms and addressed by the Apostolic Constitution could not fail to be reflected in the legal text, a compromise which was ambivalent on more than one point.[32] This reality and the doubts raised by some requests for approval made subsequent to the constitution led, along with other factors, to the promulgation in 1948 of the Motu proprio *Primo feliciter* and the Instruction *Cum Sanctissimus*. These documents, among other things, defend the special nature of this new figure, insist on secularity as the proper and distinctive note of secular institutes and regulate more strictly the procedures for obtaining approval as a secular institute. They thus restrict unwarranted uses of this title.[33]

Both of these pieces of legislation produced their effect, but they did not fully clarify the question. Why else did the Congregation feel compelled to issue in 1956 some "norms for meetings having to do with the necessary renewal of the states of perfection?"[34] It said such meetings, if they intended to deal with the internal life and the juridical condition of these institutions, required, before their celebration, the authorization of the proper papal congregation. This intervention was justified, among other reasons—as is affirmed in a commentary which appeared in the *Monitor ecclesiasticus*—by the "confusions arisen in these recent times around the concept of the state proper to the secular institutes, as well as around the juridical condition of the members of these Institutes."[35]

A year later, Fr. Larraona, then Secretary of the Congregation for Religious, spoke to the Second General Congress of States of

---

[30] A. Oberti, "Preparazione, significato e prospettive del Convegno Internazionale degli Istituti Secolari," Various authors, *Nel mondo e per il mondo. Gli Istituti Secolari, oggi*, Rome 1972, p. 18.

[31] A. Oberti, *Per una teologia degli Istituti Secolari*, Milan 1983, pp. 17-18.

[32] On this topic, see chapter V, especially section 6.

[33] See chapter VI, section 3.

[34] *AAS* 48 (1956):295-296.

[35] *Monitor ecclesiasticus*, 81 (1956):374-375; the commentary is by S. Canals, Secretary at that time of the special Commission for Secular Institutes, which had been established in the Sacred Congregation for Religious in 1947. This commentary was published also in *Apollinaris*, 29 (1956):64-73.

Perfection, celebrated in Rome from December 8 to 14, 1957. The aim of this meeting was to commemorate the 10th anniversary of the promulgation of the pontifical documents giving life to secular institutes. Fr. Larraona declared it was proper to make a "balance of the results of these ten years of agitated history of secular institutes." He reviewed various topics, dealing at length with the key notion of secularity. It was "necessary above all," he said, "to recognize that *secularity* is a very broad and very variegated concept," and consequently different understandings of secularity open a broad range of possibilities within the configuration of secular institutes. "In addition, even in the religious life, one encounters a vast multitude not only of institutes, but also of categories of religious institutes (orders, congregations, societies) which, while coinciding in the essential elements, are nevertheless so different from one another that they constitute diverse types, some of which are in fact—and could without difficulty come to be so in form—secular institutes, more secular than many true secular institutes!"[36]

Fr. Larraona's words, both because of what they imply as an invitation to reflect on the nature of secularity, as well as the recognition of the breadth of the figure of secular institute and of the absence of precise limits between secular institutes and religious institutes, were widely echoed at the time and later. In truth, it was not only the concept of secularity that was under discussion, but also others, such as consecration, consecrated life and state of perfection. This situation is reflected in both scholarly writings and the praxis of the Roman Curia.

The existence of "a certain elasticity in the form of understanding secularity allowed the approval [as secular institutes] of institutes whose inspiration was not far from that of the religious, giving rise to fears in the more clearly secular ones."[37] This fact, along with the spread of writings expanding on the concept of state of perfection, postulated a continuity between secular institutes and

---

[36] The text of this conference from 1957 has been included in the collection *Nel mondo e per il mondo . . ., op. cit.* (note 29 of this chapter) pp. 245-257; the phrases quoted are respectively on pp. 245 and 249.

[37] L. Morosini Montevecchi - S. Sernagiotto di Casavecchia, *op. cit.* (chapter V, note 49) pp. 28-29. F. Morlot, well aware of the facts, as a former official of the Section of Secular Institutes of the Sacred Congregation for the Religious, has written, "In the vacillation of the first years, the Holy See itself is not exempt from some ambiguities." During these years, "associations of all kinds presented themselves, seeking approval, of some of which it was difficult to say whether they were religious or secular institutes" (Letter published in *Dialogo*, X, no. 54, July/Sept. 1982, p. 78).

Already in 1950, J. Creusen wrote: "some [secular institutes] are differentiated from religious institutes only in the absence of a special habit" ("Instituts seculiers," in *Revue des Communautes Religieuses*, 22 (1950):29). Later, but recalling earlier times,

religious congregations.[38] The application to secular institutes of the norms proper to the law of religious was also advocated.[39] All of this generated a certain *leveling* between the two institutions, or at least an assimilation of secular institutes to religious institutes. This modified by way of practice what had been established in the papal documents.[40]

These events did not have the same effect on all secular institutes, which reacted in different ways. Neither did they exert the same influence on various writers on this topic. Among them there continued to be the two lines of interpretation we have mentioned earlier. Nevertheless, *in toto* and seen from a certain distance, the process was multifaceted and in some aspects positive. The decision to open the way for a variety of institutions, manifested in *Provida Mater Ecclesia* and confirmed by *Cum Sanctissimus*, without attempting to elaborate *a priori* a precise set of norms, allowed the birth and development of a broad range of experiences that otherwise would have been suffocated.

Nevertheless, it was obvious that this experimental phase had to give way to a process of clarification. Consequently the documents under whose auspices experiments had gone forward—*Provida Mater Ecclesia, Primo feliciter* and *Cum Sanctissimus*—had to be surpassed. This need was felt by some at the end of the 1950s, and it soon spread and intensified, above all as work proceeded with the Second Vatican Council. In general and somewhat schematically,

---

J. Beyer, referring to *Provida Mater Ecclesia* and *Primo feliciter*, wrote: "The apostolic ideal of the secular institutes was finally approved. . . . This was immediately followed by the approval of many groups that only vaguely corresponded to the ideal described in *Provida Mater Ecclesia*. . . . Thus Cardinal Larraona, when I met him for the first time in 1958, could say that some religious orders were more secular than many secular institutes recently approved" ("Secolarità e consacrazione della vita negli Istituti Secolari," various authors, *Gli Istituti secolari. Consacrazione, secolarità, apostolato*, Rome 1970, p. 53).

[38] We have referred to the beginnings of this interpretation in dealing with the first doctrinal discussions: see chapter VI, section 4. In years immediately following this first stage G. M. Benucci gives witness to this line of interpretation: "Secular institutes have been authoritatively defined as a modern and present day expression of the religious vocation." (*Gli Istituti Secolari nella nuova legislazione canonica*, Rome 1955, p. 9). Years later, J. L. Urrutia would affirm that secular institutes bring to a close the substantial evolution of the religious life. ("Evolución de la vida religiosa" in *CONFER*, Jan.-March 1963, p. 80).

[39] J. Beyer, in an article from 1969, writes: "Frequently, in the first approvals of secular institutes, the religious aspect was strengthened in the way of living the evangelical counsels, imposing reforms or corrections on the constitutions that were presented; today such corrections are considered unfortunate interventions." ("Secolarità e consacrazione . . .," *op. cit.*—note 37 of this chapter—p. 80).

[40] The phenomenon was indicated in strong terms in 1964 by J. Herranz, "La evolución de los Institutos Seculares," in *Ius Canonicum*, 4 (1964):303-333, although he refers to earlier events.

this process of clarification can be said to have given rise to three positions. Some institutes, whose inspiration was plainly religious, evolved into true religious congregations. Others sought to re-elaborate the figure, focusing on the concepts of consecration and secularity until the configuration of secular institutes defined by the 1983 Code of Canon Law was reached.[41] Finally other secular institutes manifested their dissatisfaction with that form and desired to circumvent the dislocation by a different juridical solution, more in keeping with their foundational charism. This last was the line followed by Opus Dei. Let us now see why and how, and what consequences this had.

### 3. Confronted with the insufficiency of Opus Dei's configuration as a secular institute.

The normative framework of *Provida Mater Ecclesia* made it possible for Opus Dei to obtain pontifical approval, as we have seen. In addition, the documents of approval did reflect, in ways more satisfactory than those obtainable under the 1917 Code, the spiritual and pastoral phenomenon of Opus Dei. Still the founder had to accept Opus Dei's inclusion within the framework of the states of perfection, although with special nuances and stressing its fundamental distinction from the religious state, despite its dependence on the Congregation for Religious. That explains Msgr. Escrivá's mixed feelings as seen in a text to which we now return: "We have accepted with sacrifice an unavoidable compromise that does not eclipse, however, the joy of having finally obtained a juridical path for our life. We hope, with God's grace, that the doubtful points will not remain so for long."[42]

In the negotiations preceding the promulgation of *Provida Mater Ecclesia* and those accompanying the later pontifical approvals of 1947 and 1950, the founder experienced personally the many difficulties inherent in opening new canonical paths. These new paths would require changes not only of outlook but also of the juridical and theological schemes heretofore commonly accepted.[43] Yet he also found a sympathetic hearing in those people who, with greater or lesser depth, grasped Opus Dei's message or at least recognized

---

[41] From this perspective, see Various authors, *Gli Istituti Secolari nel nuovo Codice di Diritto Canonico*, Milan 1984.

[42] *Letter*, Oct. 7, 1950, no. 20.

[43] He shows this in a letter addressed to the directors of Opus Dei who lived in Madrid on December 4, 1947: "There is much to do here: nevertheless, with work alone we will do little: pray and offer a lot of things, because it is necessary to change wills and to give light to more than one head. I will tell you everything in time" (RHF, EF-471204-1). In another one of his *Letters*, referring to this environment, he unambiguously declares: "They understood no other dedication to God than that found in the reli-

its historical importance.[44] The inadequacies of the general legislation justified certain fears with regard to future developments.[45]
Still Msgr. Escrivá thought there were sufficient guarantees—some
people reinforced this opinion, even with explicit declarations—
that the jurisprudence and subsequent legislation would not vitiate
the recently created figure.  If anything, it was surmised, future
developments should make more precise and improve the framework established by *Provida Mater Ecclesia*.[46]  This confidence—let
us underline it, even though it may seem superfluous—was not
naive.  Rather it led him to make some concessions in what he
called a "filial contention," while also prompting him to make the
precisions and juridical cautions considered in previous chapters.

At the base of everything was always an ultimate and determining concern: a desire to be fully faithful to the foundational charism,
to the reality of Opus Dei just as God had made him see it.  More
specifically he defended—this is the point to be emphasized here—
the secular condition of its members, ordinary Christians who sanctify themselves in the middle of the world.  Therefore—put in negative terms impossible to avoid owing to the circumstances of the
time—Opus Dei members were neither religious, nor equivalent in
any way to religious.

His concern to be faithful to this reality and its corollary criteria
is seen in the first juridical texts of 1941 and in all subsequent ones,
as documented in each case.  He reaffirms it also in many of his
*Letters* relating to the events of these years[47] as in the crucial docu-

---

gious state. I was obliged to use words they were capable of understanding" (*Letter*,
Dec. 29, 1947/Feb. 14, 1966, no. 168).

[44] "We will never thank our Lord enough for the understanding with which some
people of the Roman Curia have received our Work in the last months of 1946 and in
the first months of 1947.  Their understanding and affection have made it possible for
the Work to be approved as a secular institute on the 24th of February, a few days after
the promulgation of the *Provida*" (*Letter*, Oct. 7, 1950, no. 9).

[45] There is an echo of this fear in many texts, several of which we have already mentioned.  To these we could add the recently quoted letter to the directors of Opus Dei
in Madrid dated Dec. 4, 1947: "It is not possible to run in Rome: it is necessary that you
pray for the work that I came to carry out so that we manage to describe with firm
strokes the canonical figure recently born—that of secular institute—in service of our
Holy Mother the Church, because if not, working with souls will be made difficult"
(RHF, EF-471204-1).

[46] Commenting on his state of mind after the approvals of 1947 and 1950, he wrote, "I
was put at rest by the fact that in the *lex peculiaris*, as I have just said, it was repeated
that the members of these Institutes are not religious, and furthermore, authorized
persons assured me that it would be impossible for confusion to arise" (*Letter*, Dec. 12,
1952, no. 5).

[47] "Everything in our interior life and in our exterior social life," we quote a new text
taken from the *Letter* of Dec. 1949, "should be filled with naturalness: because we are

ment he addressed to the Congregation for Religious on May 3, 1950, during the negotiations for the definitive approval. The latter is worth quoting now: "I wanted to call the attention of the Sacred Congregation to a general question, and to say it in some way, to one of the principles. Namely, that the criteria to be followed for judging the constitutions and spirit of a secular institute cannot be the same as those used to pass judgment on a religious congregation. They are different phenomena, both in the field of law and in that of external life: social, professional and apostolic."[48]

In the period following the promulgation of *Provida Mater Ecclesia*, Msgr. Escrivá, conversant with the origin of the constitution, its nature as a compromise, and its consequent ambiguity, continued to defend the special nature of secular institutes as he understood them. He felt bound to avoid above all—both in scholarly views and the praxis of the Roman Curia—anything that could lead to viewing them as the last stage in the evolution of the religious state or as an attenuated form of this state. In no moment was he unaware that there existed scholars who did not share his interpretation of this figure. The views of this group could and did influence in various ways the application of the norms contained in *Provida Mater Ecclesia* and the ecclesiastical and civil environments regarding secular institutes.

The founder's sensitivity helped him to spot the process in its first steps. What he saw and foresaw if this process continued, awoke in him strong misgivings. While noting all, he reacted with prayer and deeds as well. Consistent with how he acted during the promulgation of the normative documents on secular institutes and the pontifical approvals of Opus Dei in 1947 and 1950, he sought to prevent the practical consequences that flowed from that line of interpretation from harming the Work. To that end he frankly and repeatedly voiced to Vatican authorities the same criteria he had set forth in obtaining the pontifical approvals. He also encouraged some Opus Dei members learened in theological-canonical matters to publish on the topics that could highlight—within what the circumstances allowed—the genuinely secular character of the figure created by *Provida Mater Ecclesia*. They sought to reinforce from among the possible interpretations born of the ambiguous legisla-

---

ordinary faithful, we are ordinary citizens, we are ordinary lay people or priests, and we must act like what we are, without allowing for any confusion. For this reason I have told you, and the earliest of you know it very well, that I continually affirmed: we do not want to be religious!. . . . We will defend peremptorily that we are not religious—let me repeat it—, even though we venerate the religious with all our hearts" (*Letter*, Dec. 8, 1949, nos. 43-44).

[48] With regard to this document and its context, see chapter VI.

tion those most in keeping with the underlying secularity.[49] Never-theless, he increasingly came to see that these means would not suffice.

As mentioned earlier in this chapter, these developments were simultaneous with the attempt, in 1951-52, to remove Msgr. Escrivá from Opus Dei and to divide the latter into two different institutes, one for men and another for women. Though the blow was fore-stalled by the personal intervention of the Roman Pontiff, it brought to the fore the grave insufficiency of Opus Dei as a secular institute. This figure was inadequate for defending effectively, within the framework of canon law, one of the essential characteristics of the Work's pastoral phenomenon: its institutional unity.

The affirmation and juridical recognition of this unity had been one of the fundamental concerns of Msgr. Escrivá through the ju-ridical path followed to date. One of the main objectives obtained with the configuration as a secular institute in 1947 and satisfacto-rily formulated in the documents of 1950 had been the establish-ment of an internal hierarchy distinct for each branch at all three levels of government: general or central, regional and local, united, however, in the President General at the central level and at the regional level in the Counselor, who in the women's branch acts in the name and taking the place of the President General.[50]

In the broad range of institutes where the state of perfection is professed, it is a common rule, a norm of canon law, that male and female institutes be juridically distinct entities. The 1917 Code included this prescription in paragraph 3 of canon 500.[51] The norms relating to secular institutes echo this criterion explicitly in the Instruction *Cum Sanctissimus*, although declaring that it is not di-

---

[49] He refers to this latter point in some *Letters*: "With regard to the general teaching, juridical or theological, about secular institutes some of your brothers have written and will write, prudently and freely, in order to try to make known and to emphasize the importance of the secular character of these Institutes" (*Letter*, Dec. 12, 1952, no. 19). "For this reason my teaching and that of your brothers who are canonists who have dealt with these juridical questions together with me, has been constant from the time that *Provida* was promulgated: in secular institutes it is not the canonical state of perfection that is lived, which is proper to religious, but the *juridical* or *secular* state of perfection" (*Letter*, Oct. 7, 1950, no. 23). With regard to this distinction and the corre-sponding discussions among students of the topic, see section 4 of chapter VI.

[50] For all of this we refer to what has been said in chapter VII, section 3. We recall here, among others, how the priests of Opus Dei dedicate themselves principally to the spiritual attention and formation of all members of the Work of both branches. In 1947 and 1950 the faculty had been delegated and remained sub-delegable *ad normam iuris* to hear sacramental confessions of members of both branches of the Institute (cf. chap-ter VII, note 187 and Appendix, document no. 34.).

[51] "Without a special apostolic indult, no male institute may have a religious congre-gation of women subject to it, or retain, as specially entrusted to it, the care and direction of such religious" (CIC 1917, c. 500 § 3).

rectly applicable, since it is taken from the law of religious institutes.[52]  Authorized commentary on this prescription of *Cum Sanctissimus* was made by Frs. Larraona and Gutiérrez in 1949. They agree that by special exception there may be two autonomous sections of a single secular institute, "although only in some cases after a severe trial. . . . If the difficulties and dangers are effectively avoided, it cannot be denied that it may be useful to coordinate forces for a complete and integrated apostolate."[53] The structure of Opus Dei, as regards the government of the two branches, would appear to be a special case within the common norms of secular institutes.

These events and factors led the founder to weigh possible modifications to the juridical figure assumed by Opus Dei in 1947-50. It was not only a matter of readjusting details, but also he was questioning central points of that solution and examining the need to seek formulas in a different direction. "We cannot be required— such is not our way—to live by privileges," he says in a December 1952 *Letter*. "Moreover, it couldn't make sense to turn continually to the Holy See for declarations allowing us to live in conformity with the spirit the Holy See itself has already approved many times."[54]

Do not these events document the need for Opus Dei to seek with new urgency a juridical garb whereby a structure faithful to its foundational charism is not an exception or privilege? The ultimate response of the founder would merge an ensemble of apparently dissonant principles into a unity, but at the expense of much prayer and intellectual effort. Consciousness of his duty to guard the integrity of the spirit and essential characteristics of the pastoral phenomenon of Opus Dei led him on the one hand staunchly to defend this charism. Loyalty to the Church and especially to those

---

[52] "According to art. II § 1, 2nd of the Apostolic Constitution *Provida Mater Ecclesia*, and without prejudice to art. X and art. II § 1, 1st, of the same constitution, secular institutes are not bound by the proper and particular law of religious institutes or societies of common life, nor may they live by such law, yet the Sacred Congregation may by way of exception, according to the tenor of the constitution (art. II § 1, 2nd) adapt and apply to them some particular provisions of the law of religious which may be suitable also to secular institutes, and may even prudently borrow from the aforesaid law certain more or less general criteria which are approved by experience and are in accord with the inner nature of things" (Instruction, *Cum Sanctissimus*, no. 8) A general criterion which is later expounded in more detail: "In particular: a) although the provisions of canon 500 § 3 do not strictly concern secular institutes and need not be applied to them as they stand, yet a solid criterion and clear guidance may be purposely drawn from them for the approval and ordering of secular institutes" (*Ibid.*, no. 9 § 1).

[53] Cf. "Iurisprudentiae pro Institutis Saecularibus hucusque conditae summa lineamenta," *op. cit.* (chapter VI, note 25) p. 321.

[54] *Letter*, Dec. 12, 1952, no. 9.

in the Roman Curia who had made the approvals possible moved him, on the other, to continue defending the figure of secular institute according to his understanding of it. This loyalty, allied to his prudence and sense of responsibility in matters of governance, moved him in turn to avoid polemics in this defense. His deep realism and legal background helped him finally to see there was still no adequate canonical articulation. Thus he must continue to tread the least inadequate of existing paths. Little by little, with caution and patience, without precipitating half-baked measures, new solutions must earnestly be forged.

In the oft-cited December '52 *Letter* he refers to earlier writings and successive juridical stages while stressing "the importance of reaching solutions in accordance with our spiritual characteristics." And he adds: "My way of acting is for me not only a right but a very serious duty, because nobody has lived as I have this pastoral phenomenon of Opus Dei, nobody has studied, as I have, step by step its theological core, and consequently no one is more bound than I to point out the canonical solution. For God has made me live from the outset the ascetical and apostolic problem of the Work, and he has made me tread—from that time up until now—each of its juridical steps."[55]

These words place us on the threshold of a new stage in the juridical path of Opus Dei, stemming from the deep personal reflections of the founder. He reaches the conviction that Opus Dei's good does not require any more continuing to counter interpretations of the figure of secular institute differing from what he had put forth. He believes he has done—and will continue to do, out of loyalty to the pristine figure—all within his power.[56] The next step is more radical. He now turns to finding a new juridical solution fully adequate to Opus Dei's nature by virtue of its foundational charism.

In the 1948 conference on "The Apostolic Constitution *Provida Mater Ecclesia* and Opus Dei," Msgr. Escrivá had traced the process by which religious institutes had approached the world, from the early Anchorites to recent times in which "apostolic action moves souls to launch themselves, in a tightly knit army, into the middle

---

[55] *Letter*, Dec. 12, 1952, no. 1.

[56] "For many years, out of loyalty, we have done everything possible to maintain what we thought was the genuine juridical figure of secular institutes, as it was defined in the Apostolic Constitution *Provida Mater Ecclesia*, in whose final draft, as you know, the existence and extension of our Work had some influence" (*Letter*, March 19, 1954, no. 15). At another time he wrote, "It was a joy for me to have contributed, with the grace of God, to the opening of a juridical way to which many other souls who do not have our vocation could turn" (*Letter*, Jan. 25, 1961, no. 25).

of the world. We find, as the advance party, convents established by the Holy Spirit to preach in cities. This evolution continues to the point that consecrated souls dare to go alone, as sheep in the midst of wolves. But they have always been, and remain, religious, foreigners and strangers to the world." Offering his interpretation of the figure of secular institute, he says, "Now it is from the very world itself that these apostles arise who dare to sanctify all the ordinary activities of men."[57]

Years later, those we are now considering, this thought forcefully returned to his mind as the hermeneutical key for interpreting what was happening. Experience had clearly shown him that different spiritual inspirations require also different juridical regulations.

The distinction between two spiritual developments, pointed out in the '48 conference, appears formulated with greater precision in later texts. Opus Dei in no way is another link in the evolution of the religious state or its underlying spirituality. Rather, it is a totally different phenomenon, as "old as the gospel and like the gospel new," as he said from the start. Thus it leaps over the centuries to join up with the first Christians, with those, Jews or Gentiles, who received the apostles' preaching and brought it into the ordinary framework of their lives.[58]

On March 19, 1954, he wrote: "It should not be forgotten that in general the life-giving Holy Spirit does not leap about in the historical development of the Church. Each new phenomenon he raises up has thus a certain continuity with preceding movements promoted by God: they are links of the same chain.

"Nevertheless, Church history teaches that sometimes the similarity of different links has not been perfect, and there have always been some who will not understand the reasons for new forms. It has often been said, over time, that new pastoral phenomena have been ambitious to combine the advantages of religious and those of the world. Each new arrival has aspired to a greater elasticity and accommodation in apostolate, departing from classical religious molds.

"But in our case we find ourselves before a completely different phenomenon. We are not like secularized religious, but authenti-

---

[57] J. Escrivá de Balaguer, "La Constitución Apostólica 'Provida Mater Ecclesia' y el Opus Dei," op. cit. (chapter VI, note 61) p. 17.

[58] One of the lengthiest expositions dedicated by Msgr. Escrivá to the first Christians is to be found in the Letter of Dec. 29, 1947/Feb. 14, 1960, nos. 140-146. Regarding the first Christians in the preaching of the founder, we refer to the texts and study cited in notes 43 and 44 of chapter II.

cally secular people who seek, not the life of evangelical perfection proper to religious, but Christian perfection in the world, each one in his very own state."[59]

In the writings of the founder during these years, besides general considerations, we also find doctrinal and practical determinations that are of great importance. Such, for example, is a graphic formula (in part truly a program of action) in which he summarizes the position of Opus Dei with respect to its juridical garb of the time: legally it is still a secular institute, but *de facto* it is not.[60]

Another important precision is related to how the bond is to be formalized. Faced with the interpretation of secular institutes as the latest form in the evolution of the religious state, thus making members' vows somehow public, Msgr. Escrivá manifested his decision to do away completely with bonds of this kind. In a *Letter* he writes: "We do not despise vows: we esteem them as theology teaches us. But when some seek to give public juridical acknowledgement to an act of private devotion, they get in our way; we will stay with the virtues." Later: "We are deliberately studying matters so that, in due course, private vows will be prohibited. Yet our bond with the Work will stay equally strong, mutual, full—according to each one's personal state—and supernaturally effective for all."[61]

On the thirtieth anniversary of Opus Dei in 1958, Msgr. Escrivá sums up his reflections and decisions during those years. This document resembles a declaration of motives and intentions; it is worth summarizing in four points:[62]

a) First, the *Letter* evokes some of the fundamental traits of Opus Dei's spirit and apostolate; its supernatural character, its spiritual apostolic end and means; the secular nature of its activity;[63] that Opus Dei members remain ordinary Christians and citizens, not to be confused with religious or relegated to second-class citizenship;[64] their personal freedom and responsibility in fulfilling their profes-

---

[59] *Letter*, March 19, 1954, no. 36.

[60] This formula is found in the *Letter* of Dec. 1952 following the comment that it seems incongruous to have to have recourse to exceptions to live in conformity with the spirit which the Holy See itself has approved: "The acceptance of these necessary exceptions," he adds, drawing out consequences, "with the passage of time would do no more than confirm that the Work differs radically from the juridical figure outlined by the legislation to which it has been united. This disjunction, between law and reality, is what leads me to affirm that if by law the Work is a secular institute, *in fact it is not*" (*Letter*, Dec. 12, 1952, no. 9).

[61] *Letter*, May 31, 1954, no. 9.

[62] The complete text is found in the Appendix, document no. 40. As seen later in this chapter, this *Letter* was sent by Msgr. Escrivá in 1964 to Pope Paul VI.

[63] *Letter*, Oct. 2, 1958, no. 1.

[64] *Ibid.*, nos. 2 & 3.

sional, social and other tasks;[65] the deep Christian life to which every member of the Work is called;[66] the frank simplicity, opposed to duplicity or secrecy, all ought to live;[67]

b) The *Letter's* central part, granted this secular horizon, stakes out a very clear position with regard to the relation of the state of perfection to the fundamental charism of which Msgr. Escrivá knows himself to be the depository. The only wish of Opus Dei is *"to serve the Church as she wishes to be served, within the special vocation we have received from God. For this reason, we do not desire for ourselves the state of perfection. . . .* By specific vocation, whereby we have been called to Opus Dei, God asks only that *each one seek sanctity in his own state in life*—single, married, widowed, priest—and in the practice of one's *munus publicum*, i.e., one's life's work, well known to all one's fellow citizens."[68] Thus the law for religious—as he has oft replied—should not indiscriminately be applied to Opus Dei nor should its members be likened to religious.[69]

c) Recalling the special characteristics of the Work's spirit and apostolic life, confirmed by a long experience and its juridical recognition by the Holy See,[70] the founder states: *"In fact we are not a secular institute, nor in the future should this name be applied to us."*[71]

d) Having pointed to the incongruity between the originating charism of Opus Dei and its juridical configuration as a secular institute, Msgr. Escrivá finally comments that he has entrusted to God the resolution of this spiritual concern. To this end for many years thousands of Masses have been offered, along with the professional work of members and all their apostolic work.[72] He writes, "With the same filial confidence and asking the intercession of the Blessed Virgin Mary, our Mother—*Cor Mariæ Dulcissimum, iter para tutum!*—I will inform the Holy See, at the proper time, of this situation, of this concern of mine. Then I shall indicate that we ardently desire that steps be taken to reach a proper solution, which will not constitute for us a privilege—something repugnant to our spirit and outlook. *Nor will it modify our current relations with local Ordinaries."*[73]

---

[65] *Ibid.,* no. 3.

[66] *Ibid.,* no. 4.

[67] *Ibid.,* no. 5.

[68] *Ibid.,* no. 6 (This emphasis and successive ones are Msgr. Escrivá's.)

[69] *Ibid.,* no. 7.

[70] *Ibid.,* no. 8.

[71] *Ibid.,* no. 9.

[72] *Ibid.,* no. 10.

[73] *Ibid.,* no. 11.

## 4. Consultation to the Cardinal Protector of Opus Dei

On October 28, 1958, Cardinal Angelo Roncalli, Patriarch of Venice, was elected Pope with the name of John XXIII. The new pontificate ushered in an air of renewal. This was heightened on January 25, 1959, when the Holy Father declared he would convoke an ecumenical council to rejuvenate ecclesiastical life and achieve a more decided presence of Christians in the various sectors of the contemporary world. In this context the founder deemed it opportune to raise Opus Dei's institutional problem to the Holy See and to request a revision of its juridical statute.

Confusions arisen in the common teaching and in practice with regard to the nature of secular institutes had far from disappeared. If anything, they were exacerbated by new events. Pope John XXIII, besides convoking an ecumenical council, announced his decision to reform the Code of Canon Law and to celebrate a synod for the diocese of Rome. On February 18 the Pope named the synodal council. Preparatory work began right away. Refering to this work and to the material that was being developed Oberti writes, "because of the persistent approximation of members of secular institutes to religious and priests several articles were prepared that prohibited them from entering bars, engaging in business or going to motion pictures without permission of the Cardinal Vicar. . . ."[74] This assimilation is also reflected in the index of the synodal constitutions (*Rivista Diocesana di Roma*, January/February 1960). Secular institutes were grouped with societies of common life without vows under title three of the second part *De Religiosis*, while lay people were in part three, and Associations of the faithful in part four.[75]

These general developments, displeasing of course to Msgr. Escrivá, coincided with others more directly affecting Opus Dei and its members. Thus, for example, Msgr. Escrivá was convoked by the Holy See to a meeting of Superiors General in late March 1960 to draw up a program of apostolate for religious of both sexes for Latin America.[76] Then also he learned that Opus Dei members

---

[74] A. Oberti, "Gli Istituti Secolari a vent'anni dal 'Perfectae caritatis'," in *Vita Consecrata*, 21 (1985):303. He adds: "I remember when I visited the Secretary of the Preparatory Commission to point out the incongruity of such prohibitions with regard to the nature of secular institutes, nothing was settled. It was then necessary to request, with more determination, an intervention of the Congregation for Religious, which managed to amend the text in the desired sense."

[75] *Rivista Diocesana di Roma*, 1 (1960):95-96. The promulgation of the synodal constitutions took place on June 29, 1960, by the Apostolic Constitution *Sollicitudo omnium Ecclesiarum*. All the documents of this Synod, which took place January 24-31, 1960, can be found in *Prima Romana Synodus A. D. MDCCCCLX*, Typis Polyglottis Vaticanis 1960.

[76] AGP, Sezione Giuridica, VI/15672. *L'Osservatore Romano* reported on this meeting on March 30, 1960.

in the United States had been invited to take part in a conference of persons consecrated to God in the world presided over by religious.[77] Then too he heard from Africa that an academic initiative of some members of Opus Dei was being equated to missionary activity, analogous to those carried out by members of religious congregations in this and other African countries.

In March 1959 Opus Dei's Procurator General wrote to the Secretary of the Sacred Congregation *de Propaganda Fide* to point out the harm ensuing to members when treated as missionaries or religious, a classification that could spill over onto the civil forum. The Procurator wrote: "The general law of secular institutes—*Provida Mater Ecclesia* (1947), *Primo feliciter* (1948) and *Cum Sanctissimus* (1948)—as well as our particular law from the foundation (1928) repeatedly approved by the Holy See, establish with great clarity and reaffirm the principle that members of secular institutes and specifically Opus Dei members are not religious, nor do they live *ad instar religiosorum*, nor is the law regarding religious to be applied to them nor in any way can they be equated with religious. They are ordinary citizens, whose secular character—*in quo ipsorum (Institutorum) exsistentiæ tota ratio consistit, in omnibus elucere debet* (*Primo feliciter*, II)—ought to always be clear."[78]

These errors—with their consequent protests or clarifications—as well as the hopes of renewal with the coming of John XXIII, led the founder to sound out the possibilities of requesting a revision of the juridical statute within the framework of existing law. This first sounding was a prudent move: to inform Cardinal Tardini, the Secretary of State and Protector of Opus Dei,[79] of the events and of his desire to see the statute revised. This he did on March 14, 1960. They agreed that Fr. Alvaro del Portillo should speak with Msgr. Scapinelli, Undersecretary for Extraordinary Affairs, a conversation that took place the same day. In subsequent weeks they exchanged views several times on how to focus the question. Msgr. Scapinelli made several suggestions regarding particulars, while fully concurring with the fundamental question. He agreed that the competency over Opus Dei should pass from the Congregation for Religious to the Consistorial Congregation.[80]

---

[77] AGP, Sezione Giuridica, VI/15671.

[78] The full text of this letter is found in the Appendix, document no. 41. Analogous reactions were produced in the other cases which we have mentioned.

[79] Domenico Cardinal Tardini had been named Cardinal Protector of Opus Dei in December 1959, replacing the earlier Protector, Federico Cardinal Tedeschini, who had died the month before.

[80] The Congregation was later renamed the Congregation for Bishops with the reforms established by Pope Paul VI in the Apostolic Constitution *Regimini Ecclesiæ universæ*, August 15, 1967.

Scapinelli's views were especially weighty, since in the '50s he had been Undersecretary of the Congregation for Religious. Thus encouraged, on April 9, 1960, Msgr. Escrivá sent to Cardinal Tardini not a simple report but a "consulta oficiosa," asking the Cardinal Protector to reflect on the viability of proposing to the Pope a revision of Opus Dei's juridical statute.[81]

The substance of the proposal can be summarized in four points:[82]

a) First and above all, Opus Dei would cease to depend upon the Sacred Congregation for Religious and pass to the Sacred Consistorial Congregation. It would thus find itself in the secular realm in conformity with the foundational charism and outside the framework of the states of perfection. Thus Msgr. Escrivá would be spared frequent clarifications.

b) Secondly, a prelature *nullius* would be created to depend on the Consistorial Congregation. For the land needed to be a prelature, any church in Italy with a single parish would suffice. Having a small territory in this scheme was crucial: it would have a serious impact on the juridical structure of Opus Dei and allow it to incardinate priests as occurs with the *Mission de France*;[83] they would thus be *de iure* diocesan priests.

c) Thirdly, the *Constitutions* of Opus Dei would be confirmed as already approved by the Holy See, along with all the rescripts and pontifical declarations related to the Work. This move would also reinforce the reality that the lay members of Opus Dei are ordinary faithful, ordinary citizens, and that Opus Dei priests are also, *de iure*, diocesan priests.

d) Finally, the Prelate would be the same President General of Opus Dei, who would continue to be elected in accordance with the norms in force up until then. This election would require confirmation by the Holy See, which in turn would name him Prelate *nullius* of that small territory.

Such was the sum of the consultation made to the Cardinal Protector. It consisted of a reelaboration of the formula adopted by the *Mission de France*, with appropriate changes. The priests of the *Mission de France* are incardinated in the Prelature of Pontigny, while they carry out their ministry in any French dioceses whose Ordinaries have entrusted to them various apostolates. In the proposed case of Opus Dei its priests would be incardinated in the Prelature *nullius*. As before, they would tend spiritually to the other mem-

---

[81] AGP, Sezione Giuridica, VI/15611.

[82] RHF, EF-600319-1.

[83] With regard to the origin and history of the *Mission de France*, see J. Faupin, *La Mission de France. Histoire et Institution*, Tournai 1960. The erection of the Mission de France as a Prelature *nullius* took place in 1954 with the Apostolic Constitution *Omnium Ecclesiarum sollicitudo*, August 15, 1954 (*AAS* 46 (1954):567-574)

bers of Opus Dei and collaborate in the Work's apostolic activities. Thus working together, lay people and priests of Opus Dei, they would continue to spread across environments and countries the call to holiness and apostolate amid the ordinary conditions of human life.

Msgr. Escrivá stressed that his only desire was to preserve intact the spiritual characteristics of Opus Dei and to obtain the greatest spiritual and apostolic fruit the world over for the sake of the Church and all souls.[84] From now on the founder began earnestly to seek a solution within the categories and structures belonging to the realm of ordinary ecclesiastical jurisdiction. No more would he try to maneuver within the normative framework of institutes of perfection—something that always required emphasizing Opus Dei's special characteristics and its difference from religious institutes.

What was the result? There were various conversations of the founder and Fr. Alvaro del Portillo with Msgr. Scapinelli and the Cardinal Protector. On June 27, 1960, Cardinal Tardini told Msgr. Escrivá it was not opportune at this time to present a formal petition in the sense proposed. For the moment let things stay as they are, *"siamo ancora molto lontani."*[85]

After this conversation with Cardinal Tardini Msgr. Escrivá commented: "The seed has been sown that will not fail to bear fruit."[86] It is necessary to wait, but the ideas and the focus presented will not fail to open a path. An important step had been taken by communicating in a clear and unambiguous way to the Cardinal Secretary of State in his capacity of Cardinal Protector of Opus Dei the desire to revise its juridical statute on the basis of the experiences gained during recent years and of the requirements of the spirit and apostolate proper to Opus Dei.

## 5. A letter of the founder

It is in this context that the Letter of January 25, 1961, where Msgr. Escrivá addresses some aspects of the juridical process, is situated. This text has been cited, but it is opportune now to present an overall view. It is an important testimony of the founder at the moment when the definitive juridical configuration of Opus Dei begins to take shape.

"I want to open my heart on this feast of the Apostle of the Gentiles," he opens, "so that you be filled with gratitude in considering how God has led us along this new way he has marked out by means of Opus Dei. . . .

---

[84] RHF, EF-600417-1.

[85] AGP, Sezione Giuridica, VI/15611.

[86] *Ibid.*

"When I contemplate the path we have travelled since 1928, I
see myself, my children, like a small child before a wonderful Father. A small child is not given four tasks to do at once. He is given
one, and then another, and still another one, when the previous one
is finished. Have you seen how a small child plays with his father?
The child has some wooden blocks of different shapes and col-
ors. . . . His father tells him: put this here, and that over there, and
that red one there. . . . At the end a castle! Well that, my children,
is how I see the Lord has been leading me *ludens coram eo omni
tempore: ludens in orbe terrarum* (Prov 8:30-31), like a divine game.
At the end of this marvelous game, don't you see what a marvelously beautiful fortress it is, *opus sanctum, bonum, pulchrum, amabile!*
A Work of His, with all this color, all this variety of shapes and
forms, reflecting God's Goodness."[87]

What was God's will made known in 1928? What message does
Opus Dei spread? "A novelty, as old as the gospel, that makes
available to people of all classes and conditions—with no distinction of race, nation, language—a sweet encounter with Jesus Christ
in the events of every day."[88] To proclaim this good news, to invite
souls to follow this path, and to give life to Opus Dei in the service
of this ideal, this is what God had called him to. But it was necessary to achieve a juridical recognition. Here is where troubles arose.
As a consequence of a long tradition in the Church, the pursuit of
Christian perfection was seen only as a phenomenon juridically
recognizable in the religious state. But "the religious state, my
children, I could not accept for us, because owing to its asceticism,
its means and its specific ends it is different from the asceticism,
means and ends God in his providential design has desired for his
Work."[89]

He lays a foundation for this distinction, pointing out the peculiarities of each. First, the religious state is a "fruit of the historical
evolution of some special forms of life," in which Christian perfection becomes "for the religious not only the end toward which he
tends, but also a special and typical mode of life, the object of
*profession.*" The call to perfection so understood implies "not only
an obligation to live whatever Jesus Christ has counselled, but also

---

[87] *Letter*, January 25, 1961, nos. 1-2. Then he adds: "This is the divine way of doing
things: first one thing and then another, guiding steps, using secondary causes, human
helpers. . . . Do you see? First one grace, then a task: with God choosing the time, the
ways and the circumstances. Thus God has made his Work: first one branch, then
another, and then—a new gift—the priests. And in every step of our way, on each
front that we had had to win in this beautiful war of peace, the Lord has treated me
always so: first this, afterwards that" (*Ibid.*, no. 2).

[88] *Ibid.*, no. 4.

[89] *Ibid.*, nos. 5-6.

to do so in a special way: dying to the world, and understanding by the world not only what is fostered by the three lusts, but also the state of life, the interests, work and occupations—*negotia sæcularia*—of the other faithful, who do not have this special vocation." This is the "theological foundation", to which there juridically corresponds "the creation of a *status*," that is to say, "a public state," the object of "a specific positive regulation": the religious state, just as it appears in the Code of Canon Law.[90]

Then Msgr. Escrivá turns to Opus Dei, evoking some of the expressions of the 1948 conference in a more developed form: "The Work, my children, is not a link at the end of this chain. It has not come as a new stage of the religious life or life of perfection. It is a link of another evolution: what the life-giving Holy Spirit has infused in the Catholic laity and brought to maturity: knowing itself to be called—also the simple faithful, ordinary lay people—to participate actively, in their specific way, in the single sanctifying mission of the Church. There is no need to abandon their condition as lay people nor their full involvement in the structures of the earthly city.

"God has wanted to raise up his Work as a manifestation of his divine will, as a means to make known this call to the laity's responsibility, to urge men and women of all classes and conditions to live fully their Christian vocation. He thus facilitates for them—with an especially lay spirit and a special pastoral guidance—the means together with a particular way to achieve this end, without the need to abandon the state nor the form of life that by divine disposition they have in the Church and civil society.

"Our way is not, my children, an enlargement of the religious state, *adapting it*, for pastoral reasons, to the particular circumstances which have had staying power in the world. It is something else." He explains, "We can say that, ascetically, the terms are reversed: what in religious life is an obstacle to following Jesus Christ according to that vocation, in the Work becomes *the way*: the *occupatio negotiorum sæcularium*. Precisely what hinders the religious from fulfilling his aim, is for us the means *sine qua non*, the sole means for carrying out a specific apostolate and to sanctify ourselves. . . . Work is for us the axis on which must turn all our efforts to achieve Christian perfection. . . . *The special character of the spirituality of Opus Dei is in the fact that each one ought to sanctify his own profession or occupation, his ordinary work; to sanctify himself precisely in this professional task; and through this task to sanctify others.*"[91]

---

[90] *Ibid.*, nos. 7-8.

[91] *Ibid.*, nos. 9-10. The emphasis is by Msgr. Escrivá. With regard to this topic see also nos. 14ff.

The quotation is long, but necessary to show the foundation that explains and gives meaning to the contrast between "state of perfection" and "perfection in one's own state," as Msgr. Escrivá affirmed. A vocation to Opus Dei does not create a new state, it does not lead to new conditions of life, but on the contrary, it moves one to go to the depths of his own life, to the personal conditions of his existence, of his own state, to give it a new and fuller meaning, that authorized by and communicated with the light of faith.[92] There the matter must be rooted, and from there one ought to begin.

Having elaborated this fundamental principle, Msgr. Escrivá analyzes the whole past experience and reaffirms his determination to revise the juridical statute of Opus Dei.[93]   But he does not limit himself to generalities; he specifies several implications.  We point out a few of them:

a) In referring to Opus Dei, any form of speech making reference to the state of perfection, even though attenuated, should be shunned.  More specifically, one can do without such expressions as "juridical state of perfection" or "secular state of perfection."  He knows well the origin of these terms—he had even used them; he also knows they have been used to underline the differentiation of secular institutes from the religious state.  Moreover, he is aware such expressions empty the term "state" of all content, depriving it of the technical value that, applied to persons, it has in the theological-canonical tradition.  At the same time he realizes this terminology is insufficient for attaining the end sought: every focus of the question and any terminology in any way evoking the state of perfection is bound to fail.  "Subtle distinctions will be reduced—and we will be accused of this—to mere nominalism . . . a vain verbal circumlocution."[94]  The only right way to speak is to refer not to the state of perfection, but to perfection in one's own state in life.

b) Also to be sidestepped is the expression "evangelical counsels."  Doubtless they have deep biblical roots, and the term can be used with many meanings, some even applicable to the life of ordinary Christians.  But it is also true that, canonized by history, it has been tied, in ordinary usage, to reference to the three vows poverty, chastity and obedience, understood as types, according to the experience proper to the religious state.  It is better to do without this expression, which obviously does not mean that one ceases to speak

---

[92] *Ibid.*, nos. 11-12 and *passim*.

[93] *Ibid.*, nos. 13-14 and 19ff. (In no. 19 and in some of the following ones, he comments on different stages of the preceding juridical path and some of the characteristics of the spirit of Opus Dei, underlining the secular condition of its members and apostolates.)

[94] *Ibid.*, nos. 64-66.

of these virtues. It must be, however, done in such a way as to avoid any identification with the religious state.[95]

c) Consequently the Work needs to do without any kind of vows, even private ones. He allowed members of Opus Dei to take them because of particular historical circumstances, as explained above. He always stipulated, however, that they were non-public, non-religious vows, strictly private vows, those any ordinary Christian can make. Moreover, incorporation into Opus Dei has always been accomplished with formulas devoid of any mention of vows or any kind of sacred bond. Now he saw that they must go beyond this and dispense completely with vows, even private ones: "You have heard me say we want them to disappear from our life," he writes.[96]

Msgr. Escrivá in this wide-ranging document calls for revising the juridical statute: "Now is the time to draw clearly the juridical structure of the Work. . . . My children, *omnia tempus habent!* (Ecc 3:1); everything has its moment."[97] At the end of the *Letter*, after insisting that the pastoral phenomenon of Opus Dei is born of the increased awareness of the laity's responsibility, he restates what is essential: "It cannot be denied that different ascetical and pastoral phenomena require different approaches and juridical solutions. Nobody, my children, can call us stubborn because we insist on these ideas even though to us they are so evident and elementary, that to repeat them seems to be over insisting on the same thing."[98]

## 6. Petition for a revision of the legal statute in 1962

"The seed has been planted that will not fail to bear fruit," was the founder's comment on June 27, 1960, when Cardinal Tardini said the time was not yet ripe. Meanwhile, prayer, trusting in God's providence were needed while awaiting the moment that would surely come but which he could not know.

---

[95] "The counsels of the Lord, my children, would be very difficult to enumerate. Either they are reduced to one, which is a precept and not a counsel—Love!—or it would be necessary to include for each virtue the counsel of generosity in its exercise. . . . Nevertheless, I understand very well—because I love the old tradition, the ancient wisdom of the Church, when it legislates—that these three virtues, which so directly crucify the three capital lusts, have been and are the essential nucleus and the principal instrument of the *life of evangelical perfection of the religious*. But it is God's will that in the Work these same virtues—which we love so much—be woven into the whole special fabric of our asceticism. Poverty, chastity and obedience do not have in Opus Dei—as I have reminded you—the *formal specificity* they have in the religious life" *Ibid.*, nos. 52-53.

[96] *Ibid.*, no. 15. Similar affirmations are found in the texts from which we have quoted: note 61 of this chapter, the *Letter* of May 31, 1954, no. 9.

[97] Letter, January 25, 1961, no. 28.

[98] *Ibid.*, no. 72.

On October 17, 1960, in a homily in Madrid Msgr. Escrivá invited his hearers to join him in praying for "an intention that is so great, an intention that robs me of all the energies of my soul."[99] During these years he prayed and had others pray almost incessantly for this matter, which doubtless was among his principal concerns—something he often called his "special intention."[100] Meanwhile he sought new approaches with the Holy See when circumstances required them.[101]

Cardinal Tardini died in the summer of 1961. On December 14 of the same year Cardinal Pietro Ciriaci took possession as Protector of Opus Dei. In their talks Msgr. Escrivá explained in detail both the situation of the Work and of the spread of its apostolates and the reasons of a theological, juridical and apostolic character that mandated a solution to Opus Dei's institutional problem. The 1960 consultation with Cardinal Tardini was reconstructed. Cardinal Ciriaci took a lively interest in the matter and advised Msgr. Escrivá to present the matter formally to the Roman Pontiff. The founder was hesitant to do so. Didn't the novelty of the solution suggested and recent experiences bode ill for the viability at the time of such a petition? Nevertheless, at the insistence of the Cardinal Protector, he decided to present a formal request to the Holy See.

On January 7, 1962, Msgr. Escrivá turned to the Secretary of State, Cardinal Amleto Cicognani, asking him to convey to the Holy Father John XXIII a formal petition to revise the juridical statute of Opus Dei. He pointed out the difficulties for implementing its specific apostolate that derived from the present configuration recommended this course of action, invoking a faculty formally granted to him by the Holy See on August 2, 1950, to request changes in the juridical statute that seemed to him fitting and necessary.[102]

The letter to Cardinal Cicognani was accompanied by the formal text of the petition to the Pope. The document summarized the

---

[99] RHF, 20541, p. 23.

[100] In his 1961 *Letter* he writes, "So that this situation may be set right juridically, we are offering to God Masses, communions, sacrifices, prayer and hours of this blessed professional work, the hinge of our way! I ask you now, and I will repeat it even more in this letter, that you continue praying for this intention of mine. Put faith in the Lord, who has guided us always and who has given us his fortitude to walk according to his will" (*Letter*, Jan. 25, 1961, no. 60).

[101] By way of example, see a new letter the Procurator General of Opus Dei addressed on December 30, 1960, to the Congregation for the Propagation of the Faith reiterating that the members of Opus Dei are not, nor can they ever be called, missionaries. (The complete text is found in the Appendix, document no. 42.)

[102] The letter addressed to Cardinal Cicognani is found in the Appendix, document no. 43. The document of the Sacred Congregation for Religious, August 2, 1950, to which reference is made is in the Appendix, document no. 33.

object and reasons behind the request.[103] It sets forth the hardships devolving on Opus Dei from its present juridical form. "The greatest difficulty is that many (contrary to law, but, alas, effectively) make out the members of the Institute to be the equivalent of religious, because of which they are often limited in their apostolate or even prohibited from it, under the specious pretext that certain activities are prohibited to religious." Further on, he summarizes how, on the part of some, this assimilation is derived from "the fact that the priests of *Opus Dei* are incardinated, not in a diocese or in a territory as secular priests, but in the Institute, in the same way as religious priests." And he adds: "Denying in this way the secularity of the priests of the Institute, they go on (by virtue of a false and unfounded analogy) to reject the very secularity of the lay members of Opus Dei."

To overcome these difficulties, "a new juridical configuration is necessary," one that will achieve "the definitive clarification of the secular character of the Institute (and its members) both in its external juridical structure and in what has to do with its dependence upon the congregations of the Holy See, in such a way as to make disappear the pretext of assimilation to the religious, of Opus Dei's laity and priests."

To this end, the letter suggests two possibilities that echo the proposal made to Cardinal Tardini in 1960, although with some modifications or differences not lacking in importance:

a) "Give to the Institute an organization similar, *mutatis mutandis*, to that of the *Mission de France* (cf. *AAS* 46 (1954): 567-574). That is to say, it would be a question of erecting the Institute as a Prelature *nullius*, entrusting to it a territory albeit a symbolic one, in which the priests would be incardinated; and declaring at the same time, in conformity with canon 319 § 2 (which refers to Prelatures with fewer than three parishes), that the *ius singulare*, by which the Prelature is governed, is the Constitutions (already approved) of the Institute."

b) Alternately, "Entrust to the President *pro tempore* of the Institute, who is elected *ad vitam*, a Prelature *nullius* (one already existing or one created for this purpose), endowed with the faculty of incardinating the priests of the Institute in this territory."

As can be noticed, the second proposal coincides, although expressed in a schematic way, with the one presented in 1960: the Institute, already approved, and the Prelature, to be erected, appear as two different entities, although united in the person of the Prelate. The first solution goes beyond this, since the Institute as such would be erected as a Prelature. By placing this solution first,

---

[103] The formal petition to John XXIII is found in the Appendix, document no. 44.

Msgr. Escrivá declared his preference. This formula not only underlines, the same as the second one, the secularity of Opus Dei and of each and every member, but expresses much more clearly the unity of the pastoral phenomenon as well.

Shortly thereafter, on February 13, 1962, the Vatican's Secretary of State asked Cardinal Ciriaci to give his opinion as Protector of Opus Dei on the petition presented to the Holy Father. There followed reports, conversations, more detailed information, diverse negotiations. On April 4 the Cardinal Protector had an interview with the Secretary of State. The following day Cardinal Ciriaci informed Msgr. Escrivá of the results. The doubts the founder had harbored from the beginning were not unfounded: it was seen to be difficult for the request to be accepted. Nevertheless, at Cardinal Ciriaci's behest, the founder addressed himself again on April 12 to the Secretary of State to clarify some matters and to insist on the need for a new juridical framework for Opus Dei.

What came from all this documentation presented with the formal request to the Pope on January 7, 1962? Something very significant: of the two solutions suggested in the letter, no further reference is made of the second. Rather consideration is centered on the first. It is worth while underlining the following points:

a) The request is made "to erect the Institute into a Prelature *nullius*, such as the *Mission de France*, wherein the Prelate would have ordinary jurisdiction over his own clergy and people, much like military Ordinaries over their own priests and military personnel. The proposed solution would not be something extraordinary, but rather a simple combination of the two types of interdiocesan institutions already dependent on this Sacred [Consistorial] Congregation, i.e., the military ordinariates and the *Mission de France*."[104]

b) Although the solution does have some original notes, in combining the figure of the *Mission de France* with that of the military Vicariates, it is pointed out that "there are not a few precedents, which authorize us to deem the aforesaid solution as no novelty." In effect:

- "There are many prelates in the Church (cf. *Annuario Pontificio* (1962): 1313-1314) with territorial and personal jurisdiction for the spiritual care of immigrants of different oriental rites. These prelates have sometimes for a territory—with exclusive jurisdiction— solely a church, while exercising personal jurisdiction over a territory consisting of many dioceses, plus the faculty of incardinating their own priests. (See, for example, among others, *AAS* 51 [1959]: 789)";

---

[104] RHF, EF-620308t-1, no. 13.

- "Recall also the example of the military ordinaries and of the *Mission de France*: the former for the spiritual care of groups of persons in special circumstances; the latter, for the development of a special apostolate."

- "We humbly consider," the text continues, "that in our case, there exist reasons of equal weight (the spiritual care of some lay people who carry out with a specific formation their apostolate on the cutting edge) that make advisable the adoption of a solution similar to those just mentioned."[105]

c) In addition Msgr. Escrivá points out: "The juridical configuration that I had glimpsed even from 1928 was something similar to that of the military ordinariates or vicariates, made up of secular priests, with a specific mission; and of lay people who have the need, because of special circumstances, for an appropriate juridical treatment within ecclesiastical law and for special spiritual care. In our case, the peculiarities derive from the requirements of carrying out a secular apostolate in all environments of society, in places inaccessible or prohibited to priests and religious, by means of lay people with a permanent dedication, with a specific spiritual and intellectual formation, and with a mutual bond uniting them to the Institute."[106]

d) The proposal follows the lines of a Prelature *nullius* with fewer than three parishes, governed by a special law, in accordance with canon 319.[107] In this case this law would consist of "the Con-

---

[105] RHF, EF-620412t-1, no. 1.

[106] RHF, EF-620308t-1, no. 3. One of the first members of Opus Dei, Pedro Casciaro, recalls that early in 1936 he accompanied Fr. Josemaría Escrivá to the Church of Santa Isabel in Madrid, where Msgr. Escrivá was at the time rector. While he waited, he spent time glancing at some ornamental details of the church, among them two funeral slabs placed on the ground at the foot of the presbytery. At this moment, Fr. Josemaría approached him and pointing to the slabs said: "There is the future juridical solution of the Work." After this without adding anything more—or at least Pedro Casciaro does not recall that he did—he kept on going. The two stone slabs correspond to two Spanish prelates, one from the second half of the 18th century and the other from the middle of the 19th century and beginning of the 20th century, both of them major chaplains of the king, and military vicars general, who, as such, enjoyed a special and vast personal ecclesiastical jurisdiction (RHF, T-4197). Casciaro's testimony is important and significant, because it shows that in the mind of the founder there was always present in one form or another the idea of a jurisdictional structure of a secular and personal character.

[107] CIC 1917, c. 319: "§ 1 Prelates who rule over the clergy and people of a district that is separated from every other diocese are called either abbots or prelates *nullius* (i.e. of no diocese). They are called abbots *nullius*, if their church is an abbey, and prelates *nullius*, if their church is a secular prelacy. § 2 An abbacy or prelacy *nullius* that does not consist of at least three parishes is ruled by special laws, and to such does not apply what the Canons state concerning abbacies and prelacies *nullius*."

stitutions already approved by the Holy See, with any modifications introduced by a commission of cardinals, as well as other papal documents referring to Opus Dei."[108]

e) With regard to its relationship to the Holy See, it points out that with the erection as a Prelature *nullius* Opus Dei would fall under the jurisdiction of the Sacred Consistorial Congregation.[109] With regard to the relations with local Ordinaries: "We do not desire in any way that the new solution change this dependence on them. The only change, in this aspect, would be with regard to the small territory of the Prelature: for everything else, *nihil immutetur*. In this line it should be borne in mind also that the President General of the Institute already has the faculty of giving dimissory letters for the priestly ordination of his subjects. He also has the faculty delegated by the Holy See, subdelegable *ad normam iuris*, of hearing the sacramental confessions of members of the Institute. . . .[110] For the erection of the Institute's Centers outside of the territory of the Prelature the permission of the Bishop *ad quem* would be required as is now the case."[111]

Having set forth the structural lines of the 1962 proposal, let us return to events. Msgr. Escrivá, complying again with the wishes of Cardinal Ciriaci, asked again the Cardinal Secretary of State for a new juridical structure. On April 6 he visited the shrine of Our Lady of Pompei, near Naples, to place once more in the hands of the Blessed Virgin the whole question which, as founder, he considered a serious matter of conscience. Four days later, he composed a hand-written note expressing the reasons and emotions that led him to take these steps following the insistent advice of Cardinal Ciriaci, even though in his mind he clearly saw circumstances were not such as to warrant a favorable response: "It was necessary to insist in my petition that the juridical categorization might be definitively solved for Opus Dei, lest our spirit and the efficacy of our apostolate in the service of God's Holy Church be forfeited. Both are being compromised, more each day, by our assimilation to secular institutes—I would say rather they're being confused with religious congregations.

"In me there is a grave obligation of conscience constantly urging me to avoid this assimilation. I don't want to write a history of so many years of struggle. I only want to say that I considered in my prayer before Our Lady of Pompei, the uprightness, the rectitude, the love for Holy Church and my vocation, that move me to

---

[108] RHF, EF-620308t-1, no. 13.

[109] *Ibid.*

[110] RHF, EF-620412t-1, no. 3.

[111] RHF, EF-620308t-1, no. 15.

try to have us cease being a secular institute. In this most recent effort I could affirm that my rectitude has been reinforced by obeying in something that was and is contrary to the dictates of my own mind: we have limited ourselves to obeying the Cardinal Protector, who assures that he will facilitate everything. For myself at this time, I would not have taken this step.

"With great faith in God our Lord and in the protection of our Mother Mary," he concludes, "I hope that now or in the future the formula will be found—whether what we see now or some other—so that I can present myself peacefully before the judgment seat of God, having fulfilled his holy will, despite the men, ignorant or not, who have opposed what is just and good for souls, for the Church and for the glory of God."[112]

The tone is serene, but concerned. A month later, on May 22, his negative prognosis was confirmed. A letter from Cardinal Cicognani dated two days earlier conveys the Pope's judgment, based on opinions received. The proposal of erecting Opus Dei as a Prelature *nullius* cannot be admitted, since "it does not constitute a solution," and presents "juridical and practical difficulties that are nearly insurmountable." Subsequent explanations clearly showed that the experts and authorities of the Roman Curia continued to defend a dichotomy that had dominated Canon Law for centuries: either institutions based on the concept of the state of perfection (understood in a strict manner or not), which could be granted an interdiocesan form of government and the right to have their own priests; or, on the other hand, simple associations of the faithful lacking this form of government and therefore possibility of having their own priests.[113]

On June 3 the founder acknowledged receipt of the letter from Cardinal Cicognani. He reiterates his "complete and perfect adherence to the Holy See," while he expressed that, in reading and meditating what had been transmitted to him, he could not hope less than that perhaps he had not expressed himself well. Thus in the future, "with the same filial devotion and for the tranquility of my conscience I may once again address Your Eminence in order to present to the Holy Father the object of my concerns. . . . But if this were to occur, be assured, Your Eminence, that I will do so with the sincerity of one setting forth an anxious concern of conscience, but also with the disposition which I have always had and I wish always to have of trusting and accepting beforehand whatever comes from the Holy See."[114]

---

[112] RHF, EF-620420-2.

[113] The text of the letter from the Cardinal Secretary of State is included in the Appendix, document no. 45.

[114] Complete text of this letter is in the Appendix, document no. 46.

This negative reply occasioned great sorrow for Msgr. Escrivá. He knew he was responsible before God for the future of the Work, since he had received the foundational charism. Therefore he was the one who had to transmit to successive generations an Opus Dei organized and structured with full fidelity to God's will. He was confident that, by one way or another, a solution would be reached. Shortly thereafter he personally expressed these sentiments to Pope John XXIII in a cordial audience granted to him on June 27, 1962.[115]

## 7. New reflections of the founder on the institutional question.

We earlier commented on a Letter of the founder dated January 25, 1961; now we turn to another dated May 25, 1962. Even though Msgr. Escrivá makes no explicit mention in this regard, he seemingly wanted the first steps towards a revision of the juridical structure—those of 1960 and 1962—to be accompanied by an extensive commentary. Thus he would set forth in detail his mind on the whole problem and the evaluation of historical events. The 1962 *Letter* is addressed to those in charge of directing Opus Dei.[116] Not only does he summarize the points and questions covered in earlier Letters but he unambiguously sets forth the various facets of the institutional problem of Opus Dei. He says he does so moved as on earlier occasions by the awareness of his responsibility as founder, intensified now by recent difficulties and by having reached the age of 60. He declares himself certain of the prayer of his children, who have been for some time beseeching God's mercy for the founder's special intention.[117]

"For how many days, and how many nights also, the motive of my thanksgiving has been the innumerable proofs of a universal fervor, all of you—*consummati in unum* (Jn 17:23)—beseeching the Lord that he preserve the genuine nature of our secular and lay vocation. It has nothing to do with the religious: neither by its historical origin, nor by the specific spirit given us, nor by our special mode of living; nor by the hierarchy of the Christian virtues we cultivate; nor by the manner of our apostolic actions; nor by the form of resolving the problems that come our way. When people do not grasp the nature of our Work, it might seem that all these questions are for us of the same nature, but it is not so. This misunderstanding must be confronted and resolved with quite different procedures."[118]

---

[115] RHF, EF-620712t-1.

[116] *Letter*, May 25, 1962, no. 3.

[117] *Ibid.*, no. 1.

[118] *Ibid.*, no. 2.

It is the teaching and historical experience that culminate as before in affirming the need for a new juridical solution: "Our desire, our duty of preserving intact the specific nature of the vocation God has given to us, has led us, leads us and will lead us with tireless perseverance to offer countless Masses (which can already be counted in many thousands) and innumerable personal sacrifices, plus the merit of our daily professional work, for this common intention we so ardently desire to see carried out. Namely, that our holy mother the Church give to the Work a new juridical form, so that what we are not *de facto*, a secular institute, we also cease to be *de iure*. . . . For this reason I must tell you I am moved by the fervent unity of my children, *perseverantes unanimiter in oratione* (Acts 1:14), perseveringly united in prayer and in the vigorous fidelity with which—through your ordinary occupations—you live, down to the smallest detail, the secular and lay spirituality proper to our divine call to the apostolate. . . . In the face of such fidelity, unity and refined spirit, I feel strongly the duty in conscience—which seems at the same time the charity of a father, the prudence of a man of government, and the loyalty of a man—to open my heart to you in all simplicity to make known to you the sentiments of understanding and trust with which by God's grace I feel myself filled."[119]

Opening his heart thus, he says, he will give an answer "serenely meditated in God's presence," to everything various Opus Dei members have made known to him in writing or word. He is certain these members, holding positions of government or formation, "will know how to second intelligently in the souls of all my children what I am saying to you."[120]

The breadth of the Letter, dealing as it does with previously seen topics, makes a step-by-step scrutiny unnecessary. We limit ourselves to the vision it offers of the institutional problem of Opus Dei, summarized as follows:

a) Above all he claims, the pastoral phenomenon of Opus Dei arises from the coming to consciousness of the mission proper to the laity in the Church, leapfrogging back to the first Christians; it is not within the line of the evolution of the religious life, thus repeating ideas expressed in earlier texts.[121] He writes: Opus Dei "with its universal hierarchy and its specific spirituality constitutes within the genus of lay spirituality—I think saying so is not a lack of humility, but a way of giving glory to God, from whom all good

---

[119] *Ibid.*, nos. 3-4.

[120] *Ibid.*, no. 4.

[121] In some passages, for example, in no. 45, he reproduces textually passages from the *Letter* of January 25, 1961, no. 9, that we have already quoted in section 5 of this chapter.

comes—a powerful leaven to move the Catholic laity to assume their ecclesial responsibility, that proper to them in all of the world's noble activities."[122]

He links the topic to the environment and concerns born of the advancing preparations for the ecumenical council: "In these preliminary stages of the approaching Second Vatican Ecumenical Council—for which all of us in fervent union of intentions with the Holy Father John XXIII are beseeching the special assistance of the Holy Spirit and offering our daily mortifications—particular attention is being given to the topic of the laity: to its spirituality and its apostolic mission.

"If you could see how much I rejoice that the Council is going to deal with the topics that since 1928 have filled our life! I give thanks to God our Lord for the part the Work—its life, its spirituality, its apostolates—could have had, along with other meritorious lay institutions, in provoking this theological deepening, which will undoubtedly bring great good to the Church. And I give God thanks for the opportunity for several of your brothers to cooperate directly and intensely in this work."[123]

b) These general declarations are accompanied by the reaffirmation of one of his fundamental teachings: the vocation to Opus Dei is that of ordinary Christians and ordinary citizens, each one in his own state or condition in life. The spirit of Opus Dei "is to give witness to Christ and to confess him before men, but (contrariwise from the religious) precisely by keeping intact communion with the life of ordinary faithful, your equals, so perfectly and so sincerely, that not the slightest degree of separation or segregation is allowed. . . . We do not need to do strange things in order to share, in profound human and Christian solidarity, the problems, the work, the noble ideals of men: it is enough for us to be faithful to our vocation as children of God, *personally dedicated* to the service of the Church, always *with the express condition of not being religious or considered the equivalent of religious*, in the place in life each one has, responding to a special divine call, a vocation the Holy Spirit has brought about, enriching the Church with a new charism."[124]

"The vocation to the Work—I have taught you from the beginning, and I will repeat it many times—does not take anybody out of his place. . . . Therefore this special dedication of each one of you to follow Opus Dei's apostolic goals will never signify a change of *status*—the state each one had when God's call came to him: his condition of being an ordinary member of the faithful before the

---

[122] *Letter*, May 25, 1962, no. 13.

[123] *Ibid.*, no. 92.

[124] *Ibid.*, nos. 5-6.

Church. . . . Just as the Christian vocation—baptism—does not alter or violate human nature, though it does elevate it, neither does the call to the Work—which leads simply to activating and developing the gifts received in baptism, each Christian staying in his own secular state— alter or violate our condition in life.[125] He then summarizes with an oft repeated reading: "What God asks of us is not that we change our state from being ordinary faithful (secular clerics or secular lay people) in order to assume the *status perfectionis*: but that—with God's help we will repeat these same ideas as often as necessary—each one of us seeks Christian perfection precisely within his own state and condition of life."[126]

c) He then sketches a juridical-theological characterization of Opus Dei and contrasts it with the common teaching regarding the state of perfection in which secular institutes had been placed. As if jumping over all technicalities, he cites a British journalist, who had interviewed him in 1959: Opus Dei is like "a corporate entity of mature men from many nations, inspired in principles that are both new and basic."[127] Msgr. Escrivá comments: "You know very well as I do that the richness of our vocation is found precisely in these new principles, because they differ from the common teaching with regard to the state of perfection. And they are fundamental principles, because they are based on the common human responsibility to work (since man was created *ut operaretur*: Gen 2:15) on the common call of all Christians to perfection according to the Redeemer's words: *estote ergo vos perfecti sicut et Pater vester cælestis perfectus est* (Mt 5:48); and on a simple and vibrant apostolate like the one carried out by the first faithful of the Church.

"These new and basic principles," he concludes, "are the substance of our divine call, and the object of my cares and yours, lest the fidelity we owe to what God expects of us come to nought. For me, especially, this duty of vigilance, making sure that our spirit not be denatured—destroyed—and that we live the reality of our secular vocation, is a grave obligation of conscience. I know I will have to give a strict accounting to God for this."[128] In other words: here is the root, the theological core that has always been present and must be invoked until a juridical configuration is obtained that is perfectly adequate to it.

d) In 1947 Opus Dei took advantage of the legislation creating secular institutes, obtaining "a juridical recognition that, while safeguarding the peculiarities of our secular vocation, allowed us to

---

[125] *Ibid.*, nos. 7-8.

[126] *Ibid.*, no. 91.

[127] See note 6 of this chapter; [*Also try to get the original English text!!!*]

[128] *Letter*, May 25, 1962, no. 27.

have the universal internal hierarchy needed to foster the growth and coordination of our apostolates." This juridical solution, *although a compromise,* sufficiently guaranteed then what the Work needed. And the Work grew and rapidly spread throughout the world. . . . Today—as you well realize and I am recalling once again to you in this *Letter*—this solution has proved incapable of guaranteeing the peculiar characteristics of our specific vocation."[129] Thus he reaffirms the need for an institutional change, as in many other passages: "The person who wants to go forward must sincerely count on everything that has gone before. And this past clearly shows that, while in our *ius peculiare* I have always taken pains to stress the full secularity of our vocation . . . this is not enough anymore to defend the lay nature of our spirituality and apostolate."[130]

He refers extensively to the harm that follows from this inadequate juridical form and to the uneasiness it awakens in Opus Dei members: "I understand well, for this reason, that, along with the uneasiness you experience lest the genuine nature of our vocation be changed or violated, you are also concerned about the practical difficulties you encounter in carrying out your apostolic work, whether personal or corporate, in the midst of civil society, when this society considers you religious. . . . For example I know not a few of you have been denied in your respective places of work the right to exercise your occupation or that questions about the *legitimacy* of your profession have been raised in a more or less public manner." Of course these hindrances exist so long as they are assimilated to the religious or because legislation regarding religious has been applied to them.[131]

e) This context leads him to cast the institutional question as a burning question of justice. Haven't the members of Opus Dei joined the Work with the understanding and vocation of ordinary Christians and consequently do they not justifiably resent being led along any other path? "For me . . . it is not only a question of fidelity to God's will but also of justice with all of you. . . . Before being admitted to the Work, each of you has had well and justly explained—so that your decision be conscious and free, as well as for a matter of justice—that you are not going to be religious nor people equivalent to religious. You were told you would retain in everything your personality and your condition as ordinary lay people who in nothing are going to be segregated or separated from your fellowmen, who are in the world the same as you; that in

---

[129] *Ibid.,* no. 36.

[130] *Ibid.,* no. 45.

[131] *Ibid.,* nos. 14-15. In the following numbers of the *Letter* he goes into more specific examples.

coming to Opus Dei you would not change your state, but rather keep the one you already had; and that your occupation and social responsibilities would remain an integral part of the divine vocation you have received."[132] Strongly but sincerely he adds: "How could I now commit the sin of obliging you to follow a different vocation? There is no way I could require this of you, nor could I ask you—having recourse to twisted arguments that violate the freedom of your consciences—to renew your commitment to the Work embracing a vocation different from the one we have received from God.

"I could not do this to you, nor can anyone do this to me. . . . Besides being humanly a vicious act, this would be a grave transgression of Christian morality, of positive divine law, and even of natural law itself.

"In the sweep of ecclesiastical legislation and praxis there is no norm or principle that could justify such a tyrannical deed. I beseech you to realize I speak to you in all sincerity and clarity, but also with mature thought. I'm not a young man who writes to you lightly: I have my years and *Dominus prope est* (Phil 4:5): for me the judgment of the Lord is near."[133]

"In my soul I harbor a great devotion to St. Francis, St. Dominic, St. Ignatius; but nobody in the world can force me to become a Franciscan, a Dominican or a Jesuit. Neither can anybody oblige me to get married. . . . In the spiritual life it is God's grace that counts, his will, his desire is what points out a way and a mission. . . . Who has the right to change a God-given vocation?

"Natural law, divine positive law, Christian morality and acquired rights are opposed, I repeat, to any violence of this kind and rightly defend the freedom of consciences."[134]

f) These strong, duty-bound words stem from the tension between the foundational charism and the increasingly inadequate juridical configuration. They enshrine *the* fundamental fact: fidelity to the divine vocation to do what he clearly sees God has wanted in raising up Opus Dei.

"It is you my children, filled with good spirit, tirelessly working, who have made a reality of this universal sowing of a lived teaching," he states in recalling the fruits born of the apostolic work of Opus Dei. "For these reasons, from the depths of my poor life, I limit myself to trying to love you with all my soul—I ask God to judge me only on my love for him and my love for you—and to teach you with the greatest possible solicitude, according to the

---

[132] *Letter*, May 25, 1962, no. 33.

[133] *Ibid.*, no. 34.

[134] *Ibid.*, no. 35.

teaching of Holy Scripture by which I have always measured my fidelity: 'that these words which I command you this day shall be upon your heart; and you shall teach them diligently to your children and shall talk of them when you sit in your house and when you walk by the way and when you lie down and when you rise' (Deut 6:6-7).

"Understand how much I understand you; with what great sincerity I share your vibrant desire that nothing alter or disturb the secular and lay nature of our vocation, which is the very reason for my life and yours, and the apt means for the fruitfulness of the apostolate we carry out in the Church's service and for our personal sanctity."[135]

This translates into "a grave commitment to defend the integrity of our spirituality, our secular vocation and our condition as ordinary Christians." It is not a question of vindicating rights, but of faithfully fulfilling God's will: "If I *personally* have—before the Church—*the right not to have rights*, before God our Lord *I have the obligation* of using *all* upright supernatural and human means to fulfill the holy will of God, in what concerns the foundation of his Work just as He has made me understand it."[136]

Using all the means is besides "a problem *of conscience*: I do not want to be condemned, nor you either, because I did not pray and ask in a filial way, because together we were *canes muti, non valentes latrare* (Isa 56:10); like dumb dogs afraid to bark in defending the treasure of our God."[137]

g) He concludes: We are bound "to request perseveringly for a clear juridical solution based on the Church's ordinary law—far from any privileges—that definitively guarantees the fidelity to our vocation, that assures and reinforces the spirit of Opus Dei and the fruitfulness of our apostolates in the service of the Church, the Roman Pontiff and souls."[138]

This solution, he adds, echoing as it were the difficulties encountered, is not the result of speculations in a vacuum nor a desire for novelty, but the manifestation of a desire for constant fidelity to the foundational charism, while always also respecting Church law. In the founder's words: "And if, besides spelling out this spiritual problem that affects the very essence of our vocation, we suggest and put forward the technical solution we judge most appropriate, it is because we want to avoid having anyone with only a superfi-

---

[135] *Ibid.*, no. 10.

[136] *Ibid.*, no. 26. "I cannot bury the talent (Mt 25:25), because I do not want the Lord to take it away from me, with just indignation; I cannot allow the apostolic fruit of the Work of God to be drowned or impeded" (*Ibid.*, no. 27).

[137] *Ibid.*, no. 96.

[138] *Ibid.*, no. 36.

cial appreciation for the problem include us among those whom the administrative realism of the Roman Curia sometimes calls *prophetical mysticisms*, creators of imaginary but insoluble problems. . . . No, my children: you know well that this is not our case. We do not invent problems, nor do we seek impossible solutions.

"We certainly have a clear awareness of the great charism—gift of God, *thesaurus absconditus* (Mt 13:44)—with which God's mercy has desired to fill our life and transform it. . . . But this specific secular and lay vocation is not an *imaginary construct*, nor a *false mysticism*, nor a *prophetic idea*, born and cherished in the mind of some theology scholar with no more real life than the abstraction of an idea.

"Our vocation is a living reality, incarnated in the daily existence of very many people of so many walks of life, nations, languages and races, who, the world over, work in the service of the Church; they believe, love and pray; they work and smile and, while they serve, always out of love for Jesus Christ, *they hope*.

"This is the *realism* of our vocation and, therefore, the true problem that fidelity to this vocation presents, something that leads us ardently to desire the necessary definitive juridical solution, which we humbly suggest."[139]

h) This persevering request, this solicitude to open the path, fulfilling a duty of conscience, will never be presented polemically, but with the loyalty and fidelity of a good son of the Church: "My children, you well understand that it is not a question at all of *forcing* the hand of the Holy See, nor of *engaging in polemics* with those entrusted with studying this problem. . . . My daughters and sons, I have served and loved the Church and the Pope with all the ardor of my heart. Sometimes, in God's presence, I think this love and this service—*opere et veritate* (I Jn 3:18) external proofs of reality and truth—have been as great as those of the soul who has loved most and served most."

Consequently, "nobody can honestly doubt the rectitude with which we will turn once again at the proper time to the Holy See.

---

[139] *Ibid.*, nos. 95-96. Similar thoughts about this contrast between a realism open to a new creative activity of the Holy Spirit and a short-term realism had already shown up in an earlier passage: "I do not exclude, my children, that there can be some—with an insufficient and non-scientific background in canon law—who act as though they knew and had perfectly *regulated* all of this profound and rich reality of the gifts of God, as if all of the modes of the Holy Spirit's action in the life of the Church had been already definitively *catalogued.*"

"I have to tell you, my children, that these people exist and that they are, in my judgment, the ones responsible for the bad repute, which, unfortunately, many today hold for *lex ecclesiastica*. Because these false doctors act as though charism were born of the juridical norm, as if the suit were to beget the body, as if the form preceded matter" (*Ibid.*, no. 76).

There we will present, with unlimited filial confidence, the motive and reasons behind our duty to make first viable and then ever more effective our service to the Holy Church and to souls."[140]

From beginning to end, the 1962 *Letter* betrays a keen awareness of the importance of the problem and the need to give it a prompt solution. It no less breathes a serene attitude, a tone of hope, a sure confidence that difficulties will be resolved, a complete and total surrender to the Church that guided by God will find ways to grant Opus Dei a definitive solution to its institutional problem. "It has been said, my children, that the Church is Christ *entrusted to the hands of men. . . .* It seems fitting to me to remind you now of the Church's nature, both divine and human, because we must entrust this desire for fidelity to our God-given vocation to those men in whom Christ himself has trusted. So I want you—I ask you with all my soul—to meditate as I do— on the humble and hopeful abandonment with which Christ confidently surrenders himself."[141]

Further on: "I confess that these possible difficulties have never taken away my peace. I merely ask God that, were these obstacles to arise, he grant us the chance of dialoguing, of expressing in the proper place and in the proper moment the many reasons, thank God, for showing the purity of intention that moves us, together with the effectiveness of our service and the rightness of what we seek."[142]

Towards the end Msgr. Escrivá again emphasizes this spirit: "Do not admit a single doubt or fear! Be certain: what we want is of God, and it is good for his service in all circumstances, because we are not only for this age, but for every age, for every place."[143] "Whenever I think about my littleness and the fantastic development of the Work in the world, I always reach this conclusion, which helps me so much to rest in God: no man, much less I, could do this: *digitus Dei est hic* (Ex 8:19); it is so clear that here is the hand of God.

"Once again, my children, in this crucial moment of the Work's foundation, reflecting on this reasonable way of acting to safeguard the specific nature of our vocation, God fills the soul with peace and certainty; he reminds us, *fui tecum in omnibus ubicumque ambulasti* (2 Kgs 7:9): I have always been at your side, from the first day, even in the midst of ferocious storms."[144]

---

[140] *Ibid.*, nos. 94-95.

[141] *Ibid.*, no. 60.

[142] *Ibid.*, no. 68.

[143] *Ibid.*, no. 99.

[144] *Ibid.*, no. 100.

He concludes: "My children, with renewed love for the Church, we are going to do what we humanly and supernaturally can to make available to this crowd of the Work—for which we are directly responsible—bread for their fidelity to the vocation. The Lord will do the rest! Repeat to him: *Ecce nos reliquimus omnia, et secuti sumus te, quid ergo erit nobis?* (Mt 19:27). Lord, perform one of your works: may it be seen that it is You."[145]

## 8. The early years of the pontificate of Paul VI (1963-1964)

The extensive passages from the 1962 *Letter* introduce nothing new from a technical or canonical point of view. Nevertheless they poignantly bear witness to the founder's interior attitude in the face of the last and definitive stage of Opus Dei's juridical journey. They speak of his awareness of his foundational responsibility, of his conviction that the decisive moment has come, of his acquaintance with the Church. They are reflected in all the successive steps, quite diverse one from another, as since 1963 the world, Church and Msgr. Escrivá are about to witness some transcendental events.

On June 3, 1963, John XXIII died. In the conclave celebrated a few days later the Cardinal Archbishop of Milan, Giovanni Battista Montini, was elected, taking the name of Paul VI. The election took place on June 21. Almost immediately Paul VI confirmed that not only would the Council be continued, but would do so as planned: the next session would begin in September of that year.

All of this of course affected the juridical development of Opus Dei. The work of the Second Vatican Council seemed to the founder to open in the Church's general legislation a path making possible an institutional solution for Opus Dei. Msgr. Escrivá knew moreover that the juridical configuration of Opus Dei could not be formally revised easily until the Council ended. Besides, this revision would have to be done, at the appropriate moment, taking logically into account the results of the Council. In these circumstances, both personally and through Fr. Alvaro del Portillo, he sought to make known to various members of the Roman Curia that Opus Dei's institutional question had not yet been resolved.[146]

Independently of these contacts and dealings, on October 2, 1963, the founder wrote to Paul VI proposing modifications in the 1950 *Constitutions*.[147] For some years now, beyond the reflections aimed at the new and future juridical solution, Msgr. Escrivá had been taking note of possible changes in the *Constitutions* of Opus

---

[145] *Ibid.*, no. 102.

[146] RHF, 20171, p. 1388.

[147] RHF, EF-631002-1.

Dei. From time to time he proposed some of these changes to the Holy See by virtue of the faculties granted to him on August 2, 1950;[148] others he had not raised. In the fall of 1963, he deemed the moment ripe to gather these notes and propose them to the Holy See for its approval. On October 24 the Congregation for Religious signified its agreement.[149]

In themselves these changes do not affect the general juridical configuration of Opus Dei, whose review was still pending. Hence we will merely summarize them. The main change suppressed chapters III and IV of Part II of the 1950 text, where the spirit of the Institute and some pious customs and practices are noted. Msgr. Escrivá thought the basic spirit of Opus Dei was already sufficiently covered by chapter V entitled *De pietatis officiis sociorum*. There were slight changes in the duration of positions of government and the organization of assemblies; General Workweeks were to be suppressed inasmuch as their purpose was being met by Ordinary General Congresses. Also introduced were some norms on governing the Regions in the event of impeded communication with the President General and his Council and on the general form of government when the position of President General is vacant.[150]

Following the approval of these modifications and additions, the founder revised the *Constitutions*, comprising 398 numbers, entitled *Codex Iuris Peculiaris Societatis Sacerdotalis Sanctæ Crucis et Operis Dei* and dated October 24, 1963.

A week later Msgr. Escrivá sent to Cardinal Ildebrando Antoniutti, the Prefect of the Sacred Congregation for Religious, the printed text of this *Codex*. It was accompanied by a letter where he pointed out that Opus Dei still found itself far from the desired juridical solution. "I am conscious that, as I have many times said to Your Eminence, there is still a long way to go to reach the definitive

---

[148] He had used this faculty in the request for the revision of the juridical statute presented on January 7, 1962. Furthermore, on July 16, 1953, just after the definitive approval as a secular institute, Msgr. Escrivá, invoking this faculty, had addressed Pius XII requesting some modifications in the text of June 16, 1950. He requested some 13 modifications, related to governing the women's branch, thus reinforcing the unity of Opus Dei, and also establishing in the women's branch some consulting organs parallel to those already existing in the men's branch; they were approved by the Holy See on August 12, 1953 (RHF, EF-530716-1).

[149] AGP, Sezione Giuridica, VI/15673.

[150] We point out another modification, referring to the associate and supernumerary members of the Priestly Society of the Holy Cross. The 1950 *Constitutions* established (no. 76, 3) that before requesting admission in the Priestly Society priests incardinated in dioceses should obtain permission of their respective Ordinary. This norm was suppressed in 1963, because it was no longer in conformity with the praxis of the Holy See in similar situations of other priestly associations: it is merely the application to the Priestly Society of the Holy Cross of a general criterion.

juridical solution of Opus Dei. I am comforted, nevertheless, by the certainty that God almighty, through the holy Church, will not fail to open for us the way he has desired since the far-off days of 1928 that then seemed something impossible to achieve."

He adds: "In the hope that this moment will arrive, all of my daughters and sons throughout the world continue praying for this intention, well aware that Opus Dei is by law a secular institute but in fact is not. We are in no hurry, because the Lord, in his infinite and inscrutable Wisdom, will show us the way and the opportune time for fulfilling his will with regard to Opus Dei, something—I feel obliged to say this—truly His and not the work of this poor sinner." The question, as fixed in the October 1958 *Letter* and to which he had adjusted his way of acting since then, was formally communicated to those with hierarchical authority over Opus Dei, according to the juridical configuration which he sought to overcome.[151]

Since the election of Paul VI, the Founder had evoked the figure of Msgr. Montini whom he had known in his first days in Rome in 1946. He said that his was the first friendly hand he had encountered in Rome. On January 24, 1964, Msgr. Escrivá was received in audience for the first time. In the course of the conversation Paul VI displayed to the founder and Opus Dei the affection he had always shown, and he took interest in the institutional problem of the Work.[152]

As a result of this audience, Msgr. Escrivá sent to Archbishop Dell'Acqua, the Undersecretary of State for Extraordinary Affairs,[153] a letter, dated February 14, to be presented to the Holy Father.[154] With this letter and fulfilling a request made by the Holy Father in the audience, he also sent "a small volume that contains the *Ius peculiare of Opus Dei* (Constitutions)" in its edition of October 24, 1963. He included by way of introduction the *Letter* of October 2, 1958, to which we have just referred. Also included were another small volume dealing with the spirit of Opus Dei and an extensive note—*Appunto riservato all'Augusta Persona del Santo Padre*—in which, by way of a statement of conscience, he set forth and commented some questions and desires that filled his spirit.

Among the topics dealt with in this *appunto* are references to the institutional problem of Opus Dei: "I feel obliged in conscience, before God, to do everything possible so that this universal pastoral phenomenon raised up by the Lord for the service of the Church not

---

[151] The text of this letter is found in the Appendix, document no. 47.

[152] RHF, EF-640205-1.

[153] RHF, EF-640214-1.

[154] This letter to the Holy Father can be found in the Appendix, document no. 48.

be stifled, even though He has used such a poor instrument as I."
Later on he insists: "I beseech you, Holy Father, to consider what I
have written not a desire of singling myself out; it is not a question
of pride, but of the love I owe to this Work that God has wanted to
raise up to humbly serve the Church. The same love moves me also
to seek a definitive solution, which will make it impossible to our
being considered equivalent to religious and which would avoid
the juridical and practical inclusions of Opus Dei among the states
of perfection." Then, alluding to the petition made in 1962, he
adds: "Such a solution should be sought, most certainly, in the
realm of the common law of the Church. I have already presented
some documents that at the proper time would perhaps be useful as
a basis for resolving in a clear and a just way our spiritual and
apostolic problem."[155]

In the letter to the Pope accompanying this *appunto* the founder
wrote: "In what has to do with the juridical ordering of Opus Dei,
I consider it important to reaffirm what I told Your Holiness verbally, that is to say: we are not in a rush; nevertheless, we have a
great hope for the desired definitive ordering to assure the greatest
development of our specific vocation as well as the greatest fruit of
our filial service to the Church." In sum, he did not present, either
in this letter or in the *appunto* accompanying it, a formal petition for
proceeding to a study of the institutional question of Opus Dei, but
merely opened his confident heart to the Holy Father. He well
knew (and so had been advised by several persons of the Roman
Curia) that the conclusion of the Council must be awaited before
raising again this question officially. Thus he was somewhat surprised to find out in May in talking with Archbishop Paul Philippe,
at the time Secretary of the Sacred Congregation for Religious, that
some officials of the Holy See were studying this question on the
basis of the letter and notes sent to Paul VI. The founder then
offered Cardinal Antoniutti, the Prefect of that Congregation, to
make available to him all the necessary data and explanations to do
a deeper study, if this were the case. By word of mouth and pri-
vately he was told it was not possible for the moment to go ahead
with this study.

On August 15 the founder wrote a lengthy letter from Paris to
Archbishop Dell'Acqua.[156] After expressing his joy with the encyc-

---

[155] RHF, EF-640214-2. In the *appunto*—and also in the letter that accompanies it—Msgr.
Escrivá refers to pages (photocopied) from a book of Cardinal Suenens (*Promotion
apostolique de la religieuse*, Bruges-Paris 1962, pp. 54-58), where the Cardinal speaks,
although in a theological context distinct from that of Opus Dei, of foundations that in
past centuries failed in the apostolic purpose, because of the inadequacy of the law
applied to their specific charism.

[156] This letter can be consulted in the Appendix, document no. 49.

lical *Ecclesiam suam*, the first from Paul VI, he said: "I also pray continually for the definitive juridical configuration of Opus Dei. I am not in a hurry—though the thought besieges me that at any moment God could say to me: *redde rationem villicationis tuæ*. But I think that when the Council is finished perhaps our question can be studied. Meanwhile, until the time comes to carry out this study, I consider it my obligation humbly to present the fact that Opus Dei, as you have told me more than once, is a new pastoral phenomenon, and I hope it will be studied as such."[157]

Later he adds: "In order to explain everything better—in case a commission would be set up or some persons were to be queried, whether theologians or jurists, I think that it would be most opportune that I be allowed to address them personally, not only as a theologian or a jurist, but above all (and this is not pride) as the one who best knows our life: the fruits of our service to the Church and souls granted by God over these 36 years; the difficulties we have encountered; the reasons for these difficulties; and anything else such people might want to know. I am convinced that these sought-for personal contacts and joint study would facilitate united criteria and that the persons designated to carry out this study would bless God for having promoted this apostolate of ours. In all sincerity I also think that no one could consider his opinion definitive without first hearing me, without a clarifying dialogue. Without a joint study, there could not truly be sufficient knowledge of Opus Dei without the data I in all humility ought to provide.

"In this way," he continues, "a solution could be reached that would not be an exception nor one of privilege, but one which would allow us to work in such a way that the most reverend Ordinaries whom we love *opere et veritate* are always happy with our Work; that the rights of bishops remain, as they are up to now,

---

[157] After alluding to the information received from Archbishop Philippe without mentioning its source, he insists with words taken from an earlier writing in its novelty and difference from other institutions: "It should be pointed out that, in general, the vivifying Holy Spirit does not advance in the Church by leaps, and thus each new phenomenon spurred by him has some similarity with preceding movements raised up by God: they are links of the same chain. For this reason, ecclesiastical history shows that, when the evolution is not perfectly homogeneous, some do not understand the reason for novelties. It has also been said, that with the passage of centuries, new pastoral phenomenon want to share both the advantages of religious and those of secular people. Those more recently come on the scene have wanted a greater elasticity and agility in apostolate, departing from the classical molds of religious and coming closer to the way of life of secular people. But in our case we confront a different phenomenon, because we are not secularized religious, but true secular people—diocesan priests in each diocese and ordinary laity—who do not seek *a life of evangelical perfection* proper to the religious, but *Christian perfection in the world, each one in his own state*. And nevertheless the same old criticism has been made of us."

firm and secure; and finally, that we could continue our way of love and of dedication without useless obstacles to serving the Church and therefore the Pope, the Bishops and souls."

Msgr. Escrivá was received once again by Paul VI on October 10, 1964. The audience was once more very cordial; they spoke of the institutional problem of the Work. It was obvious to both that it was more opportune to wait until the end of the Second Vatican Council to find a definitive juridical solution within the common law, appropriate to the proper charism of Opus Dei.[158]

## 9. The book "Conversations"

At this time and particularly after the audience with Paul VI, Msgr. Escrivá reached the clear conviction that before formally presenting again the proposal of a new juridical configuration for Opus Dei, with hope for success, it was better to wait beyond the end of the Second Vatican Council. He thought it would be good to let some time pass, so that the Conciliar documents and orientations could be assimilated and the Roman Pontiff could issue the necessary implementing legislation, wherever required. Meanwhile he had time to pray and prepare the future stages.

In 1966 a French journalist from the newspaper *Le Figaro* held an interview with the founder of Opus Dei. This interview was followed by others at the request of various American and European publications; they were a total of seven.[159] In 1968 a book was published with the title *Conversations with Msgr. Escrivá de Balaguer* featuring these interviews, plus the text of a homily Msgr. Escrivá gave on October 8, 1967, on the campus of the University of Navarre (Spain) before 30,000 people. This book soon found wide readership.[160] It is worthwhile examining it, since Msgr. Escrivá spoke at length about different aspects of the spirit, apostolate and nature of Opus Dei. *Conversations* in a certain way provides documentation analogous to that of the *Letters* written in the fifties and the sixties. In the latter Msgr. Escrivá explains the institutional situation of Opus Dei to members of the Institution itself. In *Conversations* he addresses the public at large, allowing us to go deeper into his teaching and to grasp how he presented Opus Dei at this critical point of its juridical history.

---

[158] With regard to this audience, see RHF, 20128, pp. 13-19 and RHF, 20129, pp. 10-11.

[159] In chronological order they were the following: *Le Figaro*, Paris, 1966; *New York Times*, 1966; *Time*, New York, 1967; *Gaceta Universitaria*, Madrid, 1967; *Palabra*, Madrid, 1967; *Telva*, Madrid, 1968; *L'Osservatore della Domenica*, Rome, 1968.

[160] In 1968, in addition to the original Spanish edition there appeared translations in Italian, English and Portuguese; in 1969 the French edition; in 1970 the German. . . . Since then there have been 41 printings in 7 different languages with a total number of books printed of 300,000.

Throughout the interviews, Msgr. Escrivá expresses himself positively, eschewing any polemics. He does not allude to the evolution of secular institutes, about which in these post-conciliar years there was considerable discussion. When directly asked, he gives his opinion that the topic of secular institutes is not now opportune, and he then turns to other points.[161]  Nor do we find any explicit reference to the decision already taken of seeking a new juridical solution, even though more than one phrase is inspired in the events and lines of action we have already referred to.

To the magazine *Palabra* he sketches the historical panorama he has been developing since 1948 to situate Opus Dei in the general context of the development of Christian spirituality, thus laying the foundation for any subsequent consideration of its statutes: "Opus Dei is not, nor can it in any way be considered, a reality tied to the evolutionary process of the 'state of perfection' in the Church. It is not a modern or up-to-date (*aggiornata*) form of that state. . . . I would simply point out, because a complete doctrinal exposition would take a long time, that Opus Dei is not interested in vows, or promises, or any form of consecration for its members, apart from the consecration accompanying baptism. Our Association[162] in no way wants its members to change their state in life, or to stop being simple faithful exactly the same as anyone else, in order to acquire a *status perfectionis*. On the contrary, what it wants and endeavors is that each should do apostolate and should sanctify himself within his own state, in the place and condition which he has in the Church and in society. We take no one out of his place, nor do we separate anyone from his work nor from his aims and noble commitments in the world. . . . Hence, the social reality, the spirituality and the action of Opus Dei fit into a quite different vein in the life of the Church. They are in the theological and vital process which is bringing the laity to assume its responsibilities in the Church fully and to participate in its own way in the mission of Christ and his Church. This has always been, during the nearly 40 years of the Work's existence, the constant, calm but forceful concern through which God has desired to channel, in my soul and in the souls of my children, the desire of serving Him."[163]

More specifically and juridically, he addresses the topic in the interview with *Time*. The journalist asks him with what institutions

---

[161] Cf. *Conversations*, no. 25.

[162] It should be pointed out that to avoid using the term secular institute—or that of Institute which could recall the former—Msgr. Escrivá started using at this time the word Association; he considered it legitimate to do so, because in accordance with his affirmation—also that of *Provida Mater Ecclesia*—secular institutes are associations of the faithful. On occasions he also used the term Institution.

[163] *Conversations*, no. 20. He develops the same ideas in the interview in the *L'Osservatore della Domenica*, *Conversations*, nos. 62 and 66.

could Opus Dei be compared: with religious orders and with secular institutes, or with Catholic associations such as for example the
Holy Name Society, the Knights of Columbus, etc.? "It is not easy
to find an answer," the founder begins. "When one compares organizations which have spiritual aims, there is always a risk of considering external features or juridical status to the detriment of
what is more important, the spirit that animates them and is the
raison d'être of their activities." Without a doubt the phrase is significant, if we recall the historical context. Furthermore, "I shall
merely say that with respect to the organizations you mentioned,
Opus Dei is very far removed from religious orders and secular
institutes and closer to institutions like the *Holy Name Society*."

The decision of always placing Opus Dei outside the state of
perfection or the religious vocation, but, as its very nature requires,
in the area of the common Christian life, has governed his answer.
Then, without comparisons, he describes Opus Dei without canonical expressions but very precisely: "Opus Dei is an international lay
organization to which a certain number of secular priests belong,
although they are a small minority. Its members are people who
live in the world and hold normal jobs. They do not join Opus Dei
to give up their job. On the contrary, what they look for in the
Work is the spiritual help they need to sanctify their ordinary work.
Thus their work becomes a means to sanctify themselves and help
others to do the same thing. They do not change their status. They
continue being single, married, widowed or priests. What they try
to do is serve God and their fellowmen in their own state in life.
Opus Dei is not interested in vows or promises," he adds introducing a more technical language. "It asks its members to make an
effort to practice human and Christian virtues, as children of God,
despite the limitations and errors that are inevitable in human life."

The long answer ends evoking a reality he often alludes to when
referring to Opus Dei, aware that this and no other historical experiences is the only adequate paradigm for understanding it: the first
Christians. "If you want a point of comparison, the easiest way to
understand Opus Dei is to consider the life of the early Christians.
They lived their Christian vocation seriously, seeking earnestly the
holiness to which they had been called by their baptism. Externally
they did nothing to distinguish themselves from their fellow citizens. The members of Opus Dei are ordinary people. They work
like everyone else and live in the midst of the world just as they did
before they joined. There is nothing false or artificial about their
behavior. They live like any other Christian citizen who wants to
respond fully to the demands of his faith, because that is what they
are."[164]

---

[164] *Conversations*, no. 24.

Throughout *Conversations* Msgr. Escrivá comments on different facets of the life, spirit and apostolate of the Work. He also replies to specific questions about Opus Dei's development in this or that country, about difficulties or misunderstandings encountered, about prospects. The image of Opus Dei emerging from the answers is one coined by Msgr. Escrivá early on: "an organized unorganization."[165] That is to say: that of a number of people, men and women of the most varied countries and social conditions, each one acting in his own environment, with complete spontaneity and freedom, according to their own personal ways of thinking. And in a parallel fashion, that of an institution, Opus Dei, whose task consists fundamentally in making available a doctrinal and theological formation and certain necessary spiritual reinforcement to those who, living in the world, aspire to act in a way consistent with the word and example of Jesus Christ.[166]

Certainly there is need to direct Opus Dei and consequently for an organization; of this Msgr. Escrivá speaks in *Conversations*, though he always stresses that it is kept to a minimum, to what is "strictly indispensable."[167] The existence of its own apostolic activities is also mentioned, which must not only have a spiritual character, but also be conceived to project a "Christian view of life."[168] They are initiatives that in various ways, each according to its mission, contribute to "help men and women to be good Christians, and therefore witnesses of Christ in the midst of their everyday occupations."[169] That is their aim. But he always insists that to understand

---

[165] He uses this phrase three times: in the interview in *Palabra*, in *Le Figaro* and in *L'Osservatore della Domenica*(*Conversations*, nos. 19, 35 and 63).

[166] Other such expressions: "We give primary and fundamental importance to the *spontaneity of the individual*, to free and responsible initiative guided by the action of the Spirit, and not to organizational structures, commands and tactics imposed from above, from the seat of government" (no. 19). "Opus Dei's main activity consists in offering its members, and other people, the spiritual means they need to live as good Christians in the midst of the world" (no. 27). "This is the fundamental mission of the directors: to help its members know and practice the Christian faith so they can make it a reality in their lives, with full individual autonomy" (no. 53). "All the activity of Opus Dei's directors is based on a great respect for the member's professional freedom" (no. 27). "Opus Dei's aims are strictly spiritual. The only thing it asks of its members, be they socially influential or not, is that they strive to lead a fully Christian life. It never gives them instructions on how to carry out their work. It does not attempt to coordinate their activities; nor does it make use of the positions they may hold" (no. 49). "Each member acts with complete personal freedom. He forms his conscience autonomously. And he tries to seek holiness and to christianize his environment, by sanctifying his own work, whether it be intellectual or manual, in all the circumstances of his life and in his own home" (no. 35).

[167] *Conversations*, nos. 19 & 63.

[168] *Conversations*, no. 18.

[169] *Conversations*, no. 51.

the breadth of Opus Dei's activity, one cannot focus only on such educational or social service activities, no matter how outstanding, but on the Christian life of those making up these undertakings: "Opus Dei's most important apostolate is the testimony of the life and conversation of each individual member in his daily contacts with his friends and fellow workers." He deals analogously with the cooperation of many other people who without belonging to the Work receive in one way or another the benefit of its spirit.[170]

One gets the impression that throughout the book Msgr. Escrivá seeks to broaden the horizons of those interviewing him. He raises their attention from questions of a more limited perspective or conjectural difficulties to the overall pastoral phenomenon represented by Opus Dei. In those moments or in general throughout his explanations, the founder repeatedly evokes that a vast variety of men and women, priests and lay people, single and married, in keeping with Opus Dei's spirit, are striving to live the Christian faith in many different countries and situations. He seems to want to go beyond making known what Opus Dei is and thus to underline its reason for being, the purpose for which God inspired it on October 2, 1928.[171]

Msgr. Escrivá frequently reaffirms the universal call to holiness. But he also seems to prolong his reflections as if to show the depth and breadth of this message and its contribution to broadening the consciousness of contemporary Christianity. Like, for instance, the growing vision of the Church "as a community made up of all the faithful," where "all share in one and the same mission, which each should fulfill according to his personal circumstances."[172] This vision of the Church has great importance for understanding Opus Dei. Hence the Church is a community where no one is passive, where all are called, whoever and wherever they may be, to ratify her mission. "Therefore the Church is present wherever there is a Christian who strives to live in the name of Christ."[173] It is a community where the priest renounces any form of clericalism and finds his greatest glory in fostering among all Christians the consciousness of their personal vocation and dignity. It is where also the layman knows himself called to fulfill a task that tran-

---

[170] *Conversations*, no. 31. The same ideas can be found in other places, for example, nos. 41 & 84.

[171] "The aim of Opus Dei is that many people all over the world should come to know both in theory and in practice that it is possible to sanctify their ordinary task, their daily work" (*Conversations*, no. 84.). "Since the foundation of the Work in 1928, my teaching has been that sanctity is not reserved for a privileged few. All the ways of the earth, every state in life, every profession, every honest work can be divine" (*Conversations*, no. 26). Similar phrases are found in other interviews.

[172] *Conversations*, no. 59.

[173] *Conversations*, no. 112.

scends any assignments entrusted to him specifically by the hierarchy. In virtue of his own baptism, inserting him into Christ and his Church, he becomes a sharer in the redeemer's mission and life.[174]

Of similar importance is the stressed Christian value of the world where man lives and out of whose structures and tasks Christian life is woven, particularly that of the ordinary lay Christian. He is to see in all such realities and his presence in the world not merely a social fact but an essential ingredient of his Christian calling. This teaching often blossoms throughout *Conversations*, but it is most persuasively expressed in the homily with which the book concludes.

It was delivered at an open-air Mass on the campus of the University of Navarre, surrounded by trees and buildings, before a large crowd of the faithful. Referring to the setting Msgr. Escrivá says, "Surely this confirms in your minds, in a tangible and unforgettable way, the fact that everyday life is the true setting for your lives as Christians. Your ordinary contact with God takes place where your fellow men, your yearning, your work and your affections are. There you have your daily encounter with Christ. It is in the midst of the material things of the earth that you must sanctify yourselves, serving God and all mankind.

"I have taught this constantly using words from Holy Scripture. The world is not evil because it has come from God's hands, because it is his creation, because Yahweh looked upon it and saw that it was good (cf. Gen 1:7ff). We ourselves, mankind, make it evil and ugly with our sins and infidelities. Have no doubt: any kind of evasion from the honest realities of daily life is for you, men and women of the world, something opposed to the will of God.

"On the contrary, you must understand now more clearly that God is calling you to serve him *in and from* the ordinary, material and secular activities of human life. He waits for us every day, in the laboratory, in the operating room, in the army barracks, in the university chair, in the factory, in the workshop, in the fields, in the home and in all the immense panorama of work. Understand this well: there is something holy, something divine hidden in the most ordinary situations, and it is up to each one of you to discover it."[175]

Finally we must mention his teaching on the ministerial priesthood and its role in the Church and every apostolic work. Msgr. Escrivá recurs to a metaphor already mentioned, that of the "sacramental wall." Each member of Opus Dei—as every Christian is indeed called to do—"strives to be an apostle in his own environment, bringing people closer to Christ by his example and word, by dialogue. But in the apostolate, in bringing souls along the paths of

---

[174] See the lengthy paragraphs in *Conversations*, nos. 58-59 and 112.

[175] *Conversations*, nos. 113-114.

interior life, they come up against the 'sacramental wall'. The sanctifying role of the lay person is incomplete without the sanctifying
role of the priest, who administers the sacrament of penance, celebrates the Eucharist and proclaims the Word of God in the name
of the Church."[176]  Then he discusses the priesthood in general,[177]
the role of priest in the Opus Dei apostolates,[178] also specifically on
the provision allowing priests incardinated in dioceses to become
members of the Priestly Society of the Holy Cross.

"The circumstances of the ecclesiastical life that gave rise to my
concern and to this apostolate of the Work were not circumstances
of a more or less accidental or transitory character, but permanent
spiritual and human needs of a spiritual and human nature, intimately related to the life and work of diocesan priests.  I refer
fundamentally to their need of being helped to find personal holiness in the exercise of their own ministry with a spirit and means
which in no way modify their status as diocesan priests."  Opus Dei
seeks to help them through the Priestly Society of the Holy Cross.
Its spirit "has as an essential characteristic that it does not take
anyone out of his place, *unusquisque, in qua vocatione vocatus est, in
ea permaneat* (I Cor 7:20), rather it leads each person to fulfill the
tasks and duties of his own state, of his mission in the Church and
in society, with the greatest possible perfection.  Therefore when a
priest joins the Work he neither modifies nor abandons any part of
his diocesan vocation.  His dedication to the service of the local
Church in which he is incardinated, his full dependence on his own
ordinary, his secular spirituality, his solidarity with other priests,
etc. are not changed.  On the contrary he undertakes to live his
vocation to the full because he knows that he must seek holiness
precisely in the exercise of his obligations as a diocesan priest."[179]

These are some of the principal ideas in *Conversations*.  It goes
without saying that Msgr. Escrivá in the interviews he granted between 1966 and 1968 had in mind not only the institutional problem
of Opus Dei, but also many other desires related to the general life
of the Church and the development of the Work's apostolate.

The points touched on here in one way or another relate to our
main topic.  They also bear witness to how Opus Dei's founder,

---

[176] *Conversations*, no. 69.

[177] *Conversations*, nos. 3, 4, 5, 7, 8, 59. We also refer the reader to a homily, *Priest Forever*
given in 1973 and found among other writings of his in *Love for the Church*, New York
1989, pp. 37-51.

[178] *Conversations*, nos. 4, 6, 24, 69, 119.

[179] *Conversations*, no. 16; see also nos. 69 & 119; he deals with the question of the
freedom of the diocesan priest to seek spiritual help according to his condition in
various kinds of institutions (see also nos. 7-8).

while awaiting the moment to begin new discussions, sought to disseminate not only to ecclesiastical authorities and Opus Dei members but also to the general public the perspectives that explain and dictate the desired change of Opus Dei's canonical status.

Furthermore, obviously both the reaffirmation of the position taken as well as the theological explanations accompanying it represent data and facts that helped to enrich and accelerate the maturing of ideas that would make it possible later to obtain a new and definitive juridical solution. The steps leading to this were about to begin. In fact they began in 1969, opening a lengthy process that would finish in 1982-1983.

# Chapter IX

## *THE SPECIAL GENERAL CONGRESS*

1. Vatican Council II: new perspectives
2. Convocation of a Special General Congress (June 25, 1969)
3. The first part of the Special General Congress (1969)

    a) Objectives of the Congress and the beginning of its sessions

    b) The work of the first part of the Congress

    c) The closure of the sessions

    d) Informing the Holy See
4. Beginning of the second part of the Special General Congress (1970)

# Chapter IX

## *THE SPECIAL GENERAL CONGRESS*

### 1. Vatican Council II: new perspectives

The general climate of renewal in the Church that followed upon the announcement of a new Ecumenical Council was a factor that made it easier for Msgr. Escrivá to take new steps towards obtaining statutes for Opus Dei which would be better adapted to its nature. Strictly speaking the requests formulated by the founder were independent of the conciliar environment, since they did no more than express the original foundational charism. But without a new attitude taking shape little by little in ecclesiastical environments and particularly in the Vatican beginning in 1959 and above all after the Council's conclusion, and without some of the Conciliar decisions and teachings, the subsequent juridical history of Opus Dei would most likely not have occurred; or rather, it would have had to adapt itself to very different requirements.

Great progress in ecclesiological teaching can be seen in the Dogmatic Constitution *Lumen gentium*, specifically in the fact that this Conciliar constitution began with a chapter dedicated to the Church as mystery. Then too a decision was taken in October 1963 placing the chapter on the People of God *before* the chapter dedicated to the hierarchy.[1] On the one hand the Constitution states— the extension of ideas already enshrined in the encyclical of Pius XII *Mystici corporis*—that the Church is no mere society, nor only an institutional depository for salvific teaching and instruments, but a

---

[1] It is not our intention here or in what follows to enter into a lengthy exposition about the history of Conciliar teaching, but only to sketch the historical context affecting our topic. Furthermore the importance of the facts we refer to was pointed out by some of the first commentaries on *Lumen gentium*: for example, a series of articles included in the collective work under the leadership of G. Barauna, *La Iglesia del Vaticano II*, Barcelona 1966 (particularly the contributions of C. Moeller, B. Rigaux and O. Semmelroth), as well as the commentary of G. Philips, *L'Église et son mystère au IIe Concile du Vatican*, Tournai 1967-1968. Subsequent scholarly works have merely reaffirmed this evaluation, adding nuances not touching our subject.

mystery, a living reality, continuing God's communication to mankind.  On the other hand it also teaches that the Church is a pilgrim community, a people pressing forward through history as a universal sacrament of salvation, endowed with a mission and called to communicate to the world the life that sustains and enlivens it.

The relation between vocation and mission, between communion with God and mission to the world, are obvious.  The traditional view that the mission had been entrusted by Jesus Christ to the ecclesiastical hierarchy who then delegate a share in the same to the laity was radically overcome.  Rather this mission is communicated directly by Christ to the whole body of the Church structured as a diversity of tasks or functions complementing each other.  The active role, the radical dignity, the vocation of the faithful Christian, that of every *christifidelis*,[2] were not only presupposed and affirmed but taken up as the inspiring criteria of every reflection on the life and activity of the Church.  As the Decree *Apostolicam actuositatem* summarizes: "There is diversity of ministry, but unity of mission."[3]

Closely deriving from this ecclesiological foundation is another major contribution of *Lumen gentium*: the proclamation in chapter five of the universal call to holiness.  Holiness, the perfection of charity, the fullness of Christian life, is not reserved to any state or condition of life, but open to all Christians.  Raised by baptism to the condition of children of God, the baptized have received the gift of the Holy Spirit and are called to follow and imitate Christ.  All are to pursue holiness, each in his own proper state and condition in life, taking occasion of every condition of life with the tasks and circumstances comprising it.  "All Christians, in the conditions, duties and circumstances of their life and through all these, will sanctify themselves more and more if they receive all things with faith from the hand of the heavenly Father and cooperate with the divine will, thus showing forth in that temporal service the love with which God has loved the world."[4]

---

[2] On the importance of the concept of Christian faithful or *christifidelis*, see the classic work of A. del Portillo, *Faithful and Laity in the Church*, Dublin 1972, (expanded edition, Pamplona 1981).  A historical study having in mind the Conciliar documents will be found in F. Retamal, *La igualdad fundamental de los fieles en la Iglesia según la Constitución dogmática "Lumen gentium". Estudio de las fuentes*, Santiago, Chile 1980.

[3] Vatican Council II, Decree *Apostolicam actuositatem*, no. 2.

[4] Vatican Council II, *Lumen gentium*, no. 41.  A first study of this chapter of *Lumen gentium* making use of the *Acta Concilii*, even though sparingly, is that of L. Ravetti, *La santità nella "Lumen gentium,"* Rome 1980.  The works cited in previous notes offer interesting data from a different perspective but for an interesting analysis of the history of chapter 5 of *Lumen gentium* see M. J. Schoenmaeckers, *Genese du chapitre VI "De Religiosis" de la constitution dogmatique sur l'Èglise "Lumen Gentium"*, Rome 1983.

The importance of these Conciliar declarations as well as the change they represent with respect to the previous theological mentality are obvious. In one of the first commentaries on this theme published by professors of the Pontifical University Theresianum, mention is made of the "renewed discovery of the universal vocation to holiness," of "a new consciousness," of "a new theological and pastoral evaluation" on the reality of this call.[5] Philips writes, "The novelty of the declaration cannot be overlooked by anyone. . . . We can even predict without fear of mistake that the insistence of the Council on proclaiming the universal call to holiness as the years pass will attract more and more attention. . . . Certainly on this topic the fathers [of the council] did not invent something unheard-of. If this truth has appeared in the light of day in our time, it is a sign that it was, at least, hidden in the substratum of the life of the Church in earlier centuries. But this is a far cry from saying that past theologians had developed it clearly and openly."[6]

Many more quotations could be given. We only wish to point out that for Msgr. Escrivá the Conciliar doctrine was joy indeed. The universal call to holiness—the authentic core of his preaching from the dawn of Opus Dei owing to which some had considered him naive and even a madman, suspected of heresy—had not only been rediscovered but had been solemnly sanctioned by the ecumenical council. How should he fail to break out in joy and thanksgiving to God? In private conversations or public statements, in meditations or homilies, he voiced these sentiments. In an interview of May 1966, dwelling on basic characteristics of the action proper to the laity, the ordinary Christian, he comments: "The important thing is not so much the dimension that I have given to these ideas, especially since 1928, but that which the Magisterium of the Church has given them. Not long ago the Council aroused, in the poor priest that I am, an emotion which is impossible to describe. For it reminded all Christians, in the Dogmatic Constitution on the Church, that they must feel their full citizenship in the earthly city—by taking part in all human undertakings with professional competence and with love for all men, by seeking that holiness to which they are called by the simple fact of their baptism."[7]

---

[5] Various authors, La santità nella costituzione conciliare sulla Chiesa, Rome 1966, p. 141.

[6] G. Philips, op. cit. (note 1 of this chapter) vol. 2, p. 98.

[7] Conversations, no. 47. From our current perspective we should point out the founder's response to these Conciliar declarations and the vistas opened to his subsequent action. It is only just to point out the decisive contribution his teaching and activity made to these declarations. Clearly Msgr. Escrivá was a forerunner of the Second Vatican Council, particularly in what has to do with proclaiming the universal call to holiness and affirming the mission of the laity. This has been recognized by various

A few years after the Council, Pope Paul VI made reference to the proclamation of the call of all Christians to holiness, to emphasize that anyone examining the totality of the work of the Council will see this as a "most special objective of the teaching of the Council and its ultimate purpose."[8] John Paul II expressed it in even stronger terms: "The tension towards sanctity is the central point of the renewal undertaken by the Second Vatican Council."[9] To proclaim the universal call to holiness forcefully points to the indispensable role every Christian plays in the life of the Church and consequently gives rise to pastoral initiatives and enriched ideas bound to have profound repercussions. In overcoming old theological positions not only was the way opened to the possibility of a clear affirmation of the original charism and message of Opus Dei, but also a process was set in motion of revising canonical schemes that would end up opening a channel for what Opus Dei sought.

Another of the underlying veins of the Council's thought led to revising juridical categories and, above all, a certain canonical mindset. The impact is most often called "pastoral." This stems from the ecclesiological perspective opened by emphasizing the concept of People of God. The Church viewed from this point of view manifests itself as a pilgrim community, a community of people treading through history, sent forth by Christ to announce to all nations and civilizations the salvation that in Christ has been communicated to all mankind. The pilgrim condition, this openness to the world, this pastoral dimension, are aspects illuminating one another, while emphasizing the need for "pastoral structures to be dynamic as well as functional."[10] These structures cannot be conceived *a priori*. Stemming from Christ's foundational will and the basic structure

---

key figures of the Second Vatican Council. For example see the declarations of Cardinal F. König, "Il significato dell'Opus Dei," in *Il Corriere della Sera*, Milan 9/9/1975; Cardinal P. Parente, "Le radici della spiritualità del fondatore dell'Opus Dei," in *L'Osservatore Romano*, 6/24/1979; Cardinal S. Baggio, "Opus Dei: una svolta nella spiritualità," in *Avvenire*, Milan 7/26/1975; Cardinal J. Rosales, "Msgr. Escrivá: Profile of a Saint," in *Philippines Evening Express*, Manila, 6/26/1976; Cardinal M. González Martín, "Cuál sería su secreto?," in *ABC*, Madrid, 8/24/1975; Cardinal A. Rossi, "Mensagem universal de Mons. Escrivá," in *O Estado de São Paolo*, São Paolo, 6/27/ 1976 and 7/4/1976; Cardinal A. Luciani, later John Paul I, "Cercando Dio nel Lavoro Quotidiano," in *Il Gazzettino*, Venice, 7/25/1978; and John Paul II, Homily given on 8/ 19/1979 and found in *L'Osservatore Romano*, 8/20-21/1979. See also A. del Portillo, "Mons. Escrivá de Balaguer, testigo del amor a la Iglesia. Una de las figuras precursoras del Concilio Vaticano II," in *Palabra*, 130 (1976):205-210.

[8] Paul VI, Motu proprio *Sanctitas clarior*, 3/9/1969, *AAS* 61 (1969):149-150.

[9] John Paul II, Angelus address, 3/29/1987, in *L'Osservatore Romano*, 3/30-31/1987.

[10] We take this expression from A. del Portillo, "Dinamicità e funzionalità delle strutture pastorali," in Various authors, *La collegialità episcopale per il futuro della Chiesa*, Florence 1969, pp. 161ff.

he established for the Church, structures must be adapted and accommodated to the times, to each historical moment, if Christian life is to be effectively spread. The organization of the Church should correspond to the demands made on its mission by successive generations throughout the history of mankind.

Whence one may doubt the sufficiency of the principle of territoriality, as the sole criteria determining the jurisdictional structures of the Church. Appeal is rightly made to an inventive capacity, to creative enterprise and more radically to the need to listen to what the Spirit is promoting in the Church. The Council did not limit itself generically to proclaiming the principles of this doctrine, nor to expressing its hopes that in post-conciliar times many concrete initiatives might arise, but it started applying it in many concrete aspects. One of these is the possibility—even suggestion or recommendation—of establishing "special dioceses or personal prelatures," when serving "special pastoral needs" recommends this, as was set forth in no. 10 of the Decree *Presbyterorum ordinis*, of December 7, 1965.[11]

---

[11] The figure that will take shape in the Decree *Presbyterorum Ordinis*, no. 10 with the name of personal prelature appeared in the work of the Council for the first time within the project *De distributione cleri*, prepared by the preparatory Commission *De disciplina cleri et populi christiani* in January 1961 (cf. *Acta et documenta Concilio Oecumenico Vaticano II apparando*, series II, vol. I, pars I, Typis Pol. Vat. 1965, pp. 563-565; see particularly no. IV, p. 564.) The solutions proposed in this project consisted in making more flexible a figure already present in the hierarchical organization of the Church, the prelature called *nullius* (cf. CIC 1917, cc. 319-327) adapting it so that, with or without its own territory, it be harmonically inserted into the pastoral life of the Church, in order to carry out special tasks. This was, then and later, the point of reference—there was no other—which was had in mind always when in the documents of that time the word *prelature* is used. (With regard to this and also the *Mission de France* in so far as it was considered in the project of the preparatory Commission of the Council, see P. Lombardía - J. Hervada, "Sobre prelaturas personales," in *Ius Canonicum*, 27 (1987):11-76.

The proposal included in the 1961 draft to which we have referred went through various stages of the Council, being successively modified and sketched out (with regard to the Conciliar evolution of the personal prelature, see J. Martínez-Torrón, *La configuración jurídica de la Prelaturas personales en el Concilio Vaticano II*, Pamplona 1986).

Number 10 of the Decree *Presbyterorum ordinis* says: "Where the nature of the apostolate demands this, not only the proper distribution of priests should be made easier but also the carrying out of special pastoral projects for the benefit of different social groups in any region or among any race in any part of the world. For this purpose there can with advantages be set up some international seminaries, special dioceses, or personal prelatures and other institutions to which, by methods to be decided for the individual undertaking and always without prejudice of the rights of the local ordinaries, priests can be attached or incardinated for the common good of the whole Church."

Less than a year after the end of the Council, on August 6, 1966, Paul VI promulgated the Motu proprio *Ecclesiæ sanctæ* to put into effect the Conciliar decrees. The first part of this document is dedicated to the provisions contained in the Decrees *Christus dominus* and *Presbyterorum ordinis*. Number 4 of the first part deals with personal prelatures specifying their purpose as "the carrying out of special pastoral or missionary tasks;" they are to be erected by the Holy See after obtaining the opinion of the episcopal conferences involved; it deals with the secular character and the specialized formation of their clergy; the government of a personal prelature is attributed to its own prelate; the possibility that some lay people may be dedicated to the service of these tasks and initiatives; relations with local ordinaries and episcopal conferences are to be governed by their proper statutes.[12]

A year later on August 15, 1967, Paul VI promulgated the Apostolic Constitution *Regimini Ecclesiæ universæ*, by which the Roman Curia was reorganized. Referring to the area of competence of the Congregation for Bishops it established, in no. 49, § 1, that it will have competence "in those things that have to do with the establishment of new dioceses, ecclesiastical provinces and regions . . . as well as the erection of military vicariates, and, having heard the episcopal conferences of the respective territory, of personal prelatures for the carrying out of special pastoral tasks on behalf of regions or

---

[12] The complete text of no. 4 reads as follows: "Furthermore, in order to accomplish special pastoral or missionary tasks for various regions or social groups requiring special assistance, prelatures may usefully be established by the Apostolic See. These would consist of priests of the secular clergy specially trained and under the rule of a prelate of their own and governed by statutes of their own.

"It would be the duty of such a prelate to erect and govern a seminary for the suitable training of students. He would have the right to incardinate such students under the title of service to the prelature and to promote them to Orders.

"The prelate should show care for the spiritual life of those he promoted under the title mentioned above and for the continuance of their special formation and their particular ministry by making arrangements with the local ordinaries to whom they are sent. He should also make provision for suitable means of living either by such agreements as are mentioned above or out of the resources of the prelature or by appropriate subsidies. He should also make provision for those who through illness or other reasons are obliged to relinquish their post.

"There is no reason why laymen, whether celibate or married, should not dedicate their professional service, through contracts with the prelature, to its works and enterprises.

"Such prelatures shall not be erected without first hearing the views of the episcopal conferences of the territory in which they will serve. In the exercise of their function care is to be shown that the rights of the local ordinaries are not infringed and that close relations are kept with the episcopal conferences at all times"   (Motu proprio *Ecclesiæ sanctæ*, I, no. 4, in *AAS* 58 (1966):760-761).

social groups in need of special help; it also deals with those things having to do with the appointment of bishops, apostolic administrators, coadjutor and auxiliary bishops, military vicars and vicars or prelates who enjoy personal jurisdiction."[13]

## 2. Convocation of a Special General Congress (June 25, 1969)

Msgr. Escrivá, as any person solicitous for the Church—and even more living in Rome—followed closely the work of the Council. He prayed for its effective development, empathizing with the problems presented to it, sharing its desires, uncertainties and hopes no less than its moments of anxiety throughout its four-year duration. He was particularly interested in those questions in some way related to the apostolate of Opus Dei, and, particularly, those relevant to its definitive juridical solution, ever one of his most heartfelt concerns.

He rejoiced with the proclamation of the universal call to holiness in the Dogmatic Constitution *Lumen gentium*. He also welcomed the Decree *Presbyterorum ordinis*, promulgated on December 7, 1965, both because of its general teaching and also its mention of personal prelatures. A few months later, on March 27, 1966, he commented colloquially with some members of Opus Dei: "How eager I am that *we eat our tail* as fish do;" that is, that the juridical process be brought to an end, reaching a solution radically tied to the original inspiration. He added: "God is listening to us: so many thousands of Masses and sufferings of all kinds offered for this intention! But it may still take another eighteen years or as long as God wants. . . ."[14]

It did not take long to reach the first milestone after which one could consider travelling the passage opened by the Council. We refer to the already mentioned Motu proprio *Ecclesiæ sanctæ*, where the juridical figure of the personal prelature is outlined with greater precision and detail than in the Conciliar Decree *Presbyterorum ordinis*. Two months later, on October 24, 1966, the founder spoke to a group of his closest collaborators of this Motu proprio: "I have to tell you that, for the present, the solution to the juridical path has already been found." Nevertheless, "It will be good to wait a little while and to continue praying as though nothing had happened."[15]

These two remarks, separated as they were by several months, show how two emotions contended in the soul of Msgr. Escrivá. On the one hand, joy at the opening of a juridical channel that could

---

[13] AAS 59 (1967):901.

[14] RHF 20171, pp. 1390-1392.

[15] *Ibid.*, p. 1392.

adjust itself to the needs of Opus Dei, a channel substantially identical to what he had requested of the Holy See in 1962; on the other, the appropriateness, confirmed by the experience gained in presenting this petition, of weighing the times and means attentively before taking another step.

Opus Dei's founder, who had defended the distinctiveness of secular institutes with respect to religious institutes and had declared that Opus Dei in fact was not a secular institute, did not at the beginning have recourse to the norms established by the Motu proprio *Ecclesiæ sanctæ*, for the implementation of the Decree *Perfectæ caritatis* of the Second Vatican Council. This council decree, dedicated to the religious life, had established several criteria renewing the life, norms and activity of religious institutes. It stipulated that "the spirit and aims of each founder should be faithfully accepted and retained, as indeed should each institute's sound traditions, for all of these constitute the patrimony of an institute."[16] On the basis of these orientations, the Motu proprio *Ecclesiæ sanctæ* recommended that religious institutes undertake the necessary process of renewal and adaptation "so that the fruits of the Council come to maturity [in them]".[17] It grants a primordial role to the institutes themselves, by means of their general chapters or assemblies, and allows them to conduct experiments, even contrary to the common law.[18] The Motu proprio itself speaks only of religious institutes. Nevertheless, some secular institutes, since they had been contemplated in the decree *Perfectæ caritatis*—"even though they are not religious institutes"[19]—invoked the principle of *favorabilia amplianda* ['favors are to be extended']. Some institutes launched gatherings and assemblies as those prescribed in the Motu proprio of Paul VI.

Msgr. Escrivá fostered ongoing studies, for which there was considerable documentation of great value born of various ordinary general congresses and regional assemblies or study weeks within Opus Dei. After various study weeks celebrated in 1968 wherever Opus Dei was at work, the founder thought that perhaps the time was ripe to ask for the application of the norms of the Motu proprio *Ecclesiæ sanctæ*. The studies underway could probably continue more effectively in this way. He was conscious of the transcendence of this step in the juridical evolution of the Work; thus he recurred as always to supernatural means, asking Opus Dei members to increase their prayer for this special intention of his. For

---

[16] Vatican Council II, Decree *Perfectæ caritatis*, no. 2.

[17] Paul VI, Motu proprio *Ecclesiæ sanctæ*, II, Introduction.

[18] *Ibid.*, II, 6.

[19] Decree *Perfectæ caritatis*, no. 11.

himself he undertook a Marian pilgrimage, visiting six shrines of the Blessed Virgin and entrusting to her his desires and resolutions. From April 22 to May 8 he betook himself to the shrines of Lourdes (France); Sonsoles, Pillar and Mercy (Spain); Einsiedeln (Switzerland) and Loreto (Italy), invocations of the Virgin related in one way or another to the history of Opus Dei. On his return to Rome he decided to gather together representatives of Opus Dei from all countries in an extraordinary and Special General Congress.

Even though the Motu proprio *Ecclesiæ sanctæ* did not require any previous authorization, Msgr. Escrivá turned to the Holy See for permission for a general congress to study the revision of its particular law in accord with the principles followed since its foundation and with its 40 years of experience. On May 20, 1969, he presented this request to the appropriate office of the Roman Curia. After noting that the Motu proprio *Ecclesiæ sanctæ* was not binding on Opus Dei because it is not a religious institute, the founder added: "On the other hand, as is well known, Opus Dei was approved on February 24, 1947 as a secular institute, and in order to achieve this it was necessary to do violence to its primitive spirit so that it might fit under the Apostolic Constitution *Provida Mater Ecclesia* which in the norms of its *lex peculiaris* did not manage to accommodate all the fundamental requirements of the spirit of our Work." Thus he pointed out once again what he had been saying by mouth and pen for some time.

He invoked the principle given in no. 2 of the Decree *Perfectæ caritatis*, "it is for the good of the Church that institutes have their own proper characters and functions;" he expressed his desire "to proceed now to the renewal and adaptation of our present particular law." He continues: "Thus even though we are not religious, we wish to follow, *congrua congruis referendo*, the procedures indicated in the aforementioned Motu proprio *Ecclesiæ sanctæ*." He requests that the period of time for the revision be computed beginning with the date of this letter.[20]

By letter of June 11, 1969, the Sacred Congregation granted the request;[21] on June 25 the founder officially convoked the Congress, to begin on September 1, 1969.[22]

---

[20] The complete text of the letter is in the Appendix, document no. 50.

[21] The reply of the Sacred Congregation is found in the Appendix, document no. 52.

[22] The day when Msgr. Escrivá convoked the Congress was the silver anniversary of the priestly ordination of the first members of Opus Dei. On this occasion Paul VI sent to the founder an affectionate telegram of congratulations. Cf. A. Vázquez de Prada, op. cit., chapter 1, note 1, p. 368.

## 3. The first part of the Special General Congress (1969)

a) *Objectives of the Congress and the beginning of its sessions*

What specific results did the founder hope to obtain from this General Congress? He obviously did not conceive it as a gathering of specialists, to carry out a detailed study of a particular canonical figure. Faithful to his conviction that life precedes juridical norms and that the latter should fully adjust themselves to the former, Msgr. Escrivá understood the Congress as a profound reflection made by everyone in Opus Dei. In close union with the founder, they would look at its essence and characteristics in the light of its 41 years of existence and its expansion to so many countries of the five continents. It was a question of synthesizing, showing how the founder's teaching had been incarnated in different places and times. The Congress had to sketch with a firm hand the proper traits of Opus Dei that needed to find in the future juridical configuration an appropriate category. At the same time it would point out other elements foreign or contrary to its nature but which had been accepted in previous stages because of the requirements of the legislation then in force, so that they might be eliminated.

All of this would influence the development of the Congress, which would end by approving orientations and fundamental criteria and entrusting to a technical commission the study of its conclusions for execution at the appropriate time. But now let us say the stated objective began to have repercussions as soon as the Congress was announced.

In communicating the convocation of the Congress Msgr. Escrivá did not merely request the members to pray for its success. He invited all who were desirous of sending communications or suggestions to do so. During the summer of 1969 many such suggestions were added to the working material already collected with the occasion of earlier studies and various regional assemblies held in 1968.

Since it was a Special and extraordinary General Congress, the founder expressly desired that representatives of the different regions, chosen from among the younger members, should be given both voice and vote. Thus the assembly was made more representative, not only with regard to countries but also to different generations. At the first session of the General Congress 192 members participated, representing more the than 50,000 people of every class, race and condition belonging at the time to Opus Dei.

Of these, 87 belonged to the men's branch and 105 to the women's. According to the general norms on such meetings, the two branches held their meetings in separate locales in Rome. Unity was fostered by the founder and President General, the Secretary General Fr.

Alvaro del Portillo, the Procurator General Fr. Daniel Cummings, plus the central Priest Secretary, Fr. Francisco Vives.[23]

The Congress opened on September 1, 1969. Msgr. Escrivá explained the reasons for which he had called the Special General Congress, as recorded in the acts of the first session: "This Special Congress of the Work has been called in order to reaffirm, first of all, the desire of living according to our genuine spirit the dedication to God of all the members—their personal sanctity—by means of the loving fulfillment of our norms and customs, which leads us to a life of continual prayer and the exercise of apostolate, each one within his or her own state and profession or occupation in the world, in the service of the Church, the Roman Pontiff, and for the good of all souls. Therefore, during this time, we will always bear in mind that the only thing that truly matters is the personal sanctity of all the members." Msgr. Escrivá concluded: "As a logical consequence of these fundamental demands of the spirit of Opus Dei, we will proceed to the revision of our particular law, in those places in which there was no other alternative but to accept provisionally certain concepts or terms proper to the law of the so-called state of perfection or the religious state."[24]

Early on the next day Fr. Alvaro del Portillo presented a preliminary motion directed to affirming that, in the lifetime of the founder, the task of revising the statutory norms pertained to him. "First of all the Father was granted by the Holy See the faculty of proposing to the Holy See any and all changes in our particular law he deemed opportune. This faculty was *ad vitam* (rescript of the S.C.R. prot. no. I.S. 1/47—August 2, 1950); and secondly both the Conciliar Decree *Perfectæ caritatis*, no. 2b, as well as the Motu proprio *Ecclesiæ sanctæ*, II, art. 12 & 13, establish that the revision of constitutions be done with the maximum fidelity to the ends and spirit given by the founder and to legitimate traditions. Since our founder continues to live, thanks be to God, he can make the whole revision of our *ius peculiare* without counting on us; he is the judge of whether or not the traditions of these 41 years of Opus Dei are legitimate or not.

"If the Father wants to call this Special General Congress we will collaborate in all joy and effort with the idea that the Father

---

[23] This brought about not only a fundamental harmony but also through the secretariats a coordination of work and a sharing of texts and documents.

[24] *Atti del Congresso Generale Speciale, Sezione maschile*, I, Sept. 1, 1969 (AGP, Sezione Giuridica, VII/15256). Hereinafter we will use ACGS-m, for the men's branch and ACGS-f for the women's branch, followed by the Roman numerals I or II, according to whether it is the first or second part of the Congress, followed by the date of the session. In the inaugural session of the meetings of the women's branch which took place on September 4, 1969, he spoke in similar terms (ACGS-f, I, Sept. 4, 1969).

will freely accept or reject what seems appropriate from among what we propose."

Those gathered agreed with the motion. Nevertheless, Msgr. Escrivá intervened to say that, although he was sincerely grateful for the filial significance of this motion, he could not accept it. The acts read: "He affirms that he does not want to accept it because, according to the spirit always lived in Opus Dei, even now he wants each of the participants in the Congress to study the various matters in depth. Each one is to feel personally responsible and to vote on the proposals with the most absolute freedom; thus the collegiality of our government will be shown in every moment."[25]

b) *The work of the first part of the Congress*

How did the work proceed? First of all there were two secretaries: for the men, Dr. Stephen Reynolds; for the women, Dr. Marie Valdeavellano. The Congress members were divided into eight commissions, four for each branch to study and evaluate the ascetical and apostolic experiences of the past 41 years and to review its law according to its foundational charism and with its historical projection as a pastoral phenomenon.[26] As the need arose, the commissions were subdivided into 29 subcommissions whose task was to fix topics and elaborate proposals, which were then presented in plenary session. There, after an explanation made by a relator, they were commented and voted on. Proposals totalling 177 were presented and voted on, 93 in meetings of the men's branch and 84 in the women's branch.

These proposals dealt with the more relevant aspects of the spirit and apostolic praxis of Opus Dei. They represent very valuable source material. Nevertheless, the nature of the Congress and its finality made advisable a new consultation via assemblies or study weeks in the various regions. From this the identification of the whole of Opus Dei with the renewal of the juridical norms would be even more patent. Thus the second part of the Congress would be called after these gatherings. For this reason, and to avoid repetitions, we will postpone our analysis of the proposals approved in the Congress' first part until after we have covered the plenary sessions of the second part. Thus we will make a global study of everything concluded in both parts of the Special General Congress.

Let us now refer, however to one proposal approved on Sept. 13, 1969, whose purpose was to evaluate the first part of the Con-

---

[25] ACGS-m, I, Sept. 2, 1969. A similar dialogue took place in the meeting of the women's branch (ACGS-f, I, Sept. 5, 1969).

[26] The four commissions of the men's branch were presided over by: Dr. Daniel Cummings, Dr. Rolf Thomas, Dr. Giuseppe Molteni and Dr. Umberto Farri (ACGS-m, I, Sept. 4, 1969); those of the women's branch were led by: Dr. Marlies Kücking, Dr. Silvia Bianchi, Dr. Marguerite Perret and Dr. Olga Marlin (ACGS-f, I, Sept. 7, 1969).

gress. It says the preparation of this Special General Congress could be said to have begun many years before, "in 1950, when our Father, with the effective help of Fr. Alvaro del Portillo, began to prepare a series of documents, some of which were opportunely transmitted to the Holy See. Their purpose was to obtain the most perfect accommodation between the law and the reality of our spirit and life as undoubtedly God wants it" in order to reach "a definitive juridical form within the common law of the Church and without privileges. These long years of work, prayer and sacrifice of our Father, plus those of Don Alvaro, have made easy and secure our task in the first part of this Special General Congress."

Congress members also evoked the motion initially presented by Fr. Alvaro del Portillo to reiterate their conviction of working not only in union with Msgr. Escrivá, but precisely at his express will in matters where he as founder had the definitive word. Nevertheless, they continued, "as recorded in the records of this first session, our founder—in keeping with our spirit of freedom and personal responsibility—has wanted to associate us to the mission God has entrusted to him, for the tasks of this Special General Congress. Fully conscious of our limitations, we have accepted in a filial spirit our Father's will, grateful for this new proof of confidence in us, while we have conscientiously tried to carry out our work. Each one of us assumes full responsibility for whatever he has said, written, signed or voted on in these days, and we bear witness to the full freedom with which we have proceeded." The unanimous motion concludes that, in any case, Msgr. Escrivá, as founder, has the right to approve whatever relates to "the spirit God has given to him to transmit to us."[27]

c) *The closure of the sessions*

On September 15, 1969, for the men's branch and the following day for the women's, the closing session of the first part of the Congress took place.

On the first day Msgr. Escrivá exhorted those present once again to "give thanks with all their hearts to the Most Holy Trinity, Father, Son and Holy Spirit, for the abundant graces granted to the Congress in which undoubtedly we have counted on the powerful intercession of the most holy Virgin, Daughter of God the Father, Mother of God the Son, Spouse of God the Holy Spirit, and queen and protectress of Opus Dei." While serious work had been achieved, he spoke of the second part, "which with God's help will be the more effective part of the whole Congress. With the material already elaborated and with the documentation awaited from all the regions during the next year, it will be possible to prepare the nec-

---

[27] ACGS-m, I, Sept. 13, 1969.

essary studies to assure the full fruits we expect from the concluding stage of the Congress. This second part will take place in the
most opportune place. . . . Meanwhile—he concluded—be serene,
trust in the Lord, certain that the infinite goodness of God, who is
our Father, will make things turn out sooner, more and better than
we think or want."[28]

The proceedings state "the decision of the Father that within a
year, in September 1970, there be celebrated the second part of this
Special General Congress." To prepare the work for the second
session, the Congress mandated "that extraordinary assemblies or
study weeks be celebrated in all the regions, and that within five
months from today the conclusion of these assemblies and the communications that all the members have made for this purpose be
sent to the General Council."[29]

Following a eucharistic act, the first session was closed. A telegram from Pope Paul VI to Msgr. Escrivá and all the participants
was also read, in which he conveyed to Opus Dei and all its members his affectionate Apostolic Blessing.

d) *Informing the Holy See*

On September 18, Fr. Alvaro del Portillo, at the founder's request, informed the Congregation for Religious and Secular Institutes of the progress of the Special General Congress and plans for
a second part.[30] On October 7 receipt of this information was acknowledged by Fr. Edward Heston, Secretary of the Congregation,
who also said the office was awaiting the modifications which as a
consequence of the Congress might be made in the particular law of
Opus Dei.[31]

On October 22 Msgr. Escrivá sent a long detailed letter to Cardinal Ildebrando Antoniutti, Prefect of the Sacred Congregation for
Religious. Let us cite some of its paragraphs, since the document
expresses precisely the mind of Opus Dei's founder and the objectives being pursued in the Special General Congress.[32]

"Even though in the phase preceding the beginning of the extraordinary Congress careful studies had been prepared following
on consultations with members, the Congress, nevertheless, limited
itself to developing general criteria to serve as the basis for a new
general consultation, in readiness for a second part of the Congress

---

[28] ACGS-m, I, Sept. 15, 1969.

[29] ACGS-m, I, Sept. 15, 1969. A similar text was approved by the women's branch in the
closing session of Sept. 16 (ACGS-f, I, Sept. 16, 1969).

[30] The letter of Fr. del Portillo to the Congregation for Religious and Secular Institutes
is found in the Appendix, document no. 52.

[31] This can be found in the Appendix, document no. 53.

[32] The complete text of this letter is included in the Appendix, document no. 54.

and thus would be better able to fulfill what is established in the Motu proprio *Ecclesiæ sanctæ*, no. 4, of the first part."[33]

These consultations were underway in preparation for the second part of the Congress. Suffice it to say now, in synthesis, that the Congress, during its first part, had reiterated that the figure of secular institute was inadequate to the reality of Opus Dei. Therefore a new canonical structure was needed, independent of the framework of the institutes of perfection. The changes to be made in the statutes of Opus Dei would consequently be profound, as the letter points out: "Some of the eventual modifications . . . could be introduced by the General Congess itself, others would require the Holy See's approval, and still others, finally, insofar as they imply a change in the nature of the institute, would require an even more solemn act of the Holy See, that is, a new erection of the institute. . . . All of this will be presented at the appropriate time to the judgment of the Sacred Congregation."

The path towards the second part of the Congress had been sketched out and its work delineated.

## 4. Beginning of the second part of the Special General Congress (1970)

a) *Preparation and beginning of the sessions*

In one way or another all the members of Opus Dei  participated. In regional assemblies or study weeks—held between September 16, 1969 and February 16, 1970—members were informed of what had transpired in the first part of the Congress, and the second part was prepared with the broadest participation possible. During these five months more than 50,710 people intervened—26,974 men and 23,736 women of 77 nationalities. Besides personally taking part in the assemblies, 54,781 written communications were generated: 25,815 from the men and 28,966 from the women.

The proposals and conclusions of these regional assemblies were forwarded to the central headquarters of Opus Dei within the time established. In Rome they were ordered and classified with a view to the second session.

While the assemblies were being carried out, Msgr. Escrivá prayed and asked for prayers. On Christmas Eve of 1969 he asked his children: "Pray a lot, well united to one another by fraternal char-

---

[33] The Motu proprio *Ecclesiæ sanctæ*, section II, "Norms for the execution of the Decree of the Second Vatican Council *Perfectæ caritatis*," establishes in norm 4 of its first part, the appropriateness of a "broad and free consultation of the members," of the institutions in question, in order to help to channel the work of the general assemblies convoked for the purpose of renewing the spiritual and apostolic spirit of the institutions and reforming the law in accordance with the teachings of the Second Vatican Council.

ity; pray besides for the Father's intention, what the Father asks for at Mass, what he is constantly beseeching of the Lord. . . . I ask Him for so many things that are necessary for the Church and the Work; I ask that He remove certain obstacles we were obliged to accept when we came to Rome."[34]

He visited several more Marian shrines. After Easter 1970, he left Rome for a pilgrimage to our Lady of the Pillar and to the Torreciudad shrine in Spain, and to Fatima in Portugal. On April 20 he was once again in Rome, but only for a few days. He decided to widen the scope of his pilgrimages by visiting our Lady of Guadelupe in Mexico. On May 14 he thus set out on his first trip beyond Europe.

At three o'clock in the morning, the next day he reached Mexico City. There, in the basilica before the image of our Lady of Guadelupe, the founder prayed for nine days—from the 16th to the 24th of May—asking for the Church and for the definitive juridical solution of Opus Dei. These were moments of intense prayer that stirred those who accompanied him. Particularly, on the fifth day of the novena Msgr. Escrivá prayed aloud to the Mother of God, opening his heart and glossing some words from the hymn *Ave Maris Stella*. Throughout his life he had used one of its phrases as an aspiration: *Monstra te esse matrem!* Now he redoubled his abandonment in the Virgin's hands.[35] His stay in Mexico lasted 40 days during which he spoke in large or small groups with more than 20,000 people. It was all quite catechetical; to people of all backgrounds he spoke of faith, of sanctifying ordinary life, of dealing with God in the middle of the world, things proper to the spirit of Opus Dei.[36]

By August 30, the day the Special General Congress was scheduled to reconvene, Msgr. Escrivá was back in Rome. He opened the second session with these words: "At the beginning of our work— a prolongation of what was done last year in the first part of the Congress and of the work carried out in this year in the special assemblies or study weeks in each region—I wish, my children, to reaffirm what has been, is, and will always be our only desire, the only purpose that moves Opus Dei and each of its members: we want to serve the Church as the Church wants and needs to be served, with full faithfulness to the Gospel and loyalty to the See of Peter, within the specific vocation God has given us.

---

[34] RHF, 20171, p. 1400.

[35] RHF, 20166, pp. 788ff.

[36] The gatherings took place not only in the capital of Mexico, but also at a conference center in the state of Morelos called Montefalco and in Guadalajara at the conference center of Jaltepec. See also information contained in A. Vázquez de Prada, *op. cit.* (chapter I, note 1), pp. 369-373.

"Our whole life is a service with supernatural objectives: to teach souls, all men—without any distinction—to find God and to learn how to become intimate with him and to love and follow him in the middle of the ordinary circumstances of life." He ended by reaffirming the fundamental aim of the Congress: "[This Congress] arises out of the firm desire and resolution all of us have to live and work—to serve, my children!—in perfect agreement with the spirit that God has wanted . . . so that what has been from the beginning the spirituality, life and apostolic mode of the Work may find an adequate and definitive juridical configuration in the law of the Church."[37]

The founder also expressed his gratitude to the regional representatives and to all Opus Dei members for showing once more in the regional assemblies their love for and exemplary fidelity to the spirit and traditions of Opus Dei and for their clear awareness of the need to revise its particular law in those points that hindered the work of Opus Dei in serving the Church and souls.[38]

b) *Development of the plenary sessions of the second part of the Congress*

The plenary sessions of the second part were organized the same way as in the first part. Again Dr. Stephen Reynolds and Dr. Marie Valdeavellano served as secretaries; the work was also done in commissions: three for the men's branch and four for the women's.[39]

On September 10 the younger representatives presented a communication expressing their satisfaction at participating and their desire that note be taken of some of their sentiments. They wished "to affirm our resolution of transmitting integrally and without stain, with God's grace the spirit of the Work we have received from the Father and from our older brothers, who with their lives have known how to make this marvelous reality of Opus Dei present in all the corners of the world." They also manifested their wish "to express our gratitude for the tireless effort of our Father to give juridical shape in a definitive way to the nature of Opus Dei and to manifest our joy for the great good that this reality will signify for the whole Church and all men."

This communication was received with applause by the other participants. Msgr. Escrivá replied to this motion presenting a synthesis of the juridical path referred to by the communication as well as underlining the enthusiasm and effort which accompanied

---

[37] ACGS-m, II, August 30, 1970. At the inaugural session of meetings of the women's branch he spoke similarly. Cf. ACGS-f, II, August 30, 1970.

[38] ACGS-m, II, August 30, 1970.

[39] The commissions of the men's branch were presided over by Drs. Fernando Valenciano, Daniel Cummings and Giuseppe Molteni; those of the women's branch by Miss Carmen Puente and Drs. Rita di Pasquale, Maria C. Wismer and Marlies Kücking.

the preparation of the General Congress.  He then concluded: "I have nothing more to say to you, except perhaps this: we have tried to see to it that in the first part of the extraordinary General Congress, and in the regional assemblies, and now, in the second part of the Congress, younger members also participate.  Let their voices be heard; that of their seniors has been heard for many years.  I am quite pleased that the work, prayer and apostolic desires of all be fused together and that the warmth of your affection be noticed as well as the effectiveness of your will to follow the love of God and to live precisely our vocation and not that of others.

"May God bless you.  The Father is grateful to all, especially to these younger sons of mine, who have always shown their desire of being united to the senior members, for the better service of the Church and souls.  May you work much, because there is much work to be done."[40]

It had been suggested in one of the resolutions of the first part of the Congress, that during the second part it would be good to count on the technical collaboration of specialists in theology and canon and civil law, who would "bring their professional help to the study of the topics the president general may indicate and in the way he considers most opportune."[41]  At the beginning of the second session Msgr. Escrivá announced the formation of a technical commission, presided over by Fr. Alvaro del Portillo and composed of two subcommissions: a juridico-canonical and a theological.  Its purpose is "to offer its scientific collaboration to the practical task of revising our particular law on the basis of the proposals the General Congress might approve."  He pointed out that "desiring first of all that this be constituted and proceeding to appoint it, I well know that I am not failing in my duties and responsibilities as founder.  On the contrary, I act as God has taught me always to do, especially in the most important moments of the Work's history.  Placing all of my confidence in the love of our Father God and of the blessed Virgin Mary, Mother of God and our Mother, and relying on the help of my children."[42]  The secretary then read the names of those appointed by the founder to make up this commission.[43]

Except for these special moments, the Congress continued its work according to plans.  The commissions examined the conclu-

---

[40] ACGS-m, II, Sept. 10, 1970.

[41] ACGS-m, I, Sept. 12, 1969.

[42] ACGS-m, II, Sept. 7, 1970.

[43] The juridical subcommission had for vice-chairman Dr. Amadeo de Fuenmayor and was made up of Drs. Xavier de Ayala, Pedro Lombardía, Salvador Canals, Umberto Farri and Joaquín Alonso.  The theological subcommission was presided by Dr. Rolf Thomas and consisted of Drs. Pedro Rodríguez, Giuseppe Molteni, Juan B. Torello,

sions of the regional assemblies and their reports which had arrived during the previous months and had been previously classified. Many of these communications stemmed from personal experiences in the Work, giving facts and concrete circumstances. Because of their outstanding value as historic documentation, these reports were properly ordered. They have been archived for the day when the history of Opus Dei would be written, along with that of the start of apostolic work in each country. Other communiqués, plus the conclusions of the preparatory regional assemblies, dealt more broadly with questions and aspects of Opus Dei's spirit and apostolate. Since they often covered topics studied and approved in the first part of the Congress, for reasons of brevity they were not made into new proposals, except when they focused on special characteristics or dealt with aspects not previously covered.

A total of 90 proposals were presented and voted on during the plenary sessions celebrated between September 10 and 14.

c) *The closure of the plenary sessions*

The closing of the plenary sessions of the second part took place on September 14. The last day was mainly dedicated to voting on the conclusions already examined by the different commissions and by each of the participants in the Congress. The conclusions, approved by participants from both branches of Opus Dei,[44] comprise a thick document regarding the most important theological and juridical issues. We will shortly examine this document. But first we might ask how the Congress' resolutions were to be executed.

Obviously a large assembly is not the proper forum for elaborating particular juridical texts. From this it was necessary to foresee an instrument or an adequate methodology such as might be a less numerous group endowed with specific professional competence. This is what led to thinking about a technical commission. Hence the fourth conclusion states: "they approved unanimously that the second part of the extraordinary General Congress of Opus Dei continue its work through a technical commission."[45]

In the closing session Msgr. Escrivá refers to this: "Today we bring to a close, my children, the plenary sessions of the second part of this extraordinary General Congress of Opus Dei. But, as you well know, this does not mean the Congress has concluded its work. The General Congress continues open.

---

Carlos Cardona and José Luis Illanes. It was foreseen that other members might be named consultors (ACGS-m, II, Sept. 7, 1970). The establishment of the technical commission was communicated to the women's branch as well (ACGS-f, II, Sept. 7, 1970).

[44] ACGS-m, II, Sept. 14, 1970 and ACGS-f, II, Sept. 14, 1970.

[45] The complete text of the conclusions are found in the Appendix, document no. 55.

"On the basis of what has been dealt with in each commission and after our plenary sessions," he continued, "you have prepared some conclusions to be submitted to the plenary session for a vote. But these conclusions, if approved do not end the work of the Congress. [These conclusions will serve] as the basis and orientation of the executive work of the technical commission, which has already been set up, with two subcommissions—theological and juridical—and which tomorrow will begin its work. Let us all ask God confidently and perseveringly that He continue to help us with His grace, that He bless the task of the technical commission. The length of its work is not known, because you and I want the work to be well done, with diligence no less than with perfection, without haste or precipitation, with love."[46]

With a liturgical ceremony consisting in Exposition and Benediction with the *Lignum Crucis*—September 14 being a feast of the Holy Cross—the sessions were concluded, and members returned to their countries and normal occupations.

## 5. United to the founder: revising the juridical status

Now let us examine the approved proposals that served as the foundation of the executive phase that began immediately thereafter. The first impression stemming from our summary, and even more from reading the acts of the Special General Congress (not to mention conversing with any of the participants) can be summarized in one word: unity. The founder of Opus Dei, at a critical moment in the juridical history of Opus Dei, wanted to listen to all the members of the Work; to share with them his ideals, desires and concerns; to take the pulse of the experience and sentiments of those incorporated to Opus Dei, both in the early years as in more recent times. The members of the Work, called by the founder and faced with their own vocation, responded by showing complete adherence not only to the one who had called them but at the same time and inseparably to the foundational charism, to the light and message that enlivened and endowed with meaning the Congress, the history and the development of Opus Dei of which this assembly was an expression.

This unity had psychological and operative manifestations: the general tenor, the trust members showed in Msgr. Escrivá and in turn Msgr. Escrivá's confidence in those who heard him. But in a final analysis this unity went even deeper: communion in the Christian faith and in the spiritual reality of Opus Dei begun on October 2, 1928, understanding of course this faith and spirit not as abstract realities but as something lived and experienced in daily life. In

---

[46] ACGS-m, II, Sept. 14, 1970.

effect the whole Work had reflected on its own way of life, comparing it with the charism or the original gift and thence evaluating the
norms and juridical framework.  It had thus confirmed and reaffirmed the need for revising its canonical status, but first and more
radically, it reinforced the validity of the pastoral phenomenon over
the years.

Text after text emphasizes that what is lived today in Opus Dei
coincides with what has been lived from the beginning and this
referring often to the words and teachings of the founder.  During
the Congress he had confirmed, in his recorded interventions, these
judgments more than once: "That is true, my children: that is what
God wanted and what with his grace we have been striving to live."
In a word the Congress did not approve a future project, but rather
certified the reality of a vocation lived with identical spirit, through
the years amid the most diverse nationalities and circumstances.  It
thus requested revision of the juridical configuration so as to achieve
one that is fully in accord with the original charism.

Although occasionally some other questions were also raised,
almost all of the Congress' proposals and interventions had been
centered on the objective for which it had been convoked: a reflection on the spirituality, life and apostolate of Opus Dei, as an organic and lived reality that later needed to be translated into a
revision of the juridical status.  This was done from many different
points of view, going back occasionally to the beginnings and fundamental perspectives and sometimes getting down to the very
particulars.  Indeed the Congress was one big vote of confidence in
the preceding discussions and in the ongoing work of the founder
to obtain a juridical solution in full conformity with the foundational charism.  Even more, it asked that these negotiations be intensified, while leaving the decision on the moment and the opportune way of doing this in the exclusive hands of the founder.

One of the first proposals approved in the plenary session of
September 1969 requests: "It seems opportune to make a detailed
study with the purpose of revising the language used in our particular law approved by the Holy See, in order to propose the necessary changes."  This resolution continues to explain the reasons.
"The text of our particular law does not properly express the secular and lay character of the Work, but rather reflects the juridical
compromise our Father had to accept at the time because of the
limitations of canon law in force and the praxis of the Holy See in
those years. . . .  We gravely urge that this work be carried out as
soon as possible out of love for the truth and for the sake of juridical precision and the effectiveness of our apostolate."[47]

---

[47] ACGS-m, I, Sept. 9, 1969. We point out once again that all of the proposals cited were
not only presented but also duly approved.

The same petition was thus formulated, taking into consideration other general and specific dimensions, in September 1970, as the first conclusion of this part: "In completing this phase of the second part of the Special General Congress . . . the participants . . . have voted and unanimously approved the following conclusions:

"1) Whereas it was the desire of the Second Vatican Ecumenical Council and of the Holy See that each institution of the Church proceed to a revision of its own law, respecting and carefully observing the spirit of its respective founder, as well as the healthy traditions that form the patrimony of each institution (cf. Decree *Perfectæ caritatis*, no. 2; Motu proprio *Ecclesiæ sanctæ*, August 6, 1966, II, art. 12, b), and

"Having considered once again, with love and a firm resolution of fidelity, the continual teaching of the founder and president general *ad vitam* of Opus Dei, who has transmitted to us a doctrine and a spirit, with a theological content and an ecclesial purpose that clearly differ from those proper to institutions professing the *state of perfection* or of *consecrated life*.

"We request that the founder and president general of Opus Dei, at the time and in the way he deems most fitting, renew before the Holy See his humble and hopeful petition that Opus Dei's institutional problem be definitively resolved, granting it—on the basis of new juridical perspectives opened by the dispositions and norms of application of the decrees of the Council—a juridical configuration different from that of secular institute: a configuration that will substantially preserve our present particular law, but will suppress those elements peculiar to institutes of perfection. . . ."[48]

This text requires little commentary. There we find not only the request for revising the juridical status, but also formulated the criteria whereby this revision ought to be carried out: to conserve substantially the specific law of Opus Dei, while eliminating whatever, out of historical necessity, was accepted in past times that introduced in some way elements in fact alien to the Work, because they were born of a configuration or terminology proper only to states of perfection.

Among the various proposals along these lines, one dated September 14, 1970 merits special mention. Its relator was Rev. Xavier de Ayala, doctor in civil and canon law, member then of the Vatican's Commission for the Revision of Canon Law and Counselor of Opus Dei in Brazil; he presented it not only in his own name, as a member of the technical commission set up during the Congress, but also of all jurists who participated in its work. "Throughout these years,

---

[48] These conclusions are included in the Appendix, document no. 55.

those of us who have lived close to the Father can verify his suffering and his concern, when, confronted with the precariousness of canonical legislation, he saw himself necessarily obliged to accept and uphold legal norms he himself well knew were not appropriate to the nature of our vocation. We have always seen in this conduct of our Father a heroic example of noble loyalty to the Holy See. The Father has been a faithful guardian of the authority Canon Law must have. Yet he experienced the profound contradiction of a jurist who must bear with a law that in many aspects is notoriously unrelated—and in some cases contrary—to the life it should serve and for which it should offer an adequate channel. We wish to make known here our gratitude to the Father for his example of heroic loyalty, always united—out of fidelity to the gift received from God—to the fortitude to know how to express clearly and to 'protest' in a filial fashion in the appropriate forum about the harm ensuing to Opus Dei from a juridical categorization that obscures the particular characteristics of our way as ordinary Christians living in the world."

These declarations opened the way to a further reflection based on the juridical experience of those who presented the proposal: "Those of us who are professionals of the law want to point out in this Congress another facet whose consideration seems a matter of justice: these sufferings of our Father, to be faithful to the gift of God and, at the same time, loyal to the Holy See, have produced—among other benefits to souls—a noticeable advance in canonical legislation itself. Many solutions opening their way today in this period of renewal in ecclesiastical legislation following on the Second Vatican Council are clearly owed to the long juridical battle of the Father to defend the particular characteristics of Opus Dei, proposing solutions to the problem not envisioned by Canon Law. It suffices to recall, for example, the criteria regarding the rights of the faithful, the rights of the laity; the juridical consequences of the freedom of Catholics in the ecclesial realm and in temporal matters; the freedom and right of association in the Church, both of lay faithful and of priests; the norms with respect to ecclesiastical goods, etc."

Proposal sponsors further declared: "We also feel filially obliged to point out the juridical sensitivity with which the Father, in difficult historical circumstances of the years 1947 and 1950 and faced with a canonical mentality completely closed to the characteristics of our path, knew how to safeguard what was essential, in spite of the impositions of the ambiguous legislation regarding secular institutes. Not only did the Father protect what was essential but— and this is what we expressly wish now to set forth for the consideration of this Congress—he had the prudence of a good jurist committed to avoiding any inadequacies of the law. He thus introduced into our specific law norms, prescriptions, clarifications and distinctions that supposed an authentic defense thereof and that neutralized in many cases the prescriptions of the norms contrary to our genuine way of being."[49]

## 6. The members of Opus Dei, ordinary Christians

The Special General Congress did not limit itself to manifesting its full communion with the Work's founder regarding the need to request and foster an adequate juridical statute for Opus Dei. It also considered various specific arguments in this regard, even though always within the same perspective: the revision of the statutory norms established in 1947 and 1950.

The affirmation of the condition of ordinary Christians proper to the members of Opus Dei underlies these considerations. "May it be clear and obvious always for the whole world that the women members of Opus Dei are ordinary persons, who strive to carry out with perfection their ordinary work, making of it a means of holiness and apostolate," we read in one of the first proposals approved by the representatives of the women's branch in the plenary session celebrated on September 9, 1969 and afterwards largely reiterated.[50]

Two days later, on September 11, the same reality was reaffirmed by a wide-ranging proposal presented by one of the commissions of the men's Congress. "God has wanted, through our Father, to promote Opus Dei as a pastoral and ascetical phenomenon that is completely new. We are not secularized religious: we are ordinary faithful, who do not seek the life of evangelical perfection specific to religious, but holiness in the world, each one in his own state and in the exercise of his own *ordinary professional work*."

The spirit of Opus Dei and the pastoral phenomenon born of this spirit is founded "on baptism and the other sacraments of Christian initiation—confirmation, holy eucharist—as a radical and specific vocation to holiness and apostolate in the middle of the world, with all the consequences deriving from this truth." Among others, it enumerates: "the general call to holiness; the revaluation of temporal tasks and structures, and very particularly of human work—intellectual or manual—as sanctifiable and sanctifying realities; in our case secularity and a *lay style*, as values of the economy of redemption; the duty of *being concerned with the meaning and reality*

---

[49] ACGS-m, II, Sept. 14, 1970. On the previous day a proposal was approved in which, referring to the fidelity to the original charism on the juridical development of Opus Dei, it was asked that "in the formation of the members of the Work, as it has been taught until now, we continue to teach everyone this clear line of the evolution of our law" (ACGS-m, II, Sept. 13, 1970).

[50] ACGS-f, I, Sept. 9, 1969.

*of one's occupation*, whatever it may be; the affirmation that it is possible and necessary to live a contemplative life amid the most intense ordinary human activity; the practical recognition of the dignity of God's children that leads to loving personal freedom and responsibility and to defending the freedom of consciences; and also, always firm in the faith of Jesus Christ sustained by the Church, to avoid any kind of fanaticism or discrimination. All of this expresses openly our condition as ordinary citizens, fully the equals of our peers, who, with them and like them, live in the middle of earthly concerns."

This theological core obviously has not only spiritual consequences but also juridical ones, to which the proposal then alludes: "This reality," evoking texts of Msgr. Escrivá already cited, "has been lived in the Work from the beginning, and our dedication to the service of God and of the Church in the Work has always been with the explicit and irrevocable condition of not ever being religious nor persons who are in any way considered the equivalent of religious, and that we never be considered under any circumstance missionaries. To say this in a graphic way, even though it be an absurd hypothesis: there is no authority on earth that can oblige us to be [religious]; natural law and positive law prohibit it, as do Christian morality and canon law, because, we repeat, we have dedicated ourselves to God *on the express condition of never being religious*."[51]

This awareness of being simply yet fully Christians who desire to sanctify themselves and to work apostolically, each one according to his own state and ordinary conditions in human life, inspires many of the proposals of the Congress. For example, we see it in those having to do with the importance of professional work, of which we will speak later. Also in those stressing the suitability of reflecting in the *Ius peculiare* the naturalness that is a trait proper to the Christian way of acting; thus any kind of clandestinity or secrecy or badly understood discretion are to be repudiated, as already discussed. Since Opus Dei and its nature are now well known, the norms of prudence required earlier are no longer necessary and were allowed to fall into disuse many years ago.[52] Secularity and

---

[51] ACGS-m, I, Sept. 11, 1969. The final declaration is echoed in one of the proposals approved by the women's Congress: "Our vocation of ordinary Christians leads us to dedicate ourselves to the service of God in the Work with the express condition of not being religious. Each member has in the Church and in civil society the state she had before belonging to Opus Dei" (ACGS-f, I, Sept. 12, 1969).

[52] After stating that "the growth and development of the Work in the whole world" have altered the historical circumstances that required these norms of prudence (see section 5 of chapter VII); and after pointing out that "for some years these regulations have not been necessary," the Congress approved that these norms "not be included in the new edition we are preparing of our law" (ACGS-m, II, Sept. 11, 1970 and ACGS-f, II, Sept. 11, 1970).

the naturalness deriving from it are reaffirmed. "Any attempt at equating this naturalness of our life as ordinary Christians with secrecy" must be repudiated. Members are ordinary Christians "who do not boast of their own spiritual life or apostolic desires."[53]

The awareness of being ordinary Christians also generated proposals that emphasize the need to shun anything possibly evoking the figure, usages or terms peculiar to the state of perfection or—as it had begun to be called at the time—the state of consecrated life. Whence follows, as we have seen, the desire to study and revise the terminology. Still other proposals—echoing the earlier teaching of the founder himself—go straight to the central question: the bond between members of Opus Dei and the Work itself is to exclude any kind of vows or analogous ties.

This point was one of those brought forth in the first of the conclusions approved at the end of the second session, on September 14, 1970. After asking for a revision of the particular law of Opus Dei, so as "to suppress from it those elements proper to the institutes of perfection," it specifies: "the profession of the three evangelical counsels of poverty, chastity and obedience (cf. Apostolic Constitution *Provida Mater Ecclesia*, art. III, §2, nos. 1°, 2°, 3° and Dogmatic Constitution *Lumen gentium*, no. 43 and Decree *Perfectæ caritatis*, no. 11) and the obligatory nature of this profession by means of bonds of a sacred character (cf. Apostolic Constitution *Provida Mater Ecclesia*, art. III, § 2, nos. 1°, 2°, 3°; and Dogmatic Constitution *Lumen gentium*, no. 44)."[54]

This petition had already been formulated in various proposals made both by the women and the men from the beginning of the Congress.[55] They had even pointed out that the evangelical counsels, which are valid or at least classic in defining the religious state, are not adequate to characterize the spirit of Opus Dei. "Traditionally, in ascetical literature and even in juridical and doctrinal texts, under the evident influence of a spirituality proper to the religious state, personal sanctification has been linked to the virtues of poverty, chastity and obedience. Clearly these three virtues—in themselves, independently of the form of living them characteristic

---

[53] ACGS-m, I, Sept. 11, 1969.

[54] See Appendix, document no. 55.

[55] This was true both generally and specifically. The latter is the case, for example, of some norms with regard to acquiring and using material goods, which, inspired in the law of institutes of perfection, had been necessary to put into the *Constitutions*. The Congress requested the suppression of these norms and their substitution by others that make clear that members of Opus Dei acquire financial rights and obligations by themselves the same as any other citizen, living detachment and cooperating in the apostolic and charitable tasks with the attitude and generosity of a good Christian (ACGS-m, II, Sept. 12 & 13, 1970). The third final conclusion deals with this same topic (see Appendix, document no. 55).

of the religious state—are necessary for sanctity, which requires all the virtues in necessary and indissoluble interconnection. It is clear also that these three virtues fulfill an ascetical function of great importance."

Nevertheless, "the doctrine of the Church and experience itself teaches us that:

"a) the essence of holiness is to be found in charity, love for God and of others out of love for God;

"b) the primacy among the virtues belongs to the theological virtues of faith, hope and charity;

"c) the cardinal virtues—prudence, justice, fortitude and temperance—have a special determinative function and an indispensable general regulating function;

"d) active presence in redeeming all temporal activities requires the constant exercise of some virtues that, following a very prevalent categorization, are usually called integral, potential or subjective parts of the four cardinal virtues; namely, industriousness, sanctified work, humility, all forms of justice, simplicity, sincerity, loyalty, naturalness, order, detachment, tenacity, optimism, modesty, decency, self-denial, docility, sobriety, hardihood, courage, considerateness, patience, spirit of initiative, affability, magnanimity, fidelity, etc.;

"e) the exercise of the supernatural and human virtues leaves us serene and cheerful, while God himself suffuses our hearts with a profound sense of divine filiation; it is thus that we sanctify ordinary professional work, sanctify ourselves in work and with our work contribute to the sanctification of others."

Summing things up, "All of this reality, which the spirit of the Work teaches, stimulates and helps us to live, cannot be expressed by the religious profession of the three virtues previously referred to." They thus conclude with the request that, in a future edition of the *Codex Iuris Particularis* of Opus Dei, the founder's teaching regarding virtues be received in all its breadth, without limiting itself to the three virtues.[56] Not surprisingly, then, the first of the final conclusions incorporates this point, which doubtless is a decisive one. Msgr. Escrivá himself had emphasized some of these institutional characteristics in the letter to Cardinal Ildebrando Antoniutti

---

[56] ACGS-m, I, Sept. 12, 1969. The women also dealt with this topic approving a similar proposal: "From now on, in order to reflect with fidelity the spiritual characteristics proper to our spirit as our founder has taught us the part of our *Ius peculiare* that specifies the way of living poverty, chastity and obedience will also speak, at even greater length, of how to live some associated virtues, which, without themselves being included in the so-called evangelical counsels, are also genuinely evangelical and have moreover a special rank within the spirit proper to Opus Dei: charity, divine filiation, sincerity, industriousness, order, loyalty, firmness, cheerfulness, etc." (ACGS-f, I, Sept. 12, 1969).

at the end of the first stage of the Congress. Summarizing the work
carried out, he stressed how the Congress had agreed on the need
to go beyond the context of the evangelical counsels. He also pointed
to the great step taken by the Second Vatican Council in opening the
door to institutions or structures of a universal or interdiocesan
character whose members were not required to profess these evangelical counsels.

The General Extraordinary Congress "first of all has pointed out,"
he wrote, "that the canonical nature of secular institute has shown
itself to be inadequate to the sociological, spiritual and pastoral reality
of Opus Dei, with respect both to the foundational charism as to the
experience of more than twenty years of pastoral work that, since
carried out the world over, has therefore a universal value."

This inadequacy of the figure of secular institute is seen, Msgr.
Escrivá continues referring to the General Congress, "when at the
time of the approval [of the Work], violence was done [forzatura
says the Italian] by including Opus Dei among the institutes of
perfection. This was inevitable, since it was the only way, according to the law in force at that time, to obtain a form of government
that was universal in character, required both by the nature and the
development already achieved by Opus Dei. . . . At that time, in
order to have juridical structures and faculties of a government of
universal scope, an indispensable condition was then thought to be
the profession of the evangelical counsels by members of the moral
entity whose erection was sought."

Has the time not come, the founder asks, to undo the forzatura
suffered earlier? "The Congress has indicated the criteria for the
legitimate separation of members' incorporation to the institute (which
by means of an appropriate juridical formula would always imply
a perpetual, mutual and full bond) from the profession, today necessary, of vows or equivalent bonds. It deems more appropriate to
the institute's nature, in resolving this problem, to recur to the first
commandment of the law of God (which manifests and contains the
universal call to holiness) and the practice of certain virtues, but
not necessarily those typified in the three evangelical counsels."

Finally, the Congress has noted "with a deep feeling of gratitude and hope that after the Second Vatican Council there can exist
within the Church's canonical legislation forms with a universal
form of government that do not require the profession of the evangelical counsels by those making up these moral persons." The
letter then points to the desired canonical figure, making express
mention of the Decree *Presbyterorum ordinis*, no. 10, and the Motu
proprio *Ecclesiæ sanctæ*, section 1, no. 4; i.e., the references to personal prelatures.[57]

---

[57] The complete text of the letter is included in the Appendix, document no. 54.

## 7. Apostolate; work; personal freedom and responsibility

"From the beginning of Opus Dei, the Father has taught us that the Work, ordinarily, does not act. It urges its members, who are ordinary citizens and faithful, to fulfill the personal obligation of each to do apostolate—in work, in the heart of family life, social environment, etc.—in such a way that this makes up the principal and most important part of the work we carry out." These are the words adopted by the General Congress in a proposal dedicated to Opus Dei's apostolate.[58] In both sessions mention was made of the apostolic initiatives of some members along with others: educational institutions, charitable or social services and so on. While recognizing the value of such undertakings—even making explicit their need and importance—the Congress insisted, as a consequence of the spirit and life of Opus Dei, on the apostolic work each member carries out in and around one's job and other circumstances of life. Thus it not only accentuated this personal responsibility, but excluded every possibility of enumerating "typical" apostolates of the institution.

Along these lines, the General Congress requested the modification of one of the compromises made necessary in earlier years: the inclusion in the *Constitutions* of certain apostolates of the male and female numeraries.[59]

"The reality, as the Father has always written and said," the proposal affirms, "is that our apostolate is a 'sea without shores.' This is due to the very nature of our vocation, which calls upon us to sanctify every upright occupation. It is thus impossible to frame the activities of Opus Dei members within a restrictive enumeration. Apostolate is not something superimposed, differentiated from the member's job and social activities. It is always coterminous with the interior life, the walk of life proper to each member and with one's external activities, in each moment of the day. We all have a clear personal experience that confirms this teaching of the Father."

The consequence was reflected in a proposal: in revising the *Ius peculiare*, "the enumeration of apostolates, which it was necessary to introduce earlier, be eliminated; or a few brief and general words be given in accordance with the reality of our life."[60] This did not exclude of course that Opus Dei members, individually or associ-

---

[58] ACGS-m, I, Sept. 12, 1969.

[59] We referred to this in section 3 of chapter VII.

[60] ACGS-m, II, Sept. 13, 1970; an analogous proposal was approved on the following day by the women (ACGS-f, II, Sept. 14, 1970).

ated with others, promote apostolic activities that could count on the ministry of priests of the Work.[61]

This and other proposals, with a directly juridical aim, speak of the apostolate of Opus Dei members, each one in his profession or occupation. These proposals were buttressed by others that deal with work from a predominantly spiritual perspective; they express the desire—logical in such a congress—of reaffirming the importance of professional work in the spirituality of Opus Dei, as confirmed by the founder's teachings and members' lives. Thus, for example, in a proposal dated Sept. 11, 1969, by one of the men's commissions, it is stated that what is proper to Opus Dei members is "to seek Christian perfection by sanctifying the ordinary work of each one, which is as it were the hinge on which all our life turns."[62] In a tone more redolent of witness, the women declare in the first part of the Congress: "Owing to our condition as ordinary Christian women, we seek holiness in the middle of the world through the professional exercise of an occupation, whether intellectual or manual. This work, besides being an ordinary means of sanctification and apostolate, is also necessary for our personal support and to further apostolic works.

"The experience of these years of work—both intellectual and manual, but always with a clearly professional aim, never that of amateurs—carried out by female members in many human fields has enabled us to verify that:

—"it has been a powerful help to the growth in spiritual life, through the habitual exercise of the virtues required by work, drawing us closer to God;

---

[61] In fact, as we said at the beginning of this section, during the Congress repeated mention was made of these activities. A great part of the references reflect experiences; others have a juridical character. Such is the case of one that bears on the topic dealt with in chapter VII in relation to the *Constitutions* of 1950. We pointed out there [see section 6 of that chapter] that the *Constitutions* dealt with corporate apostolic activities from the perspective of the legal and financial support they need from "auxiliary societies," a figure later suppressed (cf. chapter VII, note 144).

The Congress dealt with this point in the session of Sept. 12, 1970. It approved a motion where, after underlining that "Opus Dei does not manage societies," further emphasizes that the only purpose sought was: "that—with the appropriate technical formulas—the charitable will by which people are moved to make available property, whether real or personal, for apostolic purposes be assured and that the continuity in the activity be guaranteed." Thus it was proposed that in the *Ius peculiare* all reference to auxiliary societies be omitted, "so that it be clear that the material instruments used in an apostolic work are truly the property of citizens; and that the Work does not manage the corporations that citizens may establish to carry out their aim of helping in the realization of apostolic works" (ACGS-m, II, Sept. 12, 1970). In fact this was incorporated in the *Codex Iuris Peculiaris* formulated after the Congress as we will mention.

[62] ACGS-m, I, Sept. 11, 1969.

—"it has been a source of serenity and joy to live with upright intention and a spirit of responsibility the duties of one's work;

—"work well done aimed at human perfection is one of the most valuable helps that can be afforded to mankind, because it directly contributes to bettering the conditions of life that afflict some nations;

—"it constitutes a most effective means of apostolate when done with the intent of serving souls: through example and the opportunities afforded of dealing more closely with one's colleagues."[63]

Other proposals dwell on other aspects; for example, the importance of professional diligence and competency;[64] the Christian sense of work, entailing as it does presence of God and living the theological virtues, in a word, a life of prayer;[65] awareness of the value of earthly realities and respect for the nature and norms proper to each activity;[66] personal freedom and responsibility in fulfilling one's work and exercising one's civic rights and duties.

Let us pause on this last point, which is of evident juridical consequence. We limit ourselves to two texts: one from each of the two sessions. On Sept. 13, 1969, a wide-ranging proposal was approved by the men. "Incorporation to the Work—which does not change the condition of its members as ordinary Christians before the Church and of simple citizens before the state—does not dimin-

---

[63] ACGS-f, I, Sept. 12, 1969.

[64] The vocation to Opus Dei "requires that work be well done with a professional sense—without any amateurishness, with a spirit of service to society" (ACGS-m, I, Sept. 10, 1969). "All of the members of the women's branch of Opus Dei commit themselves never to abandon their occupation and to carry it out with the greatest human perfection possible. We are convinced that it is not merely a question of working much and with good will: it is necessary to work well, because the axis on which our vocation turns is ordinary work carried out with a professional outlook" (ACGS-f, I, Sept. 13, 1969).

[65] "The spirit of the Work leads us to be contemplatives in the middle of the world; to seek, find and love God through all human activities" (ACGS-m, I, Sept. 13, 1969). "Unity of life, which characterizes and is fostered by the spirit of Opus Dei, has made a reality of contemplation in the world and in and by means of work, resolving the interior conflicts many lay people have who desire a life of union with God without having to relinquish their own place and family, social and professional functions" (ACGS-m, I, Sept. 10, 1969). By means of a life of piety that is not merely devotional, but personal and alive, "one achieves an effective contemplation, perpetuated amid all activities carried out in the world, no matter how absorbing—as has been demonstrated by the universal experience of Opus Dei members of all kinds in every time and place. . . . We refer to contemplation not as an unattainable ideal; we express with this term a reality, lived in the middle of the world—'in the middle of the street,' as our Father is in the habit of telling us—and through any professional activity, since 'the unity of life of each member of Opus Dei leads him to seek God at all times and in all things'" (ACGS m, I, Sept. 11, 1969).

[66] Lay mentality and priestly soul—"which are the opposite respectively of clericalism and of secularism"—lead to dedicating "earthly reality to the service of God but with-

ish in the slightest our freedom of action in all temporal matters but rather reinforces it. The spirit of the Work, well lived, frees us from prejudices and any sort of fanaticism."

The proposal explains other aspects, some normative (respect the directors and priests must show in spiritual direction for the temporal opinions of the members), others, historical or sociological (the existence of a real pluralism of opinions among members). It ends with some conclusions and suggestions:

—"to reaffirm the freedom of all the members of Opus Dei to act on their temporal opinions in all fields: cultural, social, political and the like, and the right they have, as ordinary faithful and ordinary citizens, to act in all aspects of public life;

—"to show that in fact for each member of the Work with an important position in public life there are hundreds of others dedicated to private activities and occupations of a more humble nature;

—"to point out that the directors of the Work—following the example of our Father—have always displayed a profound respect for the freedom of their brothers, without giving an inch in the face of any slanderous campaign or other kinds of pressure;

—"to gather and present to this General Congress the experience of so many years: that Opus Dei members have never attained, exercised or retained positions of public responsibility in any nation, by exploiting either the Church or the Work. They have always acted with the most complete personal freedom and responsibility."[67]

The second text was presented personally by Msgr. Escrivá in a work session of September 1970. To grasp adequately the nature of Opus Dei, he deems it essential to heed the clear distinction between Opus Dei and other associations whose purpose is "to prepare and form, also in a political fashion, good Christians so that they defend the Church in the political realm." This is not the case of Opus Dei, which "limits itself to giving all of its members a solid doctrinal and spiritual formation, to the end that each one act as a Christian in all environments, sanctifying his profession or occupation. Then members who are professionally called to politics should form themselves and act with professional freedom in whatever environment they choose—always outside of the Work—just as other members who form themselves professionally in centers or institutions they freely select, with no further limitation than that incumbent on all Catholic citizens: the dogmatic and moral teachings of the Church.

---

out changing their nature, nor their characteristics, and without attempting to change the laws of the nature proper to these activities" (ACGS-m, II, Sept. 12, 1970).

[67] ACGS-m, I, Sept. 13, 1969.

"I ask you, therefore, my children—each one conscious of the joy and responsibility of the freedom you enjoy—that you thank God for the constant fact the Work has never entered into temporal questions open to discussion, especially those of a political nature."[68]

Another juridical suggestion of the Congress needs some historical background. During the days of the first pontifical approvals ('46-47) and the beginning of Opus Dei's international expansion, Msgr. Escrivá had asked the senior members and those called to assume tasks of government and formation to take some commitments. His aim was that the more responsible members commit themselves especially to live certain spiritual demands and thus contribute to the spiritual welfare of the Work.[69] In accordance with mentality of the time and the outlook and environment he found in the Sacred Congregation and in those people with whom he was dealing with a view to the pontifical approvals he gave these commitments the form of oaths.[70]

In subsequent years as part of the process that led him to underline more clearly the common Christian condition, Msgr. Escrivá thought it best to do without these oaths. Specifically, he proposed the suppression of numbers 20 and 58 of the *Constitutions* and their oaths. The members of Opus Dei would otherwise maintain the duty to live detachment from material goods and to form their conscience, analogous to any faithful Catholic, and to defend the Work's unity. The proposal was approved by the Congress.[71]

This decision was elaborated in the second session of the Congress. In the 1950 *Constitutions* the commitment to form one's conscience rightly was specified, as a means to reach that aim, in the form of seeking advice from the directors of the institute with respect to matters of special importance.[72] Obviously, this norm was to be understood in the context of the full freedom members have in professional questions, so proper to Opus Dei's spirit and reaffirmed so many times in the same 1950 *Constitutions*. The pre-

---

[68] The proposal was presented by the founder in plenary sessions of both branches and was approved by them (ACGS-f, II, Sept. 12, 1970; ACGS-m, II, Sept. 14, 1970).

[69] RHF, 20168, pp. 888-890.

[70] These commitments, formulated for the first time in numbers 20 and 58 of the 1950 *Constitutions*, refer to three fundamental points: to defend the unity of the Work by avoiding any desire for positions, any kind of critical gossip, but rather correcting by means of a simple and fraternal advertence the defects perceived in others, particularly in those occupying positions of government; to live a refined detachment from the material goods each person must necessarily use, especially those with an active social life and who earn their living with their work; and finally, to guarantee an upright intention when faced by major professional and social decisions and to form one's conscience well, and thus, even to seek advice if necessary.

[71] ACGS-m, I, Sept. 9, 1969; ACGS-f, I, Sept. 9, 1969.

[72] 1950 *Constitutions*, no. 58, 3°.

scribed advice looks to situations that for one reason or another have a special import (because they involve a change in a person's residence, obligations or way of life or because they have significant effects of an ethical or moral nature, etc.). But seeking advice in no way derogates the full freedom of the advice-seeker; he or she could still choose whatever option seems best. When seeking this advice, all the norms on discretion or professional confidentiality were respected. This is analogous to what happens whenever any Christian in a desire to be prudent seeks advice from a priest or another person of confidence in resolving difficult problems. Neither one nor the other thereby loses his freedom of decision or transfers his personal responsibility to the advice-giver.

The nature and scope of this norm was very clear to every member of Opus Dei. This was not be true, however, with some people who disconnected this practice from the ensemble of Opus Dei's spirit. It was hence misconstrued to imply a duty of consulting professional, social or political decisions as such and therefore as a lessening of personal freedom as well as an undue intromission of the directors of the institute in the secular activity of its members.[73] This negative experience led Msgr. Escrivá not only to declare repeatedly the members' freedom in professional, social and political matters; he reiterated explicitly that Opus Dei directors ought not nor can they give orientations in these matters.[74] He also took advantage of the Special General Congress to bear witness to the historical truth, as he did on September 13, 1970. The context was the proposition approved the previous year with regard to the suppression of the aforementioned oaths and his consequent joy. Then he referred to number 58, 3°, of the 1950 *Constitutions*, where reference is made to seeking advice. He offered a further resolution designed to uphold once again "what has been the constant tradi-

---

[73] We have alluded to this in commenting on the 1950 *Constitutions*: cf. note 32 of chapter VII.

[74] Thus for example in various texts—we have already quoted from some of them (see chapter VIII, note 166)—taken from the interviews in *Conversations*. Now we add one somewhat more extensive but very clear: "Opus Dei has nothing whatever to do with politics. It is absolutely foreign to any political, economic, ideological or cultural tendency or group. Let me repeat that its aims are exclusively spiritual and apostolic. The only thing it requires of its members is that they lead a Christian life, trying to live up to the ideal of the gospel. Therefore it never becomes involved in any temporal affair. From the moment in which they first approach the Work, all its members are fully aware of their individual freedom. If one of them ever tried to exert pressure on the others to make them accept his political opinions, or to use them for human interests, they would rebel and expel him without a second thought.

"Respect for its members' liberty is an essential condition of Opus Dei's very existence. Without it, no one would come to the Work. Even more. The Work has never intervened in politics and, with God's help, it never will; but if it were to, I would be its number one enemy" (*Conversations*, no. 28).

tion of the Work" and, therefore, the true scope of the norm. Following this he enumerated three points the assembly approved, confirming that this had always been the practice: "First, these consultations and requests for advice have always been carried out within the scope of Christian morality; second, all my children know that they can consult freely with any person outside of the Work; and third, they know that the solution each adopts depends on him and on him alone, because each is completely free to decide and to act as seems best."[75]

The proposal made in 1970 is telling, since it witnesses not only to the proper interpretation of the 1950 texts, but also to the continual practice of freedom always enjoyed by members in temporal matters. From the perspective of the juridical evolution and specifically the preparation of the definitive configuration, the 1969 proposal—presupposed and reaffirmed by the subsequent one—is more significant as it was in 1969 that the decision was made to modify the statutory texts, suppressing the obligations under oath and referring instead, to the general orientation of Msgr. Escrivá with regard to virtues and what is required in the concrete existence of each Christian.[76]

## 8. The organic unity of Opus Dei

The Congress members expressed "their unanimous conviction that in the revision of the particular law of Opus Dei it is absolutely necessary to reaffirm the constitutional importance of the perfect unity of the Work: including priest and lay members, who do not form distinct classes, whose cooperation allows for a service to the universal Church which is solidly based on an inseparable unity of vocation, spirituality and government."

Thus we read in the second of the conclusions approved on September 14, 1970. The text ends with a recognition of the benefits derived for the whole of Opus Dei from the ministerial work of its priests.[77]

---

[75] ACGS-m, II, Sept. 13, 1970; see also ACGS-f, II, Sept. 13, 1970.

[76] Since the suppression of these oaths did not constitute a modification in the structure of Opus Dei, nor was it contrary to canon law, it fell within the competence of the Special General Congress and Msgr. Escrivá decided to put it into effect immediately. This was communicated to the Holy See in a letter which Fr. Alvaro del Portillo, in his capacity of Secretary General of Opus Dei, addressed to Cardinal Ildebrando Antoniutti on March 23, 1971, in which he informed him of the progress of the second part of the Congress. Cardinal Antoniutti replied a few days later indicating his pleasure at the work accomplished. Both letters can be found in the Appendix, documents nos. 56 and 57.

[77] We recall that these conclusions are found in the Appendix, document no. 55.

The Congress thus describes a constitutional feature of Opus Dei: those who make it up are united not only in fact with the president general and among themselves by a bond of charity and a particular communion. All of them, moreover—priests and laity, men and women, married or single—have received the same unique vocation and, as a body within the Church, they form an organic unity with the same spirituality, with the same end and government and with the same means of formation. This is the organic unity for which a proper canonical configuration is sought.

This unity of vocation had been clearly affirmed from the start by the founder. He always saw to it that it was reflected in juridical texts; the 1950 *Constitutions*, as we studied, expressly affirm that the distinction between numeraries, associates and supernumeraries serves only to indicate different degrees of availability to take on tasks of government and formation, always presupposing the same vocation, spirit and intensity of dedication.[78] The Congress wanted to emphasize this reality. This it did, for example in the session celebrated by the men on September 13, 1969. There a resolution affirmed that "the members of the Work come from the most diverse and varied personal circumstances. At the same time there is a perfect and harmonious unity, a consequence of the fact that there is only one spirit and that the means and the end are the same for all the members of Opus Dei.

"There is but one vocation to Opus Dei, the same means and the same end, and all the members of the Work—celibate or married— are urged by the same call to seek holiness while each remaining in his or her own state, of bearing witness to Jesus Christ in his or her own professional or social environment and to contribute with all their strength to seconding the ends of the Work, each one within his or her own particular circumstances of life." It further asks that in the acts of the Congress and in future texts the founder's teaching be echoed according to which "all the members of the Work without exception . . . thus live *a full dedication* to their vocation and to their specific mission. In accordance with this teaching, there do not exist nor should one speak of different classes of members."[79]

In the plenary sessions of the second part participants returned to this topic. This happened, specifically, with a resolution that noted that in the assemblies celebrated in the various Regions witness had been borne once again to "the reality of this unity of vocation, in the communications of members of the Work of all condi-

---

[78] See section 3 of chapter VII.

[79] ACGS-m, I, Sept. 13, 1969. The members of the Congress dealt with this topic also in two different resolutions presented on the same day (Sept. 14, 1969) from which we cite the more significant paragraphs: "The vocation to the Work is one: the person who

tions of life: young and old, celibate, married, widowed, laity and priests." Thus it proclaims that "the vocation to the Work is one, according to which all the members of the Work seek personal sanctity with the same spirit and the same means, each one in his or her own state and through their professional work or occupation—*munus publicum*—and in all the most varied circumstances proper to them. Thus the different terms express in a simple way the degree of availability for various tasks of corporate apostolates, formation, direction or care for the other members; availability that does not affect the unity of vocation, but is conditioned by various personal, family, professional or social circumstances."[80]

The plenary session of the Congress that approved the final conclusions reaffirmed this teaching not only in the already cited second conclusion, but also in the fifth. There, speaking of the norms and practices of prayer recommended to Opus Dei members to nourish an interior life of prayer and intimacy with God, it declares these norms "are perfectly fitted to the various circumstances of life of the members who, in *unity of vocation*, strive to live as Christians, *each in his or her own state in life*, by *sanctifying ordinary professional work*, the faithful fulfillment of all their duties and the loyal exercise—personally free and personally responsible—of all their civic, social, family, professional obligations, as ordinary citizens and ordinary Christians."[81]

---

receives it from God—whatever be her state or condition in life—knows she ought to sanctify herself through the professional exercise of a job whether intellectual or manual. In Opus Dei—our founder has taught us—there are no different classes of members: there is a multitude of personal, family and social situations that configure the call each one receives to dedicate herself to the service of the Church, in the Work, and to all souls." "All of the members of the women's branch of Opus Dei know that their vocation to the Work is a vocation of service to the Church and all souls. They feel the holy pride of a divine call that has not separated them from the place and circumstances where they received it, but that has moved them to live there with a Christian sense. They feel themselves moved—whatever be their personal situation—by the same vocation: to promote Christian perfection in the middle of the world, without changing in anything one's personal status, neither in the eyes of the Church nor of the state nor of civil society" (ACGS-f, I, Sept. 14, 1969).

[80] ACGS-m, II, Sept. 12, 1970. Let us make a few brief observations with regard to this text.

a) In the approved text we have reproduced, several modifications were proposed by Msgr. Escrivá; one has particular interest here. He had added "that does not affect the unity of vocation," thus reinforcing the meaning of the text.

b) The Latin expression *munus publicum* is found in the oldest texts of the founder; it means that members of Opus Dei always have an ordinary occupation, which each one carries out in the sphere of society where he lives and by which he is identified, since it is a work well known to others.

[81] The emphasis, as seen from the Appendix, document no. 55, is found in the original.

The Congress also gave attention to other aspects of unity as reflected in the second conclusion reproduced at the beginning of this section. It reinforced the unity between priests and lay members. Here, as in all its work, the Congress first invoked the living reality of Opus Dei; it then reaffirmed it, drawing forth conclusions and proposing ways of expressing it, and, finally, noting its satisfaction or gratitude for the benefits from this lived reality.[82]

Members of the Congress wanted to leave no doubt what it meant in all of Opus Dei's apostolic works to be able to count on the help of their own priests. We quote a resolution approved by the men on Sept. 13, 1969. Echoing the writings of Msgr. Escrivá, it speaks of the tenor or spiritual attitude to be lived by the priests and what are the benefits derived therefrom: "From the start it has been our founder's desire that our priests know how to 'spend themselves completely in the service of their brothers;' having as their dominant passion to preach and to confess; serving all the others 'without tolerating that their lay brothers offer them any unnecessary services;' doing and disappearing, being 'the light that is consumed,' 'the salt that is spent,' 'the carpet on which the others tread softly;' to be the course canvas of a tapestry where their brothers and sisters can shine brightly; with 'a lay outlook that displays not the slightest trace of clericalism.' 'There are no categories to distinguish and separate into two classes the priests and the laity.' 'This represents a very special providence of God for which we ought to give thanks from the very bottom of our hearts.'"[83]

During the second part of the Congress mention was made again of this same experience and sentiments. "May it be recorded that we understand as God's gift this formation, this spirit and this work of our priests; that we are deeply grateful to the Father for having been the faithful instrument for this divine grace; and that

---

[82] For example, in a session of the men on Sept. 11, 1969, a proposal was approved to proclaim solemnly: "1. Our intimate unity around the Father, in order to give thanks with him to the Lord and his most holy Mother for the marvelous unity of the Work. 2. The desire of giving special thanks, through the Father, for the work of the women's branch for the domestic care for our Centers, contributing in a special way to making possible all our apostolates." The proposal—as the acts of the Congress show—was approved by acclamation "with an applause that lasted a long time" (ACGS-m, I, Sept. 11, 1969).

[83] ACGS-m, I, Sept. 13, 1969. In the same first session the members reaffirmed also the help that redounds to the whole Work when Christian women can count on the collaboration of priests of Opus Dei, and they approved the following resolution: "1. Our gratitude to the Father for having made available to the women's branch so valuable and effective help that leads us to bring authentically Christian criteria to all our actions. 2. The efficacy of the unity of the Work be pointed out that contributes to the improvement of the eminently lay and Christian spirit of the women members" (ACGS-f, I, Sept. 13, 1969).

we pray to God's Mother, who is also our Mother, that through her intercession all the priests of the Work, till the end of time, keep alive and operative this image of the priesthood, which the Father has transmitted to us, along with the first members who received priestly ordination in Opus Dei."[84]

These expressions of unity between the lay members and priests were echoed in the second of the final conclusions approved in 1970. As if to underline the transcendence of this trait the Congress calls it a "constitutional" character of Opus Dei. Therefore, it requests that it be reaffirmed, because it "allows for a service to the universal Church."[85] These teachings of the founder and experiences from Opus Dei's years of life join in mutual reaffirmation.[86]

We conclude our analysis of the texts that regard unity, by turning to the center of this unity. That is to say, to the president general; not only to the founder, who occupies this position at the moment, but also to his successors at the helm of Opus Dei. The whole Congress constitutes a witness in this regard: in the resolutions reference is often made to the founder, to his work of government, to his teaching, to the communion the Congress seeks to have with his intentions and desires, to the identification Opus Dei members desire between what they live and the charism Msgr. Escrivá received and transmitted from the very start. There are several proposals dealing with the office of the president general. We quote one, from the second part of the Congress, which has the value of a summary and was approved by acclamation.

"In the first part of this Special General Congress it was unanimously proposed and approved in the corresponding plenary session that the proceedings declare:

"First, that the filial affection that all the members of the Work have had and continue to have and ought to have until the end of time for the Father is a permanent and essential characteristic of our spirit;

"Second, that in the Work unity with the Father, with the directors, and among the members has never suffered the slightest weakening;

---

[84] ACGS-m, II, Sept. 12, 1970.

[85] We refer once again to the beginning of this section and to the Appendix, document no. 55.

[86] Perhaps this is the moment to make reference to another step taken by the founder with the occasion of the Congress. Msgr. Escrivá had foreseen some years before the possibility that not only numerary members be ordained priests, but also some associates. Yet the 1950 Constitutions mention only the numeraries; the time did not seem ripe for anything else. In the second part of the Congress the founder deemed the time had come to carry out this project; this he communicated to the members, who received the news with joy and warmly approved the possibility (ACGS-m, II, Sept. 13, 1970).

"Third, that our Father has always been for us a clear and sure guide watching over the good doctrine of his children and he has created in all a spirit of firm adherence to the perennial Magisterium of the Church and of filial union with the person and intentions of the Roman Pontiff.

"Reiterating these declarations from the first part of the Congress and summarizing the desires expressed by not a few communications received during this past year, it is proposed that it be mentioned in the proceedings of this second part of the Special General Congress as a witness to the experience of all members of Opus Dei, that the collective and personal unity of all—both a supernatural and human affection—with our Father is a natural and necessary consequence of our specific vocation. Besides stressing the unity of the Work, it has proven itself to be a firm support and guarantee of our unity with the Roman Pontiff: a unity we live as simple faithful and as members of the Work through our Father."[87]

## 9. In communion with the Roman Pontiff and the College of bishops

There is a last point to be examined in our attempt to sum up the deliberations of the Special General Congress: communion with the Church. Members of the Congress of course paid special heed to the Church, since Opus Dei is but a part thereof and to whose service it pledges itself. Therein it finds its reason for being. Furthermore, reflections on legal matters required such a consideration, since communion in the Church inseparably embraces spiritual, affective and hierarchical facets.

The Congress, celebrated when the Second Vatican Council was being applied and in answer to one of its decrees, above all sought to express its unanimous adherence to the Council just celebrated. A 1969 proposal affirms: "We fully accept with a humble and firm spirit whatever is contained in all the constitutions, decrees and declarations of the Second Vatican Ecumenical Council; and we express our intention to continue contributing to the application of these teachings by faithfully following all the norms of a spiritual, doctrinal and disciplinary character that have or will be given in the future by the Holy See and by the bishops in real and sincere communion with the Roman Pontiff."[88]

This full acceptance of the teaching and provisions of the Second Vatican Council did not signify anything if not a specific way of declaring unity with the Magisterium and in general with the

---

[87] ACGS-m, II, Sept. 11, 1970. A similar text was approved on the following day in the session of the women's branch (ACGS-f, II, Sept. 12, 1970).

[88] ACGS-m, I, Sept. 13, 1969.

ecclesiastical hierarchy, a unity that is coterminous with Christian life. The same day another proposal was approved: "In reference to cooperation with the local ordinary of each territorial diocese and to joining efforts with all those who work for Jesus Christ and for his Church for the good of souls, we want to point out that our founder has taught us and has moved us always to have a great love for all the bishops in communion with the Holy See. In all our corporate apostolates—for which the Work as such takes responsibility—we always act in accord with the ordinary of the territorial diocese, our desire being to reinforce his legitimate authority and to contribute to the true unity of the apostolate. . . . According to our own characteristics, with our lay and secular way of working, we contribute to the service of each diocese and to the improvement of the spiritual life of the faithful. . . . We work in all the dioceses moving in the same direction as the most reverend ordinaries, and the fruit of our work remains in the diocese."[89]

On the following day a new text points out "the firm adherence of all the members of Opus Dei to the magisterium of the pope, the successor of Peter, in his difficult task as shepherd of the universal Church," and "the certainty that is ours that this unwavering fidelity to the magisterium of Christ's Vicar reinforces, in the formation of all the members, a clarity of criteria with which each one can then carry out his own apostolic work, engaging his own personal freedom in the realization of his professional work and in the fulfillment of the duties of his state in life and his duties and rights as a citizen." It concludes: "With the occasion of the celebration of this first part of this General Congress we want the explicit witness of our sincere veneration for and our loyal firm adherence to his magisterium to be raised to the Roman Pontiff."[90]

In the final days of the first part of the Congress members reaffirmed "our full fidelity and our love for the holy Church of God, for the Roman Pontiff and the episcopal College; our fervent adherence to the magisterium of the Church, which recently has had a solemn and rich expression in the documents of the Second Vatican Council; and our firm resolution of continuing to work so that there be always fostered in the hearts of the people of God the necessary unity of faith and fraternal charity that are the distinctive signs of disciples of Jesus Christ."[91]

During the plenary sessions of the second part of the Congress similar texts were approved. We must refer only to two personal proposals of the founder. The first had to do with expanding the

---

[89] ACGS-m, I, Sept. 13, 1969.

[90] ACGS-m, I, Sept. 14, 1969.

[91] ACGS-m, I, Sept. 15, 1969; ACGS-f, I, Sept. 16, 1969.

work of Opus Dei to priests incardinated in dioceses. This was something to which Msgr. Escrivá had dedicated so many efforts, until he found a solution that made it possible for them to be incorporated into the Work without any diminution of the authority of their diocesan bishops. On the contrary this authority was reinforced. This he sought to emphasize and reiterate in the Special General Congress.

"I want to point out once again that in the Work the internal directors of the associate and supernumerary priests are never internal superiors in the juridical sense. . . . This teaching, very well known to all the members of the Work, means that all the direction given to the associate and supernumerary priests has to do with personal help to foster their piety, their culture and their pastoral charity, in circles of study, workshops and the like. Furthermore, these priests attend these activities always in ways compatible with the ministerial obedience owed to their respective bishops and always subordinated to the most perfect fulfillment of the needs of the ecclesiastical offices and of the responsibilities each one has had entrusted to him." This teaching and practice thus "avoids any problem of a possible *double obedience*." This principle should be more clearly reflected, he concludes, in the revision of the *Ius peculiare*, to be carried out at the proper time.[92]

His second proposal was read in the last plenary session on September 14, 1970. "From the very first days of the Work I have insisted by word and in writing—and you have so understood it and have always lived it—that respect, veneration and affection for bishops in communion with the Holy See are constant characteristics of our spirit since the *Spiritus Sanctus eos posuit pascere Ecclesiam Dei* (Apostolic Constitution *Lumen gentium*, no. 20)".

Msgr. Escrivá continued: "This spirit—shown in many small refinements—manifests itself moreover in the way the Work always carries out its apostolic activities in the service of the universal Church in perfect harmony with the rights of the local ordinaries.

---

[92] ACGS-m, II, Sept. 13, 1970. The importance given by the founder to this point of spirit is seen in its express mention in the letter Fr. Alvaro del Portillo sent to Cardinal Antoniutti regarding the Congress on March 23, 1971. The then Secretary General of Opus Dei writes, "The proposal to revise the formulation of the points of the *Ius peculiare* that have to do with associate priests—with this name are now called the oblates—and supernumerary priests of Opus Dei was approved by unanimity. This was done in order to reflect even more clearly and without room for erroneous interpretations, that the incorporation to the Work of these priests does not change in the least their full dependence on their respective bishop: this excludes any kind of *double obedience* or danger of conflict of authority, which has never occurred in Opus Dei. The spiritual help the Work gives to these priests has as its purpose to move them to love their own bishop more and more as well as the diocesan activities and to seek in them their own sanctification." (See the complete text of this letter in the Appendix, document no. 56.)

Before erecting a center of Opus Dei in a territorial diocese, when beginning or expanding the apostolic work proper to Opus Dei, we always request the permission of the local ordinary, who is thus kept abreast of the progress of the apostolates carried out; and our relations with these ordinaries have always been inspired by a spirit of loyal cooperation, within the special features and purposes of our specific vocation: united in the love of Jesus Christ, we always work in the same direction as they. . . . . I want this second part of our Special General Congress to bear witness in writing to this spirit of cordial veneration and this reality of service."[93]

The tone is simple and solemn. It is significant that Msgr. Escrivá sought to evoke publicly, with his authority as founder, the intimate unity that should always inspire the relations of Opus Dei with diocesan bishops.

## 10. The executive phase: the *Codex Iuris Particularis* (1974)

With the close of the plenary sessions of September 1970, the Special General Congress continued its work through a technical commission. Its mission was to prepare the way for revising the juridical status of Opus Dei. To this end it studied the documentation arising out of the Congress' proposals and conclusions, plus individual communications from Opus Dei members and the proposals and suggestions from the regional assemblies organized earlier.

These years were particularly intense for the founder. Consciousness of his age—on January 9, 1971 he celebrated his 69th birthday—accentuated by his profound sense of responsibility as the founder together with his empathy for the vicissitudes of the Church, led him to spend himself even more. To the ordinary tasks of governing Opus Dei and forming members of the Work who spent time in Rome, were added more frequent visitors,[94] as well as a series of pastoral trips that took him from one part of the world to another.

---

[93] ACGS-m, II, Sept. 14, 1970.

[94] The growth of the apostolic work of Opus Dei, combined with the ease of transportation so characteristic of our age, brought more and more people to Rome—members of Opus Dei, parents and friends. They hoped not only to be in the Eternal City and to know the pope, but also to be received by the founder of the Work.

Among these visits, some should be highlighted. There exists among German Catholics an old custom of going to Rome to celebrate the holy days of Easter. In the early 1960s some German university students associated with the apostolate of Opus Dei had gone to Rome to celebrate Easter, and were received by Msgr. Escrivá. This event was repeated and caught on elsewhere. The initial small group became thus a large pilgrimage of hundreds and even thousands of young people above all from Europe, but also from other continents. The founder always received them with great dedication and affection. With regard to these meetings, see A. Vázquez de Prada, *op. cit.* (chapter I, note 1), pp. 383-384.

A visit to Mexico in 1970 was an important milestone. On previous occasions in connection with his many trips, Msgr. Escrivá had habitually received large groups of people, belonging to Opus Dei or related in some way to its apostolates, and answered their questions. In Mexico this tradition was broadened into a true and extensive catechesis. The fruits of this preaching, the trust, attention and affection with which so many people approached the founder of Opus Dei, the later news that reached him of conversions and decisions stemming from his words—all this moved him profoundly, leading him to give thanks to God whose instrument he always considered himself to be. At the same time he saw in this experience an invitation: God was asking him to use an important part of the remaining years to teach and preach in this way, helping to make the faith more attractive and livable. In 1972, from October 4 to November 30, he visited several cities of Spain and Portugal, during which many public gatherings were organized in which more than 150,000 people participated. On May 22, 1974, he began a second trip to the Americas, visiting Brazil, Argentina, Chile, Peru, Ecuador and Venezuela in a work of teaching doctrine that lasted until August 31. From February 4-25, 1975, he was once again in the Americas, this time in Venezuela and Guatemala. Altogether he spent 122 days in the Americas, where many thousands were able to hear him.[95]

Still the search for a definitive juridical solution remained Msgr. Escrivá's main occupation and preoccupation. The technical commission was hard at work. On March 23, 1971, Fr. del Portillo, in his role as Opus Dei's Secretary General, wrote Cardinal Antoniutti, to inform him of the new phase the Special General Congress had entered. After mentioning the 54,781 communications from 50,710 members of Opus Dei that "are now the object of an attentive consideration and study," he added that "the material under study is enormous, and it is not foreseen that the work will be finished within the year 1972."[96]

Theirs was a patient and intricate work. The 1950 *Constitutions* in their 1963 version were to be reviewed, number by number, to compare them with the proposals of the 1969-1970 plenary sessions of the Congress, the recommendations of the regional assemblies and all those personal suggestions from individual members of Opus Dei—and all that to be collated with Opus Dei's spirit and praxis. The aim was to draw up, where appropriate, new formulas or drafts to be elaborated into the future Code or statutes for Opus Dei.

---

[95] With regard to these trips, see A. Vázquez de Prada, *op. cit.* (chapter I, note 1), pp. 387ff and 446ff; F. Gondrand, *op. cit.* (chapter I, note 1), pp. 321ff and 329ff.

[96] This letter is found in the Appendix, document no. 56.

On June 25, 1973, Msgr. Escrivá was received in audience by Pope Paul VI, to acquaint him with the work of the Special General Congress and the technical commission, with a view to revising the Work's juridical status. The Roman Pontiff encouraged him to continue forward.[97]

Work continued. In 1974, after his trip to South America and recovering from the tiredness it caused him,[98] the founder was able to put the finishing touches to the project of a new code of particular law for Opus Dei. On October 1 Fr. del Portillo, as Secretary General of Opus Dei and chairman of the technical commission, made a record of this approval. He describes the preceding phases of the Special General Congress and summarizes the declarations of Msgr. Escrivá at the Congress on the need to revise the juridical status of Opus Dei, as well as the conclusions approved on September 14, 1970. The technical commission had worked under the founder's "continual supervision." The document concludes: "The project elaborated by the technical commission, of which mention has been made, was presented to our founder and president general, who, after having it studied by the executive committee of the general council of the Work, has approved it in all of its parts, on this day, decreeing that to distinguish it from the Codex of 1963 it be designated with the title of *Codex Iuris Particularis* of Opus Dei."[99] Msgr. Escrivá wanted to seal it with his signature, corroborating in this way the document with his authority as founder and president general.[100]

What criteria were used in writing this *Codex Iuris Particularis* of 1974? On the one hand, in keeping with the criteria that governed writing of the 1963 *Codex Iuris Peculiaris*, an effort was made to simplify the text. Thus, as in 1963, it eliminates some chapters regarding spirit and customs, while keeping sufficient references to theological and spiritual traits to afford a description of the fundamental aspects of the spirit of Opus Dei. Some points are further synthesized to highlight fundamental characteristics. Moreover,

---

[97] RHF, 20171, p. 1266.

[98] During his stay in Peru—where he arrived on July 9—and in Ecuador—where he visited afterwards—he caught the flu with complications resulting from the altitude. Thus he had to cancel the scheduled visit to Colombia and go directly to Venezuela where at sea level he was able to recover. Even after returning to Europe at the end of August, he needed a time of rest, during which he continued, so far as his strength allowed, to work intensely.

[99] In order to avoid the use of the term "constitutions," the founder had designated the modified version of the 1950 *Constitutions* with the title of *Codex Iuris Peculiaris* which was written and approved in 1963 (see chapter VIII, section 8). Thus the new name that is still used.

[100] The document of approval is in the Appendix, document no. 58.

the structure and content of the text was profoundly revised, heeding the desideratum of the Special General Congress that the new norms be fully faithful to the foundational charism.

To better understand how these objectives were accomplished, let us recall the juridical analysis Msgr. Escrivá made in a letter to Cardinal Antoniutti on October 22, 1969, informing him about the Special General Congress.[101] After declaring that Opus Dei seeks not only a simple revision or improvement of its existing statutory norms but a change in its juridical configuration, the founder then adds: "some of the eventual modifications . . . could be introduced by the General Congress itself, others would require the Holy See's approval, and still others, finally, insofar as they imply a change in the nature of the institute, would require an even more solemn act of the Holy See, that is, a new erection of the institute." Indeed there were aspects of the 1963 *Codex Iuris Peculiaris* that the Special General Congress, with the authority conferred upon it by the common law of the Church and the presence of the founder could change directly. Other modifications exceeded the competence of the Special General Congress and therefore the Congress could but submit such proposals to the judgment of the Holy See.

These criteria are reflected in the 1974 text, about which in summary fashion we can say the following:

a) With regard to the systematic organization of the subject matter, the 1974 *Codex* distributes the subject matter in important points differently from the previous text, in order to stress even more the unity of the pastoral phenomenon. It is divided into five titles: the first deals with Opus Dei's nature and members; the second, dealing with the Priestly Society of the Holy Cross, speaks of the call to holy orders of those already belonging to Opus Dei, and later, of the possible incorporation to the Priestly Society of the Holy Cross of priests incardinated in dioceses; the third concerns the spiritual life, doctrinal-religious formation and apostolate of the members of Opus Dei; the fourth title describes how Opus Dei is governed; the fifth contains norms regarding the stability and modification of the text.[102] There is no longer a special title dedicated to the women's branch, a clear difference from the earlier text; on the other hand a title is devoted to the Priestly Society of the Holy Cross. This latter step emphasizes the unity of the pasto-

---

[101] This letter is in the Appendix, document no. 54.

[102] These titles are divided in turn into chapters: Title I comprises four chapters with these headings: the nature and aim of Opus Dei; members of Opus Dei; admission and incorporation of members; departure and dismissal of members.

Title II is divided into three chapters: the nature of the Priestly Society of the Holy Cross and of its numerary members; the call to holy orders and canonical mission of

ral phenomenon, while giving greater prominence to the role of the ministerial priesthood in the organic structure of Opus Dei.

b) Besides the simplifications and modifications already mentioned (resulting in a text comprised of 194 numbers), all expressions or formulas related to the normative systems proper to the states of perfection have been removed. In those cases where this was not possible—because they were part of the previous juridical configuration and only removable following a new erection—these terms have been retained but placed in brackets.[103] The forward points out that phrases so designated represent suppressions or modifications to be requested of the Holy See when petitioning the definitive juridical configuration.

We find ourselves before a text that goes as far as possible at the time, within the limits of law. At the same time it charts the path for the final and decisive step in the juridical development. In fact when a few years later the Holy See finally acceded to what Opus Dei's founder had sought for so many years—and officially requested in 1962—the statutes given Opus Dei will be a faithful transcription of this *Codex Iuris Particularis* of 1974, with a few necessary changes.[104]

Thus in October 1974 the study and technical execution of what had been agreed upon by the Special General Congress had been concluded. There only remained the opportune moment for presenting the Holy See with the formal request for a new juridical configuration. The founder, who had prepared everything necessary, could not, however, take this final step. A few months later,

---

the priests; the associate and supernumerary members of the Priestly Society of the Holy Cross.

Title III has three chapters: spiritual life; doctrinal-religious formation of the members; apostolate of the members.

Title IV has five chapters: governance in general of Opus Dei; central government; regional government; regional assemblies; relations with the ecclesiastical hierarchy.

Title V, because of its brevity, is not divided into chapters.

[103] Such is the case of the expression "secular institute" and references to vows or similar terms.

[104] This is the reason, furthermore, that we do not now go on to examine more carefully this code: everything to be added will be said at its proper time when in the following chapter we analyze the definitive juridical form. Nevertheless to complete the information as we did in previous chapters the text of the first chapter is included in the Appendix, document no. 59. We point out also—since it is significant both with regard to the continuity between this *Codex* and the *Statutes* of the Prelature, as well as the kinds of changes the new juridical configuration introduced—that the titles and chapters of the *Statutes* of the Prelature of Opus Dei are the very same as those of the *Codex* of 1974, with the difference that while the *Codex* calls members of Opus Dei *sociis* ("associates"), in the statutes of the Prelature the term *christifideles* is used in accordance with the nature of this juridical figure.

before initiating these negotiations with the Holy See, God called Msgr. Escrivá to his presence on June 26, 1975.

# Chapter X

## OPUS DEI, A PERSONAL PRELATURE

# Chapter X

## OPUS DEI, A PERSONAL PRELATURE

### 1. Fr. Alvaro del Portillo requests Opus Dei's transformation into a personal prelature

Barely three months after the death of Msgr. Escrivá a General Congress for the election of his successor gathered in Rome. On September 15, 1975, the Congress unanimously elected as president general Fr. Alvaro del Portillo, who for forty years had been the closest collaborator of the founder. The electors showed thus their desire for unbroken continuity with the foundational stage and complete confidence that the most appropriate choice was the person closest to the founder.[1]

---

[1] Some time after the election of Fr. del Portillo as President General of Opus Dei, Fr. Javier Echevarría—now the Vicar General of the Prelature and at the time the Secretary General of Opus Dei—published a brief but moving portrait. Among other things he said: "Don Alvaro del Portillo is 61 years old, and has been a member of Opus Dei for 40 years, lived with intensity close to the founder." He had thus not only accompanied him but had received with utmost fidelity the spiritual message to whose transmission Msgr. Escrivá dedicated all his life. Therefore "he guards in his heart a patrimony of precious value that has impregnated as it still does all his activity" (*La Vanguardia*, Barcelona, Dec. 21, 1975). The consciousness of continuity with the founder reflected in these articles sum up the sentiments that reigned in Opus Dei and doubtless in Alvaro del Portillo himself, when the first successor of Msgr. Escrivá was to be chosen. These sentiments are those that governed the remaining steps of the juridical course.

Let's note a few biographical details on Very Rev. Alvaro del Portillo. He was born in Madrid on March 11, 1914. He holds doctorates in engineering, philosophy and letters, and canon law. In 1935 he was incorporated into Opus Dei. On June 25, 1944, he was ordained a priest, one of the three first members to be so. He invariably collaborated with Msgr. Escrivá in governing the Work, especially with the successive juridical approvals.

He resided with Msgr. Escrivá in Rome from 1946 and became quickly known to the Roman Curia, having been named in the days of Pius XII a consultor to several commissions. At the convocation of the Second Vatican Council he was appointed President of the Antepreparatory Commission for the Laity and formed part in addi-

Upon taking possession of his office, Rev. del Portillo presented the Congress with some important matters that could not be put off: among others, discussions towards the new juridical configuration. The Congress signaled its agreement with what had been done until then. Pointing specifically to the founder's approval of the *Codex Iuris Particularis* in 1974, it declared it was "an approval this Congress makes its own and unanimously ratifies." It conveyed to the new president general its desire that as soon as possible and opportune to do so that the necessary steps be taken to achieve the definitive juridical configuration in accordance with the founder's will.[2]

Reflecting on these matters, Very Rev. del Portillo deemed it preferable not to open discussions at the outset of his office, lest there arise misinterpretations on the part of people outside of Opus Dei who were not cognizant of the founder's express will on this matter. He told this to Paul VI in an audience on March 5, 1976. The pope agreed with this decision and confirmed that "the matter continues to be open."[3] In a subsequent audience on June 19, 1978, Paul VI encouraged Very Rev. del Portillo to present soon the proper documentation, always faithfully following the founder's spirit in the light of the improvements to the general law of the Church that had resulted from the Second Vatican Council.[4] Nevertheless, on the following 6th of August Paul VI died before the appropriate request could be presented.

In September 1978, Very Rev. Alvaro del Portillo informed the new pope, John Paul I, elected on August 26, that the fiftieth anniversary of Opus Dei's founding was at hand, and acquainted him with the unresolved institutional problem. The Holy Father expressed his desire that the study of the sought-for jurdicial solution

---

tion of other preparatory commissions; from the course of the sessions of the Council he was Secretary of the Commission on the Discipline of the Clergy and of the Faithful Christian people and a consultor to various congregations. In 1963 he was named consultor to the Pontifical Commission for the Revision of the Code of Canon Law and at the end of the Council consultor of several congregations and commissions.

His broad curial experience, his theological-canonical studies, his profound direct and lived knowledge of the spirit and the history of Opus Dei, his broad and intense collaboration with Msgr. Escrivá made him particularly fit to succeed the founder and to conclude the final stage of the process of the definitive juridical configuration.

For further information see "Portillo, Alvaro del," in the *Gran Enciclopedia Rialp*, V. 18, Madrid 1974, pp. 800-802 and V. 25 (Suplemento), Madrid 1987, pp. 1553-1554.

[2] The acts of the session for Sept. 15, 1975, of the General Congress of Opus Dei, p. 20 in AGP, Sezione giuridica, VIII/15051.

[3] AGP, Sezione giuridica, VIII/15527, no. 41.

[4] *Ibid.*

be commenced.[5] The sudden death of the pope, however, on September 28 once again left the matter in suspense.

On November 15, 1978, John Paul II, elected Roman Pontiff on October 16, addressed to Opus Dei's president general a hand-written letter expressing his cordial sharing in the joy and thanksgiving to God with which Opus Dei celebrated the golden anniversary of its foundation. In transmitting this letter, Cardinal Jean Villot, the Secretary of State, also wrote that the Holy Father considered it "an urgent need that the question of the juridical configuration of Opus Dei be resolved."[6]

Thus we enter on to the last stage of the way leading to the definitive juridical configuration of Opus Dei. To understand the steps to be taken, let us reiterate that what Opus Dei was to request was its transformation into a personal prelature. In other words, it was not a question of creating something *ex novo* but of attributing the configuration of personal prelature to a preexisting institution. This implied the intervention of two departments of the Roman Curia. The Congregation for Bishops was competent according to the Apostolic Constitution *Regimini Ecclesiæ universæ*, in everything having to do with the erection of personal prelatures.[7] The Congregation for Religious and Secular Institutes, on which Opus Dei still depended insofar as it was *de iure* a secular institute (though *de facto* it did not so consider itself), also had competency in the matter.

Owing to the latter fact in order to put into motion the indication received from the Cardinal Secretary of State, Very Rev. del Portillo addressed himself on January 11, 1979, to the Congregation for Religious and Secular Institutes. In his letter, after pointing out the need to revise the juridical status of Opus Dei, he requested authorization to initiate the necessary discussions toward granting Opus Dei a juridical configuration distinct from that of secular institute. "Having in mind what was expressed by the Most Reverend President General of Opus Dei," the Congregation for Religious replied, "this Sacred Congregation grants the authorization requested, and recommends that for the definitive juridical configuration the spirit and indications of the founder be followed."[8]

---

[5] AGP, Sezione giuridica, VIII/15527, no. 42.

[6] AGP, Sezione giuridica, VIII/15043.

[7] Number 49 of the aforementioned Apostolic Constitution declares: "It is of the competency of the Congregation for Bishops to erect military vicariates and, having heard the opinion of the episcopal conferences of the respective territory, personal prelatures for the carrying out of special pastoral tasks on behalf of regions or social groups which have need of special help" (Paul VI, *Regimini Ecclesiæ universæ*, August 15, 1967, no. 49, in *AAS* 59 (1966):901).

[8] Both texts—the letter of Very Rev. Alvaro del Portillo and the Rescript of the Sacred Congregation—are found in the Appendix, document no. 60.

Thus Very Rev. del Portillo could turn to the Congregation for Bishops, which he did immediately. A first conversation of an informal nature took place on March 20 when the question of Opus Dei's transformation into a personal prelature was brought up. [The formal beginning of these negotiations and studies was subject to the Holy Father's expressly entrusting the matter to the Congregation for Bishops.][9] In an audience with John Paul II on February 12, Very Rev. del Portillo informed the Holy Father of the conversations with both offices and formally presented the petition that Opus Dei be transformed into a personal prelature.[10] A few weeks later, on March 3, 1979, in an audience granted to Cardinal Sebastiano Baggio the Holy Father entrusted the matter to the Congregation for Bishops under whose jurisdiction the matter fell according to its nature. It was to study the matter, having in mind all elements of law and of fact.[11] Shortly after the audience, Cardinal Baggio wrote to Very Rev. del Portillo on March 7, informing him of the charge received. On March 29, Cardinal Baggio indicated to Very Rev. del Portillo that it would be appropriate to send him an in-depth study that could serve as the basis for subsequent work. Opus Dei's President General responded with a letter dated April 27, 1979, conveying a study entitled "Trasformazione dell'Opus Dei in Prelatura personale." There he sets forth in detail both the antecedents and the content of the petition.[12] On June 2 Very Rev. del Portillo sent another letter, with further particulars on some aspects that completed the previous petition.[13] Let us examine the terms of the petition as formulated.

The study accompanying the April 27 letter is most all-encompassing; we will use it as the basis for our exposition. It is divided into three parts, which form a structured whole. They first laid down some basic principles from which the petition follows as a conclusion. Let us follow its line of argument.

a) The starting point (the first part of the study) is the consideration of the specific features and the sociological reality of Opus Dei. The writing points out that Opus Dei arose from the start with a clearly defined theological and apostolic content, founded on the

---

[9] The conversation and some of the following events are related in the study report of April 23, 1979 of which we will speak shortly and which is found in the Appendix, document no. 63.

[10] The formal petition is in the Appendix, document no. 61.

[11] Cf. S. Baggio, "A Good for the Whole Church," in *L'Osservatore Romano*, weekly edition in English, December 6, 1982.

[12] The letter of Very Rev. Alvaro del Portillo and the accompanying report are in the Appendix, document nos. 62-63.

[13] This letter is in the Appendix, document no. 64.

universal call to holiness and apostolate inherent in baptism. This call is answered with a full, personal commitment, undertaken by its members' faithful fulfillment of their family and social duties, especially their own occupation. Thus, the document adds, Opus Dei members seek their own sanctification and that of others, while each one remains in the canonical state corresponding to him, with a clearly secular and specific spirituality.

After noting the spread of Opus Dei,[14] the study highlights that the institution possesses all of the elements—its own shepherd, presbyterate and laity, who constitute a portion of the People of God hierarchically structured and organized. It is, says the document, a pastoral unity organically and indivisibly comprised of priests and lay people—men and women, celibate and married—of every social and professional condition who participate equally in the same spirit and vocation and are united under one regimen of formation and discipline. It differs, therefore, from the institutes of consecrated life as well as from pious unions or other associations of the faithful. Since Opus Dei is a new pastoral phenomenon in the life of the Church, it was understandable, the exposition concludes, that prior ecclesiastical legislation did not offer an appropriate juridical channel. From this follow the deficiencies and difficulties, born of an inadequate canonical situation, that required a compromise.

b) The conclusion of this part, an amalgam of historical, sociological and doctrinal dimensions (in fact a reaffirmation of the original charism), leads logically to the second part. It details the steps the founder took throughout Opus Dei's juridical evolution, taking whatever formulas were available at each moment; up to the petition presented to the Holy See in 1962; as well as the celebration of the Speical General Congress, leading to the accomplishment of the necessary studies to obtain a definitive juridical solution in conformity with the reality of Opus Dei and according to the canonical possibilities opened by Vatican Council II.

c) The third part points to the basis for a new juridical configuration. Logically following from its prior exposition, the study of April 1979 outlines what are called "characteristic elements" of personal prelatures, as given in the Decree *Presbyterorum ordinis* and subsequent pontifical documents (the Motu proprio *Ecclesiæ sanctæ* and the Apostolic Constitution *Regimini Ecclesiæ universæ*). These elements are the following:

—Personal prelatures are ordered to carrying out special pastoral works;

—they have a clearly secular character;

---

[14] It points out, for example, that there were then 72,375 members of Opus Dei from 87 countries.

—they are subject to the jurisdiction or government of a prelate;

—they have their own clergy, specially trained and formed to carry out their mission; the clergy are incardinated in the prelature and entrusted to the care and direction of the prelate;

—lay faithful, celibate or married, can become members of the prelature by dedicating their lives and occupations to the aims and apostolic activities of the prelature, to which they are united not by means of sacred bonds but by means of a contract or agreement that regulates the mutual exchange of services;

—they carefully respect the rights of the local ordinaries, with whom they maintain close relations;

—they are governed by their own statutes, sanctioned by the Holy See;

—they depend—as a logical consequence of their hierarchical and secular character—on the Sacred Congregation for Bishops.

This summary of the traits of personal prelatures is then matched with the spirit of Opus Dei and its social and juridical reality. Opus Dei, the document affirms, substantially possesses in fact the constitutive elements of a personal prelature. The study explains that Opus Dei is already an entity of pontifical right with a clearly secular spirituality; its president general enjoys, in what regards government and internal discipline, the attributes of the power of governance; it has its own clergy, formed in its own centers, as well as a large body of lay people; it is at work apostolically in more than 500 dioceses, in close and constant contact with the respective local ordinaries and carefully respecting their rights; it likewise has its own legal regimen, which could continue to be the statutes or particular law of the prelature, with the changes required by the new juridical form. Finally, the text adds, Opus Dei has in Rome its headquarters (domicile of the president general, offices of the general council and an international center of studies or seminary), on a small territory of its own that could constitute the necessary material foundation of the prelature.

Thus nothing seems to stand in the way of its being erected as a personal prelature; everything, rather, seems to point in that direction. The ecclesial advantages to follow from such a juridical transformation would be considerable: it would reinforce the service Opus Dei offers to the local churches; it would make available to the Holy See an apostolically effective organism made up of priests and laity trained to be a spiritual and apostolic leaven of Christian life; it would also guarantee in a definitive way the preservation of the spiritual characteristics proper to Opus Dei. Furthermore it would not constitute a disturbing precedent for other institutions of a different nature that have found their place within the confines of institutes of consecrated life or other figures foreseen by law. The study handed over on April 23, 1979, concludes by pointing out that the new juridical configuration would assure and confirm: "all the norms of a general and particular nature that regulate the present organization and government of the Work; its discipline; the thorough formation of its members (eschewing elitism and fully faithful to the ecclesiastical magisterium); their ongoing spiritual formation by their own priests; their constant, close collaboration with diocesan bishops, etc. At the same time the channels of communication and the dependence of Opus Dei on the Holy See would be reinforced, above all through the Sacred Congregation for Bishops, on which it would depend, and to which it would regularly present, among other things, the quinquennial report *de statu prelaturæ.*

The later letter of June 2, 1979, declares that the April 23 text sets forth the "fundamental dispositions" or "basic norms," whose approval would allow reaching later a more detailed normative framework covering the jurisdiction of the prelate and the relations of the prelature with diocesan bishops. To wit:

a) It specifies that the prelate's jurisdiction, analogous to the authority of the president general in the current canonical figure, will affect only the incardinated priests and the members (men and women, married and single) incorporated to Opus Dei. His jurisdiction does not extend to those persons reached by Opus Dei's apostolic work, but only those lay faithful that are contractually incorporated to the prelature.

b) Regarding relations of the prelature with local ordinaries, it insists that both the rights of the local ordinaries as well as the present norms of the particular regimen of Opus Dei would be safeguarded.[15]

c) Finally, it points out that the prelate, besides the qualities required by the common or general law in canon 331 of the Code of Canon Law then in force, should also meet the qualities prescribed by the particular law of Opus Dei (minimum age of forty, knowledge of the spirit and apostolate of Opus Dei, etc.). His election would require confirmation by the Holy Father, the usual practice in analogous cases.

If we compare these two letters of 1979 with the conclusions of the Special General Congress and with the petition the founder

---

[15] To describe this harmony between the authority of the local ordinary and that of the prelate, this letter employs the expression "accumulative jurisdiction." Its extent and meaning are made precise by Very Rev. del Portillo in another letter to Cardinal Baggio of February 6, 1980: "In everything that the common law prescribes for all the ordinary faithful, [the laity of the Work] remain under the jurisdiction of the local ordinaries; they are under the personal jurisdiction of the president general of Opus Dei only in those matters required by their specific vocation (special spiritual, formative, apostolic and disciplinary commitments to ensure a greater dedication to the service of the Church)" (AGP, Sezione giuridica, VIII/15277).

addressed to the Holy See in 1962, we observe a complete continuity in both the general orientation and in the particulars. There is, however, a greater juridical elaboration, born of the legislative advances and studies achieved since that time. This affects, above all, a central point. In 1962 Msgr. Escrivá had to move within the 1917 Code, where the only prelatures recognized were of a territorial character. Basing himself then on the precedent of the *Mission de France*, he had invoked what in a certain sense was a juridical fiction, though accepted by canon law. He had requested the erection of a territorial prelature (with a miniscule territory of a mere symbolic nature) from which would stem an apostolic action of its members—priests and lay people—in many different countries. The great step forward taken by Vatican Council II regarding the concept of prelature[16] made such a move unnecessary. It had established a new figure of a personal prelature in virtue of which lay people and priests in an organic unity carry out a particular pastoral work.

We point out also that while these letters reflect the advances made in the ecclesiological and canonical doctrine of the time, they also reflect in some points their limitations. We allude specifically to the expression *cum proprio populo*, which appears in the documents seeking the recategorization of Opus Dei. From the text it is evident that Very Rev. del Portillo wants to indicate, with terminology operative at the time, that the sought-for erection—a point of transcendental importance—refers not only to the complex made up of prelate and priests, but also to the whole of Opus Dei in its organic unity, comprising priests and laity, men and women, single and married, of all walks and social conditions. In no moment does it seek independence from the local churches. What is expressly sought is that the norms governing relations of Opus Dei with diocesan bishops should continue in force.

Thus as soon as canonists abandoned as ambiguous the expression *prelatura personal "cum proprio populo,"* Very Rev. del Portillo also ceased to use it, with the satisfaction of one who uses technically more precise terms that hold erroneous interpretations at bay. Here is his own explanation in an interview granted in 1982 whose clarity deserves extensive citation. "In 1979, at the time of these studies [those we are analyzing], experts of canon law distinguished between personal prelatures and personal prelatures *cum proprio populo*. The former were those made up only by a prelate and priests, as the prelature of Pontigny or the *Mission de France* . . . the

---

[16] For an analysis of the doctrinal development which underlies the work of the Council in order to move from the figure of the Mission de France to that of the personal prelature, we refer again to the work of P. Lombardía and J. Hervada, *Sobre prelaturas personales, op. cit.,* (chapter IX, note 11), pp. 20-34.

latter, those referred to as *cum proprio populo*, were personal prelatures also having lay members as faithful incorporated to them.

"It was logical, therefore, that, since Opus Dei was composed in great part of lay people, we should use the expression *cum proprio populo*; the contrary would have made it seem that we sought erection as a prelature of only a part of the Work—the clergy—while the lay members (more than 60,000 at the time) would continue as a secular institute.

"At the same time in these and in other documents sent to the Holy See, the very beginning of the study set forth that, even though the expression *cum proprio populo* was used to avoid the error to which we have alluded, we did not seek in any way (such was not our founder's will) that the lay faithful of the prelature should be under the complete and exclusive jurisdiction of the prelate, independent, that is, or exempt from the jurisdiction common law grants to diocesan bishops.

"Fortunately, in December 1980, the Pontifical Commission for the Revision of the Code of Canon Law in its review *Communications*, concerning the state of the work of the Commission with regard to the juridical figure of personal prelatures, made it known that the expression *cum proprio populo* had been suppressed in the draft canons, since for various technical reasons this expression was inappropriate. Logically and, I would add, with personal satisfaction, we accommodated ourselves immediately to this precise juridical and terminological norm without any need to vary the content of our petition: the same one the Holy See has now definitively sanctioned."[17]

## 2. Establishment of a technical commission to study the question

On June 28, 1979, at an ordinary meeting of the Congregation for Bishops, its cardinal and bishop members, following a study of the documentation received, examined the petition in a general way. They concluded that further study was opportune and in this regard raised some questions. Cardinal Baggio, Prefect of the Congregation, informed the Roman Pontiff of this. Msgr. del Portillo also addressed himself to the Holy Father in letters dated July 3 and July 13, 1979, indicating his full availability for whatever was needed.[18]

---

[17] Interview granted to Joaquín Navarro Valls, at the time correspondent in Rome for the Madrid daily ABC and published on Nov. 29, 1982. The decision of the Pontifical Commission for the Revision of the Code of Canon Law to which Msgr. del Portillo refers, was taken in the session of consultors of the said commission celebrated from March 10-15, 1980. The acts of this session are published in Communicationes, 12 (1980):269ff; the question to which Msgr. del Portillo refers is dealt with in pp. 275-282.

[18] AGP, Sezione giuridica, VIII/15036 and 15046.

On July 18, Cardinal Baggio sent a letter to the President General of Opus Dei.[19] After a brief factual summary, he states that, in accord with the will of the Roman Pontiff, the work is to be continued without interruption, aiming at a most thorough study. Before entering into more technical aspects, Cardinal Baggio, putting aside an official tone in order to avoid any possible misunderstandings, expressed his dispositions and those of the Holy Father: "Before all else I want to assure you that the appropriateness of a more profound study is due to the novelty and complexity of the problem and the importance which, as a precedent, it has in the institutional framework of the Church; this step does not imply any wariness with respect to Opus Dei for which the high esteem and sincere affection, many times manifested by the Roman Pontiff, is well known. I would add that in the course of the ordinary meeting of the Congregation, the value and the merits of the society you worthily preside over were unanimously recognized."

Then Cardinal Baggio, turning back to more juridical comments, noted that the Holy Father had confirmed the competence of the Congregation for Bishops with regard to the study of the topic. He enumerated a series of documents and reports he sought, for the work to go forward. The request confirms the breadth and depth with which the Congregation wished to proceed. It asked for the following: the *Statutes* of Opus Dei in force at the time; plans or norms whereby the formation of the members is carried out; a historical report on the founder's will with respect to the definitive juridical configuration of Opus Dei; a technical juridical study on the possibility of proceeding to the erection as a personal prelature on the basis of existing law (*ius conditum*); a study on the secular condition of Opus Dei and its members; a detailed analysis of the reason why Opus Dei members—clergy and laity, men and women— should depend on the prelate; a report on the criteria to be followed in the prelature's relations with territorial jurisdictions to avoid any risk of isolation or separation. Finally, since it would seem appropriate to consult the episcopal conferences involved at its proper time according to what was established in the Motu proprio *Ecclesiæ sanctæ*, a report was requested on the international expansion of Opus Dei and the spread of its apostolate to various countries.

When Msgr. del Portillo received this letter he set about preparing the material, eager to present it as soon as possible. In October 1979, however, an unexpected event occurred: two documents from the dossier (the letters from Msgr. del Portillo dated April 23 and June 2, 1979, to the Prefect of the Congregation for Bishops) fell into the hands of someone who sent them to numerous bishops and to

---

[19] This letter is found in the Appendix, document no. 65.

the media of various countries in an attempt at misrepresentation. By selective and manipulative quotations, the impression was given that Opus Dei desired to set itself up as an entity beyond any submission and accountability. The object sought by this maneuver was doubtless to awaken the fears among bishops and some sectors of the media that Opus Dei with its erection as a personal prelature sought to obtain independence from diocesan bishops. It was hoped thus to sow obstacles in the path of its erection.

Opus Dei reacted immediately denouncing this falsification.[20] The Sacred Congregation for Bishops also deplored what had happened.[21] Furthermore, this unlawful and distorted publication of documents—deplorable and distressing on many accounts—did not achieve its authors' aim; the study of the petition presented by Opus Dei went ahead. The Sacred Congregation for Bishops, moreover, moved to establish a technical commission charged with examining all the documents and related problems in order to reach a broad and diligent judgment; this step met with the Roman Pontiff's favor.

On November 17, 1979, Cardinal Baggio told the head of Opus Dei that the Pope had approved the creation of a joint study commission, made up of representatives from the Sacred Congregation and Opus Dei. From the Congregation three people had been designated: Msgr. Marcello Costalunga, undersecretary of the Congregation; Msgr. Mario F. Pompedda, auditor of the Roman Rota and consultor of the Congregation, and Msgr. Mariano Olés, a clerk of the same pontifical Congregation.[22]

On December 11, Msgr. Alvaro del Portillo informed the Congregation that on behalf of Opus Dei the members of the joint com-

---

[20] The secretariat of Opus Dei issued a press statement: "In conformity with precise indications of the Holy See, it disavows the news and information on the future juridical situation of the Work, spread recently and elaborated on the basis of an incomplete documentation brought to the public realm without respecting the dispositions of the Holy See to whom this documentation belongs.

"It communicates moreover that since this matter pertains to the exclusive competence of the Holy See, it will abstain from making any future declarations.

"At the same time this secretariat reiterates that Opus Dei, whose sole aim is the service of the Church and of souls, in all its apostolates works and seeks always to work in close and loyal communion with the most reverend bishops of the respective dioceses, whom it loves and venerates as the successors of the Apostles" (AGP, Sezione giuridica, VIII/15019).

[21] A circular letter, in which the press communication reproduced in the previous note, was sent from the Sacred Congregation to all the nuncios or apostolic delegates of the countries where the apostolate of Opus Dei was extended (of this action Cardinal Baggio informed the President General in a letter of Nov. 17, of which we will speak later in the text).

[22] AGP, Sezione giuridica, VIII/15023.

mission would be: Rev. Amadeo de Fuenmayor, dean of the faculty of canon law of the University of Navarre; Rev. Xavier de Ayala, regional counselor of Opus Dei in Brasil and consultor of the Pontifical Commission for the Revision of the Code of Canon Law, and Rev. Julián Herranz, consultor of the general council of Opus Dei.[23] Meanwhile the material requested on July 18 by the Congregation was prepared. The new commission from the start would also have the supplementary documentation, including the *Codex Iuris Particularis* of 1974.

Early in 1980, Msgr. Alvaro del Portillo began to provide this documentation accompanied by letters in which, on occasions, he commented on aspects of particular importance. In one such letter, dated February 6, 1980, he offered some considerations relevant to the methodology of the work already carried out. He begins by recalling how he had been charged by the General Congress in 1975 at his election as president general: "to carry to completion our founder's will with regard to the definitive juridical configuration of Opus Dei, in accordance with the indications he had left. . . . At the same time bearing in mind the very long period God granted me to be at our founder's side as one of his closest collaborators in governing the Work, the Congress entrusted me with the duty of pointing out, in the application of these indications of Msgr. Escrivá, were it necessary in some case, what was the exact mind of our founder in this regard." He concludes: "Through the people I have designated to represent Opus Dei and my own personal intervention as often as I deem it opportune, an old desire of our founder will be realized: to conduct an informative dialogue with experts of the Holy See in which we will supply all the clarifications, background and opportune data (which evidently only we can present *in toto*) and explain what is the reality of our vocation, our life and service to the Church; what are the difficulties, what are the reasons for these difficulties and what are the reasons—which will be obvious—for the juridical solution that we request."[24]

---

[23] AGP, Sezione giuridica, VIII/15024.

[24] AGP, Sezione giuridica, VIII/15277. One of the themes on which Msgr. del Portillo spent time in the body of this letter was the explanation of the meaning of the expression *cum proprio populo*, which he would further explain in the interview of 1982 from which we have already quoted. We reproduce the paragraphs which he dedicated to this topic even though in part we have anticipated this in note no. 15 of this chapter. "It was never the will of our founder . . . to understand this expression *cum proprio populo* in the sense of the prelatures *nullius dioecesis*, that is to say, of a territorial character, in which the *portio populi Dei* is totally exempt with regard to other ecclesiastical jurisdictions and depends in everything on the prelate.

"In our case (as I have already pointed out in what I wrote on April 23, 1979, no. 17 §§ 9-10 and no. 22, as well as in the later letter of June 2 of last year, nos. 1 and 2), it is a question of a laity, inseparably united to the presbyterate of the Work, which, in

The joint commission first met on February 27, 1980. From this date until the end of its task—February 19, 1981—it took up in twenty-five sessions all of the historical, juridical, pastoral, institutional and procedural aspects implied in the questions submitted for its study.

These different aspects affected not only Opus Dei and its members since the new juridical solution—analogous to what had happened with earlier ones—must clearly provide for the harmonious inclusion of the new prelature in the pastoral life of the universal Church and of the local churches. In fact, the work of the joint commission kept ever in mind a series of questions of particular importance:

a) With what refers to Opus Dei, the commission had to keep in mind in everything the founder's message and will—the decisive criterion in this matter, since Opus Dei did not pretend to change its way of being or its apostolic way of acting. Rather it sought to obtain the definitive expression of the foundational charism in juridical form.

b) With regard to the Holy See, the commission had to ascertain not only that the petition formulated by Opus Dei effectively corresponded to the norms of current law, but also that the transformation of Opus Dei into a personal prelature would benefit the pastoral mission of the Church—a necessary requisite for proceeding to the erection of a personal prelature, whose very reason for being is carrying out special pastoral work in the service of the whole Church.

c) With regard to the territorial hierarchy of the Church the commission had to study the harmonious workings of the new prelature with the local churches; in its relations with diocesan bishops and other territorial ecclesiastical authorities, Opus Dei must carefully respect their legitimate rights.

The joint commission worked in an environment of informative clarity and analytical rigor. Above all at the beginning, representatives of the Congregation formulated questions and expressed difficulties, while the Opus Dei representatives responded with the necessary information about the life of the Work and the spirit of the founder as well as with solutions or proposals, when needed. Thus problems and questions were clarified and, particularly, texts were drafted. In February 1981 this resulted in a conclusive report totaling 600 pages in two volumes: the first contains the study and conclusions the commission had reached; the second contains the documents making up the file, plus the material presented by Opus Dei in the course of the deliberations.

---

everything that common law prescribes for all the ordinary faithful, remains under the jurisdiction of the local ordinaries." He adds that, "in the future juridical configuration of the Work as a personal prelature the present relations of Opus Dei with the local ordinaries will remain substantially unchanged."

The joint commission's report first defines the terms of the question. To that end it summarizes the desires of Opus Dei and then expresses in precise terms the nucleus of this request. Though the quotation is a bit long, we reproduce the *status questionis*, since it acts as a framework for the whole work being carried out: "In the elaboration of this study the commission has considered it necessary to keep particularly in mind the following elements:

"a) the transformation of Opus Dei into a personal prelature is sought in order to resolve the need, deeply felt, for a juridical configuration that corresponds to the foundational charism, that is to say, to what Msgr. Josemaría Escrivá de Balaguer desired beginning in 1928, as is made clear in the complementary documentation of this study;

"b) in accordance with the foundational charism, it is a question of avoiding the inadequate assimilation of the members of Opus Dei to the members of the institutes of consecrated life or the institutions which are considered the equivalent of them;

"c) in requesting its transformation into a personal prelature Opus Dei does not wish to obtain institutionally greater power or more autonomy with respect to local ordinaries;

"d) a clearly secular juridical configuration is requested that safeguards the spirit and institutional unity of Opus Dei, plus the juridical attributions it currently enjoys, without which the apostolic service Opus Dei renders to the Church would not be possible;

"e) in addition it is a question of achieving a greater effectiveness of its service by means of an appropriate configuration of its foundational charism."[25]

The study then specifies: "With regard to the characteristics of the prelature into which Opus Dei seeks to be transformed it is fitting to make the following clarifications:

"a) it is not a question of a prelature of the type *nullius dioecesis* (cf. C.I.C., canon 319 § 1) or territorial, whose faithful would depend in everything and for everything on the exclusive jurisdiction of the prelate;

"b) nor is it a question of a prelature of the type of those of a personal diocese *ratione ritus*, which possess equally legitimate independence or complete autonomy with regard to local Churches;

"c) nor is it a question of a prelature comparable to the military vicariates, whose prelate possesses a cumulative power with local

---

[25] *Circa la trasformazione dell'Opus Dei in Prelatura personale. Studio realizzato dalla Commissione paritetica approvata da S.S. Giovanni Paolo II e composta da rappresentanti della S. C. per i Vescovi e da rappresentanti dell'Opus Dei*, Rome, February 1981, vol. I, no. 5. In the future we will refer to it as *Studio*, following the marginal numbers. A copy of the text is contained in AGP, Sezione giuridica, VIII/15531.

ordinaries, since the *ordinaria cura animarum* of the laity belonging to such a prelature has been entrusted to them;

"d) it is a question of a prelature of the type of prelatures *ad peculiaria opera pastoralia perficienda*, which are endowed with their own statutes and are foreseen in the norms of the Second Vatican Council and in the subsequent pontifical acts of application."[26]

The study then clarifies: "With what has been said before, it is clear that Opus Dei does not seek any form of exemption. In fact, it desires that the laity incorporated into it continue under the jurisdiction of the local ordinary in everything that common law establishes for all of the ordinary faithful; and that they depend upon the personal jurisdiction of the prelate solely in those matters required by their specific vocation and apostolic purpose (special spiritual formative apostolic and disciplinary commitments for a more intense dedication to the service of the Church)."[27]

Having thus framed the question, the joint commission sets for itself certain preliminary questions, which can be reduced to three: a) whether it corresponds to the thought and will of the Work's founder both the affirmation according to which the institutional problem of Opus Dei is not resolved, as well as the consequent decision of requesting its transformation into a personal prelature; b) whether the institutional problem pointed out can be resolved by recurring to one or another of the figures already foreseen in the common law of the Church other than that of a personal prelature; c) whether there exist any reasons that would, *a priori*, exclude in this particular case having recourse to the figure of personal prelature.

The analysis of the historical sources and juridical data led the commission to answer the first question affirmatively and the latter two questions negatively. In other words, it declares first that Opus Dei's founder desired the revision of the statutes of Opus Dei so as to configure it as a personal prelature. Secondly, it sees no reason in principle for not having recourse to this very figure.[28]

---

[26] *Studio*, no. 6.

[27] *Ibid*.

[28] The commission studied one of the questions put forth in earlier months and to which Cardinal Baggio makes reference in his letter of July 18, 1979. They include it among the points that, in the minds of some, had given rise to certain doubts and that therefore it was necessary to clarify, namely: if the new juridical figure of personal prelature would or would not give rise to the formation of a kind of "parallel Church."

In the commission's report the topic occupied nos. 51-56. The study points out that it would be unjust and illogical to formulate this problem based on the possible internationality of these prelatures, since there exist many ecclesiastical institutions of an international scope (entities of pontifical right), without being able to say that the fact of possessing this international character transforms them into "parallel Churches." It then goes on to consider the concrete characteristics of the institution under consid-

Thus the way is opened to passing judgment on whether Opus Dei should become a personal prelature.

Here the study divides into two parts that make up the body of the report: one dedicated to the *quæstio facti*, an analysis of the characteristics of Opus Dei as a pastoral phenomenon or social reality; the other to the *quæstio iuris*, a study of the figure of personal prelature and its applicability to Opus Dei.

The examination of the reality of Opus Dei is broad and detailed, since it covers a complete range of aspects: the unity of the pastoral phenomenon; the value of work in the spirituality and in the special aim of Opus Dei; the secular character of the members and their activities; the incorporation and bond of the members; the commitments assumed by those who are incorporated to Opus Dei; the possibility that some initiatives of a strictly apostolic nature, promoted by Opus Dei members, receive from Opus Dei a specific pastoral attention; the priests; the form of governance; relations with diocesan bishops; diocesan priests who are admitted to the Priestly Society of the Holy Cross.

The reality of Opus Dei as we have described it in this work appears throughout the whole description. We emphasize solely how clearly the conclusions of the joint commission reflect the unity of the pastoral phenomenon. The analysis of the norms and life of

---

eration, that is to say, what type of prelature it had been proposed to erect, in order to point out that it is a question not of a prelature *nullius dioecesis*, nor a jurisdictional entity to which is entrusted the *ordinaria cura animarum*, but a personal prelature in the service of a particular pastoral work, and in accordance with norms approved by the Holy See that guarantee "the necessary harmony between the power of the local ordinaries and that of the prelate."

In summary, it concludes, the jurisdiction of the prelature, "even though it be *ambitu internationalis*, insofar as it embraces members without limit of national boundaries, is nevertheless well delimited and circumscribed, with juridical norms established by its Statutes and limited to the specific end of Opus Dei. This prelature is very far from being any kind of a 'parallel Church.'" The study points out the clarifications offered by Msgr. Alvaro del Portillo in the letter addressed to Cardinal Baggio on Feb. 6, 1980—we have already made mention of this letter—and concretely to the declaration according to which "in the future juridical configuration of the Work as a personal prelature the present relations of Opus Dei with the local ordinaries will remain substantially unchanged." It analyzed afterwards the norms foreseen in the *Statutes* with regard to the relations between Opus Dei and the diocesan ordinaries, concluding by reaffirming the previous evaluation: "The commission is of the opinion that the juridical criteria necessary to avoid the constitution of a kind of 'parallel Church,' in the interior of territorial jurisdictions, are sufficiently guaranteed." The special pastoral work the prelature carries out—the text adds—that is to say, the spreading in all social environments, of the universal call to holiness and precisely through the sanctification of professional work, shows furthermore "its reason for being at the service of the local Churches and its normal and specific inclusion in the totality of the pastoral and evangelizing activity of the Church."

Opus Dei manifests it to be "a social reality already existing in the Church for over fifty years as a pastoral unity, organic and indivisible, made up by priests and laity. The consideration of this aspect seems especially important with respect to the new juridical configuration, *since a solution that was applied solely to the clergy or to the laity would be inadequate*: the specific end of Opus Dei in the service of the common good of the Church would not be attainable only by priests or only by lay people; both are necessary, because they are mutually required and mutually complement one another in carrying out their service to the Church."[29]

The *quæstio iuris* examines the figure of personal prelatures in the Second Vatican Council and in the *ius conditum* following the same. The Decree *Presbyterorum ordinis*, no. 10, is first considered, pointing out also references to personal prelatures in the Decree *Ad gentes*, no. 20, note 4, and no. 27, note 28; and later the norms contained in the Motu proprio *Ecclesiæ sanctæ*, part I, no. 4, and in the Apostolic Constitution *Regimini Ecclesiæ universæ*, no. 49, § 1, as well as the dispositions of the *Directory* on the pastoral ministry of bishops of February 22, 1973, no. 172.

After this theoretical examination, the commission analyzes the decisive question: comparing the reality of Opus Dei with the figure of personal prelature. Its judgment is: "Having in mind the norms of the *ius conditum* with regard to personal prelatures and the characteristics of Opus Dei . . ., the commission has examined the possibility of the requested transformation. In this regard it has concluded that Opus Dei—as a pastoral phenomenon already in existence—possesses the characteristics and corresponds to the requirements of the *ius conditum* with regard to being transformed into a personal prelature. All without prejudice of any kind to the local ordinaries.

"In fact the purpose of Opus Dei is a *peculiare opus pastorale*, which is carried out by means of a special *pastoral attention* of its presbyterate and a *specific apostolate* carried out by all the faithful who belong to it. This special pastoral work, of a specific character and carried out by priests and ordinary faithful, is of a clearly secular nature, by its end, by its spirituality, by the condition of the people who carry it out and by the environment in which it is carried out: the structures proper to civil society." "It is precisely to guarantee unequivocally this secular character, together with the unity of government, that its transformation into a personal prelature is sought."[30]

---

[29] *Studio*, no. 10; the question is fully dealt with in nos. 72-89. The emphasis is from the original.

[30] *Studio*, no. 20; see also nos. 204-212. Basing itself on this fact the study points out in the following sections the existence of this ecclesial opportuneness (*ratio apostolatus*),

The conclusions of the joint commission were approved unanimously and completely favored the transformation of Opus Dei into a personal prelature. But its work did not end there. It also examined the *Statutes* whereby, in accordance with current law, the prelature would be governed, in the supposition that the Roman Pontiff were finally to decide to erect it. It studied the *Codex Iuris Particularis* approved by the founder in 1974. It reached the conclusion that this text could serve as its statutes, with a few small changes. These were: suppressing terms stemming from Opus Dei's earlier configuration as a secular institute and which, in the 1974 text, had been placed in brackets by Msgr. Escrivá himself; introducing adaptations and terminological modifications required by the juridical nature of a personal prelature.

### 3. The Roman Pontiff decides to erect Opus Dei as a personal prelature

Considering its task finished, the joint commission signed two copies of the material and its conclusions—as is usual in mixed commissions—and gave one to the Prefect of the Sacred Congregation for Bishops and another to the president general of Opus Dei. The stage of technical study having come to an end, the question became once again a matter for decision.

As Cardinal Baggio has written, the first step consisted in "the examination of the conclusions of the technical commission, which comprised also the statutory norms of the prelature to be erected, by a special commission of cardinals appointed by the Holy Father, taking into consideration the purpose, the composition and the spread of Opus Dei. This commission gave its opinion on September 26, 1981."[31] With the information and opinions he had received, John Paul II, in an audience granted to Cardinal Baggio on November 7, 1981, indicated his decision to erect Opus Dei as a personal prelature, approving its statutes and commanding that everything be done required for this erection. Before making this decision public, the Pope wanted to send to all the diocesan bishops of nations where Opus Dei then had centers an informative note on its erection as a prelature. It pointed out the scope of the corresponding pontifical act and allowed recipients enough time to study and forward any observations or suggestions.

---

required by the Decree *Presbyterorum ordinis*, no. 10, for the erection of personal prelatures: thus is guaranteed an apostolic activity that represents a profound service to the Church (nos. 213-221).

[31] Card. S. Baggio, *A Good for the Whole Church, op. cit.* (note 11 of this chapter).

Cardinal Baggio officially communicated this to the President General of Opus Dei on November 9, 1981.[32] The joy of Msgr. Alvaro del Portillo was immense: finally the definitive juridical solution for which the founder of Opus Dei had worked for so many years was to see the light of day! To bear witness to his joy and to the importance of the event, he decided to write a letter to members of Opus Dei. However, given the desire of the Roman Pontiff to delay the announcement of his decision until he had heard from the bishops Msgr. del Portillo did not make the text available until later.[33]

In this letter dated December 8, 1981, Msgr. del Portillo expresses his joy and gratitude to God for the definitive juridical configuration having finally been achieved. He says it fits perfectly with the charism proper to Opus Dei. He asks all the members of the Work to unite themselves to his thanksgiving and to renew their desires of corresponding faithfully to the call they have received from God. At the same time he points out his filial sadness that the founder had not been able to see on earth the termination of this long journey for which he had prayed and caused others to pray so much and for which he had so longed.

By writing when the news had still not been made public and not knowing when they will be able to read the words addressed to them, the letter must have a general character. Thus Msgr. del Portillo limits himself to a few particularly important elements. From the historical perspective of our study, we can point out that in this decisive moment of the juridical history of Opus Dei Msgr. del Portillo selects and emphasizes those aspects he considers primordial. He wants all to reach a more profound understanding of the papal decision.

With the new form "we will see crowned the long journey of the definitive juridical configuration of our vocation, just as the Lord had inspired it in our founder on October 2, 1928. The foundational affirmation of our Father that over the years sounded to so many as an impossibility and to others as a heresy will have managed to open a way for itself: by the call we have received, we wish to dedicate our lives completely to the Lord as ordinary faithful—

---

[32] AGP, Sezione Giuridica, VIII/15027. "It is a pleasure for me to communicate to you," we read in the first paragraph of the letter, "that in an audience on the 7th of this month the Holy Father has decided to erect Opus Dei as a personal prelature in conformity with what is provided in the appropriate conciliar documents, in the Motu proprio *Ecclesiæ sanctæ* of August 6, 1966 and in the Apostolic Constitution *Regimini Ecclesiæ universæ* of August 15, 1967, and he has approved the Statutes "

[33] In accordance with what the Holy Father had decided the notification was reserved to the general council and the central advisory of Opus Dei. This letter of Don Alvaro del Portillo would reach the other members of Opus Dei only after November 28, 1982; the complete text is found in the Appendix, document no. 66.

priests and secular lay people, neither more nor less—with a spirituality, with an apostolic dedication and with a juridical bond quite
different from that proper to the state of perfection or the state of
consecrated life through the profession of the three evangelical counsels."[34]

This central statement is explained in a series of considerations
that can be reduced to three points:

a) In keeping with the founder's desire a correspondence between charism and law has been achieved, since to the condition of
personal prelature has been welcomed the reality of Opus Dei as an
organic unity, as an apostolic institution made up of priests and
laity in the service of a single mission. Opus Dei, in effect "has been
willed by the Lord to contribute, with its own spirituality, organization and apostolic modes, to reminding all men of the real demands of the universal call to holiness: that all the faithful can and
ought to sanctify themselves in the world, without changing their
state, there where the Lord has placed each one, giving due supernatural importance to ordinary life and especially to ordinary professional work raised to the order of grace and made an occasion
and instrument of apostolate."[35]

The vocation to Opus Dei does not imply, he continues, "any
change in the personal condition of those incorporated to the Work."
On the contrary, it supposes a reaffirmation of each one's secular
condition in equality of rights, duties, responsibilities, desires and
tasks with all men. He adopts and emphasizes words from the
founder: "We cannot be separated from the other faithful, our equals (I
insist), neither by the thinnest partition that could exist, not even by a
piece of cigarette paper." The members of Opus Dei are ordinary
faithful who strive to be "like the yeast in the mass, being all of us
at the same time both mass and people of God that obeys, serves,
loves, venerates and is attentive in the life of the Church to the
voice, directions and concerns of the pope and diocesan bishops."[36]

b) The new juridical configuration highlights, furthermore, the
contribution made by Opus Dei members, as ordinary Christians, to
the overall apostolate of the Church. In this vein, Msgr. del Portillo
alludes to the difficulties overcome in the course of the juridical
evolution, specifically to some in the last stages. He insists again on
the condition of ordinary faithful proper to the members of the
Work, as well as on their freedom and personal responsibility. It is
proper to the members of Opus Dei not to act as a group, but
individually, according to their own initiatives and their own loyal

---

[34] A. del Portillo, Letter, Dec. 8, 1981, no. 3.

[35] Ibid., no. 4.

[36] Ibid., nos. 4-6.

way of thinking and understanding; it is with this personal action that they thus contribute to the Church's mission of spreading the faith and the life of Christ. "Where citizens and Christian faithful live out their ordinary life, there the members of Opus Dei are present: ordinarily, each one personally—I repeat, not in a group—giving life to all these environments with apostolic drive, in the service of the universal Church and of the local Church." The configuration as a personal prelature, in juridically sanctioning this reality, will contribute to making it shine forth and will lead to the disappearance of those errors into which those with another mental frame of reference fall.[37]

c) The letter refers also to the situation of the priests belonging to the clergy from the dioceses who are also members of the Priestly Society of the Holy Cross. Because of the earlier juridical configuration, some had thought, erroneously, that such priests were subject to a double obedience: to their own ordinary and to Opus Dei directors. To avoid this false conclusion, Msgr. Escrivá had established that in the Work these priests depend upon the spiritual director, who is not among those holding a position of governance in Opus Dei. Thus with respect to such diocesan priests, there is not in Opus Dei, any internal hierarchy. The new configuration, by radically doing away with all references to schemes proper to the state of perfection, clarified things even further. The relationship between these priests and the Priestly Society of the Holy Cross has been perfectly well outlined, since they form an association of priests distinct from, though inseparably united to, the Prelature. This relationship does not lessen in any way what unites them to the diocese and their own bishop. On the contrary these links are reinforced since, as Msgr. del Portillo concludes, "the most perfect correspondence to the vocation to the Priestly Society of the Holy Cross is realized in the exact, willing and cheerful fulfillment of the indications of one's own ordinary."[38]

Meanwhile, the Sacred Congregation for Bishops, fulfilling the indications of the Roman Pontiff, had sent in November 1981 to the bishops of the countries where Opus Dei worked apostolically, the informative note to which we have referred. In all the communication reached more than 2000 bishops of 39 countries. A short time later, as the Undersecretary of the Congregation, Msgr. Marcello Costalunga relates in an article published in November 1982,[39] many responses were received. "The replies of bishops were abundant

---

[37] *Ibid.*, nos. 9-10.

[38] *Ibid.*, no. 12.

[39] M. Costalunga, "The Erection of Opus Dei as a personal Prelature, " in *L'Osservatore Romano,* weekly edition in English, December 6, 1982.

who manifested their own satisfaction with the way, in perfect agreement with the norms deriving from the Second Vatican Council, the desired solution to the institutional question of Opus Dei was reached. There were far fewer letters that set forth observations or requested clarifications: all of them have been duly taken into consideration after being properly studied, and all requests for further explanation have been answered.

"This consultation of the bishops," Msgr. Costalunga adds, "has been of great usefulness, because, as a consequence of this show of collegial affection, there was carried out a new and profound examination of the *Statutes* written by Msgr. Josemaría Escrivá de Balaguer. It has but confirmed their validity and the wisdom with which they were written, evoking appreciation for their clear witness to the foundational charism and the great love of the Servant of God for the Church."

On August 5, 1982 Cardinal Baggio in his capacity as prefect of the Congregation for Bishops was received by John Paul II. In that audience, the Holy Father established that his decision to erect Opus Dei as a personal prelature be made public and to this effect, "he approved, confirmed and commanded to be published" a declaration already prepared by the Sacred Congregation.[40] On August 23 the Vatican press office officially announced the decision of the Holy Father to erect Opus Dei as a personal prelature adding that the corresponding document would be published later. On Sunday, November 28, 1982, *L'Osservatore Romano* included on its first page, in the column "Nostra Informazione," the following words: "The Holy Father has erected the Priestly Society of the Holy Cross and Opus Dei as a personal prelature, in conformity with the Motu proprio *Ecclesiæ sanctæ*, I, no. 4, and the Apostolic Constitution *Regimini Ecclesiæ universæ*, no. 49, par. 1. His Holiness has named Prelate of the personal Prelature of the Holy Cross and Opus Dei

---

[40] The Congregation for Bishops had decided that taking into consideration the novelty of the figure of personal prelatures, created by the Second Vatican Council and still not put into practice, the notice of the erection of the first prelature be accompanied by a declaration that would present it to the whole Church. This is what the declaration *Prælaturæ personales* sought to do underlining the following reasons for the erection: "to favor the apostolic activity of the Church," causing it to "be translated into a practical and operative reality in a new pastoral instrument," which "will assure to Opus Dei an ecclesial structure fully in conformity with its foundational charism and its social reality," in such a way as to "resolve its institutional problem" and to perfect "the harmonious inclusion of this institution (i.e. Opus Dei) in the organic pastoral work of the universal Church and of the local Churches." This document goes on to explain some of the specific characteristics of the Prelature of Opus Dei.

This declaration—to which we will return—is dated August 23, 1982 and as corresponds to this type of document, it is signed by Cardinal Baggio as the Prefect of the. Congregation and certified by the Secretary Msgr. Lucas Moreira Neves, O.P. The complete text is in the Appendix, document no. 67.

the Rev. Msgr. Alvaro del Portillo, until now President General of Opus Dei."[41]

In the same issue of the *L'Osservatore Romano*, there also appears the declaration *Prælaturæ personales*, of August 23, 1982, as well as an article describing this document and the papal act erecting the Prelature written by Cardinal Baggio and entitled "Un bene per tutta la Chiesa." The continuation of these two documents, along with the article "L'erezione dell'Opus Dei in Prelatura personale" by Msgr. Costalunga, Undersecretary of the Congregation, occupies nearly the whole third page of the newspaper.

November 28, 1982, became thus a crucial date in the juridical history of Opus Dei. It is quite understandable that the former president general of Opus Dei and now prelate of the new personal prelature would feel the need to communicate with Opus Dei members. There was the letter he wrote in December 1981 obviously not yet sent. But that wasn't enough.

So opens this new letter, dated November 28, 1982: "With all our heart we give thanks to God and to the most holy Virgin." This clear spiritual tone persists to the end. Msgr. del Portillo evokes the figure of Opus Dei's founder, his abiding concern to be faithful to the mission received from God, his work and prayer—each day more intense—throughout the whole juridical journey. He recalls also the steps taken by Msgr. Escrivá towards an appropriate juridical configuration. He likewise mentions those which, following the founder's indications and spirit, it had fallen to him to give himself once elected as his successor in the office of president general. This narration and memories are mixed with invitations to cheerful thanksgiving to God for having reached the end of a long journey.

There are also considerations of a juridical character, ranging from a general description of the new statute[42] to detailing the advantages ensuing from the new juridical configuration. "My daugh-

---

[41] Following the normal practice of the Holy See, two days before on Nov. 26, the Sacred Congregation for Bishops—by means of a writing signed by its Prefect Cardinal Baggio—addressed itself to the President General of Opus Dei in the following words: "I have the pleasure of communicating to you that the Holy Father has erected the personal Prelature of the Holy Cross and Opus Dei and has named you as the first Prelate of the same." The notification included the obligation of keeping silent this news of the papal act which "will be published in the *L'Osservatore Romano* to appear on the afternoon of Saturday, November 27 next. At midday of that day therefore the bond of secrecy will cease" (AGP, Sezione Giuridica, VIII/15044). We recall that as is well known *L'Osservatore Romano* goes on sale the afternoon before its date: the news appeared then as we have said in the text in the Vatican daily dated Nov. 28.

[42] The Prelature of the Holy Cross and Opus Dei is—we read in one of the paragraphs dedicated precisely to giving a summary or synthetic description of the new juridical configuration—"a personal prelature, of the type of prelatures 'for the carrying out of special pastoral tasks' which, endowed with their own statutes, are foreseen in the documents coming from the Second Vatican Council and in successive papal acts of

ters and sons," he writes, "unite yourselves with all your soul to my
immense joy and my profound gratitude in contemplating the realization of the desires of our founder in the very way that our Father
saw God's will was to be fulfilled. Think that with the erection of
the Work as a personal prelature and with the immediate approval
of its Statutes by the Holy Father . . . the *juridical unity* of the Work
has been confirmed and reinforced with an even more solid and
secure normative structure—unity of priests and laity and of the
two branches—under the direction and government of the father, as
ordinary prelate, with power of governance." It alludes to the
events of 1951-52: "This juridical unity, based until now on a privilege granted by the Holy See—since it was a complete novelty in
Church law—could see itself threatened by external attacks, and in
fact our Father had to defend it on various occasions, with patience
and heroic energy, with the fortitude of a saint, with blood and
sufferings, under the most powerful protection of the most holy
Virgin. For this reason he went to Loreto on August 15, 1951, to
place under the protection of the most sweet heart of Mary the
precious good that is the unity of the Work."[43]

The second fruit in Msgr. del Portillo's eyes is establishing the
secular condition of the members of Opus Dei, ordinary Christians—
priests or lay people—who seek to sanctify themselves each in his
proper state and in the exercise of his profession or office. "Together with this strengthened juridical, organizational, and govern-
mental unity, our clearly secular spirit and asceticism and all the
specific means proper to the apostolate of Opus Dei have been re-
confirmed and protected forever."[44]

Secularity, as the spirit of Opus Dei understands it, "is not a
pastoral or apostolic tactic; it is specifically the place where God
has put us (while well placed in his Heart), in order to do his Work,
to sanctify this world, where we share the joys and sorrows, the
toils and distractions, the hopes and daily affairs of the other citizens our equals." He continues, "This signifies, I insist, a connatural
participation in the things that are most serious in life: in work well
done, in the faithful fulfillment of family and social obligations, in
the participation in the sorrows of mankind and the efforts to construct in peace and in God's presence the earthly city." In a word,

---

enforcement. Therefore no privilege has been granted to the Work—our founder did
not want it, nor do we want it—nor has a new juridical form been created exclusively
for us—even though Opus Dei is the first institution which the Holy See has erected
as a personal prelature—we are established therefore within the common law" (*Letter*,
Nov. 28, 1982, no. 44).

[43] *Letter*, Nov. 28, 1982, no. 47. With regard to the events of 1951-1952, see sections 1
and 3 of chapter VIII.

[44] *Letter*, Nov. 28, 1982, no. 48.

secularity consists in knowing oneself to be called by God to love him and to show to others his love in and through the world in which one lives. From this Msgr. del Portillo concludes affirming that this secularity is harmed and wasted not only "by taking up modes of life that are foreign to secular life," but also "and very gravely when this is separated from its deepest vocational sense by a life of ease: since God calls us in our place of work so that we sanctify it."[45]

It is this spiritual perspective that permits a proper evaluation of a benefit accompanying the erection as a prelature, the reaffirmation of secularity. No mere juridical quality was at risk, but rather the confirmation of a spirit, a call to sanctify oneself in and through secular realities, infusing them with the spirit of Christ and taking occasion of these activities to transmit to others the gospel message. Thus, he continues: "Each one in his own state, in the exercise of his proper profession or office amid the world we love commits himself to dedicate himself in Opus Dei to God's service and for His sake to the service of souls without excepting any. . . . Before God, before the Work, and before our conscience, we commit ourselves to be contemplatives in the middle of the world, making whatever efforts to achieve a unity of life, *simple and strong, that leads us to purify all actions, to raise them to the supernatural plane and to convert them into instruments of sanctification and of apostolate.*"[46] The text alternates between the juridical and the spiritual planes, in his call to see the erection of Opus Dei as a personal prelature, on the part of all its members, as a call to fidelity to the founder's spirit, a topic he continues to develop.

## 4. The Apostolic Constitution *Ut sit*, its execution and subsequent publication in *Acta Apostolicae Sedis*

The transformation of Opus Dei into a personal prelature was just that: a process by which in successive stages a preexisting reality acquires a new configuration. A decisive date is November 7, 1981, when John Paul II decided to erect Opus Dei as a personal prelature, with the characteristics established in the previously approved *Statutes*. Another important moment was August 5, 1982, when, following a consultation made to the episcopacy of all the countries where Opus Dei was at work, the Roman Pontiff determined his decision should be made public, approving and confirming the declaration to this effect prepared by the Congregation for Bishops. The following August 23 was another milestone, when an official (though still not formal) announcement was made of the

---

[45] *Ibid.*, nos. 22-23.

[46] *Ibid.*, no. 51 (the words emphasized are those of Msgr. Escrivá).

papal decision. But the most salient of all was November 28, 1982, when John Paul II, reaffirming definitively his earlier decision, named as prelate of Opus Dei Msgr. Alvaro del Portillo*, and the news of the erection of Opus Dei as a personal prelature was made public worldwide.

A few juridical acts still remained to complete the process of establishing the new prelature.[47] A papal decision to erect a hierarchical jurisdictional entity (as are personal prelatures), is usually formalized, in accordance with the practice of the Holy See, by means of a document of the highest category; ordinarily, an apostolic constitution written in the form of a Bull. In this both the Congregation for Bishops and the Secretariat of State intervened. In fact the document was not ready until March 1983.

Meanwhile there took place an event of great importance not only to the history we are narrating, but also to the general life of the Church: the promulgation on January 25, 1983 of the new Code of Canon Law for the Church of the Latin rite. This culminated a work begun in 1959, when John XXIII jointly announced his call for an ecumenical council and for revising the 1917 Code. There thus entered into force an instrument for the application of the Second Vatican Council, in whose teaching and orientations the new code was clearly inspired.

The promulgation of the Code of Canon Law included within the general law of the Church the figure of personal prelatures.[48] A possibility opened by the Second Vatican Council found its legislative confirmation in the Code and its first concrete realization in the Prelature of the Holy Cross and Opus Dei.

---

* (*Translator's note*: The prelate of Opus Dei, Alvaro del Portillo, was consecrated Bishop by John Paul II on January 6, 1991.)

[47] In addition to the steps already mentioned in the text it is worthwhile to point out another: the transformation of the bond of the members with Opus Dei, adapting it to the mode foreseen in the new *Statutes*. Prescinding from all reference to sacred bonds, the bond is now effected by means of a contractual exchange of wills and the assuming of mutual commitments. The second to the last disposition of the *Statutes* or *Codex Iuris Particularis* of the Prelature foresaw the date of December 8, 1982, as the moment of entering into legal force of the text with regard to the persons already incorporated in Opus Dei, both clerics as well as laity, as well as for the associate and supernumerary priests of the Priestly Society of the Holy Cross. In accordance with this prescription, the members of Opus Dei (and with respect to each one of them the prelature or in its case the Priestly Society of the Holy Cross) freely assumed over the following months the new juridical bond of a contractual nature which took the place of the former one, by means of a formal and personal act, according to the mode prescribed, that is to say, the declaration on each part, of the mutual duties and rights in the presence of two witnesses (*Codex Iuris Particularis*, nos. 27 and 64).

[48] The canons dedicated by the Code of 1983 to personal prelatures are canons 294-297; there are explicit references also in canons 265-266. With regard to personal prelatures an extensive bibliography has been published; we refer, therefore, to only a few texts

On March 5, 1983, Cardinal Baggio informed the Prelate of Opus Dei that the papal bull containing the Apostolic Constitution *Ut sit* that solemnized the papal decision to erect Opus Dei as a personal prelature was ready. Therefore it was possible to proceed to the public execution of the Bull, entrusted to the nuncio in Italy, Archbishop Romolo Carboni.[49]

The Bull *Ut sit* (designated as always by its first words) bears the date of the papal act of formalizing the erection: November 28, 1982. Its wording and style reflect the habitual practice of the Holy See in erecting institutions pertaining to the hierarchical organization of the Church.

The lengthy introduction offers a synthesis of the antecedents and the rationale. It quickly goes to the heart of the matter: by means of the juridical configuration bestowed upon Opus Dei, a perfect correspondence between charism and juridical norm, between substance and form, has been achieved. Therefore, the Apostolic Constitution refers not only to the pastoral phenomenon

---

in which furthermore reference will be found to the rest of the scientific studies; apart from the works of J. Martínez Torrón and P. Lombardía - J. Hervada already referred to (see chap. IX, note 11), we point out the following studies: P. Rodríguez, *Particular Churches and Personal Prelatures*, Dublin 1986, and also: *Consideraciones teológicas a propósito de una nueva institución canónica*, 2nd ed., Pamplona 1986; G. Lo Castro, *Le Prelature personali. Profili giuridici*, Milan 1988; E. Caparrós, "Une structure jurisdictionelle issue de la préocuppation pastoral de Vatican II: les Prélatures personnelles," in *Studia Canonica*, 17 (1983):487-531; J. Fornés, "El perfil jurídico de las Prelaturas personales," in *Monitor Ecclesiasticus*, 107 (1983):436-472; J. L. Gutiérrez, "De Praelatura personali iuxta leges eius constitutivas et Codicis Iuris Canonici normas," in *Periodica de re morali, canonica, liturgica*, 72 (1983):71-111; P. G. Marcuzzi, "Le Prelature personali nel nuovo Codice di Diritto Canonico," in *Apollinaris*, 56 (1983):465-474; D. Le Tourneau, "Les Prélatures personnelles dans la pastorale de Vatican II," in *L'Année Canonique*, 28 (1984):197-219; R. Navarro Valls, "Las Prelaturas personales en el Derecho Conciliar y Codicial," in *Estudios Ecclesiásticos*, 59 (1984):431-458; M. O'Reilly, "Personal Prelatures and Ecclesial Communion," in *Studia Canonica*, 18 (1984):439-456; P. Rodríguez - A. de Fuenmayor, "Sobre la naturaleza de las Prelaturas personales y su inserción dentro de la estructura de la Iglesia," in *Ius Canonicum*, 24 (1984):9-47; L. Spinelli, "Riflessi canonistici di una nuova struttura pastorale: le Prelature personali," in Various authors, *Raccolta di scritti in onore di Pio Fedele*, vol. I, Perugia 1984, pp. 591-612; G. Dalla Torre, "Prelato e Prelatura," in *Enciclopedia del Diritto*, vol. XXXIV, Milan 1985, pp. 973-981; R. Lanzetti, "Le Prelature personali nella missione di evangelizzazione della Chiesa," in Various authors, *Portare Cristo all'uomo. Congresso nel Ventennio del Concilio Vaticano II*, Rome 1985, pp. 597-603; W. H. Stetson - J. Hervada, "Personal Prelatures from Vatican II to the New Code: an Hermeneutical Study of Canons 294-297," in *The Jurist*, 45 (1985):379-418; A. de Fuenmayor, "Primatial Power and Personal Prelatures," in Various authors, *The New Code of Canon Law. Proceedings of the 5th International Congress of Canon Law*, Ottawa 1986, pp. 309-318; D. Le Tourneau, "Les Prélatures personnelles vues par la doctrine," in *Revue des Sciences Religieuses*, 60 (1986):235-260; J. P. Schouppe, "Les Prélatures personnelles. Reglamentation canonique et contexte ecclésiologique," in *Revue Théologique de Louvain*, 17 (1986):309-328.

[49] The text of the letter is in the Appendix, document no. 68.

that Opus Dei represents, but also to the charism from which it stems. It was *divina inspiratione ductus*, "moved by divine inspiration" that Blessed Josemaría Escrivá de Balaguer founded it in Madrid on October 2, 1928. The ecclesial intention of the document is to arrange things so that the institution born of this charism "may always be an apt and efficacious instrument of the salvific mission the Church carries out in the world."[50] *Ut sit* then describes Opus Dei's apostolic purpose: "From its beginnings in fact, this institution has striven not only to illuminate with new lights the mission of the laity in the Church and in human society but also to put it into practice; it has similarly made the effort to put into practice the teaching of the universal call to holiness and to promote among all social classes the sanctification of professional work and by means of professional work. In addition through the Priestly Society of the Holy Cross it has striven to help priests incardinated in dioceses to live the same teaching in the discharge of their sacred ministry."

Once having described the pastoral phenomenon, the apostolic constitution explains how the transformation of Opus Dei into a personal prelature is required by its distinctive features: "Since Opus Dei has grown, with the aid of divine grace, to the extent that it has spread and works in a large number of dioceses throughout the world . . . it has become necessary to give it a juridical configuration *suited to its specific characteristics.*" The new juridical form corresponds to its very nature and charism by virtue of which it presents itself "as an *apostolic organism made up of priests and laity*, both men and women, which is at the same time *organic and undivided*—that is to say, as an institution endowed with a *unity of spirit, aims, government and formation.*" The unity of the pastoral phenomenon that is Opus Dei could hardly be affirmed more strongly. The erection corresponds to the whole, not to a part, in full correspondence to the foundational charism and the life arising from that unity.

"It was the founder of Opus Dei himself," says *Ut sit* in its preamble, "who in 1962, in a humble and trusting petition, asked the Holy See to grant an appropriate ecclesial configuration to the institution, in keeping with its true nature and theological characteristics, and with a view to greater apostolic effectiveness." The Second Vatican Council had opened the canonical door. "From the time when the Second Vatican Ecumenical Council introduced into the legislation of the Church, by means of the Decree *Presbyterorum ordinis*, no. 10—which was made effective by the Motu proprio *Ecclesiæ*

---

[50] The text in the original Latin is in the Appendix, document no. 69.

(*Translator's note.* For an English version see the January 20, 1983 edition of *Origins* 12 (1983):510-512.)

*sanctæ*, I, no. 4—, the figure of personal prelatures, to carry out specific pastoral tasks, it was seen clearly that this juridical figure was perfectly suited to Opus Dei."

Then *Ut sit* summarizes the stages of study begun in the time of Pope Paul VI. The preamble twice uses the phrase "transformation" to describe the scope of the papal decision. It is not a question of introducing some modifications, of greater or less import, into the norms by which Opus Dei is governed (norms which, furthermore, have remained substantially identical following the will of the founder). Rather this is a conferral of a juridical and ecclesial form that corresponds to and ratifies its nature. Hence a transformation that has as its *terminus ad quem* a personal prelature. Opus Dei is thus incorporated to the ambit of institutions that make up the pastoral and hierarchical structure of the Church. It therefore leaves aside forms and categories appropriate to associative phenomena, within which it had been obliged to take its first steps.[51]

The Apostolic Constitution, as we have noted, puts into play two elements: a) the substance, that is to say, an institution founded under divine inspiration with its own proper and immutable charism and with a well defined apostolic purpose; and b) the form is to be attributed to the substance so that the charism and its juridical configuration dovetail perfectly and permanently, so that this Opus Dei "be always an apt and effective instrument of the salvific mission which the Church carries out for the life of the world."[52]

---

[51] The Apostolic Constitution *Ut sit* offers a datum of great hermeneutical value by pointing out that when in 1979 the Holy Father entrusted the study of the matter to the Sacred Congregation for Bishops, he did so because *res suapte pertinebat natura*: the matter corresponded to this congregation because of its very nature. That is the congregation of the Roman Curia to which (for territories of the Latin rite not depending on the Congregation *de Propaganda Fide*) corresponds everything having to do not only with dioceses but also with other entities that form part of the hierarchical and pastoral organization of the Church. The preamble of *Ut sit* says that this mandate of the Roman Pontiff prescribed that all of the data be attentively considered, both of law (conformity of the solution with the law in force and in a special way with regard to the documents of the Second Vatican Council), as in fact (possibility of applying this juridical form to the institution in question, having in mind its constitution and characteristics).

[52] Msgr. del Portillo refers to this distinction between substance and form with an analogy he used in an interview granted with the occasion of November 28, 1982. "What does it mean for the institution you head to be erected as a personal prelature?" He replies: "It is only a change of legal 'garb.' Opus Dei was a secular institute of pontifical right since 1947. Now it has been erected as a personal prelature. This change was made in answer to our petition already advanced by our founder that the juridical figure of Opus Dei should correspond to its life, its social reality and its authentic foundational spirit. Our prior legal situation was inadequate in all these respects. The new legal framework of Opus Dei makes crystal clear that its members are ordinary lay faithful or secular priests" (*Il Tempo*, Rome, Nov. 30, 1982). He expresses himself even more graphically in October 1983 in an interview granted to the

The preamble concludes reminding that the Congregation for Bishops "carefully examined the matter, taking into account the historical no less than the juridical and pastoral aspects." Thus "having completely eliminated all doubts about the basis, and the possibility, and the specific manner of granting the petition, it became abundantly clear that the desired transformation of Opus Dei into a personal Prelature was opportune and useful."[53] "Therefore," the Pope concludes, "We, with the plenitude of Our apostolic power, having accepted the opinion which Our Venerable Brother the Most Eminent and Most Reverend Cardinal Prefect of the Congregation for Bishops had expressed to Us, and making good, in so far as it is necessary, the consent of those who have, or think they have some competence in this matter, command and desire the fol-

---

*New York Times.* "How will the function of Opus Dei change as a consequence of this new status?" "This change of juridical status—I thank God for this now, as I do every day—has not produced any change in the spirit of Opus Dei, nor in its way of acting. It was requested not in order to change our mission in the Church, but rather in order to accommodate to this function the external juridical form, which was ill-suited to our true nature and way of acting. The body has not been adjusted to fit the suit, but rather we have laid aside an uncomfortable suit, putting on one that is tailor-made."

For a juridical reflection on this point, see J. L. Gutiérrez, "Unità organica e norma giuridica nella Costituzione Apostolica *Ut sit*," in *Romana*, 3 (1986):350.

[53] The cited article of Cardinal Baggio, *A Good for the Whole Church*, constitutes a commentary on all of the reasons, spiritual and ecclesial that justified the papal decision to erect Opus Dei as a personal prelature. Some of the more significant paragraphs: "The Council has reminded us, paraphrasing the words of St. Paul to the Ephesians (4:16), that 'the social structure of the Church serves the spirit of Christ who vivifies it, in the building up of the body' (*Lumen gentium*, no. 8). One can indeed say that we have now seen this happening once again. Just as it was an eminently pastoral and apostolic reason, a need of development and growth, that led to the establishment in law of the personal prelatures, so too the primary purpose of the pontifical act by which the Prelature of the Holy Cross and Opus Dei is formally erected is that of turning into a living and operative reality a new ecclesiastical structure, foreseen by the Council but which had hitherto remained simply a theoretical possibility."

Later he adds: "This measure has been taken for the good of the whole Church, and this not only as a matter of principle, but also for two other very specific reasons that are worth stressing. The first is that among the thousands of priests and laity of the prelature there are faithful of 87 nationalities and of all races, cultures and social conditions, who now see their unity of vocation and government and their foundational identity as secular priests and ordinary lay faithful fully approved, without in any way implying a lack of appreciation for the validity and worth of the consecrated secularity proper to the secular institutes and approved by solemn papal documents. The other consequence of benefit to the entire community of the Church is that this clear recognition of the foundational charism and the genuine characteristics of the spirit, organization and apostolic methods of Opus Dei cannot but further facilitate and strengthen the specific pastoral service that this well-deserving institution has now been providing for over half a century in hundreds of dioceses all the world over."

lowing to be put into practice," that is, the dispositive part of the Constitution.

Its first article reads as follows: "Opus Dei is erected as a personal Prelature, international in ambit, with the name of the Holy Cross and Opus Dei, or, in abbreviated form, Opus Dei. The Priestly Society of the Holy Cross is erected as a clerical Association intrinsically united to the Prelature."

With brief strokes the six following articles of the Apostolic Constitution detail the norms by which it is to be governed. It sanctions the *Statutes* of the Prelature; determines the scope of the jurisdiction of the prelate and the procedure for his election; establishes his dependence on the Congregation for Bishops and his relation with the other offices of the Roman Curia; fixes in Rome the seat of the central government and erects the prelatic church. We will return later to these articles; let us now make somewhat more detailed reference to the two final dispositions included also in the Apostolic Constitution: the first contains the appointment of Msgr. Alvaro del Portillo as Prelate of Opus Dei; the second prescribes how to proceed to the execution of the document. "Finally," the document lays down the last disposition, "We designate the Venerable Brother Romolo Carboni, Titular Archbishop of Sidone and Apostolic Nuncio in Italy, for the opportune execution of all the above, and confer on him the necessary and opportune faculties, including that of subdelegating—in the matter in question—in any ecclesiastical dignitary, with the obligation of sending, as soon as possible, to the Congregation for Bishops, an authentic copy of the act that testifies to the fact the mandate has been carried out."

In fact Archbishop Carboni personally fulfilled this papal mandate on March 19, 1983, with the ceremony of the inauguration of the Prelature, which took place at 5 p.m. in the Roman basilica of San Eugenio on Valle Giulia, situated close to the headquarters of the Prelature.[54]

Many cardinals, bishops and other ecclesiastical dignitaries as well as civil authorities and members of the diplomatic corps attended this event, plus many members of the faithful, most of them members of the new prelature. The mass in honor of St. Joseph patron of the universal Church and of Opus Dei, the liturgical feast of the day, was celebrated. It was concelebrated by Opus Dei's Prelate Msgr. del Portillo, the Vicar General of the Prelature Msgr. Javier Echevarría, and the regional Vicar for Italy, Rev. Mario Lantini and Revs. Rolf Thomas and Julián Herranz, members of the General

---

[54] It is suitable to underline that this last event happened in 1983; both the sending of the Bull *Ut sit* to Msgr. Carboni as well as its execution took place after the promulgation of the Code of Canon Law on Jan. 25, 1983.

Council of Opus Dei. The other members of the General Council and of the Central Advisory of the Prelature also attended.

At the beginning of the concelebration Archbishop Carboni gave an address in which he showed his delight in putting into effect *Ut sit*; he also recalled with great affection and veneration the figure of the founder, whom he had met on several occasions. This was followed by the public reading of the Apostolic Constitution and the decree of execution given by Msgr. Carboni.[55] The decree declares that "in conformity with what is established by law we declare erected the personal prelature, with all the rights and privileges personal prelatures enjoy in accordance with common law; we proclaim at the same time the Most Reverend Monsignor Alvaro del Portillo installed in the prelatic dignity and office, endowed with the rights and privileges as well as the duties and obligations according to the dispositions of the general law and of the aforementioned Apostolic Constitution, as well as those of the *Statutes* that receive the name of *Codex Iuris Particularis Operis Dei.*"

Msgr. Carboni then presented to Msgr. del Portillo, the original copy of the Papal Bull. This was accompanied by a fraternal embrace and prolonged applause.

In his homily Msgr. del Portillo said the Latin words with which the Apostolic Constitution opens had also been used for many years by Blessed Escrivá, as a brief prayer whereby he continually asked God and the most holy Virgin that God's will be fulfilled, even before he saw on October 2, 1928 what that will was. "*Ut sit*: the juridical journey of the new foundation (old as the gospel and like the gospel always new) began on October 2, 1928, itself, a journey which has evolved over the years at God's pace until it was concluded on November 28, 1982, when the Holy Father John Paul II erected Opus Dei as a personal prelature ratifying in a solemn and definitive way the foundational spirit."[56] At the end of mass the act of execution was completed with the signing of the act.[57] The Ap-

---

[55] The text is found in the Appendix, document no. 70.

[56] The original text of the address of Msgr. Carboni and of the homily of Msgr. del Portillo—together with an Italian translation of the Apostolic Constitution Ut sit and a selection of commentaries from the international press—appeared in the Italian review Studi Cattolici, 27 (1983):372-381. The homily was published in Spanish in "El Opus Dei, Prelatura personal," in Folletos Mundo Cristiano, nos. 364-365, Madrid 1983, pp. 11-12; this is a part of a volume that also contains the Spanish translation of the Apostolic Constitution Ut sit, the Declaration Praelaturae personales of the Sacred Congregation for Bishops and the articles of Cardinal Baggio and Msgr. Costalunga, as well as three interviews granted by Msgr. del Portillo with the occasion of the erection of Opus Dei as a personal prelature (ABC, Madrid, Il Tempo, Rome, and L'Osservatore Romano).

[57] The official act is in the Appendix, document no. 71.

ostolic Constitution *Ut sit* and the Declaration *Prælaturæ personales* were published in *Acta Apostolicæ Sedis*, May 2, 1983.[58] *

## 5. The Statutes of the Prelature or the *Codex Iuris Particularis Operis Dei*

Let us now speak about the *Statutes* of the Prelature, whose establishment we have already described, that personal prelatures are to have their own proper statutes was implicit in the Decree *Presbyterorum ordinis*, no. 10, where it speaks of establishing prelatures "by means to be decided for the individual undertaking and always without prejudice to the rights of local ordinaries." *Ecclesiæ sanctæ*, part I, number 4, is more explicit: personal prelatures are "governed by statutes of their own." Finally the 1983 Code of Canon Law prescribes that "personal prelatures are governed by statutes laid down by the Apostolic See."[59] *Ut sit* sanctions the *Statutes* in article two: "The Prelature is governed by the norms of general law and of this Constitution as well as by its own proper *Statutes*, which receive the name of 'Code of particular law of Opus Dei.'" Furthermore number 1, paragraph 3, of the *Statutes* establishes that it is "governed by the norms of universal law with regard to personal prelatures, as well as by these *Statutes*, and by the special prescriptions or indults of the Holy See."

These *Statutes* the Holy See has made its own, conferring on them the force and rank of papal law. Recall how *Ut sit* refers to the transformation into a personal prelature of a pre-existing reality, although with a distinct juridical configuration. This transformation inserts Opus Dei in the ecclesial role corresponding to it, while leaving unchanged its substance. On various occasions we have referred to the convergence of charism and law, between substance and form, in this regard. In fact these *Statutes* are those that Msgr. Escrivá, depository of the foundational charism, left prepared in 1974 with a view towards the definitive juridical configuration. By erecting the Prelature the Holy See adopted these Statutes, making them its own, and promulgated them with its full authority. The Holy See *sanctioned* them and thus recognized their value as the

---

[58] AAS 75 (1983):423-425 (Apostolic Constitution Ut sit) and pp. 464-468 (Declaratio Praelaturae personales).

* (*Translator's note.* It is of particular importance to add the episcopal ordination of the Prelate of Opus Dei as we conclude the study of the process of erection of Opus Dei as a personal prelature. Msgr. Alvaro del Portillo was appointed Titular Bishop of Vita on December 7, 1990 and ordained by His Holiness John Paul II on January 6, 1991, on the Solemnity of the Epiphany of Our Lord in Saint Peter's Basilica. L'Osservatore Romano, January 7-8, 1991 published a detailed report.)

[59] CIC 1983, c. 295, § 1.

expression of a charism, and it gave them to the Prelature as the papal law by which it is to be governed.

These *Statutes* retain the organization of the *Codex* of 1974. They comprise 185 numbers, grouped in five titles: nature of the Prelature and its faithful; presbyterate of the Prelature and the Priestly Society of the Holy Cross; life, formation and apostolate of the faithful of the Prelature; permanent nature and binding force of this *Codex*.

Let us make two observations to complete this general consideration of the *Statutes*: the first referring to their character; the second to the final points.

A cursory examination based on the *Codex'* name could lead to the conclusion that its norms deal exclusively with the life of the prelature itself. Nevertheless, the prescriptions contained in this *Codex Iuris Particularis* are actually of two kinds: some do deal with the organization of the prelature; others regulate the prelature's relations with local churches and episcopal conferences and, more in general, refer to its role within the organic pastoral work of the Church, both in its universal scope as well as in its particular dimensions. In dealing with a prelature of an international character that discharges special apostolic tasks within the ambit of local churches, it is logical that papal law require norms of coordination to foster a deep sense of communion with other pastors of the Church and thus favor the affective and effective union without which apostolic efforts would be sterile.

The final articles of the *Codex Iuris Particularis* contains two precepts that specify the terms of the transition to the new law of the prelature.

The first of these norms prescribes that what has been granted to Opus Dei by the Holy See and in force hitherto should continue in effect to the extent this is compatible with the new juridical form of government as a personal prelature: liturgical feasts, indulgences, and so on. Similarly, all permissions granted until then by the local ordinaries for the canonical erection of centers of Opus Dei continue to be in force as well as the respective acts by which each of these centers has in fact been erected.

The next to the last article has two paragraphs, in which the transition to the new juridical form of government with regard to persons, concretely those already belonging to Opus Dei or to the Priestly Society of the Holy Cross, is contemplated. The first paragraph prescribes that, for all, the *Codex Iuris Particularis* will enter into effect on December 8, 1982, as already pointed out. The second paragraph establishes that these same persons retain the duties and rights they had in the preceding juridical structure.

To interpret this final point, the text contains two exceptions: First, "unless the prescriptions of this *Codex* expressly establish otherwise": therefore, in the case of disagreement between the norms presently in force and the previous ones, what is established in the *Statutes* sanctioned for the prelature by the Holy See will prevail. Second, "or it is a question of things arising from the norms abrogated by this new law": the abrogated precepts are all those corresponding to the preceding configuration as a secular institute (the evangelical counsels or vows or things connected with the concept of the state of perfection). In other words, the article leaves in force only those subjective rights acquired by the faithful of the prelature during the earlier juridical configuration that are in full conformity with the new normative structure as a personal prelature. The rights and obligations proper to the previous structure that contradict the one recently inaugurated are nullified.[60]

It is a question therefore of a universal principle of law that also holds in the canonical system: when a new law enters into force, *iura quæsita integra manent*: acquired rights remain intact, except when expressly revoked.[61]

As a final note we add that Msgr. del Portillo, in conformity with what had been determined previously by the Congregation for Bishops, gave instructions to publish a volume entitled *Prælatura Sanctæ Crucis et Operis Dei. Statuta* that includes not only the *Statutes* properly speaking, but also the Apostolic Constitution *Ut sit*, the Declaration *Prælaturæ personales* of the Sacred Congregation for Bishops, the decree of execution of Archbishop Carboni, the Letter of Msgr. Escrivá of October 2, 1958, and that of Msgr. del Portillo of December 8, 1981. In April 1983 copies of this volume were sent to the Congregation for Bishops and to all the Bishops of dioceses where the prelature was at work.[62]

## 6. The mission or aim of the Prelature

Having followed the long journey traveled by Opus Dei to find its definitive canonical solution, we should now examine the principal traits of the configuration finally achieved. It is not our intention to carry out an exhaustive study, much less to present a juridical treatise of the various aspects and questions.[63] We will limit ourselves, therefore, to a commentary in broad outlines based on

---

[60] For example, the article refers to the date of admission or incorporation to Opus Dei that of course in this case will be previous to its transformation into a personal prelature, etc.

[61] Cf. can. 4 both of the 1983 Code and the 1917 Code.

[62] The text of the letter to the Sacred Congregation is in the Appendix, document no. 72. The various documents included in the volume are in the Appendix, document numbers 69, 67, 70, 40 and 66. The complete text of the *Codex Iuris Particularis Operis Dei* or Statutes of the prelature is in the Appendix, document no. 73.

[63] Besides the literature on Opus Dei as a personal prelature provoked both by the interest to explain or to analyze the definitive juridical configuration of Opus Dei or

our study heretofore.  We shall point out where and how the various historical threads are woven together.  Our exposition is based on the *Codex Iuris Particularis* or *Statutes* of the Prelature, completing it, when necessary, with references to the Apostolic Constitution *Ut sit*, the Declaration *Prælaturæ personales* of the Congregation for Bishops or other sources.[64]

---

by the desire to achieve a better understanding of the figure of personal prelatures as such, in the light of the first one to be created, is already abundant. We mention the books of D. Le Tourneau, P. Rodríguez and G. Lo Castro already cited in notes 22 of chapter II and 48 of this chapter to which can be added the following articles: A. Aranda, "El Opus Dei, Prelatura personal," in *Scripta Theologica*, 125 (1983):109-118; J. I. Arrieta, "L'atto di erezione dell'Opus Dei in Prelatura personale," in *Apollinaris*, 56 (1983):89-114; J. Fornés, "El perfil jurídico de las Prelaturas personales. Un comentario a la const. ap. 'Ut sit' del 28 de noviembre de 1982," *op. cit.* (note 52 of this chap.); A. de Fuenmayor, "La erección del Opus Dei en Prelatura personal," in *Ius canonicum*, 23 (1983):9-55; E. Caparros, "Une structure jurisdictionnelle issue de la préoccupation pastorale du Vatican II:les Prélatures personnelles," *op. cit.* (note 48 of this chap.); J. Otaduy, "Carisma y derecho en la erección del Opus Dei como Prelatura personal," in *Iglesia viva*, 184 (1983):227-238; G. W. Rutler, "The Rise of Opus Dei," in *New Oxford Review*, 6-1983, pp. 6-8; W. H. Stetson, "Opus Dei: The Church's first personal Prelature," in *Homiletic and Pastoral Review*, 7-1983, pp. 64-70; R. Schunck, "Die Errichtung der Personalprälatur Opus Dei," in *Theologie und Glaube*, 73 (1983):71-107; D. Le Tourneau, "L'Opus Dei Prélature personnelle," in *Revue du Sciences Religieuses*, 57 (1983):295-309; R. Tomassetti, "L'Opus Dei e la nuova figura giuridica delle Prelature personali," in *Aggiornamenti sociali*, 35 (1984):677-692; C. de Diego Lora, "El nou estatut de l'Opus Dei," in *Qüestions de vida cristiana*, 121 (1984):100-103; J. L. Gutiérrez, "La costituzione apostolica 'Ut sit' e la figura giuridica della Prelatura personale," in *Apollinaris*, 57 (1984):335-340; R. Ombres, "Opus Dei and Personal Prelatures," in *The Clergy Review*, 70 (1985):292-295; J. L. Gutiérrez, "Unità organica e norma giuridica nella Costituzione Apostolica *Ut sit*," *op. cit.* (note 48 of this chap.), pp. 342-351; J. Hervada, "Aspetti della struttura giuridica dell'Opus Dei," in *Il Diritto Ecclesiastico*, 97 (1986):410-430.

[64] It would be easy to annotate the exposition with texts taken from the writings of Msgr. Escrivá showing in this way the continuity between the *Statutes* of the prelature and his earlier teaching. Nevertheless, after the lengthy expositions given in previous chapters this does not seem necessary, since the continuity is obvious. On the other hand we will quote from the commentaries of Msgr. del Portillo, since they will help to reaffirm or clarify some points. These were made in three interviews published shortly after the erection of Opus Dei as a personal prelature, as well as some of an earlier date. These interviews were granted to journalists and publications as follows: to the correspondent of the Madrid paper *ABC* in Rome, Joaquín Navarro Valls, published on Nov. 29, 1982 (*Translator's note.* English version published in *Seeking God in the World*, New York 1983, pp. 15-34); to the Italian journalist Pier Giovanni Palla, published in the Rome daily *Il Tempo* on Nov. 30, 1982; the Vatican journalist Piero Monni, published in *L'Osservatore Romano*, March 25, 1983; the correspondent of the *New York Times* in Rome, Henry Kamm Oct. 22, 1983, as material for subsequent articles; to the Italian journalist Giovanni Belingardi, published in *Il Corriere della Sera*, Dec. 7, 1985; the theologian Massimo Camisasca, published in *Litteræ Communionis*, the monthly review of the movement Communion and Liberation, July-August 1985, pp. 12-15; to the writer and journalist Cesare Cavalleri, director of the Italian magazine *Studi Cattolici*, which was published in the issue of December, 1987. (31 (1987): 726-727).

The *Statutes* and *Ut sit* describe Opus Dei as a personal prelature made up of clergy and laity, who carry out a special pastoral task, under the government of its own prelate. The texts add that the Prelature of the Holy Cross and Opus Dei or, in its abbreviated form, Opus Dei, is international in scope; and its prelate or proper ordinary, with his councils, is headquartered in Rome, where is also located the prelatic church of Our Lady of Peace.[65]

This description, in part a formal one, takes on life when the mission or distinctive pastoral work that endows the prelature with meaning is made explicit, which therefore justifies its existence as a prelature as such. This goal is well known to us. Nevertheless, let us see how it is expressed by the definitive texts.

A description of the Prelature's purpose is found in *Ut sit*'s preamble, "From its beginnings, this Institution has in fact striven, not only to illuminate with new lights the mission of the laity in the Church and in society, but also to put it into practice; it has also endeavored to put into practice the teaching of the universal call to sanctity and to promote at all social levels the sanctification of ordinary work, by means of ordinary work."[66] *Prælaturæ personales* also speaks of its aim or mission: "In the aims and spirit of Opus Dei stress is laid on the sanctifying value of ordinary work, that is to say, on the obligation to sanctify work, to sanctify oneself in one's work, and to turn it into an instrument of apostolate."[67]

The *Codex* offers a detailed specification of the mission or pastoral task: "The Prelature seeks the sanctification of its faithful, in accordance with the norms of its particular law, by means of the exercise of the Christian virtues, each one in his own proper state, profession and condition of life, according to its specific spirituality, which is fully secular." It continues, "In addition the prelature seeks diligently to bring about that persons of all conditions and states in civil society, and in first place those of intellectual professions, adhere with all their heart to the precepts of Jesus Christ our Lord and that they put them into practice in the middle of the world, by means of sanctifying the professional work proper to each one, so that all things may be ordered according to the will of the Creator; and to form men and women to carry out apostolate in civil society."[68]

---

[65] Apostolic Constitution *Ut sit*, Preamble, arts. I, III, IV and VII; *Codex Iuris Particularis*, nos. 1, §§ 1 and 3; and 125 (hereinafter we will refer to this simply as *Codex*, followed by the number and paragraph).

[66] *Ut sit*, Preamble.

[67] *Prælaturæ personales*, no. II, c).

[68] *Codex*, no. 2, §§ 1 and 2.

This text repeats in their entirety expressions from earlier writings and juridical texts. It also summarizes some of the essential features of Opus Dei:

a) the universal call to holiness and apostolate, and, more particularly, the proclamation that ordinary Christians are called to sanctify themselves and to embrace all the demands of the faith in whatever state and condition as defined and situated by their human vocation and the circumstances that go to make it up;

b) an appreciation for the role of intellect, a conviction that effective Christian presence in the world requires a formed conscience and a connaturalness of the mind with the gospel; then vital attitudes and underlying convictions can configure decisions and actions so that they echo those of Jesus Christ;

c) the breadth of the pastoral task, aimed at all social conditions, professions and occupations, is, if anything, reinforced by the founder's decision in the 1930s to give special apostolic attention to people involved in the educated and academic professions (understood in the widest sense)—such vocations, even to celibacy, guaranteeing thus a greater continuity and extension in the apostolate;[69]

d) discharging this apostolic work within civil society itself: by ordinary Christians in and through their ordinary work and other circumstances of daily life; the defining element of the pastoral phenomenon of Opus Dei—why it has been erected as a prelature— is not simply spreading the teaching of sanctification amid the world, but the effective incarnation of this desire for holiness in people dedicated to secular pursuits and the transmission of this ideal by ordinary Christians who, in striving to live it, pass it on to others, who for one reason or another share their lives.[70]

Consistent with this first article, many other texts of the *Statutes* accord primacy to the redeemable and redeeming value of ordinary occupations and, consequently, stress the duty incumbent on each person to sanctify himself in his work, to sanctify that work and to

[69] This same web of ideas is also found in the chapter of the *Codex* dealing with apostolate (nos. 110ff), where reference is made to the importance of apostolate among intellectuals (no. 116), but situating this reference in the context of a universal projection: "that the faithful of the Prelature always bear in mind in their apostolate that . . . we have been established for the crowd. There is not a single soul, then, that we do not want to love and to help, making ourselves all things for all people (cf. 1 Cor. 9:22)" (no. 111, 2nd); "The apostolate of the faithful of the Prelature is directed towards all men, without any distinction of race, nation or social condition" (no. 115).

[70] This is the point Msgr. del Portillo emphasizes in the interview in *Il Corriere della Sera* (*op. cit.* note 64 of this chapter). "What is a personal prelature?" was the question addressed to him. He answered, "A hierarchical structure of the Church that gathers together priests and laity under the jurisdiction of a prelate to carry out a specific apostolic pastoral goal. In the case of Opus Dei this goal is to foster sanctity among ordinary Christians who live in the middle of the world, teaching them to transform their work into prayer and into an occasion of encounters with God."

convert it into an apostolic instrument, thus forging a unity between concern for earthly tasks and a God-centered life.

One of the more extensive and rich numbers of the *Codex* says,
"The Lord created man 'to work' (Gen 2:15); the law of work belongs, then, to the general human condition. Nevertheless, the character and special goal of the prelature leads its faithful not only to
cultivate, but also profoundly to love, ordinary work: they see in it
not only an outstanding human value, totally necessary for promoting the dignity of the human person and social progress, but also,
and principally, a marvelous occasion and means for a personal
union with Jesus Christ, imitating his hidden laborious life, generously serving his fellow men and thus cooperating in the loving
task of the creation and redemption of the world."[71]

A member of Opus Dei ought to feel called not only to work, but
also to turn his workaday occupation into an axis for his own sanctification and apostolate. Thus, echoing the founder, "the special
characteristic of Opus Dei's spirit consists in the fact that each one
is to sanctify his own professional work, sanctify himself in perfectly fulfilling his professional work and sanctify others by means
of his very own professional work."[72] Shortly after another number
says: "The proper characteristic of the vocation consists in sanctifying ordinary work."[73]

In number three the *Statutes* had already pointed out the same
idea presenting it as a means to reach the aim. Among the former,
the *Codex* first mentions spiritual life, informed by a sense of divine
filiation; then, the ascetical, doctrinal, professional and cultural growth
indispensable to the upright fulfillment of one's proper task; finally, "the imitation of the hidden life of our Lord Jesus Christ in
Nazareth, also by means of sanctifying one's own ordinary professional work."[74]

This ideal brings with it ascetical, spiritual and apostolic requirements expressly sanctioned by the juridical norms of the *Codex*.
Thus, first, the obligation the faithful of the prelature assume "never
to abandon the exercise of their professional work or some equivalent occupation, because they seek sanctification and carry out their
specific apostolate by means of this work;"[75] members have to work
intensely "always and everywhere."[76] Secondly, they dedicate themselves to acquire everything required for an adequate, responsible

---

[71] *Codex*, no. 86 § 1.

[72] *Codex*, no. 86 § 2.

[73] *Codex*, no. 92.

[74] *Codex*, no. 3 § 1, 3°.

[75] *Codex*, no. 3 § 2, 1°.

[76] *Codex*, no. 82, 4°.

and just fulfillment of one's own task. Always enjoying full freedom and personal responsibility in their professional work,[77] members, thirdly, are to carry out their work with a spirit of service to their fellows and society and, therein, to cultivate a life of growing intimacy with God.[78]

Always and everywhere they should be moved by love for God and neighbor, with a vigorous and operative faith, with the hope proper to God's children. Still they are fully to respect the proper nature of each undertaking and carefully fulfill the duties stemming from this activity.[79] Whence it follows that they ought always to acquire and improve their professional development and thus be properly prepared not only to earn their own living, but also to act in every moment with due competence.[80] They strive to work with the greatest possible perfection shouldering perseveringly, orderly and even penitentially, if need be, all its consequences, however small.[81] In this way ordinary professional work becomes a real and true witness to the Christian meaning of life. So too the task the faithful of the Prelature endeavor to sanctify becomes an occasion of apostolate in the setting proper to each, making Christianity more viable and attractive first to their colleagues.[82]

In summary, "the spirit of Opus Dei presents two aspects, ascetical and apostolic, corresponding fully to, and intrinsically and harmoniously united and intermixed with, the secular character of Opus Dei; thus there should arise a solid and simple unity of life: ascetical, apostolic, social and professional.[83] This spirit animates the activity of Opus Dei as its members strive to incarnate it and transmit it to those around them; in a word, it endows the special pastoral work to which the prelature is called with a specific character.

---

[77] Here we are dealing with a basic principle of Opus Dei which is set forth also in the *Statutes*: "With regard to professional activity and social, political doctrines, etc., each of the faithful of the prelature, within the limits of the teaching of the Catholic faith and morals, has the same freedom as other Catholic citizens. The authorities of the prelature should completely abstain even from giving advice in these matters. Therefore, this full freedom can only be diminished by the norms which in some diocese or circumscription might in some case be given by the respective bishop or episcopal conference for all Catholics; as a consequence, the prelature does not make its own the professional, social, political, financial activities of any of its faithful" (*Codex*, no. 88 § 3).

[78] *Codex*, no. 86.

[79] *Codex*, nos. 3 § 2, 2°; and 93.

[80] *Codex*, nos. 22, 94 § 2, and 112.

[81] *Codex*, nos. 92 and 93.

[82] *Codex*, nos. 113 and 117.

[83] Codex, no. 79 § 1; this paragraph is found almost textually in previous juridical documents.

## 7. The organic unity of the Prelature

The first number of the *Statutes* says "Opus Dei is a personal prelature made up of both clerics and laity."[84] Then it describes in greater detail: "The presbyterate of the prelature is comprised of those priests who are called to orders from among the lay faithful of the prelature and are incardinated in it; the laity of the prelature is formed by those faithful who, moved by divine vocation, subject themselves to the prelature by virtue of a special title, the juridical bond of incorporation."[85]

The prelature is thus formed by laity—men or women—and some priests who, already having belonged to the laity of the prelature, are, once ordained, incardinated in it.[86] With regard to the presence in the Work of men and women, this came about in 1930, and with regard to priests, this became a possibility on February 14, 1943. The *Statutes*, presupposing this history, stress forcefully that this diversity of persons—men and women, clerics and laity—is found at the core of a single spiritual and pastoral phenomenon. We find ourselves before one of the central questions of the juridical evolution described in previous chapters. How is this question resolved in the new juridical configuration?

The Apostolic Constitution *Ut sit* confronts this topic directly. The historical preamble, to document the need for a new juridical configuration, "suited to its specific characteristics," speaks of Opus Dei's growth. It works in many dioceses the world over "as an apostolic organism made up of priests and laity, both men and women, which is at the same time organic and undivided—that is to say, as an institution endowed with a unity of spirit, aims, government and formation."

---

[84] *Codex*, no. 1 § 1. *Ut sit* describes Opus Dei as an undivided apostolic organism that comprises (*constare* is the verb used) priests and laity. This number 1 § 1 of the *Codex*, in the phrase translated in the text, defines Opus Dei as a personal prelature "clericos et laicos simul complectens"; with regard to the term *complectens*, which is a precise and expressive term, see J. Hervada, *Aspetti della struttura giuridica dell'Opus Dei, op. cit.* (note 63 of this chapter), pp. 423-424.

[85] *Codex*, no. 1 § 2.

[86] Msgr. del Portillo, in the interview with *ABC* so describes the prelature: "It is made up of a prelate; of the clergy or presbyterate of the prelature, who are those priests incardinated in Opus Dei, and by the lay men and women who freely have incorporated themselves to it or will be incorporated in the future. . . . The priests come exclusively from the lay men of Opus Dei, who receive holy orders after having pursued the required ecclesiastical studies. . . . The laity of the prelature are men and women, single or married, of every race and social condition; without any kind of limitation because of reasons of health, old age, or family or professional circumstances, etc." We add that logically in the prelature of Opus Dei the proportion between clerics and laity is similar to the one found in the whole Church: the laity constitute the great majority of members.

The substantive noun used is *compages*: it has been translated as "organism." It could also have been translated by "an interconnected whole" or "a structured unity" or similar expressions. In any case it signifies a social reality made up of many persons forming a compact unity, to which each one contributes with his or her own special function. The first numbers of the *Codex Iuris Particularis* lay stress on a wide variety of persons: priests and laity, men and women, single and married, of all social conditions and occupations, quite different from one another, belong to this prelature. Yet this diversity, nevertheless, make up a single reality. All "seek the same apostolic aim, live a single spirit and an identical ascetical practice, receive a suitable doctrinal formation and priestly attention, and in what has to do with the end of the prelature they are under the power of the prelate and of his councils, according to the norms of universal law and of these Statutes."[87]

All Opus Dei members, whatever their condition, know they share in a single mission and are called to live with equal intensity the same spirit. Another consequence is the membership in Opus Dei of men and women under the same jurisdiction. The distinction between apostolic undertakings of men and women (partially rooted in human nature) is maintained in the new juridical configuration. It is one of Opus Dei's foundational elements. It stems from the markedly personal character of the formation, the primacy of personal apostolate carried out by each member, the existence of specific characteristics in each and every case, etc. Yet while men and women have their own apostolates, there is "a unity of vocation, spirit, aims and government."[88] Opus Dei's configuration as a prelature tightens the unity of the pastoral phenomenon. This is evidenced in the *Statutes*, where there is no title or special chapter dedicated to Opus Dei's men or women. The *Codex* generally covers all the faithful of the Prelature—whatever their condition be—; when necessary and that rarely, a particular norm states it applies to men or to women only.[89]

*Ut sit* not only affirms that Opus Dei is one interconnected whole, but also qualifies it with two adjectives: "undivided" and "organic." The first reinforces in a generic way the idea of unity and requires no commentary. The same is not true of the second. Organic means that component parts not only possess different functions but they contribute to a social whole thanks to diverse contributions. Thus the unity derives from the mutual complementarity of the various tasks carried out.

---

[87] *Codex*, no. 6; see also no. 4 §§ 2 and 3.

[88] *Codex*, no. 4 § 3.

[89] The last number of the *Codex* declares that all of the prescriptions formulated above apply equally to men and women (no. 185).

The theological and canonical importance of the distinction and mutual cooperation between laity and priests is obvious. What specifically makes of Opus Dei an organic unity is not distinct sociological functions, but ecclesiological ones. Diverse roles in the Church give rise to the distinction and mutual cooperation between priests and laity, between ministerial priesthood and the common priesthood of all the baptized.

This fact—as it is underlined by *Ut Sit*—requires a "suitable juridical configuration." This is achieved by means of erecting a prelature respecting the described characteristics and hence made up of priests and laity with a single vocation and complementary functions. Any other juridical solution not taking into account this historical and theological reality, would have applied only to priests or laity and therefore would have been completely inadequate; one without the other could not realize the aims of the prelature in serving the common good of the Church. They need one another mutually, since their tasks are complementary.

Anyone who would apply the term prelature to the ensemble of prelate and presbyterate, while seeing the laity as the mere object or passive subject of this priestly action, would not grasp the reality of Opus Dei. No matter how other personal prelatures which may be erected in the future are organized,[90] such a focus is utterly foreign to the spiritual and pastoral phenomenon that is Opus Dei and its juridical configuration as a prelature. Priesthood and laity in Opus Dei are complementary, as recognized by the *Statutes*. Thus the laity belong by full right to the prelature in which they are incorporated—this is the term used—[91] as members fully co-responsible for pursuing its ends. The *Statutes* read "the ministerial priesthood of the clergy and the common priesthood of the laity are intimately intertwined, (*intime coniunguntur*) mutually demand one another

---

[90] For a more detailed description of the organic cooperation in the Church (see Dogmatic Constitution *Lumen gentium*, no. 10) and the application of this concept to personal prelatures (CIC 1983, can. 296), see A. de Fuenmayor, "Los laicos en las Prelaturas personales," in Various authors, *La misión del laico en la Iglesia y en el mundo. VIII Simposio Internacional de Teología*, Pamplona 1987, pp. 733-744; J. L. Gutiérrez, "Unità organica e norma giuridica nella Costituzione Apostolica 'Ut sit'," *op. cit.* (note 48 of this chapter), pp. 342-351; J. Hervada, "Aspetti della struttura giuridica dell'Opus Dei," *op. cit.* (note 63 of this chapter), pp. 414ff; P. Rodríguez, *Particular Churches and Personal Prelatures, op. cit.* (note 48 of this chapter), pp. 122-126; G. Lo Castro, *Le Prelature personali. Profili giuridici, op. cit.* (note 48 of this chapter), pp. 122ff and 239ff.

[91] *Codex*, no. 1 § 2; the same term appears repeatedly afterwards: in addition to the name of chapter III (*De fidelium admissione et incorporatione in Prælaturam*): nos. 6; 14 § 2; 17; 23; 25; 27-30; 37 § 1; 106; 107; 125 § 2; 130 § 2; 131; etc. *Prælaturæ personales* uses this very same expression, *incorporation* to the Prelature, applied to the laity in I, b); II, b); III, b); IV, c); and in other places, referring to clergy and laity it says *qui ad Prælaturam pertinent* (II, c) and IV, a)), or it calls them *members* of the Prelature (II, d)).

and complement one another (*se invicem requirunt et complent*) in order to carry out in unity of vocation and government the end sought by the prelature."[92]

The Sacred Congregation for Bishops, in the informative note sent in November 1981 to the bishops of countries where Opus Dei had centers canonically erected, used the expression "doubly pastoral purpose." It explains: "The prelate and his presbyterate carry out a special pastoral work in the service of the prelature's laity— well circumscribed—and all the prelature—presbyterate and laity together—carry out a specific apostolate in the service of the universal Church and of the local churches.

"Thus there are two fundamental aspects of the purpose and structure of the prelature, which explain its reason for being and its natural inclusion in the totality of the pastoral and evangelizing activity of the Church:

"a) On the one hand, the special pastoral work of the prelate with the presbyterate to care for and sustain the lay faithful incorporated in Opus Dei in fulfillment of the ascetical, formative and apostolic commitments they have assumed and that are especially demanding.

"b) On the other hand, the combined apostolate of the presbyterate and laity of the prelature, which they carry out inseparably united, with the purpose of spreading in all environments of society an earnest awareness of the universal call to holiness and apostolate

---

[92] *Codex*, no. 4 § 2. The union between both priesthoods is mentioned explicitly once again in no. 79 § 2, and implicitly in many other texts. From one perspective and with a different terminology—that of *communio*—Msgr. del Portillo refers to this same theological foundation in the interview with *Studi Cattolici* (*op. cit.*, note 64 of this chapter). "A prelature is a hierarchical structure of the Church, that is to say, one of the means of self-organization the Church creates in order to attain the goals Jesus Christ assigned to it. The Second Vatican Council," he continued to explain the intrinsic configuration of structures of this type, "manifests the nature of the diocese and of other hierarchical structures that are more or less equivalent to them as Christian communities made up by their own shepherd, their own clergy and Christian people, united by bonds of the *communio fidelium* and of the *communio hierarchica*," that is to say, of a union or communion of Christian faithful in one faith and with the same apostolic goals; with a ministerial priesthood that makes present in the interior of this *communio* Jesus Christ as head. "In Opus Dei," Msgr. del Portillo continues, applying this general doctrine to the concrete reality of the Work, "there is a prelate who is the proper ordinary, a clergy incardinated in the prelature, and lay faithful—who make up the majority—in an organic and co-responsible unity, according to the particular *communio fidelium* specified by the ends of the prelature, which are the pursuit of holiness in one's own state in life and in one's own environment by means of sanctifying professional work and the apostolic spreading of the universal call to holiness. Between the prelate, the clergy and the lay faithful there are bonds of the *communio hierarchica*, always in the sphere determined by the ends of the prelature."

and, more strictly, the sanctifying value of ordinary professional work."[93]

Technically speaking, this description needs to be completed, since the laity, members of the prelature, have an active role not only in the apostolate but also in other aspects,[94] but it clearly marks both the internal and external dimensions essential to the life and mission of Opus Dei. It echoes the call to holiness and apostolate in the middle of the world, precisely through the witness of men and women, ordinary Christians, who, having come to a clear awareness of this call, share this ideal through the skein of their lives.

As faithful of the prelature, members commit themselves to a serious thoroughgoing quest for personal holiness and a full dedication to the specific apostolate of Opus Dei—the sanctification of ordinary life. To that end, they need a suitable formation and a continual pastoral attention, to which the priests incardinated in the prelature are primarily dedicated. On the one hand the priestly ministry "animates and informs" the whole of Opus Dei;[95] on the other, the apostolate proper to Opus Dei is the activity of ordinary Christians, carried out through the exercise of Christian virtues in the state, profession and condition of life proper to each one in keeping with a fully secular mode and style.[96]

In summary, the *ratio apostolatus* (contribution to the apostolic task of the Church for which Opus Dei has been erected as a prelature) is carried out in organic and necessary cooperation between clerics and laity, each one discharging the function that corresponds to him. It is a question then—if we pay attention to the work of Opus Dei as a whole—of a task that cannot be characterized in itself as either clerical or lay. Its apostolate unfolds and is structured according to the mutual relationship between ministerial priesthood and common priesthood. Being distinct in essence and not only in degree, they mutually require, and are ordered to, one another, so as to carry out together the mission Jesus Christ has entrusted to his Church.[97]

---

[93] This text was quoted by Msgr. del Portillo in *ABC*, Nov. 29, 1982 (*op. cit.*, note 64 of this chapter), adding a brief commentary.

[94] Thus, for example, they cooperate in the government and direction of the prelature at all levels (*Codex*, nos. 138 § 2; 146; 151; 157; 161 § 2; etc.); they participate in all the tasks of formation (*Codex*, nos. 8 § 1; 10 § 1; 13; etc.); they ought to feel responsible for all the other faithful of the prelature, helping one another to persevere in the commitments made, and, when necessary, practicing fraternal correction (*Codex*, no. 91), etc.

[95] *Codex*, no. 4 § 1.

[96] *Codex*, no. 2 § 1 and *passim*.

[97] In a word, and in expressing ourselves in a graphic way there is not one Opus Dei for clerics and another for laity, but both one and the other form a part of the same prelature, as occurs in any part or portion of the People of God.

## 8. The faithful of the Prelature

Let us sketch the faithful who make up the prelature Opus Dei. The *Codex Iuris Particularis* in its first title (*De Prælaturæ natura eiusdemque christifidelibus*) devotes chapter two to the faithful of the prelature (*De Prælaturæ christifidelibus*). With this same generic term—"faithful of the Prelature" (*fideles* or *christifideles*)—the *Statutes* designate who are members of Opus Dei: all those clerics and laity incorporated in the Prelature to carry out its special pastoral and apostolic work under the government of the prelate. Thus the members of Opus Dei are precisely faithful of a jurisdictional and hierarchical structure—the prelature—understood as a living and operative community of Christian faithful. In fact the generic term "faithful" is used throughout the *Statutes*.

Concretely, the faithful of the Prelature of Opus Dei are those priests incardinated in it who form its presbyterate and the lay people, men and women, single and married, of all professions and social conditions, incorporated to the prelature; all of them with a single vocation, spirit, aim and government.[98]

Number 6 of the *Codex* expressly declares: "All the faithful who are incorporated into the prelature, with a juridical bond . . . do so moved by the same divine vocation: all commit themselves to the same apostolic aim, live a single spirit and identical ascetical practices, receive a suitable doctrinal formation and priestly attention, and, in what has to do with the end of the prelature, they are under the authority of the prelate and his councils, according to the norms of universal law and of these Statutes."

The dedication required by the single vocation of all the faithful of the prelature is "full, perpetual and definitive."[99] All know themselves to be called to holiness and apostolate in their own state amid ordinary life, and all—in a way suited to their circumstances and to their personal conditions—take on the same ascetical and apostolic commitments and "participate fully in the special apostolate" of the prelature.[100]

This oneness of vocation is shown in a complete readiness to live fully the Christian vocation, with what this implies in the concrete life of each one. The faithful of the prelature—both clerics and laity—must make the effort "to put into practice in a serious and constant way according to the spirit of Opus Dei, the ascetical and apostolic requirements of the common priesthood, and, for the cler-

---

[98] Codex, nos. 1; and 4 §§ 2 and 3.

[99] *Codex*, no. 87 § 1.

[100] *Codex*, no. 11 § 1; see also nos. 10 §§ 1 and 2; 11 § 2; and the chapter on the spiritual life (nos. 79ff), equally addressed to all the faithful of the prelature.

ics, of the ministerial priesthood."[101] All must "make an effort to seek their own sanctification by means of their work or profession, without changing their canonical status," with upright intention. "With all of their strength [they] practice apostolate in conformity with the ends and means proper to Opus Dei."[102]

Within this same unity of vocation, "according to the habitual availability of each one to dedicate himself to tasks of formation and certain apostolic works of Opus Dei, the faithful of the prelature, men or women, are called numeraries, associates or supernumeraries, without thereby forming distinct classes. This availability depends on each one's circumstances of a permanent nature: personal, family, professional or other similar."[103] This availability—specified when a person seeks admission to the prelature—is discerned by the competent authority,[104] having in mind that those circumstances of each one must be permanent in character.[105]

Specifying more, the *Statutes* establish that:

a) those faithful—clerics or laity, men or women—are called numeraries who wholeheartedly dedicate themselves in apostolic celibacy and with the greatest personal availability to apostolic works proper to Opus Dei; ordinarily they live in centers of the prelature, the better to discharge these tasks and to form the other faithful of the prelature. Among the women are numerary assistants, who with full availability are dedicated principally to manual or domestic work in centers of the prelature, making these tasks their occupation;[106]

b) the faithful dedicated to the prelature's apostolic tasks in apostolic celibacy, but because of personal and permanent circumstances of a family or professional nature that ordinarily leads them to live with their own family and limits somewhat their involvement in certain apostolic or formative tasks are called associates;[107]

---

[101] *Codex*, no. 79 § 2.

[102] *Codex*, no. 18. This readiness to take on a full commitment presupposes, as this very same article indicates, not a simple appreciation or attraction, but a true vocational reality; that is to say—as Msgr. del Portillo said in *ABC* (see note 64 of this chapter)—to have "received from the Lord the specific vocation to dedicate themselves to the end proper to Opus Dei," as well as "the necessary conditions for assuming responsibly the commitments this dedication brings with it" (*ABC*, Madrid, Nov. 29, 1982). For a more detailed description of the process of admission and incorporation to the prelature, see *Codex*, nos. 17ff.

[103] *Codex*, no. 7 § 1; see also nos. 6; 21; 96; 97 *in fine*; 101 § 5; 106; 107; 132 § 4.

[104] *Codex*, nos. 19; 20 § 1, 5°.

[105] *Codex*, no. 7 § 1.

[106] *Codex*, nos. 8; 9; 13.

[107] *Codex*, no. 10.

c) those faithful of the prelature are called supernumeraries—single or married—who, with the same divine vocation, participate fully in Opus Dei's apostolate, with an availability defined by their family, professional and social obligations; they thus turn not only their life and work into a means of sanctification and apostolate—as the other faithful do—but also, similarly to the associates, they make of their home and family an occasion of holiness and apostolate.[108]

Those who collaborate in the prelature's apostolic tasks with their prayer, alms and, if possible, work can be cooperators without becoming members, while sharing in the spiritual goods of the prelature. Among them are non-Catholics and even non-Christians.[109]

The *Codex Iuris Particularis* obviously echoes expressions seen earlier. In this question, nothing needed to be changed; so nothing was changed. The *Statutes* insist that these different ways of speaking of the faithful reflect not greater or lesser subjective dispositions, but objective circumstances, a sign of God's particular will for each person. They dedicate themselves or not to certain tasks, but always with the same underlying vocational reality: the call to sanctify one's life in the world and to be an apostle there, in keeping with Opus Dei's spirit.

The condition of members has been abundantly covered in preceding chapters; so it is not necessary to lengthen this commentary. Nevertheless we should analyze in greater depth the juridical formulation of the bond. Here the *Statutes* introduce an important change, finally accommodating themselves to the founder's mind and the conclusions of the Speical General Congress.

We have seen how earlier Msgr. Escrivá, while establishing that incorporation to Opus Dei should be effected with formulas that mention neither vows nor sacred bonds, had to settle for private vows or private recognized vows. The Speical General Congress confirmed that all necessary means be exhausted to eliminate these vows, a compromise required by the previous juridical configuration. This intention is reflected in the *Codex* approved by Msgr. Escrivá in 1974; it continues to speak of vows, since such could not be avoided so long as the suitable juridical formula had not been obtained. These references to vows, however, are placed in brackets, indicating that they should be replaced by others, totally different, when the new configuration is achieved.

---

[108] *Codex*, no. 11.

[109] *Codex*, nos. 7 § 2; and 16. Religious communities can also be cooperators of the prelature; in fact many religious communities, especially those of contemplative life, have sought to be named cooperators of Opus Dei, contributing to the development of its apostolate with their prayer and sacrifice.

The solution came with the establishment of a personal prelature. As the declaration of the Congregation for bishops points out, its members take on certain "serious and qualified commitments . . . by means of a well-defined contractual bond—not by virtue of vows."[110] The "special obligations" of the prelature's faithful are assumed *Ut sit* says, "by means of a contract with the prelature."[111] The *Codex Iuris Particularis* makes no reference to sacred bonds (vows, oaths or promises); the bond between the prelature and its faithful has the nature proper to a contract.[112] By a bilateral contract or agreement, the faithful incorporated to the prelature acquire commitments, rights and duties, without any change in their condition or state: "The lay people incorporated to the prelature do not modify their own personal condition, neither theological nor canonical, of ordinary lay faithful and they act as such in all situations and specifically in their apostolate."[113]

On the other hand, the contractual nature of the bond does not mean that this contract or covenant gives rise to the prelature and constitutes it. It is not the faithful who create the prelature by means of an associative contract. The prelature was born of the act of erection by which the Holy See established a jurisdictional and hierarchical structure,[114] endowing it with statutes that specify certain rights and duties.[115] The faithful incorporate themselves to the prelature, adhere to a preexisting hierarchical reality to which, in conscience, they see themselves called and in whose mission they participate responsibly and fully with all of the duties, tasks and rights deriving therefrom.

The Declaration *Prælaturæ personales* expresses it thus: "The laity are under the jurisdiction of the prelate in everything having to do with fulfilling the specific ascetical, formative and apostolic commitments freely undertaken by means of a contractual bond whereby they dedicate themselves to serving the aims of the prelature."[116] Particularly, the person who joins Opus Dei, in full use of his freedom, makes a commitment in areas and matters that pertain by

---

[110] *Prælaturæ personales*, I, c).

[111] *Ut sit*, art. III.

[112] The *Statutes* allude to private vows and to promissory oaths in no. 27 § 4, but not with reference to the bond between the faithful and the prelature, but in a different context: this number—located in the chapter dedicated to incorporation to the prelature—establishes that the prelate can dispense the vows and oaths made by those who wish to be incorporated.

[113] *Prælaturæ personales*, II, b); see also *Codex*, nos. 18, 79 and 80.

[114] CIC 1983, can. 294.

[115] CIC 1983, canons 295-296.

[116] *Prælaturæ personales*, III, d).

their very nature to the rights of the faithful.[117] They do not thus fall under the competence of the local ordinary;[118] they are left to the faithful's discretion in the legitimate autonomy of his will.

The contractual bond is furthermore "well defined."[119] The rights and duties are assumed by both parties—the faithful and the prelature; their content is preestablished in the statutory norms. Concretely, for incorporation a person must be at least 18 years old. The incorporation is made by a mutual declaration of intent, given by the person seeking incorporation to Opus Dei and by a representative of the prelature in the presence of two witnesses. The result is a stable and mutual bond between the prelature and the faithful.[120]

As a consequence of this bond the prelature obliges itself:

a) to give to the person in question an assiduous doctrinal-religious, spiritual, ascetical and apostolic formation as well as the specific pastoral attention of the clergy of the prelature; and

b) to fulfill all the other obligations which with respect to its faithful are determined in the law governing the prelature.[121]

On the part of the person incorporated he or she manifests a firm resolution to seek holiness unstintingly and to carry out an apostolate in accord with the spirit and norms of Opus Dei, obliging themselves:

a) to be under the jurisdiction of the prelate and the other competent authorities, in order to dedicate themselves faithfully to everything related to the aim of the prelature; and

b) to fulfill all the duties stemming from the condition of numerary, associate or supernumerary and to observe the norms by which the prelature is governed, as well as the legitimate prescriptions of the prelate and the competent authorities of the prelature, in matters of governance, spirit and apostolate.[122]

---

[117] See J. Hervada, *Aspetti della struttura giuridica dell'Opus Dei, op. cit.* (note 63 of this chapter), p. 419.

[118] See M. Costalunga, *op. cit.* (note 39 of this chapter).

[119] *Prælaturæ personales*, I, c).

[120] *Codex*, nos. 6 and 27 § 1.

[121] *Codex*, no. 27 § 2.

[122] Codex, no. 27 § 3. Msgr. del Portillo in his interview in Il Tempo (op. cit. note 64 of this chapter): "The members of Opus Dei commit themselves to strive to achieve holiness and to spread it from the place each one has in the world, by means of their work and their daily occupations. To fulfill this commitment they have the right that the prelature help them by means of a continual and demanding spiritual assistance. This formation is received personally or in small groups by means of classes, talks, spiritual recollections, etc.

"The members of Opus Dei on their part make the effort to vivify their temporal obligations each day with the religious practices necessary to a contemplative life in

## 9. The spiritual life, formation and apostolate of the faithful of the Prelature

In the various regulations examined throughout the juridical development of Opus Dei, we find one permanent, basic criterion: Opus Dei does not have as a specific aim to foster or to carry out group apostolates in the areas of teaching, welfare, cultural development or any similar spiritual aim. Rather, its aim is to awaken among people of all social classes the consciousness of a mission rooted in faith and baptism. Its activity is fundamentally and foremost a "great catechesis," as Msgr. Escrivá used to say. It provides formation for individuals, so that each act freely and responsibly wherever he lives and works, striving to illuminate one's setting with the light of Christ.

This reality is reflected in the *Statutes*; it has no part entitled "activities of the prelature." This of course does not mean Opus Dei has no activity, nor that its activities are not covered by the *Statutes*. Rather, since Opus Dei is all about forming and building up members, this formative activity is covered by the *Codex* when it speaks of persons. The whole of chapter III devoted to "the life, formation and apostolates of the faithful of the prelature" is in fact full of constant references to this activity. In describing members' efforts to cultivate a spiritual life, the text also describes the means whereby the prelature transmits vigor and encouragement to them.

In general terms, here's what the prelature seeks to do:

a) to foster spiritual life among its faithful and those who in one way or another participate in its work, thus helping both to have a deeper awareness of the call to holiness;[123]

b) to educate in the Catholic faith, "so that at all levels of society there be persons intellectually well prepared who in the ordinary circumstances of daily life and work carry out simply, by word and deed, an effective apostolate of evangelization and catechesis;"[124]

c) to make available "suitable apostolic formation and the appropriate pastoral care to ensure a profound work of evangelization and catechesis, so that in the life of one and all the duty and right incumbent upon Christians to do apostolate becomes a reality."[125]

---

the middle of the world, as our vocation requires. The original thing in Opus Dei is the spirit with which all of this is carried out, in a solid unity of life in which are fused the faith professed with the lay work that each member carries out on his own personal responsibility."

[123] *Ut sit*, Preamble; *Prælaturæ personales*, II, c); *Codex*, nos. 2 §§ 1 and 2; 112; 115; with regard to the spiritual life see nos. 79-95.

[124] *Codex*, no. 96.

[125] *Codex*, no. 110.

These points correspond to the three themes enunciated in title three of the *Codex*. Let us examine in somewhat greater depth the commitments the prelature and its faithful acquire.

a) *Spiritual life*

The first of the chapters of the title III of the *Statutes* is devoted to spiritual life. Its primacy faithfully reflects the nucleus of Opus Dei's message. It brings to men and women in the midst of the world the news that precisely there they can and ought to find God. To do so they need to enter more deeply into the faith, into the awareness of God's presence and progressively to develop a God-centered life that eventually motivates all their deeds.

The faithful incorporated to the prelature commit themselves to lead an intense life of prayer and union with God, from which there stems a contemplative attitude and a genuine zeal for souls. Both aspects, together with one's occupation, are to be joined together in keeping with the secular character of Opus Dei, into a solid and thorough unity of life.[126]

The foundation of this spiritual life is a "humble and sincere sense of divine filiation in Jesus Christ."[127] Whence is born "the need and as it were the supernatural instinct of purifying all deeds, raising them to the order of grace, sanctifying and converting them into occasions for a personal union with God, fulfilling his will, and into an instrument of apostolate."[128] The unfolding and growth of this spiritual life requires a program to ensure an authentic life of faith and a real union with God in work and in the other ordinary circumstances of the Christian life. In general terms this plan for spiritual life comprises:

1. A serious sacramental life: daily participation in the sacrifice of the Mass—center and root of spiritual life—receiving, if possible holy communion daily and sacramental confession weekly;[129]

2. An equally earnest life of prayer, fostered by some periods of meditation; reading the New Testament and spiritual books; praying the rosary and other devotions to the blessed Virgin Mary, to whom members are to have recourse with the love and tenderness of children; simple dialogue with God—aspirations, acts of love, of reparation, of thanksgiving and the like—throughout the day . . .;[130]

3. Daily practices of mortification and penance, as an expression of Christian asceticism, which are indispensable to personal purification and progress in spiritual life, as well as to carry out an

---

[126] *Codex*, no. 79.

[127] *Codex*, no. 80 § 1.

[128] *Codex*, no. 80 § 2.

[129] *Codex*, nos. 81; 83 § 2.

[130] *Codex*, nos. 82 § 1; 83 § 2; 85.

effective apostolate, in imitation of Jesus Christ who won our salvation by his passion and death on the cross. A spirit of penance in Opus Dei does not exclude traditional ascetical practices; on the contrary it presupposes them. But it prompts seeking sacrifice above all in fulfilling one's own duties, sometimes onerous; perseverance in a daily toil that is constant and orderly; refined and cheerful service of others; in a word in little things, in the particulars of dedication that make up daily life.[131]

The chapter concerned with spiritual life is not limited to spiritual and ascetical practices.[132] It is largely devoted to grounding the soul in the quest for the goods that is the fruit of virtues. The *Statutes* richly review the panorama of virtues a Christian is to live: from the theological virtues of faith, hope and charity to human virtues.[133] These include humility, both personal and collective (Opus Dei's glory is to live without human glory); detachment from temporal goods, generosity to make them bear fruit for the sake of others, using them properly in the support of spiritual and apostolic activities; love for the Church and its hierarchy; obedience to all legitimate authority; temperance, chastity and so forth.[134]

In an overall consideration of the ascetical commitments acquired through incorporation to the prelature, it should be pointed out first of all that these various ascetical means belong to the common patrimony of the Church, which offers them to all the baptized, to one degree or another, although it does not require their practice, except in particular cases. The vocation to Opus Dei entails the commitment of habitually living them in accord with certain norms that specify and facilitate their fulfillment.

Furthermore, it is important to point out that the indications in the *Statutes* with regard to ascetical practices and the exhortations on the various virtues are not isolated pieces. Rather they form part of a single whole with two main threads: sense of divine filiation, the basis of a spiritual attitude that leads to referring all things to God as Father; and work, the ensemble of secular activities and

---

[131] *Codex*, nos. 83 § 1; 92.

[132] Others are, for example, daily examination of conscience, days of spiritual recollection, etc. (*Codex*, nos. 82; 83 § 2).

[133] Let us reproduce by way of example of the tone of these numbers a paragraph dedicated to these virtues: "In their professional, family and social life the faithful of the prelature diligently and constantly cultivate the natural virtues, so highly esteemed in human relations and which help so much in the development of apostolate: fraternity, optimism, daring, holy intransigence in good and noble things, cheerfulness, simplicity, nobility and sincerity, fidelity; they make the faithful effort in everything and always to supernaturalize these virtues" (*Codex*, no. 90).

[134] Reference to the various virtues occupies nos. 79-95 in the *Codex*.

duties, as the place to encounter God and to serve others, a prolongation and witness of the love discovered in God.

Previously, in discussing the mission or aim of the prelature, quoting the *Codex* verbatim,[135] we have underlined the value of work not only as an integral element in the life of men, but also as a means and occasion of a personal intimacy with Jesus Christ, as well as a means of participating in the work of creation and redemption. This awareness of the divine value of created realities leads to discovering that a God-centered life, prayer and practicing the virtues, is not juxtaposed to those tasks and desires from without but rather animates them from within. It is meant to flow from them as dimensions of a life imbued with grace. It is not strange, therefore, but consistent with what has been said, and at the same time revealing, that the first number of this chapter deals with unity of life, as a reality and criterion from which all the rest should be viewed: "The spirit and the ascetical practice proper to the Prelature have specific characteristics, well defined, ordered to achieving its proper aim. From this it follows that the spirit of Opus Dei presents two aspects, ascetical and apostolic, that fully correspond to one another. These are so intrinsically and harmonically united and penetrated with the secular character of Opus Dei that they encourage and lead necessarily to a solid and simple unity of ascetical, apostolic, social and professional life."[136]

Opus Dei helps its faithful to fulfill their ascetical commitments by offering stable spiritual direction, both individual and collective, and a specific and continual pastoral assistance.[137] In this the prelate has a particular responsibility, since his is the duty to make sure the faithful receive this spiritual help "assiduously and abundantly,"[138] a duty he shares with those who in Opus Dei have positions of direction or are priests. But to one degree or to another this is also a responsibility of all members of Opus Dei. They are to answer for the holiness of those at their side, especially of those called to the same mission.[139]

---

[135] *Codex*, no. 86 § 1.

[136] *Codex*, no. 79 § 1.

[137] *Codex*, no. 83 § 2.

[138] *Codex*, no. 132 § 2.

[139] The importance Msgr. Escrivá always gave to the practice of the ancient Christian evangelical practice of fraternal correction is a significant manifestation of this point. It is also taken up in no. 91 of the *Codex*. Having in mind the various interpretations or practical ways this evangelical norm has been lived throughout the history of the Church, perhaps it would be good to point out that it is understood and lived in Opus Dei as a dialogue in which always, one on one, with special refinement and simplicity, a careless act or a defect that could hinder one's interior life or the apostolate is pointed out by one member to another.

b) *Formation*

When speaking of the formation members of Opus Dei need—and in general any Christian called to seek holiness amid the world—Msgr. Escrivá said it comprises various facets: human, professional, spiritual, doctrinal, apostolic. None of these facets can be slighted if one is to bear witness in the world amid professional and social tasks to the truth of Christ. Such witness calls not only for real spiritual life and adequate familiarity with the doctrine of faith but also for the human and technical competence that allows for discharging one's earthly tasks with exemplarity.

Each member of Opus Dei should feel responsible for his or her own formation, of which there are appropriate reminders. Nevertheless, obviously not all aspects of this education are equally of the prelature's competence. Precisely because a call to Opus Dei does not remove anyone from his place, his human formation and the preparation required by his own profession or occupation is acquired by each in the environments where he moves. They frequent the same places—schools, shops, universities, and so forth—where their fellow citizens prepare themselves. The specific commitment of the Prelature to give formation refers then to the spiritual, doctrinal and apostolic dimensions. This training tends to improve the spiritual life of members, to enhance their knowledge of Church teachings and of Opus Dei's spirit, and to ready them to carry out with greater effectiveness an incisive and fruitful apostolate where they live and work.[140] This training, both a right and a duty of the prelature's faithful, is covered in the second chapter of title three of the *Codex*. The first deals with spiritual life and the third with apostolate. The second chapter is mainly centered on doctrinal education, though with references to other aspects, given their intimate connection. The first number stresses these links: "Under the doctrinal aspect, the formation given to the prelature's faithful aims at providing them with a thorough knowledge of the Catholic faith and Church teachings, necessary sustenance for their spiritual and apostolic life. Then in all environments of society there will be persons intellectually prepared, who in the ordinary circumstances of daily life and work, carry out simply by example and word an effective apostolate of evangelization and catechesis."[141]

Different means are used: some personal—as spiritual direction—and others collective: study courses, classes, talks, retreats, special workshops and so forth. As the vocation to Opus Dei requires sanctifying oneself in one's own environment and occupation, where members remain, this instruction must be made com-

---

[140] *Codex*, nos. 3 § 1, 2°; 27 § 2, 1°.

[141] *Codex*, no. 96.

patible, and is coordinated, with the occupations of each, calling
forth whatever practical solutions are most suitable. This is mentioned in the *Statutes*.[142]

Formation begins the very moment a person asks to be admitted
to the prelature and it never ends.[143] It is adapted to the personal
circumstances of each of the faithful;[144] it is organized for homogeneous groups particularly in the case of courses, annual workshops,
retreats and so on.[145] In any case it is demanding, as borne out by
the demand that all numeraries—plus other faithful—pursue in their
entirety a two-year curriculum of philosophy and a four year one of
theology at a post-secondary level.[146]

Apart from organizing courses and conferences, centers of studies
are to be established in each circumscription.[147] There are also interregional centers, destined primarily to prepare those who are to
take charge of formative activities in the various regions,[148] and
special centers for those called to the priesthood.[149]

The prelature discharges its formative obligation by means of
appropriate centers, suitable disciplinary norms and teachers specifically qualified for this task. The faithful of the prelature commit
themselves to attend these means, aware of their need, if they are to
shoulder suitably their vocation and Christian mission.

We conclude with two observations. The first reiterates the
integration of the various dimensions. The goal is not to transmit
certain bits of information, but rather to form persons capable of
acting with knowledge, freedom and responsibility, each on his or
her own in the various sectors of human society. Consequently the
aim is to help them forge a synthesis wherein faith illuminates all
the varied experiences of the human condition.[150]

---

[142] *Codex*, nos. 99 § 2; 101.

[143] *Codex*, nos. 106 and 107.

[144] *Codex*, no. 101.

[145] *Codex*, no. 106 § 2.

[146] *Codex*, no. 101 §§ 1, 2, 3.

[147] *Codex*, no. 97.

[148] *Codex*, no. 98.

[149] *Codex*, no. 102.

[150] In the interview published in *Litteræ Communionis* (*op. cit.* note 64 of this chapter), a
question was asked: "Is there some instructional progression [in Opus Dei]?" The
prelate replied, "Msgr. Escrivá described in a synthetic way the work of Opus Dei as
*a great catechesis* offered to men and women of all social conditions, races, languages
and cultures, so as to make it possible for them to sanctify themselves sanctifying their
own work. This pedagogy of the faith passes through the crossroads of conversion,
that is to say, of the decision to live in accordance with the gift Christ has won for us

A second observation concerns freedom in temporal matters open to discussion, so characteristic of the spirit and life of Opus Dei. This also affects theological instruction. All are to become familiar with the Catholic faith and Church teachings, without being subjected to particular opinions. The last number of the chapter dedicated to formation affirms, "Opus Dei does not have any corporate opinion or school in all theological or philosophical matters the Church has left to the free discussion of the faithful: the faithful of the prelature, within the limits established by the ecclesiastical hierarchy, guardian of the deposit of the faith, enjoy the same freedom as other Catholic faithful."[151]

c) *Apostolate*

The *Codex* chapter dedicated to apostolate begins with the assertion that the faithful of the prelature are habitually to make a reality of the duty and right incumbent on all Christians to do apostolate.[152] Then follows an exhortation, inspired in St. Paul, that each faithful of the prelature, as any other Christian, ought to feel himself sent to the crowd, invited to make himself all things for all men. "We have been constituted for the crowd. Thus there is not a single soul whom we do not want to love and help, making ourselves all things for all people (cf. I Cor 9:22). We cannot disregard the problems and needs of our fellow men, because our concern ought to be to embrace all souls. Living a life hidden with Christ in God (cf. Col 3:3), we ought to be leaven hidden in the mass of human society and made one with it until the whole mass is leavened (cf. Mt 13:33)."[153]

A subsequent number describes: "The faithful of the prelature— convinced that their special apostolate stems from interior life and love for human work—both fused and penetrated in a unity of life—must strive particularly to sanctify their own work and to perform it with the greatest human perfection possible. Thus they

---

on the cross: divine filiation. It is not a question of a merely expositive catechesis in which the content of the faith is explained, but of a true spiritual journey that echoes the invitation with which Jesus began to address men: 'Be converted and believe in the gospel' (Mk 1:15). Thus our founder gave as much importance to teaching those who followed him to be men and women of authentic interior life, souls who cultivate a constant intimacy with the three divine Persons and with the most holy Virgin, and who try to turn all the occupations of their day into prayer. This aspect is essential in the pedagogy of Opus Dei: the more a Christian is immersed in the world the more he needs to have this interior richness—a communion of life with Christ—which is only achieved with prayer and the sacraments. If not, a Christian, instead of leading the world to God, will end up letting himself become worldly."

[151] *Codex*, no. 109.

[152] *Codex*, no. 110. Chapter III, of title III, *De apostolatu*, comprises nos. 110-124.

[153] *Codex*, no. 111, 2°.

orient it in accord with God's will towards saving all souls, especially those of their colleagues."[154]

These texts presuppose the reality of Opus Dei's pastoral phenomenon: a diverse multitude of men and women, engaged in many tasks, occupations and professions, each acting with full freedom and personal responsibility in all temporal matters that make up their life,[155] but all moved by the desire of working, always and everywhere, in accord with Christ's law to make known to those around them the Good News. The *Codex* then develops some particulars.

It indicates, for example, that the apostolic endeavors of the members is directed to every class of persons, with no distinctions of race, national origin or social condition; all are to be reminded that they are called to holiness, ordinarily in the exercise of their occupation and in fulfillment of all duties proper to the state of each one.[156]

Elsewhere it emphasizes that apostolic zeal should be lived *totis viribus*: "with all one's might." It is not an activity superimposed on other activities; or rather, it is a dimension present in the whole of life.[157] It does not thus manifest itself in a uniform or typical fashion; born of a spontaneity that adapts itself to the varied circumstances of human endeavor, it is implemented among one's peers, friends and colleagues, in one's family, in the cultural and social life proper to each.[158] Therefore in a natural way it even reaches environments not ordinarily open to the pastoral work of the Church, always with utmost respect for the freedom of consciences and desirous of living peaceably with everyone.[159] It is an apostolate where a prominent place is given to witness and good example, but where the word also has a decisive role. Thus souls are drawn to God by suitable conversation, confession of faith and sharing of doctrine.[160]

The *Statutes* declare that this personal apostolate, apostolic work carried out individually by each member of Opus Dei in his own

---

[154] *Codex*, no. 113.

[155] The *Statutes* refer to this freedom in temporal matters in no. 88 § 3, already seen (note 77 of this chapter).

[156] *Codex*, nos. 112 and 115.

[157] *Codex*, nos. 2 § 2; 112; 113.

[158] *Codex*, nos. 11 *in fine*; 117; 119.

[159] *Codex*, nos. 112; 117; 118.

[160] *Codex*, nos. 113, 114, 117. Although we do so in passing, we point out that such an apostolate is rooted in the essence of the Christian vocation, with a mission derived from baptism; moreover, it redounds to the good of the Church in general and more concretely, of the local churches where it is carried out. The good of the Church as a requirement for the existence of a personal prelature is easy to see:

setting, occupies the principal place (*locus præcipuus*) in the totality of the pastoral action of the prelature.[161] This does not preclude the possibility that some faithful of the prelature, ordinarily cooperating with other people whether Catholics or not, as a consequence of their professional work, may promote initiatives of an educational, social or beneficent nature. They will have a clearly apostolic aim, but with a content that is civil and professional—not confessional. These initiatives can request spiritual help from the prelature. Even more, when certain circumstances hold, the prelature may grant to these activities a "specific pastoral assistance," which stably assures their Christian orientation and the proper spiritual attention of those to whom the activity is addressed. The criteria the prelature seeks in order to assume this specific pastoral attention are set forth in the *Codex* as follows:[162]

a) They must always be endeavors pursuing educational or social welfare goals, they can never be financial or political and the like;

b) The prelature does not assume charge of the technical or financial aspects of these activities—something that pertains fully and solely to their owners, executives and trustees;

c) The role the prelature plays is to imbue these initiatives with a Christian spirit, answering for their doctrinal-spiritual orientation and pastoral assistance, within the fullest respect for the legitimate autonomy and the civil and professional nature of each one;

d) The pastoral attention to these initiatives never becomes a primary objective of Opus Dei (foremost always is personal formation and apostolate); thus their number will always be proportionately small.[163]

---

a) through the ecclesial effectiveness ensuing from the example of a good number of the faithful—each in his own environment, striving to practice and transmit to others the demands of a Christian life lived in its fullness;

b) it contributes to helping many people to know the teachings of the Catholic Church and to put into practice the message of Jesus Christ in their professional, family and social life, to receive the sacraments frequently and to participate actively in the life of the parish, and so forth;

c) by means of this example and personal apostolate, an authentic Christian sense of life is brought to more families, from which will come in many cases vocations for the diocesan seminary and for institutes of consecrated life;

d) it will help to draw close to the Church a great number of persons—non-Catholics and non-Christians—converted as a result of the apostolate *ad fidem* so much cared for in Opus Dei; these friendships occasioned by professional and social dealings, will help to overcome prejudices and, on occasion, to bring closer the graces of conversion (*Codex*, nos. 116 § 2; 115; 118).

[161] *Codex*, no. 121 § 1.

[162] *Codex*, nos. 121-123.

[163] All of this spiritual assistance by the prelature should be carried out in accordance with the spirit of harmonious cooperation that should govern all relations between the

## 10. The Prelate and his jurisdiction

The Prelature of Opus Dei constitutes, as we have seen, a pastoral and apostolic unity, organic and indivisible, with a unity of government. In its jurisdictional structure the position of the prelate has special relevance, inasmuch as the members of the other organs of government are his vicars or are cooperating with him. Let us study the role of the prelate in greater detail.

From its outset Opus Dei shows itself to be a pastoral phenomenon with a structure united around the founder, not only as the depository of the original charism, but also the center and source of unity. This office is to be continued, therefore, in those who succeed him. The erection as a prelature assumes and confirms this reality, by means of a suitable juridical configuration.

The whole prelature is, in effect, a jurisdictional and hierarchical structure whose chief office belongs to the prelate. He governs it as its proper ordinary and pastor, with a jurisdiction circumscribed to its special pastoral apostolic mission, distinct from the ordinary pastoral care entrusted to diocesan bishops.[164] This is so established in canon 295 of the Code of Canon Law. So also says *Ut sit*: "The proper ordinary of the prelature Opus Dei is its prelate."

Since Opus Dei is an organic and indivisible unity, the jurisdiction of the prelate is exercised over this single whole. All its faithful, clerics and laity, men and women—each according to his or her respective function and position and bearing in mind the mission of the prelature—are subject to the prelate's jurisdiction. Article III of *Ut sit* describes this jurisdiction thus : "The jurisdiction of the personal prelature extends to the clergy incardinated in it, and also— only in what refers to the fulfillment of the specific obligations undertaken with the juridical bond, by means of a contract with the prelature—to the laity who dedicate themselves to the apostolic activities of the prelature: both clergy and laity are under the authority of the prelate in implementing the pastoral tasks of the prelature, as established in the preceding article."

The preceding article of the *Ut sit* establishes, in turn, the norms by which the prelature is governed: the general law, the Apostolic

---

prelature and local ordinaries, of which we will speak in a subsequent section. Nevertheless we point out now a few manifestations. There are two significant ones: a) whenever it is a question of erecting a center to give specific attention to a particular apostolic work previous permission of the local ordinary must be sought (Codex, no. 123); b) in the case of appointing teachers of religion or chaplains the local ordinary should be suitably informed (Codex, no. 121 § 2).

[164] See J. Hervada, *Aspetti della struttura giuridica dell'Opus Dei, op. cit.* (note 63 of this chapter), pp. 420-422.

Constitution *Ut sit* and the *Codex Iuris Particularis Operis Dei*. The Declaration *Prælaturæ personales* offers a summary of these norms, which determine the kind of governance of the prelate. It is a question of an "ordinary power of governance or of jurisdiction, limited to that which refers to the specific finality of the prelature." It distinguishes it from that "which belongs to the diocesan bishops in the ordinary spiritual care of the faithful."[165] Going into greater detail, it says this power "in addition to the government of the clergy of the prelature includes the general direction of the formation and of the specific apostolic and spiritual attention the laity incorporated in Opus Dei receive, to help them live a more intense dedication in the service of the Church."[166]

It also highlights the breadth of the jurisdiction and responsibility with respect to the clergy of the prelature: "Together with the right to incardinate his own candidates to the priesthood, the prelate has the obligation to attend to their specific formation in the centers of the prelature, in conformity with the norms established by the competent congregation, and to the spiritual life and the permanent formation of the priests promoted by him to holy orders. He is also obliged to provide for the proper support of his clergy and for their care in old age and in the case of illness, etc."[167]

"The laity are under the jurisdiction of the prelate in regard to what has to do with the fulfillment of the specific ascetic, formative and apostolic commitments they have freely undertaken by means of the contractual bond dedicating them to the service of the aims of the prelature."[168] "The laity incorporated in the Prelature of Opus Dei continue to be faithful of the diocese in which they have their domicile or quasi-domicile and are therefore under the jurisdiction of the diocesan bishop in what the law lays down for all the ordinary faithful."[169]

The *Codex* in turn, refers to the prelate in the first of its numbers. After affirming that Opus Dei is a personal prelature comprising both clerics and laity for the realization of a special pastoral task, it adds: "under the government of its own prelate."[170] The same number then makes reference to the first number of title four, dedicated to government, which says: "The government of the prelature is entrusted to the prelate, who is aided by his vicars and

---

[165] *Prælaturæ personales*, III, a).

[166] *Ibid.*, III, b).

[167] *Ibid.*, III, c).

[168] *Ibid.*, III, d).

[169] *Ibid.*, IV, c).

[170] *Codex*, no. 1 § 1.

councils according to the norms of universal law and of this *Codex*."[171] "The power of governance which the prelate enjoys," it adds evoking article III of *Ut sit*, "is full, both in the external forum and in the internal forum, with regard to the priests incardinated in the prelature; and with regard to the laity incorporated in the prelature this power extends only to what has to do with the special finality of the prelature itself."[172] "The power of the prelate, both over clerics and over laity," it clarifies, "is exercised in accordance with the universal law and of the law of this *Codex*."[173]

The prelate, therefore, is the ordinary and proper pastor of the prelature, endowed with the power of governance or of jurisdiction. His is ordinary power, insofar as it is joined *ipso iure* to the office. It is also proper—not vicarious—that is to say, it is exercised in his own name and not in the name of another,[174] a participation *a iure* in the power of governance of the Roman Pontiff.

The office of prelate is filled by means of a system of canonical election. Thus *Ut sit* prescribes that the prelate is to be elected "in accordance with what is established in the general and particular law."[175] This prescription is dealt with in greater detail in the *Statutes* which determine the following:

a) When the office of prelate becomes vacant, the interim government is assumed by the auxiliary Vicar, if there is one, or the Vicar General, who must convoke within a month a general elective congress, so that its celebration take place within a maximum period of time of three months from the moment when the vacancy occurred;[176]

b) Members of the Congress are appointed by the preceding prelate or prelates with the deliberative vote of his council, after having heard the corresponding regional commission, and who were congressmen in their respective circumscription. This appointment is for life and falls upon priests and laymen more than 32 years old and who have been definitively incorporated to the prelature for at least 9 years. They come from the various nations and regions where Opus Dei is apostolically at work.[177]

---

[171] *Codex*, no. 125 § 1.

[172] *Codex*, no. 125 § 2.

[173] *Codex*, no. 125 § 3.

[174] CIC 1983, can. 131 and 295.

[175] *Ut sit*, art. IV. With respect to the general law see CIC 1983 can. 164-179; in the case of a jurisdictional structure pertaining to the hierarchical organization of the Church, the election is not in this case a constitutive one, but requires confirmation (can. 178 *in fine* and 179).

[176] *Codex*, no. 149 §§ 1 and 2.

[177] *Codex*, no. 130 §§ 1 and 2.

c) In order to be elected prelate, one must be a priest member of the Congress, be 40 years old, be definitively incorporated in the prelature for at least 10 years, have been ordained priest for at least 5 years, and be possessed of the qualities that guarantee the good fulfillment of the office.[178]

d) The procedure for election begins with a meeting of the plenary committee of the Central Advisory (the council of the women's branch), with the participation of delegates of the various regional jurisdictions. In this meeting, those present formulate a proposal with the name or names of those they consider to be most worthy for the office of prelate. This slate is transmitted to the General Congress, which, having received and considered these proposals, proceeds to the election.[179]

e) Once the election has been carried out and the person elected has accepted, he, either by himself or by means of another, must request confirmation from the Roman Pontiff.[180]

f) Once the Pope has confirmed the election, the prelate, who within Opus Dei is referred to also with the name of Father,[181] has the fullness of his power of governance, which he exercises for life.[182]

The jurisdiction of the prelate is exercised over clerics and laity, in accordance with universal law and the statutes of the prelature; it encompasses everything having to do with the proper mission of Opus Dei.[183]

With respect to the priests incardinated in the prelature, this jurisdiction extends specifically to everything following on the bond of incardination: formation, discipline, canonical mission and ministerial faculties with respect to the faithful of the prelature and the mission which this carries out, etc.[184]

---

[178] *Codex*, no. 131.

[179] *Codex*, nos. 130 §§ 3 and 146.

[180] CIC 1983, can. 178-179; *Ut sit*, art. IV; *Codex*, no. 130 §§ 1 and 2.

[181] *Codex*, no. 130 § 1.

[182] *Codex*, no. 130 § 1. The Statutes foresee that if, out of old age, sickness or for some other grave cause, the prelate were incapable of governing, the General Congress would meet to elect an auxiliary vicar, to whom all the powers and rights and obligations of the prelate would pass, except the title (*Codex*, nos. 134 § 2 and 136). We point out, in passing, that apart from the auxiliary vicar named in these special circumstances, the prelate possesses in every moment the faculty to name an auxiliary vicar, who helps him in his office, delegating to him the faculties he considers appropriate (*Codex*, nos. 134 § 1 and 135).

[183] *Codex*, nos. 1, 125; 88 § 2.

[184] See *Codex*, chapt. II of title II *De promotione ad sacros Ordines et de presbyterorum missione canonica* (nos. 44ff). See also *Prælaturæ personales*, III, b) and c).

With respect to the laity incorporated to Opus Dei, the jurisdiction applies to everything related to fulfilling the serious and qualified commitments assumed with incorporation to the prelature.[185]

More particularly, the prelate's jurisdiction includes the general direction of the formation and specific pastoral attention— *peculiaris cura animarum*—of the priests and laity. The *Statutes* so state: "He shall take care above all that the priests and laity entrusted to him avail themselves assiduously and abundantly of the means and spiritual and intellectual aids, which are necessary for the support and encouragement of their spiritual life and to achieve the special apostolic aim."[186]

This pastoral solicitude also shows itself through advice and exhortations, plus laws, precepts and instructions and, in its case, sanctions. It is also the prelate's responsibility to visit by himself or by a delegate all the jurisdictions and centers, the churches of the prelature or those entrusted to it, and both with regard to persons and things.[187] He must exercise a special vigilance with regard to the observance of the law by which Opus Dei is governed as well as its legitimate customs. He fosters besides the faithful execution of the decisions of the Holy See with regard to the prelature.[188]

This power of jurisdiction of the prelate is manifested also in many other acts of government foreseen by the *Codex*. Before all else, the prelate must be for the faithful: "a teacher and father, who truly loves all with Christ's heart; forms and animates all with an overflowing charity; gladly dedicates himself and spends himself on behalf of all."[189] This spiritual norm is to inspire any and all juridical requirements.

The prelate governs the whole prelature, with both of its branches,[190] with the assistance of his vicars and councils according to the norms of universal law and the *Codex*.[191] The latter establishes, with regard to government and organization, a structure with three levels—central or universal, regional and local—with the characteristics noted earlier. There are no significant changes,

---

[185] See *Prælaturæ personales*, II, b) and d).

[186] *Codex*, no. 132 § 4 and *passim*.

[187] *Codex*, no. 132, § 5.

[188] *Codex*, no. 132 § 2. We quote also no. 184, which establishes: "It corresponds to the prelate with the deliberative vote of his council to define all of those things that refer to the practical interpretation, application and fulfillment of this *Codex*."

[189] *Codex*, no. 132 § 3.

[190] *Codex*, no. 4 § 2.

[191] *Codex*, no. 125 § 1.

except for some technical improvements and one advance—the concept of vicar—made possible by the configuration as a prelature.[192]

The prelate may erect, modify or suppress the regional circumscriptions;[193] he appoints the respective vicars, as well as those who form part of their councils.[194] His is the right to erect interregional and regional centers of studies and other centers especially destined to form those being prepared to receive holy orders.[195]

The prelate is helped in his government by other priests, as vicars. For the whole prelature the *Codex* foresees the existence, in some cases, of an auxiliary vicar,[196] and always of a vicar or general secretary and of a vicar for the women's branch. He is also helped in territorial circumscriptions by regional vicars and, where appropriate, delegate vicars.[197] The vicars enjoy general ordinary executive power; they are ordinaries of the prelature.[198] Thus not only are those with functions of government in the prelature to act in full agreement with the spirit of Opus Dei and in communion with the prelate or Father (*nomine et vice Patris*) but also must realize that the power resides in the prelate although the vicars do participate in this power, as corresponds to a hierarchical structure. Furthermore, the central role that, in the spiritual, juridical and social reality of Opus Dei the figure of the founder and of his successors has always had is thus repeated and reinforced.

Two councils cooperate in the exercise of the functions of government of the prelate. They are formed by faithful of the prelature—clerics and laity. They are called the general council for the men's branch and the central advisory for the women's branch. The general council is made up of an auxiliary vicar (if there is one), a vicar general, a vicar for the women's branch, three vice secretaries, a delegate for at least each region, a prefect of studies and a general administrator.[199] The central advisory occupies in the women's branch an analogous role with similar offices.[200]

---

[192] The three first chapters of title four of the *Codex* (nos. 125-161), deal with government at the three levels. These are completed with a fourth chapter dealing with regional assemblies (nos. 162-170); it deals with general congresses—ordinary, extraordinary and elective—in the previous numbers 130-131 and 133.

[193] *Codex*, nos. 150; 152-153.

[194] *Codex*, nos. 126; 151 § 1; 156; 157.

[195] *Codex*, nos. 97; 98; 102.

[196] See note 182 of this chapter.

[197] *Codex*, nos. 138 § 1; 146 § 1; 151 § 1; 152; 157 § 1.

[198] *Codex*, no. 125 § 4.

[199] *Codex*, no. 138.

[200] *Codex*, no. 146.

At the head of each regional circumscription is a regional vicar, who is assisted by a council for each branch—the regional commission and regional advisory (made up of as many as twelve members for each).[201] Within each region delegations can be established at the head of which is a delegate vicar, endowed with suitable faculties and helped by councils, with characteristics analogous to those of the regional commission.[202]

## 11. The presbyterate of the Prelature

After having dealt with the faithful, or the portion of Christian people incorporated to the prelature of Opus Dei, and with the chief office—the prelate—we now turn to those members who, having received holy orders, make up its presbyterate or priestly body. These cooperate in a ministerial way with the prelate by caring spiritually for the faithful of the prelature and by developing its mission.

The juridical form of prelature has not been given to Opus Dei only insofar as it contains clerics, just as the Church is not such simply because in it exists an order of priests. The presbyterate is essential, but it is not the only essential element. In Opus Dei, both the laity and the presbyterate are essential: together they constitute one organic and indivisible unity under the prelate.[203]

The *Statutes* establish: "The presbyterate of the prelature is made up of those priests who are promoted to holy orders from among the lay faithful of the prelature and are incardinated in it."[204] The first number of title two adds that these priests "are dedicated to its service," that is to say of the prelature and its mission.[205] *Prælaturæ personales* points out that thus "no candidates for the priesthood or deacons or priests are withdrawn from the local churches."[206]

The need Opus Dei has, in fidelity to its original charism, for its own priests formed in its spirit—as Msgr. Escrivá realized from the beginning—is incarnated in this definitive juridical configuration. Whence the existence of a presbyterate, placed under the full jurisdiction of the prelate and completely available to attend spiritually to all the faithful of the prelature and to participate in all of its

---

[201] Codex, nos. 151 and 157.

[202] Codex, no. 153.

[203] See the writings quoted in note 90 of this chapter.

[204] *Codex*, no. 1 § 2. We note that the incardination of the clerics in the prelature by the reception of the diaconate, leaves intact the commitments acquired by the previous incorporation to the prelature as laymen.

[205] *Codex*, no. 36 § 1; see also nos. 37 § 1; 38; 44; 45; 50 and *passim*.

[206] *Prælaturæ personales*, I, b).

apostolates.[207] The *Statutes* stipulate that, for receiving holy orders, candidates be definitively incorporated as a numerary or associate members in Opus Dei, that they be at least 25 years of age and have completed the necessary studies.[208] The prelate must recognize in them a call to the priesthood and deem necessary or suitable their ordination to address pastoral work of the prelature. Obviously anyone who feels called to priesthood should manifest this desire to the prelate, but it is the latter who makes the judgment and final decision.[209]

Besides the requirements already mentioned and those established in canon law, candidates to holy orders must possess qualities needed for effectively exercising the priestly ministry in the prelature. He is to dedicate himself first of all to tasks of spiritual and doctrinal formation: the special pastoral care of the faithful incorporated to Opus Dei and of those sharing in its apostolic work.[210] They are called to the priesthood after having worked professionally for a greater or less period of time at tasks they ordinarily renounce in order to be "priest-priests, priests a hundred percent," as the founder liked to say. Nevertheless, they may continue to exercise their profession so long as "it is in agreement with the prescription and instructions of the Holy See and is not opposed to the priestly character."[211] In any case they try always to retain the outlook and background of their professional life, qualities that obviously will help them in their priestly work with those living and working in all sectors of civil society.

Regarding the preparation of candidates to the priesthood, the norms of universal law and the particular law of the prelature are followed, namely, its *Ratio Institutionis Sacerdotalis*, approved by the Holy See.[212] There are special centers of studies established for those preparing for the priesthood and erected by the prelate.[213] Ordinarily besides the institutional studies required by law, the priests of the prelature will also earn a doctorate in an ecclesiastical discipline.[214]

At the time of ordination the prelate gives the dimissory letters; furthermore they also receive from the prelate the canonical mis-

---

[207] *Ut sit*, art. III; *Codex*, no. 125 §§ 2 and 3.

[208] *Codex*, nos. 37 § 1; and 45. The *Statutes* deal with promotion to orders and the canonical mission of the priest in nos. 44-56.

[209] *Codex*, no. 44.

[210] *Codex*, nos. 38; 39; 45; 49.

[211] *Codex*, no. 51 § 2.

[212] *Codex*, no. 46.

[213] *Codex*, no. 102.

[214] *Codex*, no. 105.

sion with the necessary ministerial faculties for celebrating Mass, preaching and hearing confessions.[215]  They also depend on him with regard to their being sent to one or another regional circumscription.[216]  The prelate must care for his priests after ordination by making available to them pastoral courses, ensuring that they take the necessary examinations and making sure they receive the means to cultivate their continuing education.[217]  It is also the prelate's mission to issue norms and instructions so that the priests receive the appropriate means to cultivate their spiritual life and the effective fulfillment of their priestly ministry; he is also charged with their support and care in the event of illness, incapacity, old age, etc.[218]

The *Codex* expressly establishes that the priests "will dedicate their activity first of all to the spiritual and ecclesiastical formation and the special pastoral care of souls—*peculiari curæ animarum*—of the faithful of both branches of Opus Dei."  These have the strict right—by virtue of the contract with the prelature—to be duly cared for by those who make up its presbyterate.[219]  To the degree they are able and with the appropriate ministerial faculties *ad normam iuris* they may also extend their ministry to other people.[220]

The declaration *Prælaturæ personales* says, "As established in the general law of the Church, and in the law of the prelature, the clergy incardinated in the prelature belong to the secular clergy to all effects."[221]  Equals among their peers, priests of the prelature strive to foster close relations of communion with the other priests of the local churches.[222]  They have an active and passive voice in the election of the corresponding presbyteral council of the local churches.[223]  Similarly they can accept offices or ecclesiastical responsibilities in the local churches with the previous consent of the prelate or, in its case of his vicar.[224]  In fulfilling these tasks they will always act "according to the will and mind" (*ad nutum e mentem*) of

---

[215] *Codex*, nos. 48; 50 §§ 2-3.  The faculty to hear confessions applies to all the faithful of the prelature and the members of the Priestly Society of the Holy Cross and to all those persons who dwell *diu noctuque* in the centers of the prelature (cf. *Codex*, no. 50 § 3).

[216] *Codex*, no. 50 § 1.

[217] *Codex*, no. 54.

[218] *Codex*, nos. 55; 132 § 4.  See also *Prælaturæ personales*, III, c).

[219] *Codex*, no. 38; as well as nos. 21 and 27 § 2, 1.

[220] *Codex*, no. 39.

[221] Declaration *Prælaturæ personales*, II, a).  See also CIC 1983, can. 294.

[222] *Codex*, nos. 41 and 56.  See also *Prælaturæ personales*, II, a).

[223] *Prælaturæ personales*, II, a).

[224] *Codex*, nos. 40 and 51.

the corresponding diocesan bishop; they will answer only to him or to the appropriate authorities of the local churches, and not to those of the prelature.[225]

Finally it should be pointed out that, when ordained, all the clerics incardinated in the prelature acquire the condition of members of the Priestly Society of the Holy Cross.[226]

## 12. The Priestly Society of the Holy Cross

Having set forth how Opus Dei has sought to put into practice the universal call to holiness and to promote it among all kinds of people, the Preamble of *Ut sit* states: "Furthermore through the Priestly Society of the Holy Cross it has helped diocesan priests to live this teaching in the exercise of their priestly ministry." In agreement with this historical background, article I of the Apostolic Constitution, after declaring erected the Prelature of the Holy Cross and Opus Dei, adds: "The Priestly Society of the Holy Cross is erected as a clerical association intrinsically united to the prelature."

The desire of extending to priests incardinated in dioceses the light and help the spirit of Opus Dei could bring to them had led Msgr. Escrivá in 1948-1950 to consider a new foundation. Then he came to see that these priests could find a place in Opus Dei, in the broader sense, more specifically, in the Priestly Society of the Holy Cross. The 1950 Constitutions said this Society was *aliquid intrinsecum Operi Dei*.[227] These Constitutions had pointed out ways by which diocesan priests might be admitted, as associate and supernumerary members, in the Priestly Society of the Holy Cross. This Society was to be made up not only of ordained Opus Dei members, but also of priests incardinated in dioceses who sought admission in it. Not for this reason were they to lose their bond of incardination; they were to continue to be fully dedicated to the service of the diocese under the government of its ordinary.

This spirit is retained in the *Statutes*, with the same theological substance. But they also feature developments and improvements that allow a new canonical configuration. The Priestly Society of the Holy Cross is no longer characterized as in 1950 by the generic expression (*quid intrinsicum*). Rather, *Ut sit* calls it an association of clerics distinct from, but intimately and inseparably united to, the prelature.

---

[225] Codex, no. 124.

[226] Codex, no. 36 § 2.

[227] Const. 1950, no. 64. These historical facts are set forth in chapter VI.

The *Statutes* define it as "a clerical association so proper and intrinsic to the prelature that with it it forms a single whole—*aliquid unum*—and cannot be separated from it."[228]  It is also established that the prelate of Opus Dei is also the president general of the Priestly Society of the Holy Cross.[229]  As we said previously, the lay men of the prelature, numeraries or associates, who receive holy orders are "from the very moment of their ordination," members of the Priestly Society of the Holy Cross.[230]

The Priestly Society offers diocesan priests the help and encouragement afforded by the spiritual message born with and lived in Opus Dei.  The *Statutes* describe its aim thus: "priestly holiness in conformity with the spirit and ascetical practice of Opus Dei, also among clerics not belonging to the prelature."[231]

Clerics incardinated in dioceses who become members of the Priestly Society of the Holy Cross as associates or supernumeraries,[232]  do so in response to a special vocation that leads them to deepen their priestly condition and to live it with the secular spirituality, that is proper to Opus Dei.  This vocation reinforces the obligation every priest has to tend towards holiness.[233]  It aids them to achieve it by means of the asceticism proper to Opus Dei; their quest for holiness takes place amid and with the realities or concrete circumstances making up the state or condition of each one. In the case of priests, the matter to be sanctified is everything ensuing from the fulfillment of their ministry and their bond to the diocese where they are incardinated.[234]

---

[228] *Codex*, no. 36 § 2.

[229] *Codex*, no. 36 § 3.

[230] *Codex*, nos. 36 § 2; and 37 § 2.

[231] *Codex*, no. 57. *Prælaturæ personales*, no. VI, expresses it in the following words: "The Priestly Society of the Holy Cross is an association inseparably united to the prelature. Priests of the diocesan clergy who wish to strive for sanctity in their ministry in accordance with the spirituality of Opus Dei may form part of this association."

[232] *Codex*, no. 58 § 1. Priests and candidates to the priesthood who have received the diaconate can be admitted to the Priestly Society of the Holy Cross as associate or supernumerary members. Other candidates to the priesthood can be received in the Priestly Society only as aspirants (*Codex*, no. 60 § 1).

[233] Vatican Council II, *Presbyterorum ordinis*, no. 12; see CIC 1983, can. 276, § 1.

[234] *Codex*, nos. 58 § 1; 61; 62. A common requirement for the priests of the Priestly Society of the Holy Cross is their total and habitual availability to seek holiness in accordance with the spirit, the asceticism and the means of formation proper to Opus Dei. For the associates, in addition, the intention is required of dedicating all their time and effort to the apostolate, in a special way spiritually helping their brothers: other diocesan priests (*Codex*, no. 61, 2°).

In joining the Priestly Society a diocesan priest exclusively seeks and receives help in the spiritual terrain. The duties stemming from his diocesan incardination remain untouched without any exception: the juridical and effective bonds with the other members of the diocesan presbyterate and the legitimate liturgical and spiritual traditions characteristic of a specific diocesan community. None of these bonds is lessened; rather, they are reinforced. The spirit these priests are exposed to in drawing close to Opus Dei leads them to seek Christian sanctity and human perfection precisely in faithfully fulfilling their priestly duties.[235] The statutory norms clearly establish that the associate and supernumerary priests who belong to the Priestly Society do not form part of the clergy of the prelature (comprised exclusively of priests incardinated in the prelature). Instead, they belong to the presbyterate of their respective dioceses.[236] The *Statutes* require, among the conditions indicative of a vocation, outstanding love for their own diocese, exemplary obedience and respect for their own diocesan bishop and fulfillment of their ministerial duties with the greatest perfection possible.[237]

The bond uniting these priests to the Priestly Society is exclusively of an associative character, whose type and aims are foreseen in the Decree *Presbyterorum ordinis*, no. 8. They do not thus belong to the prelature, nor are they under the jurisdiction of the prelate of Opus Dei;[238] the prelate, as president general of the Priestly Society of the Holy Cross, enjoys only a power proper to associations in the Church. Thus the *Statutes* declare that "even a shadow of a special hierarchy should be absolutely and carefully avoided. What is exclusively sought is the perfection of priestly life, the fruits of a diligent fidelity to interior life, a tenacious and constant effort in one's own formation and an apostolic willingness, criteria and zeal. In no way do these priests fall under the power of governance of the prelate of Opus Dei or of his vicars."[239] Thus there can never be a problem of double obedience—as emphasized in another place of the *Statutes*. In becoming members of the Priestly Society these

---

[235] *Codex*, no. 58 § 1.

[236] *Codex*, no. 58 § 1. See also *Prælaturæ personales*, VI.

[237] *Codex*, no. 59 § 1.

[238] *Codex*, no. 73 § 1.

[239] *Codex*, no. 73 § 1. For this reason the person who helps the president general and the vicars or regional counselors in the care of the supernumerary and associate priests of the Priestly Society of the Holy Cross is—as in previous regulations—a Priest Spiritual Director, who by reason of his office does not belong to the council of the prelate or the councils of his regional vicars (*Codex*, nos. 73 § 2; 148 §§ 1 and 2; 160). With the vicar or regional counselor and with the spiritual director of the region cooperate in each diocese a priest monitor and a spiritual director and their substitutes (*Codex*, nos. 73-75).

diocesan priests assume only the obligation proper to any association to observe the norms by which it is governed and which in this
case refer exclusively to spiritual and ascetical life.[240]

The Priestly Society does not interfere in the ministerial work of
the associate or supernumerary priests in the service of their respective dioceses. It limits itself to making available to them appropriate spiritual direction to intensify their interior life. Thus they
are encouraged to be united to their bishop and to obey him, and to
live a profound union with their own diocese, giving themselves
generously to serve the souls the bishop has entrusted to them and
promoting vocations to the diocesan seminary. Thus they are to
seek holiness in their priestly work.[241] They are instilled with a
refined practice of charity, especially for the other members of the
diocesan presbyterate, avoiding even a hint of division, while promoting among all a great unity.[242] An important part of their formation is insistence on their need to follow the collective spiritual
direction the diocesan bishop gives to his priests by means of pastoral letters, communications, disciplinary measures, etc. In the
personal spiritual direction they receive from the Priestly Society
these indications of the diocesan bishop are always reinforced.[243]

The members of the Priestly Society, besides making their own
the aim of Opus Dei within their own priestly condition, have as a
special goal wholeheartedly to foster  priestly holiness and a sense
of full dedication and submission on the part of the secular clergy
to the ecclesiastical hierarchy. Similarly they foster common life
among secular priests, to the extent this is deemed suitable by the
local ordinary.[244] These criteria were already present in the earliest
regulations of the Priestly Society of the Holy Cross. Here as elsewhere the new juridical configuration has wrought a greater preci-

---

[240] Codex, no. 58 § 2. With regard to this point Msgr. del Portillo insists in ABC (op. cit.,
note 64 of this chapter): "Priests incardinated in any diocese may join the Priestly
Society of the Holy Cross by means of a bond of a merely associative character. Their
membership in the Priestly Society does not place them under the power of jurisdiction
of the prelate [of Opus Dei] and they do not lose, nor in any way is weakened, the bond
that these priests have with their respective dioceses and with their own ordinary."
The Priestly Society, he continues, "gives its members the necessary spiritual and
ascetical assistance: which not only leaves intact, but reinforces the canonical obedience these priests owe to their own bishop. There is no problem of a double obedience
that can create conflicts. These priests do not have two superiors—their own bishop
and an internal superior of Opus Dei; they have but one: each his own bishop."

[241] Codex, no. 71.

[242] Codex, no. 69.

[243] Codex, no. 71; for concrete details along these lines see Codex, nos. 70 and 72, 1°.

[244] Codex, no. 68. See also Vatican Council II, Presbyterorum ordinis, nos. 7, 8, 12-17;
and also CIC 1983, can. 273, 276, 280, etc.

sion in some points and a greater adequation, where necessary, to the original charism.[245]

## 13. The insertion of the Prelature of Opus Dei in the organic pastoral work of the Church

A juridical configuration is suitable not only when it reflects the reality it aims to regulate, but also when it suitably contributes to the benefit of the social fabric. In the canonical sphere, it must answer the question: does it harmoniously join the communion with other ecclesial institutions? On occasions the universal legislation details this framework of relationships; in others it limits itself to giving some fundamental criteria, leaving further development to time and more specific regulations. This latter is what occurs, as pointed out earlier, in the case of personal prelatures. Both the Council, as later the documents that applied it—*Ecclesiæ sanctæ* and later the 1983 Code of Canon Law—give only general directives. They establish that the statutes of prelatures to be erected should include the necessary norms to guide advantageously their relations with the whole body of the ecclesiastical hierarchy, especially with the ordinaries of the dioceses where each prelature carries out its pastoral work.[246]

This was one of the points most carefully studied—as pointed out in the appropriate moment—during the sessions of the joint study commission, established by the Congregation for Bishops at the end of 1979. It concluded that the erection of Opus Dei as a prelature with a juridical configuration appropriate to its nature would also contribute, as the Preamble of *Prælaturæ personales* will say, to perfecting "the harmonious inclusion of the institution into the organic pastoral work of the universal Church and of the local churches." Furthermore, this declaration dedicates three numbers to this topic while the *Codex* devotes to it a whole chapter, besides references elsewhere. These texts, with two articles of *Ut sit*, form the basis of the following discussion.

---

[245] We recall in this regard, and in what has to do with the advantages of the new configuration, the commentaries which the then president general of Opus Dei, Don Alvaro del Portillo, made in the letter of Dec. 12, 1981 from which we have already quoted in section 3 of this chapter and which is found in the Appendix, document no. 66.

[246] Thus the Code of Canon Law, in can. 297, prescribes that the statutes of each personal prelature must determine the relations that the prelature has with the ordinaries of places in which, with the previous consent of the diocesan bishop, it exercises its special pastoral task. The universal law, therefore, prescribes: a) previous consent of the bishop before a prelature may commence its work in the diocese; b) that relations between the prelature and the local ordinaries are to be further determined in the statutes. We will see shortly how these points have been specified in the *Statutes* of the prelature of Opus Dei.

First, we note that a personal prelature—as its name indicates—is a jurisdictional and hierarchical structure of the Church of a personal and not a territorial character. As with the other jurisdictional structures—dioceses, territorial prelatures, vicariates, etc.—it is erected by the Roman Pontiff in the exercise of his function as supreme shepherd of the universal Church. The erection presupposes that the Pope, by virtue of his ministry in the service of the unity of faith and communion among all the baptized, has deemed it opportune to create a new structure to carry out a special pastoral task, for the common good of the whole Church—*in bonum commune totius Ecclesiæ*, in words of the Second Vatican Council.[247] This new pastoral service is to be exercised in a region or nation or without any geographical limits. Placing a personal prelature within the organic pastoral activity of the ecclesial community must be seen above all in light of that communion of which the Roman Pontiff is the guarantor for the whole Church.[248]

Moving from principles to practical applications, we recall that Pope John Paul II erected the Prelature of Opus Dei by a primatial act, after having heard the bishops of all the dioceses where Opus Dei was at work. In doing so, he endowed it with the characteristics and traits defined in the documents we have seen. Consequently, the prelature of Opus Dei, as established by the Apostolic See, has within the *communio*—like all other hierarchical structures—its own autonomy and ordinary jurisdiction, oriented to carrying out its special pastoral work in the service of the universal Church and of the local churches.

The *Codex Iuris Particularis* so reads in the first number of the chapter dedicated to relations with bishops: "The prelature of Opus Dei depends immediately and directly upon the Holy See, which has approved its spirit and aim and which oversees and promotes its government and discipline for the good of the whole Church."[249] *Ut sit* specifies this dependence in article V: "The Prelature is under the sacred Congregation for Bishops." This phrase also appears in number VII of *Prælaturæ personales*, which adds that the prelature, "the same as other autonomous jurisdictions, is entitled to deal directly with the relevant congregation or department of the Roman Curia, according to the nature of the matter involved in each case."[250]

---

[247] Vatican Council II, *Presbyterorum ordinis*, no. 10.

[248] Cf. J. P. Schouppe, *Les Prélatures personnelles, Réglamentation canonique et contexte ecclésiologique, op. cit.* (note 48 of this chapter), pp. 327-328.

[249] *Codex*, no. 171.

[250] See also *Ut sit*, art. V. Number VII of *Prælaturæ personales* makes reference to paragraph 1 of number 49 of *Regimini Ecclesiæ universæ*, which establishes the dependence of personal prelatures on the Congregation for Bishops, a normative criterion ratified by *Pastor bonus* of John Paul II, June 28, 1988, in *AAS* 80 (1988):880).

The *Statutes* specify, further, that it belongs to the prelate "to observe with solicitude all of the decrees, rescripts, and other indications of the Holy See that refer to the prelature." The prelate is also charged with presenting "to the Holy See, *ad normam iuris*, the appropriate information with regard to the state of the prelature and its apostolic activity."[251] With regard to this report, *Ut sit* specifies: "Through the Sacred Congregation for Bishops, the prelate will present to the Roman Pontiff, every five years, a report on the state of the prelature and on the development of its apostolic work."[252]

The faithful of the prelature, establish the *Statutes*, "are obliged to obey humbly and in everything the Roman Pontiff." It adds "This obligation of obedience as applied to all the faithful is a strong and sweet bond."[253] As a consequence that "the spirit of Opus Dei cultivates with greatest love filial union with the Roman Pontiff, the vicar of Christ," the prelate must see to it that "all the faithful of the prelature know well the documents of his magisterium and his acts with regard to the whole Church and to spread his teaching."[254]

Personal prelatures, as hierarchical structures of a personal character to carry out of a special pastoral work, are constitutionally related to structures of a territorial character for the ordinary and common *cura animarum*, that is to say, with the local churches. Because of this their proper inclusion in this sphere is necessary, requiring the formulation of norms. These are contained in the *Statutes*, whose sanctioning pertains to the Roman Pontiff, as supreme moderator of the jurisdictions of the whole Church. In fact, the *Codex*, adopted as the particular papal law for the prelature of Opus Dei, spells out in detail in title IV, chapter V the normative criteria for its correct pastoral inclusion and coordination with the local churches, respecting the legitimate rights of diocesan bishops.

Let us recall a general principle valid for every personal prelature. Since prelatures are jurisdictional structures created only to perform a specific pastoral work, the scope of their jurisdiction extends only to whatever relates to this pastoral endeavor. Therefore the jurisdiction of each is circumscribed by its mission—a mission that presupposes and harmonizes with the ordinary pastoral care given by the local ordinary. It is therefore improper to speak of a prelature's exemption, and even less of independence, with regard

---

[251] *Codex*, no. 173 § 1.

[252] *Ut sit*, art. VI. *Prælaturæ personales*, in its number VIII, repeats textually this indication of *Ut sit*, but adds that it ought to be "a detailed report from both the pastoral and juridical points of view."

[253] *Codex*, no. 172 § 1.

[254] *Codex*, no. 173 § 2.

470 TOWARDS A DEFINITIVE LEGAL SOLUTION

to other authorities; rather harmony and coordination should obtain between various hierarchical structures in the service of the common good of the Church.[255]

The criteria governing coordination with local ordinaries and the prelature's work within the local churches are the following:

a) Above all a spirit of harmony and complementarity should prevail, as the *Statutes* say: "All the apostolic work the prelature does in accordance with its own proper nature and aim, contributes to the good of each of the local churches; the prelature always cultivates due relations with the territorial ecclesiastical authority."[256]

b) At the start of apostolic work in a diocese, as for the successive development of this work, the local ordinary's permission is required to erect canonically the centers from which collective apostolate is carried out.[257] Diocesan bishops also have the right to determine whether in the prelature's canonically erected centers the prescriptions of canon law are kept with regard to the church, sacristy and place for the sacrament of penance.[258]

c) The vicar of each regional circumscription, by himself or by others in his name, maintains regular relations with the bishops in whose dioceses faithful of the prelature reside. His is the duty to make sure all the prelature's faithful are acquainted with the norms and pastoral directives laid down by the competent territorial authority for the faithful of the diocese. The vicar keeps up regular contacts with the president and offices of the episcopal conference;

---

[255] Msgr. del Portillo deals at length with this point in various interviews granted with the occasion of Nov. 28, 1982. "This transformation [erection as a prelature] does not mean any change in our juridical relations with the bishops: concretely it does not bestow upon Opus Dei a greater autonomy with regard to the diocesan hierarchy, which we have never sought. . . . We do not want nor have we ever requested a form of exemption with regard to the local hierarchy" (*Il Tempo*, op. cit., note 64 of this chapter). "Opus Dei has never sought any kind of separation or exemption with regard to the diocesan bishops. Our *raison d'être* and our spirit consist in serving the Church as the Church wants to be served and for this service to be complete and effective in each diocese where we work, we *pull the cart*—the expression frequently used by Msgr. Escrivá—in the same direction as the bishop, with our own spirit and specific apostolic way of doing things which the Holy See has approved. For this reason if in some place there were to be a conflict or a misunderstanding with the diocesan bishop, we will always follow—I say it with pride—the advice of our founder: do not argue—much less publicly; even more, we will give in always in everything that we reasonably can give in on. And I am sure that we will not regret having acted in this way. This attitude, which might seem in principle and humanly speaking to be harmful for Opus Dei, over the passage of time will always show itself to be fruitful, thank God" (*ABC*, op. cit., note 64 of this chapter).

[256] *Codex*, no. 174 § 1.

[257] *Codex*, no. 177; see also nos. 123 and 178.

[258] *Codex*, no. 179.

again he sees to it that his faithful know the dispositions and orientations the conference dictates that have a general character.[259]

d) To erect churches of the prelature or when already existing churches in the diocese are entrusted to the prelature a contract between the diocesan bishop and the prelate or the regional vicar is established.  In these churches, beyond the clauses stipulated in the contract, the general diocesan dispositions regarding secular churches are to be observed.  Regarding parishes the local ordinary might entrust to the prelature, an analogous agreement is required.[260]

The criteria to inspire relations between the faithful of the prelature—clergy and laity—with the local ordinaries are as follows:

a) The lay people incorporated to the prelature, as pointed out, do not thereby modify their personal theological or canonical status: they remain simple lay faithful.  Therefore, they continue to be faithful of the dioceses where they have their domicile or quasi-domicile; consequently, they are subject to the jurisdiction of the local ordinary no more and no less than the other faithful of the diocese, in accordance with universal law and the prescriptions of the *Codex*.[261]

b) All the prelature's faithful observe the norms in effect in the territory that refer to public order, as well as the general prescriptions of a doctrinal, liturgical and pastoral nature.  These include— and it is worthwhile to point it out since most of the members are in this situation—the general norms for the apostolate of the laity.[262] According to what is legislated in general and particular law, the clergy of the prelature's presbyterate belong to the secular clergy for all effects.  They are completely under the jurisdiction of the prelate, both in the internal and external forums, but they are to observe in each local church—general laws regarding the discipline of the clergy and general prescriptions of a doctrinal, liturgical character, etc.  In order to accept positions or ecclesiastical offices the local ordinary wishes to entrust to them, previous permission of the prelate of Opus Dei (or his vicar) is required.[263]

These norms and criteria acquire their full meaning in the context of an awareness of complementarity and mutual help among

---

[259] *Codex*, nos. 174 § 2; and 176.

[260] *Codex*, no. 180; *Prælaturæ personales*, V, b).

[261] *Codex*, no. 272 § 2; see also nos. 2 § 1; 18 and *passim*; and *Prælaturæ personales*, II, b); IV, c).

[262] *Prælaturæ personales*, II, b) and c); IV, a).  See *Codex*, no. 176.

[263] *Prælaturæ personales*, II, a); IV, a) and b); V, b).  *Codex*, nos. 40; 51 § 1.  With regard to the relations of the priests of the prelature with the local ordinary see also section 11 of this chapter.

the various hierarchical structures and a spirit of communion with all the shepherds of the Church. This is manifested not only by respecting their spheres of jurisdiction, but also through fraternity, availability for cooperation *in bonum totius Ecclesiæ* and prayer. "Besides the prayers the faithful of the prelature ought to offer up each day for the Roman Pontiff and the diocesan bishop and their intentions, they must show for them the greatest respect and affection, which they will make the effort to foster in all of those around them," we read in the *Statutes*.[264]

There is perhaps no better way to close this section than with the response of Msgr. del Portillo to a question posed by the *L'Osservatore Romano*: "In what concrete ways does Opus Dei cooperate in the diocesan pastoral plan?" He first points out it would be impossible to enumerate the many and different ways the priests and laity of Opus Dei cooperate in the hundreds of dioceses where they exercise their apostolate. Then he adds: "As a general idea, I want to say that the principal way that Opus Dei cooperates in the diocesan pastoral plan is . . . by fostering personal holiness in the middle of the world, among people of all social classes and conditions. This personal and capillary apostolate, so difficult to quantify, produces many fruits: individual conversions, vocations to the priesthood, evangelizing and creating new Christian homes, improving social structures little by little through the action of all of these persons in their professional and family life. . . . As Msgr. Escrivá liked to say, with deep gratitude to God, all of this and many other goods I cannot now detail remain in the local churches and represent a most effective contribution to the diocesan pastoral work. Many bishops from all over the world so understand it and are deeply grateful for this cooperation."[265]

---

[264] *Codex*, no. 175.

[265] *With regard to this interview see note 64 of this chapter.*

# BY WAY OF EPILOGUE

With Opus Dei's establishment as a personal prelature and the sanctioning of its *Statutes* or *Codex Iuris Particularis*, the long course traveled by Opus Dei in search of a juridical configuration suitable to the theological and pastoral substance that had defined it from its foundation came to an end. With the narration of the events of 1982 and 1983, and the analysis of the general structural lines of the *Statutes* then given by the Holy See to the new prelature, we conclude our efforts to reconstruct this path, by setting forth its various stages and highlighting the lines and underlying intentions that have governed the overall process.

Throughout this analysis we have covered the successive juridical configurations, considered in their essential characterization: pious union, society of common life without vows, secular institute, personal prelature. We have also related many aspects of Opus Dei's spirit, its government and organization, the traits of its apostolate, the life of its members, each one of which could have justified a monograph study. It was necessary to refer to them, even sometimes only schematically, in order to express what these various steps and stages of the evolution implied and, consequently, the general meaning of the process.

The fundamental point, however, is that it has been a process: not a mere juxtaposition of unrelated moments, but a true quest. It has been a journey motivated and guided by the original light received by Msgr. Escrivá on October 2, 1928, that makes explicit its potential until it achieves a juridical configuration completely fitted to it. As we reach this point, it is natural to consider the possibility, or even opportuneness, to attempt a synthesis to interpret the general affirmation we have just made. But after an attentive reflection this possibility shows itself to be a temptation that merits rejection. To synthesize the broad, complicated and profound process we have studied would involve repeating ideas already set forth and, even worse, repeating them with fewer shades of meaning.

We do underline, however, that the events and documents of 1982-83 represent a milestone of the first order in Opus Dei's history, because with the prelature's erection the definitive juridical configuration is achieved. But these events do not close the history of Opus Dei, but only one of its stages, which, given its importance, opens the way to new ones. Let us echo the current prelate of Opus Dei, Msgr. Alvaro del Portillo, in a 1985 interview with *Litteræ Communionis*: "Our founder prayed and worked so much for many years so that the Church's highest authority would thus recognize the reality and substance of the service we seek to offer, always in close union with the respective diocesan bishops," he began. "This definitive canonical *status* is certainly a point of arrival in our juridical journey, just as our founder desired. Nevertheless, I like to consider it also as a point of departure. I speak of a point of departure just to explain that the *status* of a personal prelature affords us finally the necessary juridical structure to work in the service of the Church within a canonical framework that suits its foundational charism."

The same ideas and sentiments were expressed in a letter he addressed to Opus Dei members on November 28, 1982, commenting on the news of the personal prelature. In a final analysis, the reaction springs spontaneously in anyone advancing with a determined step to bring about a truly worthwhile enterprise. Points of arrival invite one to contemplate the past, but they also lead to considering what remains to be done. Even more they prompt a recommitment to achieve it, to continue treading with the greatest determination possible the way these milestones have traced out or made more viable.

In this context the memory calls forth the great protagonist of the history we have attempted to narrate, Msgr. Josemaría Escrivá. His prolonged and persevering effort to achieve a suitable juridical solution for Opus Dei was born of a radical concern: fidelity to the charism and mission entrusted to him; specifically, finding formulas and juridical embodiments that help to guarantee a lasting fidelity throughout the future. His gaze did not rest on the mere canonical configuration; rather, through the juridical framework it reached the very message itself, "old as the gospel and like the gospel new," which God had him discover in 1928 and to whose service he dedicated all his life and energy. The universal call to holiness, the invitation to enter into a divine friendship God extends to all men, even to those in the middle of the world—such was Msgr. Escrivá's dream. That is the horizon that sealed and gave fullness of meaning to the life of Msgr. Escrivá, also as an eminent jurist. That vision strengthened throughout a lengthy process the serene hope of one who knew he was an instrument to "open the divine paths of the earth," to all men, of all races, nations and walks of life. They thus can come to know that their human paths can and ought to be made divine, since all are open to an encounter with Jesus Christ.

Appendix

# OFFICIAL DOCUMENTS

# OFFICIAL DOCUMENTS

## 1. Written petition of Rev. Josemaría Escrivá to the Bishop of Madrid-Alcalá requesting that an oratory be granted for the Residence at no. 50 Ferraz Street, Madrid, March 13, 1935.

RHF, D-15144.

José María Escrivá y Albás, pbro., Director espiritual de la Academia-Residencia D.Y.A. - Ferraz 50 - de la que es Director técnico D. Ricardo Fernández Vallespín, arquitecto, Profesor ayudante de la Escuela Superior de Arquitectura, a V.E. respetuosamente expone:

Que en la citada Academia, además de los fines culturales que le son propios, y de las clases de Religión para estudiantes universitarios que, por disposición de V.E. Rma., se vienen dando desde hace dos años, se procura hacer obras de celo con los alumnos y residentes de la Casa y con otros estudiantes de todas las Facultades y Escuelas Especiales, explicándoles el Santo Evangelio, practicando el retiro mensual, atendiendo a catequesis en los barrios extremos etc., y como, para mejor realizar dichas obras, deseamos vivamente tener, en la Casa, Capilla y Sagrario con su Divina Majestad Reservado.

Suplica a V.E. en nombre de todos estos jóvenes y en el propio se digne conceder la mencionada gracia.

Dios guarde a V.E. muchos años.

Madrid 13 de Marzo de 1935

José María Escrivá

EXMO. Y RMO. SR. OBISPO DE MADRID-ALCALA.

---

## 2. Decree of the Vicar General of the Diocese of Madrid-Alcalá erecting the semi-public oratory of the Academy-Residence DYA, Ferraz Street 50, Madrid, April 10, 1935.

AGP, Sezione Giuridica, I/08066.

En uso de las facultades que se Nos confieren en los cánones 1.192 y 1.193 C.I.C. y visto el informe favorable del Rvdo. Sr. Cura Párroco de la de

San Marcos, de esta Capital, delegado por Nos para practicar la Visita Canónica que requiere el Derecho y, una vez que el local ha sido ya bendecido; por el presente declaramos erigido en ORATORIO SEMIPUBLICO, el que a este efecto ha destinado Don Ricardo Fernández Vallespín, en la Academia-Residencia D.Y.A., en Ferraz, número cincuenta, perteneciente a la feligresía de San Marcos, y concedemos nuestra autorización y licencia para que "servatis servandis" por el tiempo de Nuestra Voluntad y sin perjuicio de los derechos parroquiales, pueda celebrarse el Santo Sacrificio de la Misa todos los días del año por cualquier sacerdote que tenga corrientes sus licencias ministeriales en este Obispado, para que los fieles asistentes al Santo Sacrificio cumplan con el precepto eclesiástico y para que en el citado Oratorio semipúblico se puedan además celebrar todas las funciones sagradas autorizadas por el Derecho a los de su clase. Asimismo, a tenor del can. 1265 C.I.C. concedemos Nuestra licencia para que pueda conservarse reservado el Ssmo. Sacramento, cuidando de observar todo lo dispuesto en el Código de Derecho Canónico y en las Sagradas Rúbricas acerca del cuidado y culto de la Sagrada Eucaristía.

Dado en Madrid a diez de Abril de mil novecientos treinta y cinco.

EL VICARIO GENERAL

L + S                              Dr. Francisco Morán

---

### 3. Written petition of Rev. Josemaría Escrivá in which he requests the transfer of the oratory of the Residence of Ferraz 50 to its new address; July 10, 1936.

RHF, D-15143.

José María Escrivá y Albás, presbítero, Director espiritual de la Academia-Residencia DYA, a V. E. respetuosamente EXPONE:

Que habiendo trasladado su domicilio la Academia-Residencia DYA, desde el número 50 de la calle de Ferraz, a la casa número 16 de la misma calle, a V. E.

SUPLICA se digne conceder el oportuno permiso, para el traslado del Oratorio semipúblico, que por V. E. fue concedido a la citada entidad DYA, al nuevo domicilio que la Academia-Residencia ocupa.

Gracia que no duda obtener del bondadoso corazón de V. E., cuya vida guarde Dios muchos años.

Madrid, 10 de Julio de 1936<br>Josemaría Escrivá

EXMO. Y RMO. SR. OBISPO DE MADRID-ALCALA

---

## 4. Written petition of Rev. Josemaría Escrivá to the Bishop of Madrid-Alcalá in which he requests the approval of Opus Dei as a Pious Union; February 14, 1941.

AGP, Sezione Giuridica, II/15075/2.

Excmo. y Rvdmo. Sr.

José María Escrivá de Balaguer y Albás, presbítero, a V. E. respetuosamente expone

Que dirige privadamente una labor de apostolado, con la denominación de "Opus Dei", iniciada en Madrid con el beneplácito y bendición de V. E. Rvma. y del Ilmo. Sr. Vicario General, el día 2 de Octubre de 1928, y que en el tiempo transcurrido hasta el presente ha dado frutos consoladores de piedad y formación cristiana y de servicio a la Iglesia; y estimando que conviene para la gloria de Dios y servicio de la Santa Iglesia dotar a esta Obra de los caracteres de estabilidad y estado oficial canónico que aseguren la permanencia de sus frutos, a V. E. humildemente

SUPLICA se digne dar canónica aprobación a la "Opus Dei" como Pía Unión, en los términos que prescribe el canon 708 del Codex Juris Canonici, y asimismo se digne aprobar benignamente los adjuntos Reglamento, Régimen, Orden, Costumbres, Espíritu y Ceremonial que informan y por los que se rige la "Opus Dei"; dejando a la consideración y resolución de V.E. designar las personas de esa Curia que hayan de conocer los Reglamentos de la "Opus Dei", dado el carácter de la Obra.

Es gracia que no duda alcanzar del corazón bondadoso de V. E. Rvma., cuya vida guarde Dios muchos años.

Madrid, 14 de Febrero de 1941

Josemaría Escrivá de Balaguer

EXMO. Y RMO. SR. OBISPO DE MADRID-ALCALA

[A first draft of this document, with some pencil and ink additions made by the Bishop of Madrid, has been preserved -AGP, Sezione Giuridica, II/15075/1-. The Bishop's comments are suggestions for corrections to the text written by the founder of Opus Dei, who noted in the margin: "Esta instancia está corregida, con lápiz y tinta, de mano del Sr. Obispo.-" These additions were referred to in note 17 of Chapter III.]

---

## 5. By-laws of Opus Dei presented to the Bishop of Madrid-Alcalá at the time of the request for approval as a Pious Union; February 14, 1941.

AGP, Sezione Giuridica, II/15076.

# REGULÆ

QUID OPUS DEI: EJUS FINES ET MEDIA.

Art. 1.

§ 1. OPUS DEI est Associatio Catholica virorum ac mulierum, qui, in medio mundo viventes, propriam ipsorum perfectionem christianam, sanctificato labore ordinario, inquirunt. Persuasi, hominem creatum fuisse "ut operaretur" (Gen. II, 15), socii OPERIS DEI, licet potenti vel œconomica vel sociali conditione pollentes, professionalem laborem aut æquivalentem haud deserere tenentur.

§ 2. Hæc autem media a sociis adhibenda obtinendo supernaturali fini sibi proposito: Interiorem et orationis et sacrificii vitam vivere, juxta regimen et spiritum ab Ecclesia Sancta adprobatos, propriaque munia professionalia et socialia, maxima rectitudine, obire.

GENERA SOCIORUM.

Art. 2.

§ 1. In OPERE DEI tria sociorum genera numerantur: inscripti, supernumerarii et numerarii.

§ 2. Socii admissi ut *inscripti* quotidianis et conscientiæ examine et dimidia orationis mentalis hora ligantur.

§ 3. *Supernumerarii* autem integra orationis mentalis quotidiana hora.

§ 4. *Numerarii*, præter integram orationis mentalis horam, onus amplectuntur fungendi muneribus dirigendi OPERIS DEI.

Art. 3.

§ 1. Nullo prætextu admittentur ut socii OPERIS DEI nec Sacerdotes sæculares, nec religiosi, nec religiosæ.

§ 2. Nullatenus pariter, rejecta qualibet excusatione, admittentur qui sint vel fuerint alumni Seminarii vel Scholæ Apostolicæ, vel in Religione conversati fuerint, licet tantummodo in Novitiatu vel Postulatu.

§ 3. Qui vero, socii OPERIS DEI, studiis ecclesiasticis operam dederint et Sacerdotes effecti fuerint, non ideo desinunt esse socii OPERIS.

ORGANA DIRECTIVA.

Art. 4.

§ 1. Organa Directiva nationalia OPERIS DEI sunt Consilium et Cœtus.

§ 2. Consilium efformant Præses, Secretarius et tres Consiliarii.

§ 3. Cœtum vero socii numerarii, e quibus, ordinarie, seligenda Consilii membra.

Art. 5.

§ 1. Consilium, singulis tribus mensibus, ordinarium conventum habebit; extraordinarium autem quoties illum tria saltem ejusdem membra exspostulaverint.

§ 2. Consilii est:

1/ Satagere ut OPUS DEI semper intra conditiones juridicas, legibus statutas, versetur.

2/ Præbere œconomica media solvendis sumptibus annuis OPERIS DEI necessaria.

3/ Præcipere ut suffragia pro sociis defunctis celebrentur.

Art. 6.

§ 1. Muneribus Consilii quæ, novem mandati annis, vacarint, tum morte tum renuntiatione, providetur de communi consilio superstitum membrorum.

§ 2. Membra Consilii poterunt in eadem munera iterum, aut pluries, eligi.

Art. 7.

Cœtus conventum habebit singulis novem annis, eoque unico scopo ut Consilium eligat. Extraordinarium vero, si universa defuerint Consilii membra, a tribus sociis numerariis convocatum, adque novum Consilium designandum procedet.

Art. 8.

Decreta, tum in Consilio tum in Cœtu, statuantur absoluta majori parte suffragiorum.

SUFFRAGIA ET INHUMATIO.

Art. 9.

§ 1. Membris OPERIS DEI cura erit testamentum in forma legali conditum habere. Modestam pro se inhumationem, absque ulla vanitate, disponere tenentur.

§ 2. Præses disponet ut celebrentur Missæ Gregorianæ statim post cognitam cujusque socii morte, quam sane reliquis sociis notam faciet, qui suffragia offerant sibi a proprio zelo inspirata.

PROVENTUS ET SUMPTUS.

Art. 10.

§ 1. Proventus œconomici OPERIS DEI, eleemosynæ sociorum.

§ 2. Nullam Consilium retinebit capitalem summam.

§ 3. Si sumptus annui inferiores proventibus erunt, summa remanens in eleemosynam tradetur Ordinario Diœcesis, ubi OPUS domicilium suum habet.

§ 4. OPUS DEI nec ulla legata recipere, nec pias fundationes sub quolibet prætextu admittere, nec bona immobilia possidere potest.

DOMICILIUM.

Art. 11.

OPUS DEI unicum habet domicilium nationale.

HUMILITAS COLLECTIVA.

Art. 12.

§ 1. Potissimum OPERIS DEI sigillum, humilitas collectiva membrorum.

§ 2. Ne autem hæc humilitas detrimentum patiatur,

1/ Prohibetur editio cujuscumque folii vel libelli publici, ut proprii OPERIS.

2/ Vetatur pariter quodlibet distinctivum vel insigne pro sociis.

3/ Suadetur sociis ne loquantur cum alienis de OPERE, quod, quippe supernaturale, tacitum esse debet et modestum.

DISSOLUTIO.

Art. 13.

Si OPUS DEI dissolvetur, ejus bona, si quæ superfuerint, in manus tradentur Rvdmi. Episcopi Diœcesis, ubi OPUS domicilium suum habeat.

---

### 6. Notification given to Rev. Josemaría Escrivá of the Decree of the Bishop of Madrid-Alcalá by which he approves Opus Dei as a Pious Union; March 19, 1941.

AGP, Sezione Giuridica, II/15075/3, 1°.

Sobre la instancia de V. de fecha 14 de febrero del corriente año, ha recaído Decreto que literalmente copiado dice así:

""Vista la precedente instancia de D. José Mª Escrivá de Balaguer, y después de examinar detenidamente el *Reglamento*, el *Régimen*, el *Orden*, las *Costumbres*, el *Espíritu* y el *Ceremonial* del *OPUS DEI*, fundado por dicho Sr. y experimentado con Nuestro beneplácito y de Nuestro Vicario General, desde el año 1928, venimos en aprobar y por el presente decreto aprobamos canónicamente el *OPUS DEI*, como Pía Unión, a tenor del Canon 708 C.I.C. vigente; y pedimos a Dios Nuestro Señor, por intercesión de San José, en cuya fiesta tenemos la satisfacción de aprobar canónicamente tan importante obra de celo, que conceda que no se malogre ninguno de los grandes frutos que de ella esperamos. Para la custodia del ejemplar del Reglamento, etc., se cumplirá lo que en Decreto especial disponemos.- Madrid, a 19 de marzo de 1941.- Hay una firma que dice: Leopoldo, Obispo de Madrid-Alcalá. - Rubricado""

Lo que traslado a Vd. para su conocimiento y satisfacción.

*Madrid 19 de marzo de 1941.*

EL CANCILLER-SECRETARIO.

L + S

Dr. Juan J. Marco

Srio.

Rvdo. Sr. D. José Mª Escrivá de Balaguer.

**7. Notification given to Rev. Josemaría Escrivá of the Decree of the Bishop of Madrid-Alcalá regarding the By-laws and accompanying documents referring to the Pious Union and being kept in the archives [of the Diocese]; March 19, 1941.**

AGP, Sezione Giuridica, II/15075/3,2°.

Sobre la instancia de Vd. de fecha, 14 de febrero de 1941 ha recaído un segundo decreto que copiado a la letra dice así:

""Aprobado canónicamente con fecha de hoy el *OPUS DEI*, Pía Unión fundada con Nuestra autorización y beneplácito el año 1928, y teniendo en cuenta la discreta reserva que para mayor gloria de Dios y eficacia de la Obra se debe guardar, disponemos que el ejemplar de su *Reglamento, Régimen, Orden, Costumbres, Espíritu* y *Ceremonial*, se custodien en Nuestro Archivo Secreto. Madrid, a 19 de marzo, fiesta del glorioso S. José de 1941.- Hay una firma que dice: Leopoldo, Obispo de Madrid-Alcalá. Rubricado.""

Lo que traslado a Vd. para su conocimiento y efectos.

*Madrid a 19 de marzo de 1941*

L + S                                             Dr. Juan J. Marco

                                                  Srio.

Rvdo. Sr. D. José Mª Escrivá de Balaguer.

---

**8. Written Petition of Rev. Josemaría Escrivá to the Bishop of Madrid-Alcalá requesting the erection of the Priestly Society of the Holy Cross as a Society of common life without vows; June 13, 1943.**

RHF, EF-430613-1.

Exc.me ac Rev.me Domine:

Infrascriptus Josephus Maria Escrivá de Balaguer et Albás, sacerdos, Piæ Unionis, "Opus Dei" dictæ, Præses, humillimo fidentique filiali animo E.V. quæ sequuntur

EXPONIT:

1°. Altera die octobris anni Domini 1928 labente, divina gratia me, licet eadem indignum, adiuvante ac prius obtentis et paterna vestra benedictione et ultro libenter mihi oblato consensu, apostolicum munus ab E.V. commissum evolvere incœpi inter iuvenes, qui discendi erudiendique causa Athænea civilia frequentant.

2°. Nec res in cassum cessit. Deus etenim, qui Apostolo docente, dives est in misericordia, quique replet nos omni benedictione spirituali in Christo Jesu, plurimorum iuvenum corda tetigit mentesque illuminavit, ac, optimis quibusve studentibus in unum undique convocatis, quod haud parvo quidem sudore vultus nostri semen in terram bonam proieceramus, in quamdam veluti magnam arborem, Deo opitulante, excrevit, ita ut formam cuiusdam piæ fidelium associationis induxerit, cui nomen "Opus Dei", et solide efformatæ et omni spe repletæ.

3°. Iam vel ipso anno Domini 1941 decurrente, ac civilium intestinarumque commotionum, quibus Hispania nostra dilaniata fuit, dolorosa æque ac gloriosa periodo clausa, quasdam directivas normas, ob eiusdem piæ associationis magnum quidem incrementum omnino requisitas, approbationi Vestræ libenti filialique animo subieci.

4°. Neque huic facto approbationis Constitutionum nostrarum ex parte E.V. alienum putamus incrementum illud, omnibus ac præsertim E.V. notum, quod horum annorum decursu, præfata dilectissima nostra pia associatio suscepit.

5°. His itaque omnibus maturo animo, coram Deo nostraque conscientia perpensis; habitoque insuper præ oculis desiderio eo, quo accendimur, magis magisque Sanctæ Catholicæ Ecclesiæ inserviendi, una cum pluribus aliis commodis quæ in maiorem diffusionem activitatis spiritualis nostræ, sodaliumque nostrorum potiorem tum scientificam tum spiritualem efformationem cederent, si Opus prædictum in fidelium associationem in communi viventium sine votis ad instar Canonis 673 et sequentium erigeretur,

omnes et singuli sodales hanc Piam Unionem constituentes, E.V. demisissime

ADPRECAMUR

ut ipsam Piam Unionem in præfatam fidelium associationem E.V. erigere dignetur, iuris quidem diœcesani, normis a Codice Iuris Canonici statutis adamussim servatis, titulo huic associationi tributo "SOCIETATIS SACERDOTALIS SANCTÆ CRUCIS", subiectæ regulis, quarum generalia delineamenta heic adnexa E.V. remittimus.

ET DEUS, ETC.

Matriti, in festo Pentecostes, die 13 iunii, anno 1943.

Pro me ac omnibus singulisque sodalibus meis, Pastorale Annulum deosculantibus paternamque Vestram benedictionem, omnium bonorum auspicatricem, petentibus.

Josemaría Escrivá de B.

---

## 9. Lineamenta generalia *of the Priestly Society of the Holy Cross as presented to the Bishop of Madrid-Alcalá at the time of requesting its erection as a Society of common life without vows, June 13, 1943.*

AGP, Sezione Giuridica, III/15079.

# SOCIETAS SACERDOTALIS SANCTÆ CRUCIS

## I

## SOCIETATIS NATURA

1. "Societas Sacerdotalis Sanctæ Crucis" est societas præferenter clericalis in communi viventium sine votis, ad normam tit. XVII, Lib. II Codicis I. Canonici constituta. Communitas autem vitæ lato sensu sumitur (Cfr. C. 487).

2. Finis ejus generalis sanctificatio membrorum per consiliorum evangelicorum exercitium et constitutionum propriarum observantiam; specificus autem, adlaborare ut pars intellectualis et directiva civilis societatis Christi Domini præceptis immo et consiliis adhæreat.

3. Ad hunc finem obtinendum "Societas Sacerdotalis S. Crucis" exigit, imprimis, in eius membris maximam animi culturam, tum in rebus spiritualibus, tum in scientiis sive ecclesiasticis sive prophanis, uti melius infra patebit; fovet perfectam adimpletionem munerum professionalium, quibus non renuntiat; utitur præsertim quadam propria apostolatus sui forma, dicta "Opus Dei", qua melius vim et efficatiam actionis apostolicæ in Societatem inducat.

4. "Opus Dei" duplicem habet sectionem, alteram ab altera penitus distinctam et separatam, hominum, nempe, et mulierum. Illa inter homines apostolatum prosequitur; hæc inter mulieres. Illa præterea, præbet Societati Sanctæ Crucis membra, ita, ut nemo in Societatem cooptari valeat qui primitus per aliquod tempus in "Opere Dei" non probe militaverit.

5. Societatis Sanctæ Crucis spiritus proprius est zelus apostolicus, pœnitentia, humilitas collectiva, submissio Auctoritati Ecclesiasticæ, æstuans erga Christum, Virginem Mariam, Romanum Pontificem amor.

6. Sodales Societatis Sanctæ Crucis religiosorum perfectionem æmulantur, quin nec illorum vota emittant nec aliquod externum signum in personis vel in domibus appareat quod religionem redoleat. Sacerdotes vestem clericalem, laici autem communes aliorum propriæ classi respondentes deferunt.

7. Societas Sacerdotalis Sanctæ Crucis habet quoque speciales patronos quos singulari devotione prosequitur, videlicet: SS. AA. Michaèl, Gabriel et Raphaèl; et SS. Ap. Petrum, Paulum et Iohannem quibus diversæ Societatis activitates singulariter consecrantur.

## II

## SOCIETATIS CONSTITUTIO ET ACTIVITAS

8. Societas Sacerdotalis Sanctæ Crucis constat duabus sectionibus, sacerdotali nempe et laicali, quin tamen veras classes diversas ad sensum juris religiosorum constituant (cfr. C. 558); quinimmo sectio laicalis est velut gradus ad sacerdotalem cum ab ipsa Sacerdotes seligantur, in eaque preparentur.

9. Utraque sectio componitur membris seu sociis *supernumerariis*, qui dum perfectioni evangelicæ acquirendæ se devovent, operibus apostolatus Societatis propriis incumbunt; *numerariis*, qui præcipuis muneribus directionis Societatis designantur; *electis*, qui voce activa ad electionem Præsidis Societatis donantur.

10. Ad Sacerdotium vocatio fit a Præside Societatis, audito suo Consilio; ordinationis autem titulus est "Societatis" (C. 982). Nemo ad ordines promovetur qui perpetuo Societati non sit adscriptus.

11. Quicumque Societati cooptatur, absque alio inter socios supernumerarios adcensetur; ad alias autem categorias accessum jubet Præses gradatim et audito proprio Consilio.

12. Ut quis *electus* designari possit requiritur: a) ut sit socius numerarius; b) ut sit triginta saltem annos natus; c) ut Societatis probe noscat historiam, spiritum et traditiones; d) ut iam a novem saltem annis in Societate militaverit; e) ut eidem servitia egregia præstiterit; f) ut homo consilii demonstretur, prudens, atque pietate solida præditus; g) denique ut cultura religiosa et propria suæ professionis præmineat.

13. Salvo præscripto can. 542, nequeunt admitti in Societatem Sacerdotes sæculares, alumni Seminariorum, religiosi et etiam qui tantum novitius vel postulans in aliqua religione fuit, aut alicuius Scholæ Ap. alumnus.

14. Item a Societate excluduntur qui adulti baptismum receperunt, et qui tribus iam generationibus, saltem ex una linea, ascendentes catholicos non habuerint.

15. Præterea ut quis in Societate admittatur requiritur præter alia requisita iuris communis et specialem ad ministerii Societatis aptitudinem, ut titulum academicum alicuius Universitatis civilis vel æquipollentis Status Facultatis possideat, necnon ut iam in ejusdem Societatis opere proprio sese exercuerit.

16. Admissio ad Societatem pertinet ad Presidem, audito eiusdem Consilio.

17. Quis Societati incorporatur *fidelitate* qua socius in perpetuum Societati se devovet. Incorporationi precedit periodus probationis decem et octo mensium, et oblatio temporaria per quinque annos renovanda.

18. Circa dimissionem sociorum, post factam incorporationem, applicantur congrua congruis referendo canones de dimissione religiosorum.

19. Societas habet domicilia in quibus socii commorantur propriam cuique activitatem apostolicam et professionalem exercentes. Sacerdotibus incumbit formatio spiritualis aliorum sociorum, directio spiritualis præsertim intellectualium; ad hoc domus exercitiorum instituunt atque alia sacerdotalia munera exercent. Laici eidem operi coadiuvant et apostolatui exemplo, conversatione, amicitia, exercitio munerum publicorum.

20. Societas prasertim incumbit constitutioni et moderationi "Operis Dei", duplici classi, hominum et mulierum, quo speciali ratione utitur ad proprium ministerium explicandum.

Hoc Opus habet propriam constitutionem; regitur specialibus statutis.

21. Socii sive numerarii sive supernumerarii cedunt Societati quidquid industria lucrantur; de administratione usu et usufructu propriorum bonorum libere disponunt, etiam favore Societatis: quæ, de cætero, sociorum familiis forte indigentibus maxima generositate providet. Eisdem sociis Societas suppeditat quidquid ad eorum victum, studium, activitatem professionalem indigent.

22. Maxima diligentia cultura sociorum exigitur: Sacerdotes una saltem laurea doctorali præditi sint oportet: laicis speciali cultura religiosa impertitur. Ad hoc singulis Territoriis centra studiorum constituuntur ubi ecclesiaticæ disciplinæ serio excoluntur.

23. Ad pietatem autem singulorum membrorum fovendam, hic ordo vitæ proponitur: *Singulis diebus:* operum Deo oblatio; oratio mentalis unius horæ spatio; Sancta Missa; Communio; Sanctissimi Visitatio; lectio spiritualis; Preces; Rosarium Mariale quindecim mysteriorum; discussio conscientiæ. *Hebdomadarie:* Confessio sacramentalis; aliqua mortificatio corporalis; recitatio sabbatina antiphonæ Salve Regina. *In mense:* recollectionis dies. *Annatim:* spiritualia exercitia. *Semper,* cura speciali fovetur: Dei præsentia; sensus filiationis divinæ; spirituales communiones; gratiarum actiones; actus reparationis; orationes jaculatoriæ; mortificatio; studium; labor; ordo; lætitia.

24. Ad accuratiorem ipsius ordinis vitæ adimpletionem, singulis hebdomadis, ubi Societas suam explicat activitatem, *Circulus brevis* habetur, qui religiosorum nonnullorum culparum capitulo quadamtenus assimilari valet.

25. Cum Societas Sanctæ Crucis ut melius suum finem prosequatur externe uti simplex societas apparet, sese ubique locorum, accomodat legibus quæ pro societatibus latæ fuerint.

## III

## REGIMEN

26. Societas Sanctæ Crucis comprehendit regimen generale, territoriale et locale. Illud Societatem universam omniaque eiusdem opera afficit; istud, socios et activitatem determinati territorii; hoc, diversa centra localia.

Universa regiminis munera temporalia; admittitur tamen reelectio.

### A. REGIMEN GENERALE

27. Universam Societatem regit Præses qui "Pater" dicitur, estque semper Sacerdos.

28. Deligitur ad normam iuris inter Sacerdotes "electos", a Consessu generali notabiliorum membrorum Societatis, id est, ab illis qui Consilium Generalem constituunt et ab omnibus sociis electis.

29. Præter requisita generalia iuris communis, sit Pater quadraginta annos natus.

30. Pater adiuvatur in ordinario regimine Societatis a Consilio, quod constat Secretario Generali, tribus Vicesecretariis, et Missis seu delegatis ex unoquoque Territorio delectis. Pater Consilium audit in præcipuis negotiis Societatis.

31. Proximus post Patrem venit Secretarius Generalis, qui specialiter eidem adsistit in expediendis negotiis Societatis, eumque in absentiis et infirmitatibus supplet. Designatur a Patre inter Sacerdotes electos, audito Consilio.

32. Vicesecretarii deliguntur inter socios electos et eodem modo designantur; possunt semper iterum ad idem munus designari. Hi præponuntur diversis activitatibus Societatis, deque eis Patri et Consilio referunt.

33. "Missi" seu delegati territoriales, item inter socios electos designantur a Patre, audito Consilio: incumbunt negotiis propriis cuiusque Territorii de quibus Patri et Consilio referunt.

34. Ut bono spirituali et corporali valetudine Patris consulant adsunt duo Custodes (admonitores) qui tamen ratione muneris Consilium non ingrediuntur. Designantur a Patre inter novem socios electos a Consilio præsentatos.

35. Vicepræses, si de judicio Patris aut Consilii necessarius sit, Patrem adjuvat et sustituit absentem aut impeditum; emortuo Patre Societatem regit ad electionem usque novi Patris. Designatur a Patre cum Consilio.

36. Ad rem œconomicam gerendam est instituta "Consultatio Tecnica Generalis" cui præest Administrator, ex sociis electis a Patre designatus, audito Consilio Generali. Ei adsistunt aliqui socii numerarii a Patre nominati, ex propositis ab ipso Administratore Generali.

37. Consultationis tecnicæ generalis est rem œconomicam administrare sub vigilantia Patris et Consilii quibus de eadem administratione sexto quoque mense refert.

38. Administrationi Generali devolvuntur: a) Contributiones Administrationum Territorialium; b) Dona Societati in genere facta; c) Summma notabilis quæ supersit Territorio quæque destinationem specialem non habuerit.

## B. REGIMEN TERRITORIALE

39. Diversæ circunscriptiones territoriales in qua Societas distribuitur, reguntur "Commissione Territoriali" sub dependentia immediata a Patre et a Consilio Generali.

40. Commissiones Territoriales constant "Consiliario", qui Commissioni præest, "Defensore" et tribus aliis membris, "Vocales" appellatis. "Missus" seu delegatus territorialis (cfr. n. 33) ius habet Commissioni proprii territorii interveniendi, et sedet post "Consiliarium".

41. "Consiliarius" nominatur a Patre, audito consilio Generali, estque socius saltem numerarius et, ut plurimum, Sacerdos.

42. "Defensor", cuius est fovere spiritum et observantiam in proprio territorio, eodem modo ac Consiliarius nominatur, estque etiam communiter Sacerdos. Speciale huius munus est referre Patri eiusque Consilio circa admissionem sociorum. In Commissione Territoriali post venit Consiliario.

43. "Vocales" designantur a Patre audito Consilio Generali, Consiliario et Defensore Territoriali.

44. Ad rem œconomicam gerendam sunt in singulis territoriis "Consultationes Tecnicæ Territoriales", quibus præsunt Administratores a Patre nominati audito Consilio inter socios numerarios.

45. Consultatio Tecnica Territorialis habet Assessores nominatos a Consiliario cum Defensore, audita Consultatione, inter numerarios Territorii.

46. Consultatio Tecnica rationes œconomicas proprii territorii tertio quoque mense ad Consultationem Tecnicam Generalem remittit.

## C. REGIMEN LOCALE

47. In omnibus domibus Societatis, ubi adest sufficiens numerus sociorum, habetur etiam regimen locale, compositum ex Directore, Digniore et Administratore.

48. Director nominatur a Consiliario, audito Consilio Territoriali, Patre probante: in negotiis alicuius momenti Dignioris consilium exquirit.

49. Dignior a Consiliario eodem modo nominatur: post venit Directori eumque supplet.

50. Administrator rei œconomicæ domi incumbit; nominatur a Consiliario, audito eius Consilio, etiam Patre approbante. Singulis mensibus ad Administratorem Territorialem rationem administrationis localis impensarum et expensarum remittit.

51. Data natura Societatis, in administrandis bonis, præter præscripta iuris communis tales societates afficientia, habentur regulæ propriæ.

52. Denique in operibus propriæ activitatis complendis Societas Sanctæ Crucis, omnimodam submissionem profitetur Ordinariis locorum, quibus efficacius quo possit adiumentum præstare cupit *"adhuc autem et animam suam"*, ad animarum salutem, ad honorem et incrementum Sanctæ Romanæ Ecclesiæ, ad laudem et gloriam Dei et Domini Nostri Jesu Christi. Amen.

---

## 10. Written petition of the Bishop of Madrid-Alcalá to the Sacred Congregation for Religious requesting the nihil obstat of the Holy See for the diocesan erection of the Priestly Society of the Holy Cross; June 22, 1943.

AGP, Sezione Giuridica, III/15078.

Emme ac Rvdme Domine:

Presbyter D. Josephus Maria Escrivá de Balaguer et Albás, post quosdam impensos apostolici laboris annos in pie efformandis alumnis Universitatum Status, meis omnimodis et adprobatione et benedictione associationem instituit huic apostolatui incumbentem, cujus specificus finis juventutem Universitariam in christiana pietate colere atque in summam studiorum professionalium perfectionem impellere; eo quidem scopo ut hi alumni dein, optima efformatione technica professionali pariterque sincera et mentis et cordis religiositate imbuti, efficacem exerceant influxum super populum e variis administrationis civilis gradibus, jugiter Sanctæ Matri Ecclesiæ inservientes et quammaxime filiali obedientia Episcopis Diœcesanis adhærentes. In omnibus quos ipsi hucusque aggressi sunt laboribus, intima semper communicatione cum Auctoritate Diœcesana, cui sane tam constanti quam filiali devotioni subduntur, processerunt.

Prospere crevit opus, magno animarum fructu tum sociorum tum etiam omnium quotquot percipiunt præclara eorundem exempla, quando, absolutis studiis, pro Ecclesia egregie adlaborant.

Hujus associationis regulæ, decennali experientia perpensæ, adprobatæ fuere a me, qui eam canonice erexi ut Piam Unionem anno 1941.

Eos vero jam protulit associatio fructus, eosque promittit in bonum animarum, ut ejusdem fundator et socii vehementer exoptent illam firmiori soliditate et altiori vita canonica munire, consulentes potissimum perfectiori sociorum christianæ efformationi et perpetuitati operis in futurum, necnon unitati methodi actionis, nullo hujus exorto detrimento ex operis extensione et dilatatione. Quem in finem constitui desiderant in Societatem juxta Tit. XVII Partis II Libri II Codicis Juris Canonici, Canones 673 &. Idque a me petunt.

Eisdem optatis et ego abundo, et firmiter credo pleniorem inde futuram vitam religiosam operis, hujus socios majori perfectione in praxim ducturos consilia Evangelica, quæ hodie fervida, exemplari vita colunt, eorumque apostolatum induturum majorem extensionem et efficaciam in salutem animarum atque Sanctæ Ecclesiæ gloriam.

Adimplendis igitur Canonibus 674 et 492, consulendi ergo, rem ad Sedem Apostolicam defero, humiliter ab ea postulans ut dignetur elargiri mihi "nihil obstat" erigendæ Societati juxta Constitutiones, quarum lineamenta generalia adnexa remitto, omnia correctioni Sanctæ Romanæ Ecclesiæ subdens dum filiali animo pando extraordinarium incepti momentum, maximam utilitatem fructuum sanctificationis in hanc diem obtentorum, et spem augmenti eorundem concessione gratiæ, ideoque ardens meum desiderium ut concedatur "nihil obstat".

Et Deus...

*Matriti, die 22 mense junio, anno 1943.*

+ Leopoldus, Ep.us Matriten.-Compluten.

Emmno ac Rvdmo Card. Præfecto
S. Congregationis *DE RELIGIOSIS.*

---

## 11. Curriculum vitæ *of the founder of Opus Dei sent to Rome by the Bishop of Madrid-Alcalá; August 28, 1943.*

AGP, Sezione Giuridica, III/15081.

OBISPADO DE MADRID-ALCALA

*REV. DUS DOMINUS JOSEPH MARIA ESCRIVÁ DE BALAGUER Y ALBÁS, RECTOR REGII PATRONATUS A SANCTA ELISABETH, MATRITI CONSTITUTI.*

Aragoniæ in Barbastrensi civitate natus die 9 ianuarii anni 1902, cuius Joseph Escrivá de Balaguer Corzán et Maria a Virgine Perdolente Albás y Blanc parentes exstiterunt.

### 1) STUDIA

Academicos gradus prolithæ ac laurea Iuris Civilis apud Cæsaraugustanam ac Matritensem Studiorum Universitates obtinuit, Summa cum laude lauream consecutus.

In Pontificia Universitate Cæsaraugustana, tunc existenti, integros quinque Sacræ Theologiæ curriculos, maximis obtentis qualificationibus, perfecit.

Nondum sacerdos sed per primam tantum tonsuram inter clericos cooptatus, ab Em.mo Cardinali Soldevila, Moderator Seminarii a Sancto Francisco de Paula renuntiatus est.

## 2) APOSTOLATUS

### a) Pauperes

Ut dissertationem ad lauream pararet, anno 1927, Matritum perrexit. Atque, sacerdotali ministerio assidue deditus, scientificis laboribus non obstantibus, ibi ab anno 1927 ad annum usque 1931 opus apostolicum exercuit inter pueros pauperes ac ægrotos egenos, quos domibus suis per miserrima civitatis suburbia quotidie invisebat.

Dein, cum operis apud Universitatis studiosos magnitudo ut illud activitatis sacerdotalis genus relinqueret, Rev.mo Episcopo approbante, coègerit, non prætermisit quin singulis dominicis ægrotos pauperes in Generali Valetudinario visitaret.

### b) Universitarii

Mense octobri anni 1928, de consensu Rev.mi Antistitis Matritensis-Complutensis, assidua oratione ac iugi pœnitentia comitantibus, intensum ac firmum laborem formationis apostolicæ inter iuvenes Universitatis auditores atque Specialium Superiorumque Scholarum alumnos, interioris vitæ et professionalis perfectionis cultu mediante, evolvere incepit. Quod quidem opus tacitum, in directum profundum validissimumque Ecclesiæ servitium ordinatum, et ab initiis a plurimis Episcopis toto ex corde benedictum.

A plurium urbium Universitatum professoribus et alumnis crebro ad exercitia spiritualia dirigenda sive spiritualis secessus dies ordinandos vocatur: notatu dignum est opus apud Universitatem Æstivam Iacensem (Cæsaraugustanam, Universitatem Status) suis conferentiis nuper peractum. Ut hic labor erga Universitatis studiosos facilior redderetur ab Apostolica Sede, rescripto diei 20 augusti 1940, privilegium Altaris Portatilis concessum fuit.

Vir quidem qui problema Hispanæ Universitatis penitus perspectum habet, dum Consilium Nationale Educationis constitueretur, Consiliarius Nationalis cooptatus est, unicus sacerdos cleri sæcularis qui, una cum tribus Rev.mis Episcopis paucisque religiosis, ad præfatum Consilium pertinet.

Mense novembri anni 1940 Magister Ethicæ ac Moralis professionalis Scholæ Periodismi (Scholæ Officialis Status) designatus fuit.

### c) Spiritualis moderatio

Multis præstantissimis personis, Actionis Catholicæ dirigentibus aliarumque nationalium activitatum catholicarum ac culturalium moderatoribus, Universitatis magistris et alumnis, sacerdotibus immo et religiosis a spiritualibus moderator exstat, quippe cui omnes assidue accedunt propterea quod eum virum dono consilii præditum habent.

Exercitia atque spiritualis secessus dies Actionis Catholicæ iuvenibus ac puellis sæpe etiam moderavit: Cæsaraugustæ, Valentiæ, Ilerdæ, Vallisoleti, Legione, Abulæ, Matriti, etc. Valentiæ, ianuario 1941, Conventus Assistentium Ecclesiasticorum A.C. Spiritualis Moderator munere functus est.

Laborem moderatoris animarum non intermisit neque Opus Dei, ipso dirigente, clam agere desivit, tempore dominationis marxistæ (durante bello Hispaniæ, 1936-1939), sub qua cum ipse tum sui discipuli acerbam passi sunt persecutionem. Cum autem in regionem regimini nationali subiectam audacter pervenire obtinuisset, vel per se vel per *Opus* suum animum erigere et auxilium afferre patienti seu prælianti studiosæ iuventuti consecutus est. Quot itinera hinc inde per diversa prælii castra, febri sæpe correptus, ut spirituale Patris munus perageret, confecit!

### d) **Exercitia spiritualia**

Alter indefessi apostolatus aspectus exstat labor a plurimis iam annis peractus, quo, Rev.mis Episcopis et Religiosorum Institutorum Superioribus postulantibus, multas exercitiorum spiritualium series sacerdotibus et religiosis moderavit. Quod etiam opus præstavit plurium Seminariorum alumnis. Hoc nempe ministerium apud diœceses Legionensem, Abulensem, Segoviensem, Victoriensem, Pampilonensem, Matritensem-Complutensem, Valentinam, Ilerdensem, etc., nuper exercuit. Anno 1940 durante supra mille sacerdotes diversarum diœcesim apud eum exercitiis spiritualibus vacavere, inter quos et ipsi Rev.mi locorum Ordinarii nonnumquam interfuerunt.

### 3) **DE EO EIUSQUE MINISTERIO IUDICIUM**

Ipsius characteris insignes sunt animi vis necnon organizationis et gubernii dotes. Occulte ac sine strepitu transire; Ecclesiasticæ Hierarchiæ obsequentissimum se præbere; amorem erga Sanctam Matrem Ecclesiam atque Romanum Pontificem palam et privatim, verbo et scripto fovere sacerdotalis eius laboris peculiarissimum est sigillum.

Rev.mus Ordinarius Diœceseos litteris 24 maii 1941 ad Rev.mum P. Abbatem Monasterii Montis Serrati, O.S.B., ita suam de P. Escrivá de Balaguer opinionem exprimebat:

"Dr. Escrivá exemplum sacerdotum est, a Deo in multarum animarum sanctificationem electus, humilis, prudens, abnegatus, Antistiti suo summe docilis, præclari intellectus, firmissimæ doctrinalis et spiritualis formationis, zelo ardentissimus, studiosæ iuventutis christianæ informandæ apostolus, nihil aliud intendens nisi ad Patriæ utilitatem et Ecclesiæ servitium ac munimen professionalium phalangem disponere, qui etiam in mundo commorantes, non tantum sancte vitam agant sed etiam apostolico labori indulgeant".

### 4) **PUBLICATIONES**

Edidit:

*Consideraciones espirituales* (Concæ, 1934)
*Santo Rosario* (Matriti, 1935)
*Estudio histórico-canónico de la jurisdicción eclesiastica "nullius diœcesis" de la Il.ma Sra. Abadesa del Monasterio de Santa María La Real de las Huelgas* (Burgis, 1938)
*Camino* (Valentiæ, 1939)
Operum "Santo Rosario" et "Camino" duæ editiones iam prodidere, immo et tertia paratur opusculi "Santo Rosario".

Matriti, die 28 mense augusto, anno 1943.

+ CASIMIRUS, Ep.us Aux.

Vic. G.ralis

## 12. Nihil obstat *of the Sacred Congregation of the Holy Office for the diocesan erection of the Priestly Society of the Holy Cross, communicated to the Sacred Congregation for Religious; September 29, 1943.*

AGP, Sezione Giuridica, III/15082.

SUPREMA SACRA CONGREGAZIONE

DEL

SANTO OFFIZIO

Prot. Num. 324/43

Dal Palazzo del S. Offizio 29 Settembre 1943.

Eccellenza Rev.ma,

Con pregiata lettera N.2777/43 in data 24 Agosto u.s., cotesta S. Congregazione domandava se da parte del S. Offizio nulla si opponeva per l'erezione della Pia Associazione dal titolo "Società Sacerdotale della Santa Croce" in Istituto di Diritto Diocesano.

Mi reco a gradita premura di comunicare all'Eccellenza Vostra Reverendissima che questa Suprema S. Congregazione, tutto considerato, ha in proposito decretato:

"EX PARTE S. OFFICII NIHIL OBSTARE".

Con sensi di ben distinta stima mi professo

dell'Eccellenza Vostra Rev.ma

Dev.mo

A. Ottaviani

assessore

A Sua Eccellenza Rev.ma
Mons. ERMENEGILDO PASETTO
Arcivescovo tit. di Iconio

Segretario della S. Congr. dei RELIGIOSI.

## 13. Nihil obstat *of the Sacred Congregation for Religious for the diocesan erection of the Priestly Society of the Holy Cross; October 11, 1943.*

AGP, Sezione Giuridica, III/15083.

EX SECRETARIA                                          N.2777-43

SACRÆ CONGREGATIONIS

DE RELIGIOSIS

Romæ die 11 octobris 1943

Rev.me ac Exc.me Domine

Sacra Congregatio de Religiosis diligenter perpendit quæ Exc. Tua exposuit de erectione canonica Instituti Clericalis, juris diœcesani, Sodalium in communi viventium sine votis, cui titulus "Societas Sacerdotalis S. Crucis", cuiusque finis specialis est "institutio catholica et professionalis adscriptorum Universitatibus Studiorum".

Pergratum itaque mihi est E.T. significare ex parte huius S. Congregationis nihil obstare, quominus juxta Can. 673 eadem E.T. ad canonicam erectionem deveniat.

Hisce autem litteris conceditur facultas ad decem annos valitura, qua E.T., prævia sanatione omnium quæ sanatione indigent et ab S. Congr. sanari solent, valeat dispensare super defectu incorporationis Societati vel ætatis, ut Sodales, qui exemplo præstiterunt observantiæ, designentur tum ad munus Præsidis tum ad alia munera majoris momenti in Societate.

Quoad incorporationem primorum Sodalium, Sodalis, servato præscripto quo dignitate sacerdotali auctus sit, qui ad munus Præsidis designatus est, fidelitatem perpetuam emittat coram Exc. T. vel Sacerdote delegato, adhibita convenienti formula; Consiliarii aliique Officiales coram Præside, ceteri autem, qui per congruum tempus ad observantiam laudabiliter incubuerunt, emittant vel oblationem temporariam vel fidelitatem perpetuam, de judicio Exc. Tuæ, audito Rev.mo Præside.

Bona temporaria in favorem Societatis forma juridice valida constituantur.

Curet Exc. Tua ut, servatis præscriptionibus Codicis J. C. ac præ oculis habito fine speciali Societatis, aptæ edantur Constitutiones.

Decreto erectionis Societatis edito ad normam Instruct. S. Congr. diei 30 nov. 1922, E.T. ad hanc S.C. exemplar transmittere non dedignetur una cum textu Constitutionum; transactis vero decem annis a die erectionis, relationem quoque de conditione disciplinari, personali et œconomica Societatis.

Cuncta fausta a Domino adprecor et permaneo Eidem Exc. Tuæ

add.mus servus

+ fr. L. E. Pasetto

Secr.

Rev.mo ac Exc.mo

Leopoldo Eijo y Garay

Archiep. Matriten in Hisp.

## 14. Decree of the Bishop of Madrid-Alcalá canonically erecting the Priestly Society of the Holy Cross; December 8, 1943.

AGP, Sezione Giuridica, III/15084.

### ERECTIO CANONICA SOCIETATIS SACERDOTALIS SANCTÆ CRUCIS

### DECRETUM

Quindecim abhinc annos pius ac zelans hujus Matriten Diœcesis Sacerdos, Doctor D. Joseph Maria Escrivá de Balaguer et Albás, favente ac benedicente Ordinario Diœcesano, Institutionem condidit, cujus sodales, præter propriam cujusque sanctificationem, servatis Evangelii consiliis in munere professionali exercendo obtinendam, hunc, quamvis non unicum, specificum finem sibi proposuerunt: enixe adlaborare ut selectam partem virorum professionum intellectualium, quibus natura competit societatem civilem dirigere, ad fidei catholicæ principia revocarent et ad Evangelicam perfectionem suaderent.

Novam hanc Institutionem -quæ, ob singularem et propriam consociationem "OPUS DEI" appellata, proprium finem omni contentione est ubique prosequuta- apprime temporum nostrorum et nostræ Patriæ necessitatibus urgentissimis respondere nemini non apparuit. Omnes enim fatentur, rei publicæ eversionem, quæ universam fere Hispaniam nuper cruentavit, desertioni a doctrina et præceptis Christi hominum "intellectualium" esse magna ex parte adstruendam, quippe qui doctrinis dissolventibus per tot lustra juventam studiosam inquinarunt.

Cui piæ Institutioni divinus favor jam inde a primordiis constans adfuit, sese præcipue manifestans tum numero et qualitate ad eadem advolantium juvenum integritate æque ac ingenio florentium, tum fructibus uberrimus ubivis ab eadem collectis, tum denique signo contradictionis, quæ operum Dei sigillum semper exstitit. At vero, succrescentibus in dies Institutionis membris, ejusdemque mirum in modum extenso activitatis ambitu, visum est, scopum, constitutionem et methodum actionis intra fines simplicis Associationis ulterius contineri non posse, sed ampliorem et firmiorem exigere rationem veræ Societatis Ecclesiasticæ legitime erectæ et constitutæ. Sic enim, dum diversæ Institutionis activitates organice coordinabuntur, ipsa Hierarchiæ intimius hærebit, necessariam internam authonomiam comparabit et firmitatem sanctionis nedum Ordinarii loci verum etiam Sedis Apostolicæ nanciscetur.

Re igitur mature perpensa, pro Nostro officio, universum negotium ad Apostolicam Sedem retulimus, a qua, per S. Congregationem de Religiosis, telegrapho prius, dein vero litteris authenticis diei 11 octobris 1943, sub nº 2777/43, responsum accepimus, nihil ab eadem Sede Apostolica obstare quominus ad optatam erectionem canonicam prædictæ piæ Associationis deveniremus.

Quapropter, facultatibus cc. 674, 492, § 1, concessis utentes, laudatam piam hucusque Associationem, a Nobis ut talem jam antea adprobatam, in veram Societatem juris Diœcesani ad normam t. XVII l. II Codicis Juris Canonici erigimus atque constituimus sub nomine SOCIETATIS SACERDOTALIS SANCTÆ CRUCIS, in finem compendio Statutorum Sanctæ Sedi submisso sat expressum et mediis *ibidem* relatis obtinendum. Hæc autem Societas Sacerdotalis Sanctæ Crucis erit ad normam juris communis Nobis Nostrisque Successoribus plane subjecta (c. 492, § 2). Ut vero efficacius intentos effectus Societas consequatur, volumus ac edicimus ut, firmo compendio Statutorum Sanctæ Sedi, ut diximus, delato, ejusdem Societatis ampliores et completiores Constitutiones exarentur Nostræ adprobationi subjiciendæ.

Hujus decreti canonicæ erectionis Societatis Sacerdotalis Sanctæ Crucis, manu Nostra subscripti Nostroque sigillo muniti, tria exscribantur exemplaria: primum ad Sedem Apostolicam remittendum, alterum Rvdo Moderatori Societatis tradendum, tertium denique in Archivo Curiæ Episcopalis ad perpetuam rei memoriam asservandum.

Matriti, in die festo Immaculatæ Conceptionis B.V.M., 8 decembris 1943.

+ Leopoldus, Episcopus Matriten.-Compluten.

L + S          J. Marco

Cancell.

---

## 15. Communication of the Bishop of Madrid-Alcalá to Rev. Josemaría Escrivá with regard to some points relative to the erection of the Priestly Society of the Holy Cross; December 8, 1943.

AGP, Sezione Giuridica, III/15142.

La Sagrada Congregación de Religiosos, por sus Letras de 11 de octubre p.p. n° 2777/43, Nos concedió facultad valedera por diez años para que, previa la sanación de cuanto la necesitase y que suela ser concedida por la misma Sagrada Congregación, pudiéramos dispensar del defecto de incorporación a la Sociedad, o de la edad, con objeto de que los socios que sobresalieron en la ejemplar observancia sean designados o para el cargo de Presidente o para los demás de mayor importancia en la Sociedad.

Haciendo uso de dicha facultad, previa dispensa y sanación de cuanto fuere necesario dispensar y sanar, V.R., designado para el cargo de Presidente, profesará la fidelidad perpetua personalmente ante Nos; y los Consejeros y oficiales mayores la profesarán ante V.R.; e igualmente lo harán ante V.R. los demás socios que durante conveniente espacio de tiempo hayan guardado laudable observancia y sean admitidos, a juicio Nuestro previa audiencia de V.R., a la oblación temporal o a la fidelidad perpetua.

Encomiendo muy especialmente a V.R. que redacte y Nos presente las Constituciones de la Sociedad Sacerdotal de la Santa Cruz canónicamente erigida por Nos el día de hoy, desarrollando como mejor convenga el boceto de Constituciones que enviamos a la Santa Sede.

Y asimismo que cuide de que los bienes temporales en favor de la Sociedad se constituyan en forma válida legalmente.

Dios guarde a V.R. muchos años.

Madrid, fiesta de la Inmaculada Concepción de Nuestra Señora y Madre la Santísima Virgen María, 8 de diciembre de 1943.

+ Leopoldo, Obispo de Madrid-Alcalá

Rev.Sr.Dr.D.José María Escrivá de Balaguer y Albás
Presidente de la Sociedad Sacerdotal de la Santa Cruz.

---

## 16. Text of the Formula used by Rev. Josemaría Escrivá for the act of incorporation to the Priestly Society of the Holy Cross.

AGP, Sezione Giuridica, III/15079.

### FORMULA FIDELITATIS

Domine Jesu: Suscipe me tibi in servum sempiternum Societatis Sacerdotalis Sanctæ Crucis, in obsequium et sacrificium laudis perpetuæ: voluntarie et in æternum meipsum, cum omnibus viribus et affectibus meis, quanto intimius valeo, offero.

Et intercedente beata et gloriosa Maria semper Virgine, cum beato Joseph, beatis Archangelis Michaèle, Gabriele et Raphaèle, ac beatis Apostolis tuis Petro, Paulo et Joanne, et omnibus Angelis Custodibus, da, Domine, pacem in diebus meis: ut ope tuæ misericordiæ adjutus, adimplere possim tuam sanctissimam voluntatem. Amen.

---

## 17. Communication of the Bishop of Madrid-Alcalá to the Sacred Congregation for Religious of the erection of the Priestly Society of the Holy Cross; December 19, 1943.

AGP, Sezione Giuridica, III/15610.

Matriti, die 19 decembris 1943

Excme ac Rvdme Domine:

Exceptis Excellentiæ Vestræ litteris diei 11 octobris hujus anni, sub n° 2777/43, ad erectionem canonicam processi *SOCIETATIS SACERDOTALIS SANCTÆ CRUCIS* per formale Decretum in scriptis datum, cujus exemplar tam in tabulario Instituti quam in Archivo Diœcesano servabitur.

Nunc vero de peracta hujusmodi erectione insto Sacram Congregationem certiorem facio, ac Decreti exemplar transmitto, ad normam Decreti ejusdem Sacræ Congregationis de Religiosis dati die 30 novembris 1922.

Facultatibus in præfatis Excellentiæ Vestræ Rvdmæ litteris mihi concessis, et, prævia sanatione eorum omnium quæ sananda fuerint et a Sacra Congregatione sanari solent, Moderator nuper erectæ Societatis Sacerdotalis Sanctæ Crucis coram me perpetuam emisit fidelitatem, quam quidem coram illo emittent Consiliarii et Officiales Majores.

Moderatori autem præscripsi ut Constitutiones Societatis exaret, apprime conformes compendio quod isti Sacræ Congregationi dedi die 22 junii elapsi.

Quæ dum isti Sacræ Congregationi refero, me profiteor Excellentiæ Vestræ Rvdmæ

addictissimum in Domino

L + S                          +Leopoldus, Ep.us Matriten.-Compluten.

Excmo ac Rvdmo D.Fr.L.E. Pasetto

Secretario S. Congregationis

DE RELIGIOSIS.

---

## 18. Decree of the Bishop of Madrid-Alcalá approving the Constitutions of the Priestly Society of the Holy Cross; January 25, 1944.

AGP, Sezione Giuridica, III/15085.

DECRETO

Por el Revmo. Presbítero Dn. José María Escrivá de Balaguer y Albás, Presidente de la Sociedad Sacerdotal de la Santa Cruz, Nos han sido presentadas las CONSTITUTIONES SOCIETATIS SACERDOTALIS SANCTÆ CRUCIS, redactadas en cumplimiento de Nuestro Decreto de 8 de diciembre de 1943, por el que fue erigida canónicamente dicha Sociedad.- Y habiendo hecho examinar las referidas Constituciones por Nuestro Fiscal General, quien las ha hallado en todo conformes a Derecho y dignas de Nuestra aprobación, y teniendo en consideración que por dichas Constituciones se reglamenta convenientemente la naturaleza, fines, actividades, prácticas ascéticas, régimen de la Sociedad y de su instrumento específico de Apostolado, llamado OPUS DEI, se ofrece un medio apto de santificación para sus miembros por el ejercicio de los consejos evangélicos y un valioso medio de apostolado para la difusión de la doctrina y virtudes cristianas entre los fieles, por el presente venimos en aprobar y aprobamos las CONSTITUTIONES SOCIETATIS SACERDOTALIS SANCTÆ CRUCIS y mandamos que sean fielmente cumplidas y observadas por todos y cada uno de los miembros de dicha Sociedad, conforme al ejemplar auténtico que, con Nuestro sello, será entregado al Presidente de la misma.

Dado en Madrid a veinticinco de enero de mil novecientos cuarenta y cuatro.

L + S                          + Leopoldo, Obispo de Madrid-Alcalá

## 19. Apostolic Brief Cum Societatis by which His Holiness Pope Pius XII grants various indulgences to the members of the Priestly Society of the Holy Cross and Opus Dei; June 28, 1946.

AGP, Sezione Giuridica, IV/12251.

PIVS PP. XII

AD PERPETUAM REI MEMORIAM

Cum SOCIETATIS SACERDOTALIS SANCTÆ CRUCIS ET "OPUS DEI", quam dilectus filius IOSEPH MARIA ESCRIVA DE BALAGUER Y ALBAS, Sacerdos, Doctor, tam magnifice constituit tamque humaniter moderatur, ardenti studio, miræ operæ laborique fructuosissimo par sit Nostra quoque fervida consensio ac propensa voluntas, periucundum nunc Nobis est hisce in Litteris, quarum tenore eiusdem piæ Societatis Sodales spiritualibus Indulgentiarum muneribus decoramus, uberrimorum repetere memoriam fructuum quos, pro Dei gloria animarumque salute, præclarus Conditor brevi temporis spatio sed constanti industria et diligentia sua percipere potuit. Nam, vehementer gratulante ac peramanter benedicente Venerabili Fratre Matritensium Episcopo, in ipsa civitate Matritensi die II mensis Octobris anno MCMXXVIII orta, eo consilio ut eius Sodales in eruditione ac doctrina præstantes præcipueque earum magistri divinis præceptis obtemperent atque, ad instar religiosorum sed in sæculo viventes, Christianæ vitæ perfectionem persequantur, Societas avide se promisit et impensius incubuit in iuvenum superiores scholas ac studiorum Universitates celebrantium mentes fingendas ad humanitatem, ad virtutem, ad religionem. Non modo intra Hispaniæ fines sed in longinquas quoque regiones, favente Deo, se pandit beneficus Sodalium labor, ut lux videlicet et veritas Christi in mentes pervaderet præcellentium eruditorum utque hi quoque vicissim lucem veritatemque Christi exemplo ac doctrina cum aliis communicarent. Nec silentio prætermittendus est apostolatus benemeriti illius Sacerdotis, qui, charitatis spiritu inflammatus, pauperibus pueris egenisque ægrotis consuluit, eorumque animos religiosis sensibus ac sana doctrina imbuendos curavit; quique fructuosissime constanterque a spiritualibus adfuit viris laicis vel sacerdotibus vel etiam religiosis, qui acres et industrii in mentis et religionis agitatione apud Hispanos fuerunt et etiamnunc exstant. Quæ cum ita sint, enixis Nos votis peramanter annuendum censemus, quæ benemeritus Præses supra laudatæ Societatis Sacerdotalis Sanctæ Crucis et "Opus Dei" ad Nos humiliter tulit, benigne quoque fervidis precibus attentis dilecti filii ALVARI DEL PORTILLO Y DIEZ DE SOLLANO, sacerdotis, doctoris, eiusdem Instituti Procuratoris Generalis. Quo tam frugifera Societas potiora capiat, opitulante Deo, incrementa, Nos, Apostolica Nostra Auctoritate, præsentium Litterarum tenore, omnibus et singulis utriusque sexus Christifidelibus, qui in prælaudatam Societatem seu Opus ascribentur, die primo eorum ingressus, si, vere pænitens et confessi, Sanctissimum Eucharistiæ Sacramentum sumpserint, PLENARIAM; -pariterque omnibus et singulis Sodalibus nunc adlectis vel in posterum ipsam in Sodalitatem sive Opus adlegendis, item pænitentibus et confessis ac Sacra Communione refectis, -quo die unusquisque eorum Sodalitati, ad tempus, se obtulerit vel fidelitatis, perpetuo, verba conceperit; -semel in mense, si ad sua liberalia opera integrum per mensem cotidie aliquam piam adiunxerit invocationem; - in festis diebus Domini Nostri Iesu Christi et Beatæ Mariæ Virginis, in Kalendario Ecclesiæ universalis significatis, Sanctorum Archangelorum Michaèlis, Gabrielis et Raphaèlis, Sanctorum Angelorum Custodum, Sancti Iosephi, Deiparæ Virginis Sponsi, Sanctorum Petri et Pauli Apostolorum, Sancti Ioannis Evangelistæ, Omnium Sanctorum; -die XIV mensis Februarii, si peculiari Sacræ functioni pro gratiarum Deo actione adstiterint, etiam PLENARIAM; -ac sodalibus nunc adlectis vel in posterum ipsam in Societatem sive Opus  adlegendis, in cuiuslibet eorum mortis articulo, si, item vere pænitentes et confessi ac Sacra Communione refecti, vel, quatenus id facere nequiverint, saltem contriti, Sanctissimum Iesu nomen ore, si potuerint, in minus corde devote invocaverint et mortem de manu Domini, tamquam peccati stipendium, patienter susceperint, PLENARIAM similiter INDULGENTIAM misericorditer in Domino concedimus. Præterea iisdem Sodalibus, qui, saltem corde contrito, in suis liberalibus operibus, ut supra, aliquam piam adiunxerint invocationem; -et qui Sanctæ Crucis signum, in oratoriis Instituti erectum, pia mente deosculati fuerint vel coram ipso aliquam piam precem iaculatoriam recitaverint, quingentos dies de iniunctis eis, seu alias quomodolibet debitis pænitentiis in forma Ecclesiæ consueta relaxamus. Quas omnes et singulas Indulgentias et pænitentiarum relaxationes, excepta plenaria Indulgentia in articulo mortis lucranda, etiam animabus Chistifidelium in Purgatorio detentis per modum suffragii applicari posse indulgemus. Contrariis quibuslibet nihil obstantibus. Præsentibus perpetuo valituris. Volumus autem ut præsentium Litterarum transumptis seu exemplis, etiam impressis, manu alicuius Notarii publici subscriptis ac sigillo personæ in Ecclesiastica dignitate vel officio constitutæ munitis, eadem prorsus fides adhibeatur, quæ ipsis præsentibus adhiberetur, si exhibitæ vel ostensæ forent.

Datum Romæ, apud Sanctum Petrum, sub anulo Piscatoris, die XXVIII mensis Iunii, in festo SS. Cordis Iesu, anno MCMXXXXVI, Pontificatus Nostri octavo.

De speciali Sanctissimi mandato
Pro Domino Cardinali a Secretis Status
L + S    Dominicus Spada
a Brevibus Apostolicis

---

## 20. Decree of the Bishop of Madrid-Alcalá by which indulgences are granted to those who kiss the wooden cross placed in the student residence at 6, Jenner Street, Madrid; March 28, 1940.

AGP, Sezione Giuridica, I/15074.

## NOS EL DOCTOR DON LEOPOLDO EIJO GARAY,

### POR LA GRACIA DE DIOS Y DE LA SANTA SEDE APOSTOLICA
### OBISPO DE MADRID-ALCALA, ETC., ETC.

*Deseando* promover en cuanto esté de nuestra parte el divino culto, y fomentar la devoción del pueblo cristiano, dando graciosamente lo que en la misma forma hemos re*cibid*o de la Divina Misericordia, sin mérito alguno nuestro, concedemos *cincuenta días* de indulgencia a todos los fieles de nuestro Obispado por cada vez que devotamente besaren *la Cruz de Palo de la Residencia de Estudiantes de Jenner 6, Madrid* y pidieren a Dios Nuestro Señor por la exaltación de nuestra Santa Fe Católica, paz y concordia entre los Reyes y Príncipes cristianos, extirpación de las herejías y demás fines piadosos de Nuestra Santa Madre la Iglesia.

Dadas en *Madrid* a *28* de *marzo* de mil novecientos *cuarenta*

+ Leopoldo, Obispo de Madrid-Alcalá.

Por mandato de S.E.R. el Obispo mi Señor

L + S       Dr. JUAN MARCO

Srio.

---

## 21. Letter Brevis sane *of the Sacred Congregation for Religious in* praise of the aims *of the Priestly Society of the Holy Cross and Opus Dei; August 13, 1946.*

AGP, Sezione Giuridica, IV/15091.

SACRA CONGREGAZIONE                                              N. 2777/43
DEI RELIGIOSI

Romæ, die 13 augusti 1946

Rev.me Pater,

brevis sane temporis lapsus pertransiit ex quo Hæc Sacra Congregatio ad Societatis Sacerdotalis Sanctæ Crucis atque Operis Dei canonicam erectionem ex actis atque satis abunde probatis veniam libenter concessit, et iam in dies ex diversis partibus copiosa et quidem certa atque authentica documenta perveniunt, quæ Institutum Tuum summopere laudant et commendant. Satis superque his documentis comprobatur quod Sacra Congregatio, re mature perpensa, censuerat circa sanctitatem, necessitatem atque opportunitatem finis et apostolatus quem Institutum Tuum sibi proposuit.

Igitur Tibi, Rev.me Pater, et tuis omnibus qui in sancto, silenti, et arduo apostolatu penetrationis sive inter scientiarum cultores, sive in publicis magisteriis, sive in civilibus omnis generis professionibus strenue adlaborant, ob copiosos iam obtentos hucusque fructus, ob celerem diffusionem quam nacti estis, ob bonum spiritum quo Institutum ducitur ex toto corde gratulamur.

Animo volenti in iis quæ fortiter incepisti perge, Rev.me Pater, et Tecum pariter pergant atque fideliter omnes, viri et mulieres, sequantur qui quæve ex divina vocatione tam nobili et sancto Operi adscripti iam sunt et in posterum adscribantur.

Dum cuncta omnia fausta prospera Tibi, Rev.me Pater, Tuoque Operi adprecor, Tui addictissimum in Domino Me profiteor

+ Al. Card. Lavitrano

Præf.

+fr. L. E. Pasetto

Secr.

Rev.mo Patri D. D. Iosepho Mariæ Escrivá de Balaguer y Albás Fundatori et Præsidi Generali Societatis Sacerdotalis Sanctæ Crucis et Operis Dei Matriti.

---

## 22. Decretum laudis *of the Priestly Society of the Holy Cross and Opus Dei as a secular institute of pontifical right; February 24, 1947*

AGP, Sezione Giuridica, IV/15092.

### DECRETUM.

Primum Institutum Sæculare, quod statim ac prodiit Constitutio Apostolica "Provida Mater Ecclesia", a SS.mo Domino Nostro Pio, Divina Providentia PP. XII, die altera Februarii huius anni subsignata, Laudis Decretum meruit, est SOCIETAS SACERDOTALIS SANCTÆ CRUCIS et OPUS DEI, breviato autem nomine Opus Dei nuncupata.

*Opus Dei* a Rev.mo D. Iosepho Maria Escrivá de Balaguer, viro tam pietate quam doctrina atque apostolico zelo insigni, exordium in Diœcesi Matritensi habuit. A primis sacerdotii sui annis, Doctor Escrivá de Balaguer, qui vix inter clericos cooptatus Moderatorem Seminarii Sancti Francisci a Paula Cæsaraugustæ egerat, in hac civitate prius, et ab anno post Christum natum MDCCCCXXVII Matriti, dum studia ad Lauream Iuris Civilis consequendam peragebat, posthac vero sine intermissione, variis ministeriis sacerdotalibus, humilioribus præcipue in suburbio, magna sui ipsius abnegatione functus est.

Dum his impigre vacabat, Divina Providentia per legitimos Superiores ecclesiasticos novum opus quasi manu ducente, Dr. Escrivá de Balaguer ad apostolatum inter laicalis Universitatis et Scholarum Superiorum Matritensium alumnos se fortiter vocatum atque suaviter motum sensit. Cum progressu temporis hanc vocationem a Domino datam esse eventus atque fructus non dubie comprobare viderentur, invocata et obtenta venia ab Exc.mo Episcopo Matritensi, die Angelis Custodibus sacra, II Octobris anni a nostra reparata salute MDCCCCXXVIII, Operis Dei ima atque solida fundamenta iacta sunt. Hoc satis felici titulo, quod omnibus humiliter fidenterque innuere volebat non de opere humano agi, sed de sacro opere Dei, parva Societas operiebatur ad apostolatum inter alumnos Universitatis atque doctiores viros exercendum, ac per ipsos deinde in totum intellectualium et dirigentium cœtum dilatandum. Satis apud omnes constat quam gravia fuerint ac difficilia tempora illa in Hispania, sive ante bellum civile, sive immani hoc bello flagrante ac persecutione religiosa acriter sæviente: verumtamen Opus Dei, ut pia consociatio benevolentia ac benedictione ecclesiasticæ Auctoritatis per plures annos (1928-1940) facto existens, ac de labore potius quam de ordinatione et formis canonicis nondum sollicita, in cœtu intellectuali prudenter selecto et accuratissime educato, spiritualem transformationem prius indeque vere apostolicam, silenter sed intense ac tenaciter perficere conabatur. Pedetentim interea Instituti character iuridice delineatus fuit. Post diuturnas moras multasque probationes Opus Dei, qua verum Dei opus (Act. V, 39), superatis non parvis neque paucis, etiam bonorum, contradictionibus, succrevit et consolidatum est. Deinceps accesserunt ecclesiasticæ recognitiones atque approbationes. Die XIX Martii anni MDCCCCXXXXI Episcopus Matritensis ad formam Piæ Unionis Opus Dei redegit, pauloque post, cum novæ satisque rapidæ in dies ascensiones et expansiones supernaturalem Instituti efficaciam confirmarent, Sancta Sede ad normam iuris consulta, Ipsiusque venia die XI Octobris anni MDCCCCXXXXIII, Maternitati Beatæ Virginis Mariæ sacra, obtenta, Ordinarius Matritensis Opus Dei in Societatem vitæ communis sine votis publicis iuris diœcesani, die VIII Decembris eiusdem anni, formaliter erexit. Postremis hisce annis, cum iam plures quam viginti domos in quatuor Europæ Statibus erectæ essent, necnon una in Africa, et fundationes in America pararentur; cumque pariter socii in dies multiplicarentur, neque solum inter medicos, advocatos, architectos, exercitus duces, cultores scientiarum atque artium, publicos scriptores, professores Universitatum et Scholarum Superiorum omne genus, etc., sed inter alumnos quoque laicalium Facultatum, qui cum collegis fructuosum apostolatum exercerent, invenirentur, haud immerito visum est tempus advenisse implorandi a Sancta Sede primam Operis Dei pontificiam approbationem. Quare Præsidis Generalis instantia SS.mo Domino Nostro exhibita est, fervida Exc.mi Ordinarii Matritensis commendatione fulta ac Litteris Testimonialibus aliorum sexaginta Ordinariorum, inter quos octo Eminentissimi Patres Cardinales recensentur et omnes Hispaniæ Metropolitani.

Dum Opus Dei has supplices Domino Nostro instanter preces exhibebat ut qua Societas vitæ communis sine votis publicis Laudis Decretum impetraret, Constitutio Apostolica "Provida Mater Ecclesia" parabatur. In tam clarissima huius Documenti luce Institutum Opus Dei eiusque Constitutiones attente in S. Congregatione perpensa sunt, speciatim illa quæ de sua interna ordinatione, de regimine, de ministeriis, de vita communi latiore sensu sumpta, ardua videbantur ac novitatis speciem referebant, et clare patuit Opus Dei præseferre exemplar germani Instituti Sæcularis ab ipsa Constitutione Apostolica proposicti. Hinc venia et iussu Sanctissimi Domini Nostri, in novo accuratiore ipsius Operis examine procedendi norma servata est, quæ in Constitutione "Provida Mater Ecclesia" (Art. VII, § 3) pro Institutorum Sæcularium approbatione præscribitur.

Die VIII Junii MDCCCCXXXXVI Commissio Consultorum coadunata fuit, habitoque huius favorabili suffragio, Congressus Plenus S. Congregationis die XIV Februarii proxime elapsa celebratus est. Huius decisio in Audientia diei XXIV eiusdem mensis ab Em.mo Cardinali Præfecto SS.mi Domini Nostri approbationi et confirmationi subiecta est, atque SS.mus ipsam ratam habuit et confirmavit.

SOCIETAS SACERDOTALIS SANCTÆ CRUCIS et OPUS DEI est Institutum Sæculare ad normam memoratæ Constitutionis Apostolicæ perfectioni christianæ in sæculo acquirendæ et apostolatui exercendo dicatum. Eiusdem finis generalis est sodalium sanctificatio, per consiliorum evangelicorum exercitium peculiarumque Constitutionum observantiam; specialis autem -arcte et intrinsece cum fine generali atque spiritu Instituti perpetuo coniunctus- est totis viribus adlaborare ut cœtus, qui intellectualis dicitur, Christi Domini præceptis, immo et consiliis, adhæreat, eademque in praxim deducat. Ad utrumque finem obtinendum Institutum exigit a propriis alumnis exquisitam animi culturam, tum in pietatis officiis tum in disciplinis sive ecclesiasticis sive profanis, ita ut sodales omnes viri Laurea doctorali in aliqua saltem disciplina ornati sint oporteat. Insuper Institutum solidam membrorum sanctitatem iugiter promovet per sanctificationem laboris ordinarii ac diligens accuratumque exercitium munerum professionalium officiorumque propriorum omnium, civilium seu politicorum, in quibus præcipue iure meritoque socii evangelicam perfectionem prosequuntur.

*Opus Dei*, etsi ex ordinaria membrorum suorum conditione, Institutum Sæculare laicale videatur (cc. 488, 4°; 673, § 2; Const. "Provida Mater Ecclesia", art. I), tamen ratione Societatis Sacerdotalis Sanctæ Crucis, quæ ipsum penitus informat, consulto in Constitutionibus (n. 2) Institutum prævalenter clericale definitum est, iuridice clericalibus Institutis æquiparandum.

*Opus Dei* ex duabus quasi sectionibus constat, virorum nempe ac mulierum, non modo ab invicem separatis, verum etiam penitus distinctis, propria cuiusque interna hierarchia, quæ regimine centrali atque etiam guberniis seu directionibus regionalibus et localibus constituitur. Ipsæ tamen sectiones in Patre seu Præside Generali uniuntur, vel in eius delegatis; ac, in unaquaque Regione, in Consiliario Regionali: atque ab ipsis tantum semper legitime repræsentantur.

Specificus sociorum Operis Dei apostolatus his præcipue exercetur: elevatione et sanctificatione proprii laboris professionalis; per exempla vitæ christianæ in propria sociali activitate; per formationem religiosam et professionalem studentium, ac præsertim alumnorum Universitatum Studiorum; in muneribus publicis exemplari fidelitate exercendis; per fidei catholicæ doctrinæ, verbo, scripto et omnibus mediis ad hoc aptis propagationem. Mulieres autem associatæ regunt domus spiritualium exercitiorum; catholicæ propagandæ orali et scriptæ incumbunt; alias mulieres instituunt, quas præparant ad opera apostolatus; modestiam christianam fovent, apud mulieres, mediis quæ ad hoc melius apta videantur; educationem puellarum promovent et residentias pro illis, quæ studiis vacant, moderantur; ac domos pariter ad præparandas ancillas servitio domestico; denique familiarem administrationem atque domesticam œconomiam omnium domorum Instituti gerunt, in loco tamen penitus separato, ita ut iure semper unica erectione, facto vero ex regula duæ semper habeantur separatæ domus in unoquoque Operis Dei domicilio. Institutum, denique, per eius sodales promptum semper ac paratum est ad illas petendas regiones in quibus Ecclesia persecutionem patiatur, vel quomodolibet ipsorum ministeria vel operam materne invocet. Attamen Opus Dei non habet specificam formam collectivæ actionis externæ: sed præprimis sodalium formationem spiritualem et apostolicam prosequitur; deinde, apostolatum sodales exercent uti quilibet alii cives. Ad professionalem actionem, itemque ad doctrinas sociales, politicas, etc., quod attinet, unusquisque Operis Dei socius, intra limites fidei et moralis catholicæ, plena gaudet libertate; nec Institutum ullius cuiusque socii labores professionales, vel activitates œconomicas, etc., suas facit.

Cum sodales Societatis Sacerdotalis Sanctæ Crucis et Operis Dei non sint religiosi ("Provida Mater Ecclesia", art. II, § 1), idcirco communem vitam religiosam non habent, neque religiosa vota emittunt, neque veste religiosa utuntur, sed externe in omnibus, quæ secularibus communia sunt et a statu perfectionis non alienis, ut alii cives propriæ conditionis ac professionis, se gerunt, vestiunt, vitam ducunt, atque hanc apostolorum vitam, orationi et mortificationi dediti hilares lætique degunt, ita ut eorum ascetismus sit revera ascetismus lætificans. Proinde sanctam lætitiam speciali ratione colere debent, quæ provenit ex generositate omnimodæ traditionis servitio Ecclesiæ. Omnes socii Operis Dei semper et ubique magnum amorem, reverentiam et obedientiam Superioribus Ecclesiasticis exhibent, memores hierarchiam unam in Ecclesia iuris divini tantum existere, scilicet, ex Romano Pontifice atque Episcopis constitutam, quos Spiritus Sanctus posuit regere Ecclesiam Dei. Quapropter id animo omnes insitum habent, internam nempe hierarchiam servitio hierarchiæ Ecclesiæ plene esse consecratam. Item omni vi contendunt ut obligationes civicas adimpleant et, iuribus propriis utentes, dum diversa apostolatus opera exercent, maximam reverentiam et obsequium demonstrant legibus civilibus propriæ regionis seu nationis, in quarum ambitu semper adlaborare intendunt.

His omnibus mature perpensis ac definitis, SS.mus Dominus Noster Pius PP. XII, attentis etiam Litteris non solum Antistitum in quorum diœcesibus Opus Dei domos habet et apostolatum exercet, sed aliorum plurium qui sponte primis in commendando hoc Instituto sese coniungere voluerunt, ipsum Opus Dei cum Societate Sacerdotali Sanctæ Crucis ut Institutum Sæculare sub auctoritate unius Superioris Generalis, cuius munus ad vitam perdurat, ad normam Const. "Provida Mater Ecclesia" propriarumque Constitutionum, quæ a Sacra Congregatione de Religiosis revisæ fuerunt et probatæ, præsentis Decreti norma, laudat atque commendat, iuris pontificii ipsum declarat, salva Ordinariorum potestate, ad eiusdem Constitutionis Apostolicæ tenorem.

Datum Romæ, ex ædibus Sacræ Congregationis, die XXIV mensis Februarii anni MDCCCCXXXXVII.

L + S

Al. Card. Lavitrano
Præf.

P. Arcadius Larraona, CMF
Subs.crius

## 23. Chapter One of the 1947 Constitutions of the Priestly Society of the Holy Cross and Opus Dei.

AGP, Sezione Giuridica, IV/15037.

### CONSTITUTIONES SOCIETATIS SACERDOTALIS SANCTÆ CRUCIS ET OPERIS DEI

CAPUT I

**De Instituti ratione et fine**

1. Institutum, cui titulus Societas Sacerdotalis Sanctæ Crucis et Opus Dei, est Institutum sæculare perfectioni christianæ adquirendæ et apostolatui in sæculo exercendo dicatum. In ipso, membra strictiore sensu sumpta, scilicet sodales omnes, clerici et laici, Societatis Sacerdotalis Sanctæ Crucis, necnon Inscripti et Numerarii Operis Dei, de quibus Constitutiones generaliter loquuntur, ab iis distinguenda sunt, qui spiritum Instituti participant et Operis Dei apostolatui efficaciter, juxta rationem infra dicendam, cooperantur.

2. Institutum prævalenter clericale eo senso dici potest, quod præcipua munera quibus regitur, plerumque ad sacerdotes pertinent.

3. Finis generalis Instituti est sanctificatio sodalium per consiliorum Evangelii exercitium harumque Constitutionum observantiam; specialis autem est totis viribus adlaborare ut classis quæ dicitur intellectualis, quæque, vel ob doctrinam, qua pollet, vel ob munera, quæ exercet, vel ob dignitatem, qua insignitur, est moderatrix societatis civilis, Christi Domini præceptis immo et consiliis adhæreat, ipsaque in praxim deducat.

4. Ad utrumque finem obtinendum Institutum exigit a propriis alumnis exquisitam animi culturam, tum in pietatis officiis tum in disciplinis sive ecclesiasticis sive profanis, uti enucleatius infra dicetur; fovet in illis perfectam adimpletionem munerum professionalium, etiam publicæ administrationis, quibus perfectio proprii status est prosequenda; promovet ac dirigit institutiones et opera, quæ ad mentem excolendam animumque perficiendum spectant, uti domus seu residentias pro scholasticis, domus spiritualium exercitiorum et alia id genus. Ad apostolatum autem exercendum utitur præcipue auxilio atque instrumento suæ internæ consociationis, quæ proprie Opus Dei appellatur.

5. Denominatio Operis Dei pertinet ad universum Institutum, sed peculiari sensu designat instrumentum eius proprium, quo classes diversas societatis civilis, apud quas activitatem suam exercet, pertingit; et etiam Opus Dei est medium ordinarium quo præparantur et seliguntur eiusdem Societatis Sacerdotalis Sanctæ Crucis membra; unde cum hac aliquid unum constituit et ab ea seiungi non potest.

6. Societatis Sacerdotalis Sanctæ Crucis et Operis Dei præcipuum propositum et peculiaris spiritus est zelus apostolicus, pœnitentia, humilitas personalis

et collectiva, submissio ecclesiasticæ Auctoritati, æstuans erga Christum Dominum, Deiparam Virginem Mariam, ac Romanum Pontificem amor.

7. Sodales Instituti evangelicam perfectionem profitentur, quin tamen religiosa vota emittant, aut aliquid externum signum' in personis vel domibus præ se ferant quod religiosam familiam demonstret. Clerici vestem clericalem communem loci, ubi commorantur, laici autem vestes apud classes eiusdem vel similis professionis, vel socialis condicionis usitatas, deferunt.

8. Societas Sacerdotalis Sanctæ Crucis nullas habebit ecclesias proprias; fundationes pias non accipiet; nullas proprias associationes fidelium fovebit; stipendia pro Missis non recipiet, neque ullam pro exercito ministerio mercedem etiam sponte oblatam aut compensationem impensarum, quas ratione itineris aliquis ex sodalibus sustinuerit. Tantum hospitium et victum, tempore alicuius ministerii spiritualis, accipere potest.

9. Societas Sacerdotalis Sanctæ Crucis et Opus Dei tamquam Patronos, quos singulari devotione prosequuntur, habent: Beatam Mariam semper Virginem, quam uti Matrem Instituti veneratur; S. Ioseph, eiusdem Beatæ Mariæ Virginis Sponsum; SS. Archangelos Michaëlem, Gabrielem et Raphaëlem; SS. Apostolos Petrum, Paulum et Ioannem, quibus universa Institutio eiusdemque singula activitatis genera specialiter consecrantur.

---

### 24. Apostolic Brief Mirifice de Ecclesia by which Pope Pius XII grants various indulgences to the members of the Priestly Society of the Holy Cross and Opus Dei; July 20, 1947.

AGP, Sezione Giuridica, IV/15094.

PIVS Pp. XII

AD PERPETUAM REI MEMORIAM

Mirifice de Ecclesia merenti Instituto, quod, SOCIETAS SACERDOTALIS SANCTÆ CRUCIS ET OPUS DEI nuncupatum, in eiusdem Ecclesiæ gremio e parvulo genitum semine brevi tempore crevit frondosæ arboris instar, laudatam itemque laudandam propter operam eius fundatoris ac supremi Moderatoris, dilecti nempe filii IOSEPH MARIÆ ESCRIVÁ DE BALAGUER ET ALBÁS, Nostri Prælati Domestici, Nos per similes Apostolicas Litteras, in festo SS. Cordis Iesu, superiore anno, sub anulo Piscatoris datas, propensam voluntatem dilectionemque Nostram præstitimus, large effuseque cælestibus Ecclesiæ thesauris a Nobis donatis Sodalibus dictæ Societatis, ut hæc "potiora caperet, opitulante Deo, incrementa". Quo autem erga tam navam industriamque Societatem benevolentia Nostra magis perspecta sit, strenuo eius labore pro Dei gloria animarumque salute perpenso, attentisque copiosis fructibus per integræ vitæ sanæque doctrinæ Sodalium apostolatum, iam ab eisdem multis in locis perceptis, Nos SOCIETATEM SACERDOTALEM

SANCTÆ CRUCIS ET OPUS DEI Decreto Laudis diei XXIV mensis Februarii vertentis anni honestavimus, Dilectumque Filium Nostrum Aloysium Sanctæ Romanæ Ecclesiæ Presbyterum Cardinalem Lavitrano ipsius Sodalitatis Patronum, seu Protectorem apud Nos et hanc Apostolicam Sedem elegimus et constituimus. Cum vero ratio atque essentia simulque peculiaris OPERIS DEI finis sanctificatio sit labore cotidiano conquirenda; eiusdemque Sodales in liberalia opera incumbentes peramplis spiritualibus indulgentiarum muneribus sint decorati, Nos, curam de omnibus Sodalibus agentes præcipueque de illis quæ Sectionem mulierum constituunt et, adhuc spe atque animo præsertim de illis cogitantes quæ Inservientes nuncupantur, quæque "ad exemplum Domini, qui ministrare venit et non ministrari (Math. XX, 28), et Beatæ Virginis Mariæ Ancillæ Domini (Lc. I, 38), vera humilitate et caritate actæ, manualia et domestica ministeria, quæ Marthæ dicuntur, interiore Mariæ spiritu animatæ, gaudentes exercent" (Ex Decreto Laudis verba istæc excerpta sunt), ut OPERIS DEI Sodales, igitur, semetipsos magis in dies sanctificare atque animabus Christifidelium igni detentis subvenire possint ac solamen afferre, benigne annuendum censemus precibus dilecti filii ALVARI Sacerdotis DEL PORTILLO ET DIEZ DE SOLLANO, Doctoris, Procuratoris Generalis eiusdem Instituti. Quapropter Nos, Apostolica Nostra Auctoritate, harum vi Litterarum, omnibus et singulis utriusque sexus Christifidelibus, nunc adlectis vel in posterum ipsam in Sodalitatem sive Opus adlegendis, qui, saltem corde contrito, cotidie, per integrum mensem, in manualibus operibus suscipiendis ac perficiendis aliquam, vel brevem, precatiunculam vel invocationem devote recitaverint, PLENARIAM INDULGENTIAM, suetis sub condicionibus lucrandam, misericorditer in Domino concedimus. Præterea supra memoratis Sodalibus, quoties, saltem corde contriti, in prædictis operibus navandis, precatiunculam vel invocationem pie pronuntiaverint, toties quadringentos dies de iniunctis eis, seu alias quomodolibet debitis pænitentiis in forma Ecclesiæ consueta relaxamus. Denique largimur Sodalibus iisdem liceat, si malint, Plenariis hisce ac partialibus Indulgentiis functorum vita labes pœnasque expiare. Contrariis quibuslibet nihil obstantibus. Præsentibus perpetuis futuris temporibus valituris.

Datum Romæ, apud Sanctum Petrum, sub anulo Piscatoris, die XX mensis Iulii, anno MDCCCCXXXXVII, Pontificatus Nostri nono.

DE SPECIALI SANCTISSIMI MANDATO

Pro Domino Cardinali a Secretis Status

L + S      Dominicus Spada

a Brevibus Apostolicis

## 25. Letter of Msgr. Montini with which he sends to Reverend Josemaría Escrivá de Balaguer the Letter of Appointment as a Domestic Prelate of His Holiness; May 25, 1947.

RHF, D-15093.

SEGRETERIA DI STATO
DI SUA SANTITÀ

Dal Vaticano, li 25 Maggio 1947

Rev.mo Signore,

Sono molto lieto di mandarLe qui unito il Diploma con il quale è conferito il titolo di Prelato Domestico di Sua Santità al Rev.mo Sac. Giuseppe Maria Escrivá de Balaguer y Albás. E' una nuova, solenne prova della stima e della benevolenza del Santo Padre verso il Fondatore dell'"Opus Dei"; ed io sono sicuro che un tale segno di considerazione da parte del Vicario di Cristo meriterà a lui ed alla sua opera nuove, copiose benedizioni di Dio.

Per parte mia sono contento di esprimere, anche in questa occasione, le mie felicitazioni e i miei auguri più sinceri.

Con cordiale ossequio

Suo dev.mo in Christo

G.B. Montini

---

## 26. Rescript of the Sacred Congregation for Religious on the equivalence [in law] of the Priestly Society of the Holy Cross and Opus Dei to clerical institutes; August 7, 1947.

AGP, Sezione Giuridica, IV/15194

Num. 6649/47

Beatissime Pater,

Procurator Generalis Instituti Sæcularis *Opus Dei*, ad Sanctitatis Vestræ pedes humiliter provolutus, hæc quæ sequuntur exponit:

Cum ad tenorem Art. VIII Constitutionis Apostolicæ "Provida Mater Ecclesia" Instituta Sæcularia, præterquam propriis legibus, ad normam iuris pro non exemptis Congregationibus et Societatibus vitæ communis vigentis, Ordinariis locorum subiecta sint; cumque consulto in nostris Constitutionibus (n. 2), a Sacra Congregatione de Religiosis probatis, *Opus Dei* "Institutum Sæculare prævalenter clericale" definitum sit, quæ verba fusius in Decreto Laudis *Operi Dei* concesso illustrantur, pariter decernendo integrum Institutum nostrum, id est, Societatem Sacerdotalem Sanctæ Crucis et Opus Dei "iuridice clericalibus Institutis æquiparandum esse": ut melius conditio nostra iuridica Ordinariis diœcesanis innotescat, S.V. humillime quærit an speciatim cc.

618, § 2 et 512, § 2, 2°, in quibus de Religionibus clericalibus agitur, Instituto nostro applicari debeant.

Et Deus...

---

Vigore facultatum a SS.mo Domino Nostro concessarum, Sacra Congregatio Negotiis religiosorum Sodalium præposita, attente perpensis expositis, rescribendum censuit: AFFIRMATIVE.

Contrariis quibuslibet non obstantibus.

Datum Romæ, die 7 augusti 1947.

L + S                                        + Fr. L. E. Pasetto

                                             Secr

                                             C. Addivinola Ad. a Studiis.

---

## 27. Rescript of the Sacred Congregation for Religious regarding territorial jurisdiction of Opus Dei; October 25, 1948.

AGP, Sezione Giuridica, V/15609.

N. 10106/48

EX SECRETARIA

SACRÆ CONGREGATIONIS

DE RELIGIOSIS

Beatissime Pater,

Alvarus del Portillo, Procurator Generalis Instituti *Opus Dei*, ad Sanctitatis Vestræ pedes humillime provolutus, fiducialiter de mandato Præsidis Generalis Instituti nostri, expostulat gratiam qua ipse Institutum non tantum in Regiones -uti iam benigne approbatum in Constitutionibus n. 276 fuit-, sed etiam in alias circumscriptiones prout infra dividi possit:

1°. Quasi-Regiones independentes, id est, quæ directe ab Instituti Præside Generali pendent. Superiores Maiores earum æquiparantur Superioribus Maioribus Regionum, et ordinaria quidem, sed vicaria Præsidis Generalis potestate propriam quique Quasi-Regionem regunt. Præses Generalis cum suo Consilio potest eas erigere et erectas supprimere vel aliter definire, auditis eis quorum intersit. Ad munera Commissionis et Assessoratus nominat Pater (Const. 277). Ipso facto erectionis Quasi-Regiones independentes iuridicam acquirunt personalitatem (c. 531).

2°. Quasi-Regiones dependentes a Consiliario Regionali, cuius Regionis hæ novæ circumscriptiones partes sunt. Superiores maiores earum habent iurisdictionem ordinariam, sed vicariam Consiliarii Regionalis, et illis insuper gaudent facultatibus quæ a Consiliario Regionali, Patre consentiente, fuerint delegatæ, Præsidis Generalis est Quasi-Regiones dependentes erigere, mutare atque supprimere, auditis Consilio Generali et Consiliario Regionali cum propria Commissione. Ad munera Commissionis et Assessoratus Quasi-Regionalis dependentis nominat Pater, audito Consiliario Regionali una cum propria Commissione vel Assessoratu.

3°. Delegationes quæ a Præside Generali immediate pendent. Erigi possunt quoties Præses Generalis cum suo Consilio id duxerit expedire. Moderator uniuscuiusque Delegationis nominatur a Patre et ab ipso delegatam illam habet potestatem, quam Pater iuxta casus, intra limites tamen facultatum Consiliariorum Regionalium, committendam censuerit.

4°. Delegationes dependentes a Consiliario Regionali, cuius Regionis partes sunt. Earum Moderatores illis tantum gaudent facultatibus, quas ipsis Consiliarius Regionalis, cum voto deliberativo suæ Commissionis et Patre probante, delegaverit. Erigi possunt a Patre, audito Consilio Generali eisque quorum intersit. Moderatores nominantur a Consiliario Regionali, de consensu Commissionis vel Assessoratus Regionis, sed designatio a Patre confirmari debet.

Et Deus, etc.

---

Vigore facultatum a SS.mo Domino Nostro concessarum, Sacra Congregatio Negotiis Religiosorum Sodalium præposita benigne annuit pro gratia iuxta preces, contrariis quibuslibet minime obstantibus.

Datum Romæ, ex Ædibus Sacræ Congregationis de Religiosis, die 25 octobris 1948.

> \+ fr. L. E. Pasetto
>
> Secr.
>
> P. Arcadius Larraona CMF
>
> Subs.

---

## 28. Rescript of the Sacred Congregation for Religious approving additions to the 1947 Constitutions of the Priestly Society of the Holy Cross and Opus Dei; January 27, 1949.

AGP, Sezione Giuridica, V/15052.

EX SECRETARIA                                              N. I.S. 1/47
SACRÆ CONGREGATIONIS
  DE RELIGIOSIS

Beatissime Pater,

Præses Generalis Operis Dei, ad Sanctitatis Vestræ pedes humiliter provolutus, expostulat ut hæc, quæ sequuntur, Constitutionibus Instituti addere possint:

N° 18. Addatur: "... Procurator Generalis, *Sacerdos Secretarius Centralis*, Vicesecretarii,..." "Defensor, *Sacerdos Secretarius Regionalis*, Vocales..."

*N° 19 bis.* Addatur: "3) Sunt etiam Adsistentes ecclesiastici a Consiliario Regionis pro uno vel diversis Cœtibus (N. 338 bis) designati, consentiente Defensore et audita Commissione Regionis. Designatio ad sui notitiam oretenus, arrepta occasione, a Consiliario vel ab alio ipsius nutu communicabitur. Eadem ratione Ordinarius opportune de designatione facta certior fieri expedit."

3) fit 4); et 4) fit 5).

In fine 5) addatur: "Tam Sacerdotes quibus Fraternitatis Litteræ concessæ fuerunt, quam etiam Adsistentes prædicti, ad propriam interiorem vitam alendam et fovendam, illud si exoptent ac petant adiutorium ab Instituto recipere valent, quod Supernumerariis præstatur."

4) incipit: "*Omnes* hi sacerdotes ..." Et tollitur "vicissim".

*N° 249.* Addere: "Ad Præsidem ... Secretario Generali, Procuratore Generali, *Sacerdote Secretario Centrali,* et tribus..." "...Consilium ad negotia... Secretario Generali, *Sacerdote Secretario Centrali,* et tribus ..."

*N° 277.* Addere: "... Defensore, *Sacerdote Secretario Regionali, Secretario Commissionis* et tribus aliis ..."

*N° 340.* Addere: "3) Socii Supernumerarii qui, mediantibus semper legitimis Instituti Superioribus, ab Ordinariis locorum, libere ad tenorem nn. 336 bis et 342, 3°, laborem commissionemve aliquam susceperint, in his exercendis, fideliter normas ab ipsis Ordinariis eorumque mentem spiritu filialis obedientiæ sequi tenentur."

---

Vigore facultatum a SS.mo Domino Nostro concessarum, Sacra Congregatio Negotiis Religiosorum Sodalium præposita, benigne annuit pro gratia iuxta preces, servatis ceteris de iure servandis. Contrariis quibuslibet minime obstantibus.

Datum Romæ, ex Ædibus Sacræ Congregationis de Religiosis, die 27 Ianuarii, anno 1949.

> \+ fr. L. E. Pasetto
> Secr
> P. Arcadius Larraona CMF
> Subs.

---

## 29. Written petition of Msgr. Escrivá de Balaguer to Pope Pius XII requesting approval of the Statute concerning a category of members of the Institute; February 2, 1948.

RHF, EF-480202-1.

Beatissime Pater,

Sacerdos Josephus Maria Escrivá de Balaguer, Præses Generalis Societatis Sacerdotalis Sanctæ Crucis et Operis Dei, ad Sanctitatis Vestræ pedes humillime provolutus, hæc, quæ sequuntur, fidenter exponit:

Ad complendam et sub omni respectu perficiendam Societatis Sacerdotalis Sanctæ Crucis et Operis Dei ordinationem atque constitutionem, valde opportunum immo fere necessarium visum fuit breve redigere Statutum, quo nostri Instituti altera membrorum categoria, de qua iam a prima ipsius Instituti delineatione cogitatum fuit, apprime defineretur et in generali ac completa Operis Dei descriptione insereretur. Ideo humilis Orator expostulare audet ut Statutum prædictum, experimenti causa, approbetur et ipsius præscripta ad correlatos Constitutionum Articulos apponi valeant.

Et Deus, etc.

Josemaría Escrivá de B.

Romæ, die altera mensis Februarii, Purificationi Beatæ<br>Mariæ Virginis sacra, an. 1948.

---

## 30. Rescript of the Sacred Congregation for Religious with some clarifications regarding the supernumerary members; September 8, 1949.

AGP, Sezione Giuridica, V/15032.

EX SECRETARIA                              N. 6592/49
SACRÆ CONGREGATIONIS
    DE RELIGIOSIS

Beatissime Pater,

Sac. Ioseph Maria Escrivá de Balaguer, Præses Generalis Instituti *Opus Dei*, ad S.V. pedes humiliter provolutus, ut vita perfecte Deo et animabus in Instituto consecrata membris sic dictis Supernumerariis plenius atque strictius extendi et applicari valeat, facultatem exposcit novam introducendi in Instituti constitutionem ac compaginem prædictorum membrorum figuram quæ satis utilis atque efficax futura prævidetur. Ipsa postquam opportuno tempore convenienter probata ac limata videbitur in Constitutionem corpus ex benigna S. V. concessione recipi valebit. Hæc nova Supernumerariorum membrorum figura his brevibus tractibus definiri clare potest:

1°. Inter membra Supernumeraria nova admittenda videtur figura seu classis, quæ nomine *Supernumeraria Interna* ab aliis discernitur.

2°. Supernumerarii Interni, illi, Superioris iudicio, viri ac mulieres in respectivis Sectionibus reddi possunt qui licet non omnia requisita forsan habeant quæ pro membris stricte dictis in Instituti Constitutionibus exiguntur, tamen cum cœlibes vel ab omni vinculo liberi vel soluti sint, vitam integram Deo et animabus ad instar Numerariorum plene consecrare solide ac fortiter volunt.

3°. Supernumerarii Interni omnia officia Numerariorum suscipiunt, et ipsorum identicis mediis asceticis ad assequendam perfectionem uti debent.

4°. Ad Admissionem recipit Consiliarius, prout fit ad complendam Admissionem Numerariorum: itemque, ad Oblationem et Fidelitatem accipit socios Supernumerarios Internos Consiliarius, servatis normis n. 325, 1°.

5°. Oblatio et Fidelitas secumferunt pro Supernumerariis Internis ea ipsa et omnia officia et obligationes quæ pro Numerariis: et vinculum quo illa membra cum Instituto ligantur est pariter mutuum ac plenum. Proinde, cum omnia requisita consecrationis vitæ pro membris stricto sensu Institutorum Sæcularium in Const. "Provida Mater Ecclesia" recensita habeant, Supernumerarii Interni in statu completo perfectionis adquirendæ de facto sunt, licet in Instituto a membris strictiore sensu ad normam n. 1 Constitutionum sumptis apte sint distinguendi.

6°. Vivere possunt privatim, ab aliis membris Instituti seiuncti, quod in genere opportunius videtur: sed etiam de iudicio Consiliarii una cum Defensore vel Sacerdote Secretario, vitam familiæ in Instituto ducere valent, in Centris aut domibus propriis, in quibus ordinarie labores apostolatus evolvuntur apud gentes propriæ classis socialis.

7°. Munera regiminis in Instituto non habent: sed Consiliarius Regionalis, una cum Defensore vel Sacerdote Secretario, inter ipsos seligere potest sic dictos Consultores, quo melius labores apostolicos in proprio uniuscuiusque Consultoris cœtu sociali evolvantur.

8°. Quoad fieri possit et in servitium Sanctæ Ecclesiæ, moderare conantur activitates -tum officiales cum privatas- sociales, professionales, œconomicas, etc., illorum qui propriæ classi et condicioni sociali pertinent.

---

Vigore facultatum a SS.mo Domino Nostro concessarum, Sacra Congregatio Negotiis religiosorum Sodalium præposita benigne annuit pro gratia iuxta preces, contrariis quibuslibet minime obstantibus.

Datum Romæ, ex Ædibus Sacræ Congregationis, die 8 Septembris 1949.

P. Arcadius Larraona

Subs.

Ph. Schioppa, Ad. a Studiis.

## 31. Decree Primum inter of definitive approval of Opus Dei and of its Constitutions, as a secular institute of pontifical right; June 16, 1950.

AGP, Sezione Giuridica, V/15097.

SEGRETERIA DELLA
SACRA CONGREGAZIONE                          Num. Prot. I. S. 1-47.
DEI RELIGIOSI

## DECRETUM

Primum inter Instituta sæcularia quod promulgata Constitutione Apostolica "Provida Mater Ecclesia", ad ipsius Apostolicæ Constitutionis normam, Laudis Decretum promeruit, indeque iuris pontificii evasit, fuit Institutum quod *Opus Dei* audit. Ipsum, Matriti anno MDCCCCXXVIII a Rev.mo Patre Domino Iosepho Maria Escrivá de Balaguer conditum, die XIX martii an. MDCCCCXXXXI ab Episcopo Matritensi ad formam Piæ Unionis redactum fuit. Postea, ita florens apparuit tum alumnorum copia, tum uberibus fructibus ubicumque collectis, ut, Sancta Sede ad normam iuris consulta (can. 492, § 1), veniaque pontificia die XI octobris an. MDCCCCXXXXIII obtenta, ipse Exc.mus Episcopus Matritensis præfatum Institutum in Societatem vitæ communis sine votis publicis, die VIII decembris eiusdem anni, canonice erexit.

Ex Laudis Decreti concessione, atque ex pontificia Constitutionum approbatione, hisce decurrentibus annis novus mirabilis expansionis impetus Instituto obvenit. Atque in primis numerus sodalium, qui Deo et animabus in Instituto plene consecrantur, ita, Dei benignitate, multiplicatus fuit, ut parvum granum sinapis in dominico agro seminatum, quasi in magnam arborem mirum in modum creverit. His viris ac mulieribus omnino Deo et Ecclesiæ consecratis addi debent non pauci qui diversis regionibus Instituto ut membra Supernumeraria addicta fuerunt, quæ strenue prœlia Domini totis viribus prœliantur. Quoad expansionem territorialem, iam plus quam centum Instituti *Opus Dei* sedes numerantur in pluribus Europæ nationibus, in Americis Septentrionali, Centrali et Meridionali, atque in Africa diffusæ.

Huic singulari diffusioni ac multiplicationi, impulsio, intentio atque efficacia ministeriorum *Operis Dei* adæquate respondent. Quibus permotus, ut necessitati atque utilitati consuleret, Rev.mus Pater Dominus Fundator preces ad SS.mum Dominum Nostrum Pium, Divina Providentia Papam XII, una cum suo Consilio Generali, supplices dedit ut, ceteris dilationibus omissis, statim Decretum definitivæ approbationis Instituti ac Constitutionum *Operi Dei* concederetur. Ad rem plenius declarandam obtulit insuper *Operis Dei* solidam atque in iure fundatam illustrationem: et pari tempore, centum ac decem Præsules, inter quos duodecim Em.mi Patres Cardinales -ex ipsis, quatuor e Curia Romana- ac sex et viginti Exc.mi Archiepiscopi, proprias Litteras Commendaticias, laudibus plenas, ad Sanctam Sedem miserunt ut SS.mus Dominus gratiam a laudato Instituto expostulatam benigne elargiri dignaretur.

Omnibus collectis paratisque documentis ad concessionem Decreti approbationis definitivæ spectantibus, ceterisque necessariis ex praxi stiloque Curiæ, res, in Commissione Consultorum semel iterumque discussa atque ad trutinam revocata, cum Consultores omnes expostulatæ concessioni favissent, ad Congressum plenum die I aprilis labentis anni Maximi Iubilæi, MDCCCCL, relata fuit.

Congressus plenus, precibus meritissimi Conditoris *Operis Dei* aures præbens, concessionem approbationis definitivæ decrevit. Ipse Congressus, præside Em.mo Sacræ Congregationis Cardinali Præfecto, voluit etiam, relate ad Constitutiones, ut quæ Institutorum novitate difficultatem quamdam offerre viderentur, audito Rev.mo Patre Domino Fundatore *Operis Dei*, ex allatis ab ipso declarationibus ac commentariis, a Commissione Consultorum dilucidarentur.

Post satis longum rerum omnium examen, quæ ratione novitatis peculiarem difficultatem præ se ferebant, Constitutiones accurate in singulis fixæ ac definitæ fuerunt. Præcipua quæ ad Instituti ordinationem, compaginem rationemque pertinent, ne dubium quodlibet in posterum remaneat, hic breviter expresse recensere visum est:

## I. NATURA ET RATIO INSTITUTI OPUS DEI.

*Opus Dei* est Institutum sæculare ad normam Const. Ap. "Provida Mater Ecclesia", cuius membra ad perfectionem evangelicam completam in sæculo adipiscendam et exercendam efficaciter tendunt et se tota apostolatui dedicant ("Provida Mater Ecclesia", Art. I). Hæc plena totius vitæ ad perfectionem atque apostolatum in sæculo consecratio, practice et efficaciter obtineri debet: per consilia evangelica votis socialibus, seu privatis recognitis, temporariis prius, perpetuis postea firmata; per virtutum moralium et christianarum exercitium, et speciatim per laboris quotidiani ordinarii et professionalis sanctificationem; et, denique, per observantiam piorum officiorum, quæ ad vota sustinenda, fovenda et exequenda necessaria moraliter sunt.

Finis Instituti *Opus Dei* aspectus genericus est Dei gloria ex filiali dilectione omni studio per Christum Dominum, cum Ipso et in Ipso, quærenda, atque sanctificatio sodalium in sæculo peragenda. Aspectus vero peculiaris, arcte atque intrinsece cum sanctificatione atque spiritu Instituti perpetuo coniunctus (Ioann. XVII, 19) est totis viribus adlaborare ut classis quæ dicitur intellectualis, quæque, vel ob doctrinam, qua pollet, vel ob munera, quæ exercet, vel ob dignitatem, qua insignitur, est moderatrix societatis civilis, Christi Domini præceptis adhæreat, ipsaque in praxim deducat: et etiam inter omnes classes civilis societatis vitam perfectionis in sæculo fovere et diffundere, atque viros ac mulieres informare ad apostolatum in sæculo exercendum.

Etsi *Opus Dei*, ex ordinaria membrorum suorum condicione Institutum laicale videtur (cc. 488, 4°; 673, § 2; Const. "Provida Mater Ecclesia", Art. I) tamen, intra ipsum, *Societas Sacerdotalis Sanctæ Crucis* quoad illa, quæ ipsam ipsorumque membra directo tangunt, Instituti clericalis figuram induit. Immo, eo quod *Societas Sacerdotalis Sanctæ Crucis* totum *Opus Dei* penitus informat et penetrat, non quidem singulis membris laicis officia, iura et privilegia clericalia applicantur: sed totum Instituti *Opus Dei* corpus, ad normam Constitutionum præscriptorumque Sanctæ Sedis, Institutis clericalibus iuridice æquiparatur.

## II. INSTITUTI ORDINATIO.

*Opus Dei* duplici veluti corpore constat, virorum scilicet et mulierum, sub unico Superiore seu Præside Generali, quem Patrem appellant.

Utrumque ex his duobus corporibus utitur propria, ideoque prorsus seiuncta hierarchia, in singulis regiminis gradibus. Inter se tamen binæ huiusmodi Instituti partes communi spiritu ascetico et apostolico, generalibus præscriptis in quibus hic communis spiritus definitur, atque efficaci virium et laborum coordinatione, arcte coniunguntur ad apostolatum unum, compactum, magisque intensum atque completum, sub unica suprema auctoritate, reddendum.

In Sectione virorum, classis sacerdotalis subnotanda est. Ob integram demissamque venerationem qua sodales omnes Sacerdotium prosequuntur, hæc sacerdotalis condicio, quamvis classis diversa iuridice in Instituto *Opus Dei* consideranda non sit, cardinale momentum in Instituto habet, præcipuas ex regula in ipso directionis functiones exercet, et merito quasi eiusdem animam constituere censetur.

Condicio tamen sacerdotalis in Instituto peculiarem categoriam atque sociale corpus constituit (Const., n. 1), quod proprio etiam nomine insignitur, scilicet: *Societas Sacerdotalis Sanctæ Crucis*. Et ex laudato erga Sacerdotium venerationis sensu, qui omnia in *Opus Dei* vivificat, communi titulo *Opus Dei* præmittitur huius Societatis Sacerdotalis denominatio, ita ut recognitus Instituti titulus completus sit: *Societas Sacerdotalis Sanctæ Crucis et Opus Dei*.

Ceterum, omnes omnino Instituti sodales eodem spiritu ascetico et apostolico vere sacerdotali informantur (I Petr. II, 5, 9), omnes in unum consummari contendunt (Ioan. XVII, 23), adeo ut condicio laicalis solidis et authenticis virtutibus sacerdotalibus informetur, sanctitatem sacerdotalem penitus colat et quodammodo veluti gradus ad Sacerdotium habeatur. Omnes igitur sodales laici Numerarii vere parati ad ipsum inveniuntur, si, sacerdotalis vocationis signis in eis legitime repertis, ad altare a Præside Generali invitentur.

In Sectione virorum, illi præ primis recensendi sunt qui ipsius membra proprio strictoque sensu dicuntur, et *Numerarii* audiunt. Ipsi, superatis omnibus præscriptis probationibus riteque emerso formationis tempore, votis socialibus Instituto incorporantur. Numerariis *Oblati* proxime accedunt. Hi, ob peculiarem suam vocationem, aut quia diversis rationibus præpediuntur quominus Numerarii evadere valeant, in hac altera categoria sodalium manent, quin proinde omnibus Numerariorum iuribus frui ipsorumve officiis singuli ligari possint. Oblati tamen omnia habent quæ in Constitutione Apostolica "Provida Mater Ecclesia" ad completam perfectionis professionem exiguntur (Art. III). Præterea, etsi vitam familiæ in Instituto ex regula non agunt, votis tamen socialibus *Operi Dei* incorporantur; et fere omnibus Constitutionum et Statutorum pro Numerariis præscriptis subiiciuntur. Oblatos sequuntur *Supernumerarii*, qui consiliorum evangelicorum in proprio statu professione, atque spiritus et apostolatus Instituti participatione, ipsi associantur.

In Sectione autem mulierum *Operis Dei* distinguendæ præ primis sunt sodales *Numerariæ*. Hæ, pari ratione ac Numerarii, votis socialibus temporariis prius et postea perpetuis, rite superatis probationibus, Instituto ligantur. Omnes vitam familiæ in *Opere Dei* ex regula ducunt, et omnibus singulisque præscriptis Constitutionum subiiciuntur. Inter Numerarias, ratione præcipue ministeriorum quibus ipsæ in Instituto occupantur, duplex sectio distinguitur, scilicet: illarum quæ simpliciter Numerariæ audiunt, et earum quæ Numerariæ *Inservientes* nuncupantur. Utraque hæc sectio in unum revera fusa et consummata prorsus est. Inservientes, ad exemplum Domini, qui ministrare venit et non ministrari (Math. XX, 28), et Beatæ Virginis Mariæ, Ancillæ Domini (Luc. I, 38), vera humilitate et charitate actæ, manualia domestica ministeria, quæ Marthæ dicuntur, interiore autem Mariæ spiritu animatæ, exercent, ipsisque speciatim destinantur: Superiorum tamen iudicio, participare poterunt labores alterius categoriæ, in apostolatus subsidium. Etiam in mulierum Sectione *Oblatæ* et *Supernumerariæ* admittuntur, eadem ratione ac Oblati et Supernumerarii in Sectione virorum.

Desiderio acta professionem authenticæ et completæ perfectionis inter sacerdotes diœcesanos excitandi, fovendi dirigendique, *Societas Sacerdotalis Sanctæ Crucis* sibi sacerdotes ut Oblatos et Supernumerarios adscribit, prout plene vel minus plene pro singulorum vocatione perfectionem in Societate ipsa profitentur, quin eorum diœcesana condicio plenaque Ordinariis subiectio quoquo modo ex hac consecratione afficiatur. Spiritus quo hi sacerdotes informantur, ita exprimi potest: "nihil sine Episcopo", quod pari prorsus modo complecti debet tam eorum Domino in Societate consecrationem, quam omnem ipsorum vitam sacerdotalem. Finis vero peculiaris horum sodalium est vitam perfectionis atque sensum plenæ Ordinariis deditionis impense in clero diœcesano promovere; et inter sacerdotes cleri diœcesani vitam communem fovere, prout Ordinario loci expedire videatur.

## III. APOSTOLATUS SODALIUM INSTITUTI RATIO ATQUE OPERA.

Instituti sodales, speciali Dei vocatione, *in sæculo* vivunt: et, sub communibus vestibus vivendique rationibus, veluti *ex sæculo* ipso apostolatum exercent. Ut id præstare valeant, externe in omnibus, quæ sæcularibus sunt communia et a statu perfectionis non aliena, ut alii cives propriæ condicionis ac professionis se gerunt, vestiunt vitamque ducunt.

Præterea, in omnibus quæ propriam sæcularem professionem ac condicionem tangunt quæque ad ipsam quoquo modo sese referunt, ut alii cives negotiantur, quin tamen ulla ratione Ecclesiam vel Institutum ad respondendum iuridice vel moraliter ex suis actibus negotiisve cogant. Omnes civiles honestas professiones maxima sollertia exercent: et quamvis profanæ sint, socii, sæpius renovata intentione, fervido interioris vitæ cultu, continua atque hilari sui abnegatione, pænitentia duri tenacisque laboris qui sub omni respectu perfectus evadat, eas sanctificare iugiter satagunt.

Leges civiles reverentur atque officia civium singula fideliter ex conscientia observare nituntur, quin ullis iustis legibus seu officiis, specioso quolibet prætextu, se subtrahere velint. Pari modo, omnia civilia politica iura, nullo imprudenter excepto, sibi vindicare debent atque ad bonum publicum tenaci animo exercere tenentur. *Opus Dei* nullam peculiarem politicam opinionem suis sodalibus imponit. Ab omnibus tamen prorsus sinceram ex conscientia Statui fidelitatem, atque ipsi in omnibus, quæ licita sunt, obedientiam exigit.

Quo melius ut sæculares atque ex sæculo apostolatum exerceant, *Operis Dei* sodales potius singillatim quam collegialiter agunt et operantur. Omnes et singuli, quin ullus ex alterius labore excusari possit, sive exemplo, quo semper et ubique inter cives, inter collegas, inter laboris socios, domi, in via, in officio, optimos sese exhibere conantur; sive actione personali; sive relationibus mentis animique contactibus omne genus, quibus fermentum in massa, sal in cibis, lux in tenebris (Math. XIII, 33; V, 13; V, 14, 16) apparent, Ecclesiæ regnique cælestis actuosi ac indefessi operarii sunt.

Formas collectivas apostolatus sodales non dedignantur, sed actionis externæ -præcipue religiosæ- formas seu associationes specificas, ex quibus Institutum publice subnotaretur, devitant. Utuntur potius, ut peculiari suæ missioni respondentibus, associationibus communibus et civilibus, ex. g. litterariis, œconomicis, industrialibus, viribus exercendis, aliisque similibus. In omnibus tamen salus animarum lex suprema esse debet, prout, Superiorum iudicio, locorum temporumque adiuncta exigere videantur.

Opera singula apprime respondent descriptæ rationi apostolatus, qui ita apparere iugiter debet, scilicet: profunde humanus, amabilis, apertus atque sincerus, etsi discretione tactuque plenus.

**In particulari, apostolatum omnes, viri præcipue, exercent:**

1.- Per elevationem humanam, socialem, thecnicam et per sanctificationem laboris professionalis, ipsum ad maiorem ædificationem maiusque semper animarum bonum convertendo, eorum præsertim qui eiusdem professionis socii sunt, illorumque etiam qui cum ipsis vel sub ipsis sodalibus laborant. Omnibus, cum quibus professionis causa vel occasione quamlibet relationem habent, sese exhibere nitantur ut vivum, practicum, constans, completum christianæ fidelitatis exemplum, cuius vexilliferi esse in sæculo revera gloriari possunt. Speciali ratione, hunc constantem plenumque apostolatum exempli attractionisque, ut veram actionem socialem exercere debent cum operariis, quos in industriis ac professionibus adiutores, collaboratores operisque socios sub se habent;

2.- Per exemplarem perfectamque munerum civilium ac politicorum omnis gradus adimpletionem, quæ publicæ legitimæ Auctoritates ipsis commiserint, vel ad quæ concivium fiducia eos vocaverit;

3.- Per assiduam et consciam collaborationem ad solidam educationem religiosam, scientificam et professionalem iuvenum, qui studiis incumbunt, præcipue in Universitatibus et Scholis Superioribus. *Opus Dei* ordinarie collegia propria privataque, in quibus sodales collective instructionem impertiantur, ut specificam suam peculiarem apostolatus rationem non respicit. Præfert, quantum potest, suam in Scholis publicis anonymam collaborationem præstare. Tamen, ubi temporum et locorum adiuncta aliud ad bonum maius animarum suadere videantur, absque difficultate quamlibet Universitatum, Collegiorum vel Academiarum formam instituere valet. Illa actio et collaboratio omnes integralis et harmonicæ educationis aspectus complectitur, nullo parvipenso vel minoris habito. Cooperantur, nempe: a) ad educationem intellectualem et professionalem, sive docendo in Universitatibus, Scholis Superioribus, etc. -dum possibile sit, publicis-; sive assistendo labori intellectuali, exercitationibus thecnicis, præparationibus scholasticis iuvenum; sive ipsos denique in Scholis applicationis, aut singillatim, ad exercitium professionum instruendo ac præparando; b) ad educationem moralem et religiosam in Collegiis ac Residentiis Universitariis, quorum regimen suscipiunt; c) ad educationem denique socialem, artisticam, physicam, etc., per societates iuvenum omne genus ad peculiares fines ordinatas;

4.- Per ministeria diffusionis ac propagationis veritatis solidæque christianæ culturæ. Omnibus, etiam modernioribus et modernissimis rationibus emissionis ac reproductionis oralis et scriptæ verbi imaginisque, ad

Ecclesiæ defensionem animarumque utilitatem promovendam *Opus Dei* uti potest ac debet;

5.- Per investigationem scientificam; per assiduam publicationem librorum, elucubrationum, opusculorum studiorumque in Ephemeridibus et Collectionibus technicis, artisticis, scientificis, etc.; per collaborationem in Congressibus scientificis; per fraternum adiutorium catholicis scriptoribus præstitum, perque alia auxilia, quæ alacrem scientiæ apostolatum constituunt;

6.- Inter peculiaria *Operis Dei* ministeria, hoc recenseri speciatim debet, quod iure meritoque Instituto carissimum est, scilicet: apostolatus ad fidem, vitam christianam, immo et piam, illos omnes trahendi et adducendi qui "ignorant et errant", vel qui a domo paterna diversimode prodigi longe absunt, aut passionibus seu præiudiciis hostes Ecclesiæ sese exhibent: præterquam aliis apostolatus rationibus, etiam ipsorum collaborationem sive professionalem sive œconomicam sive socialem prudenter quærendo ad illa Instituti opera, quæ omnibus patere possunt. Hac mente et hoc fine cooperatio petitur et ordinatur ut, ex ipsa, illi Dei gratiam ac misericordiam consequantur et ad fidem christianosque mores suaviter sed efficaciter trahantur;

7.- Denique per serenam, hilarem, perfectam omnium exsecutionem quæ ipsis Superiores ubique terrarum committere censeant, prompti semper ac parati ad illas petendas regiones, in quibus Ecclesia persecutionem patiatur vel quomodolibet ipsorum ministeria vel operam materne invocet.

Semper et ubique sodalis *Operis Dei* Christi Domini pacem ac plenam securamque in Domino lætitiam secum fert, omnibusque hominibus bonæ voluntatis amice offert; quinimmo omnes prorsus ea pace ac lætitia contagiare nititur, atque singulos ad hæc tam suavia Divinæ Bonitatis dona acceptanda atque gustanda suaviter compellit.

**Opera apostolatus Sectionis mulierum:**

Mulieres omnes ac singulæ non solum specificum apostolatum exercent, sed præterea communi apostolatui Instituti, rationibus et modis quæ donis naturæ et gratiæ ipsis a Domino largitis adæquate respondent, cooperari debent. Præter collaborationem igitur in operibus apostolatus supra descriptis -congrue tamen ac prudenter omnia ad peculiarem earum condicionem atque actionem accomodando- apostolatus mulierum Instituti hæc opera insuper, ut sibi specialiter propria, vindicat:

1.- Regunt atque administrant spiritualium exercitiorum domos;

2.- Catholicæ veritatis ac veræ solidæque culturæ diffusioni scriptæ ac pictæ per editrices domos, per officinas librarias et ope bibliothecarum, etc., incumbunt: orali vero per cursus, instructiones aliaque id genus;

3.- Alias mulieres ad diversas apostolatus formas accuratissime præparant, ope scholis, cursibus et exercitationibus;

4.- Omnibus mediis quæ apta videantur modestiam christianam mulierum indefesse fovent, defendunt, vindicant;

5.- Eadem ratione ac supra dictum est, Residentias instituunt et regunt pro puellis et iuvenibus quæ studiis vacant, earumque educationem sub omni respectu promovent;

6.- Scholas agricolas aperiunt ad christiane, socialiter et moraliter colonas instituendas, ubi in omnibus, quæ ad officia industriasque spectant et mulieribus huius condicionis utilia sunt, eas apte instruunt; pariterque domos ad ancillas servitio domestico præparandas erigere curant;

7.- Denique familiarem administrationem atque domesticam œconomiam omnium domorum Instituti gerunt, e loco tamen penitus separato, ita ut ex canonica unius domus erectione, duæ separatæ domus iure exsurgant in unoquoque *Operis Dei* domicilio.

## IV. SPIRITUS INSTITUTI OPUS DEI.

Instituti aspectus duplex, asceticus et apostolicus, ita sibi adæquate respondet, ac cum charactere sæculari *Operis Dei* intrinsece et harmonice fusus ac compenetratus est, ut solidam ac simplicem vitæ unitatem necessario secum ferre ac inducere semper videatur. Huic forti vitæ unitati, respondet spontanea magnanimitas, perpetuo renovata, in omnibus patens, omnibusque manifesta. Ex ipsa, ut *Operis Dei* sodalis, speciali vocatione signatus, Christi Iesu fidelis miles in sæculo evadat (II Tim. II, 3), debet se totum et omnia sua in holocaustum offerre: "in simplicitate cordis mei lætus obtuli universa" (I Par. XXIX, 17).

Fundamentum solidum quo omnia in *Opere Dei* constant, radixque fœcunda singula vivificans est sensus humilis ac sincerus filiationis divinæ in Christo Iesu. Donum pietatis ad omnia utile (I Tim. IV, 8), ex quo dulciter creditur charitati paternæ quam habet Deus in nobis (I Io. IV, 16), ex quo Christus Dominus, Deus homo, ut frater primogenitus ineffabili sua bonitate sentitur, omnes sodales fraterna veraque pietate adstringit. Sensus gustatus paternitatis divinæ, adoptivæ filiationis ac fraternitatis in Christo, naturales veluti fructus in *Opere Dei* producit: amorem orationis et spiritum precum (Zac. XII, 10), ardorem et sitim interioris vitæ, fiduciam filialem in paterna Dei Providentia atque deditionem serenam et iucundam divinæ Voluntati.

Pietas *Operis Dei* simplex, sobria et virilis est in omnibus: deinde doctrinalis, perfecte assimilata ac renovata ex perpetuo et practico religionis studio; delectatur S. Liturgia, ipsamque et suaviter gustat et amice componit cum solidis formis, quæ eam applicant vel complent, atque cum exercitiis personalibus meditationis ac contemplationis, examinum, mortificationum aliorumque similium.

Ex plena magnanimitate ac profunda vitæ unificatione -Domino et Patri per Christum Dominum, cum unctione doni pietatis, totaliter consecratæ et fratribus in communionem perpetuo traditæ-, nascitur necessitas et veluti instinctus supernaturalis omnia purificandi, elevandi ad ordinem gratiæ, sanctificandi et convertendi in instrumentum apostolatus. Hinc magna cura virtutum moralium, harmonica educatio humana, digna et nobilis socialis conversatio: "omnia autem vestra sunt, vos autem Christi" (I Cor. III, 23; Phil. III, 8). Breviter nempe: spiritus *Operis Dei* est supernaturalis, sincerus ac profundus, simplex, perfecte assimilatus et veluti connaturalis effectus, qui omnia penetrat, purificat et, quin deformet, in veram substantiam sanctificationis et apostolatus transformat: "vos autem Christi", et ad exemplum Christi et cum Christo, Dei (Phil. *ihid.*).

Ut insidiæ vincantur triplicis concupiscentiæ, superbiæ vitæ speciatim, quæ ex doctrina, ex condicione sociali et ex muneribus ali posset, ascetismus sapienti firmitate plenus impense in Instituto colitur. Hic ascetismus nititur:

humilitate, quam a summo mane, fronte ad pulverem usque prona, omnes profitentur sub lemmate "serviam"; obedientia absoluta; sui abnegatione et frequentibus mortificationibus, etiam corporis. Hæc omnia scienter curantur ut media non solum purificationis, sed præterea veri et solidi progressus spiritualis, iuxta illud bene probatum ac comprobatum verbum: "tantum proficies quantum tibi ipsi vim intuleris"; curantur etiam ut authentica demonstratio et exercitatio effectivi et practici amoris Christi, qui "dilexit me et tradidit semetipsum pro me" (Gal. II, 20); et denique, ut præparatio ad omnem apostolatum eiusque perfectum exercitium: "Adimpleo ea quæ desunt passionum Christi in carne mea pro corpore suo, quod est Ecclesia" (Col. I, 24).

Renovatus sensus filiationis divinæ in Christo Iesu, necessario in *Opere Dei* vertitur et practice traducitur in ardens desiderium et sincerum studium, vere tenerum simulque profundum, imitandi Deum ut filii carissimi (Eph. V, 1) et -ad exemplum Christi, Unigeniti Patris et Primogeniti in multis fratribus, qui in omnibus via et exemplar est- plene et totaliter propriam vitam conformandi ad christianam perfectionem (Rom. VIII, 29), in sæculo quidem et in propria cuiusque professione.

Hoc ascetismi exemplar aliquibus tractibus completur: tenera devotione et deditione erga Beatissimam Virginem Mariam; pio amore erga Sanctam Matrem Ecclesiam, omniumque ad illam quoquo modo pertinentium; sincera veneratione, dilectione atque docilitate erga Summum Pontificem et ecclesiasticam ordinariam Hierarchiam; fideli ac perpetuo sensu humilitatis externæ et intrinsecæ, non tantum individualis sed etiam collectivæ; candore connaturalis simplicitatis; familiari et nobili agendi ratione; et, denique, expressione iugis serenæ lætitiæ.

## V. FORMATIONIS RATIO, GRADUS, NOTÆ AC CHARACTERES.

Attento *Operis Dei* fine, candidatorum severissima fit selectio atque, iam veluti ad ianuas, eliminatio. Non raro inter Supernumerarios provide et amice retinentur qui iudicati sunt ad plenam consecrationem non vere vocati.

Præter illa communia impedimenta, quæ Institutis sæcularibus etiam applicantur, et præter requisita generalia, ad *Opus Dei*, ex ipsius natura atque ratione apostolatus, non immerito requisita nonnulla exiguntur et aliqua imponuntur particularia impedimenta. Attenditur sane ad personæ condicionem, etiam socialem, ipsiusque qualitates et exigitur ingenium capax superioris formationis; quoad animi dotes, pro omnibus et singulis candidatis, necessarius reputatur character sincerus, rectus, sociabilis, virilis, ad actionem et apostolatum individualem exercendum idoneus et aptus. Candidati debent esse tenaces, dociles, ad profundam formationem et transformationem dispositi. Denique, pro Numerariis, studia in aliqua Universitate iam peracta vel cum fructu peragenda requiruntur.

Ut educatio possit profunde a candidatis assimilari et ulteriore formatione et transformatione novi homines verique apostoli ex ipsis creari queant, arduum opus quadam veluti præformatione incipiendum est. Nemo sane ad *Opus Dei* ut verum ipsius membrum directo admittitur. In cœtibus per quos apostolatum "operis S. Raphaëlis" sodales exercent, candidatus iuvenis probatur, educatur, præparatur. Qui vocatus præsumi potest, quia impedimentis caret, requisitis et qualitatibus ornatur et bonum de se specimen dedit, in Collegiis et Residentiis *Operis Dei*, cum studiis vacat vel ipsa complet, in contactu gradatim ponitur cum spiritu intrinseco Instituti et pedetentim in diversis apostolatus operibus exercetur. Interea candidatus lente experitur et ipsius probatio completur.

Quando iam hæc individualis probatio absoluta censeri potest, quando iuvenis culturam religiosam claram et profundam acquisivit suamque vere et practice fecit, tunc candidatus ad *Opus Dei* admittitur. Postea incipiunt formalis probationis cursus, quibus superatis, ascensio ad diversos gradus, qui sapienter in *Opere Dei* distinguuntur, fieri valet. Post primam huiusmodi formationem, candidatus sui ipsius *Oblationem* Domino et Instituto facit. In ipsa, vota socialia ad annum emittuntur et per quinque saltem solidos annos renovari debent. Ex Oblatione ad *Fidelitatem* transitus et gradus fit, quo pulchro nomine perpetua consecratio designatur.

Inter perpetuo Fidelitate incorporatos, seliguntur qui accurate ulterius probati et formati, ad munera regiminis atque educationis apti declarantur voceque, ut dicunt, passiva fruuntur et *Inscripti* nuncupantur. Voce etiam activa in supremis Instituti Congressibus, præsertim vero in electivis, ex quo *Electores* dicuntur, pauci post severam præparationem donantur.

Clericalis sacerdotum institutio omnibus modis fovetur ac severissime exigitur. Sub respectu ecclesiasticæ culturæ, non solum ab omnibus completum curriculum, ad normam iuris communis peculiarisque *Societatis Sacerdotalis Sanctæ Crucis*, ad unguem requiritur, sed præterea una saltem doctoralis ecclesiastica laurea, in Athæneis Romanis ex regula consequenda, ab omnibus et singulis expostulatur. Ecclesiastica vero spiritualis formatio accuratissime in cursibus Collegiisque ad hoc destinatis et ordinatis præbetur ac impertitur.

## VI. REGIMEN INSTITUTI.

Duæ hierarchiæ internæ pro viris et mulieribus diversæ, in omnibus gradibus regiminis distinguuntur. Ipsæque in Patre eiusque delegatis ac, in unaquaque Regione, in Consiliario uniuntur: atque ab ipsis tantum sive Institutum sive singulæ eius Regiones legitime repræsentatur. Consiliarius tamen, quoad mulierum Sectionem, vice et nomine Patris agit.

Hierarchia tribus gradibus constat: generali, regionali et locali, in quibus interna munera atque officia sociis Numerariis semper reservantur.

Supremus Moderator seu Præses Generalis Instituti ad vitam eligitur et plena potestate fruitur. *Operis Dei* ratio atque intima ipsius ad modum familiæ constitutio; membrorum Numerariorum condicio quæ, cum omnes intellectuales sint talis evadit ut auctoritas, si discutiatur, periclitetur; denique natura et character apostolatus sodalium, suadere visa sunt ut Pater omnia in manibus habeat, ita ut Congressus, Consilia ac munera ipsum adiuvare debeant, atque non nisi in casibus gravioribus, ad normam iuris et Constitutionum, votum deliberativum in regimine præcipue generali admittatur. Rationes quibus hæc absoluta auctoritatis ratio vindicabatur severe ad trutinam non semel revocatæ sunt: et post diligens earum examen in Commissionibus Consultorum prius, et postea in Congressibus plenis, a S. Congregatione probatæ et, præcipue quoad graviora, etiam SS.mo Domino Nostro Papæ subiectæ sunt.

Corpora moralia, quibus Patris electio aliorumque generalium munerum utriusque Sectionis Instituti provisio reservantur, sunt *Congressus Electorum* et *Congressus Electricum*. Præter facultates electivas, ipsis, in unaquaque Sectione competit participatio quædam in supremo regimine, ad normam Constitutionum. Congressus ordinarius singulis quinquenniis convocatur, ut de Instituti statu iudicium proferat et futuræ actioni regiminis opportunas normas suadere valeat. Convocari insuper Congressus Sectionis virorum debet quando Patris officium vacat: et etiam convocandus extra ordinem est, cum rerum adiuncta quoquo modo ad normam Constitutionum id postulent.

Inter Congregationes, quæ in regiminis ordinatione notatu dignæ sunt, recenseri debent *Hebdomadæ Laboris*, generales et regionales. Ipsæ ad internæ experientiæ lectiones diligenter colligendas, et ad progressum ordinate promovendum in methodis et instrumentis ad apostolatum adhibendis dedicantur, in utraque *Operis Dei* Sectione. Ad Hebdomadas Laboris sodales omnes Instituti seu Regionis Fidelitate *Operi Dei* perpetuo incorporati collaborare valent, etsi non omnes ipsis adsistere queunt.

Cum iam ergo omnia ad Institutum et Constitutiones *Operis Dei Societatisque Sacerdotalis Sanctæ Crucis* spectantia accurate perpensa sub omni versu haberi valeant, et clare solideque constent, Hæc Sacra Congregatio Negotiis Religiosorum Sodalium præposita, vigore specialium facultatum a SS.mo Domino Nostro Pio, Divina Providentia Papa XII, occasione Anni Maximi Iubilæi concessarum, Ipsiusque nomine et auctoritate, quæ sequuntur statuere decrevit:

1.um.—Institutum *Societas Sacerdotalis Sanctæ Crucis et Opus Dei* ut Institutum sæculare, ad normam Constitutionis Apostolicæ "Provida Mater Ecclesia", definitive approbatur et confirmatur;

2.um.—Constitutiones Instituti sæcularis *Societas Sacerdotalis Sanctæ Crucis et Opus Dei*, prout in hoc textu adsunt cuius autographum in Archivo Sacræ Congregationis conservatur, definitive approbantur.

Contrariis quibuslibet minime obstantibus.

Datum Romæ, ex Ædibus Sacræ Congregationis de Religiosis, die XVI iunii an. Maximi Iubilæi MDCCCCL, Sanctissimo Divinoque Cordi Iesu sacra.

L + S

+ Al. Card. Lavitrano

Præf.

+ fr. L. E. Pasetto

Secr.

## 32. Chapter One of the 1950 Constitutions of the Priestly Society of the Holy Cross and Opus Dei.

AGP, Sezione Giuridica, V/15034.

## CONSTITUTIONES SOCIETATIS SACERDOTALIS SANCTÆ CRUCIS ET OPERIS DEI

### CAPUT I

**De Instituti ratione et fine**

1. Institutum, cui titulus Societas Sacerdotalis Sanctæ Crucis et Opus Dei, breviatum autem nomine Opus Dei, est Institutum sæculare perfectioni christianæ in sæculo adquirendæ et apostolatui exercendo dicatum. Denominatio Operis Dei pertinet ad universum Institutum: in eo tamen est quædam coadunatio sociorum, cui nomen Societas Sacerdotalis Sanctæ Crucis, constans Instituti sacerdotibus nonnullisque laicis, qui Patris iudicio specialiter magis dispositi æstimantur ad sacerdotium aliquando suscipiendum.

2. Societas Sacerdotalis Sanctæ Crucis proprio spiritu universum Opus Dei vivificat atque ita informat, ut ipsum clericale eo sensu reddat quod præcipua regiminis munera plerumque sacerdotibus reserventur; sacerdotum categoria ut verum clericale Institutum, quoad illa omnia quæ vitam clericalem respiciunt, habeatur; totumque demum Operis Dei corpus veris Institutis clericalibus, ad normam tantum harum Constitutionum et iuxta Sanctæ Sedis specialia præscripta vel indulta, quæ Instituto concessa fuerunt vel in posterum forsitan concedantur, æquiparetur, quin ea de causa socii laici iuribus et privilegiis clericorum, ut singuli, gaudeant, neque umquam clericalibus officiis subiiciantur.

3. § 1. Aspectus genericus finis Instituti est sanctificatio sodalium per consiliorum Evangelii exercitium harumque Constitutionum observantiam.

   § 2. Specificus autem est totis viribus adlaborare ut classis quæ dicitur intellectualis, quæque, vel ob doctrinam, qua pollet, vel ob munera, qua exercet, vel ob dignitatem, qua insignitur, est moderatrix societatis civilis, Christi Domini præceptis adhæreat, ipsaque in praxim deducat: et inter omnes classes civilis societatis vitam perfectionis in sæculo fovere et diffundere, atque viros ac mulieres informare ad apostolatum in sæculo exercendum.

4. § 1. Hic finis obtinetur per sanctificationem laboris ordinarii et per exercitium muneris professionalis vel alterius æquipollentis, quod consociati eo non deserunt, quia per ipsum sanctificationem persequuntur.

   § 2. Propterea, Institutum exigit a propriis alumnis exquisitam animi culturam, tum in pietatis officiis tum in disciplinis sive ecclesiasticis sive profanis; fovet in illis perfectam adimpletionem munerum professionalium et socialium etiam publicæ administrationis, quibus perfectio proprii status est prosequenda; promovet ac dirigit institutiones et opera, quæ ad mentem excolendam animumque perficiendum spectant, uti domus seu residentias pro scholasticis, domus spiritualium exercitiorum et alia id genus.

§ 3. Media igitur, quæ membra Operis Dei præferunt, et quibus potiore ratione uti debent, sunt: vita orationis et sacrificii iuxta spiritum Instituti, et quam maxima fidelitas in adimpletione actionis seu professionis socialis cuiusque propriæ.

5. Sodales Instituti evangelicam perfectionem profitentur, quin tamen religiosa vota emittant, aut aliquid externum signum in personis vel domibus præ se ferant quod religiosam familiam demonstret. Clerici vestem clericalem communem loci, ubi commorantur, laici autem vestes apud classes eiusdem vel similis professionis vel socialis condicionis usitatas, deferunt.

6. Opus Dei profitetur humilitatem collectivam, quapropter nequit edere folia et cuiusque generis publicationes nomine Operis, nisi interne ad usum sodalium; eius membra nullum signum distinctivum deferunt; caute loquuntur de Opere Dei cum extraneis, nam actio modesta esse debet et non apparens; ad nullum actum socialem Opus Dei, ut plurimum, intervenit vel in eo repræsentatur.

7. Opus Dei non habet generatim specificam formam collectivæ actionis externæ. Præprimis curare sodalium formationem spiritualem et apostolicam debet. Apostolatum autem peragunt sodales per exercitium munerum et publicorum officiorum, vel per associationes legitime constitutas, prout adiuncta temporum vel locorum postulare videantur, ac summam habent reverentiam etiam pro legitimis societatis civilis legibus.

8. Socii Operis Dei suam impendunt actionem in tria opera, quæ singula sub Patronis sunt constituta, scilicet habetur:

1°. Opus S. Raphaèlis et S. Ioannis, ad excolendos iuvenes: hic labor Operis Dei propriissimus est, et veluti Instituti seminarium;

2°. Opus S. Gabrielis et S. Pauli, ad socios Supernumerarios instituendos atque eorum observantiam fovendam, confirmandam et in dies profundiorem reddendam: necnon, ope ipsorum sodalium Supernumerariorum, ad diversas civilis societatis classes criterio catholico professionali et sociali imbuendas;

3°. Opus S. Michaèlis et S. Petri, ad Numerariorum et Oblatorum formationem promovendam, et ad quærendam opportuniorem solutionem quæstionibus scholasticis, socialibus, professionalibus, etc. boni animarum gratia.

9. Socii Operis Dei operantur sive singillatim, sive ope associationum, quæ vel culturales esse possunt, vel artisticæ, pecuniariæ, etc., et quæ Societates Auxiliares nuncupantur. Hæ pariter societates, in earum actione, auctoritati hierarchiæ Instituti prorsus obnoxiæ sunt.

10. § 1. Institutum, nisi aliud ad ministeria et opera sustinenda vel fovenda necessarium videatur, nullas habebit ecclesias proprias; nullas

proprias associationes fidelium fovebit; stipendia pro Missis non recipiet, neque ullam pro exercito ministerio sacerdotali mercedem, etiam sponte oblatam, aut compensationem impensarum, quas ratione itineris aliquis ex sodalibus sustinuerit. Tantum hospitium et victum sacerdotes Instituti, tempore alicuius ministerii spiritualis, accipere possunt. Tamen Opus Dei acceptat legata cuiusvis generis ad finem Instituti persequendum, sed ipsum bona immobilia ordinarie non possidet.

§ 2. Si in his omnibus aliquam, gravibus de causis, exceptionem admittere in Domino opportunum videatur, Pater ex Consilii voto deliberativo, donec necessitas seu magna utilitas perduret, eam decernere potest.

11. Si rerum adiuncta postulent ut in diversis Regionibus Opus Dei vel Societas Sacerdotalis Sanctæ Crucis sese constituat in societatem civilem, Consiliarius Regionalis designare ad nutum poterit organum directivum seu Consilium nationale, a Directore, Secretario et tribus Vocalibus constitutum. Huius Consilii erit satagere ut Opus Dei semper leges civiles regionis seu nationis fideliter observet, atque intra terminos ab ipsis constitutos sese contineat atque operetur; œconomica media sustinendis sumptibus annuis Operis Dei necessaria, colligere ac suppeditare; necnon aliis officiis forsan ab ipso Consiliario Regionali iniunctis, operam fideliter navare.

12. Societas Sacerdotalis Sanctæ Crucis et Opus Dei tamquam Patronos, quos singulari devotione prosequuntur, habent: Beatam Mariam semper Virginem, quam uti Matrem Institutum veneratur; S. Ioseph, eiusdem Beatæ Mariæ Virginis Sponsum; SS. Archangelos Michaëlem, Gabrielem et Raphaëlem; SS. Apostolos Petrum, Paulum et Ioannem, quibus universa Institutio eiusdemque singula actionis genera specialiter consecrantur.

## 33. Letter of the Sacred Congregation for Religious to Msgr. Escrivá de Balaguer granting him special faculties; August 2, 1950.

RHF, D-15184.

EX SECRETARIA
SACRÆ CONGREGATIONIS                          N. I. S. 1/47
   DE RELIGIOSIS

Rev.me Pater,

Sacra Congregatio, dum Instituti sæcularis "Societas Sacerdotalis Sanctæ Crucis ac Opus Dei", cui Paternitas Tua, cum instrumentum a Domino electum pro ipsius fundatione iam fuerit, nunc pari zelo ac prudentia præsidet, approbatas definitive Constitutiones transmittit, hæc quæ sequuntur quoad approbationis vim ac peculiares facultates Tibi, vita durante, concessas et quoad ipsarum Constitutionum exsecutionem Tibi communicare opportunum ducit:

1) Quoad approbationem definitivam Constitutionum: etsi plene definitiva ad normam iuris ipsa habenda est, Hæc Sacra Congregatio, dum uti mos est ordinarias ipsius Sacræ Congregationis facultates circa Institutorum Constitutiones sibi reservat, libenter Paternitati Tuæ tuoque Consilio facultatem concedit mutationes, declarationes, complementa proponere quæ evolutioni ac necessitatibus Instituti suique tam singularis atque eximii apostolatus intensioni atque extensioni, opportuna seu utilia quavis ratione videantur.

2) Quoad Constitutionum exsecutionem, in iis præcipue quæ ad regiminis installationem spectant, annus integer post mensem a momento computandus in quo typis impressæ Constitutiones vobis habere præ manibus licebit, Tuæ Paternitati conceditur. Intra annum ita computandum commode res ordinare libere poteris.

Dum cuncta fausta prospera Paternitati Tuæ tuoque Instituto ex corde adprecor

addictissimum in Christo me profiteor

+ fr. L. E. Pasetto

Seg.

Datum Romæ, ex Ædibus Sacræ Congregationis, die 2 augusti, an. 1950.

Ill.mo ac Rev.mo Domino
Iosepho M. Escrivá de Balaguer
Fundatori ac Generali Præsidi Instituti sæcularis

Societas Sacerdotalis Sanctæ Crucis ac Opus Dei

## 34. Rescript of the Sacred Congregation for Religious regarding the faculty to hear the confessions of the members of the Institute; June 20, 1950.

AGP, Sezione Giuridica, V/15183.

SEGRETERIA

DELLA

SACRA CONGREGAZIONE                    N. 6158/50

DEI RELIGIOSI

Beatissime Pater,

Procurator Generalis Instituti Secularis OPUS DEI, ad Sanctitatis Vestræ pedes humiliter provolutus, expostulat pro Præside Generali Instituti facultatem delegatam, subdelegabilem ad normam iuris, audiendi confessiones sodalium Instituti: quæ facultas a Consiliariis Regionalibus, de consensu Præsidis Instituti, iterum subdelegari valeat.

Et Deus, etc.

Vigore specialium facultatum a SS.mo Domino Nostro concessarum, Sacra Congregatio Negotiis religiosorum sodalium præposita, mature perpensa peculiari Instituti natura, benigne annuit pro gratia iuxta preces, ita ut petita facultas extendatur ad sodales Numerarios, Oblatos et Supernumerarios utriusque Operis Dei sectionis, Societatis Sacerdotalis Sanctæ Crucis, necnon ad convictores ad normam can. 514 § 1, et servatis omnibus de iure servandis. Contrariis quibuslibet minime obstantibus.

Datum Romæ, ex Ædibus Sacræ Congregationis de Religiosis, die 20 junii an. 1950.

L + S                                  + fr. L. E. Pasetto

                                       Secr

                                       C. Addivinola Ad. a Studiis.

## 35. Decree of erection of the Roman College of the Holy Cross; June 29, 1948.

RHF, D-15096.

### Societas Sacerdotalis Sanctæ Crucis

### et

### Opus Dei

Ut ad cathedram Petri, Christi Vicarii, cuius dignitas in Beatissimo Domino Nostro, Ipsius herede, quin deficiat claris fulgoribus perpetuo splendet (cfr. S. Leo, Sermo II, in Anniversario Assumptionis suæ), et ad gloriosum S. Pauli, Doctoris gentium, sepulchrum, superædificatum super fundamentum Apostolorum Ipsique Angulari lapidi Christo Iesu firmiter inhærens (Eph. II, 20) solidum ac securum ædificium crescat nostræ catholicæ et apostolicæ culturæ ac formationis tam in illis dilectis filiis nostris, qui ad sacerdotium destinantur, quam in aliis qui divina vocatione prælia Domini ubique omnibusque modis et armis sæculari nobili ratione præliari debent, auditis et consentientibus nostris Consultoribus, Collegium ex omni natione Operis Dei in Urbe constituere decrevimus.

Quam ob rem, Christo Salvatore ac Domino Nostro suppliciter fidenterque invocato, Beatæ Mariæ Virginis, dulcissimæ Matris nostræ, tutelæ ac præsidio re commendata, atque Sanctorum Archangelorum Michaèlis, Gabrielis et Raphaèlis, et Sanctorum Apostolorum Petri, Pauli et Ioannis patrocinio confisi, hoc nostro decreto, Collegium ex omni natione Operis Dei, quod ad omnes effectus, qui ex nobis pendent, hodie erigimus atque erectum declaramus.

Quod Collegium Romanum Operis Dei, in cuius præparatione et erectione suavem providamque æterni Numinis opem persensimus et experti sumus, ut in dies vigeat, crescat, floreat fructusque optimos edat, paterno animo ominamur incensaque prece a Deo efflagitamus. 6

Dabamus Romæ ad limina Apostolorum, in festo SS. App. Petri et Pauli, die XXIX iunii, anno MDCCCCXXXXVIII.

L + S                                      Josemaría Escrivá de B.

## 36. Decree of erection of the Roman College of St. Mary, December 12, 1953.

RHF, D-15098.

**Opus Dei**

Cum formationem Sodalium Sectionis Mulierum Operis Dei semper corde habeamus, cumque magna Nobis sit cura, ut omnia ipsis præbeantur subsidia, quæ arctiorem earum unionem cum Deo fovere valeant easque magis in dies paratas efficiant ad gentes universas continua et supernaturali apostolica actione Deo lucrandas, apta doctrina ad omniumque aures quam maxime accommodata vias Domini in lætitia docentes, audito et consentiente Assessoratu Centrali, Collegium ex omni natione in Urbe, Catholicæ Ecclesiæ centro atque capite, quæ et sedes exstat Beati Petri, Christi Vicarii, eiusque Successorum, constituere decrevimus, quod Collegium ad Apostolorum limina consistens peculiare esset pro Opere Dei instrumentum unitatis et cohæsionis.

Quapropter, re mature perpensa, Christo, Dei Filio et Salvatore nostro, suppliciter fidenterque invocato, præsidio Beatissimæ semper Virginis Mariæ, Operis Dei Reginæ, Matris Dei et Matris nostræ tota re commendata, atque intercessione confisi Sanctorum Archangelorum Michaèlis, Gabrielis et Raphaèlis, Sanctorum Apostolorum Petri, Pauli et Ioannis et omnium Angelorum Custodum, hoc Nostro decreto Collegium Romanum ex omni natione Operis Dei, quoad omnes effectus, qui ex Nobis pendent, hodie erigimus atque erectum declaramus, et in signum amoris et devotionis erga Deiparam Virginem Mariam, quæ Associationi Nostræ materna cura prospicere ac providere nunquam destitit, volumus ut in posterum Collegii Romani Sanctæ Mariæ nomine decoretur.

Quo magis tandem hoc Collegium, in servitium Sanctæ Ecclesiæ constitutum, fructus opimos producat, atque ibi Operis Dei Sodales Sectionis Mulierum ita animarum siti accendantur, ut pacem et gaudium seminantes, gentes quam plurimas suaviter atque efficaciter ad Dominum trahant, fervidas Deo effundimus preces et Beatæ Mariæ Virginis patrocinium enixe expostulamus. 7

Dabamus Romæ, ex ædibus Domus Nostræ Generalis, die XII, mensis decembris, an. a rep. sal. MDCCCCLIII.

L + S                                        Iosephmaria Escrivá de B.

## 37. Letter of Federico Cardinal Tedeschini, Apostolic Datary and Cardinal Protector of Opus Dei to Msgr. Escrivá on the occasion of the 25 anniversary of the foundation of Opus Dei; September 24, 1953.

RHF, D-15036

DATARIA APOSTOLICA

Roma, 24 de septiembre de 1953.

Muy venerado Padre y estimadísimo amigo,

Alegría grande me træ la próxima fiesta del día 2 de octubre, por evocar ella el acontecimiento que tan grabado está en nuestros corazones, y que no ha podido transcurrir sin que la mano de nuestro amadísimo Padre Santo se levantara a bendecir una vez más y de la manera más expresiva lo que Su paternal corazón tantas veces había delante de mí bendecido con palabras reveladoras del consuelo, que el Pontífice experimentaba, y de las esperanzas que las conseguidas realidades permitían concebir.

El cumplirse cinco lustros desde la fundación de un Instituto, pocas veces llama la atención, y menos aún despierta interés, dado que veinticinco años sólo pueden bastar para comienzos y nunca para progresos.

*El Opus Dei*, con la Sociedad Sacerdotal de la Santa Cruz, nació en cambio grande y maduro, por la inspirada oportunidad de la idea, oculta antes en el anhelo de los tiempos, y confiada ahora por Dios a la virtud sacerdotal y al prestigio personal del egregio Fundador: se abrió el camino a través de dos guerras, la Hispana y la segunda mundial; renovó, como en el Evo Medio, su llamada, no ya a una clase, sino a toda la sociedad, empezando por los selectos, intelectuales, y descendiendo a la universalidad del pueblo cristiano y de las cristianas familias; ganó la difícil simpatía de los jóvenes estudiosos y aún de los más favorecidos por su posición en el mundo, y los llevó, como en los admirables tiempos de San Benito, de Santo Tomás de Aquino y de San Bernardo, con fuerza irresistible, a dejarlo todo, nombre, familia, bienestar, porvenir, por amor de Dios, en forma sin embargo tan acertadamente singular que la acogida tomó aspecto de fenómeno social nuevo.

Y me place recordar, pues presente era yo, que brotó el *Opus Dei* en el silencio; se reveló sin ruido; se extendió sin fatiga; y llenó en pocos años, más que los Claustros, el mundo, arrastrando cuantos había de generosos, de abnegados, de entusiastas.

Somos de ayer y lo hemos llenado todo, decían los primeros cristianos, y lo repiten hoy los hijos del P. Escrivá. Lo que para los extraños es asombro, para ellos es naturalidad; y para la Iglesia es orgullo y consuelo.

¡Oh! ¡cuántas y cuáles vocaciones! Yo las conozco: yo puedo compararlas; puedo admirarlas. Lo que no puedo, es contarlas. De donde menos era de esperar, naciones, carreras, oficios, de ahí más espontáneas, y, lo que más importa, más espirituales han venido los reclutas; y cuantos más instantes para ellos, (por no desertar ni ambiente, ni profesiones, ni hábitos de aquel mundo que hay que curar), los peligros, tantos más adiestradas las legiones, y más interiores las armaduras de los nuevos ejércitos.

La Iglesia ha mirado complacida, pero también sorprendida, el avanzar y el estrecharse a su maternal regazo, de tantos y tan inesperados soldados, y ha creído en la *caridad* que los animaba y los ha reconocido por los frutos. Y no esto sólo: sino que ha visto, por ellos, brotar de sus antiguas, maternales y tan fecundas entrañas, una fuerza nueva, desconocida antes, y claramente necesaria ahora; y de la fuerza, una idea y un rumbo, santos y saludables; y estos ha recogido como una joya más, que añadir a su celestial Corona: la idea y el rumbo de los Institutos seculares: tan dignos de consideración, tan prometedores de bienes, tan consentáneos a la época, y, aún más, tan por la época exigidos, que no ha podido menos que injertarlos en sus leyes, como un Capítulo notable y nuevo, y como manantial del más fecundo porvenir.

Con la Santa Iglesia y con el Augusto Pontífice, sólo Usted, querido Padre, tiene hoy el honroso derecho de elevar la mirada al Cielo, con la más fervorosa y más debida acción de gracias.

Pero no le extrañará que yo también encuentre especialísimos motivos de agradecer la magna Obra al Santo y Divino Espíritu, y de presentar enhorabuenas a usted, al Instituto, a la Iglesia y a España.

Surgió en efecto, la Obra en el medio de mi Nunciatura: el año 1928; entre el 1921 y el 1936, confines de mi Misión.

Considero el *Opus Dei* como la flor más bella, más olorosa, y más consoladora de aquel período de mi vida, en que la Providencia me dio a conocer cual fuerza se esconde y cual dinamismo se perpetúe en la vieja y siempre nueva y juvenil pujanza de España. Y una vez los dos, yo y ella, en Roma, y nombrado yo Protector, una nueva vocación, esto es una nueva invitación divina, ha venido a añadirse al antiguo Nuncio, para que no interrumpa sus destinos españoles: seguir, abarcar, entender y comprender los designios de Dios sobre la Obra; acompañarlos con sus solicitudes; ampararlos contra los peligros propios de toda novedad y de toda grandeza; animar y confortar, con el afecto de la primera hora, a los dirigentes, a los Numerarios, a los Oblatos y a los Supernumerarios; y decir en todo instante a Dios, al Vicario de Cristo, a España y al mundo: he amado y amo lo que es digno de amor; protejo lo que veo conducir más almas a Dios; leo en los corazones, valientes y nobles, del Fundador, de esta magnífica juventud y de los sacerdotes que la cuidan, el más puro amor a la Iglesia; y por lo tanto, doy todo lo que está en mi pecho para que esta *armada*, la verdaderamente invencible, sea mina inagotable de Apóstoles, seculares, como los primeros de Cristo, y Romanos, como los eternos del Papa!

Bendigo con toda el alma a Usted, querido Padre, y a todos los Hijos, suyos y míos; y me reitero, con votos de incesante avanzar, y con siempre más cálido corazón.

afectísimo amigo

+ Federico Card. Tedeschini

Obispo Suburbicario de

Frascati

Protector

**38. Letter of Valerio Cardinal Valeri, Prefect of the Sacred Congregation for Religious to Msgr. Escrivá on the occasion of the 25 anniversary of the foundation of Opus Dei; September 25, 1953.**

RHF, D-15012.


SACRA CONGREGAZIONE                     Roma, lì 25 settembre 1953
    DEI RELIGIOSI

                                             Num. Prot. I. S. 1/47

Ill.mo e Rev.mo Monsignore,

abbiamo appreso con viva soddisfazione che il prossimo 2 ottobre, festività dei SS. Angeli, la S. V. Ill.ma e Rev.ma s'appresta a celebrare, nel silenzio e nell'umile prece, in intima unione coll'eletto e numeroso stuolo dei Suoi Figli e delle Sue Figlie, sparsi ormai in tante parti del mondo, il venticinquesimo dalle prime origini dell'Opus Dei.

La Sacra Congregazione dei Religiosi che ha dovuto, per ragioni di ufficio, seguire da vicino lo sviluppo, l'espandersi della fiorente Opera, e che è stata l'Organo della Santa Sede nella concessione delle successive approvazioni ottenute dall'Istituto, si congratula cordialmente, nella fausta ricorrenza, con la Signoria Vostra Ill.ma e Rev.ma e con i membri delle due Sezioni, maschile -sacerdoti e laici- e femminile; con i sodali tutti, Numerari, Oblati e Soprannumerari; con i sacerdoti diocesani della Società Sacerdotale della Santa Croce: con tutti quelli cioè che costituiscono l'organismo agile e compatto, la milizia forte ed ordinata -*acies ordinata*- dell'Opus Dei.

E' doveroso e veramente giusto e degno che la S. V. con tutti i Suoi, pieni di fedele e devota gratitudine, ringrazino con tutto il cuore la bontà di Dio, che, per l'intercessione della Vergine Madre, al Cui materno Cuore è stato filialmente consacrato l'Istituto, e dei SS. Patroni e Protettori, amati e continuamente invocati, ha colmato l'Istituto con copiose benedizioni di dolcezza e di efficacia apostolica.

Mentre l'Opus Dei inizia l'ascesa verso le nozze d'oro, la Sacra Congregazione Gli augura felice la continuazione del Suo rapido incremento numerico e della sua fortunata diffusione, nonché di quella soda individuale formazione ascetica, culturale, professionale ed apostolica che incomincia su solide basi e continua, poi, ininterrotta per tutta la vita.

Questa Sacra Congregazione si compiace, finalmente, per il provvidenziale e svariato apostolato individuale dell'Opus Dei, attraverso l'irradiamento della cultura, a mezzo dell'esercizio delle diverse professioni e dell'audace lavoro sociale, nonché per le diverse forme dell'apostolato collettivo e corporativo dell'Istituto.

Invocando sulla S. V. Ill.ma e Rev.ma e su tutto l'Opus Dei le più sante ed elette benedizioni e grazie di santità, di apostolato, di diffusione ed incremento, mi professo

> della Signoria Vostra Ill.ma e Rev.ma
> devotissimo nel Signore
> Valerio Card. Valeri
> Prefetto
> Giovanni Battista Scapinelli
> Sottosegretario

---

Ill.mo e Reverendissimo
> Mons. Giuseppe Maria Escrivá de Balaguer
> Presidente Generale della Società Sacerdotale
> della Santa Croce e Opus Dei.

---

**39. Letter of Giuseppe Cardinal Pizzardo, Secretary of the Sacred Congregation of the Holy Office and Prefect of the Sacred Congregation for Seminaries and Universities, to Msgr. Escrivá on the occasion of the 25 anniversary of the foundation of Opus Dei; September 24, 1953.**

RHF, D-15189.

SACRA CONGREGATIO
> DE SEMINARIIS
ET DE STUDIORUM UNIVERSITATIBUS

---

Num. Protoc. 1128/53

> Roma, 24 settembre 1953
> Festa di Maria SS.ma della Mercede

Illustrissimo e Reverendissimo Monsignore,

la fausta ricorrenza del venticinquesimo anniversario della fondazione dell'Opus Dei -che si celebrerà il prossimo 2 ottobre, nella festa dei Santi Angeli Custodi- è per questa Sacra Congregazione circostanza gradita, anzi desiderata, per rivolgere una parola di lode alla Signoria Vostra Reverendissima.

Ella, illustre e benemerito Fondatore dell'Opus Dei, ha saputo compiere, non senza speciale aiuto di Dio, il sapiente ordinamento delle Costituzioni dell'Istituto, specie per quanto riguarda la sana e profonda formazione dei Sodali, come universitari e studiosi non solo di tutte le scienze e professioni civili, ma anche delle ecclesiastiche.

E' infatti a conoscenza di questa Sacra Congregazione che, in applicazione dei criteri sanciti dalle Costituzioni dell'Istituto, è stata adottata una "Ratio studiorum", corroborata ormai da una felice esperienza, secondo la quale tutti i Sodali Numerari laici hanno l'obbligo di seguire, oltre il biennio filosofico, anche il quadriennio completo di Sacra Teologia, secondo lo spirito della Costituzione Apostolica "Deus scientiarum Dominus", con quei complementi che si addicono alle peculiari necessità dell'Opus Dei.

A nessuno dovrà destar meraviglia il fatto che ai laici dell'Istituto venga richiesto il non lieve onere dello studio anche delle discipline ecclesiastiche alla stregua dei Sacerdoti: certamente ciò costituisce una perfezione che vorremmo dire ideale, da proporsi a modello a quanti desiderano unire la solida preparazione professionale -tale da affermarli nei diversi campi del sapere umano- con quella seria formazione dottrinale religiosa, che ne completi al massimo lo sviluppo della personalità. L'unire le discipline cosiddette profane con quelle ecclesiastiche, mentre le integra e le completa tra loro, offre ai Sodali dell'Istituto armi più efficaci per la loro azione apostolica, ed eleva le loro anime verso il Signore di tutte le scienze.

Ottima, a tal fine, la prassi vigente presso i Centri di Studi dell'Istituto di far seguire ad ognuno dei corsi quadrimestrali, nei quali si articolano il biennio di filosofia e il quadriennio di teologia, un periodo di tempo nel quale il Sodale, pur continuando l'esercizio delle sue professioni civili, matura le cognizioni acquisite, mediante lo studio e la riflessione personale per diversi mesi, sotto l'immediata e vigile guida del Direttore degli studi, armonizzando così le proprie esigenze professionali con quelle degli studi ecclesiastici.

Con particolare dilezione pensiamo ai Sacerdoti Numerari, che dopo aver svolto da laici un lungo periodo d'apostolato specifico dell'Opus Dei in mezzo alla società civile, son chiamati al Sacerdozio dal Presidente Generale, e tutti conseguono una laurea ecclesiastica. E ci è caro rilevare che non solo i Sacerdoti, ma anche tutti i membri laici destinati ad essere docenti nei Centri di formazione dell'Opus Dei convengono a Roma per conseguire il grado ecclesiastico superiore in uno degli Atenei dell'Urbe. Saggia e lungimirante è stata la prudenza della Signoria Vostra Reverendissima che a questo scopo, senza risparmiare fatiche e sofferenze, ha eretto nell'Urbe, nell'anno 1948, il Collegio Romano della Santa Croce, che nel prossimo anno giubilare dell'Istituto raggiungerà la consolantissima cifra di circa 150 alunni provenienti da diverse Nazioni d'Europa e di America.

Questa Sacra Congregazione, mentre si compiace per tutte le iniziative promosse dall'Opus Dei nel campo degli studi, è ben lieta di costatare la mirabile diffusione dell'Opera nel mondo, l'abbondanza di così scelte vocazioni e i consolanti frutti di apostolato finora raccolti.

In unione alla Signoria Vostra Reverendissima e ai Sodali dell'Istituto, eleviamo fervide preghiere all'Altissimo per ringraziarLo dei copiosi doni elargiti ed invocare da Lui grazie sempre più abbondanti per la prosperità dell'Istituto nel servizio della Santa Chiesa.

Mi valgo della circostanza per dirmi

della Signoria Vostra Reverendissima

devotissimo nel Signore

G. Cardinale Pizzardo

Igino Cecchetti,

Sottosegretario

---

Ill.mo e Rev.mo Sig
Mons. GIUSEPPE MARÍA ESCRIVA DE BALAGUER
Presidente Generale dell'Opus Dei
**ROMA**

---

## 40. Letter of Msgr. Escrivá to the members of Opus Dei on the institutional question; October 2, 1958.

RHF, EF-581002-1.

1. No ignoráis, hijas e hijos queridísimos, *que el fin y los medios de la Obra de Dios son plena y exclusivamente sobrenaturales, espirituales y apostólicos:* queremos promover vocaciones de cristianos, que se obliguen a buscar la santidad en el mundo, cada uno en su propio estado, de modo que conviertan en apostolado toda su vida.

   El apostolado nuestro, con el que cooperamos en la misión salvífica de la Iglesia, tiene un carácter y un modo *seculares:* no porque busquemos fines *seculares* o *temporales,* sino porque el apostolado de la Obra de Dios, teniendo un fin sobrenatural, debe dirigirse a personas que viven en el mundo, y debe hacerse por personas que trabajan libremente en las mismas condiciones y circunstancias temporales que los demás, sin querer distinguirse en nada de sus compañeros.

2. *No somos religiosos, ni se nos puede llamar religiosos o misioneros.* Todos los socios del Opus Dei ejercen su profesión de médico, de abogado, de obrero, de campesino, u otra cualquiera, del mismo modo que los demás ciudadanos: procurando a la vez ganar almas para la Iglesia Santa, mediante el ejercicio de su tarea profesional, y con frecuencia en lugares y circunstancias difícilmente accesibles a los sacerdotes y a los religiosos.

3. Tampoco somos ciudadanos *de segunda categoría: gozáis de una libertad completa y sois personalmente responsables de vuestros actos,* no sólo en el ejercicio del trabajo profesional, sino también en vuestra acción social, cultural o política, que son cosas que tenéis en común con los demás ciudadanos de vuestra nación; de ahí que tengáis también los mismos derechos y deberes.

En las cosas temporales, nunca los Directores de la Obra pueden imponer una opinión determinada sobre aquellas materias que Dios Nuestro Señor deja a la libre discusión de los hombres: cada uno de vosotros actúa siempre con plena libertad, según su conciencia.

Si alguna vez fuera necesario, en bien de las almas, establecer y determinar alguna norma en estos asuntos, dar ese criterio corresponderá exclusivamente al Ordinario del lugar, como parte de su ministerio pastoral; y en cada caso, será deber vuestro secundar las normas que el Revdmo. Ordinario diocesano dicte, con espíritu de obediencia ante Dios y ante los hombres.

4.  Aunque vivimos en el mundo y participamos de todos los afanes y trabajos de la sociedad, *nuestra vocación es necesariamente contemplativa:* estamos en continua, sencilla y filial unión con Dios, nuestro Padre. Si no fuéramos realmente contemplativos, sería difícil que pudiéramos perseverar en el Opus Dei.

5.  Hemos de vivir con naturalidad y sencillez nuestra personal unión con Dios. No ocultamos nuestra condición, *ni usamos de misterio o secreteo, que no necesitamos nunca.*

Sin embargo, debemos preservar la intimidad de nuestro amoroso trato con el Señor de la curiosidad indiscreta de otros, por la misma razón y con el mismo cuidado con que todo el mundo evita que se difunda o divulgue sin motivo lo que pertenece a la intimidad de su familia.

6.  Nuestro único afán es *servir a la Iglesia, como Ella quiere ser servida, dentro de la peculiar vocación que hemos recibido de Dios.* Por eso, *no deseamos para nosotros el estado de perfección.* Lo amamos, para los religiosos y para los que pertenecen a los que ahora se denominan Institutos Seculares, porque es propio de su vocación.

A nosotros, en cambio, por la vocación específica, con la que hemos sido llamados al Opus Dei, Dios nos pide solamente que *cada uno busque la santidad en el propio estado* -soltero, casado, viudo, sacerdote- y en el ejercicio de su *munus publicum,* o sea, de su trabajo profesional, bien conocido por todos sus conciudadanos.

7.  No queremos, por tanto, que se nos aplique indiscriminadamente el derecho propio de los religiosos, ni que en modo alguno se nos equipare o, más o menos, se nos identifique con ellos.

De lo contrario, no podríamos ayudarles ni defenderlos como lo hacemos; se haría más difícil nuestro eficaz servicio a la Iglesia Santa de Dios, que debe realizarse sin ruido; y, sobre todo, nos resultaría imposible conservar el espíritu que Dios quiere para nosotros.

8.  Las características peculiares del espíritu y de la vida apostólica de la Obra de Dios -que han sido confirmadas ampliamente por una larga experiencia, desde el año 1928-, junto con el *Ius peculiare* que nos ha sido concedido (*Decretum laudis*, 24-II-1947, y Decreto de aprobación definitiva, 16-VI-1950; además de los Breves Apostólicos *Cum Societatis*, 28-VI-1946, y *Mirifice de Ecclesia*, 20-VII-1947), confieren a nuestra Obra una personalidad ciertamente especialísima -sin soberbia alguna, debemos reconocerlo y manifestarlo-, que la diferencia claramente de los actuales Institutos Seculares: porque éstos -sean o no secretos- tienen características

que los hacen muy semejantes a las Congregaciones religiosas o a las comunes Asociaciones de fieles, de las que frecuentemente es difícil distinguirlos, tanto por su espíritu como por su modo de vida.

9. *De hecho no somos un Instituto Secular, ni en lo sucesivo se nos puede aplicar ese nombre:* el significado actual del término difiere mucho del sentido genuino, que se le atribuía cuando la Santa Sede usó esas palabras por primera vez, al concedernos el *Decretum laudis* en el año 1947.

   Tampoco puede confundirse el Opus Dei con los llamados *movimientos de apostolado*. Lo impiden sus características peculiares: el vínculo mutuo y sobrenatural, con el que cada uno de los socios se une al Opus Dei; nuestra dedicación plena y completa a Dios; nuestra formación doctrinal, sólida y constante, que nunca damos por terminada, sino que procuramos mejorar continuamente durante toda la vida; nuestra jerarquía interna, que es universal, para que sea más eficaz nuestro trabajo en servicio de la Iglesia; la atención, solícita y delicada, que prestamos a los socios enfermos y ancianos; etc.

10. Hasta tal punto *deseamos que esta situación se arregle,* que desde hace muchos años se han celebrado y se continúan celebrando miles de misas por esta intención. Y con el mismo fin todos rezamos constantemente, ofreciendo también a Dios con amor el cumplimiento del trabajo profesional, y de toda la labor apostólica.

    Haciendo esto, depositamos nuestra confianza filial en Dios, para que se digne poner fin a esta preocupación espiritual.

11. Con la misma confianza filial, y pidiendo la intercesión de la Bienaventurada Virgen María, Madre nuestra -*Cor Mariæ Dulcíssimum, iter para tutum!*-, informaré a la Santa Sede, en el momento oportuno, de esa situación, de esa preocupación. Y a la vez manifestaré que deseamos ardientemente que se provea a dar una solución conveniente, que ni constituya para nosotros un privilegio -cosa que repugna a nuestro espíritu y a nuestra mentalidad-, *ni introduzca modificaciones en cuanto a las actuales relaciones con los Ordinarios del lugar.*

12. *Es sólo nuestro amor* a Jesucristo Señor Nuestro, a la Santa Madre Iglesia, y al Romano Pontífice -amor manifestado y expresado siempre con obras de servicio-, lo que nos mueve a procurar con todas las fuerzas que se asegure nuestro espíritu y se refuerce la eficacia del apostolado de la Obra.

    Movidos -repito- solamente por ese amor, deseamos también que la Iglesia sancione con la correspondiente declaración jurídica nuestra peculiar vocación, plenamente secular, es decir, propia de sacerdotes seculares y de laicos o fieles corrientes.

    Por la misma razón y con el mismo deseo, para que no pudiera originarse ni difundirse ninguna falsa opinión sobre nuestra vocación específica, nunca quisimos -con conocimiento de la Santa Sede- formar parte de las federaciones de religiosos, o asistir a los congresos o asambleas de los que se dice que están en *estado de perfección.*

13. Entretanto, hijas e hijos míos, nuestro *Ius peculiare* está clarísimo, y ha sido repetidamente confirmado por los documentos pontificios: cumplidlo -vividlo- con fidelidad. Y con sentido sobrenatural también, observad

diligentemente vuestros deberes civiles, y ejerced libremente vuestros derechos de ciudadanos.

14. Encarecidamente os pido que no tengáis ningún temor a que la Santa Madre Iglesia, contra nuestra voluntad, quiera hacernos religiosos o equipararnos de algún modo a los religiosos, no siendo ésta la vocación que Dios nos ha dado.

Tened *una confianza plena y una firmísima esperanza*; seguid rezando sin interrupción, ofreciendo a Dios cada día vuestro trabajo y vuestro sacrificio, para que, finalmente, pueda llegarse a una solución conveniente.

Cariñosamente os bendice en el Señor vuestro Padre

Josemaría

Roma, 2 de octubre de 1958

## 41. Letter of the Procurator General of Opus Dei to the Sacred Congregation de Propaganda Fide, March 2, 1960.

AGP, Sezione Giuridica, VI/15662.

**Società Sacerdotale della Santa Croce**

e

**Opus Dei**

**Il Procuratore Generale**                    Roma, 2 marzo 1960

Eccellenza Reverendissima,

la prassi ordinariamente seguita dall'Autorità Ecclesiastica nel Kenya, per trattare con quel Governo gli argomenti concernenti l'istruzione, è sempre quella di giovarsi dell'intervento di Fr. O'Meara, Segretario dell'"Educazione delle Missioni Cattoliche".

A causa della recente indisposizione dello stesso Fr. O'Meara, e con l'approvazione dell'Arcivescovo di Nairobi, il Consigliere dell'Opus Dei in Kenya ha trattato direttamente con le locali autorità civili diversi problemi attinenti il costituendo "Higher Certificate School" di Nairobi.

Tali contatti sono stati utili, anche a confermare il grande interesse che il Governo di Kenya ha verso la realizzazione di detto centro d'istruzione interrazziale e la sua favorevole disposizione a sovvenzionarlo generosamente.

Si è potuto, inoltre, rilevare, sempre attraverso i rapporti diretti, la gradita sorpresa ricevuta dal Governo nell'apprendere che il corpo insegnante dell'"Higher Certificate School" sarà costituito da professionisti laici; dato che la mediazione della Curia diocesana, nelle relazioni con le autorità civili, aveva fatto sì che il dipartimento governativo dell'educazione ci considerasse come "un gruppo religioso missionario".

Per la considerazione di cui sopra, i nostri docenti, laici laureati nelle Università di lingua inglese, sarebbero equiparati ai religiosi che svolgono la loro opera missionaria nelle scuole elementari e medie; questo equivoco si rifletterebbe nella partecipazione economica del Governo per la retribuzione degli insegnanti, giacché, se dovessero considerarci come "un gruppo religioso missionario", la sovvenzione per i nostri professori sarebbe solamente del 50% di quella assegnata ai laici.

Se il pregiudizio economico che deriverebbe in questa ipotesi concreta nel Kenya è di per se stesso interessante, per noi è molto più pregiudizievole che ci si confonda con i religiosi, nonostante la profonda venerazione che per essi nutriamo.

Il diritto generale degli Istituti Secolari -C.A. *Provida Mater Ecclesia* (1947), il motu proprio *Primo feliciter* (1948) e l'istruzione *Cum Sanctissimus* (1948)- così come il nostro diritto particolare dalla fondazione (1928), in seguito ripetutamente approvato dalla Santa Sede, pongono con grande chiarezza e ribadiscono il principio che i membri degli Istituti Secolari, e concretamente quelli dell'*Opus Dei*, non sono religiosi, non vivono *ad instar religiosorum*, né si applica nei loro confronti il diritto dei religiosi e, neanche, in maniera alcuna, possono essere equiparati ai religiosi: sono cittadini ordinari, il cui carattere secolare -"in quo ipsorum (Institutorum) exsistentiæ tota ratio consistit, in omnibus elucere debet" (Primo feliciter, II)- deve sempre rimanere chiaro.

Trattare dunque, i membri dei *veri* Istituti Secolari come se fossero religiosi, o religiosi *lato sensu*, è voler distruggere "*ipsorum Institutorum exsistentiam*"; per di più, quando si tratti concretamente dell'Opus Dei è far sì che vada dispersa gran parte della loro efficacia apostolica.

Questa confusione implica, inoltre, una mancanza di giustizia, perché le migliaia di anime che si sono consacrate al servizio di Dio e della Chiesa nell'Opus Dei, dall'anno 1928 in poi, lo han fatto secondo alcune forme giuridiche, che assicurano -per questa consacrazione- la *conditio sine qua non* di non essere religiosi, né di essere equiparati in alcun modo ai religiosi, come è stato innanzi esposto.

Mi dà grande gioia far presente all'Eccellenza Vostra che il nostro Fondatore ha posto come parte principale del nostro spirito, particolarmente, quell'affanno di anime, che ci fa essere missionari non soltanto in terre di Missione, ma nel mondo intero.

Cosicché, un avvocato, un medico, un operaio, un professore dell'Opus Dei, fanno il proprio lavoro come ciascun altro cittadino, procurando con il loro operato professionale di guadagnare anime alla Chiesa, in qualsiasi parte del mondo essi si trovino.

Pertanto, incaricato dal nostro Presidente Generale, Mons. Escrivá de Balaguer, prego l'Eccellenza Vostra che, nei casi in cui il nostro lavoro sia svolto in pæsi di missioni, perché si possa rendere alle anime un più efficace servizio, voglia codesta Sacra Congregazione indicare ai Reverendissimi Ordinari tutte queste caratteristiche essenziali dell'Opus Dei e, anche, la necessità, assai conveniente per la Santa Chiesa -e, conseguentemente, per i Reverendissimi Ordinari ed i fedeli- che i Superiori dell'Istituto possano rivolgersi direttamente alle autorità civili, sempre che lo ritengano opportuno.

Voglia perdonare se mi sono permesso disturbare per iscritto l'Eccellenza Vostra, ripetendo quanto, in altre circonstanze, ho già avuto l'onore di esporLe a voce.

Mi è gradito, ancora una volta, ringraziare l'Eccellenza Vostra Reverendissima, dell'affetto che dimostra per il nostro Istituto e della simpatia con cui guarda i nostri specifici mezzi di apostolato, valendomi dell'occasione per professarmi, con i più deferenti ossequi.

dell'Eccellenza Vostra Rev.ma

dev.mo nel Signore

Sac. Pietro Casciaro

Proc. Gen.

A Sua Eccellenza Rev.ma
Mons. Pietro Sigismondi
Arcivescovo Tit. di Neapoli di Pisidia
**Segretario della S. C. de Propaganda Fide**
**ROMA**

## 42. Letter of the Procurator General of Opus Dei to the Sacred Congregation de Propaganda Fide, December 30, 1960.

AGP, Sezione Giuridica, VI/15663.

**Società Sacerdotale della Santa Croce**

e

**Opus Dei**

**Il Procuratore Generale**                                    Roma, 30 dicembre 1960

Eccellenza Reverendissima,

Il *Consejo Superior de Misiones* -organismo ufficiale alle dipendenze del *Ministerio de Asuntos Exteriores* di Spagna- si è ripetutamente rivolto alla nostra Curia Generale chiedendo dati sull'attività che l'*Opus Dei* svolge nei Pæsi di Missione. Recentemente ha insistito ancora, ed in modo scortese, nella richiesta, per poter includere tali dati in un annuario missionario del Ministero.

Già in numerose occasioni abbiamo avuto l'onore di esporre all'E. V. - ed Ella lo ha sempre compreso con una chiara visione giuridica ed apostolica- che i soci dell'*Opus Dei* non si chiamano mai missionari, e che il fatto che i loro nomi appaiano negli annuari missionari deformerebbe e sarebbe di ostacolo al lavoro che svolgono in servizio della Chiesa nei suddetti Pæsi: per questo, mi rivolgo all'E. V. e La prego caldamente affinché codesto Sacro Dicastero si degni dichiarare: 1) che i membri dell'*Opus Dei* non si chiamano, né possono essere chiamati missionari; 2) che né l'*Opus Dei*, né i suoi membri possono essere inclusi negli elenchi di missionari.

Mi è gradito cogliere l'occasione per rinnovarLe i sensi della mia più profonda stima e dirmi dell'Eccellenza Vostra Reverendissima.

dev.mo in Domino

Sac. Pietro Casciaro

Proc. Gen

A Sua Eccellenza Rev.ma
Mons. Pietro Sigismondi
Arcivescovo Tit. di Neapoli di Pisidia
**Segretario della S. C. de Propaganda Fide**
**ROMA**

## 43. Letter of Msgr. Escrivá de Balaguer to the Secretary of State Amleto Cardinal Cicognani; January 7, 1962.

RHF, EF-620107t-1.

**Società Sacerdotale della Santa Croce**

e

**Opus Dei**

**Il Presidente Generale**                          Roma, 7 gennaio 1962

Eminenza Reverendissima,

mi consenta di deporre nelle Sue mani l'unita supplica, con preghiera di volerla umiliare al Santo Padre.

La supplica in parola concerne una domanda volta ad ottenere una nuova sistemazione dell'Opus Dei, che sembrerebbe essere postulata da alcune notevoli difficoltà che l'Istituto ha purtroppo riscontrato, nell'esercizio del suo specifico apostolato di permeare, a mezzo di anime consacrate al servizio di Dio, i diversi ambienti della società civile.

Ardisco elevare la predetta supplica al Santo Padre: sia per un senso di filiale fiducia verso il Vicario di Cristo, Cui senza veli sento di dover sottoporre le difficoltà che l'Istituto incontra; sia perché la paterna benevolenza che la S. Sede ha accordato sempre all'Istituto, si manifestò anche nei miei riguardi, col concedermi, all'atto della approvazione definitiva dell'Istituto e delle sue Costituzioni, una particolare facoltà, che riterrei ora di dover invocare.

La Sacra Congregazione dei Religiosi, infatti, nell'approvare definitivamente le Costituzioni dell'Opus Dei, mi accordava, con lettera del 2 agosto 1950, di prot. n. I.S. 1/47, la facoltà del seguente tenore: ". . . libenter Paternitati Tuæ tuoque Consilio facultatem concedit mutationes, declarationes, complementa proponere, quæ evolutioni ac necessitati Instituti suique tam singularis atque eximii apostolatus intensioni atque extensioni, opportuna seu utilia quavis ratione videantur".

Nella speranza che l'Eminenza Vostra Reverendissima Si degni accogliere la presente domanda e umiliarla al Santo Padre, mi chino al bacio della Sacra Porpora e con sensi di profonda venerazione mi professo

dell'Eminenza Vostra Reverendissima

dev.mo nel Signore

Josemaría Escrivá de B.

A Sua Eminenza Reverendissima
il Sig. Card. Amleto Giovanni Cicognani
Segretario di Stato di Sua Santità
**Città del Vaticano**

## 44. Letter of Msgr. Escrivá de Balaguer to His Holiness, Pope John XXIII in which he requests the revision of the juridical status of Opus Dei; January 7, 1962.

RHF, EF-620107t-2.

**Opus Dei**                                             Roma, 7 gennaio 1962

Beatissimo Padre,

La Divina Provvidenza e l'appoggio e la benevolenza della Santa Sede hanno dato all'Opus Dei uno sviluppo veramente notevole, nonostante che l'Istituto abbia cercato sempre di lavorare nella maniera meno appariscente possibile: cosa che, per quanto da alcuni sia stata criticata, ho sempre modestamente ritenuto conforme all'umiltà del Vangelo.

Ancora una volta dal piccolo seme si è silenziosamente sviluppato il grande albero, alla cui ombra molti vengono a rifugiarsi e si moltiplica così quel bene delle anime e della Chiesa santa di Dio, che è l'unico scopo dell'Opus Dei.

Questo bene potrebbe essere ancora maggiore, se taluni inconvenienti, risultanti dal presente ordinamento giuridico dell'Istituto ed appalesatisi nel corso di questi anni, che datano dall'approvazione definitiva, non ne turbassero e compromettessero l'armonioso sviluppo.

L'inconveniente maggiore è che da molti (sia pure illegalmente, ma purtroppo efficacemente) i membri dell'Istituto vengono assimilati ai religiosi, per cui si vedono spesso limitare o addirittura interdire il loro apostolato, sotto lo specioso pretesto che certe attività sono proscritte ai religiosi.

Ad esempio, mentre i laici dell'Istituto dovrebbero aver aperto per Costituzioni, e nell'intento di arrivare a santificare con l'esempio e con l'apostolato individuale, ogni genere di onesta professione (alla stregua dei comuni laici), si vedono invece precluse alcune di queste prospettive apostoliche, perché vengono accomunati ai religiosi: fatti oggetto di critiche, taluni dei membri dell'Istituto, sono stati ostacolati o si sono addirittura visti sollevare delle eccezioni circa il legittimo esercizio delle loro attività professionali o sociali, perché -secondo quanto asserivano quelli che muovevano le difficoltà- si trattava, nel caso, di religiosi, cui siffatte attività sono per diritto interdette.

A confortare la predetta equiparazione (pregna di gravi conseguenze per l'apostolato di penetrazione dell'Istituto) si adduce da taluni come prova il fatto che i sodali sacerdoti dell'*Opus Dei*, sono incardinati, non ad una diocesi o territorio come i sacerdoti secolari, bensì all'Istituto, alla stregua dunque dei sacerdoti religiosi.

Negando così la secolarità ai sacerdoti dell'Istituto, si passa poi (in virtù di una falsa e infondata analogia) a rifiutare la secolarità stessa ai laici dell'Opus Dei. E tale è la precipua sorgente dei mali e delle difficoltà sopra specificate, con le gravi conseguenze anche indicate sopra.

Ad eliminare, per l'avvenire, simili gravi inconvenienti, occorrerebbe dare all'Istituto un nuovo assetto giuridico, corrispondente ai seguenti criteri:

chiarire definitivamente il carattere secolare dell'Istituto (e dei suoi membri) anche nella struttura giuridica esterna e nella dipendenza dai Dicasteri della S. Sede, di modo che si tolga il pretesto di assimilazione ai religiosi, sia dei laici che dei sacerdoti dell'Opus Dei; da notare peraltro che ha favorito finora l'equivoco la dipendenza esclusiva dalla S. Congregazione dei Religiosi, pur tanto benemerita verso il nostro Istituto.

Per la realizzazione di questo scopo, si prospetterebbero queste due vie:

a) Dare all'Istituto una organizzazione simile,*mutatis mutandis*, a quella della Mission de France (cfr. A.A.S. 46 (1954), 567-574). Si tratterebbe cioè di erigere in Prelatura *nullius* l'Istituto, fornendogli un territorio, sia pure simbolico, cui i sacerdoti sarebbero incardinati; e dichiarando insieme, in armonia con il can. 319 § 2 (riguardante le Prelature di meno di tre parrocchie) che lo *ius singulare*, da cui deve essere retta la Prelatura, sono le Costituzioni (già approvate) dell'Istituto.

b) Affidare al Presidente pro tempore dell'Istituto, che è eletto *ad vitam*, una Prelatura *nullius*, (già esistente o da crearsi), con annessa facoltà di incardinare i sacerdoti dell'Istituto al predetto territorio.

Per il territorio che sia in una che nell'altra soluzione sarebbe necessario (*necessitate iuris*), si indicano a titolo esemplificativo, e subordinatamente: il piccolo territorio dell'attuale sede della Casa Generalizia (Viale Bruno Buozzi 73, Roma); un piccolo territorio in una delle diocesi più o meno vicine a Roma, ma sempre in Italia, perché ciò sembra postulare la natura universale (e spiccatamente romana) dell'Istituto.

Le due soluzioni prospettate non vogliono essere, naturalmente, che a titolo di esempio. La Santa Sede, infatti, nella alta sapienza, saprà anche eventualmente scegliere quelle altre soluzioni che ritenga atte al raggiungimento degli scopi sopra enunciati.

Allo scopo si renderebbe comunque necessario un atto pontificio: o Costituzione Apostolica o Breve pontificio.

E' perciò che l'umile sottoscritto, nella sua qualifica di Fondatore e Presidente Generale dell'Istituto, si rivolge fiduciosamente alla Santità Vostra, perché, completando l'opera del venerato Predecessore di Vostra Santità, Pio XII, di f. m., Si degni, con questo nuovo atto, di voler dare la definitiva necessaria struttura al nostro Istituto, confacente ai tempi ed alle moderne finalità, per il maggior bene delle anime e più efficace servizio della Chiesa.

Della Santità Vostra

dev.mo umil.mo aff.mo figlio

Josemaría Escrivá de B.

A Sua Santità
il Santo Padre Giovanni XXIII
**Città del Vaticano**

## 45. Letter of the Secretary of State, Amleto Cardinal Cicognani, to Msgr. Escrivá regarding the revision of the juridical status of Opus Dei; May 20, 1962.

AGP, Sezione Giuridica, VI/15007.

SEGRETERIA DI STATO
DI SUA SANTITA

N. 4244/62

Dal Vaticano, 20 Maggio 1962

Ill.mo e Rev.mo Signore,

Con stimata Lettera del 7 gennaio u.s., la Signoria Vostra Illustrissima e Reverendissima presentava, perché fosse sottoposta alla augusta considerazione del Santo Padre, una istanza, nella quale implorava una nuova sistemazione giuridica della Società Sacerdotale della Santa Croce ("Opus Dei").

Ella mi ha fatto avere altresì un Appunto, datato 4 aprile, riguardante il medesimo argomento.

E' stata mia premura di portare a conoscenza di Sua Santità quanto Ella esponeva.

In esecuzione delle sovrane disposizioni, la questione, trattandosi di cosa nuova e delicata, è stata attentamente esaminata anche col parere dei Sacri Dicasteri competenti ed interessati.

Sono, adesso, a significare alla Signoria Vostra che, tutto maturamente considerato, e tenuto conto degli avvisi espressi, il Sommo Pontefice Si è degnato di manifestare l'augusta Mente.

La proposta di erigere l'"Opus Dei" in Prelatura "nullius" non può accogliersi, perché è lontana dal presentare una soluzione, e invece, incontra difficoltà pressoché insuperabili, giuridiche e pratiche. Anziché diminuire gli inconvenienti lamentati, li accrescerebbe, facendo sorgere problemi nuovi e minando lo stesso carattere di secolarità dell'Istituto.

E' da richiamare che l'"Opus Dei" è il primo degli Istituti Secolari che ha ottenuto, con l'ordinamento da esso richiesto, l'approvazione della Santa Sede dopo la Costituzione Apostolica "Provida Mater"; come tale è stato anche arricchito di privilegi, che presentemente si avrebbe difficoltà a concedersi; e infine, una modificazione di simile situazione, implicherebbe conseguenze e ripercussioni di pregiudizio alla buona disciplina.

La Signoria Vostra voglia credere -e lo confido- come la sovrana decisione sia nell'interesse e per il maggior bene dell'"Opus Dei".

Come Istituto secolare e stato di perfezione, esso dipende dalla Sacra Congregazione dei Religiosi; togliere via questa sua caratteristica sarebbe ridurlo a semplice associazione di sacerdoti e laici, con perdita dei suoi privilegi: un cambiamento radicale, e cioè da stato di perfezione a semplice movimento di apostolato.

Profitto della circostanza per formulare fervidi voti di sempre maggiore fecondità spirituale per le attività del benemerito Istituto, e con sensi di distinta stima mi confermo

della Signoria Vostra Ill.ma e Rev.ma

dev.mo nel Signore

A.G. Card. Cicognani

Il.mo e Rev.mo Signore
Monsignor GIUSEPPE M. ESCRIVÁ DE BALAGUER
Presidente Generale dell'"Opus Dei"

**ROMA**

## 46. Letter of Msgr. Escrivá to Cardinal Amleto Cicognani; June 3, 1962.

RHF, EF-620603t-1.

**Opus Dei**

---

**Il Presidente Generale**                    Roma, li 3 giugno 1962

Eminenza Reverendissima,

con la più sincera venerazione mi onoro accusare ricevimento della lettera dell'Eminenza Vostra Reverendissima, in data 20 maggio u. s., con cui la stessa Eminenza Vostra mi dà comunicazione della Mente della Santa Sede, nella questione concernente la desiderata nuova sistemazione giuridica dell'Istituto.

Per quanto tale venerata Mente sia stata contraria a quelle che erano le mie personali vedute, non posso che ringraziare sinceramente l'E. V. Rev.ma per avermela comunicata, giacché così mi ha dato modo di mostrare ancora una volta la mia completa e perfetta adesione alla Santa Sede.

Per nulla celare delle disposizioni del mio animo, devo anche manifestare all'E. V. Rev.ma che, nel leggere e meditare la venerata Mente, mi è venuto talvolta di pensare -con filiale pensiero- di non essermi espresso bene, nel formulare le mie ansietà e nell'esporre le difficoltà riscontrate dal mio Istituto nello svolgimento del lavoro di apostolato. Se tale pensiero seguitasse ad affiorare alla mia mente, forse mi permetterei, con la stessa filiale devozione, e per tranquillità della mia coscienza, di ricorrere di nuovo alla benevolenza dell'E. V. Rev.ma, per sottoporre al Santo Padre l'oggetto delle mie preoccupazioni.

Ma qualora ciò dovesse avvenire, sia certo, Eminenza, che lo farei con la sincerità di chi espone una angoscia di coscienza, ma anche con la disposizione, che ho sempre avuto e che desidero sempre avere, di fiduciosa previa accettazione di quanto viene dalla Santa Sede.

Mentre mi chino al bacio della S. Porpora, profitto della circostanza per dirmi, con sensi di profonda venerazione

dell'Eminenza Vostra Rev.ma

dev.mo nel Signore

Josemaría Escrivá de B.

---

A Sua Eminenza Rev.ma il Sig.
Card. Amleto Giovanni Cicognani
Segretario di Stato di Sua Santità

**CITTA' DEL VATICANO**

## 47. Letter of Msgr. Escrivá to the Prefect of the Sacred Congregation for Religious, Ildebrando Cardinal Antoniutti, October 31, 1963.

RHF, EF-631031-2.

**Società Sacerdotale della Santa Croce**

**e**

**Opus Dei**

**Il Presidente Generale**

Roma, 31 ottobre 1963

Eminenza Reverendissima,

mi pregio di allegare alla presente una copia dello *Ius Peculiare* dell'Opus Dei, che ho preparato in esecuzione del Rescritto di codesta S. C. per i Religiosi, IS 1/47, del 24 ottobre 1963, dopo aver chiesto ed ottenuto di introdurre le modifiche ed i chiarimenti pertinenti per meglio adeguare quel testo giuridico alla realtà della vita apostolica ed ascetica dell'Opera.

Sono consapevole che, come ho manifestato parecchie volte a V. E., manca ancora molto per arrivare alla soluzione giuridica definitiva dell'Opus Dei. Mi conforta, però, la certezza che Iddio Onnipotente, tramite la sua Chiesa Santa, non mancherà di aprirci la strada che Lui ha voluto fin dal lontano 1928 e che allora sembrava qualcosa di impossibile da realizzare.

In attesa che giunga quel momento, tutti i miei figli e figlie, sparsi in tutto il mondo, continuano a pregare per questa intenzione, perché son ben consci che l'Opus Dei è di diritto un Istituto Secolare, ma non lo è *di fatto*. Non abbiamo fretta, perché il Signore nella sua infinita ed inscrutabile Sapienza, ci mostrerà la strada ed il tempo opportuni per compiere la sua Volontà riguardo all'Opus Dei, che -mi preme dirlo- è veramente Suo e non di questo povero peccatore.

Mi è grato profittare della circostanza per manifestare a V. E. i sensi della mia stima, e confermarmi

dell'Eminenza Vostra Rev.ma

dev.mo in Domino

Josemaría Escrivá de B.

A Sua Eminenza Rev.ma il Sig.
Card. Ildebrando Antoniutti
Prefetto della S.C. dei Religiosi

**ROMA**

## 48. Letter of Msgr. Escrivá to His Holiness Paul VI; February 14, 1964.

RHF, EF-640214t-2.

Opus Dei
_____

**Il Presidente Generale**                              Roma, li 14 febbraio 1964

Beatissimo Padre,

con cuore grato e commosso sono a ripeterLe la gioia e i sentimenti di filiale e devoto affetto per la recente Udienza accordatami.

L'averLa potuta avvicinare e ascoltare, l'aver sentito il Suo sguardo paterno e amabile, l'aver raccolto la Sua benedizione per tutta l'Opera, ben mi hanno ripagato dei 36 anni di servizio alla Santa Madre Chiesa attraverso la mia vocazione all'Opus Dei. Mi sembrava di rivedere l'amabile sorriso e di riascoltare le benevole parole d'incoraggiamento -furono le prime che ascoltai nel Vaticano- di S. E. Mons. Montini, nel già lontano 1946: ma adesso era Pietro a sorridere, a parlare, a benedire!

Sono lieto d'inviarLe, secondo il desiderio espressomi, un volumetto contenente lo *Ius peculiare dell'Opus Dei* (Costituzioni), al quale mi compiaccio di unirne un altro riguardante lo spirito dell'Opera, affinché meglio possa conoscerne il tessuto interiore che l'anima.

Unisco altresì un appunto, nel quale si mettono brevemente in risalto alcune note caratteristiche e salienti dell'Associazione e si registrano alcune esperienze, che ritengo doveroso segnalare all'attenzione della Santità Vostra. Come allegato a questo appunto, penso infine opportuno rimetterLe, per le interessanti riflessioni che vi sono contenute, fotocopia di qualche pagina del libro del Card. Suenens "Promotion apostolique de la religieuse", recentemente dato alla stampa. Invio il tutto con gioia e con spirito di obbedienza.

Per quanto concerne l'assetto giuridico dell'Opus Dei, tengo a ribadire quanto ebbi occasione di dirLe a viva voce e cioè che non abbiamo fretta: tuttavia è grande la nostra speranza nel definitivo auspicato ordinamento, per assicurare la migliore esplicazione della nostra specifica vocazione nonché il miglior rendimento del nostro servizio filiale alla Chiesa. La nostra ansia spirituale è perfettamente compatibile con la pace e la fiducia derivanti dalla fede, dall'amore e dalla speranza nella Santa Chiesa di Dio e nel Papa.

L'occasione mi fa ardito -consapevole come sono della reale difficoltà dell'accoglimento della mia preghiera- per dire alla Santità Vostra che sarebbe un grande conforto e un grande beneficio, per l'anima mia e per i molti figli dell'Opus Dei, se mi fosse data di quando in quando occasione di una viva Sua parola d'incoraggiamento e di guida, come mi venne offerta nella recente indimenticabile Udienza.

Mentre invoco dalla Santità Vostra il conforto della benedizione apostolica su tutti i Suoi figli dell'Opus Dei e su tutti gli apostolati perseguiti dall'Opera, assicurando la costante preghiera di tutti per la Sua Persona e per le Sue intenzioni, mi confermo della Santità Vostra

devotissimo e ubbidientissimo figlio

Josemaría Escrivá de B.

A Sua Santità il
Santo Padre Paolo VI
**CITTA' DEL VATICANO**

---

### 49. Letter of Msgr. Escrivá to Archbishop Angelo Dell'Acqua, Undersecretary of State; August 15, 1964.

RHF, EF-640815t-2.

Parigi, lì 15 agosto 1964

Reverendissima e cara Eccellenza,

E' sempre per me un motivo di grande gioia il rivolgermi, sia pure per iscritto, all'E. V. Ma oggi la gioia è ancor più intensa, perché ho testé letto il testo integro dell'Enciclica *Ecclesiam Suam*, e, essendomisi presentata la possibilità di inviarLe questa lettera a mano, dalla *douce France*, non posso non dire a V. E. quanto ho goduto leggendo e meditando le illuminate parole del S. Padre, così piene di spirito soprannaturale e di saggezza umana; e che tanto bene si addicono ai membri dell'Opus Dei, il cui spirito e la cui maniera di agire sembrano come dipinti con vigorose ma dolci pennellate nel Documento del nostro Padre Comune: la priorità dell'interiorità spirituale; la carità ordinata; la vita contemplativa, che suona come antinomia di quella attiva, e che è tuttavia assolutamente necessaria per poter perseverare nell'Opus Dei; il desiderio di dialogo con tutti, per portare tutti alla vera dottrina di N. Signore; la povertà personale amata e vissuta; l'essere nel mondo senza essere del mondo; l'importanza santificante del lavoro (*Opus Dei*, per noi, è *lavoro di Dio*: l'uomo fu creato *ut operaretur*); il bisogno di comprendere tutti, per servire tutti. E soprattutto, mi ha riempito di allegria la chiarezza dei concetti sul Pontefice Romano, e sul vero significato dell'aggiornamento - continuo ringiovanirsi- della Santa Chiesa di Dio. Posso pregarLa, Eccellenza, di voler porgere al S. Padre l'espressione della mia filiale adesione al Suo alto insegnamento, e il mio ringraziamento per così sana dottrina, ottimo alimento per me e per i membri tutti dell'Opus Dei, e valido sprone che ci rassicura nel nostro cammino? Se ritiene riguardoso farlo, La pregherei inoltre di aggiungere che ogni giorno chiedo al Signore tante cose nella S. Messa e lungo tutta la giornata, per la Persona e per le intenzioni del Papa, per il Suo Pontificato, e per il felice esito del Concilio.

Vorrei dirLe ancora, Eccellenza carissima, che prego anche continuamente per la sistemazione giuridica definitiva dell'Opus Dei. Non ho fretta -anche se mi preme il pensiero che, in qualsiasi momento, potrà dirmi il Signore: *redde rationem villicationis tuæ*-, ma penso che, a Concilio finito, forse si potrebbe studiare la nostra questione. E già sin d'ora, per quando arriverà l'occasione di fare tale studio, credo mio obbligo far umilmente presente che l'Opus Dei, come ebbe a dirmi V. E. più di una volta, è un fenomeno pastorale nuovo, e come tale quindi amo sperare che sia studiato.

Se, come di prassi, si chiederà allora -quando si farà tale studio- il parere di alcune persone della Curia, non mi potrebbe affatto recar meraviglia che queste, in perfetta buona fede, e pur essendo degli ottimi specialisti in Sacra Teologia o in Diritto, arrivassero a delle conclusioni contrarie, anzi contraddittorie -anche riguardo a dei fatti concreti-, se si basassero soltanto sui documenti che ho inviato al S. Padre: e ciò per il fatto che non conoscerebbero bene la nostra vita vissuta; la realtà della nostra dedizione specifica, in mezzo al mondo; lo spirito peculiare; le difficoltà che riscontriamo, ecc. Cose tutte che evidentemente non ho potuto mettere per iscritto, perché ne sarebbe venuto fuori un documento troppo lungo che non avrei avuto l'ardire di inviare al S. Padre.

A modo di esempio, per illustrare quanto ho or ora affermato, ritengo opportuno dirLe che pochi giorni prima della mia partenza da Roma, venne da me un Prelato della Curia -non italiano, né spagnolo-, e parlai a lungo con lui, leggendogli qualche mio vecchio documento indirizzato ai miei figli. Mentre io leggevo e commentavo quello scritto, lui, con grandissimo interesse e con sorpresa, che non cercava di dissimulare, mi faceva delle domande, ed alla fine mi disse: "Peccato! Qualche tempo fa ho dovuto esprimere un mio parere su alcune cose attinenti l'Opus Dei, e vedo che mi sono sbagliato in pieno, che non ho interpretato bene quello che adesso, dopo questo dialogo con Lei, capisco benissimo!".

Simili sbagli, che facilmente si possono prevedere, sono dovuti -ripeto- alla mancanza di dati sulla nostra non breve esperienza apostolica e sulla nostra peculiare spiritualità: e, d'altra parte, alla stessa accennata novità del fenomeno pastorale dell'Opus Dei, che non può essere giudicato, né capito, con la mentalità di chi è abituato a studiare problemi della vita clericale, o religiosa, ma che non è solito ricercare o immedesimarsi nei problemi dei laici, i quali devono vivere sì staccati dal mondo, ma nel mondo, inseriti nelle strutture temporali: esercitando per esigenza della loro vocazione secolare, da veri professionisti, il lavoro ordinario del proprio mestiere, del quale vivono, e del quale avrebbero vissuto pure se non fossero stati membri dell'Opus Dei: non come dilettanti, alla maniera in cui alcuni religiosi o sacerdoti esercitano mestieri secolari, o coltivano scienze profane. Lavoro professionale o mestiere che i membri dell'Opus Dei cercano di rendere santificato e santificante, onde poter svolgere con efficacia l'apostolato dell'amicizia e dell'esempio fra i colleghi. Con una mentalità non abituata a valutare gli sforzi apostolici del laicato, è oltremodo facile per esempio che la perseveranza nell'esercizio del lavoro professionale -senza badare a fatiche o a stanchezze- venga addirittura scambiata per il desiderio di salire, di avere cariche, di ambirle, quando invece si tratta soltanto di santificarsi con tale lavoro, fatto con grande slancio e generosità -e con la maggiore possibile perfezione, anche umana- per amore di Dio e per attirare le anime a Cristo ed alla Sua Chiesa, in difficile, abnegata ed umile missione di servizio.

E' pure da notare che in generale lo Spirito Santo Vivificatore, non procede nella Santa Chiesa per salti, e così ciascun nuovo fenomeno da Lui suscitato ha qualche rassomiglianza con altri movimenti precedentemente promossi da Dio: sono anelli della stessa catena. Per questo motivo, la Storia Ecclesiastica insegna che, nel vedere che la rassomiglianza tra i diversi anelli non è perfetta, alcuni non capiscono il motivo delle novità, e molto spesso si è detto, col passare dei secoli, che i nuovi fenomeni pastorali ambivano avere i vantaggi dei religiosi e quelli dei secolari: e ciò perché i nuovi arrivati volevano avere una maggiore elasticità ed agilità nell'apostolato, allontanandosi così dai moduli religiosi classici, per avvicinarsi a quelli secolari. Ma nel caso nostro siamo di fronte ad un fenomeno diverso, perché noi non siamo come religiosi secolarizzati, ma dei veri secolari -preti diocesani in ciascuna diocesi, e laici comuni- che non cercano la *vita di perfezione evangelica* propria dei religiosi, ma la *perfezione cristiana nel mondo, nel proprio stato*. Eppure, anche di noi si è fatta da anni quella vecchia critica.

Onde poter spiegare meglio tutto -qualora si formasse una Commissione, o si interpellassero alcune persone, sia teologi che giuristi- penso quindi che sarebbe sommamente opportuno che io potessi spiegare personalmente a ciascuna di esse, non solo come teologo e come giurista, ma soprattutto (non è superbia) come quello che più conosce la nostra vita: i frutti del nostro servizio alla Chiesa ed alle anime, concessi dal Signore in questi 36 anni; le difficoltà riscontrate; i motivi di queste difficoltà, e quanto di più quelle persone volessero sapere. Sono certo che, con questi augurabili contatti personali, con questo studio comune, si potrebbe arrivare ad una unità di criterio, e che le persone eventualmente designate per fare tale studio benediranno Iddio, perché ha voluto promuovere questo nostro apostolato. Con tutta sincerità, penso ugualmente che nessuno potrebbe considerare il suo parere come definitivo senza sentirmi prima, senza un chiarificatore dialogo, perché senza questo studio fatto insieme non potrebbe certamente avere sufficiente conoscenza dell'Opus Dei, mancandogli i dati che io umilmente dovrei fornire.

In questa guisa si potrà arrivare ad una soluzione che non sia di eccezione, né di privilegio, ma che ci permetta lavorare in tale maniera che i Rev.mi Ordinari che noi amiamo *opere et veritate*, siano sempre contenti del nostro lavoro; che i diritti dei Vescovi continuino ad essere, come adesso, ben saldi e sicuri; e, finalmente, che noi possiamo seguire il nostro cammino, di amore e di dedizione, senza inutili ostacoli a questo servizio alla Chiesa, e cioè, al Papa, ai Vescovi, alle anime.

Oso sperare che il grande cuore del S. Padre, in cui entriamo tutti -cattolici, fratelli separati, non cristiani, e anche gli atei e i persecutori della Chiesa-, permetterà questo mio dialogo con chi debba studiare la nostra questione: dialogo che da tanto tempo mantengo io, come pure tutte queste migliaia di figli di 62 nazioni, con Dio Nostro Signore, affinché Egli si degni dare la sistemazione giuridica definitiva a quest'Opera Sua, per garantirne sempre lo spirito soprannaturale e l'efficacia apostolica. Forse quello che ardisco chiedere è fuori della *prassi*: ma penso solo al bene della Chiesa, e ciò mi incoraggia a sperare che Sua Santità, Che con la Sua paterna bontà sta superando tante cose, vorrà esaudire questi desideri dell'ultimo Suo figlio, e mi concederà l'occasione di intervenire nello studio di questo problema.

Nei primi di settembre sarò di nuovo a Roma -adesso lascio Parigi-, e farò avvertire il Suo Segretario del mio arrivo, affinché, quando V. E. possa, mi voglia concedere il piacere di salutarLa di persona.

Mi scusi, cara Eccellenza, di questa lunga lettera. Io prego ogni giorno per V. E. : preghi pure per me, facendo con la mia persona questo grande *divinum commercium!*

Con grande affetto, sono sempre di V. E.

dev.mo in Domino

Josemaría Escrivá de B.

---

## 50. Letter of Msgr. Escrivá to Cardinal Antoniutti, Prefect of the Sacred Congregation for Religious and Secular Institutes with regard to the convocation of a Special General Congress of Opus Dei; May 20, 1969.

RHF, EF-690520t-2.

*Società Sacerdotale della Santa Croce*

*e*

*Opus Dei*

---

Roma, 20 maggio 1969

Eminenza Reverendissima,

il Decreto *Perfectæ Caritatis* esige che gli istituti religiosi provvedano all'aggiornamento voluto dal Concilio Vaticano II, secondo lo spirito dei Fondatori e le fonti autentiche degli stessi istituti; e con il *Motu Proprio Ecclesiæ Sanctæ*, nella Sezione intitolata *Normæ ad exsequendum Decretum ss. Concilii Vaticani II "Perfectæ Caritatis"* vengono stabiliti la procedura ed i tempi con cui portare a termine detto aggiornamento.

Poiché tali obblighi non concernevano l'Opus Dei, non essendo esso un istituto religioso, non abbiamo mai fatto nulla in tal senso. D'altro canto, come è noto, l'Opus Dei venne approvato il 24 febbraio 1947 come Istituto Secolare, e, per poter fare ciò, si dovette forzare il suo spirito primitivo in modo che si adeguasse alla C. A. *Provida Mater Ecclesia*, che nelle disposizioni della sua *Lex Peculiaris* non riusciva ad accogliere tutte le esigenze fondamentali dello spirito della nostra Opera.

In considerazione di quanto sopra, ed appellandoci al principio generale, enunciato nel n. 2 del succitato Decreto, che cioè *in ipsum Ecclesiæ bonum cedit ut instituta peculiarem suam indolem ac munus habeant,* desidereremmo ora procedere al rinnovamento ed adattamento del nostro attuale diritto peculiare. In tal senso, pur non essendo religiosi, vorremmo seguire, *congrua congruis referendo,* la procedura indicata nel surriferito M. P. *Ecclesiæ Sanctæ,* chiedendo al tempo stesso a codesta Sacra Congregazione autorizzazione affinché, per quanto riguarda il periodo di tempo stabilito per portare a termine detta revisione, esso venga computato a partire dalla data odierna.

Con l'occasione, mi è grato rinnovarLe i sensi della mia profonda considerazione, mentre mi confermo volentieri,

dell'Eminenza Vostra Rev.ma

dev.mo in Domino

L + S

Josemaría Escrivá de B.

Pres. Gen.

A Sua Eminenza Rev.ma il Sig.
Card. Ildebrando Antoniutti
Prefetto della S.C. per i Religiosi
e gli Istituti Secolari
ROMA

## 51. Letter of Cardinal Antoniutti to Msgr. Escrivá in reply to his letter of May 20; June 11, 1969.

AGP, Sezione Giuridica, VII/15135.

SACRA CONGREGAZIONE
PER I RELIGIOSI                     Roma, 11 Giugno 1969
E GLI ISTITUTI SECOLARI

Prot. N. I.S. 1/47
Reverendissimo Monsignore,

Prendo atto della Sua comunicazione del 20 Maggio concernente la revisione del diritto particolare della Società Sacerdotale della Santa Croce e Opus Dei, e desidero comunicarLe che, in virtù del Motu Proprio "Ecclesiæ sanctæ", possono essere portati a termine i lavori del Congresso anche dopo la data dell'undici Ottobre, secondo lo spirito dei documenti pontifici pel miglior bene dell'Opera cui Ella presiede.

Con i migliori auguri e con sensi di distinta considerazione, mi confermo

Suo dev.mo in Domino

E. Heston, csc.          I. Card. Antoniutti

Segr.                    Pref.

Reverendissimo Signore
Mons. JOSEMARÍA ESCRIVÁ DE BALAGUER
Presidente della Società Sacerdotale
della Santa Croce e Opus Dei
ROMA

## 52. Letter of Rev. Alvaro del Portillo, Secretary General of Opus Dei to Cardinal Antoniutti regarding the progress of the Special General Congress; September 18, 1969.

AGP, Sezione Giuridica, VII/15276.

*Opus Dei*

*Il Segretario Generale*                    Roma, 18 settembre 1969

Eminenza Reverendissima,

per incarico del nostro Presidente Generale, mi pregio di informarLa che, d'accordo con quanto disposto nel M.P. *Ecclesiæ Sanctæ* e con quanto comunicatoci da codesta Sacra Congregazione con lettera prot. N.I.S. 1/47, dell'11/6/69, nei giorni 1-15 del mese in corso hanno avuto luogo in Roma, in separate sedi, la prima parte dei Congressi Generali Speciali rispettivamente della Sezione Maschile e della Sezione Femminile dell'Opus Dei, per la revisione del nostro *Ius Peculiare*.

Questa prima fase è stata preceduta da molta preghiera e mortificazione, nonché da uno studio approfondito che ha dato origine ad un numero assai abbondante di consulte e richieste di comunicazioni, provenienti da tutte le parti del mondo dove l'Opera è estesa, e che sono poi state elaborate dai partecipanti ai Congressi.

Accludo, per una più ampia informazione di codesto Sacro Dicastero, due relazioni riassuntive del lavoro svolto nelle due Sezioni dell'Opera.

Ora, continuerà lo studio di alcuni punti trattati nei Congressi e di altri che momentaneamente non si sono potuti ancora affrontare: il che darà luogo ad ulteriori richieste di comunicazioni, provenienti da una base amplissima di soci e di associate dell'Opus Dei di 73 nazionalità, dei più svariati mestieri e professioni, e che verranno elaborate nella 2ª parte dei Congressi. In tal modo contiamo di poter terminare, con l'aiuto di Dio, il lavoro di aggiornamento dell'*Ius Peculiare* entro l'anno prossimo.

Con l'occasione, mi è grato porgerLe i sensi della mia piú alta considerazione, e confermarmi

dell'Eminenza Vostra Reverendissima

dev.mo nel Signore

Alvaro del Portillo

Segr. Gen.

A Sua Eminenza Rev.ma
il Sig. Card. Ildebrando Antoniutti
*ROMA*

**53.** *Letter of Father Edward Heston, secretary of the Sacred Congregation for Religious and Secular Institutes to Rev. Alvaro del Portillo, in which he acknowledges receipt of the letter of September 18; October 7, 1969.*

AGP, Sezione Giuridica, VII/15389.

SACRA CONGREGAZIONE                        Roma, 7 Ottobre 1969
  PER I RELIGIOSI
E GLI ISTITUTI SECOLARI
      ———————

   Prot. N. I.S. 1/47

  Reverendissimo Signore,

   E' pervenuto a questa Sacra Congregazione il Rapporto trasmesso dalla Signoria Vostra in data 18 Settembre p.p., circa la celebrazione dei Congressi Generali Speciali rispettivamente delle sezioni maschile e femminile dell'Opus Dei, che hanno avuto luogo recentemente in accordo con le disposizioni del Motu Proprio "Ecclesiæ Sanctæ".

   E' stato preso atto delle eccellenti disposizioni che hanno dimostrato i partecipanti ai citati Congressi, e si attende di conoscere le proposte che verranno avanzate per la revisione del "Ius Peculiare" dell'Istituto.

   RingraziandoLa dei Suoi cortesi uffici, con i migliori auguri mi confermo

        Suo devotissimo

        E. Heston, csc.

        Segr.


  ———————————

  Reverendissimo Signore
  D. ALVARO DEL PORTILLO
  Segretario Generale dell'Opus Dei
  *ROMA*

## 54. Letter of Msgr. Escrivá to Cardinal Antoniutti with respect to the Special General Congress and its aims; October 22, 1969.

RHF, EF-691022t-1.

*Opus Dei*

_____

*Il Presidente Generale*                                        Roma, 22 ottobre 1969

Eminenza Reverendissima,

mi è pervenuta la lettera di codesta S. Congregazione, in data 8 ottobre u.s., in cui si accusa ricevimento della Relazione inviata dopo la conclusione della prima parte del Congresso Generale Straordinario dell'Opus Dei, che ha avuto luogo a Roma, nello scorso mese di settembre.

Nella medesima lettera, l'Ecc.mo Segretario di codesta S. Congregazione si dichiara in attesa di conoscere le modifiche giuridiche che, in forza delle facoltà concesse dal M. P. "Ecclesiæ Sanctæ", verranno introdotte dal detto Congresso Straordinario, nel nostro "Ius peculiare".

In riferimento alla predetta domanda, devo far presente all'E. V. di essere in grado di poter fornire soltanto le linee ed i criteri generali di dette modifiche. Ciò in quanto, pur essendo stati preparati, nella fase precedente l'inizio del Congresso Straordinario, studi accurati dopo consultazione dei soci, detto Congresso nella sua prima parte ha ritenuto opportuno limitarsi ad elaborare dei criteri generali, onde poter indire, prima della seconda parte, una nuova consultazione generale, per un adempimento il più completo possibile di quanto disposto nel citato M.P. "Ecclesiæ Sanctæ", al n. 4 della parte prima.

Ora noi ci troviamo in questa fase, preparatoria della seconda parte, che sarà quella conclusiva. Comunque, per quanto riguarda le linee ed i criteri generali delle eventuali modifiche, il Congresso Generale Straordinario ha constatato ed auspicato quanto segue.

Ha rilevato innanzitutto che la natura canonica di Istituto Secolare si è dimostrata inadeguata alla realtà sociologica, spirituale e pastorale dell'Opus Dei, sia secondo il carisma fondazionale, che secondo una esperienza ultra ventennale di lavoro pastorale, che essendo stata collaudata in tutto il mondo ha, per ciò stesso, valore universale.

Ha preso atto che al momento dell'approvazione fu operata una forzatura, includendo l'Opus Dei fra gli Istituti di perfezione: e ciò per forza di cose, in quanto che quella era l'unica via, nel diritto allora vigente, per poter usufruire di un regime a carattere universale, postulato sia dalla natura che dallo sviluppo già allora raggiunto dell'Opus Dei.

Allora infatti, com'è a tutti noto, per poter porre giuridicamente in essere le strutture e i poteri che sorreggono un regime a carattere universale, era condizione necessaria la professione dei consigli evangelici da parte dei membri della persona morale erigenda.

Il Congresso ha perciò espresso il criterio di poter giungere legittimamente a separare l'incorporazione dei sodali all'Istituto (che con un'apposita formula giuridica porrebbe sempre in essere un vincolo perpetuo, mutuo e pieno) dalla emissione, oggi necessaria, dei voti o vincoli equipollenti: in quanto troverebbe più consono alla natura dell'Istituto il risolvere questo problema sulla base del primo comandamento della legge di Dio (che esprime e contiene la chiamata universale alla santità) e sulla pratica di determinate virtù, ma non necessariamente tipificate nei tre consigli evangelici.

Risulta peraltro al Congresso che il desiderio di uscire dal quadro giuridico degli Istituti di perfezione è una necessità avvertita, sia pure per diversi motivi, non solo da diversi Istituti Secolari, ma anche da alcune Società di vita comune. Saremmo dunque innanzi ad un problema ecclesiale, sul quale dovrebbero soffermarsi gli organi legislativi e di governo della Chiesa. Il Congresso ha voluto comunque prendere atto che, nel caso dell'Opus Dei, questo desiderio di uscire dal quadro giuridico degli Istituti di perfezione viene avvalorato, oltre che dalla situazione citata, comune ai suddetti Istituti che professano lo stato di perfezione, anche dal fatto che, come esposto più sopra, l'inclusione dell'Opus Dei fra detti Istituti di perfezione -e conseguentemente la sua dipendenza dalla S.C. dei Religiosi- è stata una forzatura dovuta all'insufficienza dell'ordinamento canonico vigente, ma non rispondente alla reale natura dell'Opus Dei.

Il Congresso ha espresso ancora il voto che si studi il modo di mettere più efficacemente in risalto il carattere secolare dell'Istituto e dei suoi membri, che non mutano condizione in seno all'ordinamento giuridico della Chiesa.

La perfetta e piena secolarità dei membri è stata infatti catalogata come vera *conditio sine qua non*, per il lavoro sociale e professionale che gli stessi membri, per dovere di vocazione, debbono esercitare in seno alla società, e in tutte le sue strutture, che è peraltro il loro specifico mezzo di santificazione e di apostolato.

Il voto di ubbidienza, benché la sua materia sia perfettamente delimitata in modo da salvare accuratamente e pienamente la personale libertà dei membri in materia professionale, sociale e politica, crea tuttavia degli equivoci nella mentalità corrente, ignara, quando non prevenuta, di questi problemi.

La stessa efficacia del lavoro pastorale dello Opus Dei è spesso ostacolata, quando non compromessa, dall'idea ormai acquisita presso l'opinione pubblica circa la natura degli Istituti Secolari, che vengono di fatto -anche se erroneamente- equiparati ai Religiosi.

La predetta arbitraria equiparazione (della quale è difficile aver ragione) è particolarmente nociva e stridente nel caso nostro -come ha voluto sottolineare il Congresso-, in quanto che il lavoro che svolge sia l'Istituto che i suoi membri non è un lavoro ecclesiastico, bensì laicale e secolare; e così pure i beni di cui l'Opera si serve per il proprio lavoro, non sono ecclesiastici, sia per la titolarità della loro proprietà che per l'origine dei medesimi.

Nell'Istituto, infine, prevale il carattere secolare ed apostolico su quello di perfezione, inteso nel senso di uno stato di vita tipificato dalla professione dei tre consigli evangelici.

Il Congresso ha preso finalmente atto, con vivo senso di gratitudine e di speranza, che dopo il Concilio Ecumenico Vaticano II possono esistere in seno all'ordinamento della Chiesa, altre forme canoniche, con regime a carattere universale, che non richiedono la professione dei consigli evangelici, da parte dei componenti la persona morale (cfr. n. 10 del Dec. "Presbyterorum Ordinis" e n. 4 del M. Pr. "Ecclesiæ Sanctæ").

Ecco, Eminenza, le linee generali e sintetiche del panorama giuridico che è stato prospettato nella prima parte del Congresso Straordinario dell'Opus Dei, e sul quale si sta svolgendo una nuova consultazione generale.

Come V. E. stessa potrà rilevare, alcune di queste eventuali modifiche (che sono tuttora allo stato di proposte), potrebbero essere introdotte dallo stesso Congresso Generale, altre richiederebbero un'approvazione della S. Sede, ed altre, infine, in quanto comporterebbero un cambiamento di natura dell'Istituto, postulerebbero addirittura un atto più solenne della S. Sede, cioè una nuova erezione dell'Istituto.

Tutto ciò verrà naturalmente sottoposto, al momento opportuno, al giudizio di codesta S. Congregazione.

Chino al bacio della Sacra Romana Porpora, colgo l'occasione per dirmi con sensi di alta e profonda stima

dell'Eminenza Vostra Reverendissima

dev.mo in Domino

Josemaría Escrivá de B.

A Sua Eminenza Rev.ma il Sig.
Card. Ildebrando Antoniutti
Prefetto della S.C. per i Religiosi
e gli Istituti Secolari
ROMA

## 55. Conclusions of the Special General Congress of Opus Dei; September 14, 1970.

AGP, Sezione Giuridica, VII/15256.

Al finalizar esta fase de la Segunda Parte del Congreso General Especial, en el que el Fundador y Presidente General del Opus Dei ha querido solicitar expresamente el libre parecer de todos los participantes sobre el grave problema institucional de nuestra Asociación, al haber tenido que aceptar en 1947 -por razones de todos bien conocidas- la legislación propia de los Institutos Seculares de perfección, los Representantes de las Regiones presentes ahora en Roma -unidos a todos los participantes en la Primera Parte de este Congreso y a todos los que han intervenido en las especiales Semanas Regionales de Trabajo tenidas en el primer trimestre de este año- después de reiterar el profundo amor de todos a la Iglesia y su unión al Papa y al entero Colegio Episcopal, han votado y aprobado unánimemente las siguientes conclusiones:

1ª)  -Teniendo en cuenta el deseo del Concilio Ecuménico Vaticano II y de la Santa Sede de que se proceda a la revisión del derecho propio de cada asociación de la Iglesia, respetando y observando cuidadosamente el espíritu del respectivo Fundador, así como las sanas tradiciones que constituyen el patrimonio de cada institución (cfr. Decr. *Perfectæ caritatis*, n. 2; Motu pr. *Ecclesiæ Sanctæ*, del 6-VIII-1966, II, Art. 12, b), y

-Habiendo considerado una vez más, con amor y con firme propósito de fidelidad, las continuas enseñanzas del Fundador y Presidente General *ad vitam* del Opus Dei, que nos ha transmitido una doctrina y un espíritu, con un contenido teológico y una finalidad eclesial netamente diversos de los que son propios de las instituciones que profesan el *estado de perfección* o de *vida consagrada,*

Ruegan al Fundador y Presidente General de la Obra que, en el momento y forma que él considere más oportunos, renueve ante la Santa Sede su humilde y esperanzada petición para que se resuelva definitivamente el problema institucional del Opus Dei, otorgándole -en base a las nuevas perspectivas jurídicas que han abierto las disposiciones y las normas de aplicación de los Decretos conciliares- una configuración jurídica diversa de la de *Instituto Secular*: la cual conserve substancialmente nuestro actual derecho peculiar, pero permita suprimir de él los elementos propios de los Institutos de perfección, es decir, la profesión de los tres consejos evangélicos de pobreza, castidad y obediencia (cfr. Const. Ap. *Provida Mater Ecclesia*, Art. I, III y *passim*; Const. dogm. *Lumen Gentium*, n. 43 y Decr. *Perfectæ caritatis*, n. 11) y la obligatoriedad de esa profesión mediante vínculos de carácter sagrado (cfr. Const. Ap. *Provida Mater Ecclesia*, Art. III, § 2, nn. 1°, 2°, 3°; Const. dogm. *Lumen gentium*, n. 44).

2ª) Expresan al Padre la unánime convicción de que en la revisión del derecho particular del Opus Dei es absolutamente necesario que venga reafirmada la importancia constitucional de la perfecta unidad de la Obra: que, incluyendo socios sacerdotes y laicos, que no forman clases distintas, permite realizar un servicio a la Iglesia universal sólidamente apoyado en esta inseparable unidad de vocación, de espiritualidad y de régimen.

Recuerdan que esta unidad de la Obra fue ya sancionada en 1943, en el Decreto de erección diocesana del Opus Dei, concedido por el Obispo de Madrid con el *nihil obstat* de la Santa Sede y reafirmada sucesivamente en el Decreto de erección pontificia, otorgado en 1947, y en el Decreto con el que la misma Santa Sede aprobó el Derecho particular del Opus Dei en 1950.

Testimonian -recogiendo la experiencia de toda la vida de la Obra- la gran utilidad y conveniencia que tiene el hecho de que todos los socios laicos del Opus Dei hayan contado siempre con la insustituible ayuda del ministerio doctrinal y sacramental de los sacerdotes de la Obra, gracias a que estos sacerdotes, que proceden a su vez de entre los mismos socios laicos, reciben una formación pastoral específica para ese ministerio, al cual son destinados por el Presidente General del Opus Dei.

3ª) Se unen también plenamente al deseo de nuestro Fundador de que, volviendo a lo que es el espíritu genuino y las tradiciones de la Obra desde su Fundación el 2 de octubre de 1928, se eliminen las normas sobre la administración de bienes, que resultan inadecuadas a nuestro espíritu, ya que en 1943 y en 1947 hubo que aceptar disposiciones canónicas que no se acomodaban a lo que se venía viviendo en la Obra desde el principio.

Desean, a la vez, que se redacten nuevas normas administrativas -deben ser poquísimas y muy concisas-, y se refleje también de modo claro el criterio que en la Obra se ha vivido siempre con respecto a la naturaleza y a la titularidad civil de los bienes que se utilizan por los socios -ciudadanos corrientes-, para realizar labores de apostolado.

Simultáneamente subrayan también el valor y la eficacia apostólica que tiene la generosidad con que los socios de la Obra -siguiendo el ejemplo del Padre y de los primeros- han procurado vivir totalmente desprendidos de los bienes terrenos, y la alegría con que han llevado las consecuencias de este desprendimiento, por amor a Jesucristo y a las almas.

4ª) Reiteran su aprobación a todas las demás Propuestas sancionadas en las Sesiones plenarias del Congreso, con criterios y directrices para la revisión de nuestro *Ius peculiare* y para la ampliación del volumen *De Spiritu.*

Aprueban a la vez unánimemente que se continúe esta Segunda Parte del Congreso General Especial del Opus Dei a través del trabajo de la Comisión Técnica -con las dos Subcomisiones jurídica y teológica-, que ha sido constituida por nuestro Fundador en aplicación de las resoluciones tomadas en la Primera Parte del Congreso (Sesión 10ª, Propuesta n. 13, 1º).

5ª) Reafirman una vez más la plena actualidad y eficacia espiritual de todas las Normas y Costumbres de piedad, que se adecúan perfectamente a las diversísimas circunstancias de la vida de los socios que, en *unidad de vocación*, procuran vivir cristianamente, *cada uno en su propio estado*, por la *santificación del trabajo profesional ordinario*, el fiel cumplimiento de todos sus deberes y el leal ejercicio -personalmente libre y personalmente responsable- de todos sus derechos civiles, sociales, familiares, profesionales, etc., como ciudadanos y cristianos corrientes.

A la vez, hacen constar la perfecta vigencia de la formación espiritual y doctrinal-religiosa que la Obra imparte a sus socios; con alabanza expresa de las características de esa formación y de los medios que se vienen empleando para este fin.

6ª) Desean manifestar, finalmente, que estas Conclusiones y todas las Propuestas formuladas son fruto de la enseñanza y de la dedicación con que el Presidente General ha formado a todos sus hijos. Como muchas veces han utilizado incluso sus mismas palabras sin hacerlo constar, todos los participantes en los trabajos del Congreso desean también pedir perdón por esta negligencia filial, que tiene como único atenuante el deseo de todos de corresponder a la gracia de Dios en el Opus Dei, siguiendo generosamente los caminos que ha enseñado a los socios de la Obra su Fundador, que con tanto amor, claridad y desvelo dirige el Opus Dei.

## 56. Letter of Rev. Alvaro del Portillo to Cardinal Antoniutti informing him of the progress in the executive phase of the conclusions of the Special General Congress; March 23, 1971.

AGP, Sezione Giuridica, VII/15026.

*Opus Dei*

---

*Il Segretario Generale*                    Roma, 23 marzo 1971

Eminenza Reverendissima,

nel corso della prima parte del Congresso Generale Straordinario dell'Opus Dei, sul cui svolgimento ebbi già occasione di informare codesto Sacro Dicastero con lettera del 18 settembre 1969, fu deciso, per espresso desiderio del nostro Fondatore e Presidente Generale, di approfondire ulteriormente le consultazioni da farsi in tutte le Regioni, allo scopo di preparare nel migliore dei modi la 2ª parte del Congresso Straordinario delle due Sezioni dell'Opera.

Così, infatti, è avvenuto e da parte di 50.710 soci di 77 nazionalità sono state presentate 54.781 comunicazioni, che sono ora oggetto di attenta considerazione e studio. Poi, come ci è stato confermato per iscritto dell'Ecc.mo Segretario P. Heston, al termine di tutto il lavoro, che attualmente procede in sede di commissioni tecniche, sarà nostra premura comunicare tempestivamente a codesto Sacro Dicastero le decisioni e proposte approvate dal Congresso in ordine alla revisione dell'attuale *Ius Peculiare* dell'Opus Dei.

Tuttavia, poiché il materiale di studio è enorme e si prevede che i lavori difficilmente potranno essere ultimati entro il 1972, desidererei informare nel frattempo codesta Sacra Congregazione circa due fra le decisioni di maggior rilievo adottate nel corso della prima parte del Congresso Generale Straordinario, anche se nessuna di esse comporta mutamenti della struttura dell'Opera o delle norme di diritto comune.

La prima si riferisce ai giuramenti di cui ai numeri 20 e 58 dello *Ius Peculiare*. Il nostro Fondatore e Presidente Generale ha fatto presente che, dalla fondazione dell'Opera, i soci hanno sempre agito in ogni campo seguendo il dettato della propria coscienza rettamente formata, e che l'esperienza di tutti questi anni ha dimostrato che i giuramenti in oggetto non sono necessari per conservare il nostro peculiare carisma fondazionale. Ha quindi proposto che, in considerazione di ciò, detti giuramenti venissero soppressi: proposta che è stata approvata all'unanimità.

Pure all'unanimità è stata approvata la proposta di rivedere la formulazione dei punti dello *Ius Peculiare* che facciano riferimento ai sacerdoti Aggregati -con questo nome vengono ora designati i soci Oblati- e Soprannumerari dell'Opus Dei. Ciò allo scopo di riflettere ancor più chiaramente, e senza che possa in alcun modo darsi adito ad interpretazioni equivoche, che l'incorporazione all'Opera di questi sacerdoti non cambia minimamente la loro piena dipendenza dal rispettivo Vescovo: il che esclude ogni sorta di *doppia obbedienza* o pericolo di conflitto di autorità, che mai si è verificato nell'Opus Dei. Scopo, infatti, dell'aiuto spirituale che l'Opera presta a quei sacerdoti è di spingerli ad amare sempre più il proprio Vescovo e le attività diocesane ed a cercare in esse la propria santificazione.

Gradisca i miei migliori ossequi, mentre, con sensi della più alta considerazione, mi confermo ben volentier

dell'Eminenza Vostra Reverendissima

dev.mo nel Signore

Alvaro del Portillo

A Sua Eminenza Rev.ma il Sig.
Card. Ildebrando Antoniutti
Prefetto della S. C. per i Religiosi e
gli Istituti Secolari
ROMA

---

## 57. Letter of Cardinal Ildebrando Antoniutti to Rev. Alvaro del Portillo in reply to his of March 23; March 31, 1971.

AGP, Sezione Giuridica, VII/15035.

SACRA CONGREGAZIONE                           Roma, 31 Marzo 1971

PER I RELIGIOSI

E GLI ISTITUTI SECOLARI

Prot. n. I.S. 1/47

Reverendo Don Alvaro,

Con pregiata lettera del 23 corr. mese Ella mi ha cortesemente informato dell'andamento dei lavori del Congresso generale straordinario dell'Opus Dei.

Mentre La ringrazio dell'apprezzata comunicazione desidero esprimerLe il mio vivo compiacimento per l'impegno con il quale si procede nello studio dei diversi argomenti presentati dai Soci di numerose nazioni.

Mi è grato inoltre significarLe che ho preso atto con soddisfazione di alcune opportune modifiche allo Statuto, già decise dai partecipanti alla recente Sessione del Congresso.

In attesa di conoscere le questioni che saranno ulteriormente studiate e risolte formulo i migliori auguri perché i lavori del detto Congresso proseguano nello spirito di fervore e di fruttuosa collaborazione che caratterizza la fiorente Istituzione dell'Opus.

Con sensi di distinto ossequio mi confermo

devotissimo in Domino

I. Card. Antoniutti

Pref.

Reverendo Signore
Don ALVARO DEL PORTILLO Y DIEZ DE SOLLANO
ROMA

## 58. Act approving the Codex Iuris Particularis of Opus Dei drawn up in conformity with the conclusions of the Special General Congress; October 1, 1974.

AGP, Sezione Giuridica, VII/15050.

El que suscribe, Alvaro del Portillo y Diez de Sollano, Secretario General del Opus Dei, Presidente de la Comisión Técnica -que abarca las Subcomisiones jurídica y teológica- por mandato de su Fundador y Presidente General, Excelentísimo y Reverendísimo Monseñor Josemaría Escrivá de Balaguer y Albás, extiende la presente acta para dejar constancia de la aprobación del Codex Iuris Particularis del Opus Dei, de los antecedentes de su redacción y de la fuerza obligatoria que se atribuye a las normas que lo integran.

I

Con la *venia* de la Santa Sede y dentro de las finalidades y términos, *congrua congruis referendo*, del Decreto *Perfectæ caritatis* del Concilio Vaticano II, así como del Motu pr. *Ecclesiæ Sanctæ*, del 6 de agosto de 1966, que determinan las normas de aplicación del citado Decreto Conciliar, se celebró el Congreso General Especial del Opus Dei, para la revisión de su *Ius peculiare*. Las sesiones plenarias del Congreso tuvieron lugar en Roma -en sedes separadas para la Sección masculina y para la Sección femenina de la Obra- y se celebraron en dos Partes: la primera, durante los días 1 a 15 de septiembre de 1969; y la segunda, durante los días 30 de agosto a 14 de septiembre de 1970. Con anterioridad al Congreso, y como preparación a cada una de sus Partes, se celebraron en los diversos países, en 1968 y en el primer trimestre de 1970, las Semanas de Trabajo Regionales, precedidas en cada lugar de una extensa consulta hecha a todos los socios de la Obra, según el deseo expreso de nuestro Fundador, que quiso que todos sus hijos del Opus Dei fuesen invitados a participar en estas tareas preparatorias del Congreso.

II

Por su particular importancia y por el singular valor que tienen, para la determinación del íntimo sentido que debe inspirar el Derecho particular del Opus Dei y de las finalidades a que sus normas deben servir para ser fieles al carisma fundacional, se transcriben seguidamente algunas declaraciones de nuestro Fundador en las sesiones plenarias del Congreso:
a)   En la sesión inaugural de la primera Parte del Congreso, nuestro Fundador pone de relieve "que se ha reunido este Congreso Especial de la Obra para reafirmar, en primer lugar, el deseo de vivir de acuerdo con nuestro espíritu genuino la dedicación al Señor de todos los socios -su santidad personal-, mediante el cumplimiento amoroso de nuestras Normas y Costumbres, que nos lleva a una vida de oración continua, y el ejercicio del apostolado, cada uno dentro de su estado y en su propia profesión u oficio en el mundo, en servicio de la Santa Iglesia, del Romano Pontífice, y en bien de todas las almas. Por eso, durante este tiempo, tendremos siempre presente que lo único que verdaderamente importa es la santificación personal de todos los socios. En segundo lugar,  y como una lógica consecuencia de esas exigencias fundamentales del espíritu

del Opus Dei, se procederá a la revisión de nuestro derecho particular, en aquellas partes en las que no hubo más remedio que aceptar provisionalmente conceptos o términos propios del llamado estado de perfección o estado religioso" (Sesión de 1-IX-1969).

b) En la séptima sesión plenaria de la Parte Primera del Congreso, nuestro Fundador -al comentar la propuesta n. 1, de la Comisión I, acerca de la revisión de nuestro Derecho particular- "confirma que, efectivamente, para poder obtener la necesaria y urgente aprobación de la Santa Sede en 1947 y 1950, no hubo más remedio que incluir en nuestro Derecho particular algunas expresiones o normas, propias de la parte general de la Constitución Apostólica *Provida Mater Ecclesia*, aceptando un ropaje jurídico que no respondía a la naturaleza de nuestro espíritu, pero con ánimo de recuperar -también en sede de derecho- nuestra fisonomía plenamente secular. De ahí, aclara también el Presidente General, las fuertes contradicciones jurídicas que, a un examen atento, aparecen en nuestro *Ius peculiare*: de una parte, lo que tuvimos que aceptar como consecuencia del forzado estatuto jurídico que se podía entonces obtener; de otra parte, claras y repetidas afirmaciones -en el mismo texto del *Ius peculiare*-, en abierta contradicción con lo anterior" (Sesión del 9-IX-1969).

c) En la décima sesión plenaria de la Parte Primera, en la propuesta n. 15 de la Comisión I, se sugiere que la "enseñanza de nuestro Padre sobre las virtudes que nuestra vocación exige, encuentre también su expresión en la estructura del capítulo de nuestro *Codex Iuris Peculiaris*, en que se trata de la pobreza, de la castidad y de la obediencia". Al exponer el Relator los diversos puntos de la motivación de esta propuesta, comenta nuestro Fundador que "la imposibilidad de incluir la ascética de la Obra dentro de la tipificación de las virtudes cristianas propias de la teología del estado religioso, la ha puesto de manifiesto en numerosas ocasiones, entre otras en diversas Cartas suyas, antes y después de haber tenido que adaptar forzosamente nuestro *Ius peculiare* al esquema habitual del *status perfectionis*, que está presente en la Cosntitución Ap. *Provida Mater Ecclesia*" (Sesión del 12-IX-1969).

d) En la siguiente sesión plenaria, el Presidente Genral interviene "para recordar que, al mismo tiempo que -por lealtad- defendíamos por escrito y de palabra la figura jurídica de los Institutos Seculares, ya nuestro Fundador, con la ayuda de D. Alvaro del Portillo, iba recogiendo documentación y preparando material de trabajo, para tratar de resolver satisfactoriamente la situación jurídica de la Obra" (Undécima sesión plenaria de la Parte Primera, del 13-IX-1969).

e) Al iniciarse la Segunda Parte del Congreso, hace notar el Presidente General que, dentro precisamente del afán de servicio a la Iglesia y a la humanidad entera -que realizamos con lealtad y firme adhesión al Papa y a los Obispos en comunión con el Sucesor de Pedro-, se comprende perfectamente bien la misma finalidad fundamental de este Congreso General Especial. "Porque obedece -concluye nuestro Fundador- al deseo y firme propósito que todos tenemos de vivir y trabajar -¡de servir, hijos míos!- en perfecto acuerdo con el espíritu que Dios ha querido para nuestra Asociación: de modo que lo que ha sido desde el principio la espiritualidad, la vida y el modo apostólico de la Obra encuentre una adecuada y definitiva configuración jurídica en el derecho de la Iglesia" (Sesión plenaria del 30-VIII-1970).

f) En la citada sesión inaugural, el Presidente General "agradece a los Representantes de las Regiones y, a través de ellos, a los Directores Regionales y a todos los socios de la Obra, el que hayan demostrado una vez más -durante las especiales Semanas de Trabajo Regionales celebradas en preparación de esta Segunda Parte del Congreso- su amor y ejemplar fidelidad al espíritu y tradiciones del Opus Dei, y la clara conciencia que todos tienen sobre la necesidad de que sea revisado nuestro actual derecho particular sobre aquellos puntos en los que no hubo más remedio que aceptar -concediendo, pero sin ceder y con ánimo de recuperar- conceptos o términos propios del llamado estado de perfección, que dificultan nuestra tarea de servicio a la Iglesia y a las almas" (Sesión del 30-VIII-1970).

g) En la octava sesión plenaria de la Parte Segunda, se expone la propuesta n. 1 de la Comisión I, en la que se dice: "rogamos a nuestro Fundador que -en el momento y en la forma que considere más oportunos- solicite nuevamente a la Santa Sede, junto con una configuración jurídica de la Obra diversa de la de Instituto Secular, la autorización para suprimir de nuestro derecho particular las normas que se refieren a la profesión de los consejos evangélicos: de modo que se termine de una vez el sufrimiento de nuestro Fundador, y de todos nosotros con él, por la falta de correspondencia que actualmente existe entre esas normas jurídicas propias del estado de "vida consagrada" que hubo que admitir por motivos ajenos a nuestra voluntad, y la substancia teológica del carisma fundacional del Opus Dei". Después de ser aprobada la propuesta por unanimidad, nuestro Fundador interviene para decir que agradece con toda el alma la sugerencia que se le hace: prueba evidente de cómo sus hijos han sabido aprender y vivir, con la gracia de Dios, el genuino espíritu del Opus Dei. "La urgencia -continúa- de solucionar graves poblemas vitales de la Obra (la incardinación de sacerdotes, el hecho de tener una organización de régimen universal y centralizado y la necesidad de obtener una sanción pontificia que frenase la incomprensión y persecución de que la Obra era objeto) nos obligaron en 1943 y en 1947 a aceptar unas formas jurídicas inadecuadas a nuestro espíritu. No cedimos: concedimos, con ánimo de recuperar. No había posibilidad de obrar de otra manera. Hubimos de acogernos a las soluciones menos inadecuadas -las únicas- que el derecho común eclesiástico ofrecía: y -¡bien lo sabéis, hijos míos!- hemos rezado, estamos rezando y rezaremos mucho, en espera confiada de poder ir por el camino jurídico que conviene al espíritu de la Obra" (Sesión plenaria del 11-IX-1970).

h) En la novena sesión plenaria de la Segunda Parte del Congreso, nuestro Fundador se refiere a las diversas etapas del *iter* jurídico de la Obra, y dice: "Hijos míos, el Señor nos ha ayudado siempre a ir, en las diversas circunstancias de la vida de la Iglesia y de la Obra, por aquel concreto camino jurídico que reunía en cada momento histórico -en 1941, en 1943, en 1947- tres características fundamentales: ser un camino posible, responder a las necesidades de crecimiento de la Obra y ser -entre las varias posibilidades jurídicas- la solución más adecuada, es decir, la *menos inadecuada* a la realidad de nuestra vida" (Sesión del 12-IX-1970).

i)   En la sesión que se acaba de citar, nuestro Fundador formula también la siguiente declaración: "todos los socios de la Obra buscan la santidad personal con el mismo espíritu y los mismos medios, cada uno en su propio estado, a través de su trabajo profesional u oficio -*munus publicum*- y en las circunstancias diversísimas que le son propias: de manera que las distintas denominaciones empleadas expresan sencillamente el grado de disponibilidad para determinadas tareas de apostolado corporativo, de formación, de dirección o atención de los demás socios; disponibilidad que no afecta a la unidad de vocación, sino que depende de diversas circunstancias personales, familiares, profesionales o de estado" (Sesión plenaria del 12-IX-1970).

### III

1.   A la presente acta se une -como Anexo n° 1-trascripción literal de las Conclusiones finales del Congreso General Especial, aprobadas unánimemente el día 14 de septiembre de 1970, hallándose presente nuestro Fundador, bajo cuya presidencia se celebró también la última sesión plenaria[1].

2.   En estas Conclusiones se reitera la aprobación de todas las propuestas sancionadas en las sesiones plenarias del Congreso, con criterios y directrices para la revisión de nuestro *Ius peculiare*, y se aprueba también "unánimemente que se continúe esta Segunda Parte del Congreso General Especial del Opus Dei a través del trabajo de la Comisión Técnica -con las dos Subcomisiones jurídica y teológica- que ha sido constituida por nuestro Fundador en aplicación de las resoluciones tomadas en la Primera Parte del Congreso".

3.   En la sesión citada del 14 de septiembre fue aprobada, también con voto unánime, la siguiente Propuesta, para ser tenida en cuenta "en la labor de orden ejecutivo encomendada a la Comisión Técnica";

"Que, cuando nuestro Derecho particular quede definitivamente y perfectamente acomodado a la realidad de nuestro espíritu, y cuando esa acomodación haya sido ya aprobada en la medida que sea necesario por la Santa Sede (de modo que nuestro Fundador considere satisfactoriamente concluido este largo camino institucional del Opus Dei), se establezca que:

1°)  ese *Ius peculiare* del Opus Dei, que recogerá todas las normas constitutivas de la Obra, habrá de considerarse dotado del máximo grado de estabilidad legal;

2°)  cualquier cambio, adición, supresión o suspensión temporal de alguna norma podrá hacerse únicamente por decisión del Congreso General del Opus Dei, supremo órgano de gobierno, y con arreglo a normas particulares que deberán detallarse en el mismo texto legal;

3°)  la decisión no será válida hasta haber re*cibido* la aprobación de la Santa Sede, si así lo requiere por derecho común la naturaleza concreta de la norma que se desea cambiar, añadir, suprimir o suspender *ad tempus*".

---

\* For these conclusions, see no. 55 of this Appendix (Official Documents, p. 560).

## IV

Al término del trabajo que le había sido encomendado, la Comisión Técnica hace constar en su informe que el texto del "Codex Iuris Particularis Operis Dei" por este organismo elaborado bajo la continua dirección del Fundador, y que somete a la aprobación del mismo Fundador de la Obra, es fruto de un detenido estudio en el que se han tenido en cuenta los siguientes criterios:

1.  La Comisión Técnica ha tenido clara conciencia de que -como declaró el Presidente de la misma Comisión ante el Pleno del Congreso, en la sesión séptima de la Parte Segunda, el día siete de septiembre de 1970- su función tenía "carácter puramente instrumental: al servicio del carisma fundacional de la Obra, del que el Padre es, por voluntad divina, el solo y exclusivo depositario". Por eso ha sido para los miembros de la Comisión motivo de especial confianza y seguridad, el haber realizado su trabajo bajo la directa e inmediata inspiración de nuestro Fundador.

2.  El articulado del proyecto de Codex se formula en cumplimiento de los Acuerdos del Congreso General Especial, siguiendo las orientaciones del Motu pr. *Ecclesiæ Sanctæ*, del 6 de agosto de 1966, y dentro de los límites establecidos en estas Letras Apostólicas. En efecto:

    a)  Partiendo del texto del *Codex Iuris Peculiaris* del Opus Dei, reelaborado por nuestro Fundador en 1963, y que ya había recibido las primeras aprobaciones de la Santa Sede en 1947 y en 1950, se ha procurado (con absoluta fidelidad a la substancia de este nuestro actual Derecho peculiar), aligerar el texto, no acogiendo en él las disposiciones caídas en desuso o que jamás de hecho han tenido vigor.

    b)  Para superar la falta de correspondencia que actualmente existe entre las normas jurídicas propias del "status perfectionis", que hubo que admitir en el Codex que ha regulado el Opus Dei como Instituto Secular, y la substancia teológica del carisma fundacional del Opus Dei, se hacen figurar entre corchetes aquellas normas -todavía vigentes- relativas a la profesión de los consejos evangélicos de castidad, pobreza y obediencia, cuya supresión será solicitada a la Santa Sede cuando se ruegue al Santo Padre que sea concedida al Opus Dei la adecuada configuración jurídica, distinta de la de Instituto Secular.

    c)  En el texto aparecen no sólo normas jurídicas, sino también elementos de naturaleza teológica y espiritual, especialmente los que hacen referencia a aspectos fundamentales de nuestro espíritu. Se ha recogido, con particular relieve, la constante enseñanza de nuestro Fundador acerca de la necesidad de vivir las virtudes teologales y las virtudes humanas sobrenaturalizadas, haciendo especial hincapié en la santificación del trabajo ordinario, puesto que en la obligación de santificar cada socio los deberes de su propio estado, los de su propia profesión u oficio, los de su trabajo ordinario, se puede resumir el carácter peculiar de la espiritualidad del Opus Dei.

    d)  En los pocos puntos en que se introduce alguna novedad, siempre se hace respetando el fin, la naturaleza y el carácter del Opus Dei, según el Codex de 1963, y permaneciendo dentro de los límites obligados del derecho común. Entre estas novedades, merecen citarse las dos siguientes, por ser las de mayor relieve:

d') La supresión de los juramentos regulados en los números 20 y 58 del Codex de 1963, aprobada unánimemente por el Congreso General Especial, a propuesta de nuestro Fundador, quien hizo presente que, desde la fundación de la Obra, los socios han obrado siempre en todos los campos siguiendo el dictamen de la propia conciencia rectamente formada, y que la experiencia ha demostrado que los citados juramentos no son necesarios para conservar nuestro peculiar carisma fundacional.

d'') Por unanimidad fue también aprobada por el Congreso la propuesta de revisar la formulación de los puntos del Codex de 1963 que hacen referencia a los sacerdotes Agregados -nombre con el que ahora se designan los socios Oblatos- y Supernumerarios de la Sociedad Sacerdotal de la Santa Cruz. Y esto con el fin de reflejar aún más claramente, y sin que pueda darse lugar en modo alguno a interpretaciones equívocas, que la incorporación a la Obra de estos sacerdotes no cambia en lo más mínimo su plena dependencia del respectivo Obispo: lo que excluye toda suerte de *doble obediencia* o peligro de conflicto de autoridad, que nunca se ha verificado en el Opus Dei. La ayuda espiritual que la Obra presta a esos sacerdotes tiene por fin moverles a amar siempre más al propio Obispo y las actividades diocesanas y a buscar en ellas la propia santificación.

V

El proyecto elaborado por la Comisión Técnica, de que se viene haciendo mención, fue presentado a nuestro Fundador y Presidente General, quien -tras haberlo hecho examinar por la Comisión permanente del Consejo General de la Obra- lo ha aprobado en todas sus partes, en el día de hoy, disponiendo que, para distinguirlo del Codex de 1963, se le designe con el título de "Codex Iuris Particularis" del Opus Dei, y sea debidamente autenticado su texto original, para su archivo en la Secretaría de su Consejo. Este Codex será presentado a la Santa Sede en el momento de solicitar la nueva configuración jurídica que se desea para la Obra, dentro de las perspectivas abiertas por las disposiciones y las normas de aplicación de los Decretos emanados del Concilio Vaticano II. Entonces se solicitará a la Santa Sede la supresión de las normas relativas a la profesión de los consejos evangélicos y la aprobación de las acomodaciones que sea imprescindible introducir en el "Codex Iuris Particularis", en cuanto exigidas por la nueva configuración jurídica. Todo ello según lo expresamente previsto en la Disposición final del Codex.

Y para la debida constancia, suscribo la presente acta, en Roma, en la sede del Consejo General del Opus Dei, el día 1 de octubre de mil novecientos setenta y cuatro.

Alvaro del Portillo

Josemaría Escrivá de B
Pres. Gen.

## 59. *Chapter One of the 1974 version of the* Codex Iuris Particularis *of Opus Dei.*

AGP, Sezione Giuridica, VII/15661.

SOCIETAS SACERDOTALIS SANCTÆ CRUCIS ET OPUS DEI

### CODEX IURIS PARTICULARIS

CAPUT I

DE NATURA ET FINE OPERIS DEI

1. Institutum, cui titulus Societas Sacerdotalis Sanctæ Crucis et Opus Dei, breviato autem nomine Opus Dei, est [Institutum sæculare] iuris pontificii, clericis et laicis simul compositum, sanctitati in mundo promovendæ et apostolatui exercendo dicatum. Societas Sacerdotalis Sanctæ Crucis, quæ sacerdotibus Institutionis constituitur, proprio spiritu et ministerio universum Opus Dei vivificat atque ita informat, ut ipsum clericale eo sensu reddat quod præcipua regiminis munera plerumque sacerdotibus reserventur. Institutio est proinde clericalis ad normam huius Codicis et iuxta Sanctæ Sedis specialia præscripta vel indulta, quin ea de causa socii laici iuribus et privilegiis clericorum gaudeant neque umquam clericalibus officiis subiiciantur.

2. § 1. Aspectus genericus finis Operis Dei est sociorum sanctificatio per exercitium in proprio cuiusque statu, professione ac vitæ condicione [consiliorum Evangelii ceterarumque] virtutum christianarum, secundum ius peculiare ipsius Operis Dei eiusque spiritualitatem, prorsus sæcularem.

   § 2. Specificus autem est totis viribus adlaborare ut personæ omnium condicionum et statuum civilis societatis, et in primis quæ intellectuales dicuntur, Christi Domini præceptis integro corde adhæreant ipsaque, etiam ope sanctificationis proprii uniuscuiusque laboris professionalis, in praxim deducant, in medio mundo, ut omnia ad Voluntatem Creatoris ordinentur; atque viros ac mulieres informare ad apostolatum item in mundo exercendum.

3. Media quæ, ad hos fines supernaturales obtinendos, socii Operis Dei adhibent, hæc sunt:

   1° impensa vita spiritualis orationis et sacrificii, iuxta spiritum Operis Dei: ipsorum enim vocatio est essentialiter contemplativa, fundatur in humili ac sincero sensu filiationis divinæ et subridenti ascetismo constanter sustinetur;

   2° profunda ac continua institutio ascetica et doctrinalis religiosa, ad personalia cuiusque adiuncta accommodata atque in ecclesiastico Magisterio solide innixa, necnon constans studium adquirendi et perficiendi necessariam formationem professionalem propriamque animi culturam;

3° imitatio vitæ absconditæ Domini Nostri Iesu Christi in Nazareth, etiam in sanctificatione proprii laboris professionalis ordinarii, quem, exemplo et verbis, convertere satagunt in instrumentum apostolatus, unusquisque propriam attingens actionis sphæram, prout sua cuiusque cultura et aptitudo expostulant, sciensque se esse debere tamquam fermentum in massa humanæ societatis latens; item, seipsos sanctificent socii in perfecta adimpletione huius laboris, peracti quidem in constanti unione cum Deo; necnon per ipsum laborem alios sanctificent;

4° omnes Operis Dei socii se obligant ad exercitium laboris professionalis vel alterius æquipollentis non derelinquendum, quia per ipsum sanctificationem persequentur;

5° quam maxima fidelitas in adimplendis officiis proprii status necnon in actione seu professione sociali cuiusque propria, summa semper cum reverentia pro legitimis societatis civilis legibus; itemque in laboribus apostolicis perficiendis, a Directoribus ipsis commissis.

4. § 1. Sacerdotium ministeriale clericorum et commune sacerdotium laicorum intime in Opere coniunguntur atque se invicem requirunt et complent, ad exsequendum in unitate vocationis et regiminis, finem quem Opus Dei sibi proponit.

§ 2. In utraque pariter Operis Dei Sectione, virorum scilicet ac mulierum, eadem est unitas vocationis, spiritus, finis et regiminis, etsi unaquæque Sectio proprios habeat apostolatus.

5. Opus Dei tamquam Patronos habet Beatam Mariam semper Virginem, quam uti Matrem veneratur, et S. Ioseph, eiusdem Beatæ Mariæ Virginis Sponsum. Peculiari devotione socii prosequuntur SS. Archangelos Michaëlem, Gabrielem et Raphaëlem, atque SS. Apostolos Petrum, Paulum et Ioannem, quibus universa Institutio eiusdemque singula actionis genera specialiter consecrantur.

---

**60. Written request of Very Rev. Alvaro del Portillo to the Sacred Congregation for Religious and Secular Institutes seeking authorization to initiate the process of obtaining a definitive juridical configuration for Opus Dei; together with the reply of the Congregation; January 11 and 12, 1979.**

AGP, Sezione Giuridica, VIII/15028.

*Opus Dei*                                                    Roma, 11 gennaio 1979

*Il Presidente Generale*

Eccellenza Reverendissima,

L'Em.mo Card. Segretario di Stato, nel trasmettermi in data 18 novembre u.s. una Lettera Autografa di Sua Santità con cui partecipava alla nostra gioia spirituale per il 50° Anniversario dell'Opus Dei, mi ha gentilmente comunicato che il Santo Padre considera anche "una indilazionabile necessità che sia risolta la questione della sistemazione giuridica dell'Opus Dei", in maniera cioè adeguata al suo carisma fondazionale ed alla sua realtà sociale.

La graditissima indicazione di Sua Santità è stata per noi motivo di vivi ringraziamenti al Signore, anche perché essa concorda pienamente con i desideri a suo tempo espressi dal nostro venerato Fondatore; e siamo sicuri che potrà favorire molto l'efficacia apostolica dell'Opera ed il suo ancora più pieno inserimento nella Comunità ecclesiale.

Volendo pertanto procedere al riguardo con la sollecitudine che ci è stata richiesta, mi premuro di sottoporre alla Sua considerazione l'unito esposto. Mi sembra infatti doveroso chiedere l'autorizzazione di codesto Sacro Dicastero per fare quei passi chiarificatori che si renderanno opportuni affinché possa essere accordata all'Opera una sistemazione giuridica diversa da quella di Istituto Secolare.

Nel ringraziarLa vivamente fin d'ora, profitto ben volentieri della circostanza per confermarmi, con sensi di profondo ossequio,

dell'Eccellenza Vostra Reverendissima

dev.mo nel Signore

Alvaro del Portillo

Pres. Gen.

Atteso quanto esposto dal Rev.mo Presidente Generale dell'Opus Dei, questa Sacra Congregazione concede l'autorizzazione richiesta, e raccomanda che per la definitiva sistemazione giuridica siano fedelmente seguiti lo spirito e le indicazioni del Fondatore.

L + S        12 gennaio 1979

+ Agostino Mayer

Segr.

A Sua Eccellenza Rev.ma
Mons. Augustin Mayer, O.S.B.
Arcivescovo tit. di Satriano

Segretario della S.C. per i Religiosi e gli Istituti Secolari

**61. Letter of Very Rev. Alvaro del Portillo to His Holiness John Paul II requesting the erection of Opus Dei as a personal prelature; February 2, 1979.**

AGP, Sezione Giuridica, VIII/15029.

*Opus Dei*

---

*Il Presidente Generale*                    Roma, 2 febbraio 1979

Beatissimo Padre,

Con grande gioia e fervidi ringraziamenti al Signore, non appena l'Em.mo Card. Segretario di Stato mi comunicò in data 18 novembre 1978 che Vostra Santità riteneva che era una indilazionabile necessità risolvere la questione della sistemazione giuridica dell'Opus Dei, ho proceduto immediatamente a dare i passi necessari per portare a compimento il venerato incarico.

Grazie alle molte orazioni ed al grande lavoro di preparazione che il nostro amatissimo Fondatore aveva fatto, non è stato per noi difficile proporre, in fedeltà allo spirito del nostro Fondatore e tenendo conto degli arricchimenti apportati dal Concilio Vaticano II al diritto generale della Chiesa, una concreta formula giuridica per detta soluzione. Le motivazioni di tale scelta si espongono nell'unito *Appunto* (Allegato I).

In merito a tale *Appunto*, ed in via riservata, ho chiesto il consiglio di persone assai qualificate che conoscono molto bene sia la Curia Romana -di cui fanno parte- che l'Opus Dei, il cui spirito e la cui realtà sociale ed apostolica sono per esse da lungo tempo familiari. Unisco, perciò, assieme al parere di Sua Eccellenza Mons. Andrzej Deskur (che lo ha apposto in calce ad una fotocopia dell'*Appunto*: cfr. Allegato II), anche quello di Sua Eminenza il Card. Franz König (Allegato III).

Inoltre, poiché l'auspicata soluzione giuridica comporterebbe l'erezione dell'Opus Dei in Prelatura personale "cum proprio populo", mi è sembrato doveroso rivolgermi anche ai due competenti Dicasteri della Curia Romana: prima, alla Sacra Congregazione per i Religiosi e gli Istituti Secolari, che, attese le ragioni da noi addotte, ci ha autorizzato a cercare la soluzione del nostro problema istituzionale fuori dell'ambito di competenza e di dipendenza di quella Congregazione (Allegato IV); e poi alla S. Congregazione per i Vescovi, il cui Em.mo Card. Prefetto si è dichiarato pienamente favorevole all'erezione dell'Opus Dei in Prelatura personale "cum proprio populo" (Allegato V).

Santo Padre, tenendo conto di tutti questi autorevoli consigli e pareri, e considerando altresì che la realtà sociale dell'Opera (unità pastorale organica e indivisibile, composta da 2.248 sacerdoti e 70.127 laici) non potrebbe trovare una adeguata sistemazione giuridica sotto la dipendenza del Pontificio Consiglio per i Laici né della S. Congregazione per il Clero, mi permetto pertanto di domandare umilmente quanto segue: *che la Santità Vostra si degni far dipendere l'Opus Dei dalla S. Congregazione per i Vescovi erigendolo in Prelatura personale "cum proprio populo"; e che a questo scopo voglia disporre che detta Sacra Congregazione proceda a preparare i relativi atti giuridici secondo la* mens *espressa nei nn. 5, 6 e 8,b) dell'unito Appunto (Allegato I).*

Da parte mia, posso assicurare Vostra Santità che sarà nostra premura metterci subito a disposizione dei Superiori del medesimo Sacro Dicastero, ed offrire loro ogni necessaria od utile collaborazione. Sono infatti pienamente convinto, come lo era il nostro Fondatore, che tale sistemazione giuridica dell'Opus Dei, mentre salvaguarderebbe in modo inequivocabile la sua identità e fisionomia spirituale, rafforzerebbe moltissimo la sua efficacia apostolica al servizio della Santa Sede e delle Chiese locali dei cinque continenti in cui si lavora. Ciò garantirebbe a tutti i livelli l'ancora più pieno inserimento dell'Opera nella Comunità ecclesiale.

Nella filiale speranza che la paterna bontà di Vostra Santità vorrà accogliere benignamente questa nostra fiduciosa richiesta, Le chiedo per me e per tutti i Suoi figli dell'Opus Dei l'Apostolica Benedizione, e sono lietissimo di confermarmi

L + S

di Vostra Santità

obb.mo, um.mo e dev.mo figlio

Alvaro del Portillo

Pres. Gen.

Javier Echevarría

Segr. Gen.

A Sua Santità
il Papa Giovanni Paolo II
CITTA' DEL VATICANO

## APPUNTO PER IL SANTO PADRE

(Circa la desiderata soluzione giuridica definitiva dell'Opus Dei)

L'Opus Dei, fondato il 2 ottobre 1928, è nato con un contenuto teologico ed apostolico chiaramente definito, che, approvato dalla Gerarchia sin dall'inizio, si è poi visto abbondantemente confermato dal Magistero solenne del Concilio Vaticano II, e particolarmente dalla Cost. dogm. "Lumen gentium", Cap. II-V. Il suo Fondatore, il Servo di Dio Mons. Josemaría Escrivá de Balaguer, pose infatti come fondamento dottrinale dell'Opera la chiamata universale alla santità ed all'apostolato insita nel Sacramento del Battesimo, asserendo che i soci dell'Opera dovevano vivere e diffondere le esigenze ascetiche ed apostoliche delle promesse battesimali con un impegno personale pieno, ciascuno nel proprio stato di vita e nella propria condizione -senza cambiare, cioè, il rispettivo stato canonico- e secondo una spiritualità specifica nettamente secolare. Questa pone l'accento sulla necessità di cercare la pienezza della vita cristiana -la santità- e la diffusione del messaggio evangelico - l'apostolato- attraverso il fedele adempimento dei doveri familiari e sociali, e in modo particolare mediante la perfetta realizzazione -per amore a Dio ed al prossimo- del rispettivo lavoro professionale od officio, fino a farlo diventare -come il divino Redentore a Nazareth- lavoro di Dio, *operatio Dei*, *opus Dei*.

L'Opera, a cui apartengono attualmente fedeli di 87 nazionalità, rappresenta di fatto, più che una società od associazione, una vera "portio

Populi Dei". L'Opus Dei, infatti, costituisce un'unità pastorale, organica e indivisibile -con unità di spirito e di vocazione, di regime e di apostolato-, che è integrata da sacerdoti (2.248 ) e da laici (70.127) di ogni stato di vita e di ogni condizione sociale e professionale: uomini e donne, celibi e sposati, intellettuali e operai, ecc.

Sia le caratteristiche del suo spirito fondazionale che quelle della sua realtà sociale hanno qualificato l'Opus Dei come una realtà ecclesiale diversa dagli Istituti clericali o laicali che assumono il peculiare stato di "vita consacrata per la professione dei consigli evangelici", e che dipendono dalla S. Congregazione per i Religiosi e gli Istituti Secolari. Allo stesso tempo, l'Opera rappresenta -per la sua solidità organizzativa a struttura internazionale e centralizzata; per il suo ordinamento giuridico di ente clericale di diritto pontificio con facoltà di formare e di incardinare i propri candidati al sacerdozio; per le conseguenti attribuzioni di potestà del suo Presidente Generale; per la piena dedicazione apostolica di tutti i soci, e per la svariata molteplicità delle sue attività apostoliche- un'Istituzione assai diversa dalle Pie unioni e dalle altre Associazioni di fedeli che dipendono dal Pontificio Consiglio per i Laici e dalla S. Congregazione per il Clero.

Le considerazioni sopra brevemente esposte possono meglio illustrare quanto segue, in vista dell'auspicata soluzione del problema istituzionale dell'Opera:

1.  L'Opus Dei costituisce -come è stato pienamente riconosciuto- un fenomeno pastorale assolutamente nuovo nella vita della Chiesa, paragonabile soltanto alla realtà di spirito e di attività apostolica dei fedeli, chierici e laici, delle prime comunità cristiane. Era quindi comprensibile che la legislazione generale della Chiesa, vigente cinquant'anni fa ed anche quella degli anni successivi, prima dell'applicazione dei Decreti del Conc. Vaticano II, non prevedesse la possibilità per l'Opus Dei di una sistemazione giuridica adeguata, rispondente cioè pienamente alle caratteristiche dell'Opera. Ciò, però, ha significato per l'Opus Dei il dover affrontare durante tutta la sua vita delle gravi e frequenti difficoltà, che erano motivo continuo di sofferenza per il nostro Fondatore, perché ostacolavano e riducevano sensibilmente la portata del servizio dell'Opera alla Chiesa ed alle anime.

2.  Il nostro Fondatore (per motivi di urgente necessità che minacciavano lo sviluppo e per fino la stessa esistenza dell'Opera) si vide costretto a dover ricorrere provvisoriamente a formule giuridiche inadeguate -Società di vita comune senza voti, Istituto Secolare-, che consentissero di avere, assieme alle necessarie facoltà giuridiche, l'imprescindibile approvazione della Santa Sede. Tutto ciò, in attesa che lo sviluppo futuro della legislazione ecclesiastica potesse offrire la possibilità di una sistemazione giuridica definitiva, non privilegiata, capace di favorire la massima efficacia apostolica dell'Opus Dei e di salvaguardare la sua identità fondazionale.

3.  Nel 1964, il Fondatore dell'Opera, in uno scritto di coscienza -un'apertura della sua anima al Papa- nel quale trattava svariati argomenti, prospettò anche, *per incidens*, la necessità di procedere più avanti, quando fossero maturate le disposizioni giuridiche della Chiesa, a dare all'Opus Dei una sistemazione giuridica adeguata "che non fosse singolare né di privilegio".

Il Santo Padre Paolo VI gli confermò che -come del resto ben sapeva il nostro Fondatore- non era possibile trovare in quel momento nel diritto vigente della Chiesa la formula conveniente; e che nulla vietava di riprendere in esame la questione, quando fosse opportuno.

Più tardi, in un'Udienza che il Santo Padre gli concesse il 25 giugno 1973, il nostro Fondatore precisò che nel frattempo, all'uopo di preparare i documenti necessari per chiedere l'auspicata soluzione giuridica d'accordo con la nuova legislazione, aveva convocato un Congresso Generale Speciale dell'Opus Dei. Ma il venerato Fondatore morì due anni dopo, senza aver avuto il tempo di presentare i nuovi documenti, anche se aveva lasciato precise indicazioni in merito. Egli, infatti, oltre ad essere stato in molti aspetti un vero precursore del Concilio Vaticano II, seguì attentamente i suoi lavori e le successive norme applicative dei suoi Decreti.

4. Il Santo Padre Paolo VI confermò anche a me, in due Udienze concessemi il 5 marzo 1976 ed il 19 giugno 1978, che "la questione rimaneva aperta" in attesa di darle una soluzione quando io ne facessi la domanda. Sua Santità Giovanni Paolo I manifestò poi nel settembre 1978 la sua volontà che si procedesse a dare l'auspicata soluzione al nostro problema istituzionale; ed infine il 18 novembre u.s., nel trasmettermi la Vostra graditissima Lettera Autografa augurale per il 50° anniversario dell'Opera, l'Em.mo Card. Segretario di Stato mi comunicò che Sua Santità considerava "una indilazionabile necessità che sia risolta la questione della sistemazione giuridica dell'Opus Dei".

5. In effetti, ciò appare oggi cosa facilmente realizzabile, senza necessità alcuna di forzature giuridiche, grazie agli importanti arricchimenti pastorali ed alle innovazioni che negli anni posteriori al 1964 sono state introdotte nel diritto della Chiesa. Per cui, come segnalò opportunamente lo stesso Fondatore dell'Opus Dei, attualmente nel Decr. *Presbyterorum Ordinis*, n. 10 § 2, nel Motu pr. *Ecclesiæ Sanctæ*, I, n. 4 e nella Cost. Ap. *Regimini Ecclesiæ universæ*, n. 49 § 1, si trovano già tutte le norme giuridiche generali, entro le quali si potrebbe risolvere adeguatamente il problema della definitiva sistemazione giuridica dell'Opus Dei.

6. L'erezione, infatti, dell'Opus Dei in una Prelatura personale "cum proprio populo" (a norma dei predetti documenti conciliari e pontifici, le cui disposizioni si raccolgono anche negli schemi del nuovo Codice di Diritto Canonico: cfr. "De Populo Dei", can. 217 § 1 e 219 § 2) permetterebbe di sancire definitivamente, senza ulteriori equivoci, che nell'Opus Dei i sacerdoti sono sacerdoti pienamente secolari, diocesani, e che i laici dell'Opera sono fedeli comuni, il cui stato canonico non cambia per il fatto dell'incorporazione all'Opus Dei. Al tempo stesso, si assicurerebbero altre tre cose fondamentali: e cioè,

a) che l'Opus Dei rimanga nella sua condizione di Ente con personalità canonica pubblica di diritto pontificio, con la facoltà, di cui è già in possesso, di incardinare i propri chierici -formati all'interno, cioè nei Seminari dell'Opera-; di Ente, però, nettamente diverso dagli Istituti Secolari o da qualsiasi altra forma di Istituto di "vita consacrata", e perciò non dipendente dalla Sacra Congregazione per i Religiosi e gli Istituti Secolari, ma dalla Sacra Congregazione per i Vescovi;

b)   che, salvo quelle riguardanti la professione dei consigli evangelici
     -cosa estranea al nostro carisma fondazionale-, vengano confermate
     nel nuovo Statuto giuridico dell'Opus Dei tutte le norme di diritto
     generale e particolare che regolano: l'attuale regime dell'Opera, a
     carattere internazionale e centralizzato, con sede a Roma; le facoltà
     giuridiche del suo Presidente Generale, che è già in possesso di una
     vera potestà ordinaria di regime; la disciplina e la profonda formazione
     ascetica e dottrinale dei soci, secondo una apposita *Ratio studiorum*
     più volte lodata dalla Santa Sede; la continua cura spirituale e pastorale
     dei soci, da parte dei sacerdoti incardinati all'Opera, che hanno
     ricevuto negli stessi Seminari dell'Opus Dei la necessaria formazione
     specifica, ecc.;

c)   che si ottenga un ancor più efficace servizio apostolico dell'Opera
     nell'ambito della Comunità ecclesiale, in stretta e continua
     collaborazione con gli Ecc.mi Vescovi diocesani -senza la cui previa
     autorizzazione nessun Centro dell'Opus Dei viene né verrebbe eretto
     in alcuna diocesi-, e potendo essere seguita l'Opera ancor più da
     vicino dalla Santa Sede, e concretamente dalla Sacra Congregazione
     per i Vescovi, alla quale, tra l'altro, verrebbe regolarmente presentata
     la usuale relazione quinquennale *ad normam iuris*.

7.   L'erezione dell'Opus Dei in Prelatura personale "cum proprio populo"
     dovrebbe avvenire tramite una particolare Costituzione Apostolica,
     secondo la prassi ordinaria della Santa Sede in casi simili (Vicariati
     Castrensi, Mission de France, ecc.); mentre la definizione concreta del
     suo Statuto giuridico dovrebbe essere sancita, sempre secondo la prassi,
     da un apposito Decreto della Sacra Congregazione per i Vescovi.

8.   L'elaborazione di tali atti giuridici (Costituzione Apostolica e Decreto
     da sottoporre all'approvazione del Santo Padre) potrebbe essere fatta in
     uno di questi due modi:

a)   affidando detto incarico ad una Commissione mista, presieduta
     dall'Ecc.mo Sostituto della Segreteria di Stato e composta dai Segretari
     della Sacra Congregazione per i Vescovi e della Sacra Congregazione
     per i Religiosi e gli Istituti Secolari, nonché dal Segretario Aggiunto
     della Pontificia Commisione per la Revisione del Codice di Diritto
     Canonico, che vanta una particolare competenza in merito. Fra i
     membri della stessa Commissione potrebbe essere annoverato, per
     eventuali delucidazioni e chiarimenti che si rendessero necessari, il
     Presidente Generale dell'Opus Dei od un suo delegato. L'elaborazione
     degli atti si farebbe in base ai principi esposti ai nn. 5 e 6, e tenendo
     inoltre presente che, nel caso dell'Opus Dei, potrebbe considerarsi
     in effetti come già adempiuto il requisito, previsto dal Decreto *Ecclesiæ
     Sanctæ*, di chiedere il voto consultivo delle Conferenze Episcopali
     dei territori in cui si lavora: ciò perché l'Opus Dei, che fin dal 1947
     è *de iure* un ente di diritto pontificio, a cinquant'anni dalla sua
     fondazione svolge la propria attività in molte nazioni dei cinque
     continenti sempre con la previa *venia* ed approvazione di tutti gli
     Ordinari dei luoghi interessati, i cui diritti peraltro rimarrebbero
     intatti anche nella nuova sistemazione giuridica dell'Opera;

b) oppure, elaborando sempre gli atti in base ai principi esposti ai nn. 5 e 6 e considerando già adempiuto -come nel caso precedente- il requisito, previsto dal Decreto *Ecclesiæ Sanctæ*, di chiedere il voto consultivo delle Conferenze Episcopali dei territori in cui si lavora, per render più agile lo studio dei due Documenti sopraddetti, basterebbe che il Santo Padre affidasse la pratica alla Sacra Congregazione dei Vescovi, con la collaborazione del Segretario Aggiunto della Pontificia Commissione per la Revisione del Codice di Diritto Canonico, e, per i possibili chiariamenti, del Presidente Generale dell'Opus Dei o di un suo delegato.

Roma, 26 dicembre 1978

Alvaro del Portillo          Javier Echevarría          L + S
Pres. Gen.                   Segr. Gen.

---

## 62. Letter of the Very Reverend Alvaro del Portillo to the Prefect of the Sacred Congregation for Bishops, Sebastian Cardinal Baggio, together with a memorandum on the transformation of Opus Dei into a personal prelature; April 23, 1979.

AGP, Sezione Giuridica, VIII/15030.

*Opus Dei*

---

*Il Presidente Generale*                           Roma, 23 aprile 1979

Eminenza Reverendissima,

In risposta alla gentile lettera dell'Eminenza Vostra Reverendissima in data 7 marzo u.s. ed in seguito alla nostra gradita conversazione del 29 s.m., mi pregio di inviarLe come d'accordo lo studio qui allegato.

In esso sono stati esposti, secondo la venerata Mente del Santo Padre, illustratami ulteriormente da V.E. nel predetto incontro, i nuovi dati di fatto e di diritto in base ai quali potrebbe avvenire la concreta trasformazione giuridica dell'Opus Dei in Prelatura personale "cum proprio populo".

Nella fiducia che l'approvazione delle predette norme basilari del nuovo statuto giuridico dell'Opera, sostanzialmente corrispondenti alla sua realtà sociale ed apostolica, possa finalmente portare all'auspicata soluzione del nostro problema istituzionale, in fedeltà allo spirito e ai desideri dell'amatissimo Fondatore dell'Opus Dei, mi onoro di confermarmi con sentimenti di cordiale amicizia e profonda venerazione

L + S                        di Vostra Eminenza Reverendissima
                             dev.mo nel Signore
                             Alvaro del Portillo          Javier Echevarría
                             Pres. Gen.                   Segr. Gen.

---

A Sua Eminenza Reverendissima il Sig.
Card. Sebastiano Baggio
Prefetto della S. Congregazione per i Vescovi
ROMA

---

## 63. Memorandum sent to Cardinal Baggio with the previous letter; April 23, 1979.

AGP, Sezione Giuridica, VIII/15031.

### TRASFORMAZIONE DELL'OPUS DEI
### IN PRELATURA PERSONALE

1.· **Caratteristiche specifiche e realtà sociale dell'Opus Dei.**

1.  L'Opus Dei, fondato il 2 ottobre 1928, è nato con un contenuto teologico ed apostolico chiaramente definito, che, approvato dalla Gerarchia sin dall'inizio (1), si è poi visto ampiamente confermato dal Magistero solenne del Concilio Vaticano II, e in particolare dalla Cost. dogm. "Lumen gentium", cap. II-V.

    Il suo Fondatore, il Servo di Dio Mons. Josemaría Escrivá de Balaguer, pose infatti come fondamento dottrinale dell'Opera la chiamata universale alla santità ed all'apostolato, insita nel Sacramento del Battesimo, e un impegno personale pieno dei soci -ciascuno nel proprio stato canonico, con la espressa conditio sine qua non di non diventare "persona consacrata per la professione dei consigli evangelici"- a vivere e a diffondere le esigenze ascetiche ed apostoliche delle promesse battesimali, secondo una spiritualità specifica nettamente secolare.

    Questa pone l'accento sulla necessità di cercare la pienezza della vita cristiana -la santità- e la diffusione del messaggio evangelico -l'apostolato- attraverso il fedele adempimento dei doveri familiari e sociali e in particolare mediante lo svolgimento il più perfetto possibile, per amore a Dio e al prossimo, del proprio lavoro professionale. Esso, infatti, nell'Opera è oggetto di speciali esigenze ascetiche, formative e apostoliche (tra l'altro, per i soci laici dell'Opera è condizione irrinunciabile, per poter corrispondere alla propria vocazione, l'esercizio costante di un lavoro professionale civile da normale cittadino), che sono ordinate a farlo diventare, come quello del divino Redentore a Nazareth, un lavoro di Dio, operatio Dei, opus Dei.

2.  L'Opus Dei, a cui appartengono attualmente 72.375 fedeli di 87 nazionalità, di cui il 2% circa sacerdoti, si configura giuridicamente, più che come una società, un movimento o una associazione, come una vera "portio

---

(1) Fondato a Madrid, l'Opus Dei ebbe fin dalla sua nascita l'incoraggiamento del Vescovo di quella diocesi, Mons. Eijo y Garay. Ricevette il Decreto di erezione diocesana, con il "nihil obstat" della Santa Sede, l'8 dicembre 1943; il Decreto di erezione pontificia il 24 febbraio 1947, ed il Decreto di approvazione da parte della Santa Sede del suo diritto particolare il 16 giugno 1950.

Populi Dei" (2) gerarchicamente ordinata (3), molto assomigliante a una Chiesa particolare o diocesi di carattere personale secondo la definizione data dal Concilio (4). Infatti, nell'Opus Dei esistono:

1°) un Ordinario o pastore proprio (il Presidente Generale), a cui è già stata attribuita da parte della Santa Sede, iure communi et particulari, la necessaria potestà di règime o di giurisdizione per il governo e la disciplina interna dell'Opera;

2°) un presbiterio, composto da sacerdoti secolari incardinati all'Opus Dei. Essi provengono dagli stessi laici dell'Opera, ricevono nei Seminari dell'Opus Dei (Centri di Studi) una completa formazione filosofica e teologica unitamente alla preparazione pastorale specifica -tutti, inoltre, compresi coloro che provengono da un ambiente operaio o rurale, conseguono una laurea ecclesiastica-, e vengono destinati dal Presidente Generale specialmente, anche se non esclusivamente, alla cura ministeriale dei soci laici;

3°) un laicato composto da semplici fedeli e comuni cittadini, uniti dalla medesima vocazione specifica rite probata, assistiti spiritualmente dai sacerdoti dell'Opera e tutti pienamente dedicati, ciascuno nella propria condizione di vita secolare e attraverso il proprio lavoro professionale, al raggiungimento delle finalità apostoliche proprie dell'Opus Dei, nel servizio del bene comune della Chiesa universale e, in concreto, delle Chiese particolari, giacché in esse rimane il frutto della loro attività apostolica.

---

(2) Cfr. Concilio Vaticano II, Cost. dogm. "Lumen gentium", n. 23; Decr. "Christus Dominus", n. 11. Si tratta, infatti, di sacerdoti secolari e di comuni fedeli laici, giacché, pur dedicandosi tutti ai fini apostolici dell'Opera e ricevendo perciò una formazione ed una cura spirituale specifica, nessun socio dell'Opus Dei cambia di stato canonico personale -non diventa cioè religioso o "persona consacrata"- per il fatto della sua incorporazione all'Opera, e tanto meno cambia la sua condizione civile di normale cittadino: "ut alii cives propriæ condicionis ac professionis se gerunt, vestiunt vitamque ducunt" (Decr. di approvazione pontificia del diritto particolare).

(3) "Sacerdotalis condicio, quamvis classis diversa in Opere Dei iuridice non sit, cardinale momentum in Instituto habet, præcipuas ex regula in ipso directionis functiones exercet, et merito quasi eiusdem animam constituere censetur" (Decr. di approvazione pontificia del diritto particolare).

(4) "Diœcesis est Populi Dei portio, quæ Episcopo cum cooperatione presbyterii pascenda concreditur" (Decr. "Christus Dominus", n. 11). Si mettono così in rilievo i tre elementi sostantivi e realmente costitutivi della diocesi: 1°) la comunità di fedeli o "Populi Dei portio", che viene spiritualmente curata; 2°) il Pastore proprio, che nel caso di una diocesi o Chiesa particolare è sempre un Vescovo; 3°) il presbiterio o corpo sacerdotale, che collabora con il Vescovo nella cura spirituale dei fedeli. "Definitionem realem diœcesis potius ex intrinsecis ipsius elementis quam ex territoriali structura conati sumus statuere, unde hæc quæ sequuntur commoda obtineri posse censemus: a) theologia quædam Ecclesiæ particularis, iuxta plurium Patrum postulata, veluti in nuce præbetur; b) clarius episcopalium munerum finis elucescit; c) notio diœcesis etiam ad 'personales' quas vocant diœceses æquo iure extenditur" (Relatio prior de capite II, art. I et II, in Schema Decreti de pastorali Episcoporum munere in Ecclesia, textus emendatus et relationes, Tipografia Poliglotta Vaticana 1964, p. 51).

3. Perciò, dal punto di vista sia giuridico che di fatto, vale a dire come realtà sociale esistente nella Chiesa da più di 50 anni, l'Opera costituisce un'unità pastorale, organica e indivisibile, che è integrata da sacerdoti e da laici di ogni stato di vita e condizione sociale e professionale: uomini e donne, celibi e sposati, intellettuali e operai, ecc., tutti partecipi dello stesso spirito e vocazione, e uniti sotto lo stesso regime, formazione e disciplina.

4. Sia le caratteristiche del suo spirito fondazionale -n. 1- che quelle della sua realtà giuridica e sociale -nn. 2 e 3-, hanno qualificato l'Opus Dei come un'entità ecclesiale diversa dagli Istituti clericali o laicali che assumono il peculiare stato di "vita consacrata per la professione dei consigli evangelici" e che dipendono dalla S. Congregazione per i Religiosi e gli Istituti Secolari. "L'Opus Dei -ripeteva il suo Fondatore- non è né può essere considerato come un fenomeno relativo al processo evolutivo dello 'stato di perfezione' nella Chiesa; non è una forma moderna o 'aggiornata' di questo stato. In effetti, la spiritualità e il fine apostolico che Dio ha voluto per la nostra associazione non hanno nulla a che fare con la concezione teologica dello status perfectionis (che San Tommaso, Suárez ed altri autori hanno configurato in termini definitivi nella dottrina), né con le diverse concretizzazioni giuridiche ("Instituta religiosa", "Instituta ad consilia evangelica profitenda", "Instituta vitæ consecratæ", ecc.) che sono o possono essere derivate da questo concetto teologico" (5).

5. Allo stesso tempo l'Opera -per la sua solidità organizzativa a struttura internazionale e centralizzata, per il suo ordinamento giuridico di ente clericale di diritto pontificio con facoltà di formare e di incardinare i propri candidati al sacerdozio, per le attribuzioni di potestà giurisdizionale attribuite al suo Presidente Generale, per la piena dedicazione apostolica di tutti i soci e per la svariata molteplicità delle sue attività apostoliche -ha una natura assai diversa da quella delle Pie Unioni e delle altre Associazioni di fedeli anche a carattere internazionale e misto (composto cioè da chierici e laici), che dipendono dal Pontificio Consiglio per i laici (6).

6. L'Opus Dei rappresenta perciò -com'è stato pienamente riconosciuto- un fenomeno pastorale nuovo nella vita della Chiesa, unicamente paragonabile alla realtà di spirito e di attività apostolica dei fedeli, chierici e laici, delle prime comunità cristiane. Questa novità era ancor più evidente al momento della nascita dell'Opera. Era quindi comprensibile che la legislazione generale della Chiesa, vigente in quegli anni, non prevedesse la possibilità per l'Opus Dei di una sistemazione giuridica adeguata, rispondente cioè pienamente alle sue reali caratteristiche. Ciò, però, ha comportato per l'Opus Dei il dover affrontare durante tutta la sua vita delle gravi e frequenti difficoltà, che erano motivo continuo di sofferenza per il nostro Fondatore, perché

---

(5) Mons. Escrivá de Balaguer, Colloqui, Milano 1968, p. 30.

(6) Cfr. Paolo VI, Motu pr. "Apostolatus peragendi", del 10 dicembre 1976, VI, 3: AAS 68 (1976), pp. 696 ss.

ostacolavano e riducevano sensibilmente la portata del servizio dell'Opera alla Chiesa ed alle anime (7).

## II. Ricerca di una sistemazione giuridica adeguata. Precedenti

7. Il Fondatore dell'Opus Dei (per motivi di urgente necessità che minacciavano lo sviluppo e perfino la stessa esistenza dell'Opera) si vide costretto a dover ricorrere provvisoriamente a formule giuridiche inadeguate -Pia Unione, Società di vita comune senza voti, Istituto Secolare-, che consentissero di avere, assieme alle necessarie facoltà giuridiche, l'imprescindibile approvazione della Santa Sede. Lo fece suo malgrado, perché tali formule non erano consentanee alla natura dell'Opus Dei, e non nascose mai all'Autorità ecclesiastica questo suo convincimento. Tutto ciò, in attesa che lo sviluppo futuro della legislazione ecclesiastica potesse offrire la possibilità di una sistemazione giuridica definitiva, non privilegiata, capace di favorire la massima efficacia apostolica dell'Opus Dei e di salvaguardare la sua identità fondazionale.

8. Nel 1962 il Fondatore dell'Opera prospettò alla Santa Sede l'eventuale soluzione del problema istituzionale dell'Opus Dei mediante la sua trasformazione in una Prelatura "nullius" in base al can. 319 § 2 del C.I.C. Come si sa, detto canone stabilisce che una Prelatura di questo tipo "tribus saltem parœciis non constans" si regge mediante un diritto peculiare ("singulari iure regitur"). Lo "ius singulare" della Prelatura sarebbe stato, con gli imprescindibili accomodamenti, lo stesso "ius peculiare" dell'Opus Dei, già approvato dalla Santa Sede; mentre la natura nettamente secolare di tale figura giuridica avrebbe anche assicurato il carattere pienamente secolare e diocesano dei sacerdoti e dei laici dell'Opus Dei. Il Fondatore era ben edotto del fatto che la predetta norma del can. 319 § 2 del C.I.C. riguardava soltanto le Prelature a carattere territoriale; ma ubbidì all'allora Card. Protettore dell'Opera, il Card. Pietro Ciriaci, che lo incoraggiò a prospettare ugualmente tale soluzione, perché pensava all'eventualità di un'applicazione estensiva del dettato codiciale. Il Santo Padre Giovanni XXIII fece rispondere che la richiesta non poteva essere accolta, perché allora presentava difficoltà pressoché insuperabili; ed il nostro Fondatore, che del resto capì sin dal primo momento tali difficoltà giuridiche, fece sapere che in coscienza avrebbe riprospettato il problema non appena si fosse aperto nella legislazione della Chiesa il cammino opportuno, che già in forma più evidente si veniva maturando nei lavori conciliari.

---

(7) Tale mancanza di corrispondenza tra il carisma fondazionale dell'Opus Dei e la sua qualificazione giuridica come Istituto Secolare o "Istituto di vita consacrata" ha dato luogo, infatti, a gravi e crescenti difficoltà, non ultima la pesante discriminazione dei laici dell'Opera (perché considerati persone non libere, in quanto legate da un voto di ubbidienza) negli ambienti professionali civili in cui debbono lavorare. Questa ed altre continue difficoltà che riguardano l'insieme dello spirito e dell'apostolato dell'Opera si sono accentuate con il trascorrere del tempo, fino a costringere il Fondatore dell'Opus Dei a dover ricorrere più volte al Santo Padre e a diversi Dicasteri della Curia Romana, domandando filialmente di voler intervenire, di fronte a singoli problemi e circostanze, con atti singolari di governo (chiarimenti, dispense, ecc.), che salvaguardassero il più possibile la natura propria dell'Opera e la sua efficacia apostolica.

9.  Il Santo Padre Paolo VI, infatti, nell'anno 1964, anche se confermò al Fondatore dell'Opus Dei che non era ancora possibile trovare nel diritto vigente la formula adeguata, aggiunse che nulla vietava di riprendere in esame la questione più tardi, alla luce cioè dei Decreti del Concilio Vaticano II, allora in fase di svolgimento.

    D'accordo con le possibilità offerte dal Motu proprio Ecclesiæ Sanctæ (6 agosto 1966), il nostro Fondatore, dopo di averne informato la Santa Sede, convocò il 25 giugno 1969 un Congresso Generale Speciale, allo scopo di fare gli studi necessari per chiedere l'auspicata soluzione giuridica d'accordo con la nuova legislazione, successiva al Concilio.

    Posteriormente, in un'Udienza che il Santo Padre gli concesse il 25 giugno 1973, il venerato Fondatore informò di nuovo Sua Santità sulla buona marcia del Congresso: il Santo Padre ne fu lieto, ed incoraggiò il nostro Fondatore ad andare avanti con il Congresso Generale. Ma Mons. Escrivá de Balaguer morì due anni dopo, senza aver avuto il tempo di presentare i nuovi documenti, anche se aveva lasciato precise indicazioni in merito. Egli, infatti, oltre ad essere stato in molti aspetti un vero precursore del Concilio Vaticano II, ne seguì attentamente i lavori e le successive norme applicative dei suoi Decreti.

10. Il Santo Padre Paolo VI confermò a me, nella prima Udienza che mi concesse come Presidente Generale dell'Opus Dei, il 5 marzo 1976, che "la questione rimaneva aperta", in attesa di darle una soluzione quando io ne facessi la domanda: io risposi a Sua Santità che, anche se il Congresso Generale aveva pressoché finito il suo studio, in considerazione del fatto che la scomparsa del Fondatore era così recente avrei preferito lasciare passare alcun tempo, prima di inoltrare detta domanda, a meno che il S. Padre non mi dicesse di procedere subito. Il S. Padre si disse d'accordo con il mio suggerimento. In un'altra Udienza, concessami il 19 giugno 1978, Sua Santità mi ripetè che "la questione rimaneva aperta", e mi incoraggiò a presentare la relativa domanda, onde ottenere la soluzione giuridica auspicata. Io mi ripromisi di farlo post aquas, ma il Santo Padre Paolo VI morì prima che io potessi fare nulla.

    Sua Santità Giovanni Paolo I manifestò poi nel settembre 1978 la sua volontà che si procedesse a dar "l'auspicata soluzione" al nostro problema istituzionale. Ed infine, il 15 novembre 1978, nel trasmettermi una Lettera Autografa augurale del Santo Padre Giovanni Paolo II per il 50° anniversario dell'Opera, il compianto Em.mo Card. Segretario di Stato mi comunicò che Sua Santità considerava "una indilazionabile necessità che sia risolta la questione della sistemazione giuridica dell'Opus Dei".

11. Attese le ragioni d'ordine fondazionale, teologico e giuridico da noi sollecitamente esposte in ossequio al desiderio di Sua Santità, la S. Congregazione per i Religiosi e gli Istituti Secolari autorizzò l'Opus Dei a fare, in fedeltà allo spirito ed alle indicazioni del Fondatore, gli ulteriori passi -al di fuori dell'ambito di competenza di detto S. Dicastero- che si rendessero necessari per arrivare ad una sistemazione giuridica dell'Opus Dei diversa da quella di Istituto Secolare.

    Il primo contatto con codesta Sacra Congregazione per i Vescovi ebbe luogo il 20 gennaio 1979. In esso fu già prospettata, in maniera soltanto interlocutoria, subordinata cioè all'eventuale affidamento formale della pratica alla S. Congregazione per i Vescovi da parte del Santo Padre, la trasformazione giuridica dell'Opus Dei in una Prelatura personale.

12. Nell'Udienza concessami il 12 febbraio u.s. informai il Santo Padre del risultato dei passi fatti sia nel Dicastero a quo (S. Congregazione per i Religiosi e gli Istituti Secolari) che nel Dicastero ad quod (S. Congregazione per i Vescovi), in vista dell'auspicata soluzione giuridica del nostro problema istituzionale. Allo stesso tempo, ed a nome anche del Consiglio Generale dell'Opera -il quale si era dichiarato unanimemente favorevole, sapendo che era questo il desiderio del nostro Fondatore- domandai formalmente al Santo Padre la predetta trasformazione dell'Opus Dei da Istituto Secolare in Prelatura personale "cum proprio populo", tenendo conto della realtà sociale dell'Opera e dei nuovi elementi giuridici contenuti nella legislazione applicativa dei Decreti conciliari, particolarmente nel Motu pr. Ecclesiæ Sanctæ, I, n. 4.

Sua Santità accolse benignamente la richiesta; mi disse che nel futuro questa soluzione potrebbe essere utile anche per qualche altra istituzione che avesse elementi fondazionali con caratteristiche analoghe a quelle dell'Opera; e mi assicurò che avrebbe incaricato la Sacra Congregazione competente di compiere lo studio necessario per la concreta definizione del nuovo statuto giuridico dell'Opera come Prelatura personale "cum proprio populo". Tale incarico è stato infatti affidato all'Em.mo Card. Prefetto della S. Congregazione per i Vescovi nell'Udienza "di tabella" avuta il 3 marzo u.s. Lo stesso Em.mo, con lettera del 7 marzo u.s. ed in successiva conversazione avuta il 29 s.m., mi ha gentilmente confermato essere Mente del Santo Padre che si faccia uno studio tenendo conto di tutti i nuovi dati di fatto e di diritto, e che tale studio sia concretamente ordinato alla determinazione del quomodo -vale a dire, in base a quali precise norme giuridiche- debba avvenire la richiesta trasformazione dell'Opus Dei in Prelatura personale.

### III. Individuazione delle basi per la nuova sistemazione giuridica

A. *Le Prelature personali del Concilio Vaticano II:elementi caratteristici*

13. In effetti, la concreta definizione del nuovo statuto giuridico appare oggi cosa facilmente realizzabile senza ulteriori dilazioni né inutili forzature giuridiche, grazie agli arricchimenti pastorali e normativi che sono già stati introdotti dal Concilio Vaticano II nel diritto della Chiesa. Lo stesso Fondatore dell'Opus Dei, prima di lasciare questa terra, ci aveva segnalato espressamente che nel Decr. Presbyterorum Ordinis, nel Motu pr. Ecclesiæ Sanctæ e nella Cost. Ap. Regimini Ecclesiæ universæ si trovano già tutte le norme necessarie, in base alle quali si possono stabilire le linee fondamentali del nuovo statuto giuridico dell'Opera. E ciò in perfetta corrispondenza al suo spirito ed alla sua realtà sociale, di regime e di organizzazione apostolica.

14. Il Decreto conciliare Presbyterorum Ordinis, n.10 § 1 sancì esplicitamente l'esistenza di "Prelaturæ personales", che potranno essere utilmente costituite ("utiliter constitui possunt") per la realizzazione di peculiari opere pastorali ("ad peculiaria opera pastoralia perficienda") nel servizio della Chiesa universale ("in bonum commune totius Ecclesiæ"), secondo norme particolari da stabilirsi per ognuna di queste istituzioni ("modis

pro singulis inceptis statuendis") e restando sempre salvi i diritti degli Ordinari del luogo ("salvis semper iuribus Ordinariorum locorum").

15. Successivamente, il Motu pr. Ecclesiæ Sanctæ, I, n. 4, nell'applicare il predetto Decreto conciliare ha configurato tali Prelature personali con norme più concrete e dettagliate, e cioè:

1°) si tratta di Prelature erette dalla Santa Sede a carattere nettamente secolare (ben diverse perciò dagli Ordini religiosi, monacali o meno, il cui Superiore supremo compare a volte nel diritto sotto il nome di "Prelato" -cfr. can. 110 C.I.C.- ed ha comunque la qualifica di Ordinario: cfr. can. 198 C.I.C.);

2°) sono sottoposte alla giurisdizione o regime (alla potestà cioè legislativa, giudiziale e amministrativa) di un proprio Prelato; il Motu proprio rimanda invece alla legge particolare il compito di determinare nei singoli casi se l'Ordinario della Prelatura dovrà avere o meno carattere episcopale;

3°) hanno un proprio clero in possesso di una formazione particolare, adeguata cioè alla specifica finalità pastorale ed apostolica propria di ciascuna Prelatura;

4°) per la formazione dei propri candidati al sacerdozio, le Prelature hanno seminari nazionali od internazionali, che sono eretti dal Prelato, al quale corrisponde il compito della suprema direzione disciplinare, dell'ordinamento degli studi, ecc.;

5°) il Prelato ha il diritto di incardinare gli alunni formati nei seminari della Prelatura e di promuoverli agli Ordini con il titolo di "ad servitium Prælaturæ" (conseguentemente, è pure il Prelato che, sempre nel dovuto rispetto dei diritti degli Ordinari del luogo, conferisce a ciascun sacerdote della Prelatura la relativa missione canonica e le facoltà ministeriali nei limiti del proprio ambito di giurisdizione);

6°) tra gli altri doveri inerenti al suo munus pastorale, il Prelato ha quello particolare di curare la vita spirituale dei suoi sacerdoti, di perfezionare continuamente la loro formazione speciale e di provvedere in base al patrimonio della Prelatura, od eventualmente talvolta anche mediante opportuni accordi con gli Ordinari del luogo, all'onesto sostentamento dei medesimi sacerdoti ed alla loro previdenza sociale;

7°) oltre ai sacerdoti formati ed incardinati nelle Prelature, nulla vieta che in alcune di esse ci possano essere anche dei fedeli laici, sia celibi che coniugati, che dedichino la loro vita ed il loro lavoro professionale ai fini ed alle attività apostoliche proprie della Prelatura;

8°) contrariamente a quanto succede negli "Istituti di vita consacrata", religiosi o secolari, l'incorporazione di questi fedeli alla Prelatura non avviene mediante l'assunzione o la professione di voti o di altri vincoli di carattere sacro, ma mediante opportuni contratti o convenzioni, che regoleranno la mutua prestazione di servizi;

9°) nello svolgimento della loro missione, le Prelature rispetteranno accuratamente i diritti degli Ordinari del luogo, con i quali avranno stretti e continui rapporti;

10°) ciascuna Prelatura si reggerà d'accordo con uno statuto proprio o legge particolare sancita dalla Santa Sede, secondo cioè le sue concrete finalità e caratteristiche organizzative (di ambito nazionale o internazionale, "cum proprio populo" o senza di esso, ecc.).

16. La Cost. Ap. Regimini Ecclesiæ universæ, nel riordinare in seguito al Concilio Vaticano II le competenze proprie dei vari Dicasteri della Curia Romana, ha sancito esplicitamente la dipendenza delle Prelature personali dalla S. Congregazione per i Vescovi (cfr. n. 49 § 1), il che peraltro già avveniva precedentemente nel caso delle Prelature personali, con o senza proprio popolo, costituite "iure extraordinario" prima del Concilio, dal diritto cioè post-codiciale (8).

B. *Conformità di questo quadro giuridico alla realtà ed allo spirito dell'Opus Dei*

17. Come si è accennato all'inizio di questo esposto (cfr. n. 2), l'Opus Dei riunisce sostanzialmente tutti gli elementi costitutivi delle Prelature personali -strutture giurisdizionali equiparate alle diocesi-, che sono previsti nel Motu pr. Ecclesiæ Sanctæ. Infatti:

1°) l'Opus Dei è già un Ente con personalità canonica pubblica di natura clericale e di diritto pontificio, eretto dalla Santa Sede nel 1947, ed ha una spiritualità nettamente secolare e diocesana (proprio per garantire in maniera inequivocabile quest'ultima caratteristica, insieme alla necessaria unità di regime, si desidera la trasformazione in Prelatura);

2°) l'Opera si trova sotto la giurisdizione del suo Presidente Generale (assistito da un Consiglio Generale), cui è già stata attribuita dalla Santa Sede, per quanto riguarda il governo e la disciplina interna, la potestà di regime nel foro sia esterno che interno, propria di un Ordinario;

3°) l'Opus Dei ha un proprio clero proveniente dagli stessi soci laici dell'Opera, il quale ha ricevuto la preparazione dottrinale, ascetica ed apostolica necessaria per la realizzazione della specifica attività pastorale ad esso richiesta;

4°) eretti dal Presidente Generale, l'Opus Dei ha un Seminario (Centro di Studi) internazionale a Roma ed altri nelle singole Regioni o Nazioni dove l'Opera lavora da tempo; lo stesso Presidente Generale esercita la suprema direzione disciplinare e determina l'ordinamento degli studi, secondo una "Ratio studiorum" più volte lodata dalla Santa Sede;

5°) il Presidente Generale ha il diritto di incardinare all'Opus Dei i candidati al sacerdozio formati nei predetti Seminari, e di promuoverli agli Ordini per il servizio dell'Opera, concedendo loro le relative lettere dimissorie; lo stesso Presidente Generale affida a questi

---

(8) E' il caso degli Ordinariati militari o Vicariati castrensi (Prelature personali "cum proprio populo", a volte distribuite in più Nazioni e continenti), della Prelatura di Pontigny o "Mission de France" e di altre istituzioni simili per la cura pastorale specializzata di determinati gruppi di persone.

sacerdoti i diversi compiti ministeriali e concede loro le facoltà ministeriali interne;

6°)   parimenti, e sempre a norma del diritto particolare dell'Opus Dei, il Presidente Generale cura la vita spirituale e la continua e specifica formazione dei sacerdoti, in ordine soprattutto alla cura ministeriale dei soci laici; l'Opera provvede pure all'onesto sostentamento dei propri sacerdoti e alle loro necessità in caso di malattia, invalidità o vecchiaia;

7°)   nell'Opus Dei la stragrande maggioranza dei soci è composta da fedeli laici, uomini e donne, sia celibi che coniugati, i quali (con unità di vocazione, di spirito e di regime e con una profonda formazione ascetica e dottrinale) si dedicano pienamente al raggiungimento delle finalità apostoliche dell'Opera, attraverso soprattutto il libero lavoro professionale o mestiere proprio di ciascuno;

8°)   questa dedicazione personale dei laici ascritti all'Opus Dei ha la forma di una prestazione di servizi, che genera mutui obblighi, non essendo adeguato alla spiritualità e alle finalità dell'Opus Dei (come è già stato esposto alla S. Congregazione per i Religiosi e gli Istituti Secolari: cfr. n. 11) un vincolo mediante voti od altri sacri legami ad essi equiparati;

9°)   nelle più di cinquecento diocesi in cui svolge il suo lavoro apostolico tra persone di tutte le razze e condizioni sociali, l'Opus Dei mantiene stretti e continui contatti con gli Ordinari del luogo, i cui diritti vengono sempre accuratamente rispettati e senza la cui previa autorizzazione nessun Centro è stato né sarà mai eretto; ugualmente si procede sempre tramite apposite convenzioni con i Vescovi diocesani, quando su loro richiesta si accetta l'affidamento di chiese pubbliche (che rimangono comunque chiese secolari), cappellanie od altri uffici ecclesiastici diocesani;

10°) l'Opus Dei ha, infine, un proprio diritto particolare approvato dalla Santa Sede, che potrebbe continuare ad essere lo statuto o legge particolare della Prelatura, con i leggeri accomodamenti richiesti dalla nuova veste giuridica; in tale diritto particolare, infatti, si contengono tutte le norme sopra esposte (di struttura organizzativa, regime, disciplina e apostolato), e che sono richieste dalla stessa legge generale istitutiva delle Prelature personali.

18. Appare infine opportuno considerare che:

a)   l'Opus Dei ha un regime a carattere personale di ambito internazionale ma centralizzato, con la sua sede centrale a Roma (residenza del Presidente Generale, uffici del Consiglio Generale, e Centro internazionale di studi); essa si trova in un piccolo territorio proprio, che offre già l'imprescindibile base materiale della Prelatura;

b)   il requisito della previa consultazione delle Conferenze Episcopali interessate, onde procedere alla trasformazione dell'Opus Dei in Prelatura personale, risulta di fatto già adempiuto, poiché l'Opus Dei lavora già in tutte le nazioni con l'approvazione e la *venia* previa degli Ordinari del luogo interessati (cfr. n. 17, 9°), secondo una

norma che continuerebbe a praticarsi anche in futuro. Inoltre, una ripetizione di questo adempimento non sembra necessaria (né sarebbe pratico farlo, dato che, attesa l'estensione dell'ambito apostolico dell'Opera, bisognerebbe rivolgersi a tutte le Conferenze Episcopali, allungando di molto l'iter della nuova sistemazione giuridica) anche per diverse altre ragioni: non si tratterebbe di costituire ex novo, ma di trasformare (peraltro, senza sostanziali cambiamenti di regime e di organizzazione: cfr. n. 17, 10°) il carattere di una persona giuridica clericale di diritto pontificio già esistente; l'Opus Dei svolge il suo lavoro apostolico -che continuerebbe ad essere lo stesso- da ormai più di 50 anni, e si tratta di un lavoro ampiamente collaudato e ben conosciuto sia dalla Santa Sede che dai Vescovi diocesani; il clero della Prelatura non si costituirebbe sottræm
ndolo al clero secolare o ai seminaristi di nessuna diocesi (come avviene, ad esempio, nel caso dei Vicariati castrensi); ecc.

C. *Vantaggi di carattere ecclesiale dell'auspicata sistemazione giuridica*

19. La trasformazione dell'Opus Dei da Istituto Secolare in Prelatura personale "cum proprio populo" in base alle predette norme giuridiche fondamentali sopra esposte (cfr. nn. 14-18), mentre rafforzerebbe ulteriormente il servizio dell'Opera alle singole Chiese locali, offrirebbe alla Santa Sede la possibilità di disporre con maggiore efficacia di un corpo mobile di sacerdoti e di laici (accuratamente preparati), che sarebbero ovunque possente fermento spirituale ed apostolico di vita cristiana, e ciò soprattutto in ambienti della società civile e in attività professionali dove spesso non è facile oggi arrivare in maniera apostolicamente incisiva con i comuni mezzi che la Chiesa ha a sua disposizione.

20. Per dare al riguardo un'idea, anche se succinta, si pensi che, oltre all'apostolato personale con i propri parenti, amici, ecc., i soci dell'Opera già lavorano -pur essendo attualmente ostacolati dalle gravi difficoltà sopra accennate: cfr. n. 6- nelle seguenti attività professionali, fra le molte di altro genere che si potrebbero elencare: in 479 Università e Scuole Superiori dei cinque continenti; in 604 giornali, riviste e pubblicazioni scientifiche; in 52 emittenti di televisione e radio, 38 agenzie di informazione e pubblicità e 12 case produttrici e distributrici cinematografiche, ecc. Inoltre gli stessi soci, assieme ad altri normali cittadini, cattolici come pure non cattolici e non cristiani, hanno promosso in 53 Nazioni -sempre con carattere professionale e civile- svariate attività apostoliche d'indole educativa, assistenziale, sociale, ecc. : Scuole di ogni grado ed Istituti tecnici, Clubs per ragazzi, Centri di qualificazione professionale per operai e contadini, Scuole alberghiere e di economia domestica, Cliniche e ambulatori medici, e così via (9).

---

(9) Tutto ciò senza contare l'apostolato di penetrazione che, attraverso e con occasione di normali attività professionali (corsi di specializzazione e scambi culturali, incontri internazionali e congressi, inviti a operatori economici, tecnici, docenti, ecc.), si cerca di sviluppare in Nazioni sottoposte a regimi totalitari di carattere anticristiano o ateo o comunque di acceso nazionalismo, i quali rendono difficile e spesso impossibile, de iure o de facto, l'azione dei missionari e dei religiosi, e perfino una presenza organizzata e attiva della Chiesa come istituzione.

21. Ma soprattutto, ed insieme ai vantaggi d'ordine apostolico, la predetta soluzione del problema istituzionale dell'Opus Dei -prospettata già in vita dallo stesso suo Fondatore, che era convinto della perfetta corrispondenza di tale soluzione con quanto il Signore voleva da Lui- garantirebbe definitivamente nel futuro la conservazione (che sarebbe, invece, in pericolo, se non si trovasse la sistemazione giuridica adeguata al carisma fondazionale) dell'autentica fisionomia spirituale dell'Opera e la corretta qualificazione canonica dei suoi soci. Permetterebbe cioè di sancire in forma inequivocabile, conservando l'Opera allo stesso tempo l'imprescindibile unità di regime e di apostolato, che i sacerdoti dell'Opus Dei sono sacerdoti pienamente secolari, diocesani, e che i laici sono fedeli comuni e non "laici consacrati". Proprio perché si tratta di assicurare così l'identità fondazionale dell'Opus Dei, è evidente che tale soluzione giuridica al suo problema istituzionale non potrà costituire precedente per altre istituzioni di natura diversa (Ordini e Congregazioni Religiose, Istituti Secolari, ecc.), le quali sono state giuridicamente configurate come "Istituti di vita consacrata" proprio in ossequio al loro carisma fondazionale.

22. Infine, nella nuova veste giuridica dell'Opus Dei come Prelatura personale in base alle norme sopraddette sarebbero assicurate e confermate -come si è detto al n. 17, 10°)- tutte le norme di diritto generale e particolare che regolano l'attuale organizzazione e regime dell'Opera; la disciplina; la profonda formazione dei soci (senza "elitismi", ma di piena fedeltà al Magistero ecclesiastico); la loro continua cura spirituale da parte dei propri sacerdoti; i rapporti di costante e stretta collaborazione con i Vescovi diocesani, ecc. Al tempo stesso, si rafforzerebbero ancora di più i contatti informativi e la dipendenza dell'Opus Dei dalla Santa Sede, tramite soprattutto la S. Congregazione per i Vescovi, da cui dipenderebbe e alla quale verrebbe regolarmente fatta, tra l'altro, la dettagliata relazione quinquennale "de statu Prælaturæ".

## CONCLUSIONE

Atteso che il Santo Padre ha benignamente accolto la richiesta presentata per l'adeguata soluzione del problema istituzionale dell'Opus Dei (cfr. n. 12), si chiede sommessamente a codesto Sacro Dicastero di voler approvare i lineamenti giuridici dettagliati ai nn. 17-18 come base per la trasformazione dell'Opus Dei in una Prelatura personale.

Roma, 23 aprile 1979

Alvaro del Portillo

Pres. Gen.

L + S

Javier Echevarría

Segr. Gen.

## 64. Letter of the Very Reverend Alvaro del Portillo to Cardinal Baggio in which he clarifies some points of the petition; June 2, 1979.

AGP, Sezione Giuridica, VIII/15039.

**Opus Dei**

**Il Presidente Generale**                    Roma, 2 giugno 1979

Eminenza Reverendissima,

In ossequio al venerato desiderio del Santo Padre circa la sistemazione giuridica dell'Opus Dei come Prelatura personale "cum proprio populo", ho avuto l'onore di sottoporre a codesta Sacra Congregazione, in data 23 aprile c.a., l'esposto in cui si propongono, corredate dai relativi elementi di diritto e di fatto, le basi giuridiche dell'auspicato statuto definitivo dell'Opera.

Dette norme contengono le disposizioni fondamentali di diritto che configurerebbero nei loro tratti sostanziali lo spirito e la natura giuridica, la finalità pastorale ed apostolica, la struttura e il regime della Prelatura, nonché le sue relazioni con la Santa Sede e con gli Ordinari del luogo. In tal modo, se, come noi con fiducia filiale ci auguriamo, dette norme basilari venissero positivamente accolte da codesto Sacro Dicastero ed approvate dal Santo Padre, sarebbe in seguito possibile procedere alla loro applicazione particolareggiata a livello di concreta applicazione tecnica.

Mi sembra tuttavia forse utile, perché si tratta di questioni di rilievo, riguardanti la giurisdizione e la nomina del Prelato, precisare ulteriormente i seguenti quattro punti:

1)  Non è nostra intenzione, né sembrerebbe opportuno, che la giurisdizione del Prelato venga estesa oltre l'ambito di persone sulle quali il Presidente Generale dell'Opus Dei ha già una potestà ordinaria di regime, vale a dire i sacerdoti incardinati all'Opera e i laici (uomini e donne, celibi e sposati) ad essa appartenenti. E questo, sia per elementari ragioni di certezza giuridica riguardo ai destinatari della potestà del Prelato, che per lo spirito del Fondatore dell'Opera, che sempre desiderò servire la Chiesa come lievito, con caratteristiche proprie ben determinate, in tutte le Diocesi dove si lavora.

Pertanto sarebbero fedeli della Prelatura, costituirebbero cioè il suo "proprio popolo", non le persone destinatarie del lavoro apostolico dell'Opus Dei e del ministero dei suoi sacerdoti, ma soltanto quei laici che, previa convenzione con la Prelatura, vorranno (di fatto già lo sono) incorporarsi giuridicamente ad essa, impegnandosi al servizio del suo specifico compito apostolico con una piena dedicazione personale, che trascende di gran lunga le limitate prestazioni di servizi di altri tipi di possibili convenzioni anch'esse contemplate nel Motu pr. "Ecclesiæ Sanctæ", I, n. 4 (cfr. esposto "Trasformazione dell'Opus Dei in una Prelatura personale", nn. 7° e 8°). Sono infatti questi laici i fedeli che, per poter dovutamente ed efficacemente adempiere il loro pieno impegno apostolico negli ambienti laicali e professionali in cui si muovono, hanno bisogno e diritto alla continua formazione specializzata, ascetica e apostolica ed alla sollecita cura pastorale specifica da parte dei sacerdoti dell'Opus Dei (della Prelatura). Giova notare la corrispondenza esistente tra questa realtà e la seguente norma che -nello sviluppare il Motu pr. "Ecclesiæ Sanctæ", I, n.4- è prevista nel progetto del nuovo C.I.C. : "*Prælatura tamen cum* proprio populo item haberi potest cum portio populi Dei, Prælati curæ commissa, indolem habeat personalem, complectens nempe *solos fideles speciali quadam ratione devinctos*" (Schema "De Populo Dei", can. 219, § 2).

2) Dovendo essere il regime e governo della Prelatura a carattere personale e non territoriale, è pacifico che la potestà ordinaria del Prelato, alla stregua di quanto avviene nel caso dei Vicariati castrensi e di altre simili giurisdizioni ecclesiastiche, avrà nelle singole diocesi e riguardo a svariate materie (disposizioni dottrinali e liturgiche, disciplina generale del clero, attività esterne di apostolato, ecc.) il carattere di giurisdizione cumulativa. Proprio per il ruolo di particolare inserimento dell' apostolato che i soci dell'Opera svolgono al servizio delle Chiese locali, la regolamentazione particolareggiata di tale potestà salvaguarderà sempre accuratamente, come si dice nel precitato esposto (cfr. n. 17, 9°), sia i diritti degli Ordinari locali che le norme del diritto particolare dell'Opus Dei già approvato dalla Santa Sede.

3) Il Prelato dovrà avere tutte le qualità personali di pietà, prudenza, dottrina, ecc. richieste dal diritto generale della Chiesa (cfr. C.I.C., can. 331), più quelle che sono stabilite nel diritto particolare dell'Opus Dei riguardo al Presidente Generale (tra le altre, età minima di 40 anni, approfondita conoscenza ed esperienza dello spirito e della prassi apostolica dell'Opera).

4) La elezione del Prelato da parte del Congresso Generale -procedura questa che garantisce il massimo grado di accettazione e di autorità morale della persona designata- richiederebbe giuridicamente la conferma del Santo Padre, come è norma di diritto in questi casi (cfr. C.I.C., cann. 329, § 3; 321; Schema "De Populo Dei" del nuovo C.I.C., can. 228, § 1).

Profitto volentieri della circostanza per confermarmi con sentimenti di profonda venerazione

dell'Eminenza Vostra Reverendissima

dev.mo nel Signore

L + S       Alvaro del Portillo

Pres. Gen.

Javier Echevarría

Segr. Gen.

A Sua Eminenza Reverendissima il Sig.
Card. Sebastiano Baggio
Prefetto della Sacra Congregazione per i Vescovi
ROMA

## 65. Letter of Sebastiano Cardinal Baggio requesting additional information; July 18, 1979.

AGP, Sezione Giuridica, VIII/15041.

SACRA CONGREGAZIONE                        Roma, 18 Luglio 1979
    PER I VESCOVI
    ─────────────────

Prot. n. 317/62

Reverendisimo Presidente Generale,

nella nostra conversazione del 9 di questo mese Le comunicavo che il voto degli Em.mi ed Ecc.mi Padri della nostra Congregazione circa la proposta erezione della Società della Santa Croce, Opus Dei, in prelatura personale "cum proprio populo", nella Riunione Ordinaria del 28 giugno precedente, era stato "Dilata et compleantur acta" e che il Santo Padre lo aveva fatto Suo "ad mentem". Compio ora il venerato incarico di parteciparLe il tenore dell'augusta Mente.

Anzitutto, però, voglio assicurarLa che l'approfondimento dello studio si deve alla novità ed alla complessità del problema ed all'importanza del precedente che esso viene a costituire nel quadro istituzionale della Chiesa; non già a restrizioni nei confronti dell'Opus Dei, verso il quale è nota la grande stima ed il sincero affetto professato e più volte attestato dal Sommo Pontefice. Aggiungerò che nel corso dell'Adunanza Ordinaria della Congregazione è stato unanime il riconoscimento dei pregi e dei meriti della Società che Ella degnamente presiede, al di sopra di certe critiche e perplessità che non potevano non affiorare.

Prima ancora che la Presidenza dell'Opus Dei proceda alla formulazione della "Lex particularis" che dovrebbe definirne la fisionomia proposta di Prelatura "cum proprio populo", è volontà del Papa che questo sacro Dicastero, al quale Egli ha confermato la competenza in materia, perfezioni lo studio generale previo che consenta di sciogliere ogni riserva, sollecitando a questo scopo anche l'apporto della sacra Congregazione per i Religiosi e gli Istituti Secolari, nel cui alveo l'Opera ha sviluppato finora la sua esistenza canonica.

A tal fine sarebbe necessario che questa nostra Congregazione conoscesse i vigenti Statuti dell'Opus Dei e possibilmente anche quelli originali, nonché la "ratio studiorum" e gli atti di approvazione pontificia di tali documenti. Interesserebbe inoltre, nei limiti del possibile, una documentazione storica della volontà del Fondatore circa la configurazione ecclesiale dell'Opera, particolarmente con anteriorità al 7 gennaio 1962, data in cui venne inoltrata al Segretario di Stato di Sua Santità la prima istanza di erezione in Prelatura. Parimenti si vorrebbe che venisse fugato ogni dubbio sulla possibilità di procedere nel senso desiderato in base al "jus conditum", senza che sia necessario riferirsi al "jus condendum" ed anticiparlo.

E poiché Sua Santità ha accolto il voto della grande maggioranza dei Padri sull'opportunità di consultare le Conferenze Episcopali maggiormente interessate, occorrerebbe altresì conoscere la consistenza dell'Opus Dei, nelle sue diverse categorie, nei vari pæsi.

Anche dopo l'esame da parte del collegio dei Membri della sacra Congregazione degli ampi esposti da Lei presentati in data 23 aprile e 2 giugno 1979 e dopo lo studio delle lettere da Lei dirette al Santo Padre il 2 febbraio scorso e il 3 e il 13 del presente mese di luglio, che Sua Santità si è degnato di mettere a mia disposizione, rimane qualche incertezza che sarebbe necessario chiarificare, cioè:

1) la specifica secolarità dell'Opus Dei in quanto la contraddistingue dagli Istituti Secolari e differenzia i suoi membri dagli altri battezzati;

2) la "specialis ratio devinctionis" o di sudditanza al Prelato di chierici e laici, uomini e donne, nei diversi gradi della loro appartenenza all'Opus Dei, in rapporto con la loro qualità di soci o di aggregati;

3) i criteri concreti intesi a prevenire la costituzione di una "Chiesa parallela" all'interno delle giurisdizioni territoriali, praticamente in tutto il mondo.

In assidua comunione di preghiera "cum Maria, matre Jesu" e in ecclesiale spirito di fraternità, mi è caro ripetermi

di Lei, carissimo Presidente Generale,
aff.mo
+ S. Card. Baggio
Prefetto

Rev.mo Don Alvaro del Portillo
Presidente Generale dell'Opus Dei
ROMA

## 66. Letter of the Very Reverend Alvaro del Portillo to the members of Opus Dei; December 8, 1981.

AGP, Sezione Giuridica, VIII/15064.

Queridísimos: ¡que Jesús me guarde a mis hijas y a mis hijos!

1. Me ha sido comunicado oficialmente, hace poco, que el Santo Padre ha deliberado erigir el Opus Dei en Prelatura personal, como había solicitado nuestro queridísimo Fundador, aprobando los Estatutos que había dejado preparados nuestro Padre. *Deo Gratias!*

Ha de pasar algún tiempo antes de que se publique esta noticia, porque el Papa desea oír a todos los Obispos de las diócesis y de las naciones en las que trabajamos: por ahora, el Santo Padre ha dispuesto que esta buena nueva, tan esperada, y por la que desde hace tantos años rezó y nos hizo rezar nuestro queridísimo Fundador, quede reservada al Consejo General y a la Asesoría Central de la Obra.

No sé, por lo tanto, cuándo podré enviaros estas líneas que, como las redacto cuando aún no se conoce la decisión pontificia, han de tener necesariamente un carácter general: voy a limitarme en este momento a fijar sobre el papel sólo tres o cuatro ideas importantes, que me llevan a dar gracias a Dios de todo corazón. Pero ya desde ahora os adelanto que, cuando se haga pública la noticia, os comunicaré en otra carta, si Dios quiere, todos los detalles que lógicamente deseáis saber, porque amáis con toda el alma vuestra vocación y anheláis por encima de todo que se cumpla la Voluntad de Dios, tal como se manifestó a nuestro Padre desde el comienzo de la Obra. Entretanto, os escribo con un sentimiento de profunda alegría en el alma, porque ya se ve el final del largo y difícil camino que hemos debido recorrer para que la Obra alcanzara la configuración jurídica prevista por nuestro santo Fundador. Tengo el gozo inmenso de confirmaros que ha sido nuestro Padre, mientras estaba con nosotros, el que -sabiendo lo que el Señor quería que fuese el Opus Dei, y movido por una esperanzada intuición del desarrollo general de la Iglesia- ha marcado todos los pasos que hemos ido dando.

2. Al mismo tiempo, y permitidme que os abra enteramente mi corazón, pruebo la tristeza filial de pensar que ha sido necesario el holocausto de su vida santa, para que sus hijos camináramos por ese camino seguro y llegáramos a este gozoso final, que tanto esperó nuestro Padre. Así se condujo siempre nuestro Fundador, plantando generosamente este árbol de Dios, que es la Obra, con la ilusión sobrenatural y humana de que los demás se cobijaran a su sombra.

Ayudadme, hijas e hijos, a dar gracias a la Trinidad Beatísima; gracias a Santa María y a San José, su Esposo; gracias a nuestros demás Patronos e Intercesores; gracias a nuestro Padre, instrumento fiel para que el Opus Dei se realice a lo largo de los siglos, tal y como el Cielo lo ha querido.

\* \* \*

3. Con esta nueva forma, señalada y deseada por nuestro Padre, que el Papa, después de un largo y profundo estudio, ha decretado otorgar al Opus Dei, se verá coronado el largo itinerario de la definitiva configuración jurídica de nuestra vocación, tal como el Señor la había inspirado a nuestro Fundador aquel 2 de octubre de 1928.

Se habrá conseguido abrir camino aquella afirmación fundacional de nuestro Padre que, a lo largo de tantos años, sonaba para muchos como un imposible y para otros como herejía: que, por la llamada que habíamos recibido, deseábamos dedicar enteramente nuestra vida al Señor como fieles corrientes -sacerdotes o laicos seculares, nada más y nada menos-, con una espiritualidad, con una entrega apostólica y con un vínculo jurídico muy diversos de los que son propios del *estado de perfección* o *estado de vida consagrada* por la profesión de los tres consejos evangélicos.

4. El Opus Dei, que, a partir del momento de la erección en Prelatura personal, contará con un reconocimiento jurídico, teológico y pastoral plenamente adecuado a su naturaleza, ha sido querido por el Señor para que contribuya, con su propia espiritualidad, organización y modos apostólicos, a recordar a los hombres las exigencias reales de la llamada universal a la santidad: que todos los fieles pueden y deben santificarse en el mundo, sin cambiar de estado, allí donde el Señor ha colocado a

cada uno, dando todo el relieve sobrenatural a la vida corriente y especialmente al ordinario trabajo profesional elevado al orden de la gracia, y hecho ocasión e instrumento de apostolado.

No implica, pues, nuestra vocación ningún cambio en la condición personal de quienes se incorporan a la Obra. Somos -cada una, cada uno- lo que éramos antes: mujeres corrientes, hombres de la calle -solteros, casados, viudos-, intelectuales, empleados, obreros, campesinos, etc., que adquieren el compromiso maravilloso de hacer divinos los caminos de la tierra, esos caminos que recorremos con nuestros iguales, los otros ciudadanos.

5. Fijaos en que he escrito -siguiendo la afirmación tajante de nuestro Padre- que recorremos los caminos *con nuestros iguales*, los otros ciudadanos, fieles corrientes, y que no he puesto que ellos son *como nosotros*, sino que son *nuestros iguales*. No era una sutileza jurídica esa precisación de nuestro Padre, era la expresión lógica y la defensa leal de lo que el Señor le había pedido, porque -como afirmaba- *no puede separarnos de los otros fieles* -insisto: *nuestros iguales-, ni el tabique más fino que pueda existir, ni una hoja de papel de fumar*. Si lo tolerásemos, estaríamos traicionando a la Voluntad de Dios.

6. El Señor nos quiere como fermento en la masa, siendo nosotros a la vez masa y Pueblo de Dios que obedece, sirve, ama, venera y atiende, en la vida de la Iglesia, la voz, las directrices y las preocupaciones del Papa y de los Obispos diocesanos. Hacemos nuestros, con sinceridad y con agradecimiento, estimulados y guiados en ese empeño por las normas propias de nuestro espíritu y de nuestro derecho, todos los planes de los Pastores diocesanos; y, allí donde está cada uno de nosotros, tratamos de ponerlos por obra y nos esforzamos por meterlos -con un apostolado continuo- en la existencia de los que nos rodean, nuestros iguales -¡dejadme que repita machaconamente!-: en nuestras familias, parientes, amigos, colegas de trabajo, compañeros de distracción, etc.

\* \* \*

7. No imagináis qué duro ha sido el camino que tuvo que recorrer nuestro Padre: hubo de sufrir -y sufrió con gozo, sin rencor, sin juzgar a nadie- una auténtica discriminación, una dura marginación, pues llegaron a decir que *venía a destruir la Iglesia*. No me importa confiaros que por ese camino de sufrimiento hemos seguido andando, al dar esta batalla final, para conseguir el reconocimiento jurídico adecuado.

Nos han achacado -os lo cuento porque ha sido público, y porque hemos perdonado desde el primer instante- que queríamos ser independientes de los Obispos, o que buscábamos estar al margen de la Jerarquía, o que no estábamos insertados en las Iglesias locales.

No comprendían quizá que lo único que nos interesaba era que se nos reconociera como lo que somos: sacerdotes plenamente seculares y fieles corrientes, que constituyen ciertamente a nivel internacional una unidad jurisdiccional de espíritu, de formación específica y de régimen, pero que -de igual modo que los otros fieles- siguen gustosamente dependientes de los Obispos en todo lo que se refiere a la *cura pastoral ordinaria*, la misma que cada Obispo ejercita con todos los otros laicos de su diócesis.

Una particularidad quizá nos distingue: que, en medio de nuestras flaquezas personales, intentamos siempre ser los súbditos más fieles y leales que tengan los Obispos: ¡con cuánta alegría rezamos y nos mortificamos a diario, de modo expreso y varias veces cada día, por la persona y las intenciones del Pastor diocesano!

8. Hemos sufrido, ¡y no poco!, porque esa calumnia ha dejado su poso, y algunos Reverendísimos Ordinarios -casi exclusivamente de diócesis en las que no trabajamos todavía, o bien Obispos nuevos de diócesis en las que desde hace mucho tiempo trabajamos- han adoptado una postura distanciada, de cierta desconfianza hacia la Obra.

El equívoco estaba en que -por no conocer suficientemente la naturaleza propia de la Obra- algunos querían tratarnos como a los religiosos, o como a miembros de asociaciones o movimientos eclesiales que actúan siempre en grupo, en las estructuras eclesiásticas o en la vida civil. Y cuando aclarábamos que los miembros del Opus Dei actúan personal y libremente, veían esa afirmación bajo la luz tenebrosa de la calumnia que nos achacaban.

No entendían que lo nuestro -a pesar de la solidez de formación y régimen- no es, de ordinario, trabajar como un grupo más entre los existentes, sino *abrirnos en abanico*, esforzándose cada uno por ser fermento o sal allá donde tiene su labor profesional, y en su familia, y entre sus amigos.

9. Algunos no comprendían tampoco que para *hacer apostolado* no sacásemos - no podemos hacerlo - al obrero de su lugar de trabajo; a los padres y madres de familia de sus hogares; a los estudiantes de sus Facultades o Centros académicos; a los enfermos de sus camas; a los médicos de las clínicas, etc.

Y al no vernos como un grupo más, entre los que trabajan en la diócesis, sin darse cuenta de que queríamos ser -repito- fermento o sal, que desaparecen en la masa, pensaban que no queríamos colaborar, y que estábamos al margen de la pastoral diocesana. No se percataban de que a través de los cauces ordinarios por donde transcurre la vida secular, profesional y familiar, estáis presentes, hijos míos, en todas partes: en los ambientes académicos y en el mundo del trabajo, en las parroquias, en las asociaciones diocesanas, en las iniciativas civiles, educativas, asistenciales, etc. Allí donde desarrollan los ciudadanos y fieles cristianos su existencia corriente, los miembros del Opus Dei están presentes: de ordinario, cada uno personalmente -repito, no en grupo-, vivificando todos esos ambientes con vibración apostólica, al servicio de la Iglesia universal y de la Iglesia local.

10. Pienso, y doy gracias a Dios, que con este acto de la Santa Sede, que vendrá a sancionar jurídicamente lo que hemos querido ser siempre - como lo quería y lo quiere Dios-, se desvanecerán esas falsas interpretaciones de mirarnos como a un grupo aparte; y pienso también que los Obispos diocesanos, cuya inmensa mayoría, gracias a Dios, nos entiende bien, tocarán con las manos que cuentan con fieles ejemplares -los laicos de la Prelatura- que, convencidos de su debilidad personal,

tienen el afán de servir a la Iglesia, a la diócesis, en el lugar que les corresponda en la sociedad civil, animando de vida cristiana todas las profesiones humanas honradas.

* * *

11. Me imagino, hijas e hijos, la sonrisa de agradecimiento y la alabanza a Dios de nuestro Padre, al ver entonces cumplido otro gran deseo suyo, con esta próxima aprobación de la Santa Sede: que los sacerdotes Agregados y Supernumerarios no tendrán más superior en su ministerio sacerdotal que el propio Ordinario diocesano. Quedará, si cabe, más claro aquel *nihil sine Episcopo*, que ha definido siempre la condición de los sacerdotes Agregados y Supernumerarios de la Sociedad Sacerdotal de la Santa Cruz.

    Hasta ahora, como bien sabéis, con una norma que nos impusieron desde la Congregación de Religiosos -otro de los puntos en los que nuestro Fundador hubo de conceder, sin ceder, con ánimo de recuperar-, se disponía que estos sacerdotes debían tener un Superior interno en el Opus Dei. ¡Cuánto padeció nuestro Padre y con qué interés buscó la fórmula que menos perjudicara a los Obispos y a la condición diocesana de esos sacerdotes!

12. Con la ayuda de Dios, nuestro Padre dispuso que dependieran del Director Espiritual de la Obra, que no tiene rango de cargo de gobierno en el Opus Dei, y estableció que no se ejercitara nunca el título de mandato con los sacerdotes Agregados y Supernumerarios y que no hubiera *ni la sombra de una jerarquía interna de la Obra*, para estos sacerdotes, puesto que lo único que se pretendía era ayudarles con la dirección espiritual, que ellos deseaban, sin darles jamás indicaciones o directrices de ninguna clase, para su ministerio sacerdotal, que sólo depende del Ordinario del lugar.

    Más aún, quiso que se comprometieran a dejar todos sus cargos y beneficios eclesiásticos en manos del propio Obispo; y determinó que -en la asistencia espiritual a estos sacerdotes, pues sólo en esto consiste, de hecho, su unión a la Obra- se les recordara constantemente que la respuesta más perfecta a su vocación a la Sociedad Sacerdotal de la Santa Cruz se realiza en el cumplimiento exacto, gustoso y alegre, de las indicaciones del propio Ordinario.

13. Jamás se opuso nuestro Padre a que los Ordinarios conocieran qué sacerdotes de sus respectivas diócesis querían asociarse a la Sociedad Sacerdotal de la Santa Cruz; no sólo no se opuso, sino que indicó que, antes de comenzar el apostolado específico de la Sociedad Sacerdotal de la Santa Cruz en cualquier diócesis, se explicase detalladamente la labor al Obispo respectivo, y sólo se empezaba esa labor si el Ordinario del lugar estaba de acuerdo y daba su expresa aprobación.

    Además, deseando que esos sacerdotes demostrasen su leal servicio al Ordinario diocesano y a la diócesis, estableció que hablasen de su nueva llamada con el propio Obispo, y así se hizo hasta que desde la Santa Sede nos comunicaron que no se podía imponer esa obligación. A pesar de todo, siempre hemos aconsejado a los sacerdotes Agregados y

Supernumerarios que huyan de todo lo que pueda significar secreteos o falsas discreciones sobre su adhesión espiritual a la Obra.

14. Ahora, con la nueva forma que nos dará la Santa Sede, se vendrá a confirmar que estos sacerdotes ni cambiarán de situación jurídica, ni tendrán Superiores en la Prelatura: se habrá cumplido así el deseo de nuestro Fundador de que, con esta llamada a la Sociedad Sacerdotal de la Santa Cruz, que se une a su vocación sacerdotal, se sientan más sacerdotes de su propio Obispo, más entregados a su diócesis, más hermanos de sus hermanos los sacerdotes, más amantes del Seminario y de las obras diocesanas y más servidores de las almas.

Por eso, y sé que no hago más que llevar a la práctica los deseos de nuestro Fundador, aconsejaré a esos sacerdotes que expliquen al Obispo su nueva dedicación a su sacerdocio, pues no buscan más que gastar su vida entera en la entrega que se comprometieron a llevar a cabo con su incardinación a la diócesis.

\* \* \*

15. *Cor Iesu Sacratissimum et misericors, dona nobis pacem!; Cor Mariæ dulcissimum, iter para tutum!* Con éstas y con otras jaculatorias, nuestro Fundador se dirigió confiadamente al Cielo, para que la Obra se realizara. Ahora, con la intervención directísima de nuestro Padre, llegaremos a puerto. Nos toca, a cada una y a cada uno, recoger este preciosísimo legado que es Voluntad de Dios, para trasmitirlo por los siglos.

Meditad lo que tantas veces -como fruto de su inmensa humildad y rectitud de intención- fue tema de oración de nuestro Padre: *si la Obra no es para servir a la Iglesia, ¡destrúyela, Señor!* Continuad, pues, alimentando cada vez más en vuestras almas el afán de trabajar por la Iglesia, con lealtad, con finura, con exigencia, allí donde el Señor os ha colocado y os ha buscado, sin abandonar ese puesto, sirviendo al Papa, a los Obispos diocesanos y a las almas, como fieles ejemplares, conscientes de sus miserias personales y sabedores de que el Señor cuenta con nosotros.

16. Ayudadme ahora y siempre a dar gracias a Dios, durante toda nuestra vida, haciendo eco a la eterna acción de gracias de nuestro Fundador, con una mayor entrega al Señor, a través de la vida corriente, ordinaria, cada uno en el lugar donde Dios le ha llamado, y que no podemos abandonar.

Os bendice vuestro Padre

Alvaro

Roma, 8 de diciembre de 1981

## 67. *Declaration* Prælaturæ personales *of the Sacred Congregation for Bishops regarding the Prelature of the Holy Cross and Opus Dei; August 23, 1982.*

*AAS* 75 (1983): 464-468.

ACTA SS. CONGREGATIONUM

_____

SACRA CONGREGATIO PRO EPISCOPIS

_____

DECLARATIO

### De Prælatura Sanctæ Crucis et Operis Dei.

Prælaturæ personales, quas ad "peculiaria opera pastoralia" perficienda Concilium Vaticanum II voluit (Decr. *Presbyterorum Ordinis*, n. 10 § 2) quæque dein iuridicam obtinuerunt ordinationem in legibus pontificiis ad exsequenda eiusdem Concilii Decreta latis (cfr. Motu pr. *Ecclesiæ Sanctæ*, Pars I, n. 4), aliud constituunt signum ac testimonium sollicitæ illius curæ qua peculiaribus nostri temporis necessitatibus in re pastorali atque in suo evangelizationis munere exercendo Ecclesia respondet. Quamobrem pontificia decisio qua "Opus Dei" in Prælaturam personalem, sub nomine "Sanctæ Crucis et Operis Dei", erigendum est, apostolicæ operositatis Ecclesiæ efficacitatem directe et imprimis respicit; qua ratione ad effectum re et opere adducitur novum instrumentum pastorale, hactenus in iure quidem desideratum ac prævisum, idque fit per institutionem quæ probatas exhibet cautiones quoad doctrinam, disciplinam et apostolicum vigorem.

Simul vero, huiusmodi decisio "Operi Dei" confert ecclesialem ordinationem suo ipsius charismati fundationali atque germanæ naturæ sociali plene accommodatam, ita ut, dum problema eius institutionale apte solvit, harmonicam insertionem huius institutionis in actionem pastoralem organicam Ecclesiæ universalis et Ecclesiarum localium apprime compleat efficaciusque eius servitium reddat.

Ut clare patet ex normis Santæ Sedis istiusmodi Prælaturæ structuram atque apostolicam operositatem regentibus -congrua quidem servata observantia legitimo Episcoporum diœcesanorum iuri debita-, notæ præcipuæ quibus constituta Prælatura insignitur hæ sunt:

### I. Quod ad eius structuram attinet:

a)   Prælatura "Opus Dei" ambitu internationalis est habenda; Prælatus, qui est Ordinarius proprius, sedem centralem cum suis Consiliis Romæ habet;

b)   Prælaturæ clerus, eidem incardinatus, ex laicis provenit ipsi incorporatis: nullus proinde candidatus ad sacerdotium, diaconus vel presbyter Ecclesiis localibus subtrahitur;

*c)* illi laici -cum viri tum mulieres, sive cælibes sive matrimonio iuncti, ex qualibet professione vel condicione sociali- qui servitio finis apostolici Prælaturæ proprii sese dedicant, graves et qualificatas obligationes ad hoc assumentes, id efficiunt non vi votorum, sed vinculi contractualis iure definiti.

## II. Prælatura "Opus Dei" est structura iurisdictionalis sæcularis, et ideo:

*a)* clerici eidem incardinati quoad omnes effectus pertinent ad clerum sæcularem, iuxta præscripta iuris generalis atque iuris Prælaturæ proprii; arctas igitur relationes fovent unitatis cum sacerdotibus sæcularibus Ecclesiarum localium et, quod ad constitutionem attinet Consiliorum presbyteralium, voce activa et passiva gaudent;

*b)* laici Prælaturæ incorporati non mutant suam condicionem personalem, sive theologicam sive canonicam, communium fidelium laicorum, et qua tales in omnibus se gerunt ac, reapse, in exercitio sui apostolatus;

*c)* spiritus ac finis "Operis Dei" in lucem proferunt vim sanctificantem ordinarii laboris professionalis propriam, munus nempe sese in eo absolvendo labore sanctificandi, immo ipsum laborem sanctificandi eumque convertendi in apostolatus instrumentum; eorum ergo qui ad Prælaturam pertinent opera et apostolatus præcipue exercentur in locis, adiunctis atque structuris sæcularis societatis propriis, attentis normis generalibus quæ pro apostolatu laicorum dentur sive a Sancta Sede sive ab Episcopis diœcesanis;

*d)* quod ad optiones spectat in re professionali, sociali, politica, etc., laici fideles ad Prælaturam pertinentes, intra limites videlicet catholicæ fidei et christianorum morum atque Ecclesiæ disciplinæ, eadem gaudent libertate qua ceteri fruuntur catholici, quorum sunt concives: Prælatura igitur suorum membrorum labores professionales, sociales, politicos, œconomicos, etc., suos omnino non facit.

## III. Relate ad Prælati potestatem:

*a)* ipsa est potestas ordinaria regiminis seu iurisdictionis, ad id circumscripta quod finem respicit Prælaturæ proprium, et ratione materiæ substantialiter differt a iurisdictione quæ, in ordinaria cura pastorali fidelium, Episcopis competit;

*b)* præter regimen proprii cleri, generalem secum fert directionem tum institutionis doctrinalis tum peculiaris curæ spiritualis et apostolicæ quas laici "Operi Dei" incorporati recipiunt, quo impensius ad Ecclesiæ servitium sese dedant;

*c)* simul cum iure incardinandi proprios candidatos ad sacerdotium, Prælatus obligatione tenetur curandi peculiarem eorum institutionem in Centris Prælaturæ, iuxta normas a competenti Sacra Congregatione latas, necnon vitam spiritualem ac permanentem institutionem eorum sacerdotum quos ipse ad sacros Ordines promoverit, ac præterea eorum congruam sustentationem atque convenientem assistentiam ob infirmam valetudinem, senectutem, etc.;

*d)* laici iurisdictioni Prælati obnoxii sunt in iis quæ pertinent ad adimpletionem peculiarium obligationum, vitam spiritualem, doctrinalem institutionem atque apostolatus exercitium respicientium, quas ipsi libere sibi sumpserunt vinculo deditionis ad finem Prælaturæ proprium.

**IV. Quoad dispositiones ecclesiasticas territoriales atque legitima Ordinariorum locorum iura:**

*a)* qui ad Prælaturam pertinent, iuxta iuris præscripta, normis territorialibus tenentur quæ tum dispositiones generales respiciunt indolis doctrinalis, liturgicæ ac pastoralis tum leges ordini publico consulentes; sacerdotes præterea generalem cleri disciplinam servare debent;

*b)* Prælaturæ sacerdotes facultates ministeriales petere debent, a competenti auctoritate territoriali concedendas ut suum ministerium erga personas ad "Opus Dei" non pertinentes exercere possint;

*c)* laici Prælaturæ "Operis Dei" incorporati fideles esse pergunt earum diœcesium in quibus domicilium vel quasi-domicilium habent, et subsunt igitur iurisdictioni Episcopi diœcesani in iis omnibus quæ iure statuuntur quoad communes fideles.

**V. Quod ad pastoralem præterea attinet coordinationem cum locorum Ordinariis atque ad proficuam insertionem Prælaturæ "Operis Dei" in Ecclesias locales, hæc statuuntur:**

*a)* ad unumquodque Prælaturæ Centrum erigendum, prævia semper requiritur venia sui cuiusque Episcopi diœcesani, cuius est præterea ad normam iuris visitare huiusmodi Centra, de quorum actuositate regulariter certior fit;

*b)* relate ad parœcias vel templa, sive rectoralia sive non, aliaque officia ecclesiastica quæ ipsi Prælaturæ vel sacerdotibus eidem incardinatis a loci Ordinario concredita sint, fiet singulis in casibus conventio inter loci Ordinarium et Prælatum "Operis Dei" eiusve Vicarios;

*c)* omnibus in nationibus Prælatura debitas relationes servabit cum Præside et organismis Conferentiæ episcopalis, necnon frequenter cum Episcopis earum diœcesium in quibus ipsa operatur.

**VI.** Cum Prælatura inseparabiliter iungitur Societas Sacerdotalis Sanctæ Crucis, ad quam illi sacerdotes e clero diœcesano pertinere possunt, qui sanctitatem in exercitio sui ministerii consequi desiderent, iuxta spiritum et praxim asceticam "Operis Dei". Vi tamen huius adscriptionis ipsi non efficiuntur membra cleri Prælaturæ, sed quoad omnes effectus sub regimine manent proprii Ordinarii, quem, si id desideret, de prædicta adscriptione certiorem reddent.

**VII.** Prælatura dependet a Sacra Congregatione pro Episcopis (cfr. Const. A. *Regimini Ecclesiæ universæ*, n. 49 § 1) et, haud secus atque aliæ iurisdictiones autonomæ, capacitate gaudet ut, attenta materia de qua singulis in casibus agatur, quæstiones tractet cum competentibus Sanctæ Sedis Dicasteriis.

VIII. Per Sacram Congregationem pro Episcopis, singulis quinquenniis Prælatus Romano Pontifici subiiciet diligentem relationem de Prælaturæ statu, sub respectu sive pastorali sive iuridico, deque eius specifici laboris apostolici exsecutione.

*Declarationem hanc de Prælatura "Sanctæ Crucis et Operis Dei" Summus Pontifex Ioannes Paulus divina Providentia Pp. II, in audientia concessa infrascripto Præfecto Sacræ Congregationis pro Episcopis, d. 5 m. augusti a. 1982, ratam habuit, confirmavit atque evulgari iussit.*

Datum Romæ, ex Ædibus Sacræ Congregationis pro Episcopis, d. 23 m. augusti a. 1982.

+ SEBASTIANUS Card. BAGGIO, *Præfectus*

+ Lucas Moreira Neves, Archiep. tit. Feraditanus maior, *a Secretis*

---

## 68. Letter of Sebastiano Cardinal Baggio to Msgr. Alvaro del Portillo regarding the Papal Bull erecting the Prelature and its execution; March 5, 1983.

AGP, Sezione Giuridica, VIII/15045.

**SACRA CONGREGATIO**                    Roma, 5 marzo 1983
**PRO EPISCOPIS**

Prot. N. 317/62

Reverendissimo Monsignor Prelato,

sono lieto di significarLe che la Bolla Pontificia, da tempo attesa, dell'erezione dell'Opus Dei in Prelatura personale, finalmente è pronta.

La Congregazione ha provveduto ad inoltrare il documento al Nunzio Apostolico in Italia, incaricato della sua esecuzione, chiedendogli di mettersi in contatto con Lei.

Tanto Le comunico per sua opportuna conoscenza e norma.

Profitto ben volentieri della circonstanza per confermarmi, con sensi di distinto ossequio

dev.mo nel Signore
+ S. Card. Baggio
Pref.

Rev.mo Signore
Mons. ALVARO del PORTILLO
Prelato dell'Opus Dei

**69. Apostolic Constitution Ut sit of Pope John Paul II erecting Opus Dei as a personal prelature of universal extension; November 28, 1982.**

AAS 75 (1983): 423-425.

CONSTITUTIO APOSTOLICA

SANCTÆ CRUCIS ET OPERIS DEI

**Opus Dei in Prælaturam personalem ambitus internationalis erigitur.**

IOANNES PAULUS EPISCOPUS
SERVUS SERVORUM DEI
AD PERPETUAM REI MEMORIAM

Ut sit validum et efficax instrumentum suæ ipsius salvificæ missionis pro mundi vita, Ecclesia maternas curas cogitationesque suas maxima cum spe confert in Opus Dei, quod Servus Dei Ioseph Maria Escrivá de Balaguer divina ductus inspiratione die II Octobris anno MCMXXVIII Matriti inivit. Hæc sane Institutio inde a suis primordiis sategit missionem laicorum in Ecclesia et in humana societate non modo illuminare sed etiam ad effectum adducere necnon doctrinam de universali vocatione ad sanctitatem re exprimere atque sanctificationem in labore et per laborem professionalem in quolibet sociali cœtu promovere. Idem pariter efficiendum curavit per Societatem Sacerdotalem Sanctæ Crucis quoad sacerdotes diœcesibus incardinatos in sacri ministerii exercitio. Cum Opus Dei divina opitulante gratia adeo crevisset ut in pluribus orbis terrarum diœcesibus extaret atque operaretur quasi apostolica compages quæ sacerdotibus et laicis sive viris sive mulieribus constabat eratque simul organica et indivisa, una scilicet spiritu fine regimine et spirituali institutione, necesse fuit aptam formam iuridicam ipsi tribui quæ peculiaribus eius notis responderet. Idemque Operis Dei Conditor, anno MCMLXII, a Sancta Sede humili cum fiducia suppliciter postulavit ut, natura theologica et primigenia Institutionis perspecta eiusque maiore apostolica efficacia considerata, consentanea configuratio ei inveniretur. Ex quo autem tempore Concilium œcumenicum Vaticanum Secundum, Decreto *Presbyterorum Ordinis*, n. 10 per Litteras "motu proprio" datas *Ecclesiæ Sanctæ*, I n. 4 rite in actum deducto, in ordinationem Ecclesiæ figuram Prælaturæ personalis ad peculiaria opera pastoralia perficienda induxit, visa est ea ipsa Operi Dei apprime aptari. Quapropter anno MCMLXIX Decessor Noster felicissimæ recordationis Paulus Sextus petitioni Servi Dei Ioseph Mariæ Escrivá de Balaguer benigne annuens potestatem illi dedit Congressum generalem specialem convocandi, cui cura esset, ipso duce, ut studium iniretur de Operis Dei transformatione, eius ipsius indoli et Concilii Vaticani Secundi normis magis consentanea. Quod omnino studium explicate iussimus Nos ipsi continuari atque anno MCMLXXIX Sacræ Congregationi pro Episcopis, ad quam res suapte pertinebat natura, mandatum dedimus ut, cunctis elementis sive iuris sive facti attente consideratis, formalem petitionem ab Opere Dei exhibitam examini subiceret. Profecto eadem Congregatio huic negotio vacans quæstionem sibi propositam accurate investigavit ratione cum historica tum iuridica et pastorali ita ut, quolibet sublato dubio circa fundamentum possibilitatem et concretam rationem postulationi obsecundandi, plane pateret opportunitas atque utilitas optatæ transformationis Operis Dei in Prælaturam personalem. Idcirco Nos de apostolicæ plenitudine potestatis Nostræ, adsensi interea consilio, Nobis dato, Venerabilis Fratris Nostri S.R.E. Cardinalis Præfecti Sacræ Congregationis pro Episcopis ac suppleto, quatenus necessarium sit, eorum consensu quorum interest vel qui sua interesse existimaverint, hæc quæ sequuntur decernimus fierique volumus.

I.   Opus Dei in Prælaturam personalem ambitus internationalis erigitur sub nomine Sanctæ Crucis et Operis Dei, breviato autem nomine Operis Dei. Simul vero erigitur Societas sacerdotalis Sanctæ Crucis qua Adsociatio Clericorum Prælaturæ intrinsecus coniuncta.

II.  Prælatura regitur normis iuris generalis et huius Constitutionis necnon propriis Statutis, quæ "Codex iuris particularis Operis Dei" nuncupantur.

III. Prælaturæ iurisdictio personalis afficit clericos incardinatos necnon, tantum quoad peculiarium obligationum adimpletionem quas ipsi sumpserunt vinculo iuridico, ope conventionis cum Prælatura initæ, laicos qui operibus apostolicis Prælaturæ sese dedicant, qui omnes ad operam pastoralem Prælaturæ perficiendam sub auctoritate Prælati exstant iuxta præscripta articuli præcedentis.

IV.  Prælaturæ Operis Dei Ordinarius proprius est eius Prælatus cuius electio iuxta præscripta iuris generalis et particularis facta Romani Pontificis confirmatione eget.

V.   Prælatura a Sacra Congregatione pro Episcopis dependet et pro rei diversitate quæstiones pertractabit cum ceteris Romanæ Curiæ Dicasteriis. VI. Prælatus singulis quinquenniis per Sacram Congregationem pro Episcopis relationem Romano Pontifici exhibebit de Prælaturæ statu deque modo quo eius apostolatus procedit. VII. Prælaturæ sedes gubernii centralis in Urbe posita est. In ecclesiam prælatitiam erigitur oratorium Sanctæ Mariæ de Pace apud sedem centralem Prælaturæ. Præterea Reverendissimus Alvarus del Portillo, die XV mensis Septembris anno MCMLXXV Præses Generalis Operis Dei rite electus, confirmatur atque nominatur Prælatus erectæ Prælaturæ personalis Sanctæ Crucis et Operis Dei. Denique ad hæc omnia convenienter exsequenda destinamus Nos Venerabilem Fratrem Romulum Carboni, Archiepiscopum titulo Sidoniensem et in Italia Apostolicum Nuntium, dum necessarias ei atque opportunas tribuimus facultates, etiam subdelegandi ad effectum de quo agitur quemlibet virum in ecclesiastica dignitate constitutum, onere imposito ad Sacram Congregationem pro Episcopis quam primum remittendi verum exemplar actus ita impletæ exsecutionis. Contrariis quibusvis rebus minime obstantibus.

Datum Romæ, apud S. Petrum, die XXVIII mensis Novembris, anno MCMLXXXII, Pontificatus Nostri quinto.

AUGUSTINUS Card. CASAROLI    + SEBASTIANUS Card. BAGGIO
a publicis Ecclesiæ negotiis    S. Congr. pro Episc. Præfectus
                                Iosephus Del Ton, Proton. Apost.
                                Marcellus Rossetti, Proton. Apost.

Loco + Plumbi

In Secret. Status tab., n. 101486.

## 70. Decree of Archbishop Romolo Carboni, Papal Nuncio in Italy, executing the Bull Ut sit; March 19, 1983.

AGP, Sezione Giuridica, VIII/15048.

NUNZIATURA APOSTOLICA
IN ITALIA
PROT. N. 15431/83

### DECRETUM

De Apostolica sub plumbo Constitutione "Ut sit", qua Opus Dei in Prælaturam personalem erigitur, perficienda.

---

Summus Pontifex Joannes Paulus, Divina Providentia PP. II, Apostolicis sub plumbo Litteris, quarum initium "Ut sit", die XXVIII mensis novembris, anno MCMLXXXII, Pontificatus anno quinto, Opus Dei in Prælaturam personalem ambitus internationalis erexit sub nomine Sanctæ Crucis et Operis Dei, breviato autem nomine Operis Dei.

Idem Summus Pontifex, auctoritate Sua Apostolica, nobis, Romulo Carboni, Archiepiscopo titulo Sidoniensi et in Italia Nuntio Apostolico, memoratarum Apostolicarum Litterarum munus perficiendi benigne tribuit.

Easdem, itaque Nos, præ manibus tenentes Litteras, easdemque Prælato personali Operis Dei Reverendissimo Domino Alvaro del Portillo, officio fungentes, statim offerentes, ipsam Prælaturam personalem, uti statutum est, constitutam declaramus cum omnibus iuribus et privilegiis quæ, ad normam iuris communis, Prælaturæ gaudent personales, simulque Reverendissimum Dominum Alvarum del Portillo Prælatitia dignitate et gradu insignitum, iuribus et privilegiis ornatum, oneribusque pariter et obligationibus ligatum, ad normam iuris generalis et prædictæ Constitutionis Apostolicæ, necnon propriorum Statutorum, quæ -"Codex iuris particularis Operis Dei"- nuncupantur, renunciamus.

Mandamus denique ut quæ constituta et declarata sunt, ab iis, quorum interest, adamussim serventur.

Datum, Romæ, in Basilica Sancti Eugenii, die 19 mensis Martii, Anno Domini MCMLXXXIII.

+ Romulus Carboni
Archiepiscopus titulo Sidoniensis
In Italia Nuntius Apostolicus

## 71. Official Act of the ceremony executing the Bull Ut sit by Archbishop Carboni; March 19, 1983.

AGP, Sezione Giuridica, VIII/15049 .

*Prelatura della Santa Croce e Opus Dei*

Il giorno 19 del mese di marzo dell'anno 1983, a Roma, nella Basilica parrochiale di S. Eugenio a Valle Giulia, alle ore 17, S.E.R. Mons. Romolo Carboni, Arcivescovo tit. di Sidone e Nunzio Apostolico in Italia, secondo il mandato conferitogli dal Santo Padre Giovanni Paolo II, ha dato esecuzione a quanto prescritto nella Costituzione Apostolica Ut sit, del 28 novembre 1982, mediante la quale il Sommo Pontefice felicemente regnante si è degnato di erigere l'Opus Dei in Prelatura personale, con il nome completo di Prelatura della Santa Croce e Opus Dei, conferendogli così l'auspicata configurazione giuridica per la quale pregò e fece pregare durante lunghi anni il Servo di Dio Mons. Josemaría Escrivá de Balaguer y Albás, suo Fondatore, offrendo la vita al Signore per questa intenzione. Con lo stesso atto, il Santo Padre ha nominato Prelato della medesima Prelatura il Rev.mo Mons. Alvaro del Portillo.

Il solenne atto si è svolto alla presenza di Eminentissimi e Reverendissimi Cardinali, del Rappresentante dell'Eminentissimo e Reverendissimo Signor Cardinale Segretario di Stato, di Ecc.mi Arcivescovi e Vescovi ed altri dignatari ecclesiastici, nonché di Autorità civili e di Rappresentanti Diplomatici.

Con il Rev.mo Mons. Prelato dell'Opus Dei erano presenti il Vicario Generale della Prelatura, Rev.do Mons. Javier Echevarría, i componenti il Consiglio Generale e l'Assessorato Centrale dell'Opus Dei, il Vicario dell'Opus Dei per l'Italia, Rev.do Don Mario Lantini, e numerosi fedeli dell'eretta Prelatura, che hanno assistito alla cerimonia in spirito di vivo ringraziamento a Dio Onnipotente e Misericordioso e alla Vergine Santissima, Madre e Regina della Chiesa, Madre e Regina dell'Opus Dei, ed in filiale unione all'Augusta Persona del Sommo Pontefice.

La cerimonia ha preso avvio con la celebrazione della Santa Messa. Con Monsignor Prelato, hanno concelebrato Monsignor Vicario Generale della Prelatura, il Vicario Regionale della Prelatura per l'Italia ed i Rev.di Don Rolf Thomas e Don Julián Herranz, del Consiglio Generale dell'Opus Dei.

Subito dopo il saluto iniziale della Santa Messa, S.E.R. Mons. Romolo Carboni si è rivolto a Monsignor Prelato, alle Autorità presenti ed a tutti i fedeli che assistevano, manifestando la propria profonda gioia per aver ricevuto dal Santo Padre il graditissimo incarico di dare esecuzione alla Bolla di erezione della Prelatura dell'Opus Dei. Ha desiderato ricordare alcuni suoi incontri con il Fondatore dell'Opus Dei, Mons. Josemaría Escrivá de Balaguer, sia con motivo dell'espletamento di suoi incarichi -in occasione dell'avviamento della Prelatura di Yauyos nel Perù, affidata a sacerdoti dell'Opus Dei-, sia in altre circonstanze, in un rapporto di sacerdotale amicizia e di viva venerazione per il Servo di Dio, di santa memoria. Infine, S.E.R. Mons. Romolo Carboni ha concluso esprimendo la propria ferma convinzione che l'Augusta decisione del Santo Padre di erigere l'Opus Dei in Prelatura Personale è foriera di grandi beni per tutta la Santa Chiesa.

Successivamente, per ordine di S.E.R. il Nunzio Apostolico in Italia, si è proceduto alla lettura della Costituzione Apostolica Ut sit, del 28 novembre 1982, nel testo italiano.

Immediatamente dopo, S.E.R. Mons. Romolo Carboni ha fatto leggere il testo italiano del Decreto di esecuzione, da Lui stesso emanato, in lingua latina, in data odierna.

Dopodiché, S.E.R. Mons. Romolo Carboni ha consegnato nelle mani del Rev.mo Prelato, Mons. Alvaro del Portillo, la Bolla Pontificia con la Costituzione Apostolica Ut sit ed il relativo Decreto di esecuzione, dando così compimento al mandato ricevuto da Sua Santità Giovanni Paolo II.

E' quindi proseguita la celebrazione della Santa Messa. L'omelia è stata tenuta dal Rev.mo Prelato, Mons. Alvaro del Portillo, che ha invitato i presenti a stringersi intorno a San Giuseppe, Sposo di Maria, custode e protettore di Gesù, Patrono della Chiesa universale -la cui festa liturgica ricorre oggi-, per innalzare i propri cuori a Dio Padre misericordioso, in unione con lo Spirito Santo. Ha ricordato poi, con profonda commozione, perché si toccava la presenza del Servo di Dio Mons. Josemaría Escrivá de Balaguer, le parole Ut sit, con cui inizia la Costituzione Apostolica, che per tanti anni furono usate come giaculatoria dal Fondatore dell'Opus Dei, per affrettare il compimento della Volontà di Dio nei suoi confronti. Successivamente, il Rev.mo Prelato dell'Opus Dei ha esternato il vivissimo ringraziamento suo personale e di tutti i fedeli della Prelatura per l'avvenuta erezione, nonché la loro ferma unione al Santo Padre, alla Curia Romana e a tutti gli Ecc.mi Vescovi Ordinari dei luoghi. Ha ricordato quanto il Fondatore dell'Opus Dei, Mons. Escrivá de Balaguer, avesse desiderato il compimento -ora avvenuto- della sua costante petizione al Signore, accompagnata da innumerevoli orazioni e sacrifici, perché si pervenisse alla configurazione giuridica definitiva dell'Opus Dei. Ha anche sottolineato, con particolare vigore e con gioia, uno degli aspetti fondamentali dello spirito dell'Opus Dei: quello di una profonda decisione di servire la Chiesa come essa desidera essere servita, secondo le caratteristiche della vocazione con cui il Signore chiama i membri dell'Opus Dei. Infine, ha concluso rivolgendo di nuovo il pensiero a San Giuseppe, Mæstro di vita interiore, perfetto esempio della devozione mariana, che amava Gesù e Maria senza distogliersi dal suo duro lavoro, ed ha affidato a questo venerato Patrono dell'Opus Dei la rinnovata determinazione di tutti i membri dell'Opus Dei di ricercare la santità nella vita quotidiana.

Al termine della Santa Messa, nella Sagrestia della Basilica parrocchiale, è stato letto il presente processo verbale.

Sia reso a Dio perenne ringraziamento a Sua lode e gloria.

Io, Rev.do Don José Luis Gutiérrez, Cancelliere della Curia Prelatizia dell'Opus Dei, ho redatto il presente documento, che viene firmato dal Nunzio Apostolico in Italia, S.E.R. Mons. Romolo Carboni, dal Rev.mo Prelato della Prelatura dell'Opus Dei, Mons. Alvaro del Portillo, dal Rev.do Vicario Generale della Prelatura, Mons. Javier Echevarría, e dalle Autorità presenti.

Alvarus del Portillo
+ S. Card. Baggio
+ Silvius Card. Oddi
James Card. Knox
+ Umberto Card. Mozzoni
Petrus Card. Palazzini
Opilius Card. Rossi
Luigi Card. Ciappi, O.P.

+ Romolo Carboni, Nunzio Apostolico
+ Agostino Mayer O.S.B. Arciv. tit. di Satriano
+ Fiorenzo Angelini
+ Pietro Rossano
Battista Re
+ Joseph Cardinale Slipyj
Javier Echevarría
+ Mario Schierano Arciv. tit. di Acrida

[the signatures of another 52 persons follow and include diplomats, civic and ecclesiastical figures, as well as some of the faithful of the prelature]

Roma, 19 marzo 1983

L + S

In fede

José Luis Gutiérrez

Cancelliere della Curia

Prelatizia dell'Opus Dei

---

## 72. Letter of Msgr. Alvaro del Portillo to the Sacred Congregation for Bishops informing that he has sent the Statutes to the bishops of the dioceses in which Opus Dei is established; April 5, 1983.

AGP, Sezione Giuridica, VIII/15053.

Prelatura della Santa Croce e Opus Dei

*Il Prelato*

Roma, 5 aprile 1983

Eminenza Reverendissima,

in seguito all'esecuzione della Bolla Pontificia di erezione di questa Prelatura ed in base agli accordi precedentemente presi con l'Eminenza Vostra Rev.ma, è stato stampato un volume dal titolo "Prælatura Sanctæ Crucis et Operis Dei. Statuta". Mi premuro ora di enviarLe, qui uniti, sei esemplari di tale volume, destinati a codesta Sacra Congregazione.

Nel libro sono stati raccolti, insieme agli Statuti -di cui si trova già copia nel vostro archivio-, la Costituzione Apostolica di erezione della Prelatura con il relativo Decreto esecutorio, la Dichiarazione esplicativa di codesto Sacro Dicasterio pubblicata sull'*Osservatore Romano* del 28 novembre 1982, e due documenti interni che ci è sembrato opportuno includere per una ancora più completa informazione.

Sono inoltre lieto di comunicare all'Eminenza Vostra che ho già dato le debite disposizioni, affinché venga consegnata una copia di questo volume a tutti gli Ecc.mi Vescovi delle diocesi in cui la Prelatura è stabilita: sono già state spedite da Roma, e portate a mano, tutte le relative copie.

Profitto volentieri della circostanza per confermarmi, con sensi di profonda venerazione,

dell'Eminenza Vostra Rev.ma

dev.mo in Domino

Alvaro del Portillo

A Sua Eminenza Rev.ma il Sig.
Card. Sebastiano Baggio
Prefetto della Sacra Congregazione per i Vescovi
*ROMA*

---

## 73. Statutes *of the Prelature of the Holy Cross and Opus Dei; Codex iuris particularis Operis Dei.*

AGP, Sezione Giuridica, VIII/15660.

### CODEX IURIS PARTICULARIS OPERIS DEI

#### TITULUS I

#### DE PRÆLATURÆ NATURA

#### EIUSDEMQUE CHRISTIFIDELIBUS

#### CAPUT I

#### DE PRÆLATURÆ NATURA ET FINE

1. § 1. Opus Dei est Prælatura personalis clericos et laicos simul complectens, ad peculiarem operam pastoralem perficiendam sub regimine proprii Prælati (cfr. n. 125).

   § 2. Prælaturæ presbyterium constituunt illi clerici qui ex eiusdem fidelibus laicis ad Ordines promoventur et eidem incardinantur; laicatus Prælaturæ ab iis fidelibus efformatur qui, vocatione divina moti, vinculo iuridico incorporationis speciali ratione Prælaturæ devinciuntur.

   § 3. Prælatura, quæ Sanctæ Crucis et Operis Dei, breviato autem nomine Operis Dei nuncupatur, est ambitu internationalis, sedem suam centralem Romæ habet atque regitur normis iuris universalis Prælaturarum personalium necnon horum Statutorum, et iuxta Sanctæ Sedis specialia præscripta vel indulta.

2. § 1. Prælatura sibi proponit suorum fidelium, iuxta normas iuris particularis, sanctificationem per exercitium in proprio cuiusque statu, professione ac vitæ condicione virtutum christianarum, secundum specificam ipsius spiritualitatem, prorsus sæcularem.

§ 2. Item Prælatura intendit totis viribus adlaborare ut personæ omnium condicionum et statuum civilis societatis, et in primis quæ intellectuales dicuntur, Christi Domini præceptis integro corde adhæreant ipsaque, etiam ope sanctificationis proprii uniuscuiusque laboris professionalis, in praxim deducant, in medio mundo, ut omnia ad Voluntatem Creatoris ordinentur; atque viros ac mulieres informare ad apostolatum item in societate civili exercendum.

3. § 1. Media quæ, ad hos fines supernaturales obtinendos, christifideles Prælaturæ adhibent, hæc sunt:

    1°   impensa vita spiritualis orationis et sacrificii, iuxta spiritum Operis Dei: ipsorum enim vocatio est essentialiter contemplativa, fundatur in humili ac sincero sensu filiationis divinæ et subridenti ascetismo constanter sustinetur;

    2°   profunda ac continua institutio ascetica et doctrinalis religiosa, ad personalia cuiusque adiuncta accommodata atque in ecclesiastico Magisterio solide innixa, necnon constans studium adquirendi et perficiendi necessariam formationem professionalem propriamque animi culturam;

    3°   imitatio vitæ absconditæ Domini Nostri Iesu Christi in Nazareth, etiam in sanctificatione proprii laboris professionalis ordinarii, quem, exemplo et verbis, convertere satagunt in instrumentum apostolatus, unusquisque propriam attingens actionis sphæram, prout sua cuiusque cultura et aptitudo expostulant, sciensque se esse debere tamquam fermentum in massa humanæ societatis latens; item, seipsos sanctificent christifideles in perfecta adimpletione huius laboris, peracti quidem in constanti unione cum Deo; necnon per ipsum laborem alios sanctificent.

§ 2. Propterea omnes Prælaturæ christifideles:

    1°   se obligant ad exercitium laboris professionalis vel alterius æquipollentis non derelinquendum, quia per ipsum sanctificationem et peculiarem apostolatum persequentur;

    2°   quam maxima fidelitate adimplere satagunt officia proprii status necnon actionem seu professionem socialem cuiusque propriam, summa semper cum reverentia pro legitimis societatis civilis legibus; itemque labores apostolicos perficiendos, a Prælato ipsis commissos.

4. § 1. Sub regimine Prælati, presbyterium suo ministerio sacerdotali universum Opus Dei vivificat atque informat.

§ 2. Sacerdotium ministeriale clericorum et commune sacerdotium laicorum intime coniunguntur atque se invicem requirunt et complent, ad exsequendum, in unitate vocationis et regiminis, finem quem Prælatura sibi proponit.

§ 3. In utraque pariter Operis Dei Sectione, virorum scilicet ac mulierum, eadem est unitas vocationis, spiritus, finis et regiminis, etsi unaquæque Sectio proprios habeat apostolatus.

5. Prælatura tamquam Patronos habet Beatam Mariam semper Virginem, quam uti Matrem veneratur, et S. Ioseph, eiusdem Beatæ Mariæ Virginis Sponsum. Peculiari devotione christifideles prosequuntur SS. Archangelos Michaëlem, Gabrielem et Raphaëlem, atque SS. Apostolos Petrum, Paulum et Ioannem, quibus universum Opus Dei eiusdemque singula actionis genera specialiter consecrantur.

CAPUT II

DE PRÆLATURÆ CHRISTIFIDELIBUS

6. Cuncti christifideles qui Prælaturæ incorporantur, vinculo iuridico de quo in n. 27, hoc faciunt eadem divina vocatione moti: omnes eundem finem apostolicum prosequuntur, eundem spiritum eandemque praxim asceticam colunt, congruam recipiunt doctrinalem institutionem et curam sacerdotalem atque, ad finem Prælaturæ quod attinet, subsunt potestati Prælati eiusque Consiliorum, iuxta normas iuris universalis et horum Statutorum.

7. § 1. Pro habituali cuiusque disponibilitate ad incumbendum officiis formationis necnon aliquibus determinatis Operis Dei apostolatus inceptis, fideles Prælaturæ, sive viri sive mulieres, vocantur Numerarii, Aggregati vel Supernumerarii, quin tamen diversas classes efforment. Hæc disponibilitas pendet ex diversis uniuscuiusque permanentibus adiunctis personalibus, familiaribus, professionalibus aliisve id genus.

   § 2. Quin Prælaturæ fideles efficiantur, ipsi aggregari valent associati Cooperatores, de quibus in n. 16.

8. § 1. Vocantur Numerarii illi clerici et laici qui, speciali motione ac dono Dei cœlibatum apostolicum servantes (cfr. Matth. XIX; 11), peculiaribus inceptis apostolatus Prælaturæ totis viribus maximaque adlaborandi personali disponibilitate incumbunt, et ordinarie commorantur in sedibus Centrorum Operis Dei, ut illa apostolatus incepta curent ceterorumque Prælaturæ fidelium institutioni se dedicent.

   § 2. Numerariæ familiarem insuper administrationem seu domesticam curam habent omnium Prælaturæ Centrorum, in loco tamen penitus separato commorantes.

9. Admitti possunt qua Numerarii ii omnes fideles laici qui plena gaudeant disponibilitate ad incumbendum officiis formationis atque laboribus apostolicis peculiaribus Operis Dei, quique, cum admissionem expostulant, ordinario præditi sint titulo academico civili aut professionali æquipollenti, vel saltem post admissionem illum obtinere valeant. Præterea, in Sectione mulierum, Numerariæ Auxiliares, eadem disponibilitate ac ceteræ Numerariæ, vitam suam præcipue dedicant laboribus manualibus vel officiis domesticis, quæ tamquam proprium laborem professionalem voluntarie suscipiunt, in sedibus Centrorum Operis.

10. § 1. Vocantur Aggregati illi fideles laici qui vitam suam plene Domino tradentes in cœlibatu apostolico et iuxta spiritum Operis Dei, curam tamen impendere debent in suas concretas ac permanentes necessi-

tates personales, familiares vel professionales, quæ eos ordinarie ducunt ad commorandum cum propria ipsorum familia. Hæc omnia determinant simul eorum dedicationem aliquibus officiis apostolatus vel formationis Operis Dei perficiendis.

§ 2. Aggregati, nisi aliud pro eis specialiter caveatur, omnia officia seu obligationes suscipiunt ac Numerarii, et ipsorum identicis mediis asceticis ad assequendam sanctitatem et apostolatum exercendum uti debent.

11. § 1. Vocantur Supernumerarii ii omnes fideles laici, cœlibes et etiam coniugati, qui, eadem vocatione divina ac Numerarii et Aggregati, peculiarem apostolatum Operis Dei plene participant, ea quidem disponibilitate quoad incepta apostolica, quæ sit compatibilis cum adimpletione suarum obligationum familiarium, professionalium ac socialium; quique non solum suam vitam suamque professionem convertunt, sicut et ceteri alii Prælaturæ christifideles, in medium sanctificationis et apostolatus, verum etiam, non aliter ac Aggregati, propriam domum propriasque familiares occupationes.

§ 2. Supernumerarii de eodem spiritu vivunt, et pro viribus easdem servant consuetudines ac Numerarii et Aggregati.

12. Inter Aggregatos et Supernumerarios recipi valent etiam chronica aliqua infirmitate laborantes.

13. Numerarii specialiter dicati muneribus regiminis vel formationis residere debent in sede Centrorum quæ ad hunc finem destinantur.

14. § 1. Candidatus qui litteras scripserit expostulando admissionem in Opus Dei qua Numerarius vel Aggregatus, cum ipsi ordinarie per competentem Directorem significetur suam petitionem dignam, quæ examinetur, habitam fuisse, eo ipso inter Supernumerarios admissus manet, quoadusque eidem concedatur admissio quam exoravit.

§ 2. Si quis ante incorporationem ut Numerarius vel Aggregatus videtur ad hoc idoneitate carere, potest in Opere Dei retineri qua Supernumerarius, modo requisitas condiciones habeat.

15. Possunt Supernumerarii inter Numerarios vel Aggregatos recipi, modo tamen requisitis polleant qualitatibus.

16. § 1. Cooperatores, assiduis precibus ad Deum effusis, eleemosynis, et quatenus possibile etiam proprio labore, collaborationem præstant operibus apostolicis et bona spiritualia Operis Dei participant.

§ 2. Sunt etiam qui a domo paterna diversimode longe absunt vel veritatem catholicam non profitentur, qui attamen adiumentum Operi Dei proprio labore aut eleemosynis præstant. Hi iure meritoque Operis Dei Cooperatores nuncupari quoque possunt. Cuncti Prælaturæ fideles, oratione, sacrificio, conversatione, ita cum his Cooperatoribus laborare debent ut, Beatissima Virgine intercedente, a misericordia divina indeficiens lumen fidei pro ipsis consequantur, eosque ad christianos mores suaviter et efficaciter trahant.

## CAPUT III

### DE FIDELIUM ADMISSIONE ET INCORPORATIONE IN PRÆLATURAM

17. Adscriptio tres gradus comprehendit: simplicis Admissionis, quam facit Vicarius Regionalis, audita sua Commissione; incorporationis temporaneæ, quæ Oblatio dicitur, post annum saltem ab Admissione; incorporationis definitivæ seu Fidelitatis, post quinquennium saltem ab incorporatione temporanea transactum.

18. Admissionem postulare valet, habita quidem Directoris localis licentia, quilibet laicus catholicus qui, præter ætatem et alias qualitates requisitas, de quibus in n. 20, recta intentione moveatur ex vocatione divina ad enixe prosequendam suam sanctificationem, mediante proprio labore vel professione, quin ideo mutet suum statum canonicum, velitque totis viribus incumbere apostolatui exercendo, iuxta fines ac media Operis Dei propria, et ad eiusdem onera ferenda eiusdemque peculiares labores exercendos sit idoneus.

19. Candidatus expostulare tenetur suam admissionem mediantibus litteris ad competentem Prælaturæ Ordinarium inscribendis, in quibus manifestet suum desiderium ad Opus Dei pertinendi qua Numerarius, Aggregatus vel Supernumerarius.

20. § 1. Ut quis possit ad Prælaturam admitti requiritur:

    1°   ut ætatem saltem decem et septem annorum compleverit;

    2°   ut in sanctificationem personalem incumbat, enixe colendo virtutes christianas, iuxta spiritum et praxim asceticam quæ Operis Dei sunt propria;

    3°   ut vitæ spirituali prospiciat, per frequentem receptionem Sacramentorum SS. Eucharistiæ et Pænitentiæ et per exercitium orationis mentalis quotidianæ aliarumque normarum pietatis Operis Dei;

    4°   ut antea in apostolatu peculiari Operis Dei, per dimidium saltem annum, sub ductu auctoritatis competentis sese exercuerit; nihil obstat quominus candidatus iam prius per aliquot tempus ut adspirans habeatur, quin tamen ad Prælaturam adhuc pertineat;

    5°   ut ceteris qualitatibus personalibus sit præditus, quibus experimentum præbeat se recepisse vocationem ad Opus Dei.

    § 2. Ab Opere Dei arcentur qui alicuius Instituti religiosi vel Societatis vitæ communis fuerit sodalis, novitius, postulans vel alumnus scholæ apostolicæ; et qui in aliquo Instituto sæculari qua probandus degerit vel admissionem expostulaverit.

    § 3. Præterea, ne diœceses priventur propriis vocationibus sacerdotalibus, ad Prælaturam non admittuntur alumni Seminariorum, sive laici sive clerici, neque sacerdotes alicui diœcesi incardinati.

21. Candidati, ex quo admissionem expostulent eisque significetur suam petitionem dignam, quæ examinetur, habitam esse ad normam n. 14 § 1, ius habent recipiendi congrua formationis media necnon curam ministerialem sacerdotum Prælaturæ.

22. Edocendus est candidatus, antequam admittatur, spiritum Operis Dei exigere ut unusquisque vitam agat impensi laboris, utque, mediante exercitio propriæ professionis vel actuositatis, sibi procuret media œconomica: ea nempe quæ sunt necessaria non solum ad suipsius et, si res id ferat, suæ familiæ sustentationem, sed etiam ad contribuendum generose et iuxta propria personalia adiuncta operibus apostolicis sustinendis.

23. Incorporatio, tum temporanea tum definitiva, requirit præter liberam et expressam candidati voluntatem, opportunam concessionem Vicarii Regionalis cum voto deliberativo sui Consilii; si vero de incorporatione definitiva agatur, necessaria est insuper Prælati confirmatio.

24. § 1. Cuncti Prælaturæ fideles necessarias assumere debent assecurationes seu cautiones, quas civiles leges pro casibus defectus vel impossibilitatis laboris, infirmitatis, senectutis, etc., prævident.

    § 2. Quoties, attentis adiunctis, id requiratur, Prælaturæ officium est subveniendi necessitatibus materialibus Numerariorum et Aggregatorum.

    § 3. Fidelium, de quibus in paragrapho præcedenti, parentibus forte indigentibus, Prælatura, qua par est caritate et generositate providet, quin ex hoc iuridica quælibet obligatio umquam oriri possit.

25. Incorporatio temporanea singulis annis ab unoquoque fideli singillatim renovatur. Ad hanc renovationem requiritur et sufficit licentia Vicarii Regionalis, qui, in casu dubii, suam Commissionem et Directorem localem cum eius Consilio audire potest. Si nullum dubium subsit circa Vicarii renovationi contrariam voluntatem, et nihil ex parte Directoris obsit, licentia iure præsumitur et incorporatio temporanea renovari potest; iure item præsumitur renovationem tacite factam fuisse si fidelis prius non manifestaverit suam voluntatem renovationi contrariam; ipsa vero renovatio subiicitur condicioni resolutivæ si Vicarius de ea certior factus, una cum Defensore et audita sua Commissione, contradicat.

26. Quando aliquis Supernumerarius devenerit Aggregatus aut Numerarius, potest totaliter vel partialiter dispensari circa tempus requisitum pro nova incorporatione temporanea vel definitiva, sed a speciali formatione nullatenus dispensatur.

27. § 1. Pro incorporatione temporanea vel definitiva alicuius christifidelis, fiat a Prælatura et ab eo cuius intersit formalis declaratio coram duobus testibus circa mutua officia et iura.

    § 2. Prælatura, quæ in casu ab eo repræsentatur, quem Vicarius respectivæ circumscriptionis designaverit, a momento incorporationis eiusdem christifidelis eaque perdurante, se obligabit:

    1° ad præbendam eidem christifideli assiduam institutionem doctrinalem religiosam, spiritualem, asceticam et apostolicam, necnon peculiarem curam pastoralem ex parte sacerdotum Prælaturæ;

    2° ad adimplendas ceteras obligationes quæ, erga eiusdem christifideles, in normis Prælaturam regentibus statuuntur.

    § 3. Christifidelis vero suum firmum propositum manifestabit se totis viribus dicandi ad sanctitatem prosequendam atque ad exercendum apostolatum iuxta spiritum et praxim Operis Dei, seque obligabit, a momento incorporationis eaque perdurante:

1° ad manendum sub iurisdictione Prælati aliarumque Prælaturæ competentium auctoritatum, ut fideliter sese impendat in iis omnibus quæ ad finem peculiarem Prælaturæ attinent;

2° ad adimplenda omnia officia quæ secum fert condicio Numerarii vel Aggregati vel Supernumerarii Operis Dei atque ad servandas normas Prælaturam regentes necnon legitimas præscriptiones Prælati aliarumque competentium auctoritatum Prælaturæ quoad eius regimen, spiritum et apostolatum.

§ 4. Quod attinet ad Prælaturæ fideles, potest Ordinarius Prælaturæ, iusta de causa, vota privata itemque iusiurandum promissorium dispensare, dummodo dispensatio ne lædat ius aliis quæsitum. Potest quoque, quoad eosdem fideles, adscriptionem alicui tertio Ordini suspendere, ita tamen ut ipsa reviviscat si, qualibet de causa, vinculum cum Prælatura cesset.

## CAPUT IV

### DE FIDELIUM DISCESSU ET DIMISSIONE A PRÆLATURA

28. § 1. Antequam aliquis temporaliter Prælaturæ incorporetur, potest quovis momento libere ipsam deserere.

§ 2. Pariter auctoritas competens, ob iustas et rationabiles causas, valet eum non admittere, aut ei discedendi consilium dare. Hæ causæ præsertim sunt defectus spiritus proprii Operis Dei et aptitudinis ad apostolatum peculiarem fidelium Prælaturæ.

29. Perdurante incorporatione temporanea vel iam facta definitiva, ut quis possit Prælaturam voluntarie relinquere, indiget dispensatione, quam unus Prælatus concedere potest, audito proprio Consilio et Commissione Regionali.

30. § 1. Fideles temporarie vel definitive Prælaturæ incorporati nequeunt dimitti nisi ob graves causas, quæ, si agatur de incorporatione definitiva, semper ex culpa eiusdem fidelis procedere debent.

§ 2. Infirma valetudo non est causa dimissionis, nisi certo constet eam, ante incorporationem temporaneam, fuisse dolose reticitam aut dissimulatam.

31. Dimissio, si opus sit, fiat maxima caritate: antea tamen suadendus est is cuius interest ut sponte discedat.

32. Dimissio a Prælato vel, in sua circumscriptione, a Vicario, semper cum voto deliberativo proprii Consilii, est decernenda, causis ei cuius interest manifestatis dataque eidem plena respondendi licentia, et post binas monitiones incassum factas, salvo semper iure fidelium ad Prælatum vel ad Sanctam Sedem recurrendi. Si recursus interpositus fuerit intra decem dies, effectus iuridicus dimissionis suspenditur donec responsio a Prælato vel, in casu, a Sancta Sede prodierit.

33. Exitus legitimus ab Opere Dei secum fert cessationem vinculi, de quo in n. 27, necnon officiorum atque iurium, quæ ex ipso profluunt.

34. Qui qualibet ratione Prælaturæ valedicat vel ab ea dimittatur, nihil ab ea exigere potest ob'servitia eidem præstita, vel ob id quod, sive industria sive exercitio propriæ professionis, sive quocumque alio titulo vel modo, eidem rependerit.

35. Clericus Prælaturæ incardinatus, ad normam n. 36, nequit ipsam deserere donec Episcopum invenerit, qui eum in propria diœcesi recipiat. Quodsi non invento Episcopo exierit, nequit interim suos Ordines exercere, donec Sancta Sedes aliter providerit.

## TITULUS II

### DE PRÆLATURÆ PRESBYTERIO DEQUE SOCIETATE SACERDOTALI SANCTÆ CRUCIS

### CAPUT I

### DE COMPOSITIONE PRESBYTERII ET SOCIETATIS SACERDOTALIS SANCTÆ CRUCIS

36. § 1. Prælaturæ presbyterium ab illis clericis constituitur, qui, ad sacros Ordines a Prælato promoti ad normam nn. 44-51, Prælaturæ incardinantur eiusque servitio devoventur.

§ 2. Hi sacerdotes, ex ipso suæ ordinationis facto, fiunt socii Numerarii vel, iuxta infra dicenda (n. 37 § 2), Coadiutores Societatis Sacerdotalis Sanctæ Crucis, quæ est Associatio clericalis Prælaturæ propria ac intrinseca, unde cum ea aliquid unum constituit et ab ea seiungi non potest.

§ 3. Prælatus Operis Dei est Præses Generalis Societatis Sacerdotalis Sanctæ Crucis.

37. § 1. Ut quis sacros Ordines recipere valeat in servitium Prælaturæ, requiritur ut sit eidem definitive incorporatus qua Numerarius vel Aggregatus, atque ut periodum formationis compleverit, quam omnes laici Numerarii, necnon Aggregati illi qui ad sacerdotium destinantur perficere tenentur, ita ut nemini immediate in Prælatura qua sacerdos Numerarius vel respective Aggregatus Operis Dei incardinari liceat.

§ 2. Quo aptius a sociis Aggregatis Societatis Sacerdotalis Sanctæ Crucis, de quibus in nn. 58 et sequentibus, iure distinguantur, Aggregati laici Operis Dei, qui sacerdotium in servitium Prælaturæ suscipiunt, in Societate ipsa Coadiutores seu simpliciter sacerdotes Aggregati Operis Dei vocantur.

38. Hi sacerdotes operam suam præ primis navabunt formationi spirituali et ecclesiasticæ atque peculiari curæ animarum ceterorum fidelium utriusque Sectionis Operis Dei.

39. Sacerdotes Operis Dei cum aliis quoque fidelibus ministeria Ordinis sacerdotalis propria exercebunt, semper quidem habitis licentiis ministerialibus ad normam iuris.

40. Si, ratione officii ecclesiastici vel personalis competentiæ, hi sacerdotes ad Consilium presbyterale aliaque organa diœcesana invitantur, pro

posse participare debent, præhabita tamen licentia Prælati Operis Dei vel eius Vicarii.

41. In cunctis diœcesibus in quibus suum ministerium exercent, hi sacerdotes apostolicæ caritatis nexibus coniunguntur cum ceteris sacerdotibus presbyterii uniuscuiusque diœcesis.

42. Præter clericos de quibus in nn. 36 et 37, ipsi Societati Sacerdotali Sanctæ Crucis adscribi etiam valent, ad normam n. 58, tam socii Aggregati quam socii Supernumerarii, quin tamen inter Prælaturæ clericos adnumerentur, nam unusquisque pertinere perget ad suum presbyterium diœcesanum, sub iurisdictione unius respectivi Episcopi.

43. Societati Sacerdotali Sanctæ Crucis adnumerari etiam possunt, ut associati Cooperatores, alii clerici alicui diœcesi incardinati, qui Societati adiumentum præstant oratione, eleemosynis et, si fieri possit, etiam proprio cuiusque ministerio sacerdotali.

CAPUT II

DE PROMOTIONE AD SACROS ORDINES<br>ET DE PRESBYTERORUM MISSIONE CANONICA

44. Illi tantum Numerarii et Aggregati Operis Dei ad sacros Ordines promoveantur, quos Prælatus vocatione ad sacerdotium ministeriale præditos noverit et Operi Dei eiusque ministeriis necessarios vel congruentes iudicaverit. Qui autem Ordines appetere exoptant, desiderium suum Prælato exponere possunt, sed eius decisioni acquiescere debent.

45. Ut quis Numerarius vel Aggregatus ad Ordines promoveri valeat, præter carentiam irregularitatum aliorumque impedimentorum, de quibus in iure universali, requiritur -servato quoque præscripto n. 37- ut sit speciali aptitudine ornatus ad munera sacerdotalia prout in Prælatura exercenda sunt, et sit saltem viginti quinque annos natus antequam presbyteratum recipiat.

46. Ad formationem quod attinet candidatorum ad sacerdotium, accurate serventur normæ iuris universalis et proprii Prælaturæ.

47. Adscriptio inter candidatos per liturgicum admissionis ritum, ministeriorum collatio necnon promotio ad sacros Ordines Prælato reservantur, post præviam uniuscuiusque candidati declarationem propria manu exaratam et subscriptam, qua testificetur se sponte ac libere sacros Ordines suscepturum atque se ministerio ecclesiastico perpetuo mancipaturum esse, insimul petens ut ad Ordinem recipiendum admittatur.

48. Litteras dimissorias pro ordinatione dat Prælatus Operis Dei, qui potest promovendos ab interstitiis necnon a defectu ætatis his in Statutis requisitæ dispensare, non tamen ultra annum.

49. Qui ad sacros Ordines vocantur, non modo requisita a canonibus præscripta habere debent, præsertim specialem in disciplinis ecclesiasticis cognitionem, verum etiam emineant pietate, vitæ integritate, animarum zelo, erga SS. Eucharistiam fervido amore, ac desiderio imitandi quod quotidie tractare debent.

50. § 1. Cum sacros Ordines recipiunt, clerici ad nutum Prælati manent quoad primam et ulteriores destinationes ad unam vel aliam Operis Dei circumscriptionem.

   § 2. Missio canonica sacerdotibus confertur a Prælato, per se vel per respectivos Vicarios circumscriptionum, semper quidem iuxta normas a Prælato statutas, ipsis concedendo opportunas licentias ministeriales, Sacrum nempe litandi, Verbum Dei prædicandi atque confessiones excipiendi.

   § 3. Hæc facultas audiendi confessiones, quæ ab Ordinario Prælaturæ presbyteris quibuslibet conferri potest, extenditur ad omnes fideles Prælaturæ atque Societatis Sacerdotalis Sanctæ Crucis socios secundum tenorem ipsius concessionis, necnon ad illos omnes qui in Centris Operis Dei diu noctuque degunt.

51. § 1. Sacerdotes presbyterii Prælaturæ munia et officia ecclesiastica quælibet, etsi cum propria condicione et munere pastorali in Prælatura compatibilia, absque Prælati Operis Dei expressa venia admittere non valent.

   § 2. Non tamen ipsis prohibetur exercere actuositatem professionalem sacerdotali characteri, ad normam iuris Sanctæque Sedis præscriptorum atque instructionum, non oppositam.

52. Sacerdotum Prælaturæ ius est et officium, cum periculum mortis immineat, infirmis Numerariis Sacramenta ministrare, quod etiam facere possunt Aggregatis necnon omnibus in Centris Operis Dei versantibus. Agonia autem superveniente, commendatio animæ fiat, adstantibus, quoad fieri possit, omnibus fidelibus Centro adscriptis, et orantibus ut Deus infirmum soletur, ei festivus occurrat eumque in Paradisum perducat.

53. Iusta funebria tam pro Numerariis quam pro Aggregatis et Supernumerariis ex regula in parœcia, ad normam iuris, persolvantur. Celebrari autem possunt per exceptionem in sede alicuius Centri, saltem quando ipsum habeat ecclesiam adnexam, vel agatur de Centro maiore.

54. Post receptam sacram Ordinationem, sacerdotes periodice frequentabunt cursus theoreticos et practicos de re pastorali, collationes, conferentias aliaque id genus, atque statuta examina post presbyteratum et pro licentiarum ministerialium prorogatione subibunt, iuxta normas a Prælato determinatas.

55. Prælato officium est providendi, mediantibus opportunis normis, honestæ sustentationi clericorum qui sacros Ordines receperint in servitium Prælaturæ, necnon congruæ eorum assistentiæ in casibus infirmæ valetudinis, invaliditatis et senectutis.

56. Prælatus eiusque Vicarii fovere enitantur in omnibus Prælaturæ sacerdotibus fervidum spiritum communionis cum ceteris sacerdotibus Ecclesiarum localium, in quibus ipsi suum exercent ministerium.

## CAPUT III

### DE SOCIIS AGGREGATIS ET SUPERNUMERARIIS
### SOCIETATIS SACERDOTALIS SANCTÆ CRUCIS

57. Societas Sacerdotalis Sanctæ Crucis, de qua in n. 36, constituitur in Associationem, quo melius suum sanctificationis sacerdotalis finem etiam inter clericos ad Prælaturam non pertinentes prosequatur iuxta spiritum et praxim asceticam Operis Dei.

58. § 1. Socii Aggregati ac Supernumerarii Societatis Sacerdotalis Sanctæ Crucis, qui quidem membra non efficiuntur cleri Prælaturæ, sed ad suum cuiusque presbyterium pertinent, sunt sacerdotes vel saltem diaconi alicui diœcesi incardinati, qui Domino in Societate Sacerdotali Sanctæ Crucis iuxta spiritum Operis Dei, peculiari superaddita vocatione, sese dicare volunt, ad sanctitatem nempe in exercitio sui ministerii pro viribus prosequendam, quin tamen eorum diœcesana condicio plenaque proprio uniuscuiusque Ordinario subiectio quoquo modo ex hac dedicatione afficiantur, sed contra, iuxta infra dicenda, diversis respectibus confirmentur.

§ 2. In Societate Sacerdotali Sanctæ Crucis non sunt Superiores interni pro Aggregatis et Supernumerariis, quapropter, cum ipsi obœdire tantum debeant proprio loci Ordinario, ad normam iuris, nulla omnino exsurgit quæstio de duplici obœdientia: nulla enim viget obœdientia interna, sed solummodo normalis illa disciplina in qualibet Societate exsistens, quæ provenit ex obligatione colendi ac servandi proprias ordinationes; quæ ordinationes, hoc in casu, ad vitam spiritualem exclusive referuntur.

59. § 1. Qui admitti volunt, eminere debent in amore diœceseos, obœdientia ac veneratione erga Episcopum, pietate, recta in scientiis sacris institutione, zelo animarum, spiritu sacrificii, studio vocationes promovendi, et desiderio adimplendi cum maxima perfectione officia ministerialia.

§ 2. Pro incorporatione in Societatem Sacerdotalem Sanctæ Crucis nullus viget limes maximus ætatis, et admitti quoque possunt clerici chronica aliqua infirmitate laborantes.

60. § 1. Alumni Seminariorum nondum diaconi non possunt in Societatem recipi. Si vocationem persentiunt antequam ordinentur, ut Adspirantes haberi et admitti valent.

§ 2. Iure etiam a Societate arcentur qui alicuius Instituti religiosi vel Societatis vitæ communis fuerit sodalis, novitius, postulans vel alumnus scholæ apostolicæ; et qui in aliquo Instituto sæculari qua probandus degerit vel admissionem expostulaverit.

61. Ut quis qua Aggregatus admittatur, divina vocatio requiritur secum ferens totalem et habitualem disponibilitatem ad sanctitatem quærendam iuxta spiritum Operis Dei, qui exigit:

1° imprimis studium perfecte adimplendi munus pastorale a proprio Episcopo concreditum, sciente unoquoque se soli Ordinario loci rationem reddere debere de huiusmodi muneris adimpletione;

2° propositum dedicandi totum tempus totumque laborem ad apostolatum, spiritualiter præsertim adiuvando confratres sacerdotes diœcesanos.

62. Ut quis recipi possit qua Supernumerarius, eadem vocatio divina requiritur ac pro Aggregatis, necnon plena disponibilitas ad sanctitatem quærendam iuxta spiritum Operis Dei, licet Supernumerarii, propter suas condiciones personales, familiares aliasque id genus, habitualiter in activitatem apostolicam incumbere non valent totaliter et immediate.

63. Admissio petitur litteris ad Præsidem Generalem inscriptis, in quibus candidatus manifestet suum desiderium sese incorporandi Societati Sacerdotali Sanctæ Crucis qua socius Aggregatus vel Supernumerarius.

64. Pro admissione ac incorporatione clericorum inter Aggregatos vel Supernumerarios Societatis Sacerdotalis Sanctæ Crucis, eædem normæ et agendi ratio servari debent, quæ pro admissione et incorporatione Aggregatorum et Supernumerariorum Operis Dei præscribuntur, etiam relate ad tempus peculiaris formationis spiritualis et ad media quæ candidatis præbentur, ut eorum spiritualis vita alatur.

65. Qui admissionem qua Supernumerarii expostulaverint, possunt postea inter Aggregatos recipi, modo tamen requisitis polleant qualitatibus.

66. Si quis ante incorporationem ut Aggregatus videtur necessaria disponibilitate carere, potest retineri qua Supernumerarius, modo requisitas condiciones habeat.

67. Quoad egressum et dimissionem, eadem vigent ac tenenda sunt, congrua congruis referendo, quæ pro egressu et dimissione Aggregatorum ac Supernumerariorum Operis Dei statuuntur.

68. Præter finem Operis Dei, quem hi socii in propria condicione suum faciunt, hunc ut peculiarem propriumque vindicant, scilicet: sanctitatem sacerdotalem atque sensum plenæ deditionis ac subiectionis Hierarchiæ ecclesiasticæ in clero diœcesano impense promovere; et inter sacerdotes cleri diœcesani vitam communem fovere, prout Ordinario loci expedire videatur.

69. Spiritus quo Aggregati et Supernumerarii Societatis Sacerdotalis Sanctæ Crucis informari in omnibus debent, his præprimis continetur:

1° nihil sine Episcopo agere, quod quidem complecti debet omnem ipsorum vitam sacerdotalem atque animarum ministeria;

2° propriam condicionem diœcesanam non derelinquere, sed contra, ipsam maiore semper Dei amore exercere;

3° maxima quidem semper et ubique naturalitate inter confratres sacerdotes se gerant, et nullo modo secretos sese exhibeant, cum nihil in ipsis inveniri debeat quod ita celari oporteat;

4° a confratribus sacerdotibus nullo modo distingui velint, sed totis viribus uniri cum ipsis nitantur;

5° cum ceteris membris presbyterii cuiusque proprii ita fraterna caritate pleni sint, ut quamlibet prorsus divisionum umbram vitent, specialibus apostolicæ caritatis et fraternitatis nexibus coniungantur, et inter omnes omnino sacerdotes maximam unionem studeant.

70. Aggregati et Supernumerarii Societatis Sacerdotalis Sanctæ Crucis, præter clericorum obligationes in iure universali statutas aliasque quas pro omnibus suis sacerdotibus singuli Episcopi præscribere possint, pietatis officia colunt praxis asceticæ Operis Dei propria; cursus vero recessus spiritualis ipsi peragere debent cum ceteris suæ diœcesis sacerdotibus, loco et modo ab Ordinario proprio determinatis.

71. Sacerdotes Aggregati et Supernumerarii ad christianas virtutes tam theologales quam cardinales specialiter colendas dicantur, unusquisque in proprio labore et munere pastorali, a suo cuiusque Episcopo sibi concredito.

72. Spiritus Operis Dei fovet, in Aggregatis et Supernumerariis Societatis Sacerdotalis Sanctæ Crucis, necessitatem ardenter obsecundandi atque ad effectum deducendi directionem spiritualem collectivam, quam Episcopus diœcesanus suis sacerdotibus impertit litteris pastoralibus, allocutionibus, provisionibus disciplinaribus aliisque mediis. Hunc sane in finem, et sine ulla umquam interferentia cum indicationibus diœcesanis vel cum temporibus ad eas adimplendas præscriptis, Societas Sacerdotalis Sanctæ Crucis Aggregatis et Supernumerariis præbet peculiaria media formationis, quorum præcipua sunt sequentia:

1° periodicæ collationes, in quibus directio spiritualis personalis recipitur, et studiorum Circuli, quibus præsunt Zelatores ad spiritum sociorum fovendum: quæ quidem omnia ita ordinari debent, quoad durationis tempus, absentiam e propria diœcesi diebus festis, aliaque similia, ut sacerdotes omnes eisdem assistentes præprimis muneribus in diœcesi sibi commissis commode satisfacere valeant;

2° alia omnia media, industriæ, instrumenta ascetica piæque praxes Operis Dei;

3° expolitio atque opportuna, prout in Domino videatur, intensio et ampliatio culturæ et formationis scientificæ, quatenus ipsæ sunt medium ad ministerium exercendum.

73. § 1. Absolute accurateque vitanda est in diœcesi, quoad Aggregatos et Supernumerarios, vel umbra specialis hierarchiæ Societatis propriæ; quod enim unice quæritur, hoc esse debet: perfectio vitæ sacerdotalis ex diligenti fidelitate vitæ interiori, ex tenaci constantique studio formationis, atque ex mente, criterio et ardore apostolicis, quin hi clerici ullo modo subsint potestati regiminis Prælati Operis Dei eiusque Vicariorum.

§ 2. Ad Aggregatos et Supernumerarios Regionis adiuvandos, Vicarius Regionalis utitur ministerio Sacerdotis Rerum Spiritualium Præfecti, quocum collaborant in unaquaque diœcesi Admonitor et Director spiritualis cum propriis ipsorum substitutis.

74. Pro illis omnibus cum Episcopo locive Ordinario tractandis vel expediendis, quæ ad Aggregatos et Supernumerarios in propria uniuscuiusque diœcesi spectant, Societas ex regula Admonitore eiusve substituto utitur, nisi Vicarius Regionalis, vel ipse directo, vel per specialem suum delegatum aliqua negotia agere seu expedire maluerit.

75. § 1. Vicarius Regionalis sacerdotes Admonitores, Directores spirituales eorumque substitutos ad quinquennium designat.

§ 2. Hæc munera quamlibet potestatis regiminis formam seu speciem vitare prorsus debent.

§ 3. Designationes factas quantocius opportune Episcopo diœcesano locive Ordinario communicare Vicarius Regionalis satagat.

76. Sacerdotes Aggregati et Supernumerarii Societatis Sacerdotalis Sanctæ Crucis in Cœtibus componuntur ac ordinantur, qui specialibus Centris personalibus adscribuntur. Unum idemque Centrum diversos huiusmodi Cœtus adscriptos, etiam per varias diœceses, prout magis expedire videatur, distributos, habere valet.

77. Societas nullam peculiarem œconomicam administrationem habere debet. Ipsa ordinaria fidelium Operis Dei administratione, si qua egeat, utitur.

78. In illis quæ hic expresse præscripta non sunt, congrua congruis referendo et dummodo condicioni sacerdotali conveniant, ea omnia sacerdotibus Aggregatis ac Supernumerariis applicantur, quæ pro Aggregatis et Supernumerariis Operis Dei ordinata sunt, eorumque bona spiritualia et facultates ipsi participant.

## TITULUS III

## DE VITA, INSTITUTIONE ET APOSTOLATU FIDELIUM PRÆLATURÆ

## CAPUT I

## DE VITA SPIRITUALI

79. § 1. Spiritus et praxis ascetica propria Prælaturæ specificos characteres habent, plene determinatos, ad finem proprium prosequendum. Unde spiritus Operis Dei aspectus duplex, asceticus et apostolicus, ita sibi adæquate respondet, ac cum charactere sæculari Operis Dei intrinsece et harmonice fusus ac compenetratus est, ut solidam ac simplicem vitæ -asceticæ, apostolicæ, socialis et professionalis- unitatem necessario secum ferre ac inducere semper debeat.

§ 2. Ut exigentiæ asceticæ et apostolicæ sacerdotii communis et, pro clericis, sacerdotii ministerialis iuxta spiritum Operis Dei in praxim serio et continuo deducantur, utque ita Prælaturæ fideles efficax fermentum sanctitatis et apostolatus inter ceteros clericos et laicos sæculares esse possint, intensa vita orationis et sacrificii præprimis ab omnibus requiritur, iuxta pietatis officia hoc in Codice statuta ceteraque ad traditionem Operis Dei pertinentia.

80. § 1. Fundamentum solidum, quo omnia in Opere Dei constant, radixque fecunda singula vivificans, est sensus humilis ac sincerus filiationis divinæ in Christo Iesu, ex quo dulciter creditur caritati paternæ quam habet Deus in nobis; et Christus Dominus, Deus homo, ut frater primogenitus ineffabili sua bonitate sentitur a Prælaturæ fidelibus, qui Spiritus Sancti gratia Iesum imitari conantur, in memoriam præsertim revocantes mirum exemplum et fecunditatem operosæ eius vitæ in Nazareth.

§ 2. Hac ratione, in vita fidelium Prælaturæ, qui sicut ceteri clerici sæculares et laici, sibi æquales, in omnibus se gerunt, nascitur necessitas et veluti instinctus supernaturalis omnia purificandi, elevandi ad ordinem gratiæ, sanctificandi et convertendi in occasionem personalis unionis cum Deo, cuius Voluntas adimpletur, et in instrumentum apostolatus.

81. § 1. Vitæ spiritualis fidelium Prælaturæ radix ac centrum Sacrosanctum Missæ est Sacrificium, quo Passio et Mors Christi Iesu incruente renovatur et memoria recolitur infiniti eius amoris salvifici erga universos homines.

§ 2. Omnes proinde sacerdotes Sacrosanctum Missæ Sacrificium quotidie celebrent eique cuncti laici devotissime assistant, Corporis Christi Dapem sacramentaliter vel spiritualiter saltem participantes. Præterea Christum in SS. Sacramento alio diei tempore visitent.

82. Exemplum imitantes Apostolorum, qui erant perseverantes unanimiter in oratione, atque communitatum primævorum christianorum, Prælaturæ fideles, dum ordinariis vitæ ac laboris quotidiani vicissitudinibus se dedicant, continuam suæ animæ contemplativæ unionem et conversationem cum Deo curare debent. Ad hunc finem necessario custodiendum ac fovendum:

1° singulis diebus, mane, post oblationem suorum operum Deo factam, orationi mentali spatio semihoræ vacabunt; vespere autem aliam semihoram orationi dedicabunt. Præterea lectioni Novi Testamenti et alterius libri spiritualis per aliquot temporis spatium vacent, et Preces communes Operis Dei recitent;

2° singulis mensibus spirituali recessui unam dedicent diem;

3° singulis annis longiori per aliquot dies recessui spirituali vacent;

4° semper et ubique recolant Dei præsentiam; meminerint filiationis divinæ; communiones spirituales iterent; item gratiarum actiones, actus expiationis, orationes iaculatorias; foveant impensius mortificationem, studium, laborem, ordinem, gaudium.

83. § 1. Ut insidiæ vincantur triplicis concupiscentiæ, superbiæ vitæ speciatim, quæ ex doctrina, ex condicione sociali et ex professionalibus laboribus ali posset, ascetismi christiani exigentiæ a Prælaturæ fidelibus firmiter et impense colendæ sunt. Hic ascetismus nititur fideli ac perpetuo sensu humilitatis externæ et intrinsecæ, non tantum individualis sed etiam collectivæ; candore connaturalis simplicitatis; familiari et nobili agendi ratione; expressione iugis serenæ lætitiæ, labore, sui abnegatione, sobrietate, actibus sacrificii atque statutis exercitiis mortificationis etiam corporalis singulis diebus et hebdomadis peragendis, iuxta uniuscuiusque ætatem et condicionem. Hæc omnia curantur ut media non solum purificationis personalis, sed præterea veri ac solidi progressus spiritualis, iuxta illud bene probatum et comprobatum verbum: "tantum proficies quantum tibi ipsi vim intuleris". Curantur etiam ut necessaria præparatio ad omnem apostolatum in societate peragendum eiusque perfectum exercitium: "adimpleo ea quæ desunt passionum Christi in carne mea pro corpore eius, quod est Ecclesia" (Col. I, 24).

§ 2. Hic ascetismus et spiritus pænitentiæ alias quoque exigentias in vita fidelium Prælaturæ secum fert, præsertim quotidianam conscientiæ discussionem, directionem spiritualem et praxim hebdomadariam confessionis sacramentalis.

84. § 1. Ament Prælaturæ fideles et diligentissime custodiant castitatem, quæ homines Christo eiusque castissimæ Matri reddit gratissimos, pro certo habentes operam apostolatus castitate suffultam esse debere.

§ 2. Ad præsidium huius thesauri, qui vasis fertur fictilibus, summopere conferunt fuga occasionum, modestia, temperantia, corporis castigatio, SS. Eucharistiæ frequens receptio, ad Virginem Matrem adsiduus ac filialis recursus.

85. Tenero amore et devotione Beatissimam Virginem Mariam, Domini Iesu Christi Matrem et nostram, Prælaturæ fideles colant. Quotidie quindecim mysteria marialis Rosarii contemplentur, quinque saltem mysteria vocaliter recitantes, vel, iis in locis in quibus pia hæc praxis usualis non sit, aliam æquipollentem marialem precationem pro hac recitatione substituentes. Ipsam Deiparam, uti mos est, salutatione Angelus Domini vel antiphona Regina cœli filiali devotione honorare ne omittant; et die sabbato mortificationem aliquam faciant, recitentque antiphonam Salve Regina vel Regina cœli.

86. § 1. Dominus hominem creavit "ut operaretur" (Genes. II, 15), ideoque hæc laborandi lex pertinet ad generalem humanam condicionem. Attamen peculiaris character ac finis Prælaturæ eius fideles ducit non solum ad colendum, verum etiam ad profunde amandum ordinarium laborem: in ipso enim vident tum insignissimum valorem humanum, necessarium quidem ad tuendam humanæ personæ dignitatem et societatis progressionem, tum præcipue miram occasionem atque medium unionis personalis cum Christo, imitantes eius operosam vitam absconditam generosi servitii aliorum hominum et ita cooperantes operi amore pleno Creationis et Redemptionis mundi.

§ 2. Peculiaris proinde character spiritus Operis Dei in eo consistit, quod unusquisque suum laborem professionalem sanctificare debet; in sui laboris professionalis perfecta adimpletione, sanctificari; et per suum laborem professionalem, alios sanctificare. Unde multæ oriuntur concretæ exigentiæ in vita ascetica et apostolica eorum qui ad opera peculiaria Prælaturæ dicantur.

87. § 1. Prælatura Operis Dei tota devota est servitio Ecclesiæ, pro qua fideles Prælaturæ -plena, perpetua ac definitiva Christi Domini servitio deditione sese mancipando- relinquere parati semper erunt honorem, bona, adhuc autem et animam suam; numquam Ecclesiam sibi inservire præsumant. Sit ergo firmus ac exemplaris pius amor erga Sanctam Matrem Ecclesiam omniaque ad illam quoquo modo pertinentia; sint sinceræ dilectio, veneratio, docilitas et adhæsio Romano Pontifici omnibusque Episcopis communionem cum Apostolica Sede habentibus, quos Spiritus Sanctus posuit Ecclesiam Dei regere.

§ 2. Præter orationes quæ in Sacrosancto Eucharistico Sacrificio et in Operis Dei Precibus quotidianis pro Summo Pontifice et pro Ordinario uniuscuiusque Ecclesiæ localis effunduntur, omnes fideles quotidie intentiones eorundem Domino specialiter commendare ne omittant.

88. § 1. Prælatura fovet in suis fidelibus necessitatem speciali sollertia colendi obœdientiam illam illudque religiosum obsequium, quæ christiani universi exhibere debent erga Romanum Pontificem et Episcopos communionem cum Sancta Sede habentes.

§ 2. Omnes fideles tenentur præterea humiliter Prælato ceterisque Prælaturæ auctoritatibus in omnibus obœdire, quæ ad finem peculiarem Operis Dei pertinent. Hæc obœdientia sit penitus voluntaria, ob motivum divini amoris et ut imitentur Christum Dominum, qui cum esset omnium Dominus, semetipsum exinanivit formam servi accipiens, quique factus est "obœdiens usque ad mortem, mortem autem crucis" (Philip. II, 8).

§ 3. Ad professionalem autem actionem quod attinet, itemque ad doctrinas sociales, politicas, etc., unusquisque Prælaturæ fidelis, intra limites utique catholicæ doctrinæ fidei et morum, eadem plena gaudet libertate qua ceteri gaudent cives catholici. Auctoritates vero Prælaturæ a quibuslibet vel consiliis dandis his in materiis omnino abstinere debent. Proinde illa plena libertas tantum minui poterit a normis quas forsan dederint pro omnibus catholicis, in aliqua diœcesi aut ditione, Episcopus vel Episcoporum Conferentia; quapropter Prælatura labores professionales, sociales, politicos, œconomicos, etc., nullius omnino sui fidelis suos facit.

89. § 1. Omnes Prælaturæ fideles diligant atque foveant humilitatem non modo privatam, sed etiam collectivam; ideo numquam Operi Dei gloriam quærant, quinimmo hoc unum animo alte defixum habeant: gloriam Operis Dei summam esse sine humana gloria vivere.

§ 2. Quo efficacius suum finem assequatur Opus Dei, uti tale, humiliter vivere vult: quare sese abstinet ab actibus collectivis, neque habet nomen vel denominationem communem quibus Prælaturæ fideles appellentur; nec ipsi aliquibus publicis manifestationibus cultus, uti processionibus, intererunt collective, quin ex hoc occultent se ad Prælaturam pertinere, quia spiritus Operis Dei, dum fideles ducit ad humilitatem collectivam enixe quærendam, quo impensiorem atque uberiorem efficaciam apostolicam attingant, omnino simul vitat secretum vel clandestinitatem. Quapropter universis in circumscriptionibus omnibus nota sunt nomina Vicariorum Prælati necnon eorum qui Consilia ipsorum efformant; et Episcopis petentibus nomina communicantur non solum sacerdotum Prælaturæ, qui in respectivis diœcesibus suum ministerium exercent, sed Directorum etiam Centrorum quæ in diœcesi erecta habentur.

§ 3. Huius humilitatis collectivæ causa, Opus Dei nequit edere folia et cuiusque generis publicationes nomine Operis.

90. In sua vita professionali, familiari et sociali, fideles Prælaturæ virtutes naturales, quæ in humano consortio magni æstimantur et ad apostolatum peragendum iuvant, diligenter et fortiter colant: fraternitatem, optimismum, audaciam, in rebus bonis ac rectis sanctam intransigentiam, lætitiam, simplicitatem, nobilitatem ac sinceritatem, fidelitatem; sed eas semper et in omnibus supernaturales fideliter reddere curent.

91. Prælaturæ fideles, memores normarum caritatis et prudentiæ, exercere tenentur correctionem fraternam, ut, in casu, sese mutuo amoveant a moribus, qui spiritui Operis Dei repugnent.

92. Omnes maxima cura res etiam parvas cum spiritu supernaturali perficiant, eo quod vocationis ratio in diurno labore sanctificando consistit. Non semper res magnæ occurrunt; parvæ utique, in quibus Iesu Christi amor sæpius demonstrari potest. Hæc est una ex manifestationibus spiritus pænitentiæ Operis Dei proprii, quæ potius in parvis et ordinariis rebus est quærenda et in labore quotidiano, constanti, ordinato.

93. In hoc suo ordinario labore adimplendo, maximo cum amore Dei et proximi, fidem vivam et operantem necnon filialem spem omnibus in adiunctis Prælaturæ fideles colant; quæ virtutes omnia superare faciunt obstacula in Ecclesiæ animarumque servitio forte obvenientia: "omnia possum in eo qui me confortat" (Philip. IV, 13). Nihil ergo aut neminem formident: "Dominus illuminatio mea et salus mea, quem timebo?" (Ps. XXVI, 1).

94. § 1. Prælaturæ fideles plena vivant personali cordis a bonis temporalibus libertate, unusquisque iuxta suum statum et condicionem, animis ab omnibus, quibus utuntur, alienatis; sobrie semper in vita sua personali et sociali iuxta spiritum et praxim Operis Dei se gerentes; omnem sollicitudinem de rebus huius sæculi in Deum proiicientes; atque in hoc mundo tamquam peregrini, qui civitatem futuram inquirunt, commorantes.

§ 2. Suo ordinario labore professionali, peracto cum mente et animo patris familiæ numerosæ ac pauperis, omnibus Prælaturæ fidelibus officium est providendi propriis necessitatibus œconomicis personalibus et familiaribus atque, in quantum ab ipsis fieri possit, iuvandi sustentationem apostolatus Prælaturæ, remedium afferentes indigentiæ spirituali ac materiali plurimorum hominum. Gaudeant simul quando effectus experiantur carentiæ mediorum, scientes numquam in necessariis providentiam Domini defecturam, qui nos monuit ut primum Regnum Dei et iustitiam eius quæramus, si volumus ut cetera omnia nobis adiiciantur.

§ 3. Prælatura tamen curat ne suis fidelibus necessarium adiutorium spirituale desit, atque Prælatus, per se vel per suos Vicarios, paterno affectu eos fovet, ab unoquoque ea ratione exigendo, prout varia cuiusque adiuncta suadeant. Propterea, quod attinet ad Prælaturæ fideles atque personas, quæ diu noctuque in Centris Operis Dei degunt, potest Prælaturæ Ordinarius, iusta de causa, dispensationem concedere ab obligatione servandi diem festum vel diem pænitentiæ, aut commutationem eiusdem in alia pia opera.

95. Præter festa Domini, Beatæ Mariæ Virginis et Sancti Ioseph, a Prælaturæ fidelibus speciali devotione celebrantur festa Exaltationis Sanctæ Crucis; SS. Archangelorum Michaëlis, Gabrielis et Raphaëlis atque Apostolorum Petri, Pauli et Ioannis; aliorum Apostolorum et Evangelistarum; dies secunda octobris seu Angelorum Custodum festivitas, et decima quarta februarii. Hæ postremæ dies, pro Opere Dei, dies actionis gratiarum sunto.

## CAPUT II

### DE INSTITUTIONE DOCTRINALI RELIGIOSA

96. Sub aspectu doctrinali religioso, institutio quæ fidelibus Prælaturæ impertitur ipsis profundam cognitionem Fidei catholicæ et Magisterii ecclesiastici, alimentum quidem necessarium suæ vitæ spiritualis et apostolicæ, præstare contendit, ut in quocumque societatis ambitu personæ adsint intellectualiter præparatæ, quæ, cum simplicitate, in ordinariis adiunctis quotidianæ vitæ atque laboris, exemplo ac verbis efficacem apostolatum evangelizationis et catecheseos exerceant.

97. In qualibet regionali circumscriptione a Vicario Regionali, de consensu sui Consilii et Prælato confirmante, erigantur, prout opus fuerit, Studiorum Centra pro omnibus cuiusque Regionis fidelibus, ut institutio doctrinalis religiosa impensa et assidua ad vitam spiritualem sustinendam et ad finem apostolicum Prælaturæ proprium prosequendum cunctis congrue præbeatur.

98. Potest etiam Prælatus, audito suo Consilio, Interregionalia Centra Studiorum erigere, a seipso dependentia, ut in his instituantur Prælaturæ fideles ab ipso Prælato selecti sive directe, sive respectivis circumscriptionum Vicariis id proponentibus. Hæc Centra specialiter destinari possunt ad fideles, sacerdotes vel laicos, præparandos, qui formationis officiis in diversis Regionibus incumbant.

99. § 1. Institutio doctrinalis religiosa, præsertim quod attinet ad disciplinas philosophicas ac theologicas, impertietur a professoribus Centrorum Studiorum Regionalium vel Interregionalium quæ hunc in finem eriguntur, quæque diversa habentur pro viris et pro mulieribus.

§ 2. Programmata cyclica ita componentur, ut institutio continue impertiri ac perfici valeat, quin unusquisque fidelis, in adimpletione officiorum professionalium et familiarium, detrimentum patiatur.

100. § 1. Prælaturæ fideles tempus institutionis perficere possunt extra Centra Studiorum iuridice erecta, si, attentis circumstantiis, audito proprio Consilio, Vicarius Regionalis hoc disposuerit.

§ 2. Tempore hoc perdurante, formationem accipiunt a professore vel professoribus a Vicario Regionali delectis.

§ 3. Iidem autem periculum debent postea subire in aliquo Centro iuridice erecto.

101. § 1. Omnes Numerarii, necnon illi Aggregati quorum personalia adiuncta id suadeant, integra studia biennii philosophici et quadriennii theologici peragant.

§ 2. Singuli anni biennii atque quadriennii dividuntur in duos cursus semestrales, quorum duratio, numerus nempe horarum quæ lectionibus dedicantur, æquivalere debet illi cursuum semestralium apud Pontificias Romanas studiorum Universitates, quorumque programmata eadem amplitudine qua in iisdem studiorum Universitatibus explicentur.

§ 3. Duodecim curriculis semestralibus persolvendis, de quibus in §§ præcedentibus, unusquisque alumnus tot annis incumbat, quot necessarii sint, iuxta adiuncta sua personalia atque sui laboris professionalis.

§ 4. Pro mulieribus Numerariis Auxiliaribus, Centra Studiorum cursus disponunt institutionis philosophicæ ac theologicæ ad earum personalia adiuncta accommodatos. Huiusmodi cursus non necessario amplecti debent integrum curriculum philosophicum-theologicum.

§ 5. Pro ceteris vero Prælaturæ fidelibus institutio doctrinalis complectitur etiam congruam formationem doctrinalem religiosam, quæ eos idoneos reddat ad suum apostolatum exercendum.

102.§ 1. Pro Numerariis qui ad sacerdotium destinantur sunt specialia Centra Studiorum a Prælato erecta, ubi tamen semper alii Numerarii qui sacerdotes non erunt commorari debent, propriam ipsorum institutionem accipientes et vitam cum primis ducentes, quia una eademque pro omnibus spiritualis formatio requiritur.

§ 2. Attamen, post hoc satis longum tirocinium in Centris Studiorum peractum, durante uno tantum sacræ theologiæ studiorum anno, candidati ad sacerdotium commorantur in Centro speciali ad ipsos solummodo destinato.

§ 3. Quoad Aggregatos qui pro sacerdotio recipiendo instituuntur, eædem normæ applicari possunt, congrua tamen congruis referendo.

103.Philosophiæ rationalis ac theologiæ studia, et alumnorum in his disciplinis institutionem, professores omnino pertractent ad Angelici Doctoris rationem, doctrinam et principia, eaque sancte teneant, iuxta normas a Magisterio Conciliorum et Sanctæ Sedis traditas vel tradendas.

104.Quoad illos omnes, qui in posterum ad sacerdotium destinentur, studia de quibus in n. 101, ad normam iuris et Sanctæ Sedis instructionum peracta, publica habenda sunt.

105.Omnes sacerdotes Prælaturæ præditi sint oportet laurea doctorali in aliqua disciplina ecclesiastica.

106.§ 1. Cuncti qui Prælaturæ incorporari desiderant, ex quo admissionem expostulant, formationem doctrinalem religiosam, quæ prævia vocatur, recipiant necesse est antequam eisdem incorporatio concedatur.

§ 2. Post incorporationem vero, perficere tenentur studia de quibus in n. 97. Hunc in finem frequentabunt cursus pro cœtibus homogeneis dispositos, et assistent coadunationibus, conferentiis aliisque id genus.

107.Expletis respectivis studiis institutionis doctrinalis religiosæ, quam recipiunt post incorporationem in Prælaturam, omnes suam institutionem modo permanenti et per totam vitam continuabunt iuxta rationem cyclicam repetitionis et adæquationis ad recens adquisitas cognitiones, quo profundius in dies suam formationem doctrinalem ipsi perficiant.

108.Pro Cooperatoribus catholicis, necnon pro aliis Cooperatoribus qui Ecclesiæ Catholicæ doctrinam cognoscere desiderent, cursus, coadunationes aliaque similia promoveantur de re dogmatica ac morali deque ascetica christiana, ita ut ipsi formationem doctrinalem sibi adquirant vel perficiant.

109. Opus Dei nullam habet propriam sententiam vel scholam corporativam in quæstionibus theologicis vel philosophicis quas Ecclesia liberæ fidelium opinioni relinquit: Prælaturæ fideles, intra limites statutos ab ecclesiastica Hierarchia, quæ Depositum fidei custodit, eadem libertate gaudent ac ceteri fideles catholici.

## CAPUT III

## DE APOSTOLATU

110. Prælatura sollicite suis fidelibus tradit congruam formationem apostolicam ac necessariam assistentiam pastoralem ad impensum laborem evangelizationis et catecheseos exsequendum, ita ut in vita omnium atque singulorum constanter ad effectum deducatur officium et ius christianorum exercendi apostolatum.

111. Hæc semper Prælaturæ christifideles in apostolatu meminerint:

1° zelus quo adurimur hoc unum quærit, nempe ut omnes cum Petro ad Iesum per Mariam quasi manu ducamus;

2° pro multitudine constituti sumus. Nulla igitur est anima quam diligere et adiuvare non velimus, omnia omnibus nos facientes (cfr. I Cor. IX, 22). Vivere nequimus prætermittentes omnium hominum curas atque necessitates, quia nostra sollicitudo omnes animas amplectitur: vitam agentes absconditam cum Christo in Deo (cfr. Col. III, 3), esse debemus tamquam fermentum in massa humanæ societatis latens et ipsi se immiscens donec fermentata sit tota (cfr. Matth. XIII, 33).

112. Prælaturæ fideles sibi proponant, semper et super omnia, ad effectum deducere suum finem personalem sanctificationis et apostolatus, fideliter adimplentes normas asceticas, formativas ac disciplinares Operis Dei, quibus adiuvantur in nisu perfecte exsequendi propria officia professionalia, familiaria et socialia, constans ita testimonium christiani sensus vitæ humanæ præbentes, et nuntium Christi diffundentes apud omnes societatis ambitus, iis non exclusis ad quos ordinarius labor apostolicus sacerdotum ac religiosorum difficile pervenit.

113. Prælaturæ fideles, persuasum habentes suum peculiarem apostolatum procedere ex propria vita interiore atque ex amore erga humanum laborem, quæ fundi ac compenetrari debent in unitate vitæ, speciatim enitantur ut suum laborem sanctificent ipsumque quam maxima possint perfectione humana exsequantur, secundum divinam voluntatem ordinent atque ad animarum salutem dirigant, in primis vero suorum in professione collegarum. Ideo eorum actuositas apostolica non habet modum se manifestandi uniformem vel exclusivum, quia radicatur in ipsa circumstantiarum varietate, quam humanus labor secum fert.

114. Præter apostolatum testimonii atque exempli, per congruentem vitam personalem unionis cum Domino exhibiti, fideles Prælaturæ eniti debent ut aperto etiam sermone de Deo loquantur, veritatem cum caritate diffundentes constanti apostolatu doctrinali et catechetico, accommodato ad peculiaria adiuncta personarum cum quibus laborant et convivunt.

115. Apostolatus fidelium Prælaturæ ad cunctos homines dirigitur, sine distinctione stirpis, nationis vel condicionis socialis, ut christiani invitentur, edoceantur atque adiuventur ad respondendum vocationi universali ad sanctitatem in exercitio suæ professionis et in officiorum proprii status adimpletione, utque illi etiam qui Christum nondum agnoscunt testimonium de Ipso exemplo et verbis recipiant, et ita disponantur ad fidei gratiam recipiendam.

116. Sua divina vocatione, Prælaturæ christifideles ad ordinem supernaturalem evehere satagunt sensum servitii erga homines atque societatem, quo labor quilibet professionalis exercendus est. Continenter præ oculis habebunt fecunditatem apostolatus apud personas condicionis intellectualis, quæ, ob doctrinam qua pollent, vel ob munera quæ exercent, vel ob dignitatem qua insigniuntur, magni sunt ponderis pro servitio societati civili præstando: ideo totis viribus Prælaturæ fideles adlaborabunt ut etiam illæ personæ Christi Domini doctrinæ et præceptis adhæreant ipsaque in praxim deducant.

117. Prælaturæ fideles qui ad apostolatum efficaciorem reddendum, exemplum christianum in exercitio proprii uniuscuiusque laboris professionalis, necnon in proprio ambitu familiari, culturali et sociali, dare conabuntur, suum personalem apostolatum exercent præsertim inter pares, ope præcipue amicitiæ et mutuæ fiduciæ. Omnes nos amici sumus -"vos autem dixi amicos" (Ioann. XV, 15)-, immo eiusdem Patris filii ac proinde in Christo et Christi una simul fratres: peculiare igitur Prælaturæ fidelium apostolatus medium est amicitia et assidua cum collaboratoribus consuetudo, quin tamen ad hoc speciales associationes actionis externæ religiosæ constituantur.

118. Peculiaris etiam nota, qua labor apostolicus fidelium Prælaturæ insignitur, est amor libertatis personalis cunctorum hominum, cum accuratissimo obsequio erga libertatem conscientiarum et desiderio cum omnibus convivendi. Quo spiritu fideles ducuntur ad sinceram caritatem semper colendam erga eos qui Christum sequuntur, quia pro Ipso laborant; necnon ad eos diligendos, recte quoque eorum mentes æstimantes, qui Christum nondum sectantur, exemplo ac doctrina eos ad Dominum trahere satagentes.

119. Prælatura a suis fidelibus quærit impensam et constantem actuositatem apostolicam personalem, in ipso labore et ambitu sociali uniuscuiusque propriis exercendam, liberam ac responsabilem, spontaneitate plene imbutam, quæ fructus sit actionis gratiæ quæque sese accurate accommodet fidei et moribus christianis atque Ecclesiæ Magisterio.

120. In hac continua actuositate apostolatus personalis, Prælaturæ fideles adhibent etiam, pro cuiusque peritia, media illa atque incepta quæ in societate civili communia sunt, nempe circulos studiorum, coadunationes, frequentes conventus, sessiones, conferentias, cursus studiorum aliaque similia, modo quidem accommodato ad diversos ambitus civiles in quibus ipsi vitam agunt.

121. § 1. Præter apostolatum personalem, quem Prælatura in suis fidelibus fovet cuique profecto locus præcipuus competit, Prælatura qua talis specificam assistentiam pastoralem præstat laboribus et inceptis

indolis civilis ac professionalis, non confessionalis, persequentibus fines educativos, assistentiales, etc.

§ 2. Prælaturæ Ordinarius, necessitate ductus adimplendi suam specificam missionem utque peculiaris Prælaturæ finis quam melius in praxim deducatur, maxima cura eos seliget qui cappellanorum atque religionis magistrorum munere fungentur, tum in inceptis ab Opere Dei qua tali promotis, tum in iis quæ a Prælaturæ fidelibus una cum aliis suscitantur et pro quibus adiutorium spirituale ab Opere Dei postulant. In nominandis vero his cappellanis et religionis magistris, Prælaturæ Ordinarius suum Consilium audire numquam omittat, atque nominationes ita factas loci Ordinario opportune communicet.

122. Prælatura numquam sibi assumit aspectus technicos et œconomicos inceptorum de quibus in n. 121, neque de iisdem respondet; hi enim pertinent ad eorum proprietarios et gestores, utentes bonis et opibus ex propria industria vel aliis mediis similiter civilibus obtentis vel obtinendis. Ordinarie Prælatura non est proprietaria instrumentorum materialium eorum inceptorum, quorum spiritualem curam acceptat.

123. Pars Prælaturæ in inceptis de quibus in numero præcedenti consistit in eorum christiana vivificatione, per opportuna media orientationis atque formationis doctrinalis ac spiritualis, necnon per congruam assistentiam pastoralem, accurate quidem servata alumnorum, convictorum ceterorumque omnium legitima conscientiarum libertate. Ad hanc curam de unoquoque incepto apostolico exercendam, Centrum Operis Dei erigetur, prævia opportuna venia Ordinarii loci, melius in scriptis data.

124. Cum aliquis Prælaturæ christifidelis, ad Ordinarii loci petitionem et servata Prælaturæ disciplina, adiutorium directe præstat in laboribus diœcesanis, idem incumbit illis laboribus explendis ad nutum et mentem eiusdem Ordinarii, ipsique tantum de peracto labore rationem reddit.

## TITULUS IV

## DE REGIMINE PRÆLATURÆ

## CAPUT I

## DE REGIMINE IN GENERE

125. § 1. Prælaturæ regimen committitur Prælato, qui suis Vicariis et Consiliis adiuvatur iuxta normas iuris universalis et huius Codicis.

§ 2. Potestas regiminis qua gaudet Prælatus est plena in foro tum externo tum interno in sacerdotes Prælaturæ incardinatos; in laicos vero Prælaturæ incorporatos hæc potestas ea est tantum quæ spectat finem peculiarem eiusdem Prælaturæ.

§ 3. Prælati potestas, sive in clericos sive in laicos, ad normam iuris universalis et huius Codicis exercetur.

§ 4. Nomine Ordinarii Prælaturæ iure intelleguntur et sunt Prælatus necnon qui in eadem generali gaudent potestate exsecutiva ordinaria, nempe Vicarii pro regimine tum generali cum regionali Prælaturæ constituti.

126. Prælatura distribuitur in circumscriptiones regionales, quarum unamquamque moderatur Vicarius, qui Consiliarius Regionalis appellatur, cuique respectiva Consilia assistunt.

127. Excepto Prælati officio, quod est ad vitam, alia omnia munera Prælaturæ sunt temporaria; admittitur tamen iterata eorundem nominatio.

128. Universa Prælatura eiusque partes tantum a Prælato vel eius delegatis, etiam in omnibus negotiis iuridicis, legitime repræsentantur; munere autem Prælati vacante vel impedito, ab eo qui regimen assumit ad normam n. 149 §§ 1 et 4; unaquæque vero Operis Dei circumscriptio regionalis, etiam a proprio Vicario.

129. § 1. Prælatura eiusque circumscriptiones personalitate iuridica præditæ adquirunt, possident, administrant et alienant bona temporalia ad normam iuris, iuxta præscripta a Prælato statuta.

§ 2. Ex omnibus bonis, undecumque ipsa proveniant, quæ Prælaturæ adscribi possunt, illa tantum ut vere ecclesiastica ad normam iuris habenda sunt, quæ de facto ipsi Prælaturæ a Prælato adscripta iam fuerint.

§ 3. Prælatura vel circumscriptiones de quibus in § 1 respondent de obligationibus quas respective contraxerint, atque semper legitimas leges civiles regionis vel nationis de qua agatur fideliter observant, intra terminos ab ipsis constitutos operando.

## CAPUT II

### DE REGIMINE CENTRALI

130. § 1. Prælatus, qui interne dicitur Pater cuiusque officium est ad vitam, seligitur excluso compromisso a Congressu Generali electivo hunc in finem convocato; electio vero Romani Pontificis confirmatione indiget.

§ 2. Congressus Generalis constituitur a Congressistis, qui etiam vocantur membra Congressus. Sunt Congressistæ illi sacerdotes vel viri laici, triginta duos saltem annos nati et iam a novem saltem annis Prælaturæ definitive incorporati, qui inter fideles ex diversis nationibus vel regionibus, in quibus Opus Dei suum laborem apostolicum exercet, nominantur ad vitam a Prælato, cum voto deliberativo sui Consilii, auditis etiam Commissione Regionali et Congressistis respectivæ Regionis.

§ 3. Congressus, antequam ad Prælati electionem procedere iure valeat, requirere et recipere debet, ab omnibus atque singulis membris Consilii Centralis de quo in n. 146, propositiones circa nomen seu nomina illius illorumve quos ad supremum Prælaturæ munus digniores et aptiores censeant.

§ 4. Acceptatione ab electo rite habita, ipse confirmationem electionis a Romano Pontifice per se vel per alium petere debet.

131. Ut quis possit Prælatus eligi requiritur:

1° ut sit sacerdos membrum Congressus Generalis, iam a decem saltem annis Prælaturæ incorporatus, et a quinquennio saltem in presbyteratus Ordine constitutus, filius legitimi matrimonii, bona existimatione gaudens et natus saltem annos quadraginta;

2° eluceat praeterea prudentia, pietate, erga Ecclesiam eiusque Magisterium exemplari amore et obœdientia, erga Opus Dei devotione, erga Praelaturae fideles caritate, erga proximos zelo;

3° praeditus sit speciali cultura etiam profana, immo laurea doctorali in aliqua ecclesiastica disciplina, aliisque qualitatibus ad agendum necessariis.

132.§ 1. Praelatus, sicut christifidelibus suae curae commissis auctoritate praeest, unde etiam Praeses Generalis nuncupari potest, prae ceteris ipsum etiam excellere virtutibus et qualitatibus decet, iis praesertim quae propriae sunt Operis Dei, quaeque eiusdem spiritum consequuntur.

§ 2. In exercitio sui muneris pastoralis, Praelatus specialiter curare debet ut universum ius quo regitur Opus Dei ac omnes eiusdem legitimae consuetudines adamussim serventur, atque fideliter promovere exsecutionem dispositionum Sanctae Sedis Praelaturam respicientium.

§ 3. Sit ergo omnibus Praelaturae fidelibus magister atque Pater, qui omnes in visceribus Christi vere diligat, omnes effusa caritate erudiat atque foveat, pro omnibus impendatur et superimpendatur libenter.

§ 4. Curet praesertim ut sacerdotibus ac laicis sibi commissis assidue et abundanter praebeantur media et auxilia spiritualia atque intellectualia, quae necessaria sunt ad eorum vitam spiritualem alendam ac fovendam eorumque peculiarem finem apostolicum exsequendum.

§ 5. Pastoralem suam sollicitudinem manifestet consiliis, suasionibus, immo et legibus, praeceptis et instructionibus, atque si id requiratur, congruis sanctionibus; necnon visitationibus sive per se sive per alios a se delegatos peragendis, in circumscriptionibus ac Centris, in ecclesiis Praelaturae vel eidem commissis, et circa personas et res.

§ 6. Ut bono spirituali Praelati et eiusdem valetudini consulant, sint duo Custodes seu admonitores qui tamen, ratione huius muneris, Consilium Generale non ingrediuntur. Designantur ad periodum octo annorum ab eodem Praelato inter novem Praelaturae fideles de quibus in n. 13, a Consilio Generali praesentatos. Convivunt in eadem cum Praelato familia.

133.§ 1. Praeter Congressum Generalem electivum, octavo quoque anno celebrari debent Congressus Generales ordinarii a Praelato convocati, ut de Praelaturae statu iudicium proferant et futurae actioni regiminis opportunas normas suadere valeant. Congressui praeest Praelatus vel, eius delegatione, dignior Consilii Generalis.

§ 2. Congressus Generalis extra ordinem convocandus est, cum rerum adiuncta de iudicio Praelati cum voto deliberativo sui Consilii id postulent; et ad Vicarium auxiliarem seu Vicepraesidem designandum vel revocandum, ad normam nn. 134 § 2 et 137 § 2.

§ 3. Pro Sectione mulierum adsunt etiam Congressus Generales tum ordinarii cum extra ordinem convocati, non autem Congressus electivi.

His Congressibus præest Prælatus, cui assistunt Vicarius auxiliaris, si adsit, atque Vicarii Secretarius Generalis et Sacerdos Secretarius Centralis. Congressistæ nominantur pari ratione ac viri Congressistæ.

§ 4. Audita Commissione permanenti sui Consilii, de qua in n. 138 § 2, Prælatus convocare potest Prælaturæ fideles non Congressistas, diversis in materiis peritos, qui Congressui Generali intersint qua collaboratores, cum voce sed sine voto; quod etiam valet pro mulieribus, in propria Sectione.

134.§ 1. Si Prælatus opportunam seu convenientem in Domino censeat Vicarii auxiliaris ad normam n. 135 designationem, libere, audito suo Consilio, ipsum nominare potest. Consilium Generale plenum poterit etiam Prælato sincere suggerere opportunitatem Vicarii auxiliaris designationis, qui ipsum in regimine adiuvare ad octo annos valeat. Prælatus, nisi graves obsint rationes, Consilio facile morem gerat.

§ 2. Si vero Prælatus illo Vicario auxiliari egere videatur de quo in n. 136, tunc Consilium plenum, post rei maturam in Domino considerationem, Congressum convocare poterit, cui huius Vicarii auxiliaris designatio ad normam n. 136 exclusive reservatur. Ut vero Consilium iure Congressum, hunc in finem, convocare possit, formalis requiritur deliberatio in qua duæ tertiæ partes Consilii pleni prædictam nominationem postulent et unus ex Custodibus. Tunc Vicarius Secretarius Generalis convocare tenetur Congressum extra ordinem Generalem, cui ipse Vicarius Secretarius Generalis præsit.

§ 3. In Vicario auxiliari, excepta ætate, eædem requiruntur qualitates ac in Prælato.

135. Vicarius auxiliaris, si detur Prælato habili, hunc adiuvat, ipsum supplet absentem vel impeditum: alias autem facultates non habet nisi quas, vel habitualiter vel ad casum, Prælatus delegaverit. De omnibus peractis Prælato rationem fideliter reddat.

136.§ 1. Si Prælatus senio, infirmitate aliave gravissima causa ad gubernandum, etiam ordinario Vicario auxiliari adiutus de quo in n. 135, certo incapax ita evadere videatur ut ipsius regiminis continuatio in damnum Prælaturæ practice converteretur, tunc Vicarius auxiliaris eligi a Congressu potest in quem omnia Prælati iura et officia, excepto tamen titulo, transferantur; electus confirmationem electionis a Sancta Sede per se vel per alium petere debet.

§ 2. Iudicium de exsistentia et gravitate causarum ad designationem huius Vicarii auxiliaris, ipsiusque si casus ferat electio, vel, ex adverso, iudicium de opportunitate Vicarii auxiliaris ordinarii designationis, vel mutationis, si hoc nempe sufficere videretur, Congressui reservatur, qui duabus ex tribus suffragiorum partibus quod magis, omnibus ponderatis, Prælaturæ bono conveniat decidere debet.

137.§ 1. Vicarius auxiliaris ordinarius ad nutum Prælati revocabilis est. Opportune Prælatus, sicut in nominatione, de qua in n. 134 § 1, ita etiam in revocatione suum Consilium Generale audire poterit.

§ 2. Vicarius auxiliaris vero qui in regimine Prælatum substituit usque ad novum ordinarium Congressum perdurat. Poterit tamen Congressus extra ordinem convocatus ipsum revocare: et tam ordinarius quam extraordinarius Congressus, speciatim si rationes suspensionis regiminis Prælati non necessario perpetuæ æstimari valeant, Consilio Generali pleno facultatem delegare ut ex morali unanimitate Prælati regimen, revocato Vicario auxiliari, instaurare possit; quæ Sanctæ Sedi communicentur.

138.§ 1. Ad Prælatum adiuvandum in dirigenda atque gubernanda Prælatura est Consilium Generale, constans e Vicario auxiliari, si adsit, Vicario Secretario Generali, Vicario pro Sectione mulierum, qui Sacerdos Secretarius Centralis nuncupatur, tribus saltem Vicesecretariis, uno saltem Delegato cuiusque Regionis, Studiorum Præfecto et Administratore Generali, qui constituunt Consilium plenum et vocantur Consultores.

§ 2. Prælatus, Vicarius auxiliaris, si adsit, Secretarius Generalis, Sacerdos Secretarius Centralis et, prout casus ferant, vel unus e Vicesecretariis vel Studiorum Præfectus aut Administrator Generalis, constituunt Commissionem permanentem Consilii. Huius Commissionis aliqua membra laici esse valent, pro negotiis tractandis quæ characterem Ordinis sacri non requirant; sed Vicarius auxiliaris, Secretarius Generalis et Secretarius Centralis, qui sunt etiam Vicarii Prælati, semper inter sacerdotes nominentur.

§ 3. Ad Consilium Generale admitti semper debent, ad normam tamen n. 139, Consultores illi, qui præsentes sunt. Invitari possunt, iudicio Prælati, et invitati assistere debent etiam illi qui ex munere absunt.

139.§ 1. Ad negotia illa resolvenda, pro quibus ad normam iuris requiritur votum deliberativum Consilii Generalis, invitari semper debent illi saltem Consultores qui non sunt absentes ex munere: et ad validam Consilii decisionem quinque saltem ipsius membra adesse necesse est. Si quinque Consultores invitari non possint, vel invitati adesse non valeant, Prælatus cum præsentibus aliquem vel aliquos designare ex Congressistis possunt, qui absentes pro illa vice substituant.

§ 2. Pro aliis vero quæstionibus Consilium competens est eiusdem Consilii Generalis Commissio permanens.

140.§ 1. Munera Consilii Generalis hac ratione provideri debent: Prælatus statim ac sua electio a Romano Pontifice confirmata fuerit informationes, quibus in Domino egere censeat, accurate colligit indeque per ordinem singillatim nomina candidatorum ad diversa munera Congressui proponit. Proposito a Prelato unoquoque nomine, Congressus, ad normam iuris universalis, suffragium secretum fert. Si propositum nomen a Congressu non probetur, aliud usque ad optatum suffragationis exitum proponere Prælatus debet.

§ 2. Octavo quoque anno, Prælato excepto, munera regiminis generalis omnia et singula Congressus revisioni, eadem servata ratione, subiicienda sunt. Possunt iidem ad idem aliudve munus generale absque limitatione eligi. Magni tamen interest ut ex regula aliqua nova membra ad Consilium Generale designentur.

141. Vacante, qualibet canonica ratione, Consultoris alicuius munere, Prælatus ad Consultoris munus Consilio Generali candidatum proponit, quod suo secreto suffragio, ipsum, eadem ratione ac in Congressu Generali, acceptare vel reiicere poterit. Hac occasione Prælato liberum relinquitur, audito Consilio, munera aliqua Consultoribus adnexa, si opportunum videatur, inter Consultores mutare.

142. Secretarius Generalis, Sacerdos Secretarius Centralis et Administrator Generalis debent esse membra Congressus. Ad cetera munera Consilii Generalis tantummodo habiles sunt Prælaturæ fideles de quibus in n. 13. Præ aliis debent prudentia, cultura et Operi Dei devotione fulgere.

143. Licet munus ad octo annos perduret, possunt nihilominus Consultores ob iustas causas et quoties bonum maius Prælaturæ requirat, a Prælato, ceteris auditis, removeri. Liberum quoque sit omnibus muneri renuntiare, verum renuntiatio effectum nullum habeat donec a Prælato admittatur.

144. § 1. Inter Consultores primus est Secretarius Generalis. Est semper sacerdos, post Prælatum venit, si Vicarius auxiliaris non adsit, eumque absentem vel quocumque modo impeditum supplet. Prælatum præterea specialiter adiuvat tum in iis quæ ad regimen et incepta universæ Prælaturæ, tum in iis quæ ad res œconomicas attinent, sed illis tantum facultatibus gaudet, quas vel habitualiter vel ad casum Prælatus delegaverit.

   § 2. Secretarius Generalis ad criteria, mentem et praxim Prælati, in quantum fieri possit, negotia gerat atque expediat: nihil proinde eorum, quæ a Prælato gesta vel præscripta sunt, innovare valeat, sed semper Prælato et Consilio erit quam maxime fidelis.

   § 3. Eius insuper est labores inter membra Consilii distribuere, ab eisque fidelem muneris adimpletionem exigere.

145. § 1. Ut Prælato adiumentum specialiter præstet in moderanda Sectione mulierum Operis Dei (cfr. n. 4 § 3), est Vicarius, qui Sacerdos Secretarius Centralis nuncupatur.

   § 2. Post Secretarium Generalem venit et illis facultatibus gaudet, quas vel habitualiter vel ad casum Prælatus delegaverit. Debet esse quadraginta saltem annos natus.

146. § 1. Sectio mulierum regitur a Prælato cum Vicario auxiliari, si adsit, Vicario Secretario Generali, Vicario Secretario Centrali et Consilio Centrali, quod Assessoratus Centralis appellatur, et eundem locum habet in Sectione mulierum ac Consilium Generale in Sectione virorum.

   § 2. Assessoratus Centralis constat e Secretaria Centrali, Secretaria Assessoratus, tribus saltem Vicesecretariis, una saltem Delegata cuiusque Regionis, Studiorum Præfecta, Præfecta Auxiliarium et Procuratrice Centrali.

   § 3. Ad munera Assessoratus Centralis nominat Prælatus in Congressu mulierum, eadem ratione ac in Congressu virorum vocat ad munera Consilii Generalis. Secretaria Centralis et Procuratrix Centralis seligantur inter Congressistas; ad alia munera Assessoratus vocentur Numerariæ de quibus in n. 13.

147.§ 1. Pro quæstionibus œconomicis, Prælato assistit Consilium ab ipso nominatum, quod vocatur Consultatio Technica cuique præest Prælatus vel, eius delegatione, Administrator Generalis.

§ 2. Rei œconomicæ rationes, saltem semel in anno, ab Administratore Generali subsignatæ, Prælato eiusque Consilio sunt exhibendæ.

§ 3. Consilium simile habetur pro quæstionibus œconomicis Sectionis mulierum.

148.§ 1. Quin ratione muneris Consilium Generale ingrediantur, adsunt etiam Procurator seu Agens precum, qui debet esse semper sacerdos, quique Prælaturam apud Sanctam Sedem ex delegatione habituali Prælati repræsentat; necnon Sacerdos Rerum Spiritualium Præfectus, qui directioni spirituali communi omnium Prælaturæ fidelium, sub ductu Prælati et Consilii, præponitur.

§ 2. In cura spirituali Aggregatis et Supernumerariis Societatis Sacerdotalis Sanctæ Crucis præstanda eius Præsidem Generalem Præfectus adiuvat, iuxta facultates habitualiter vel ad casum ipsi a Præside delegatas.

§ 3. Procurator et Præfectus a Prælato, audito Consilio, ad octo annos nominantur.

149.§ 1. Vacante munere Prælati, regimen tenet Vicarius auxiliaris, si sit; aliter Secretarius Generalis vel, post eum, Vicarius Secretarius Centralis; iisque omnibus deficientibus, sacerdos Congressista maiore suffragiorum numero ab iis designatus, quibus ius est constituendi Commissionem permanentem Consilii Generalis.

§ 2. Qui regimen assumit, tenetur obligationibus et gaudet potestate Prælati, iis exclusis quæ ex rei natura vel iure Prælaturæ excipiuntur. Congressum Generalem electivum convocare tenetur intra mensem a muneris vacatione, ita ut intra tres menses ab eadem vacatione celebretur, aut, si maiore de causa intra statutum tempus coadunari nequeat, statim ac causa impediens cessaverit.

§ 3. Vacante munere Prælati, qui muneribus funguntur regiminis, tum generalis Prælaturæ tum circumscriptionum, in exercitio suorum munerum pergunt, donec, post novum electum Prælatum, in ipsis confirmentur vel substituantur.

§ 4. Prælato impedito, iuxta normas in § 1 statutas procedendum est; si vero, in gravioribus rerum adiunctis, eædem servari nequeant, coadunentur membra Consilii Generalis quæ id facere valeant, sub moderatione dignioris, et sacerdotem quoad fieri possit membrum Congressus designent, qui regimen Prælaturæ ad interim assumat.

## CAPUT III

### DE REGIMINE REGIONALI ET LOCALI

150. Prælati de consensu sui Consilii est circumscriptiones regionales, quæ vocantur Regiones vel Quasi-Regiones, erigere, mutare, aliter definire, et etiam supprimere.

151. § 1. Regimini uniuscuiusque Regionis præponitur Vicarius, qui Consiliarius Regionalis nuncupatur, quemque nominat Prælatus cum voto deliberativo sui Consilii; Consiliario assistit Consilium, quod vocatur Commissio Regionalis, constans membris usque ad duodecim, designatis inter Prælaturæ fideles de quibus in n. 13 pariterque nominatis a Prælato audito suo Consilio, cuius consensus requiritur in casibus de quibus in nn. 157 § 1 et 159.

§ 2. Inter membra Commissionis peculiarem locum obtinet Defensor, cuius munus est adimpletionem normarum huius Codicis fovere.

152. § 1. Quando non sint omnia elementa necessaria ad novas Regiones constituendas, possunt etiam Quasi-Regiones a Prælato, cum voto deliberativo sui Consilii, erigi. Eas moderantur Vicarii, qui Vicariis Regionalibus iure æquiparantur.

§ 2. Potest etiam Prælatus, audito suo Consilio, Delegationes erigere directe a se dependentes, Vicario delegato conferens facultates quas, iuxta casus, intra limites tamen facultatum Consiliariorum Regionalium, committendas censuerit.

153. Ad meliorem curam exercendam laboris apostolici in aliqua circumscriptione, Prælatus, audito suo Consilio eisque quorum intersit, erigere potest Delegationes a Commissione eiusdem circumscriptionis dependentes, quarum unicuique præponatur Vicarius delegatus, cum proprio Consilio, opportunis facultatibus præditus.

154. Ipso facto erectionis, Regiones, Quasi-Regiones et Delegationes a Prælato dependentes iuridicam adquirunt personalitatem. Delegationes in circumscriptione regionali constitutæ donari possunt personalitate iuridica in erectionis decreto.

155. Circumscriptiones personalitate iuridica gaudentes, de quibus in n. 154, quoad negotia iuridica et, in genere, quoad quæstiones omnes, repræsentantur, præterquam a Prælato eiusque delegatis, tantummodo a respectivis Vicariis, qui agere possunt per se vel per alios opportuno mandato præditos.

156. § 1. Munera regionalia conferuntur a Prælato, audito Consilio, exceptis tamen Consiliario, Sacerdote Secretario Regionis et Administratore Regionali, qui nominari debent ad normam nn. 151, 157 § 1 et 159, et durant ad quinquennium, nisi pro omnibus vel pro aliquibus Commissionis membris tempus in munere ad octo annos prorogetur. Pro Delegatis autem Regionalibus valet præscriptum n. 140 §§ 1 et 2.

§ 2. Ad munera Commissionis in Quasi-Regionibus et Delegationibus vocat Prælatus, audito suo Consilio.

157.§ 1. In singulis Regionibus, nomine et vice Prælati semperque ad ipsius mentem, respectivus Vicarius Consiliarius Regionalis cum alio sacerdote, qui Sacerdos Secretarius Regionalis vocatur, nominato a Prælato cum voto deliberativo sui Consilii et audito Assessoratu Centrali, Sectionem mulierum moderantur, una cum Consilio regionali mulierum, quod Assessoratus Regionalis appellatur et eundem locum habet in Sectione mulierum ac Commissio Regionalis in virorum Sectione.

§ 2. Assessoratus Regionalis constare potest membris usque ad duodecim, selectis inter Numerarias de quibus in n. 13; nominatur a Prælato, audito Assessoratu Centrali, cuius consensus requiritur pro muneribus Secretariæ Regionalis et Procuratricis Regionalis.

§ 3. Ad munera Assessoratus in Quasi-Regionibus et Delegationibus vocat Prælatus, audito Assessoratu Centrali.

158. Si quando in aliqua Regione impedimentum obstiterit, quod impossibilem reddat cum Prælato eiusque Consilio communicationem et, perdurante hac impossibilitate, defuerit aliquod Commissionis membrum, ad eius munus ipsa Commissio alium Numerarium per maiorem suffragiorum partem eliget. Cum autem plus quam tria Commissionis membra defuerint vel cum ipsa Commissio, expleto tempore sui mandati, renovanda sit, Numerarii ad munera vocabuntur maioritate item suffragiorum a speciali coadunatione constituta ex omnibus Regionis Congressistis non impeditis omnibusque membris Commissionis, cui coadunationi præerit Congressista ordine præcedentiæ senior. Quodsi, quavis de causa, tres saltem Congressistæ coadunationi adesse non potuerint, vocandi erunt etiam tres Numerarii ex iis de quibus in n. 13, ordine præcedentiæ seniores Regionis, non impediti: absentibus Congressistis, præerit ordine item præcedentiæ senior inter præsentes. Paritatem suffragiorum dirimet præses coadunationis.

159.§ 1. In unaquaque Regione, pro rebus œconomicis, Vicario Regionali assistit Consilium œconomicum, seu Consultatio Technica, cuius membra ab eodem Vicario designantur, cuique præest Administrator Regionalis, a Prælato nominatus cum voto deliberativo proprii Consilii.

§ 2. Consultatio similis habetur pro quæstionibus œconomicis Sectionis mulierum.

160. In unaquaque circumscriptione, quin ratione muneris ad Commissionem pertineat, est Sacerdos Rerum Spiritualium Præfectus Regionalis, ad vitam spiritualem omnium Prælaturæ fidelium sub ductu Consiliarii fovendam. Consiliario insuper adiumentum præstat in cura spirituali Aggregatis et Supernumerariis Societatis Sacerdotalis Sanctæ Crucis danda, iuxta facultates habitualiter vel ad casum ipsi a Consiliario delegatas. A Prælato, auditis Consiliario et Defensore Regionis, ad quinquennium nominatur.

161.§ 1. In singulis circumscriptionibus Centra erigantur, ad normam n. 177.

§ 2. Regimen locale constituitur a Directore cum proprio Consilio. Munera sunt ad triennium, et conferuntur a Consiliario, audito suo Consilio.

§ 3. Conceptus Centri, hoc in Codice, potius personalis est quam territorialis, et potius regionalis quam localis.

§ 4. Ut apta habeatur Prælaturæ fidelium cura, ad idem Centrum adscribi possunt fideles, vel etiam fidelium Cœtus, qui sive in eadem civitate sive in diversis civitatibus vel diœcesibus commorentur.

§ 5. Sunt proinde in Prælatura Centra autonoma et Centra ab aliis dependentia, quia adhuc canonice non sunt erecta.

## CAPUT IV

### DE ADUNATIONIBUS REGIONALIBUS

162. Ad impensiorem formationem fidelium Prælaturæ et ad meliorem evolutionem actionis apostolicæ, decimo quoque anno, in singulis Regionibus, Adunationes de more celebrentur, in quibus transactæ periodi experientiæ habitæ perpendantur.

163. Præter Adunationes ordinarias, possunt etiam extraordinariæ celebrari, in una vel in pluribus circumscriptionibus, quoties Prælatus, auditis Consilio Generali et Commissione Regionali, id expedire duxerit.

164. Adunationem, de mandato Prælati, convocat Vicarius circumscriptionis designans locum et tempus sessionis, tribus saltem mensibus ante eiusdem celebrationem.

165. Adunationibus præsunt Prælatus vel eius delegatus, cui assistunt Vicarius et Delegatus circumscriptionis. A secretis est iunior laicus præsens.

166. § 1. Adunationi cuiusque circumscriptionis interesse debent:

    1° omnes qui in Commissione aliquo munere funguntur, vel functi sunt;

    2° omnes Congressistæ circumscriptioni adscripti;

    3° omnes eiusdem Regionis sacerdotes aliique fideles Prælaturæ, qui; cuncti inter eos de quibus in n. 13 adnumerentur;

    4° Directores Centrorum Studiorum;

    5° item, a Prælato designati, Directores locales.

§ 2. Vocari etiam possunt ad Adunationem alii Prælaturæ fideles, diversis in materiis periti, ut eidem intersint qua collaboratores.

167. § 1. Fovenda est quam maxima omnium Prælaturæ fidelium participatio in Adunationibus, requirendo eorum communicationes, notulas de experientiis habitis aliaque id genus.

§ 2. Eadem de causa, si adiuncta id suadeant, haberi queunt plures cœtus diversis in sedibus, quo maior harum Adunationum efficacitas obtineatur.

§ 3. Notæ vel schedæ de experientiis habitis postulari quoque possunt ab Operis Dei Cooperatoribus, etiam non catholicis, qui suggestiones præbeant pro studio thematum laboris.

168. Omnes ad Adunationem convocati, mense saltem ante eiusdem celebrationem, mittant ad secretarium notas, schedas, animadversiones,

etc., quas proponere conveniens eis videatur; ex ipsis autem atque ex omnibus propositionibus Adunationi transmissis (n. 167), commissio, a præside nominata, elenchum quæstionum iis qui intersint submittendarum conficiat.

169.Conclusiones Adunationis vim præceptivam non habent quousque adprobationem receperint Prælati, audito suo Consilio, nisi ex rei natura votum deliberativum ipsius Consilii requiratur. Ipse Prælatus opportunas etiam feret instructiones per organa directionis ordinaria.

170.Adunationes Sectionis mulierum celebrentur, congrua congruis referendo, iuxta normas in n. 162 et sequentibus traditas.

## CAPUT V

### DE RELATIONIBUS CUM EPISCOPIS DIŒCESANIS

171.Prælatura Operis Dei immediate et directe subiicitur Sanctæ Sedi, quæ eius spiritum et finem probavit et eius quoque regimen ac disciplinam tuetur et promovet in bonum Ecclesiæ universæ.

172.§ 1. Cuncti Prælaturæ christifideles tenentur humiliter Romano Pontifici in omnibus obœdire: hæc obœdiendi obligatio fideles omnes forti ac dulci vinculo obstringit.

§ 2. Ordinariis quoque locorum subiiciuntur ad normam iuris universalis, eadem ratione ac ceteri catholici in propria diœcesi, iuxta præscripta huius Codicis.

173.§ 1. Prælati est sollicite exsecutioni mandare omnia decreta, rescripta aliasque dispositiones Sanctæ Sedis quæ Prælaturam respiciant, itemque eidem Sanctæ Sedi opportunas relationes præbere, ad normam iuris, de statu Prælaturæ deque eiusdem apostolica activitate.

§ 2. Ipse Prælatus curabit, etiam quia spiritus Operis Dei maximo amore filialem unionem cum Romano Pontifice, Christi Vicario, colit, ut eiusdem Magisterii documenta et acta universam Ecclesiam respicientia ab omnibus Prælaturæ fidelibus accurate cognoscantur, utque eorum doctrinam ipsi diffundant.

174.§ 1. Universus labor apostolicus quem Prælatura, iuxta propriam naturam propriumque finem, exsequitur, ad bonum singularum Ecclesiarum localium confert, atque Prælatura debitas cum Auctoritate ecclesiastica territoriali relationes semper colit.

§ 2. Curet præterea Prælatus ut, singulis in circumscriptionibus, Vicarius competens, per se vel per alios eiusdem Vicarii nomine, habituales relationes servet cum Episcopis in quorum diœcesibus Prælaturæ christifideles resideant, et præsertim ut frequenter colloquatur cum illis Episcopis locorum in quibus Opus Dei Centra erecta habet, necnon cum iis qui muneribus directivis funguntur in respectiva Conferentia Episcopali, ad illas indicationes ab iisdem Episcopis suscipiendas, quas Prælaturæ fideles filiorum animo in praxim deducant (cfr. n. 176).

175. Præter orationes quas pro Romano Pontifice et Episcopo diœcesano eorumque intentionibus quotidie Prælaturæ fideles recitare tenentur, maximam eis reverentiam et amorem demonstrabunt, quæ etiam impense apud omnes fovere contendant.

176. Singulis in circumscriptionibus, auctoritates Prælaturæ curent ut eiusdem fideles bene cognoscant normas directivas pastorales a competenti ecclesiastica Auctoritate territoriali, nempe a Conferentia Episcopali, ab Episcopo diœcesano, etc., statutas, ut unusquisque, iuxta propria adiuncta personalia, familiaria et professionalia, eas ad effectum deducere et in ipsis cooperari valeat.

177. § 1. Ut labor apostolicus Prælaturæ in aliqua diœcesi incipiat, mediante canonica erectione primi Centri, ex quo exerceri possit apostolatus collectivus, debet prius informari loci Ordinarius, cuius venia requiritur, melius scripto data.

§ 2. Quoties laboris progressus aliorum Centrorum erectionem in diœcesi suadeat, procedendum semper est ad normam paragraphi præcedentis.

§ 3. Simplex mutatio domicilii alicuius Centri Prælaturæ, intra terminos eiusdem civitatis, si Centrum non habeat adnexam ecclesiam, communicari debet in scriptis loci Ordinario, etsi novam veniam non requirat.

178. § 1. Erectio Centri secum fert potestatem erigendi aliud Centrum pro mulieribus fidelibus Prælaturæ Administrationi prioris Centri addictis, ita ut de iure et de facto duo sint Centra in unoquoque Operis Dei domicilio (cfr. n. 8 § 2).

§ 2. Secum fert pariter facultatem oratorium pro usu fidelium Prælaturæ aliorumque in unoquoque Centro ad normam iuris habendi, ibique SS.mum Sacramentum asservandi atque functiones pro labore apostolico opportunas peragendi. In oratoriis sollemnis Sanctissimi Sacramenti expositio nocte primam feriam sextam uniuscuiusque mensis præcedenti fieri saltem debet.

§ 3. Concedere potest Ordinarius Prælaturæ ut sacerdotes, iusta de causa, bis in die, immo, necessitate pastorali id postulante, etiam ter in diebus dominicis et festis de præcepto Sanctam Missam celebrent, ita ut non solum fidelium Prælaturæ necessitatibus, sed etiam aliorum diœcesis fidelium, dum possibile sit, satis faciant.

179. Episcopus diœcesanus ius habet visitandi singula Centra Prælaturæ canonice erecta (cfr. n. 177) in iis quæ ad ecclesiam, sacrarium et sedem ad sacramentum Pænitentiæ pertinent.

180. Ad erigendas ecclesias Prælaturæ vel, si res ferat, ad eidem committendas ecclesias in diœcesi iam exsistentes, fiat singulis in casibus opportuna conventio, ad normam iuris, inter Episcopum diœcesanum et Prælatum vel competentem Vicarium Regionalem. Iis in ecclesiis, una cum normis in unaquaque conventione statutis, servabuntur dispositiones generales diœcesis ecclesias sæculares respicientes.

## TITULUS V

## DE STABILITATE ET VI HUIUS CODICIS

181.§ 1. Hic Codex fundamentum est Prælaturæ Operis Dei. Ideo sanctæ eius normæ habeantur, inviolabiles, perpetuæ, unique Sanctæ Sedi reservatæ tam quoad mutationem quam quoad novorum præceptorum inductionem.

§ 2. Tantummodo mutationem alicuius Codicis præscripti, seu in eius corpus aliquam innovationem, aut denique temporariam vel perpetuam alicuius normæ suspensionem vel expunctionem a Sancta Sede poscere valet Congressus Generalis Prælaturæ, dummodo hic certitudinem habeat de necessitate huius mutationis, innovationis, suspensionis vel expunctionis.

§ 3. Ut hæc certitudo iuridice exsistat, si agatur de textus expunctione, innovatione vel indefinita suspensione, requiritur diuturnum experimentum, duorum ordinariorum Congressuum Generalium auctoritate confirmatum, quod tertio ordinario Congressui Generali subiiciatur et duabus saltem ex tribus suffragiorum partibus comprobetur.

§ 4. Si agatur vero de temporaria alicuius Codicis præscripti suspensione, Prælatus, cum voto deliberativo unius tantummodo Congressus Generalis, a Sancta Sede eam exposcere valet: requiritur tamen ut plane Sanctæ Sedi manifestetur tempus ad quod postulata suspensio est protrahenda.

182.§ 1. Auctoritates Prælaturæ omnibus modis Codicis applicationem fovere, ipsamque prudenter et efficaciter exigere tenentur, scientes illum medium esse certum sanctificationis fidelibus Prælaturæ: quapropter adversus ipsum Codicem nec consuetudo aliqua, nec desuetudo, prævalere umquam poterunt.

§ 2. Facultas dispensandi ab adimpletione disciplinari Codicis, in his quæ dispensari valent et non manent Sanctæ Sedi reservata, competit tantummodo Prælato cum voto consultivo sui Consilii, si de rebus magni momenti agatur, vel dispensatio universæ Prælaturæ sit concedenda: secus, sufficit decretum Vicarii Regionalis, de consensu proprii Consilii.

183.§ 1. Præscripta Codicis quæ leges divinas vel ecclesiasticas referunt, propriam quam ex se habent obligationem retinent.

§ 2. Codicis præscripta, quæ regimen spectant; item, quæ definiunt regiminis necessarias functiones aut munera quibus exercentur, quoad nempe ipsorum cardinales normas; pariterque præscripta quæ naturam et finem Prælaturæ statuunt et consecrant, in conscientia, pro gravitate materiæ, obligant.

§ 3. Præscripta denique mere disciplinaria vel ascetica, quæ sub præcedentibus paragraphis huius numeri non cadunt, per se sub reatu culpæ directo non obligant. Insuper, quælibet ex ipsis, vel minimis, ex formali contemptu violare, peccatum est; quod si transgressio ex ratione vel fine non recto fiat, vel ad scandalum moveat, peccatum contra respondentes virtutes secum fert.

184. Prælati cum voto deliberativo sui Consilii est illa omnia definire quæ ad practicam huius Codicis interpretationem, applicationem et adimpletionem spectant.

185. Quæ de viris hoc in Codice statuuntur, etsi masculino vocabulo expressa, valent etiam pari iure de mulieribus, nisi ex contextu sermonis vel ex rei natura aliud constet aut explicite specialia præscripta ferantur.

## DISPOSITIONES FINALES

1. Quæ ad hæc usque tempora ab Apostolica Sede in favorem Operis Dei concessa, declarata vel approbata sunt, integra manent, quatenus cum eius regimine iuridico Prælaturæ personalis componuntur. Pariter vim suam retinet venia ad hæc usque tempora concessa a locorum Ordinariis, ut Operis Dei Centra canonice erigantur necnon successivus actus erectionis.

2. Hic Codex, quoad omnes fideles Operi Dei iam incorporatos, tum sacerdotes tum laicos, necnon quoad sacerdotes Aggregatos et Supernumerarios Societatis Sacerdotalis Sanctæ Crucis, vim exserere incipiet a die 8 decembris an. 1982.

   Hi omnes iisdem obligationibus tenentur et eadem servant iura, quæ habebant in regimine iuridico præcedenti, nisi aliud expresse statuant huius Codicis præscriptiones vel de iis agatur quæ ex normis novo hoc iure abrogatis proveniebant.

# OFFICIAL DOCUMENT INDEX

# INDEX OF NAMES*

* Numbers indicate pages; when numbers appear in italics they refer to footnotes.